Contents

www.philips-maps.co.uk

First published in 2006 by Philip's
a division of Octopus Publishing Group Ltd,
Endeavour House, 189 Shaftesbury Avenue
London WC2H 8JY
www.octopus-publishing.co.uk
An Hachette UK company
www.hachette.co.uk

Fifth edition 2010
First impression 2010

Cartography by Philip's
Copyright © 2010 Philip's

Data for the speed cameras provided by **PocketGPSWorld.com** Ltd.

Information for National Parks, Areas of Outstanding Natural Beauty, National Trails and Country Parks in Wales supplied by the Countryside Council for Wales.

Information for National Parks, Areas of Outstanding Natural Beauty, National Trails and Country Parks in England supplied by Natural England. Data for Regional Parks, Long Distance Footpaths and Country Parks in Scotland provided by Scottish Natural Heritage.

Gaelic name forms used in the Western Isles provided by Comhairle nan Eilean.

Data for the National Nature Reserves in England provided by Natural England. Data for the National Nature Reserves in Wales provided by Countryside Council for Wales. Darparwyd data'n ymwneud â Gwarchodfeydd Natur Cenedlaethol Cymru gan Gyngor Cefn Gwlad Cymru.

Information on the location of National Nature Reserves in Scotland was provided by Scottish Natural Heritage.

Data for National Scenic Areas in Scotland provided by the Scottish Executive Office. Crown copyright material is reproduced with the permission of the Controller of HMSO and the Queen's Printer for Scotland. Licence number C02W0003960.

Printed in China

Route-finding system

Town names printed in yellow on a green background are those used on Britain's signposts to indicate primary destinations. To find your route quickly and easily, simply follow the signs to the primary destination immediately beyond the place you require.

Below Driving from St Ives to Camborne, follow the signs to Redruth, the first primary destination beyond Camborne. These will indicate the most direct main route to the side turning for Camborne.

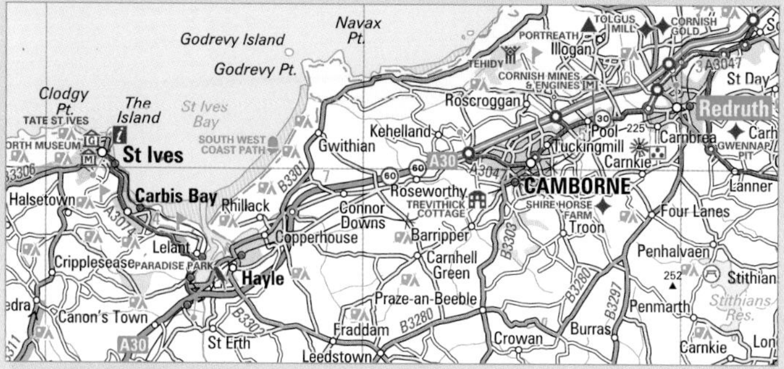

Speed Cameras

Fixed camera locations are shown using the ⓐ symbol.

In congested areas the ⓐ symbol is used to show that there are two or more cameras on the road indicated.

Due to the restrictions of scale the camera locations are only approximate and cannot indicate the operating direction of the camera.

Mobile camera sites, and cameras located on roads not included on the mapping are not shown. Where two or more cameras are shown on the same road, drivers are warned that this may indicate that a SPEC system is in operation. These cameras use the time taken to drive between the two camera positions to calculate the speed of the vehicle.

Road map symbols

Symbol	Description
M6	Motorway, toll motorway
4 5	Motorway junction – full, restricted access
S S	Motorway service area – full, restricted access
	Motorway under construction
A453	Primary route – dual, single carriageway
	Service area, roundabout, multi-level junction
4 5	Numbered junction – full, restricted access
	Primary route under construction
	Narrow primary route
Derby	Primary destination
A34	A road – dual, single carriageway
	A road under construction, narrow A road
B2135	B road – dual, single carriageway
	B road under construction, narrow B road
	Minor road – over 4 metres, under 4 metres wide
	Minor road with restricted access
2	Distance in miles
	Scenic route
49 49	Speed camera – single, multiple
TOLL	Toll, steep gradient – arrow points downhill
	Tunnel
	National trail – England and Wales
	Long distance footpath – Scotland
	Railway with station
	Level crossing, tunnel
	Preserved railway with station
	National boundary
	County / unitary authority boundary
	Car ferry, catamaran
	Passenger ferry, catamaran
	Hovercraft
CALAIS 1:30 Ferry	Ferry destination, journey time – hrs : mins
	Car ferry – river crossing
	Principal airport, other airport
	National park
	Area of Outstanding Natural Beauty – England and Wales National Scenic Area – Scotland forest park / regional park / national forest
	Woodland
	Beach
	Linear antiquity
	Roman road
X 1066	Hillfort, battlefield – with date
795	Viewpoint, nature reserve, spot height – in metres
	Golf course, youth hostel, sporting venue
	Camp site, caravan site, camping and caravan site
P&R	Shopping village, park and ride
29	Adjoining page number – road maps

Tourist information

✝ Abbey / cathedral / priory	⚓ Historic ship	ℹ Tourist information centre – open all year
🏛 Ancient monument	🏠 House	ℹ Tourist information centre – open seasonally
⚲ Aquarium	🏡 House and garden	🐻 Zoo
🏛 Art gallery	🏎 Motor racing circuit	✦ Other place of interest
🐦 Bird collection / aviary	🏛 Museum	
🏰 Castle	Ⓟ Picnic area	
⛪ Church	🚂 Preserved railway	
🎪 Country park – England and Wales	🏇 Race course	
🏴 Country park – Scotland	🏛 Roman antiquity	
🐄 Farm park	V Safari park	
✿ Garden	🎡 Theme park	

Road map scale: 1: 265 320, 4·2 miles to 1 inch

0 1 2 3 4 5 6 7 8 9 miles
0 1 2 3 4 5 6 7 8 9 10 11 12 13 14 15km

Relief

Feet	metres
3000	914
2600	792
2200	671
1800	549
1400	427
1000	305
0	0

Route planning

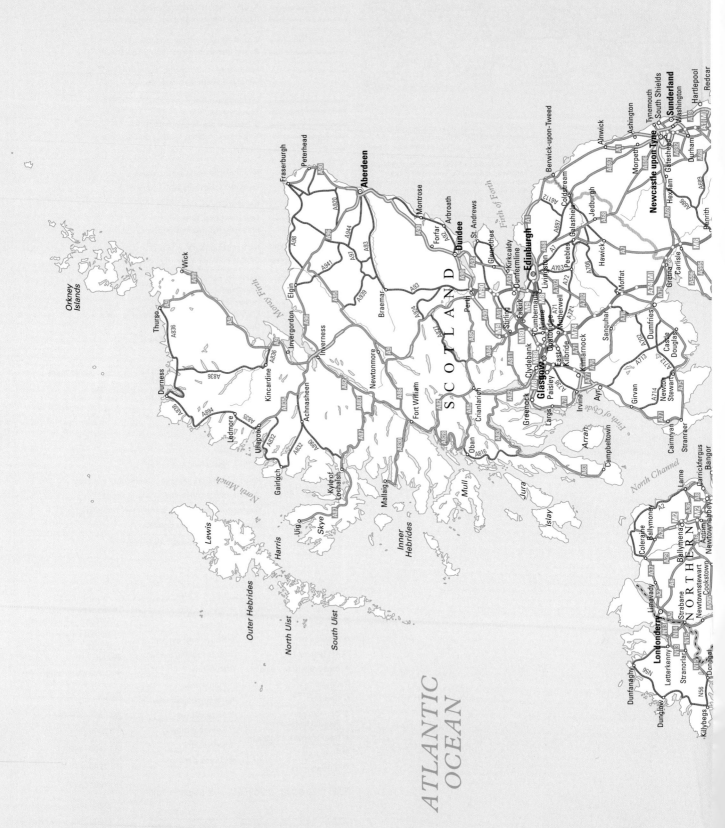
NORTH SEA
ATLANTIC OCEAN
SCOTLAND
NORTHERN
Orkney Islands
Wick
Thurso
Durness
Moray Firth
Firth of Forth
Firth of Clyde
North Minch
North Channel
Fraserburgh
Peterhead
Aberdeen
Elgin
Invergordon
Inverness
Kincardine
Achnasheen
Ullapool
Ledmore
Gairloch
Kyle of Lochalsh
Mallaig
Fort William
Newtonmore
Braemar
Montrose
Arbroath
Forfar
Dundee
St. Andrews
Glenrothes
Kirkcaldy
Dunfermline
Perth
Stirling
Falkirk
Edinburgh
Livingston
Cumbernauld
Airdrie
Coatbridge
Motherwell
East Kilbride
Glasgow
Clydebank
Paisley
Greenock
Largs
Irvine
Kilmarnock
Ayr
Girvan
Cairnryan
Stranraer
Newton Stewart
Castle Douglas
Dumfries
Sanquhar
Moffat
Peebles
Galashiels
Jedburgh
Hawick
Coldstream
Berwick-upon-Tweed
Alnwick
Ashington
Morpeth
Tynemouth
South Shields
Sunderland
Washington
Newcastle upon Tyne
Gateshead
Hexham
Durham
Hartlepool
Redcar
Penrith
Carlisle
Gretna
Crianlarich
Oban
Campbeltown
Arran
Jura
Islay
Mull
Inner Hebrides
Skye
Uig
Lewis
Harris
Outer Hebrides
North Uist
South Uist
Larne
Carrickfergus
Bangor
Antrim
Newtownabbey
Ballymena
Ballymoney
Coleraine
Limavady
Londonderry
Strabane
Cookstown
Newtownstewart
Letterkenny
Stranorlar
Donegal
Dunfanaghy
Dungloe
Killybegs

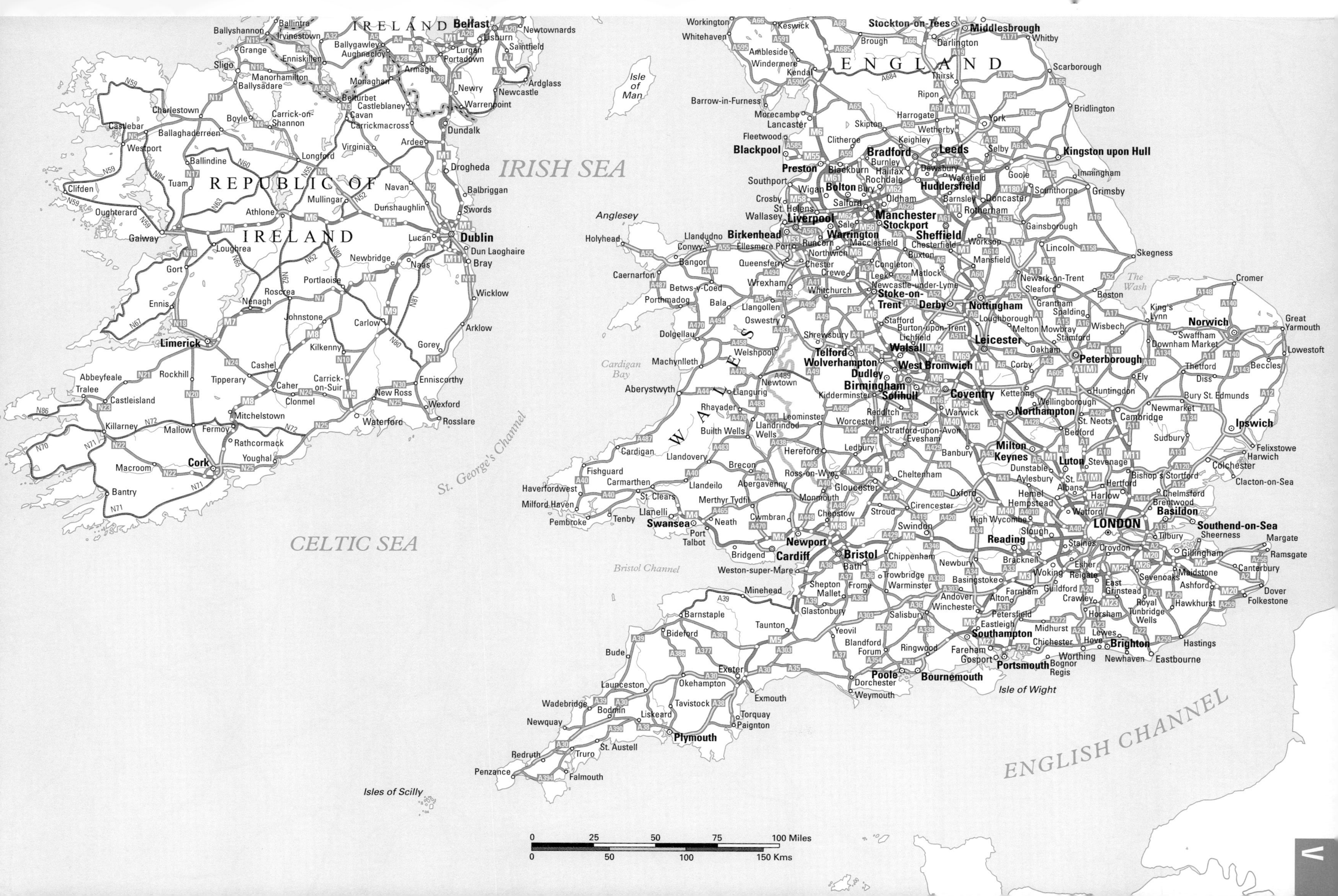

IRELAND
REPUBLIC OF IRELAND
ENGLAND
WALES
IRISH SEA
CELTIC SEA
ENGLISH CHANNEL
St. George's Channel
Bristol Channel
Cardigan Bay
The Wash
Isle of Man
Anglesey
Isle of Wight
Isles of Scilly
Belfast
Dublin
Cork
Limerick
Galway
Waterford
Wexford
Dundalk
Drogheda
Sligo
Kilkenny
Stockton-on-Tees
Middlesbrough
Kingston upon Hull
Blackpool
Preston
Bradford
Leeds
Bolton
Huddersfield
Manchester
Stockport
Liverpool
Birkenhead
Warrington
Sheffield
Stoke-on-Trent
Derby
Nottingham
Leicester
Norwich
Peterborough
Telford
Wolverhampton
Walsall
West Bromwich
Dudley
Birmingham
Solihull
Coventry
Northampton
Ipswich
Milton Keynes
Luton
Basildon
Southend-on-Sea
LONDON
Reading
Swansea
Newport
Cardiff
Bristol
Southampton
Portsmouth
Brighton
Poole
Bournemouth
Plymouth
0 25 50 75 100 Miles
0 50 100 150 Kms
V

Borehamwood
Elstree
Aldenham
Arkley
Barnet
East Barnet
Underhill
New Barnet
Chipping Barnet
Ducks Island
Rowley Green
Oxhey
Bushey
Watford Heath
Bushey Heath
Caldecote Hill
Merry Hill
Carpenders Park
South Oxhey
Harrow Weald Common
The Kiln
Bentley Priory
Brockley Hill Fm
Stanmore Hall
Deacons Hill
Bury Fm
London Gateway Services
Barnet Gate
Hyver Hall
Totteridge Park
Totteridge
Oak Lodge
Highwood Hill
Whetstone
Oakleigh Park
Oak Hill Park
Osidge
Friern Barnet
Brunswick Park
Edgware
Collegiate School
Canons Park
Stanmore
Harrow Weald
Hatch End
Eastbury
Pinnerwood Ho
Pinnerwood Park
Pinner Green
Pinner
Northwood Hills
Mill Hill
Mill Hill Broadway
Mill Hill East
Woodside Park
North Finchley
Colney Hatch
Finchley
Church End
Holders Hill
Little Stanmore
Burnt Oak
Belmont
Colindale
Queensbury
Headstone
Wealdstone
Harrow
Nower Hill
Eastcote Village
Eastcote
North Harrow
Greenhill
Kenton
Kingsbury
The Hyde
Hendon
West Hendon
Cool Oak Br
Brent Res
Welsh Harp
Hampstead Garden Suburb
Golders Green
Fortis Green
Cranley Gardens
Muswell Hill
East Finchley
Highgate
Highgate Ponds
Kenwood Ho
Hampstead Heath
Vale of Health
Parliament Hill
Dartmouth Park
Highgate Cemy
North End
Child's Hill
Hampstead
West Hampstead
Rayners Lane
West Harrow
Harrow on the Hill
Harrow School
Preston
South Kenton
North Wembley
Fryent Barn Hill
Ruislip Manor
Ruislip Gardens
South Ruislip
Roxeth
South Harrow
Wembley
Wembley Park
Neasden
Dollis Hill
Cricklewood
Dudden Hill
Tokyngton
Conference Centre
Sudbury
Horsenden Hill
Northolt
Downe Barns Fm
Church End
Willesden
Willesden Green
Brondesbury Park
Brondesbury
Kilburn
Kensal Rise
Kensal Green
South Hampstead
Primrose Hill
Camden
London Zoo
Regent's Park
St John's Wood
Maida Vale
Alperton
Perivale
Greenford
Stonebridge
Harlesden
Park Royal
Lower Place
College Park
West Kilburn
Westbourne Green
Paddington
Madame Tussauds
British Library
Lisson Grove
Marylebone
North Acton
Old Oak Common
HM Prison Wormwood Scrubs
Kensal Town
North Kensington
Yeading
Hayes
Hayes Town
Southall
Dormer's Wells
Hanwell
Ealing
West Ealing
Castle Bar Park
Drayton Green
Hangar Lane
West Acton
Acton
East Acton
Shepherd's Bush
Notting Hill
Bayswater
Kensington Gardens
Hyde Park
Mayfair
Royal Academy of Arts
Ealing Common
Acton Green
South Acton
Bedford Park
Hammersmith
Kensington
Holland Park
West Kensington
Earl's Court
Knightsbridge
Belgravia
Buckingham Palace
Apsley House
Natural History & Science Mus
Victoria & Albert Museum
Chelsea
Gunnersbury
Gunnersbury Park Mus
Chiswick
Chiswick Ho
Hogarth's Ho
Kew Br
Kew
Kew Gardens
National Archives
Brentford
Brentford End
Osterley Park
Osterley
Heston
Heston Services
Harlington
Cranford
Norwood Green
North Hyde
Spring Grove
Syon House
Royal Botanic Gardens
Isleworth
Lampton
Hounslow
Hounslow West
Hounslow Heath
Hatton
North Feltham
Woodlands
North Sheen
Mortlake
Barnes
Wetlands Centre
Craven Cottage
Fulham
Hammersmith Bridge
Parsons Green
Sands End
Putney Bridge
Walham Green
West Brompton
Battersea
Battersea Park
Chelsea Physic Gdn
Carlyle's Ho
Clapham
Richmond
East Sheen
St Margarets
Twickenham
Marble Hill Ho
Mus of Rugby
Whitton
The Stoop
East Sheen Common
Roehampton Gate
Grove Ho
Roehampton
Putney
Putney Heath
Wandsworth
Wandsworth Common
West Hill
Southfields
Earlsfield
Balham
Feltham
Bog Lodge
Richmond Park
White Lodge
Pen Ponds
Petersham
Pembroke Lodge
Ham House
Ham
Ham Common
Strawberry Hill
Hanworth Park
Lower Feltham
Hanworth
Teddington
Isabella Plantn
Thatched House Lodge
HM Prison
Putney Vale
Kingston Vale
Caesar's Camp
Warren Ho
Wimbledon Common
Copse Hill
Wimbledon
Wimbledon Park
Summerstown
Upper Tooting
Tooting Graveney
Furzedown
South Wimbledon
Crooked Billet
Cottenham Park
Coombe
Norbiton
Hampton Hill
Hampton
Kempton Park
Feltham Hill
Sunbury Common
Sunbury-on-Thames
Sunbury Court
Upper Halliford
Bartons Cott
Bushy Park
Hampton Wick
Kingston upon Thames
Merton
Mitcham
Collier's Wood
Raynes Park
Merton Park
Morden Hall Park
Morden
West Molesey
Hurst Park
East Molesey
Hampton Court Palace
Hampton Court Park
Molesey Reservoirs
Sunbury Lock
Seething Wells
Berrylands
New Malden
Motspur Park
West Barnes
Bushey Mead
Cannon Hill
Thames Ditton
Queen Elizabeth
Island Barn Res
Mitcham Junction
St Helier
Croydon

London approaches

Scale

1:100000, 1cm = 1km, 1 inch = 1.58 miles

0   1   2   3 miles
0   1   2   3   4   5 km

Distance table

How to use this table

Distances are shown in miles and, in *italics*, kilometres.
For example, the distance between Aberdeen and Bournemouth is 564 miles or *908* kilometres.

Supporting

THINK!

Travel safe –
Don't drive tired

The distance table is a triangular mileage chart. For each city the top figures are miles and the lower *italic* figures are kilometres.

From	Distances (miles / *km*) to preceding cities
London	—
Aberdeen	517 / *832*
Aberystwyth	445 211 / *716 340*
Ayr	317 183 394 / *510 295 634*
Berwick-upon-Tweed	134 311 182 352 / *216 501 293 567*
Birmingham	274 289 114 420 117 / *441 465 183 676 188*
Blackpool	123 181 180 153 308 226 / *198 291 290 246 496 364*
Bournemouth	270 147 412 436 207 564 107 / *435 237 663 702 333 908 172*
Braemar	524 281 385 148 143 405 59 482 / *843 452 620 238 230 652 95 776*
Brighton	534 92 286 163 409 446 253 573 52 / *859 148 460 262 658 718 407 922 84*
Bristol	147 477 82 204 81 362 370 125 493 122 / *237 768 132 328 130 583 595 201 793 196*
Cambridge	169 116 438 154 208 100 306 357 214 471 54 / *272 187 705 248 335 161 493 575 344 758 87*
Cardiff	190 45 182 483 117 209 103 368 382 105 505 157 / *306 72 293 778 188 336 166 592 615 169 813 253*
Carlisle	289 264 277 370 196 343 87 196 87 93 224 221 301 / *465 425 446 596 316 552 140 315 140 150 360 356 484*
Doncaster	142 209 116 175 236 310 235 94 184 235 176 344 171 / *229 336 187 282 380 499 378 151 151 296 378 283 554 275*
Dover	242 389 238 125 202 82 553 174 312 194 424 478 297 588 71 / *390 626 383 201 325 132 890 280 502 312 683 769 478 947 114*
Dundee	523 275 152 441 406 517 52 495 239 349 117 574 642 381 374 448 / *842 443 245 710 654 692 832 84 797 385 562 182 188 605 108 721*
Edinburgh	56 462 219 96 385 345 373 456 91 439 183 292 57 73 320 125 390 / *90 744 352 154 620 555 600 734 146 707 295 470 92 117 515 201 628*
Exeter	450 518 248 251 353 121 249 76 184 550 82 282 157 428 446 201 569 181 / *724 834 399 404 568 195 401 122 296 885 132 454 253 689 718 323 916 291*
Fishguard	230 399 460 331 247 297 112 270 154 291 493 222 209 170 371 373 56 504 260 / *370 642 740 533 398 478 180 435 248 468 794 357 336 274 597 600 90 811 418*
Fort William	486 560 144 127 596 357 206 485 479 575 125 539 296 665 205 308 665 205 149 510 / *782 901 232 204 959 575 332 781 771 782 926 201 867 476 631 306 214 692 240 821*
Glasgow	101 376 449 44 83 488 249 96 385 372 373 468 110 439 183 292 101 33 320 145 397 / *163 605 723 71 134 786 401 154 620 599 600 753 177 707 295 470 163 53 515 233 639*
Gloucester	346 454 153 111 349 410 191 150 247 56 123 35 159 443 99 174 56 318 330 102 468 109 / *557 731 246 179 562 660 307 241 398 90 198 56 256 713 159 280 90 512 531 164 753 175*
Great Yarmouth	225 419 527 366 335 386 484 185 167 320 284 82 275 180 477 240 252 180 345 402 294 517 128 / *362 674 848 589 539 621 779 298 269 515 457 132 443 290 768 386 406 290 555 647 473 832 206*
Harwich	82 196 432 543 337 279 413 469 125 194 336 246 67 217 128 504 387 372 425 281 535 76 / *132 316 695 874 542 449 665 755 201 312 541 396 108 349 206 811 301 443 269 599 684 452 861 122*
Holyhead	349 334 191 330 438 167 282 333 394 360 181 231 216 270 206 334 426 288 141 148 311 305 111 439 269 / *562 538 307 531 705 269 454 536 634 580 291 372 348 435 332 538 686 463 227 238 501 491 179 707 433*
Inverness	474 569 553 504 166 66 542 618 158 132 622 383 262 549 505 539 617 75 372 458 114 357 588 52 / *763 916 890 811 267 106 872 995 254 212 1001 617 422 884 813 867 993 121 961 560 737 346 320 782 169 885*
John o' Groats	129 603 693 677 628 295 195 671 744 285 259 746 507 391 680 630 668 741 202 724 478 574 342 328 601 232 663 / *208 970 1116 1090 1011 475 314 1080 1197 459 417 1201 816 629 1094 1014 1075 1193 325 1165 769 924 550 528 967 373 1067*
Kingston upon Hull	518 394 231 196 207 169 254 369 280 309 234 295 256 47 377 394 127 204 216 298 404 359 586 / *834 634 372 316 333 272 409 594 451 497 377 475 412 76 254 393 224 375 394 526 425 204 216 298 404 359 586*
Kyle of Lochalsh	445 189 84 514 611 602 528 179 79 567 628 216 186 671 432 275 564 555 552 651 159 618 372 471 263 212 499 189 586 / *716 304 135 827 983 969 850 288 127 913 1011 348 299 1080 695 443 908 893 888 1048 256 995 599 758 423 341 803 304 943*
Land's End	763 421 868 741 405 390 446 235 123 574 642 381 378 922 1104 568 198 924 1033 613 602 768 394 602 322 496 1070 330 652 281 552 / *1228 678 1397 1193 652 628 718 378 922 1104 568 198 924 1033 613 602 768 394 602 322 496 1070 330 652 452 888 917 504 1114 478*
Leeds	405 394 55 487 360 176 223 196 174 215 329 237 270 202 258 260 29 119 232 145 194 260 293 255 72 113 156 212 169 327 189 / *652 634 89 784 579 283 359 315 280 346 530 381 435 325 415 418 47 192 373 233 312 419 472 410 116 182 251 341 272 526 304*
Leicester	95 320 500 102 588 461 190 147 140 85 314 422 209 196 296 349 185 74 206 154 68 120 166 389 158 140 39 252 299 153 414 97 / *153 515 805 164 947 742 306 237 225 137 505 679 336 315 477 562 298 119 332 248 109 193 267 626 254 225 63 406 481 246 666 156*
Lincoln	51 68 371 476 44 554 427 216 155 128 159 291 399 272 247 258 314 202 39 191 208 85 183 197 357 209 128 90 224 274 396 383 131 / *82 109 597 766 71 892 687 348 249 206 256 468 642 438 398 415 505 325 63 307 335 137 295 317 575 336 206 145 360 441 320 616 211*
Liverpool	129 130 75 361 407 130 511 382 102 265 240 140 216 329 160 237 216 286 289 86 120 166 389 158 273 381 348 460 481 138 193 272 312 259 / *208 209 121 581 655 209 822 615 164 427 386 225 348 530 257 381 348 460 481 138 193 272 312 259 438 512 377 79 150 352 343 167 549 325*
Manchester	35 84 92 40 406 95 500 373 124 228 212 126 215 329 197 236 215 285 266 61 119 183 165 161 257 318 252 48 80 196 212 129 340 / *56 135 148 64 581 654 153 805 600 200 367 341 203 346 530 317 380 346 459 444 98 192 295 266 259 414 512 365 77 129 315 341 208 547 298*
Newcastle upon Tyne	132 168 159 187 92 498 318 132 395 268 272 308 281 266 148 253 329 364 110 166 358 114 17 325 241 299 352 201 347 129 207 64 149 257 235 / *212 270 256 301 148 802 512 212 636 431 438 496 452 428 238 407 529 586 177 267 576 183 92 523 388 481 567 323 558 208 333 103 240 414 378 460*
Norwich	264 185 220 105 119 176 421 582 149 65 529 311 73 20 204 385 504 343 308 366 422 174 147 289 262 62 252 175 457 214 232 166 328 382 276 496 114 / *425 298 354 169 192 283 678 937 240 1053 852 501 117 32 328 620 811 552 496 589 679 280 237 465 422 100 406 282 735 344 373 267 528 615 444 798 183*
Nottingham	130 157 73 98 35 25 70 345 479 90 557 430 185 150 153 110 293 401 220 221 262 328 205 43 94 192 83 145 193 353 183 111 50 221 274 164 393 122 / *209 253 118 158 56 40 113 555 771 145 896 692 298 241 246 177 472 646 354 358 422 528 330 69 312 277 134 233 311 568 295 179 80 356 441 264 633 196*
Oban	390 492 233 307 308 387 419 307 665 128 346 244 117 427 524 515 441 92 49 481 594 123 117 528 346 188 477 468 465 565 141 530 285 384 180 94 412 178 499 / *628 792 375 494 496 623 674 494 1070 206 557 393 188 687 843 829 710 148 79 774 884 198 188 942 557 303 768 753 748 910 227 853 459 618 290 151 663 286 803*
Oxford	462 109 145 260 144 172 137 73 168 274 550 192 656 532 238 145 200 52 356 472 205 156 372 433 141 145 260 108 82 74 108 465 90 187 64 325 154 483 / *744 175 233 418 232 277 221 117 270 441 885 309 1056 856 383 233 322 84 573 760 330 251 599 697 227 233 418 174 134 119 174 749 145 301 103 521 248 777*
Plymouth	199 587 267 343 410 283 283 293 242 316 95 495 595 264 46 496 552 300 297 399 167 293 122 224 587 128 328 203 474 615 / *320 945 430 552 660 455 455 472 389 509 143 1085 571 1271 1069 528 497 588 253 797 958 425 74 798 888 483 478 642 269 472 196 361 945 206 528 327 763 792 990 351*
Portsmouth	176 77 545 191 207 337 236 254 201 162 257 259 633 269 737 613 311 166 221 119 448 555 251 135 453 514 130 348 142 232 156 77 881 84 547 227 645 692 357 901 113 / *283 124 877 307 333 542 380 409 323 261 414 417 1019 433 1186 987 501 267 356 192 721 893 404 217 729 827 209 560 229 373 251 124*
Sheffield	230 283 135 339 37 146 125 38 62 361 427 105 837 623 270 301 166 203 399 560 346 381 378 468 394 29 245 312 193 259 364 515 348 138 122 306 394 256 579 256 / *370 455 217 546 60 235 201 61 116 74 100 53 581 687 105 837 270 301 166 203 399 560 346 381 378 468 394 29 245 312 193 259 364 515 348 138 122 306 394 256 579 256*
Shrewsbury	82 207 225 106 364 93 201 69 58 133 84 109 303 451 169 567 438 113 240 225 77 272 382 145 179 274 330 251 109 176 119 159 163 265 269 77 399 160 / *132 333 362 171 586 150 330 323 111 93 214 135 175 488 726 272 912 705 182 386 362 124 438 615 233 288 441 531 404 175 283 191 256 262 427 433 124 642 258*
Southampton	185 199 21 151 64 530 176 260 324 221 239 204 135 228 618 256 723 818 609 412 289 354 169 697 541 235 169 705 805 230 336 521 195 238 122 98 856 140 50 404 206 624 671 323 880 124 / *298 320 34 243 103 853 283 332 521 356 385 328 220 373 367 995 412 1164 963 472 264 354 169 697 541 235 169 705 805 230 336 521 195 238 122 98 856 140 50 404 206 624 671 323 880 124*
Stranraer	445 277 263 461 500 379 314 290 403 158 220 221 298 330 220 585 263 306 379 342 338 410 426 343 84 195 392 454 124 167 496 257 101 390 379 375 194 444 188 297 170 73 507 194 / *716 446 423 742 805 610 238 467 649 254 354 356 480 531 354 942 423 492 610 422 544 660 686 552 135 314 631 731 200 478 274 82 523 367 610 608 761 613 715 303 478 274 82 523 367 194*
Swansea	417 161 182 166 158 182 195 233 177 248 385 176 248 201 189 217 330 261 287 194 250 282 34 121 244 165 622 285 269 96 130 148 214 195 319 207 / *671 259 190 349 293 332 227 815 309 485 559 301 314 375 285 399 459 956 425 1120 921 296 430 530 143 658 798 108 259 663 761 441 373 497 66 365 137 357 813 269 348 192 616 610 117 816 312*
York	272 222 258 133 52 278 333 181 309 77 181 84 64 99 75 108 24 411 407 37 479 352 204 228 201 189 217 330 261 287 194 250 282 34 121 244 165 622 285 269 96 130 148 214 195 319 207 / *438 357 415 214 84 448 536 291 497 124 291 135 103 159 121 174 39 661 655 60 771 566 328 367 323 304 349 531 420 462 312 402 454 55 195 393 266 443 458 154 209 238 344 314 513 333*

Key to road map pages

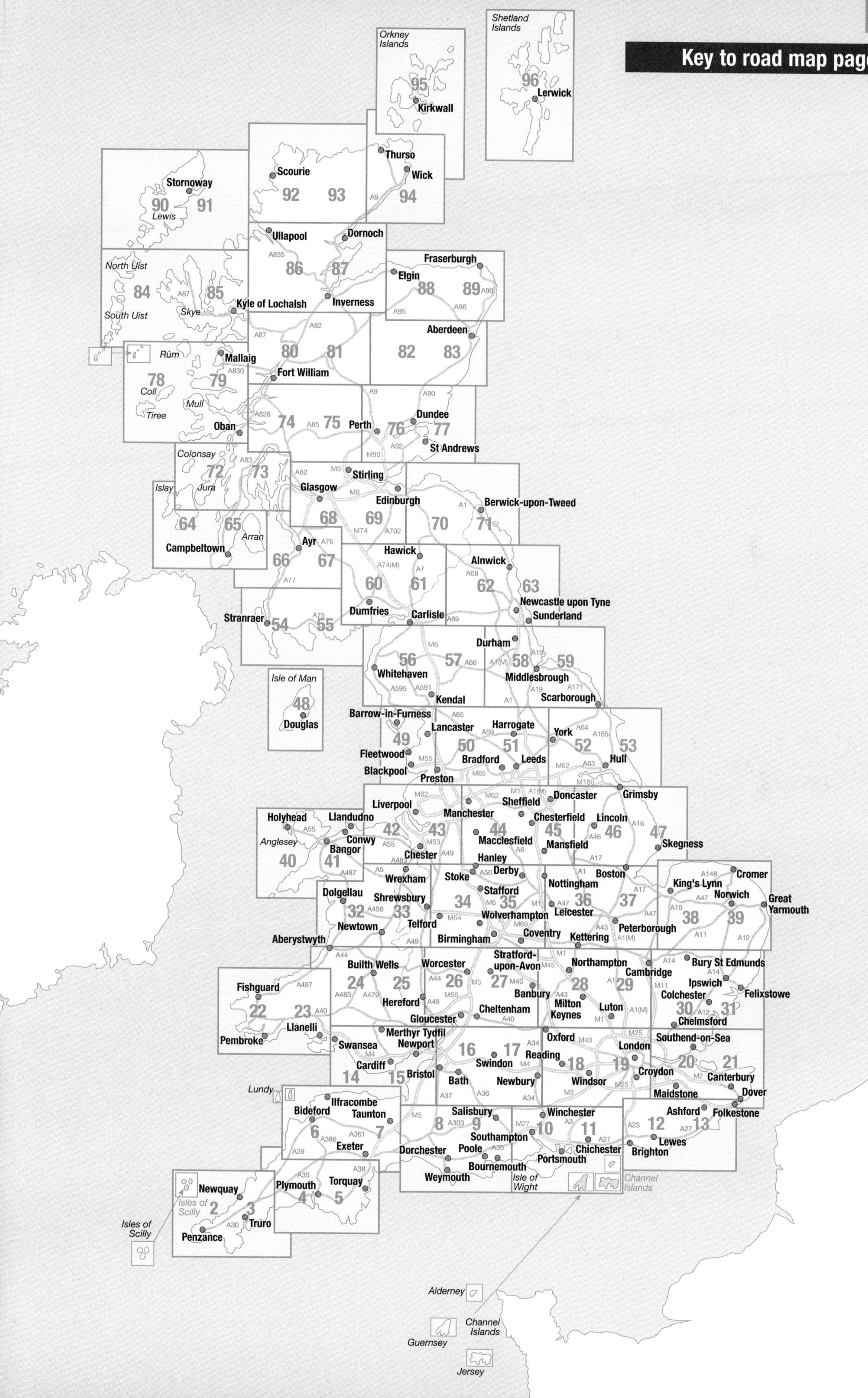
Orkney Islands
95
Kirkwall
Shetland Islands
96
Lerwick
Thurso
Wick
94
A9
Scourie
92
93
Stornoway
90
91
Lewis
Ullapool
Dornoch
A835
86
87
Fraserburgh
Elgin
88
89
A90
A96
A95
Inverness
North Uist
84
85
A87
Skye
South Uist
Kyle of Lochalsh
Aberdeen
A87
A82
80
81
82
83
Rùm
Mallaig
A830
Fort William
78
Coll
79
Mull
Tiree
A828
74
A85
75
Perth
76
77
Dundee
A9
A90
A92
M90
St Andrews
Oban
Colonsay
72
73
A83
Jura
Islay
A82
M9
Stirling
Glasgow
M8
Edinburgh
A1
Berwick-upon-Tweed
64
65
Arran
68
69
70
71
M74
A702
Campbeltown
Ayr
A76
66
67
A77
Hawick
A74(M)
A7
60
61
Alnwick
A68
62
63
Newcastle upon Tyne
Sunderland
Stranraer
54
A75
55
Dumfries
Carlisle
A69
Durham
M6
56
57
A66
A1(M)
58
A19
59
Whitehaven
Middlesbrough
A595
A591
Kendal
A1
A19
A171
Scarborough
Isle of Man
48
Douglas
Barrow-in-Furness
A65
Lancaster
Harrogate
A59
York
A64
A165
49
50
51
52
53
Fleetwood
M55
Bradford
Leeds
M62
A63
Hull
Blackpool
Preston
M65
M180
M62
M1
A1(M)
Doncaster
Grimsby
Liverpool
M62
Manchester
Sheffield
Chesterfield
Lincoln
A16
Holyhead
A55
Llandudno
42
43
44
45
46
47
Conwy
Macclesfield
Mansfield
A46
Skegness
Anglesey
A55
M53
A6
40
41
Bangor
A483
Chester
A49
Hanley
A17
A487
A5
Wrexham
Stoke
A50
Derby
A1
Boston
A148
Cromer
Nottingham
A17
King's Lynn
Dolgellau
Shrewsbury
Stafford
A47
Norwich
Great Yarmouth
32
A458
33
34
M6
35
M1
A47
36
37
A10
38
39
Leicester
A47
Newtown
Telford
M54
Wolverhampton
M69
A43
Peterborough
A11
A12
Aberystwyth
A49
Birmingham
Coventry
Kettering
A1(M)
A44
Builth Wells
Worcester
Stratford-upon-Avon
M45
M1
Northampton
A14
Bury St Edmunds
Cambridge
A14
Fishguard
A487
24
25
A44
26
M5
27
M40
28
A1
29
M11
Ipswich
A483
A479
Hereford
M50
Banbury
A43
Colchester
Felixstowe
22
23
A40
A49
Cheltenham
Milton Keynes
Luton
A1(M)
30
A12
31
Llanelli
Gloucester
A40
M1
Chelmsford
Pembroke
Merthyr Tydfil
Oxford
M40
M25
Southend-on-Sea
Swansea
Newport
16
17
A34
London
M4
Cardiff
Swindon
M4
Reading
18
19
20
21
14
15
Bristol
Croydon
M2
Canterbury
Lundy
Bath
Newbury
Windsor
M25
M3
Maidstone
Ilfracombe
A37
A36
A34
Dover
Bideford
Taunton
Salisbury
Winchester
Ashford
Folkestone
A361
M5
8
A303
9
M27
10
A3
11
A23
12
A27
13
6
7
A386
Southampton
A27
Lewes
A39
Exeter
Dorchester
Poole
A35
Chichester
Brighton
A30
A38
Bournemouth
Portsmouth
Newquay
Plymouth
Torquay
Weymouth
Isle of Wight
Channel Islands
Isles of Scilly
2
3
4
5
A30
Truro
Penzance
Isles of Scilly
Alderney
Channel Islands
Guernsey
Jersey

Isles of Scilly
SV
St Helens
White Island
St Martin's
Bryher
New Grimsby
Higher Town
Tresco
Samson
Eastern Isles
Newford
Maypole
Hugh Town
St Mary's
Old Town
Crim Rocks
Annet
St Agnes
Gugh
Bishop Rock
SW
CORNWALL
MOUNT'S BAY
St Ives
Carbis Bay
Hayle
CAMBORNE
Redruth
Penzance
Newlyn
St Just
LAND'S END
Helston
Porthleven
Mullion
LIZARD POINT
St Agnes
Marazion
Mousehole
Sennen
Zennor
Lizard

3
6
7
8
9
10
11
Camelford
Delabole
Valley Truckle
Helstone
St Clether
Laneast
Polyphant
Altarnun
Trewint
Lewannick
High Moor
ROUGH TOR
BROWN WILLY
Congdon's Shop
Trebartha
North Hill
Codda
Bolventor
MUSEUM OF SMUGGLING
BODMIN MOOR
Dozmary Pool
Colliford Lake
Henwood
KILMAR TOR
Upton Cross
THE HURLERS STONE CIRCLES
Minions
Siblyback Lake
Darite
Commonmoor
GOLITHA FALLS
KING DONIERT'S CIRCLE
Tremar
St Cleer
Merrymeet
Liskeard
Dobwalls
Doublebois
St Pinnock
East Taphouse
West Taphouse
LANHYDROCK HOUSE
Trebyan
RESTORMEL CASTLE
Lostwithiel
Braddock
Herodsfoot
St Keyne
MUSIC MACHINES
Trewidland
Duloe
Sandplace
Morval
Muchlarnick
Pelynt
Looe
East Looe
West Looe
OLD GUILDHALL
Looe Bay
St George's or Looe I.
Talland Bay
Polperro
HERITAGE MUSEUM
Lansallos
Lanreath
Trenewan
Lanteglos Highway
Penpoll
St Veep
Lerryn
Bocaddon
Couch's Mill
Milltown
Golant
Tywardreath
Fowey
Bodinnick
Polruan
Pencarrow Hd.
Gribbin Hd.
Polkerris
Menabilly
ST CATHERINE'S CASTLE
SOUTH WEST COAST PATH
Par
Boscoppa
Carclaze
St Blazey
EDEN PROJECT
Penpillick
Luxulyan
Lanlivery
Sweethouse
Redmoor
Bodmin
BODMIN TOWN MUSEUM
BODMIN AND WENFORD RAILWAY
Lanivet
Nanstallon
St Lawrence
Bodmin Forest
Cardinham
Mount
Warleggan
St Neot
CARNGLAZE SLATE CAVERNS
Ley
Maidenwell
Millpool
Temple
Blisland
Helland
Wenfordbridge
Bradford
St Breward
Row
Michaelstow
Trevighan
St Teath
Port Gaverne
Pendoggett
Port Isaac
Port Isaac Bay
Port Quin
Port Quin Bay
LONG CROSS
Trelights
St Endellion
Trelill
St Tudy
St Kew
St Kew Highway
St Mabyn
PENCARROW HOUSE
Washaway
Wadebridge
Egloshayle
Burlawn
St Breock
Bodieve
Trevanson
Whitecross
Chapel Amble
Trewethern
St Minver
Pityme
Rock
Polzeath
New Polzeath
Trebetherick
Padstow Bay
Pentire Pt.
Gulland Rock
Gunver Hd.
TREVOSE HEAD
Crugmeer
PRIDEAUX PLACE
Trevone
Padstow
NATIONAL LOBSTER HATCHERY
Constantine Bay
Treyarnon
St Merryn
Shop
Porthcothan
Park Hd.
Penrose
St Ervan
Rumford
St Issey
Little Petherick
Tredinnick
St Jidgey
CREALY GREAT ADVENTURE PARK
ST BREOCK DOWNS MONOLITH
St Eval
Trenance
Berryl's Pt.
Trevarrian
St Mawgan
CORNISH BIRDS OF PREY CENTRE
SPIRIT OF THE WEST
Rosenannon
Rutherbridge
Withiel
St Wenn
Talskiddy
Tregurrian
WATERGATE BAY
NEWQUAY
St Columb Major
Tregonetha
Belowda
Victoria
CASTLE AN DINAS
SPRINGFIELDS FUN PARK & PONY CENTRE
Ruthvoes
Towan Hd.
Newquay Bay
Fistral Bay
Porth
St Columb Minor
NEWQUAY ZOO
Trebudannon
Colan
Pentire
Kelsey Hd.
BLUE REEF AQUARIUM
Newquay
Quintrell Downs
Mountjoy
Trevarren
Indian Queens
GOSS MOOR
Tregoss
Roche
Lockengate
Bilberry
Bugle
West Pentire
Crantock
Lane
St Columb Road
Kestle Mill
DAIRY LAND FARM WORLD
Fraddon
Penhale
Trezaise
Hensbarrow Downs
St Dennis
Whitemoor
Stenalees
Penwithick
Trethurgy
HOLYWELL BAY FUN PARK
Holywell
Carines
Cubert
TRERICE
Gummow's Shop
St Newlyn East
LAPPA VALLEY STEAM RAILWAY
St Enoder
Retew
Treviscoe
Nanpean
CHINA CLAY
Carthew
WHEAL MARTYN CHINA CLAY HERITAGE CENTRE
Mount
Rejerrah
Summercourt
Penhale Sands
Rose
PERRAN ROUND
Perranporth
Goonhavern
Newlyn Downs
Mitchell
Brighton
Trethosa
Foxhole
High Street
St Austell
Bolingey
MINIATURA PARK
Carland Cross
Trelassick
St Stephen
Trewoon
Holmbush
SHIPWRECK & HERITAGE CENTRE
Charlestown
ST AUSTELL BREWERY
Zelah
Perranzabuloe
New Mills
Coombe
St Mewan
Polgooth
Porthpean
ST. AUSTELL BAY
St Allen
Callestick
CORNISH CYDER FARM
St Erme
Trispen
Ladock
Grampound Road
Sticker
Hewas Water
TORTOISE GARDEN
Tenarren
Black Hd.
Marazanvose
Allet
Probus
Grampound
TREWITHEN
Creed
THE LOST GARDENS OF HELIGAN
Pentewan
Mevagissey Bay
Shortlanesend
Tresillian
St Ewe
Kestle
WORLD OF MODEL RAILWAYS
Mevagissey
Truro
Kenwyn
CATHEDRAL
Merther
Tresawle
Polmassick
Tregony
Portmellon
Chapel Pt.
Chacewater
Threemilestone
ROYAL CORNWALL MUS
Baldhu
St Clement
Kea
Malpas
Ruan Lanihorne
Trevarrick
Gorran Churchtown
St Michael Caerhays
Gorran Haven
Twelve Heads
Bissoe
Playing Place
Old Kea
St Michael Penkevil
Lamorran
Treworga
Portholland
Boswinger
Penare
Dodman Pt.
Carnon Downs
Trelissick
Philleigh
Veryan Bay
Perranarworthal
Penpol
Devoran
Feock
TRELISSICK
Veryan
Portloe
Treworlas
Carne
Gerrans Bay
Nare Hd.
Ponsanooth
Burnthouse
Mylor Bridge
St Just in Roseland
Trewithian
Gerrans
Portscatho
Penryn
Flushing
Mabe Burnthouse
Falmouth
NATIONAL MARITIME
ART GALLERY
St Mawes
Bohortha
Greeb Pt.
Budock Water
Treverva
Pendennis Pt.
PENDENNIS CASTLE
Zone Pt.
Penjerrick
Falmouth Bay
Mawnan Smith
Rosemullion Hd.
GLENDURGAN
TREBAH
Mawnan
Helford Passage
Helford River
Helford
St Anthony-in-Meneage
Nare Pt.
Manaccan
Porthallow
Tregidden
Porthoustock
St Keverne
Manacle Pt.
The Manacles
Lowland Pt.
Coverack
COVERACK
Chynhalls Pt.
Black Hd.
C O R N W A L L
SX
A30
A38
A39
A390
A391
A392
A3058
A3059
A3075
A3076
A3078
A3082
A389
B3266
B3267
B3268
B3269
B3274
B3275
B3276
B3279
B3285
B3287
B3289
B3314
B3359
C
D
E
F
G
H

4
BUDE
BAY
Widemouth Bay
Widemouth Sand
Dizzard Pt.
CORNWALL
Cambeak
Fire Beacon Pt.
Boscastle
Tintagel Hd.
Tintagel
Start Pt.
Port Isaac Bay
Port Gaverne
Camelford
Delabole
Trevalga
Bossiney
Treknow
Trewarmett
Trebarwith
Davidstow
Davidstow Moor
Crowdy Res.
High Moor
Rough Tor
Brown Willy
Garrow Tor
BODMIN MOOR
Dozmary Pool
Colliford Lake
Siblyback Lake
Bolventor
Altarnun
Trewint
Five Lanes
Codda
Temple
Blisland
St Breward
St Tudy
St Kew
St Kew Highway
St Mabyn
Helland
Wenfordbridge
Michaelstow
St Teath
Helstone
Valley Truckle
Bodmin
Bodmin Forest
Nanstallon
Washaway
St Lawrence
Lanivet
Lanhydrock House
Cardinham
Warleggan
Mount
St Neot
Ley
Millpool
Maidenwell
Minions
Upton Cross
Rilla Mill
Henwood
Kilmar Tor
Caradon Hill
Darite
Commonmoor
Tremar
St Cleer
Dobwalls
Doublebois
Liskeard
East Taphouse
West Taphouse
Braddock
Lostwithiel
Restormel Castle
Lanlivery
Luxulyan
Lockengate
Bilberry
Stenalees
Penwithick
Trethurgy
St Blazey
Par
St. Austell
Charlestown
Holmbush
Boscoppa
Carclaze
Porthpean
ST. AUSTELL BAY
Gribbin Hd.
Fowey
Polruan
Bodinnick
Golant
Tywardreath
Pencarrow Hd.
Trenarren
Black Hd.
Pentewan
Mevagissey
World of Model Railways
Chapel Pt.
Gorran Haven
Lerryn
Penpoll
St Veep
Lanteglos Highway
Bocaddon
Lanreath
Herodsfoot
St Keyne
Trewidland
Duloe
Sandplace
Morval
Muchlarnick
Pelynt
Trenewan
Lansallos
Polperro
Talland Bay
Looe
East Looe
West Looe
Looe Bay
St George's or Looe I.
St Martin
Monkey Sanctuary
Downderry
Seaton
Hessenford
Widegates
Tideford
Tideford Cross
Menheniot
Pengover Green
Merrymeet
Quethiock
St Ive
Pensilva
Gang
Callington
Kelly Bray
Kit Hill
St Ann's Chapel
Gunnislake
Drakewalls
Albaston
Harrowbarrow
Calstock
St Dominick
Cotehele
Bere Alston
TAMAR VALLEY
Weir Quay
Bere Ferrers
Tamerton Foliot
Landulph
Cargreen
Botusfleming
Hatt
Pillaton
St Mellion
Newbridge
Landrake
Trematon
Saltash
St Stephens
St Germans
St Erney
Polbathic
Sheviock
Crafthole
Portwrinkle
Whitsand Bay
Antony
Torpoint
Devonport
St John
Millbrook
Freathy
Kingsand
Cawsand
Rame
Rame Hd.
Penlee Pt.
Cremyll
Mount Edgcumbe
Drake's I.
The Sound
Plymouth
Plymstock
Plympton
Staddiscombe
Hooe
Bovisand Bay
Down Thomas
Heybrook Bay
Wembury
Wembury Bay
Great Mew Stone
Roscoff 6:00
Santander 20:00
(Mar-Nov)
Launceston
Tregadillett
St Stephen's
Dutson
Polyphant
Lewannick
South Petherwin
Daw's House
Trewen
Laneast
St Clether
Tresmeer
Treneglos
Hallworthy
Warbstow
Canworthy Water
Otterham
Marshgate
Trelash
Trespararrett
Tresparrett Posts
Crackington Haven
St Gennys
Rosecare
Jacobstow
Wainhouse Corner
Trewint
Tregole
Poundstock
Millook
Coppathorne
Treskinnick Cross
Week St Mary
Whitstone
North Tamerton
Marhamchurch
Bridgerule
Pyworthy
Holsworthy
Derril
Derriton
Chasty
Whimble
Hollacombe
Brandis Corner
Highampton
Graddon Moor
Halwill Junction
Halwill
Beaworthy
Northlew
Oak Cross
Patchacott
Ashbury
BROADBURY
Leworthy
Clawton
Quoditch
Tetcott
Lana
Luffincott
Ashwater
Henford
Chapmans Well
Virginstow
Germansweek
Eworthy
Boasley Cross
Thorndon Cross
Sourton
Roadford Res.
Gnnacombe Moor
Bratton Clovelly
Northcott
East Panson
St Giles on the Hth.
Gridley Corner
Broadwoodwidger
Boyton
Bennacott
Brazacott
Maxworthy
West Curry
South Wheatley
Langdon
North Petherwin
Bridgetown
Werrington
Yeolmbridge
Egloskerry
Langore
Tregeare
Piper's Pool
Cold Northcott
Tremaine
Liftondown
Lifton
Tinhay
Portgate
Stowford
Thrushelton
Lewdown
Lewtrenchard
Bridestowe
Shortacombe
Lydford
Coryton
Chillaton
Kelly
Bradstone
Lawhitton
Milton Abbot
Dunterton
Rezare
Trekenner
Lezant
Treburley
Trebullett
Coad's Green
Congdon's Shop
Trebartha
North Hill
Bathpool
Bray Shop
Linkinhorne
Stoke Climsland
South Hill
Golberdon
Trevigro
Haye
Downgate
Luckett
Latchley
Chilsworthy
Horsebridge
Sydenham Damerel
Lamerton
Tavistock
Gulworthy
Whitchurch
Grenofen
Mary Tavy
Peter Tavy
North Brentor
Black Down
Willsworthy
Horndon
Cudliptown
Wilminstone
Merrivale
Sampford Spiney
Higher Walreddon
Horrabridge
Walkhampton
Buckland Monachorum
Crapstone
Yelverton
Milton Combe
Lopwell
Clearbrook
Shaugh Prior
Bickleigh
Roborough
Lydford Gorge
Sourton Cross Services
Tamar Otter & Wildlife Centre
Hidden Valley Discovery Park
Trethorne Leisure Farm
Dingle's Fairground Heritage Centre
Launceston Steam Railway
The Arthurian Centre
Cornwall at War
Museum of Smuggling
The Hurlers Stone Circles
Golitha Falls
King Doniert's Circle
Trethevy Quoit
Carnglaze Slate Caverns
Bodmin Town Museum
Bodmin and Wenford Railway
Magnificent Music Machines
Shipwreck & Heritage Centre
St Austell Brewery
Eden Project
St Catherine's Castle
Old Guildhall
Heritage Museum
Penhallam
Winsford Walled Garden
Old Post Office
Saltash Services
Mary Newman's Cottage
Antony House
Merchant's House
Royal Citadel
Saltram
South West Coast Path
0 1 2 3 4 5 6 miles
0 1 2 3 4 5 6 7 8 9 10 km

5
Okehampton
Exbourne
Jacobstowe
Honeychurch
Sampford Courtenay
North Tawton
Zeal Monachorum
Down St Mary
Copplestone
Newbuildings
Sandford
Nymet Tracey
Bow
Coleford
Colebrooke
Knowle
Crediton
THE COLLEGIATE CHURCH OF THE HOLY CROSS
Yeoford
Hillerton
Uton
Hookway
Venny Tedburn
Newton St Cyres
Hittisleigh
Spreyton
Itton
Taw Green
Inwardleigh
Folly Gate
DARTMOOR RAILWAY
Sticklepath
FINCH FOUNDRY
South Tawton
South Zeal
Belstone
Whiddon Down
Cheriton Bishop
Crockernwell
Tedburn St Mary
Whitestone
Meldon
Okehampton Camp
CASTLE
BRACKEN TOR
Okehampton Common
COSDON HILL
YES TOR
HIGH WILLHAYS
Drewsteignton
CASTLE DROGO
Sandypark
Easton
Wonson
Gidleigh
Murchington
Chagford
Teigncombe
Frenchbeer
Longdown
Dunsford
Doccombe
Moretonhampstead
Bridford
Bridfordmills
Christow
Doddiscombsleigh
Higher Ashton
Lower Ashton
Trusham
OKEMENT HILL
HANGINGSTONE HILL
DARTMOOR
DARTMOOR NATIONAL PARK
Lettaford
THE MINIATURE PONY CENTRE
North Bovey
CUT HILL
SITTAFORD TOR
GRIMSPOUND
HAMELDOWN TOR
Manaton
Lustleigh
Water
POSTBRIDGE INFORMATION CENTRE
Postbridge
ROUGH TOR
HOUND TOR
EAST DARTMOOR WOODS & HEATHS
CANONTEIGN FALLS
Hennock
Bovey Tracey
Chudleigh Knighton
Chudleigh
UGBROOKE HOUSE
Bellever
WISTMAN'S WOOD
GT. MIS TOR
PREHISTORIC SETTLEMENT
Two Bridges
Rundlestone
HIGH MOORLAND VISITOR CENTRE
Princetown
Widecombe in the Moor
Bonehill
Haytor Vale
HAYTOR INFORMATION CENTRE
Brimley
Ilsington
RIPPON TOR
Heathfield
CRAFT CENTRE
Liverton
Coldeast
STOVER
TRAGO MILLS
Sigford
Ponsworthy
Dartmeet
Hexworthy
Poundsgate
Buckland in the Moor
Whiteworks
Bickington
Kingsteignton
Highweek
NEWTON ABBOT
BRADLEY
Wolborough
RIVER DART ADVENTURES
Ashburton
West Ogwell
East Ogwell
PRICKLY BALL HEDGEHOG HOSPITAL
DECOY
Abbotskerswell
Holne
Woodland
Denbury
Burrator Res.
Sheepstor
RYDER'S HILL
BUCKFAST ABBEY
Buckfast
Forder Grn.
Torbryan
Ipplepen
North Whilborough
UPPER PLYM VALLEY
Buckfastleigh
Landscove
BUCKFAST BUTTERFLIES & DARTMOOR OTTER SANCTUARY
Broadhempston
Dean
Staverton
Dean Prior
PENNYWELL FARM & WILDLIFE CENTRE
Dartington
DARTINGTON CIDER PRESS CENTRE
DARTINGTON HALL
SHELL TOP
Ugborough Moor
DENDLES WOOD
Didworthy
Wotter
Lee Moor
Rattery
Shinner's Bridge
SOUTH DEVON RAILWAY
Totnes
CASTLE
Cott
Tigley
Berry Pomeroy
BERRY POMEROY CASTLE
South Brent
Drakeland Corner
Lutton
Cornwood
Harford
UGBOROUGH BEACON
Cheston
Bittaford
Avonwick
Lincombe
Harberton
Belsford
Sparkwell
Lee Mill
Ivybridge
Ugborough
North Huish
Diptford
Harbertonford
Ashprington
Tuckenhay
Cornworthy
Crabadon
Washbourne
Dittisham
Westlake
Ermington
Curtisknowle
Halwell
Allaleigh
Capton
Brixton
Yealmpton
Brownston
Modbury
Moreleigh
WOODLANDS LEISURE PARK
Blackawton
Dartmouth
Kingswear
NEWCOMEN ENGINE HOUSE
Woodford
Millcombe
Warfleet
BAYARDS COVE FORT
DARTMOUTH CASTLE
Holbeton
Luson
Battisborough Cross
Mothecombe
Loddiswell
Woodleigh
East Allington
Bowden
Stoke Fleming
Kingston
St Ann's Chapel
Aveton Gifford
SORLEY TUNNEL ADVENTURE WORLDS
Strete
Blackpool
Ringmore
Bigbury
SOUTH WEST COAST PATH
Stoke Pt.
Goveton
Churchstow
West Alvington
Kingsbridge
Harleston
Slapton
Sherford
Frittiscombe
SLAPTON LEY
Stokenham
Frogmore
Chillington
Charleton
Slapton Sands
Torcross
Bigbury on Sea
Burgh I.
BIGBURY BAY
Bantham
Buckland
Thurlestone
South Milton
Woolston
Kernborough
Beeson
Beesands
Galmpton
Hope
Malborough
South Pool
Kellaton
Bolt Tail
Bolberry
Salcombe
East Portlemouth
South Allington
Hallsands
Soar
OVERBECKS MUSEUM AND GARDEN
START POINT
East Prawle
Lannacombe Bay
Bolt Hd.
Prawle Pt.
START BAY
SOUTH DEVON
Exeter
EXETER
CATHEDRAL
St Thomas
Alphington
Countess Wear
Ide
Wheatley
Cowley
Exwick
Pinhoe
Whipton
Heavitree
Upton Pyne
Brampford Speke
Stoke Canon
Rewe
Poltimore
Thorverton
Up Exe
Nether Exe
Efford
Shute
Shobrooke
Sweetham
Stockleigh Pomeroy
FURSDON HOUSE
Silverton
Bradninch
Ellerhayes
KILLERTON HOUSE
Hele
Westcott
Langford
Clyst Hydon
Tale
Colestock
Clyst St Lawrence
Budlake
Westwood
Talaton
Broadclyst
ESCOT PARK
Dog Village
Jack in the Green
Whimple
Rockbeare
Clyst Honiton
EXETER INTERNATIONAL
Sowton
EXETER SERVICES
Clyst St Mary
Marsh Green
West Hill
Aylesbeare
Farringdon
Venn Ottery
Harpford
Clyst St George
ADVENTURE PARK
CREALY
Woodbury Salterton
Hawkerland
Ebford
Woodbury
Colaton Raleigh
Topsham
MUS.
Exton
Exminster
Shillingford St George
Kennford
Kenn
Powderham
ROWDERHAM CASTLE
Kenton
Starcross
Lympstone
A LA RONDE
BLACK HILL
BICTON PARK
Yettington
Otterton
Withycombe Raleigh
Knowle
Budleigh
Budleigh Salterton
FAIRLYNCH ARTS CENTRE AND MUSEUM
Littleham
Exmouth
WORLD OF COUNTRY LIFE
EXMOUTH MODEL RAILWAY
Straight Pt.
EXETER
Cockwood
DAWLISH WARREN
Dawlish Warren
Ashcombe
Ideford
Luton
Little Haldon
Dawlish
Holcombe
Bishopsteignton
Teignmouth
Shaldon
SHALDON WILDLIFE TRUST
Preston
Teigngrace
Combeinteignhead
Netherton
Stokeinteignhead
PLANT WORLD
SOUTH WEST COAST PATH
BABBACOMBE BAY
Coffinswell
Kingskerswell
Maidencombe
Barton
Watcombe
MODEL VILLAGE
Babbacombe
Shiphay
Torquay
Torre
TORRE ABBEY
KENT'S CAVERN PREHISTORIC CAVES
Wellswood
Hope's Nose
LIVING COASTS
Compton
COMPTON CASTLE
Cockington
Marldon
OLDWAY MANSION
Hollicombe
Blagdon
Torbay
KIRKHAM
Paignton
PAIGNTON & DARTMOUTH STEAM RAILWAY
TORBAY
TOR BAY
Collaton St Mary
ZOO
Stoke Gabriel
Goodrington
GOLDEN HIND
Brixham
BERRY HEAD
Berry Head
Galmpton
Churston Ferrers
St Mary's Bay
RIVER DART
Sharkham Pt.
Hillhead
Scabbacombe Hd.
COLETON FISHACRE
Mew Stone
D
E
F
G
H
6
7
8
9
10
11

6
1
2
3
4
5
A
B
C
D
E
F
G
H
North West Point
North East Point
LUNDY
LUNDY MARINE NATURE RESERVE
142
ILFRACOMBE 2:00
BIDEFORD 2:00
South West Point
Surf Point
SWANSEA 0:50
LUNDY 2:00
OLD CORN MILL
Rillage Pt.
Combe Martin Bay
Ilfracombe
ILFRACOMBE MUSEUM
WATERMOUTH CASTLE
Hele
Girt Down
Highveer Pt.
Woody Bay
CLIFF RAILWAY
Lynton
Trentishoe
Martinhoe
Heale
LYNTON AND BARNSTAPLE RLY
Barbrook
East Ilkerton
Martinhoe Cross
Shallowford
Bull Pt.
Rockham Bay
Lee
Whitestone
Slade
Berrynarbor
Combe Martin
Sterridge
WILDLIFE & DINOSAUR PARK
Paracombe
Morte Point
Mortehoe
Woolacombe
Trimstone
Cheglinch
Berry Down
Berry Down Cross
Patchole
Kentisbury
Kentisbury Ford
Blackmoor Gate
EXM
Challacombe Common
Challacombe
MORTE BAY
Woolacombe Sand
SOUTH WEST COAST PATH
Dean
Bittadon
West Down
East Down
Churchill
Arlington
ARLINGTON COURT
EXMOOR ZOO
Baggy Pt.
Putsborough
Pickwell
North Buckland
Croyde Bay
Georgeham
Croyde
Nethercott
Darracott
Halsinger
Milltown
Muddiford
Loxhore
Knightacott
Shoulsbarrow Common
Leworthy
Lobb
Saunton
Knowle
Braunton
Pippacott
Marwood
Guineaford
Kingsheanton
BROOMHILL
Shirwell
Shirwell Cross
Bratton Fleming
Stoke Rivers
Benton
Lydcott
ELLIOT GALLERY
MARWOOD HILL GARDENS
Heanton Punchardon
Prixford
Wrafton
TOLL
Saunton Sands
Braunton Burrows
Chivenor
Ashford
Burridge
Goodleigh
Brayford
High Bray
Barnstaple
Pilton
MUSEUM OF NORTH DEVON
Westacott
Gunn
Charles
Fremington
Yelland
Bickington
Bickleton
Newport
P&R
Landkey
Swimbridge Newland
Swimbridge
NORTH DEVON FARM PARK
West Buckland
East Buckland
Bishops Tawton
NORTH DEVON MARITIME MUSEUM
NORTHAM BURROWS
Instow
BIDEFORD BAY
NORTH DEVON
Appledore
TAPELEY PARK GDNS
Westleigh
Westward Ho!
Northam
Tawstock
Filleigh
HARTLAND POINT
Windbury Pt.
Orchard Hill
Eastleigh
Horwood
Newton Tracey
Ensis
Herner
Cobbaton
QUINCE HONEY FARM
Titchberry
THE BIG SHEEP
Abbotsham
Bideford
BURTON ART GALL & MUS
East-the-Water
Woodtown
Hiscott
Chapelton
COBBATON COMBAT COLL
East Stowford
Chittlehampton
HARTLAND ABBEY
CLOVELLY VILLAGE
Clovelly
Handy Cross
Alverdiscott
Fishleigh Barton
South Molton
Stoke
Hartland Quay
Buck's Mills
Fairy Cross
ATLANTIC VILLAGE
Ford
Landcross
Umberleigh
Clapworthy
Hartland
Higher Clovelly
Horns Cross
Woodtown
Yarnscombe
Atherington
173
SOUTH WEST COAST PATH
DOCTON MILL
Philham
Littleham
Warkleigh
George Nympton
Milford
Eddistone
THE MILKY WAY ADVENTURE PARK
Buck's Cross
Goldworthy
Langridge Ford
Satterleigh
ELMSCOTT
Elmscott
Tosberry
Woolfardisworthy
Parkham
Weare Giffard
High Bullen
Sherwood Green
High Bickington
Chittlehamholt
Parkham Ash
Buckland Brewer
Monkleigh
DARTINGTON CRYSTAL
South Hole
Hartland Forest
Alminstone Cross
216
St Giles in the Wood
King's Nympton
Knaps Longpeak
Welcombe
235
Frithelstock
Frithelstock Stone
Great Torrington
Kingscott
Roborough
Cadbury Barton
Tythecott
Taddiport
R.H.S. GARDEN ROSEMOOR
Meddon
Ashmansworthy
Little Torrington
205
Burrington
Elstone
Gooseham
Woolley
East Putford
Eastcott
Youlstone
West Putford
Langtree
Beaford
Higher Sharpnose Pt.
Morwenstow
Dinworthy
GNOME RESERVE & GARDEN
Riddlecombe
Chulmleigh
Shop
Bulkworthy
Stibb Cross
Woodford
Peters Marland
Ashreigney
BROCKLANDS ADVENTURE PARK
Bradworthy
Bradworthy Cross
Abbots Bickington
Newton St Petrock
Woollaton
Winswell
Dolton
Chawleigh
Merton
Huish
Ashley
Coombe
Kilkhampton
Alfardisworthy
Sutcombe
Venn Green
Milton Damerel
Hollocombe
Stibb
Soldon Cross
Buckland Filleigh
170
Petrockstow
Dowland
Wembworthy
DUNSDON
Shebbear
Meeth
138
Iddesleigh
Winkleigh
Brushford
Coldridge
Poughill
Hersham
Holsworthy Beacon
Thornbury
Bradford
Flexbury
1643
Grimscott
Woodacott
Sheepwash
Broadwood Kelly
Bude Haven
Stratton
Chilsworthy
Black Torrington
Monkokehampton
West Leigh
Bude
Pancrasweek
Cookbury
Holemoor
Bondleigh
East Leigh
Launcells
Highampton
Hatherleigh
Zeal Monachorum
Upton
Marhamchurch
Bridgerule
Derril
Derriton
Holsworthy
Brandis Corner
Graddon Moor
Pyworthy
162
Chasty
Whimble
Hollacombe
150
Exbourne
Honeychurch
204
Widemouth Bay
Chilla
193
WINSFORD WALLED GARDEN
Jacobstowe
North Tawton
Sampford Courtenay
Halwill Junction
Coppathorne
Leworthy
Halwill
Beaworthy
Northlew
Inwardleigh
Itton
Clawton
Oak Cross
DARTMOOR RAILWAY
Treskinnick Cross
Whitstone
Patchacott
Ashbury
Folly Gate
Taw Green
Week St Mary
North Tamerton
Quoditch
BROADBURY
Spreyton
PENHALLAM
Tetcott
Lana
Okehampton
Ashwater
Jacobstow
Luffincott
Eworthy
Sticklepath
South Tawton
FINCH FOUNDRY
South Zeal
Henford
Germansweek
Boasley Cross
Thorndon Cross
Belstone
Whiddon Down
South Wheatley
West Curry
Chapmans Well
Virginstow
OKEHAMPTON (Dartmoor)
Maxworthy
Northcott
East Panson
Roadford Res.
Meldon
CASTLE
Okehampton Camp
Bennacott
Boyton
Grinacombe Moor
Bratton Clovelly
SOURTON CROSS SERVICES
BRACKEN TOR
Okehampton Common
550 COSDON HILL
Throwleigh
Canworthy Water
Brazacott
St Giles on the Hth.
Warbstow
TAMAR OTTER & WILDLIFE CENTRE
Langdon
Gridley Corner
619 YES TOR
Sourton
Wonson
Tremaine
Bridgetown
Broadwoodwidger
Bridestowe
BLACKATOR COPSE
621 HIGH WILLHAYS
Gidleigh
North Petherwin
Murchington
Hallworthy
Treneglos
Werrington
Cross Green
Thrushelton
Bridestowe and Sourton Common
585
566 OKEMENT HILL
Chagford
Tresmeer
Yeolmbridge
DINGLE'S FAIRGROUND HERITAGE CENTRE
Stowford
Lewdown
262
Teigncombe
Tregeare
Egloskerry
Langore
Dutson
Liftondown
Portgate
Lewtrenchard
Shortacombe
604 HANGINGSTONE HILL
Frenchbeer
Cold Northcott
HIDDEN VALLEY DISCOVERY PARK
St Stephen's
LAUNCESTON STEAM RAILWAY
Lydford
THE MINIATURE PONY CENTRE
Piper's Pool
Launceston
Lifton
Tinhay
LYDFORD
DARTMOOR
Lettaford
TRETHORNE LEISURE FARM
Tregadillett
CASTLE
St Clether
Laneast
Coryton
LYDFORD GORGE
DARTMOOR
604 CUT HILL
537 SITTAFORD TOR
North Brentor
Black Down
Willsworthy
Lawhitton
Kelly
Chillaton
South Petherwin
FOREST
GRIMSPOUND
0 1 2 3 4 5 6 miles
0 1 2 3 4 5 6 7 8 9 10 km

6
7
8
9
10
11
A
B
C
D
E
F
G
H
Lynmouth Bay
Foreland Pt.
Countisbury
Lynmouth
WATERSMEET HOUSE
Brendon
Malmsmead
Oare
CULBONE HILL
TOLL
Porlock Weir
Porlock Bay
Porlock
Bossington
Hurlstone Pt.
SOUTH WEST COAST PATH
EXMOOR FALCONRY
SELWORTHY BEACON
Allerford
Selworthy
Woodcombe
Minehead
WEST SOMERSET RAILWAY
BUTLINS
Alcombe
West Luccombe
Luccombe
Wootton Courtenay
Periton
Marsh Street
DUNKERY VINEYARD
DOLL MUS.
MINEHEAD
Dunster
DUNSTER CASTLE
MILL & YARN MARKET
Blue Anchor Bay
Blue Anchor
BRIDGWATER
BAY
STERT
Cheriton
Furzehill
EXMOOR
Brendon Common
Holnicote Estate
HAWKCOMBE WOODS
DUNKERY BEACON
THE DUNKERY & HORNER WOOD
OOR FOREST
Pinkworthy Pond
Exe Plain
NATIONAL
Simonsbath
Exe
B3223
Edgcott
Exford
EXFORD
Luckwell Bridge
B3224
Cowbridge
Timberscombe
Cutcombe
Wheddon Cross
BRENDON
FOREST
CROYDON HILL
Carhampton
Withycombe
Old Cleeve
Washford
CLEEVE ABBEY
Bilbrook
Rodhuish
Watchet
MARKET HOUSE MUS
TROPIQUARIA
West Quantoxhead
Williton
Quantoxhead
East
Staple
Kilton
Lilstock
Shurton
Burton
Stolford
Stockland Bristol
Stogursey
Otterhampton
Kilve
Stringston
Holford
Nether Stowey
Fiddington
COLERIDGE COTTAGE
Over Stowey
CANNINGTON COLLEGE
QUANTOCK FOREST
Spaxton
Charlynch
Four Forks
Sampford Brett
Bicknoller
Yard
Monksilver
Vellow
Stogumber
WEST SOMERSET RAILWAY
Crowcombe
Flaxpool
Somerset
Somerset
BRENDON HILLS
Luxborough
Roadwater
Kingsbridge
LYPE HILL
Treborough
COMBE SYDENHAM
Elworthy
Lower Vexford
Willett
Lydeard St Lawrence
West Bagborough
Lower Aisholt
Courtway
Enmore
TEMPLE OF HARMONY
FYNE COURT
Broomfield
Cothelstone
Withypool
Withypool Common
HORSEN HILL
Barle
North Radworthy
North Heasley
South Radworthy
Heasley Mill
WINSFORD HILL
Winsford
Exton
PARK
Liscombe
TARR STEPS
Bridgetown
Hawkridge
Brompton Regis
Withiel Florey
B3224
Clatworthy Res.
Brompton Ralph
Tolland
GAULDEN MANOR
Tarr
East Combe
Combe Florey
Cushuish
Molland Common
Twitchen
Dane's Brook
North Molton
Anstey Common
West Anstey
Molland
East Anstey
Dulverton
B3222
Battleton
Wimbleball Lake
HADDON HILL
Upton
Huish Champflower
Clatworthy
Langley Marsh
Maundown
HEYDON HILL
Wiveliscombe
Fitzhead
Ash Priors
Bishops Lydeard
Fulford
Pickney
Kingston St Mary
HESTERCOMBE GARDENS
Nailsbourne
West Monkton
Cheddon Fitzpaine
Mole
Yeo
Yeo Mill
Nightcott
Brushford
Bury
Skilgate
Chipstable
VALE OF TAUNTON DEANE
Halse
Heathfield
Preston Bowyer
Milverton
Hillcommon
Oake
Norton Fitzwarren
Staplegrove
Bathpool
Bish Mill
Newtown
B3227
Oldways End
Exebridge
Morebath
Petton
Waterrow
Bishops Nympton
Alswear
Ash Mill
Knowstone
Roachill
Bampton
Shillingford
Clayhanger
Bathealton
Hillfarance
East Nynehead
Bradford-on-Tone
Bishop's Hull
Taunton
SOMERSET CRICKET MUS
Mariansleigh
Rose Ash
Oakfordbridge
Oakford
Kittisford
Langford Budville
Nynehead
Runnington
Wellington
SHEPPY'S CIDER
Trull
Staplehay
TAUNTON DEANE SERVICES
Orchard Portman
Thurlbear
Romansleigh
Meshaw
Huntsham
Appley
COTHAY
Thorne St Margaret
Ashbrittle
Rockwell Green
Holywell Lake
West Buckland
Pitminster
Corfe
Creacombe
Rackenford
STOODLEIGH BEACON
Stoodleigh
Cove
Hockworthy
Holcombe Rogus
Sampford Arundel
Wrangway
Ford Street
Angersleigh
Blagdon Hill
Staple Fitzpaine
Week
Lutworthy
Queen Dart
Loxbeare
Washfield
EXE VALLEY
East Mere
Westleigh
Burlescombe
Nicholashayne
BLACKDOWN HILLS
STAPLE HILL
West Worlington
East Worlington
Witheridge
Templeton Bridge
Chevithorne
KNIGHTSHAYES COURT
Bolham
Whitnage
Uplowman
Appledore
Clayhidon
Churchstanton
Fyfett
Rosemary Lane
Culmstock
Culm Valley
Drayford
Nomansland
Templeton
Calverleigh
TIVERTON CASTLE
Chettiscombe
A361
Sampford Peverell
Halberton
Uffculme
COLDHARBOUR MILL
Hemyock
Stapley
Churchinford
Bishopswood
Cheldon
Thelbridge Barton
Washford Pyne
B3137
Cruwys Morchard
Withleigh
Cotteylands
Cowleymoor
Tiverton
GRAND WESTERN CANAL
Craddock
HACKPEN HILL
Bolham Water
Pennymoor
Way Village
Ash Thomas
Smithincott
Ashill
Abbey
Smeatharpe
Marsh
Filleigh
Black Dog
Puddington
Well Town
Willand
DIGGERLAND
Howley
Eastington
Poughill
Blackborough
Newcott
Yarcombe
Lapford
Morchard Bishop
Woolfardisworthy
Upham
Cadeleigh
Butterleigh
BICKLEIGH MILL
Sheldon
Dunkeswell
CULLOMPTON SERVICES
Cullompton
Kentisbeare
Kennerleigh
Stockleigh English
BICKLEIGH CASTLE
Bickleigh
DEVON RAILWAY CENTRE
BLACK DOWN
Upottery
Oldborough
Cheriton Fitzpaine
Luppitt
Rawridge
Ash Bullayne
East Village
Cadbury
FURSDON HOUSE
Colebrook
Dulford
Kerswell
Beacon
Down St Mary
Newbuildings
Stockleigh Pomeroy
Bradninch
Mutterton
Westcott
Broadhembury
Stockland
Millhayes
Copplestone
Sandford
Upton Hellions
Silverton
Norman's Green
Wick
Monkton
Knowle
Thorverton
Up Exe
Hele
Langford
Plymtree
Combe Raleigh
Heathstock
Coleford
THE COLLEGIATE CHURCH OF THE HOLY CROSS
Shobrooke
Efford
Shute
Ellerhayes
Clyst Hydon
Tale
Payhembury
Awliscombe
Buckerell
Cotleigh
Colebrooke
Crediton
Nether Exe
KILLERTON HOUSE
Clyst St Lawrence
Colestocks
Dalwood
Wilmington
Rewe
Sweetham
Brampford Speke
Budlake
Westwood
Talaton
ESCOT PARK
Feniton
Honiton
Offwell
BURROW FARM
Yeoford
Uton
Hookway
Fenny Bridges
Alfington
Gittisham
Venny Tedburn
Newton St Cyres
Stoke Canon
Upton Pyne
Broadclyst
Whimple
Fairmile
Ottery St Mary
Church Green
EAST DEVON
Shute
Kilmington
Hittisleigh
Cowley
Poltimore
Dog Village
Jack in the Green
Northleigh
Farway
Whitford
Tedburn St Mary
Pinhoe
Clyst Honiton
Rockbeare
West Hill
Broad Down
Southleigh
Colyton
Cheriton Bishop
Whitestone
Exwick
Whipton
EXETER INTERNATIONAL
A30
EXETER
CATHEDRAL
Sowton
EXETER SERVICES
Marsh Green
Wiggaton
Crockernwell
Heavitree
Aylesbeare
Tipton St John
Sidbury
BLACKBURY CAMP
Colyford
Drewsteignton
Longdown
B3212
Wheatley
St Thomas
Clyst St Mary
Farringdon
Venn Ottery
Harcombe
Axmouth
Countess Wear
Ide
CREALY
Harpford
Bowd
Sidford
Teign
Dunsford
Alphington
ADVENTURE PARK
Clyst St George
Woodbury Salterton
Newton Poppleford
Weston
Vicarage
BEER QUARRY CAVES
PECORAMA
Seaton
Beer
MARINE HOUSE
Seaton Bay
Shillingford St George
Topsham
Hawkerland
Sid
Salcombe Regis
Branscombe
Beer Hd.
Doccombe
Bridfordmills
Exminster
Woodbury
Colaton Raleigh
Cotmaton
Sidmouth
Moretonhampstead
Bridford
Kennford
Ebford
Exton
BICTON PARK
Yettington
Doddiscombsleigh
Christow
Higher Ashton
Kenn
Otterton
Ladram Bay
Lower Ashton
Powderham
Lympstone
A LA RONDE
East Budleigh
OTTERTON MILL
North Bovey
SOUTH WEST COAST PATH
ROWDERHAM CASTLE
Kenton
Withycombe Raleigh
Knowle
CANONTEIGN FALLS
Trusham
Starcross
Exmouth
Littleham
Budleigh Salterton
Danger Pt.
FAIRLYNCH ARTS CENTRE
Lustleigh
Hanaton
River Exe
A38
A380
A396
A39
A373
A375
A3052
M5
15
8
5

Bawdrip
Stawell
Catcott
POLDEN HILLS
Shapwick
Glastonbury
West Pennard
Pylle
Evercreech
Batcombe
Chilton Trinity
Wembdon
Chedzoy
Sutton Mallet
Moorlinch
Greinton
Ashcott
Walton
Street
Northover
Edgarley
West Bradley
East Pennard
Ditcheat
Lamyatt
Milton Clevedon
North Brewham
South Brewham
Bridgwater
Four Forks
Durleigh
Pedwell
Overleigh
Butleigh Wootton
Parbrook
Ham Street
Baltonsborough
Wraxall
Alhampton
Bruton
Hardway
Enmore
Goathurst
North Petherton
Huntworth
Westonzoyland
Middlezoy
King's Sedge Moor
Butleigh
Hornblotton Green
Sutton
Ansford
Cole
Redlynch
Stoney Stoke
Pitcombe
Temple of Harmony
Fyne Court
Broomfield
Northmoor Green or Moorland
North Newton
Othery
Pathe
Henley
Dundon
Compton Dundon
Barton St David
Southwood
West Lydford
East Lydford
Alford
Castle Cary
Shepton Montague
Charlton Musgrove
Kingston St Mary
Hestercombe Gardens
Thurloxton
High Ham
Stembridge Tower Mill
Littleton
Kingweston
Keinton Mandeville
Lydford-on-Fosse
Lovington
Galhampton
Hadspen Garden
Bratton Seymour
Bayford
Leigh Common
Hedging
Lyng
Burrow-bridge
Stathe
Aller
Low Ham
Charlton Adam
Babcary
North Barrow
Haynes Motor Mus
Yarlington
Wincanton
West Monkton
Durston
Athelney
West Lyng
Pitney
Somerton
Stoke Trister
Cheddon Fitzpaine
Monkton Heathfield
Creech Heathfield
Stoke St Gregory
Langport
Charlton Mackerell
Lytes Cary Manor
South Barrow
North Cadbury
Holton
Staplegrove
Bathpool
North End
Willows & Wetlands Visitor Centre
West Sedge Moor
Huish Episcopi
Sparkford
Maperton
Lattiford
Creech St Michael
Knapp
Curry Rivel
Langport & R Parrett Visitor Centre
Long Sutton
Kingsdon
Cary Fitzpaine
South Cadbury
Compton Pauncefoot
Blackford
North Cheriton
South Cheriton
Taunton
Somerset Cricket Mus
Ruishton
Thornfalcon
North Curry
Drayton
Muchelney
Podimore
West Camel
Queen Camel
Sutton Montis
Horsington
Henlade
Fivehead
Isle
Long Load
Northover
Ilchester
Yeovilton
Fleet Air Arm Mus
Bridgehampton
Chilton Cantelo
Marston Magna
Corton Denham
Charlton Horethorne
Abbas Combe
Stoke St Mary
West Hatch
Wrantage
Hatch Beauchamp
Curry Mallet
Isle Brewers
Isle Abbotts
Hambridge
Kingsbury Episcopi
Stapleton
Limington
Ashington
Rimpton
Sandford Orcas Manor House
Stowell
Temple Combe
Yenston
Henstridge Marsh
Orchard Portman
Thurlbear
Corfe
Beercrocombe
Westport
West Lambrook
East Lambrook
Coat
Martock
Ash
Tintinhull
Tintinhull Garden
Chilthorne Domer
Adber
Mudford
Sandford Orcas
Poyntington
Milborne Wick
Henstridge Ash
Henstridge
Milborne Port
Stalbridge
Staple Fitzpaine
Hatch Green
Puckington
Barrington Court
Barrington
South Petherton
Hurst
Bower Hinton
Stoke sub Hamdon
Montacute House
Yeovil Marsh
Trent
Nether Compton
Over Compton
Oborne
Sherborne
Sherborne Castle
Goathill
Purse Caundle
Stalbridge Weston
Bickenhall
Curland
Staple Hill
Ilton
Ashill
Stocklinch
Shepton Beauchamp
Stoke-sub-Hamdon Priory
Montacute
Preston Plucknett
Yeovil
Windmill Hill
Broadway
Ashwell
Seavington St Michael
Norton sub Hamdon
Odcombe
Brympton
North Wootton
Haydon
Stourton Caundle
Horton
Ilminster
Seavington St Mary
Over Stratton
Ham Hill
Chiselborough
West Coker
Barwick
Bradford Abbas
Alweston
Bishop's Caundle
Lydlinch
Fyfett
Buckland St Mary
Donyatt
Perry's Cider
Lopen
West Chinnock
North Coker
East Coker
Stoford
Thornford
Folke
BLACKMOOR VALE
Crock Street
Dowlish Wake
Kingstone
Dinnington
East Chinnock
Hardington Moor
Hardington Mandeville
Ryme Intrinseca
Lillington
Longburton
Holwell
Woodbridge
King's Stag
Churchinford
Bishopswood
Combe St Nicholas
Hinton St George
Merriott
Beer Hackett
Yetminster
Crouch Hill
Marsh
Whitestaunton
Hornsbury Mill
Cricket Malherbie
Chillington
Cudworth
Haselbury Plucknett
Pendomer
Closworth
Holnest
Wadeford
Chaffcombe
North Perrott
Hardington Marsh
Newcott
Howley
Cricket St Thomas
Wildlife Park
Crewkerne
Leigh
Glanvilles Wootton
Pulham
Hazelbury Bryan
Yarcombe
Wambrook
Chard
Hewish
Misterton
Chetnole
Halstock
Melbury Osmond
Hermitage
Middlemarsh
Whatley
Wayford
Winsham
Clapton
South Perrott
Westfields
Forton
Tatworth
Seaborough
Mosterton
Chedington
Corscombe
West Chelborough
Melbury Sampford
Melbury Bubb
Hilfield
Lyon's Gate
Dungish
Mappowder
South Chard
Drimpton
Evershot
Buckland Newton
Stockland
Furley
Chardstock
Forde Abbey and Gardens
Minterne House & Gardens
Millhayes
Membury
Tytherleigh
Thorncombe
Burstock
Holywell
Minterne Magna
Batcombe
Alton Pancras
Heathstock
Alston
Holditch
The Craft and Design Centre
Broadwindsor
Holm Park
Beaminster
Rampisham
Frome St Quintin
Up Cerne
Plush
Cotleigh
Churchill
Birdsmoorgate
Up Sydling
Cerne Abbas Giant
Cerne Abbas
Dalwood
Smallridge
Hawkchurch
Stoke Abbott
Wraxall
Cattistock
Sydling St Nicholas
Piddletrenthide
Burrow Farm
Weycroft
Marshalsea
Bettiscombe
Netherbury
Mapperton
Hooke
Chilfrome
Axminster
Marshwood
Pilsdon
Melplash
Toller Porcorum
Maiden Newton
Nether Cerne
White Lackington
Piddlehinton
Shute
Kilmington
Shute Barton
North Poorton
Toller Fratrum
Hog Cliff
Godmanstone
Broad Oak
Salwayash
West Milton
Powerstock
Wootton Fitzpaine
Forston
Whitford
Whitchurch Canonicorum
Ryall
Dottery
Nettlecombe
Wynford Eagle
Frampton
Charlton Down
Eggardon Down
Grimstone
Musbury
Morcombelake
Bradpole
Loders
West Compton
Colyton
Uplyme
Charmouth
Symondsbury
Bridport
Uploders
Askerswell
Mucklefold
Stratton
Charminster
Combpyne
Charmouth Heritage Coast Centre
Chideock
Eype
Walditch
Bothenhampton
Kingston Russell
Compton Valence
Bradford Peverell
Dorchester
Stinsford
Colyford
Rousdon
Lyme Regis
Aquarium
Dinosaurland
Seatown
South West Coast Path
Shipton Gorge
Chilcombe
Long Bredy
Winterbourne Abbas
The Tutankhamun Exhibition
Kingston Maurward
Axmouth
Seaton Tramway
Axmouth to Lyme Regis Undercliffs
West Bay
Litton Cheney
Poor Lot Barrows
Nine Stones
Military Museum
The Dinosaur Museum
West Stafford
Pecorama
Seaton
Charlton Bay
Burton Bradstock
Littlebredy
Winterbourne Steepleton
Martinstown
Maiden Castle
Whitcombe
Beer
Marine House
Seaton Bay
LYME BAY
Puncknowle
Valley of Stones
Black Down
Hardy Monument
Winterborne Monkton
Winterborne Herringston
Beer Hd.
Swyre
Kingston Russell Stone Circle
Broadmayne
West Bexington
Portesham
South West Coast Path
SY
Abbotsbury
Sub Tropical Gardens
Abbotsbury Children's Farm
St Catherine's Chapel
Swannery
Rodden
Upwey
Bincombe
White Horse
Poxwell
Preston
Broadwey
Littlemoor
Langton Herring
Nottington
Overcombe
Osmington
Jordan Hill Roman Temple
Osmington Mills
Radipole
CHESIL BEACH
Chickerell
Bennetts Water Gardens
Sea Life
Melcombe Regis
Westham
Weymouth
Charlestown
Nothe Fort
Brewer's Quay and Timewalk
Rodwell
Wyke Regis
Portland Harbour
Weymouth & Portland National Sailing Academy
Portland Castle
Fortuneswell
Grove
Easton
PORTLAND
Weston
Museum
Southwell
Bill of Portland
Somerset
Dorset
Devon
Black Down Hills
East Devon
ST
0 1 2 3 4 5 6 miles
0 1 2 3 4 5 6 7 8 9 10km

CRANBORNE CHASE
VALE OF WARDOUR
WEST CHASE
CRANBORNE CHASE
WILTSHIRE DOWNS
Dorset
NEW FOREST NATIONAL PARK
ISLE OF PURBECK
PURBECK HILLS
POOLE BAY
SU
SZ
Maiden Bradley
Brixton Deverill
Monkton Deverill
Kingston Deverill
Kilmington
Norton Ferris
Great Ridge
Pertwood
Keysley Down
Chicklade
Stourhead
Stourton
Stourton House
White Sheet Hill
Mere
Zeals
Penselwood
Bourton
Queen Oak
Bush Farm Bison Centre
West Knoyle
The Green
Hindon
Berwick St Leonard
Fonthill Bishop
Fonthill Gifford
Barrow Street
East Knoyle
Huntingford
Milton on Stour
Sedgehill
Gillingham
Ham Common
Elm Hill
Cucklington
Wyke
Buckhorn Weston
Motcombe
Kington Magna
Knap Corner
West Stour
East Stour
Shaftesbury
Ivy Cross
Cann
Cann Common
Fifehead Magdalen
Stour Provost
Stour Row
Guy's Marsh
Todber
Pillwell
Marnhull
Margaret Marsh
East Orchard
West Orchard
Bedchester
Compton Abbas
Melbury Abbas
Melbury Down
Ashmore
Fontmell Magna
Sutton Waldron
Hinton St Mary
Manston
Sturminster Newton
Fiddleford Manor
Fiddleford
Hammoon
Iwerne Courtney or Shroton
Iwerne Minster
Child Okeford
Hambledon Hill
Shillingstone
Okeford Fitzpaine
Fifehead Neville
Broad Oak
Newton
Kingston
Woolland
Ibberton
Turnworth
Durweston
Stourpaine
Pimperne
Blandford Forum
Blandford St Mary
Bryanston
Stoke Wake
Higher Ansty
Hilton
Winterborne Houghton
Winterborne Stickland
Winterborne Clenston
Charlton Marshall
Thorncombe
Milton Abbey
Milton Abbas
Whatcombe
Melcombe Bingham
Charlton Down
Winterborne Whitechurch
Cheselbourne
Dewlish
Winterborne Kingston
Winterborne Zelston
Milborne St Andrew
Anderson
Almer
Bere Regis
Tolpuddle
Puddletown
Burleston
Affpuddle
Athelhampton
Turners Puddle
Briants Puddle
Lane End
Wareham Forest
Woodsford
Moreton
Bovington Camp
Tank Museum
Monkey World
Trigon Hill
Crossways
Mill House Cider Museum
Warmwell
East Burton
Wool
Owermoigne
East Stoke
Stokeford
West Holme
East Knighton
Winfrith Newburgh
Coombe Keynes
Holworth
Chaldon Herring or East Chaldon
Chaldon Down
Lulworth Castle
East Lulworth
West Lulworth
Lulworth Cove
Durdle Door
Heritage Centre
Worbarrow Bay
Tyneham
Kimmeridge
Kimmeridge Bay
Grange Heath
Wareham
Stoborough
Stoborough Green
Ridge
Middlebere Heath
Wytch Heath
Norden Heath
East Creech
Corfe Castle
Church Knowle
Steeple
Model Village & Gardens
Nine Barrow Down
Kingston
Harman's Cross
Langton Matravers
Acton
Worth Matravers
St Alban's Head
Swanage
Swanage Railway
Peveril Pt.
Durlston Head
Tilly Whim Caves
New Swanage
Ulwell
Studland
Studland Bay
Studland Beach and Nature Reserve
Newton Heath
The Foreland
South West Coast Path
Sandbanks
Brownsea I.
Poole Harbour
Arne
Arne Toy Mus
Northport
Sandford
Holton Heath
Lytchett Minster
Lytchett Matravers
Upton
Hamworthy
Poole
Parkstone
Lilliput
Canford Cliffs
Compton Acres
Branksome
Branksome Park
Westbourne
Bournemouth
Oceanarium
Boscombe
Southbourne
Pokesdown
Christchurch
Mudeford
Hengistbury Head
Christchurch Bay
Highcliffe
Barton on Sea
Milford on Sea
New Milton
Ashley
Old Milton
Hordle
Downton
Everton
Walkford
Hinton
Bransgore
Burton
Winkton
Sopley
Neacroft
Godwinscroft
Avon
Ripley
Thorney Hill
Bashley
Wootton
Sway
Jumpers Green
Holdenhurst
Hurn
Adventure Wonderland
Parley Cross
West Parley
Ensbury
Kinson
Talbot Village
Moordown
Winton
Bear Cross
Bearwood
Canford Magna
Merley
Oakley
Broadstone
Corfe Mullen
Hill View
Morden
East Morden
Slepe
Bloxworth
Canford Heath
Waterloo
Newtown
Wimborne Minster
Walford Mill
Colehill
Hampreston
Longham
Stapehill
Canford Bottom
Ferndown
Trickett's Cross
West Moors
St Leonards
St Ives
Ashley Heath
Three Legged Cross
Moors Valley
Ringwood
Moortown
Kingston
Burley
Burley Street
Bisterne Close
Picket Post
Linford
Burley Lodge
Emery Down
Brockenhurst
Minstead
Stoney Cross
Newtown
Fritham
Bramshaw
Brook
Furzey Gdns
Crockford
Rockford
Moyles Court
Linwood
Mockbeggar
Ibsley
Broomy Lodge
South Gorley
North Gorley
Hungerford
Hyde
Stuckton
Blissford
Godshill
Bickton
Fordingbridge
Ashford
Sandleheath
Alderholt
Alderholt Mill
Charing Cross
Verwood
Ringwood Forest
Blashford
Woodlands
Horton
Chalbury Common
Chalbury
Mannington
Hinton Martell
Gaunt's Common
Holt
Holt Heath
Stanbridge
Broom Hill
Clapgate
Hillbutts
Pamphill
Kingston Lacy
Shapwick
Sturminster Marshall
Spetisbury
Tarrant Crawford
Tarrant Keyneston
Tarrant Rushton
Tarrant Rawston
Tarrant Monkton
Royal Signals Museum
Tarrant Launceston
Tarrant Hinton
Tarrant Gunville
Witchampton
Manswood
Long Crichel
Moor Crichel
Gussage St Michael
Gussage All Saints
Knowlton
Knowlton Church
Wimborne St Giles
Cripplestyle
Edmondsham
Heavy Horse Centre
Cranborne
Manor Gardens
Monkton Up Wimborne
Cashmoor
Chettle
Chettle House
Stubhampton
Farnham
Dean
Sixpenny Handley
Larmer Tree Gardens
Woodcutts
Tollard Royal
Deanland
Woodyates
Pentridge
Pentridge Hill
Martin
Martin Down
Tidpit
Martin Drove End
Rockbourne
Rockbourne Down
Damerham
Whitsbury
Breamore House & Museum
Upper Street
Outwick
Roman Villa
Burgate
Breamore
Woodgreen
Hale
North Charford
Hamptworth Lodge
Nomansland
Landford Manor
Plaitford
Canada
Redlynch
Lover
Downton
Woodfalls
Morgan's Vale
Newhouse
Langley Wood
Newton
Whiteparish
Charlton-All-Saints
Wick
Wick Down
Win Green
Charlton
Ludwell
Woodminton
Bowerchalke
Ebbesbourne Wake
Alvediston
Berwick St John
West End
White Sheet Hill
Donhead St Andrew
Donhead St Mary
Milkwell
Ansty
Swallowcliffe
Old Wardour Castle
Semley
Sutton Mandeville
Fovant
Prescombe Down
Fifield Bavant
Broad Chalke
Mount Sorrel
Bishopstone
Stoke Farthing
Croucheston
Stratford Tony
Coombe Bissett
Homington
Odstock
Nunton
Bodenham
Whaddon
Alderbury
Britford
Salisbury
East Harnham
West Harnham
Netherhampton
Wilton
Wilton House
Burcombe
Quidhampton
Bemerton
Milford
Laverstock
Old Sarum
Stratford sub Castle
Ditchampton
Compton Chamberlayne
Barford St Martin
Dinton
Baverstock
Teffont Magna
Teffont Evias
Chilmark
Farmer Giles Farmstead
Chicksgrove
Tisbury
Hatch
Newtown
Ridge
Grovely Wood
Wylye Down
Wylye
Wylye Valley
Hanging Langford
Little Langford
Steeple Langford
Stapleford
Deptford
Stockton
Sherrington
Boyton
St James
Great Wishford
Little Wishford
Stoford
South Newton
Chilhampton
Lake
Great Durnford
Upper Woodford
Middle Woodford
Lower Woodford
Boscombe
Allington
Idmiston
Porton
Gomeldon
Winterbourne Dauntsey
Winterbourne Gunner
Winterbourne Earls
Firsdown
Lopcombe Corner
East Winterslow
Middle Winterslow
West Winterslow
The Common
Pitton
Farley
East Grimstead
West Grimstead
West Dean
Lockerley
East Dean
Pepperbox Hill
Guernsey 2:40
Jersey 3:00
St. Malo 4:35
Cherbourg 2:15
(Apr-Oct)
(May-Sept)
Guernsey 2:10
Jersey 3:25
St. Malo 5:15
A303
A350
A30
A36
A354
A338
A31
A35
A351
A352
A348
A347
A341
A3049
A3060
A337
B3081
B3078
B3082
B3075
B3074
B3072
B3073
B3055
B3058
B3069
B3070
B3071
B3351
6
7
8
9
10
11
A
B
C
D
E
F
G
H
16
10

Hampshire
Winchester
Southampton
SOUTHAMPTON
EASTLEIGH
Romsey
Totton
Lyndhurst
Brockenhurst
LYMINGTON
New Milton
Barton on Sea
Milford on Sea
Fareham
GOSPORT
Portsmouth
PORTSMOUTH
Southsea
HAVANT
Waterlooville
Emsworth
Hayling Island
South Hayling
Bishop's Waltham
Wickham
New Alresford
Alton
Kings Worthy
Twyford
Hedge End
Netley
Hythe
Fawley
Beaulieu
Stockbridge
Isle of Wight
NEWPORT
Cowes
East Cowes
RYDE
Sandown
Shanklin
Ventnor
Yarmouth
Totland
Freshwater
Bembridge
The Needles
St Catherine's Point
THE SOLENT
SPITHEAD
SOUTHAMPTON WATER
NEW FOREST NATIONAL PARK
FOREST OF BERE
Christchurch Bay
Sandown Bay
Brighstone Bay
Chale Bay
Osborne Bay
Stokes Bay
Gilkicker Pt.
Needs Ore Pt.
Stone Pt.
Atherfield Pt.
Culver Cliff
Foreland
The Undercliff
SU
SZ
17
18
9
GUERNSEY 7:00 JERSEY 10:30
BILBAO 35:00 SANTANDER 24:00 (Mar-Nov)
0 1 2 3 4 5 6 miles
0 1 2 3 4 5 6 7 8 9 10 km

East Worldham
Kingsley
Sleaford
Bowlhead Green
Hambleden
Cranleigh
Walliswood
Ockley
Oakwoodhill
Rusper
Lambs Green
Ifield
Beacon Hill
Hindhead
Brook
Sandhills
Oakhurst Cottage
Loxhill
Dunsfold
Kingsfold
Lindford
Arford
Combe Common
Oakhanger
Bordon Camp
Headley
Grayshott
Gibbet Hill
Chiddingfold
Alfold Crossways
Ellen's Green
Faygate
Crawley
Bordon
Whitehill
Standford
Grayswood
Ramster Garden
Rowhook
Tilgate
Blackmoor
Bramshott
Shottermill
Haslemere
Alfold
Rudgwick
Warnham
Buchan
Pease Pottage
Conford
Hammer
Ramsnest Common
Alfold Bars
Tisman's Common
Bucks Green
Strood Green
Broadbridge Heath
Roffey
Colgate
Greatham
Liphook
Camelsdale
Empshott
Longmoor Camp
Linchmere
Fisherstreet
Loxwood
Park Street
Slinfold
Horsham
St Leonard's Forest
Plaistow
Ifold
The Haven
Kingsley Green
Hollycombe Steam Collection
Liss Forest
Langley
Black Down
Fernhurst
Northchapel
Mackerel's Common
Roundstreet Common
Itchingfield
Ashfold Crossways
Handcross
Nymans Garden
West Liss
East Liss
Liss
Rake
Five Oaks
Southwater Street
Mannings Heath
Monk's Gate
Slaugham
Staple
Steep Marsh
Milland
Hill Brow
Lurgashall
Ebernoe Common
Balls Cross
Kirdford
Wisborough Green
Newpound Common
Barns Green
Southwater
Nuthurst
Lower Beeding
Leonardslee Lakes & Gardens
Warninglid
Henley
Borden
Lickfold
Strood Green
Billingshurst
Parbrook
Brooks Green
Copsale
Crabtree
Sheet
Petersfield
South Downs
West Sussex
Rogate
Chithurst
Iping
Woolbeding
Easebourne
Lodsworth
Halfway Bridge
Upperton
Petworth HO
Petworth
Bedham
Adversane
Coneyhurst
Maplehurst
Bolney
Dumpford
Trotton
Stedham
Midhurst
South Ambersham
Selham
Tillington
Byworth
Broadford Bridge
Coolham
Coolham Airfield D-Day Memorial
Shipley
Whitehill
West Grinstead
Cowfold
Kent Street
Nyewood
Minsted
Codmore Hill
North Heath
Gay Street
Broomer's Corner
Nursted
East Harting
National Park
West Lavington
Stopham
Nutbourne
Hickstead
Wineham
Twineham
South Harting
Elsted
Didling
Fittleworth
Pulborough
West Chiltington
Goose Green
Dial Post
Partridge Green
Burgess Hill
Treyford
Bepton
Heyshott
Coates
Marehill
Spear Hill
Common
Uppark
Linch Down
Cocking
Graffham
Duncton
Coldwaltham
Hardham
West Chiltington Common
Wiggonholt
Thakeham
North Marden
East Lavington
Barlavington
South Downs Way
Greatham
Ashington
West End
Blackstone
Albourne
Washbrooks Farm Centre
Compton
Up Marden
Chilgrove
Sutton
Roman Villa
Watersfield
Henfield
Woodmancote
Ashurst
West Marden
East Marden
Upwaltham
Bignor
Rackham
Cootham
Parham
Storrington
Rock
Wiston
Singleton
Charlton
West Burton
Amberley
Bury
Sullington
Washington
Small Dole
Poynings
Forestside
Kingley Vale
West Dean
West Dean Gardens
Weald and Downland Open Air Museum
East Dean
Houghton
Amberley Mus
Kithurst Hill
Steyning
Bramber
Fulking
Stoughton
Goodwood
St. Roche's Hill
Bow Hill
Madehurst
North Stoke
South Stoke
Harrow Hill
North End
Upper Beeding
Truleigh Hill
Edburton
Saddlescombe
Devil's Dyke
Stansted Park
Walderton
Eartham
Arundel Park
Burpham
Findon
St Mary's House
Botolphs
Woodend
West Stoke
Mid Lavant
East Lavant
Goodwood House
Halnaker
Offham
The Wildfowl and Wetlands Centre
Arundel
Coombes
Brighton & Hove
Westbourne
Funtington
Woodmancote
East Ashling
West Ashling
Strettington
Boxgrove
Fontwell
Slindon
Walberton
Patching
High Salvington
Mile Oak
Portslade
Westdene
Hambrook
Summersdale
Westerton
Denmans
Fontwell Park
Museum and Heritage Centre
Crossbush
Hammerpot
Clapham
North Lancing
Hermitage
Nutbourne
Chichester
Westhampnett
Tangmere
Aviation Mus
Norton
Eastergate
Aldingbourne
Nyton
Westergate
Tortington
Poling
Angmering
Salvington
Durrington
Sompting
Kingston by Sea
Southwick
Southbourne
Broadbridge
Fishbourne
Bosham
Oving
Woodgate
Barnham
Yapton
Ford
Lyminster
Wick
Hangleton
Broadwater
Lancing
Shoreham-by-Sea
Portslade-by-Sea
Hove
Chidham
Bosham Walk
Fishbourne Palace
Apuldram
Pallant House
Colworth
Climping
Rustington
East Preston
Ferring
Goring-by-Sea
West Worthing
Worthing
East Worthing
South Lancing
Marlipins Museum
Chichester Harbour
West Thorney
Donnington
North Mundham
Runcton
Merston
North Bersted
Shripney
Flansham
Bilsham
Littlehampton
Kingston Gorse
West Itchenor
Shipton Green
Hunston
Sussex Falconry Centre
South Mundham
South Bersted
Middleton-on-Sea
Harbour Park
Birdham
Street End
Nyetimber
Felpham
Acre Street
Rose Green
Aldwick
Southcoast World
Bognor Regis
West Wittering
Somerley
Highleigh
Earnley Butterflies and Gardens
Sidlesham
Pagham
East Wittering
Earnley
Bracklesham
Norton
Church Norton
Selsey
Selsey Bill
Caen 6:00
Le Havre 5:30
St. Malo 9:00
Caen 3:45 (April-Sept)
Cherbourg 3:00 (April-Nov)
TV
Alderney
4½ miles to 1 inch
Dielette 0:45
St. Peter Port 1:00 (Apr-Oct)
Brehou
Braye
Quesnard Pt.
Clonque Bay
Longis Bay
St Anne
Alderney
Telegraph Bay
Guernsey
4½ miles to 1 inch
Poole 2:30 (Apr-Oct)
Weymouth 2:10
Portsmouth 7:00
L'Ancresse Bay
Le Plomb
Grand Havre
La Fontenelle
Sark 0:45
Guernsey
St Sampson
Shell Beach
L'Islet
Cobo Bay
Herm
Vazon Bay
Belle Greve Bay
Lihou I.
Le Villocq
Museum & Art Gall.
Beau Sejour Centre
Mont Saint
Victor Hugo's House
St Peter Port
Jethou
Rocquaine Bay
Castle Cornet
The Little Chapel
Carmel
Fort George
Pleinmont Pt.
Guernsey
St. Helier 2:00
Mouilpied
Le Planel
La Planque
St Martin's Pt.
St. Helier 0:55
St. Malo 1:45
Moulin Huet Bay
Pointe de la Moye
Icart Pt.
Dielette 1:00
Carteret 1:00 (Apr-Oct)
Alderney 1:00
Jersey
4½ miles to 1 inch
Plémont Pt.
Sorel Pt.
Ronez Pt.
Grosnez Pt.
St John's Bay
Belle Hougue Pt.
Carteret 0:45
St. Peter Port 1:10 (Apr-Oct)
North Coast Visitor Centre
St John's
Bouley Bay
Tour de Rozel
St Mary's
Trinity
Rozel
La Coupe Pt.
Jersey
St Ouens
Durrell Wildlife Conservation Trust (Zoo)
Kempt Tower Visitor Centre
Carrefour Selous
St Martin's
St Ouen's Bay
St Peter's
La Hougue Bie
St Catherine's Bay
Jersey
Five Oaks
Mont Orgueil Castle
Red Houses
Gorey
Corbière Pt.
St Aubin
Jersey Museum
Grouville
Royal Bay of Grouville
Sark 0:50 (Apr-Oct)
St Brelade
St Helier
St Aubin's Bay
St Clements
St Brelades Bay
Elizabeth Castle
Fort Regent Leisure Centre
St. Peter Port 0:55
Weymouth 3:25
Poole 3:00 (Apr-Oct)
Noirmont Pt.
Le Nez Pt.
St Clements Bay
La Rocque Pt.
Granville 1:00
St. Peter Port 1:00 (Apr-Oct)
Carteret 1:00
St. Peter Port 2:00
Portsmouth 10:30
St. Malo 1:15

Merstham
Redhill
Reigate
Limpsfield
Oxted
Westerham
Godstone
Sevenoaks Weald
Hildenborough
TONBRIDGE
Edenbridge
Lingfield
Horley
GATWICK AIRPORT
Southborough
ROYAL TUNBRIDGE WELLS
Pembury
East Grinstead
Three Bridges
Crawley
Forest Row
Crowborough
ASHDOWN FOREST
Wadhurst
Mayfield
Balcombe
Cuckfield
HAYWARDS HEATH
Lindfield
Uckfield
Heathfield
BURGESS HILL
Hurstpierpoint
Ditchling
Lewes
Hailsham
Battle
Brighton and Hove
BRIGHTON
HOVE
Southwick
SHOREHAM-BY-SEA
Woodingdean
Peacehaven
Newhaven
Seaford
Polegate
Willingdon
Eastbourne
BEXHILL
Pevensey Bay
BEACHY HEAD
East Sussex
THE WEALD
SOUTH DOWNS
DIEPPE 4:00
TQ
TV

Shepway
Otham
Stoneacre
Leeds
Leeds Castle
Harrietsham
Broomfield
North Downs Way
Warren Street
Stalisfield Green
Leaveland
Badlesmere
Shottenden
Chilham
Shalmsford Street
Garlinge Green
Nackington
Street End
Lower Hardres
Bridge
Bishopsbourne
Adisham
Aylesham
Nonington
Snowdown
Tilmanstone
Loose
Boughton Monchelsea
Langley
Langley Heath
Kingswood
Sandway
Lenham
Lenham Heath
M20
A20
A252
Molash
Challock
Godmersham
Petham
Upper Hardres Court
Kingston
Barham
Womenswold
Elvington
Linton
Chart Corner
Chart Sutton
Boughton Monchelsea Place
Sutton Valence
Warmlake
Grafty Green
Boughton Malherbe
Charing
Charing Heath
Westwell Leacon
Westwell
Boughton Aluph
Bilting
Sole Street
Crundale
Waltham
Bossingham
Derringstone
Barfrestone
Eythorne
Ulcombe
Rabbit's Cross
Egerton
Egerton Forstal
Little Chart
Ram Lane
Goat Lees
Boughton Lees
A28
Hassell Street
Wye
Wye Crown
Stelling Minnis
Elham Valley Vineyard
Denton
Wingmore
Woolage Green
Coxhill
Shepherdswell
Coldred
Wootton
Lydden
Cross-at-Hand
Milebush
Southernden
Hawkenbury
Headcorn
Pluckley
Pluckley Thorne
Hothfield
Godinton House
Kennington
Brook
Hastingleigh
Bodsham
Elmsted
Lyminge Forest
Selsted
St John's Commandery
Lydden Temple Ewell
Ewell Minnis
Marden Thorn
Staplehurst
Iden Croft Herbs
Farm Mus
Knox Bridge
Sinkhurst Green
Frittenden
Smarden Bell
Smarden
Haffenden Quarter
Lashenden
Maltman's Hill
Great Chart
Ashford
Willesborough
Sevington
Wissenden
Hinxhill
Willesborough Lees
Brabourne
Lymbridge Green
Rhodes Minnis
Elham
Butterfly Centre
Swingfield Street
Swingfield Minnis
Ottinge
Densole
Alkham
Drellingore
Farthingloe
Collier's Green
Cranbrook Common
Sissinghurst Castle
Three Chimneys
Standen
Biddenden
Bethersden
Stubbs Cross
Kingsnorth
Mersham
Brabourne Lees
Stowting
Smeeth
Sellindge
Postling
Lyminge
Kent Battle of Britain Museum
Paddlesworth
Hawkinge
West Hougham
Etchinghill
Channel Tunnel
Capel-le-Ferne
East Cliff & Warren
East Wear Bay
Wilsley Pound
Cranbrook Museum
Union Mill
Sissinghurst
Tanden
Shadoxhurst
Cheeseman's Green
Aldington Frith
Clap Hill
Aldington
Stop 24 Services
Sellindge Lees
Stanford
Beachborough
Newington
Cheriton
Folkestone
Biddenden Vineyard
High Halden
Henghurst
Bromley Green
Bonnington
Newingreen
Pedlinge
Saltwood
Elham Valley Rly Mus
Sandgate
Rotunda
Cliff Lift
Cranbrook
East End
St Michael's
Kent & East Sussex Railway
Shirkoak
Orlestone
Ham Street Woods
Court-at-Street
Lympne
Port Lympne Wild Animal Park and Gardens
Hartley
Parkgate
Woodchurch
South of England Rare Breeds Cen
Ruckinge
Bilsington
Brockhill
Hythe
West Hythe
Royal Military Canal
Palmarsh
Benenden
Tenterden
Brook Street
Kenardington
Hamstreet
Warehorne
Newchurch
Burmarsh
Gill's Green
Iden Green
Dingleden
Rolvenden
Colonel Stephens Railway Museum
Leigh Green
Small Hythe
Reading Street
Appledore Heath
Horne's Place Chapel
Snave
Romney Marsh
Romney, Hythe and Dymchurch Light Railway
Hawkhurst
Four Throws
Rolvenden Layne
Smallhythe Place
Isle of Oxney
Appledore
Peening Quarter
St Mary in the Marsh
Dymchurch
Martello Tower
The Moor
Sandhurst
Linkhill
Newenden
Wittersham
Stone
Snargate
Sandhurst Cross
Rother
Ham Green
The Stocks
Brenzett
Aeronautical Museum
Ivychurch
Romney Warren
St Mary's Bay
Bodiam
Great Dixter
Rother Levels
Farm World
Northiam
Brookland
Old Romney
Ewhurst Green
Beckley
Four Oaks
Littlestone on Sea
TR
Millcorner
Clayhill
Iden
Houghton Green
Walland Marsh
New Romney
Romney Sands
Staple Cross
Horns Cross
Peasmarsh
Rye Foreign
Playden
Greatstone on Sea
Cripp's Corner
East Guldeford
Lydd
Lydd (London Ashford)
Vinehall Street
Broadland Row
Tillingham
Rye
Lydd on Sea
Broad Oak
Udimore
Rye Heritage Centre
Camber
Denge Marsh
Lydd International Raceway
Sedlescombe
Brede
Rye Harbour
Whatlington
Sedlescombe Street
Brede Steam Engine
Winchelsea
Camber Castle
Dungeness
Denge Beach
Dungeness Power Station & Information Centre
The Old Lighthouse
Rye Bay
Guestling Thorn
Winchelsea Court Hall Museum
Winchelsea Beach
Icklesham
Kent Street
Three Oaks
Westfield
Pett
Baldslow
Guestling Green
Cliff End
Crowhurst
Hollington
St Helen's
Ore
Fairlight
Fairlight Cove
Hastings
Silverhill
St Clement's Caves
St Leonards
Underwater World
Bulverhythe
West Marina
ENGLISH CHANNEL
Kent
North Downs
6
7
8
9
10
11
C
D
E
F
G
H

Swansea
Clydach
Pontardawe
Pontarddulais
Gorseinon
Loughor
Gowerton
Dunvant
Killay
Sketty
Brynmill
Mumbles Hd.
Black Pill
West Cross
Mayals
Bishopston
Newton
The Mumbles (Y Mwmbwls)
Mumbles Hd. Trwyn yr Mwmbwls
SWANSEA BAY
BAE ABERTAWE
CORK 10:00
ILFRACOMBE 0:50
Swansea (Abertawe)
Port Tennant
Morriston
Llansamlet
Skewen
Neath
Neath (Castell-Nedd)
Port Talbot (Castell-Nedd Port Talbot)
Port Talbot
Aberavon
Baglan
Briton Ferry
Margam
Tonna
Resolven
Glyn-neath (Glynedd)
Ystalyfera
Seven Sisters
Crynant
Cilfrew
Aberdulais
Melincourt
Glyncorrwg
Cymer
Maesteg
Bridgend (Pen-y-bont ar Ogwr)
Bridgend
Pyle (Y Pîl)
Kenfig
Porthcawl
Tusker Rock
Pencoed
Laleston
Ogmore
Ogmore-by-Sea
St Brides Major
Southerndown
Nash Pt. Trwyn yr As
Llantwit Major (Llanilltud Fawr)
St Donat's
Cowbridge (Y Bont-Faen)
Vale of Glamorgan (Bro Morgannwg)
Rhondda Cynon Taff (Rhondda Cynon Taf)
Treorchy (Treorci)
Treherbert
Ferndale
Tonypandy
Porth
Pontypridd
Llantrisant
Aberdare (Aberdâr)
Hirwaun
Mountain Ash (Aberpennar)
Merthyr Tydfil (Merthyr Tudful)
Treharris
Abercynon
Rhoose (Y Rhws)
Breaksea Pt. Trwyn Breaksea
MÔR HAFREN
BRISTOL CHANNEL
Foreland Pt.
Highveer Pt.
Lynmouth
Lynton
Countisbury
Combe Martin
Parracombe
Porlock
Hurlstone Pt.
Minehead
Dunster
Blue Anchor Bay
Watchet
Exmoor Forest
EXMOOR NATIONAL PARK
Brendon Common
Simonsbath
Exford
Withypool
Wheddon Cross
Brendon Hills
Barnstaple
SS
SN
0 1 2 3 4 5 6 miles
0 1 2 3 4 5 6 7 8 9 10km

15
Monmouthshire
(Sir Fynwy)
Torfaen
(Tor-faen)
Caerphilly
(Caerffili)
Newport
(Casnewydd)
Cardiff
(Caerdydd)
North
Somerset
Bristol
Somerset
ABER HAFREN
MOUTH OF THE SEVERN
ST
SO
Blaina
Abertillery
Abersychan
Pontypool
Cwmbran
Usk
Caerleon
Chepstow
Caldicot
Risca
Machen
Caerphilly
Penarth
Barry
Portishead
Clevedon
Nailsea
Yatton
Weston-super-Mare
Burnham-on-Sea
Highbridge
Bridgwater
Cheddar
Wells
Glastonbury
Street
Shepton Mallet
Filton
Patchway
Avonmouth
Thornbury
Lydney
Keynsham
Flat Holm
Steep Holm
Sully Island
Ynys Sili
Brean Down
POLDEN HILLS
QUANTOCK FOREST
BRIDGWATER BAY
STERT FLATS
BERROW FLATS
M4
M5
M48
M49
M32
25
16
7
8

Gloucestershire
South Gloucestershire
Bristol
Bath and N.E. Somerset
Chepstow (Cas-gwent)
Lydney
Stroud
Stonehouse
Nailsworth
Dursley
Tetbury
Malmesbury
Wotton-under-Edge
Thornbury
Yate
Chipping Sodbury
Filton
Patchway
Mangotsfield
Kingswood
Keynsham
Avonmouth
Portishead
Nailsea
Long Ashton
Chippenham
Corsham
Bath
Bradford-on-Avon
Melksham
Trowbridge
Westbury
Warminster
Frome
Radstock
Midsomer Norton
Paulton
Peasedown St John
Wells
Shepton Mallet
Glastonbury
Street
Cheddar
Evercreech
Bruton
Castle Cary
Mere
Caldicot
Frampton on Severn
Berkeley
Severn Beach
Wrington
Holt
The Noose
Oakley Wood
Summer Down
Cranborne Chase
Bruton Forest
Battery Pt.

Cirencester
Fairford
Lechlade-on-Thames
Carterton
Faringdon
ABINGDON
Didcot
Wantage
Swindon
Cricklade
Highworth
Wootton Bassett
Stratton St Margaret
Purton
South Cerney
Calne
Marlborough
Hungerford
Newbury
Thatcham
Devizes
Pewsey
Tidworth
Ludgershall
Andover
Amesbury
Durrington
Whitchurch
Overton
Stockbridge
Kings Worthy
Wilton
Lambourn
VALE OF WHITE HORSE
LAMBOURN DOWNS
MARLBOROUGH DOWNS
VALE OF PEWSEY
Savernake Forest
Collingbourne Forest
Harewood Forest
Berkshire
West Berkshire
Hampshire
Wiltshire
SALISBURY PLAIN
NORTH WESSEX DOWNS
Thames or Isis
THE RIDGEWAY
STONEHENGE
UFFINGTON CASTLE
MUSEUM OF ARMY FLYING

Oxford
Headington
Wheatley
Cowley
Kennington
Abingdon
Didcot
Wallingford
Thame
Chinnor
Princes Risborough
Wendover
Berkhamsted
Chesham
Great Missenden
Amersham
Chesham Bois
Prestwood
High Wycombe
Beaconsfield
Marlow
Henley-on-Thames
Maidenhead
Slough
Windsor
Eton
Datchet
Reading
Caversham
Woodley
Tilehurst
Twyford
Wokingham
Bracknell
Crowthorne
Sandhurst
Camberley
Frimley
Farnborough
Aldershot
Fleet
Farnham
Guildford
Godalming
Milford
Haslemere
Hindhead
Grayshott
Liphook
Bordon
Alton
Basingstoke
Hook
Tadley
Thatcham
Newbury
Overton
Whitchurch
Goring
Pangbourne
Streatley
Sunninghill
Ascot
Bagshot
Windlesham
Yateley
Thatcham
Kingsclere
Wantage
West
Berkshire
Wokingham
Bracknell Forest
Windsor and Maidenhead
Hampshire
North
Surrey
Micheldever Forest
Chobham Ridges
Great Park
Kennet
Oxford Services
Reading Services
Fleet Services
Winchester Services
Micheldever Services
Chieveley Services
Beaconsfield Services
SP
SU
28
17
10
11
0 1 2 3 4 5 6 miles
0 1 2 3 4 5 6 7 8 9 10 km

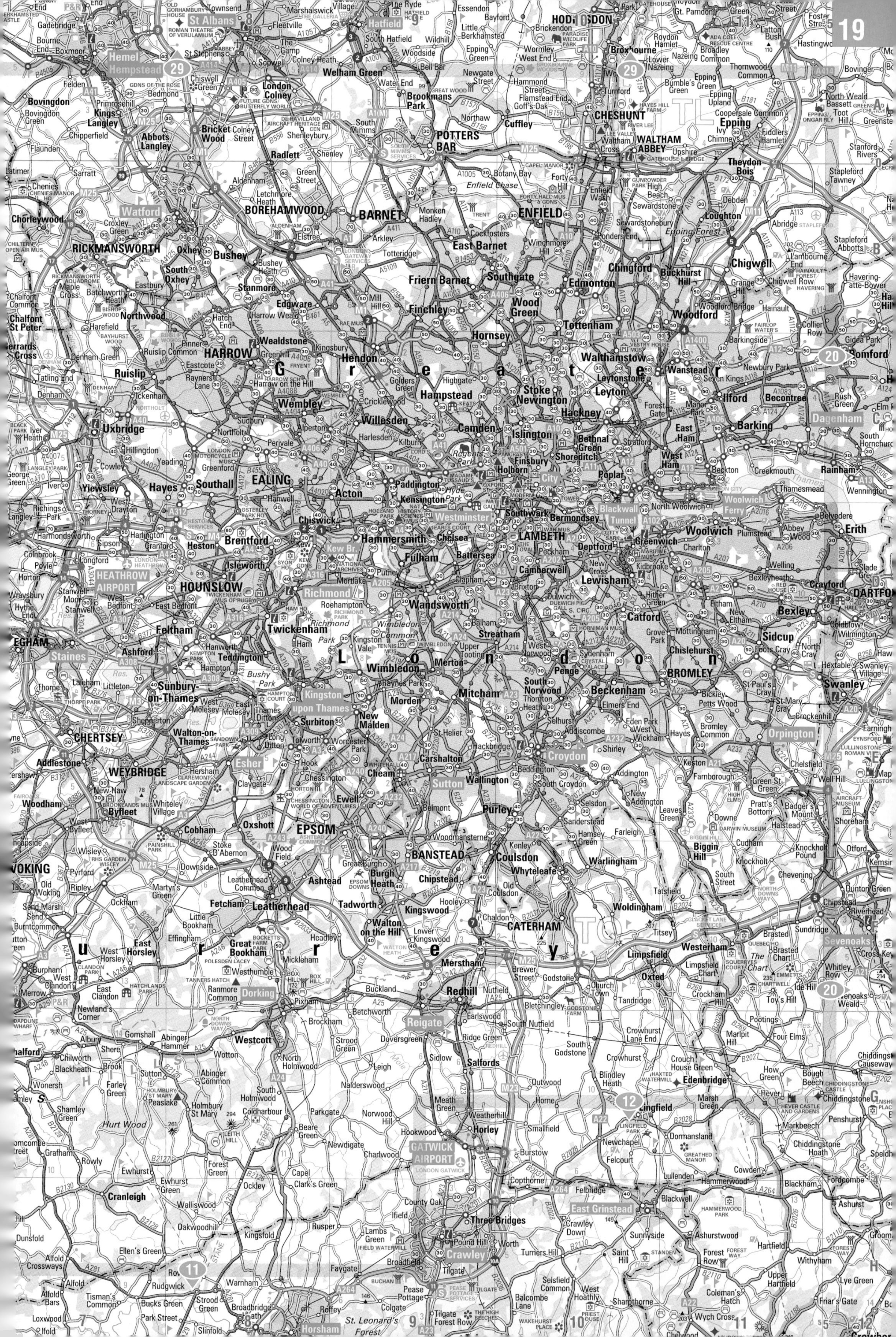
St Albans
Hatfield
Hemel Hempstead
Welham Green
Hoddesdon
Broxbourne
Cheshunt
Waltham Abbey
Epping
Potters Bar
Watford
Rickmansworth
Borehamwood
Barnet
Enfield
Loughton
Chigwell
Bushey
Stanmore
Edgware
Finchley
Southgate
Edmonton
Chingford
Woodford
Harrow
Wealdstone
Hendon
Hornsey
Tottenham
Walthamstow
Romford
Ruislip
Wembley
Hampstead
Stoke Newington
Hackney
Leyton
Ilford
Barking
Dagenham
Uxbridge
Willesden
Camden
Islington
Ealing
Southall
Hayes
Acton
Paddington
Kensington
Westminster
Holborn
City
Chiswick
Hammersmith
Chelsea
Southwark
Bermondsey
Blackwall Tunnel
Woolwich
Woolwich Ferry
Erith
Brentford
Fulham
Lambeth
Deptford
Greenwich
Heathrow Airport
Hounslow
Richmond
Battersea
Camberwell
Lewisham
Wandsworth
Dartford
Feltham
Twickenham
Streatham
Catford
Bexley
Sidcup
Staines
Egham
Wimbledon
Mitcham
Penge
Beckenham
Bromley
Swanley
Kingston upon Thames
Surbiton
Morden
Croydon
Orpington
Chertsey
Weybridge
Esher
Sutton
Epsom
Purley
Banstead
Coulsdon
Caterham
Leatherhead
Woking
Sevenoaks
Dorking
Redhill
Reigate
Oxted
Edenbridge
Lingfield
Gatwick Airport
Crawley
Three Bridges
East Grinstead
Horsham
Cranleigh
Horley
Greater London
Surrey

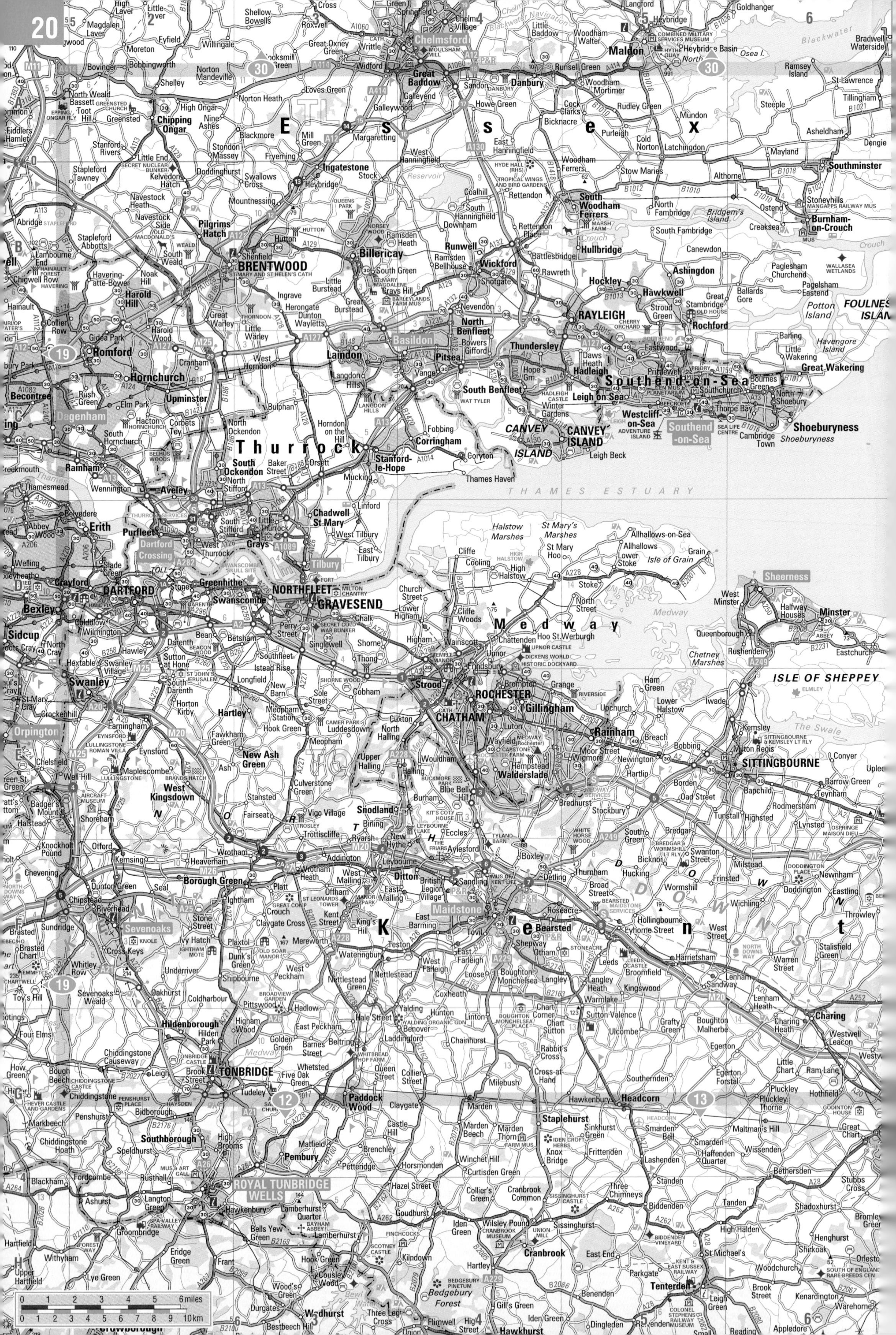

Essex
Thurrock
Medway
Kent
Chelmsford
Maldon
Great Baddow
Danbury
Chipping Ongar
Ingatestone
Billericay
BRENTWOOD
Wickford
South Woodham Ferrers
Burnham-on-Crouch
Southminster
Hullbridge
RAYLEIGH
Rochford
Basildon
Laindon
Pitsea
Romford
Hornchurch
Upminster
Dagenham
Becontree
Rainham
Thundersley
Hadleigh
Southend-on-Sea
Leigh on Sea
Westcliff-on-Sea
Shoeburyness
Great Wakering
CANVEY ISLAND
Stanford-le-Hope
Corringham
South Benfleet
Grays
Tilbury
Aveley
Purfleet
Erith
Dartford Crossing
DARTFORD
Bexley
Sidcup
Swanley
Orpington
NORTHFLEET
GRAVESEND
Swanscombe
Greenhithe
THAMES ESTUARY
Isle of Grain
Sheerness
Minster
Queenborough
ISLE OF SHEPPEY
The Swale
Strood
ROCHESTER
CHATHAM
Gillingham
Walderslade
Rainham
SITTINGBOURNE
Snodland
West Malling
Ditton
Maidstone
Sevenoaks
Borough Green
Hildenborough
TONBRIDGE
Southborough
ROYAL TUNBRIDGE WELLS
Paddock Wood
Pembury
Staplehurst
Headcorn
Cranbrook
Tenterden
Charing
Harrietsham
Hawkhurst
Bedgebury Forest
FOULNESS ISLAND

0 1 2 3 4 5 6 miles
0 1 2 3 4 5 6 7 8 9 10 km

7
8
9
10
11
A
B
C
D
E
F
G
H
TM
TR
31
ST PETERS ON THE WALL
Bradwell on Sea
DENGIE
Ray Sand
Montsale
Deal Hall
Foulness Sand
Foulness Pt.
Courtsend
Churchend
MAPLIN SANDS
Warden Pt.
Warden
Leysdown-on-Sea
Isle of Harty
Shell Ness
THE SWALE
WHITSTABLE
Tankerton
Swalecliffe
HERNE BAY
Seasalter
Chestfield
Greenhill
Herne
Beltinge
Broomfield
RECULVER
RECULVER TOWERS AND ROMAN FORT
Reculver
Hillborough
Minnis Bay
Birchington
Westgate on Sea
Margate
THE SHELL GROTTO
Cliftonville
Foreness Pt.
Kingsgate
NORTH FORELAND
Northdown
St Peter's
BROADSTAIRS
BLEAK HOUSE
DICKENS HOUSE MUSEUM
Dumpton
Newington
Ramsgate
MARITIME MUSEUM
OOSTENDE 4:00
BOULOGNE 1:15
QUEX HOUSE
Isle of Thanet
SPITFIRE AND HURRICANE MEM.
Acol
Northwood
Manston
St Nicholas at Wade
Sarre
Monkton
Minster
Cliffsend
Pegwell
SANDWICH & PEGWELL BAY
ST. AUGUSTINE'S CROSS
Pegwell Bay
Boyden Gate
Hoath
Chislet
Upstreet
Calcott
South Street
Yorkletts
Oare
Graveney
CHART GUNPOWDER MILLS
Faversham
FLEUR DE LIS HERITAGE CENTRE
Goodnestone
Dargate
Hernhill
Preston
FARMING WORLD
MOUNT EPHRAIM
Boughton Street
Dunkirk
Honey Hill
Blean
Rough Common
Tyler Hill
Hales Place
Broadoak
Sturry
Fordwich
Hersden
West Stourmouth
Stour
East Stourmouth
Grove
STODMARSH
Preston
Westbere
Stodmarsh
Elmstone
Westmarsh
Ware
Hoaden
RICHBOROUGH CASTLE
AMPHITHEATRE
Great Stonar
Canterbury
P&R
Wickhambreux
WINGHAM BIRD PARK
Ickham
Littlebourne
Wingham
Guilton
Ash
Sandwich
Sandwich Bay
ROYAL ST. GEORGE'S
TOLL
Marshborough
Woodnesborough
Stone Cross
North Street
South Street
Harbledown
ST. AUGUSTINE'S ABBEY
Sheldwich
Selling
Oversland
Chartham Hatch
Thanington
CANTERBURY TALES
HOWLETTS WILD ANIMAL PARK
Bekesbourne
Bramling
Staple
Worth
Old Wives Lees
Chartham
Patrixbourne
Goodnestone
GOODNESTONE PARK
Eastry
Gore
Ham
Finglesham
Badlesmere
Shottenden
Chilham
Shalmsford Street
Nackington
Street End
Adisham
Bridge
Lower Hardres
Bishopsbourne
Aylesham
Chillenden
Knowlton
Betteshanger
Sholden
MARITIME AND LOCAL HISTORY MUSEUM
DEAL
DEAL CASTLE
THE DOWNS
Molash
Garlinge Green
Petham
Kingston
Nonington
Easole Street
Northbourne
Snowdown
Tilmanstone
Elvington
Great Mongeham
Walmer
WALMER CASTLE AND GARDENS
NORTH DOWNS WAY
Godmersham
Upper Hardres Court
Barham
Derringstone
Womenswold
Barfrestone
EAST KENT RLY.
Eythorne
Ripple
Sutton
East Studdal
Ringwould
Kingsdown
Bilting
Sole Street
Crundale
Bossingham
Waltham
ELHAM VALLEY VINEYARD
Woolage Green
Shepherdswell
Coxhill
West Langdon
Martin
Boughton Aluph
Boughton Lees
Hassell Street
WYE CROWN
Wye
Stelling Minnis
Denton
LYDDEN
Wingmore
Wootton
Coldred
East Langdon
Martin Mill
Whitfield
Guston
St Margaret's at Cliffe
THE BAY MUSEUM
St Margaret's Bay
West Cliffe
THE PINES GARDEN
Kennington
Brook
13
Bodsham
Elmsted
Lyminge Forest
Selsted
ST JOHN'S COMMANDERY
Lydden
LYDDEN TEMPLE EWELL
Temple Ewell
Ewell Minnis
Swingfield Street
Elham
BUTTERFLY CENTRE
CRABBLE CORN MILL
Buckland
Hinxhill
Lymbridge Green
Rhodes Minnis
Swingfield Minnis
Alkham
ROMAN PAINTED HOUSE
SOUTH FORELAND
WHITE CLIFFS
CASTLE & HELLFIRE CORNER
Maxton
Willesborough Lees
Brabourne
Ottinge
Densole
Drellingore
Farthingloe
CALAIS 1:30
DUNKERQUE 1:45
Willesborough
Sevington
Brabourne Lees
Stowting
KENT BATTLE OF BRITAIN MUSEUM
Lyminge
Paddlesworth
Hawkinge
West Hougham
DOVER
Mersham
Smeeth
Etchinghill
Postling
Aycliff
DE BRADELEI WHARF
SAMPHIRE HOE
BOULOGNE 1:45
Cheeseman's Green
Sellindge
STOP 24 SERVICES
Sellindge Lees
Stanford
Beachborough
CHANNEL TUNNEL
Capel le Ferne
EAST CLIFF & WARREN
East Wear Bay
Aldington Frith
Clap Hill
Aldington
E. Stour
FOLKESTONE
Newingreen
Newington
Folkestone
CHANNEL TUNNEL
Bonnington
Court-at-Street
Lympne
PORT LYMPNE WILD ANIMAL PARK AND GARDENS
Pedlinge
Saltwood
ELHAM VALLEY RLY MUS
Cheriton
ROTUNDA
CLIFF LIFT
Sandgate
Bilsington
HAMSTREET WOODS
West Hythe
Canal
Military
BROCKHILL
Hythe
Palmarsh
Burmarsh
Newchurch
ROMNEY, HYTHE AND DYMCHURCH LIGHT RAILWAY
12

Pembrokeshire
(Sir Benfro)
SM
SR
PEMBROKESHIRE COAST
ARFORDIR PENFRO
ST. BRIDES BAY
BAE SAIN FFRAID
MYNYDD PRESELI
ROSSLARE 3:30
ROSSLARE 1:50
(May-Sept)
ROSSLARE 3:45
Cardigan I.
Ynys Aberteifi
Cemaes Head
Pen Cemaes
Strumble Head
Pen Caer
Dinas Head
Newport Bay
Bae Trefdraeth
Fishguard Bay
Bae Abergwaun
ST. DAVID'S HEAD
PENMAEN DEWI
Whitesand Bay
Porth-mawr
Ramsey Island
Ynys Dewi
Ramsey Sound
Skomer Island
Ynys Skomer
NATIONAL NATURE RESERVE
Broad Sound
Tower Point
Trwyn Twr
Wooltack Point
Trwyn Wooltack
Gateholm Island
Ynys Gateholm
Skokholm Island
Ynys Skokholm
St Ann's Hd.
Pentir St. Ann
MILFORD HAVEN
ABERDAUGLEDDYF
Sheep Island
Ynys y Defaid
Freshwater West
Angle Bay
Bae Angle
Linney Hd.
Pentir Linney
The Wash
Stackpole Hd.
Pen Stackpole
St Govan's Hd.
Pen St Gofan
Trewent Pt.
Trwyn Trewent
Old Castle Hd.
Caldey Sound
Caldey Island
Ynys Bŷr
Chapel Pt.
Trwyn Capel
Giltar Pt.
Cardigan
(Aberteifi)
Fishguard
(Abergwaun)
Goodwick
(Wdig)
Newport
(Trefdraeth)
St David's
(Tyddewi)
Haverfordwest
(Hwlffordd)
Milford Haven
(Aberdaugleddau)
Pembroke Dock
(Doc Penfro)
Pembroke
(Penfro)
Neyland
Narberth
(Arberth)
Tenby
(Dinbych-y-Pysgod)
Saundersfoot
Kilgetty
Solva
Newgale
Crymych
St Dogmaels
Moylgrove
Nevern
Eglwyswrw
Dinas Cross
Lower Town
Scleddau
Mathry
Croes-goch
Letterston
Wolf's Castle
Roch
Simpson Cross
Broad Haven
Little Haven
Marloes
Dale
St Ishmael's
Hakin
Angle
Castlemartin
Bosherston
Lamphey
Manorbier
Penally
Carew
Llawhaden
Clunderwen
Whitland
Maenclochog
Rosebush
New Inn
Puncheston
Fishguard
Johnston
Hook
Freystrop
Llangwm
Burton
Lawrenny
Templeton
Amroth
Jeffreyston
Begelly

23
7
8
9
10
11
12
A
B
C
D
E
F
G
H
New Quay
(Ceinewydd)
Cei-bach
Maen-y-groes
Gilfachrheda
Cwmtudu
Cwmtydu
Cross Inn
Nanternis
Caerwedros
Llwyndafydd
Ynys-Lochtyn
Llangrannog
Blaencelyn
Synod Inn
Pontgarreg
Plwmp
Pentregat
Penbryn
Tresaith
Aberporth
Parcllyn
Felinwynt
Penmorfa
Brynhoffnant
Sarnau
Blaenannerch
Tremain
Aberporth West Wales Airport
Tan-y-groes
Glynarthen
Blaenporth
Penparc
Bettws Ifan
Rhydlewis
Hawen
Beulah
Pantgwyn
Ponthirwaun
Bryngwyn
Brongest
Troedyraur
Capel Tygwydd
Llandygwydd
Llechryd
Cilgerran Castle
Carreg-wen
Cwm-cou
Cenarth
Abercych
Coracle Centre & Flour Mill
Newcastle Emlyn
(Castell Newydd Emlyn)
Newchapel
Clynfyw
Boncath
Cilwendeg
Penrherber
Cheese Farm
Bwlchygroes
Cwmcych
Star
Clydey
Cwmorgan
Tegryn
Hermon
Llanfyrnach
Hen-feddau fawr
Dinas
Trelech
Blaen-waun
Welsh Chocolate Farm
Cwmbach
Cwmfelin Mynach
Llanboidy
Gellywen
Llanwinio
Pen-y-bont
Blaen-y-coed
Talog
Ty-hen
Abernant
Dyffryn
Meidrim
Merthyr
Llangynin
Sarnau
Bancyfelin
Pwll-trap
St Clears
(Sanclêr)
Backe
Afon Taf
Llanddowror
Halfpenny Furze
Red Roses
Llandawke
Dylan Thomas Boathouse
Laugharne
Llansadurnen
Brook
Broadway
Museum of Speed
Pendine
East Marsh
Pendine Sands
Traeth Pentywyn
Marros
Llanybri
Llansteffan
Castle
Morfa Bach
Llangynog
Llangain
Afon Tywi
Ferryside
Broadlay
Llansaint
Kidwelly Industrial Museum
Kidwelly
(Cydweli)
Pembrey Forest
Pembrey
Burry Port
(Porth Tywyn)
Millennium Coastal Park Discovery Centre
Carmarthen
Bay
Bae Caerfyrddin
SS
SN
Ceredigion
Carmarthenshire
(Sir Gaerfyrddin)
Swansea
(Abertawe)
Llanarth
Llwyncelyn
Oakford
Llanerchaeron
Cilcennin
Ciliau Aeron
Newbridge
Afon Aeron
Dihewyd
Mydroilyn
Ystrad Aeron
Felinfach
Temple Bar
Caledrhydiau
Talgarreg
Gorsgoch
Capel Cynon
Rhos Llawr Cwrt
Bwlch-y-fadfa
Castell-Howell
Aber
Cwrt-newydd
Ffostrasol
Maesymeillion
Pont-siân
Llanwnnen
Cwmsychpant
Penrhiw-pâl
Coed-y-bryn
Maesllyn
Tregroes
Croes-lan
Rhydowen
Llanwenog
Dre-fach
Alltyblaca
Prengwyn
Capel Dewi
Rock Mill Woollen Mill
Maesycrugiau
Brynteg
Rhuddlan
Llanybydder
Horeb
Llandysul
Landyfriog
Aber-banc
Penrhiw-llan
Teifi Valley Railway
Pentrecagal
Henllan
Aber-Arad
National Wool Museum
Llangeler
Drefach
Felindre
Drefelin
Cwmhiraeth
Cwmpengraig
Capel Iwan
Moelfre
Pentre-cwrt
Saron
Rhôs
Bancyffordd
Llanfihangel-ar-arth
Llanllwni
Aber-Giâr
Pencader
New Inn
Gwyddgrug
Dolgran
Tanglwst
Bryn-Iwan
Hermon
Cwmduad
Alltwalis
Mynydd Rhos-wen
Brechfa Forest
Llanpumsaint
Llanllawddog
Cynwyl Elfed
Pontarsais
Horeb
Brechfa
Afon Duad
Gwili Railway
Rhydargaeau
Bwlchnewydd
Newchurch
Bronwydd Arms
Ffynnon ddrain
Tre-vaughan
Tanerdy
Carmarthen
(Caerfyrddin)
Abergwili
Carmarthen
Peniel
Capel Gwyn
Llanfihangel-uwch-Gwili
Felingwm isaf
Felingwm uchaf
White Mill
Nantgaredig
Pont-ar-gothi
Pant-teg
Llanllwch
Cors Goch Llanllwch
Johnstown
Pensarn
Llangunnor
Capel Dewi
Nantycaws
The National Botanic Garden of Wales
Cwmffrwd
Croesyceiliog
Idole
Bancycapel
Llangendeirne
Llanddarog
Cwmisfael
Porthyrhyd
Gwendraeth Fach
Pontantwn
Crwbin
Llandyfaelog
Meinciau
Pontyberem
Bancffosfelen
Four Roads
Pontyates
Pont-Henri
Mynyddygarreg
Carway
Ffos Las
Five Roads
Trimsaran
Pinged
Waun-y-clyn
Cynheidre
Sylen
Horeb
Llannon
Achddu
Cwmbach
Pwll
Furnace
Llanelli
Sandy
Machynys
Wildfowl and Wetlands Trust
Morfa
Llwynhendy
Bynea
Dafen
Felinfoel
Llangennech
Bryn
Gorsgoch
Lampeter
(Llanbedr Pont Steffan)
Maestir
Cribyn
Ffynnon-oer
Llangybi
Silian
Betws Bledrws
Olwen
Cellan
Cwmann
Pentre-bach
Parc-y-rhôs
Pencarreg
Glan-Duar
Ty Mawr
Mynydd Pencarreg
Esgairdawe
Rhydcymerau
Llidiad Nenog
Llansawel
Edwinsford
Abergorlech
Gwernogle
Nant-y-ffin
Pen-y-garn
Talley
Talley Abbey
Cynros
Cwm-byr
Cwmdu
Soar
Llanfynydd
Capel Isaac
Pant-glas
Salem
Pantgwyn
Pentrefelin
Broad Oak
Court Henry
Llangathen
Cilsan
Aberglasney
Dinefwr Park
Llandeilo
Ffairfach
Vale of Tywi
Dyffryn Tywi
Felindre
Dryslwyn
Llanegwad
Llanarthne
Golden Grove
Gelli Aur
Penrhiwgoch
Maesybont
Temple Bar
Milo
Carmel
Foel-gastell
Llyn Llech Owain
Cefneithin
Gorslas
Pen-y-groes
Cwm-y-glo
Cwm-mawr
Cross Hands
Tumble
Drefach
Pentre
Cwmgwili
Capel Hendre
Saron
Penybanc
Llyn-tegg
Llwyn-teg
Pont Abraham Services
Llanedi
Sardis
Fforest
Hendy
Pontarddulais
Allt
Waungron
Llangennech
Grovesend
Pontlliw
Pengelly
Penllergaer
Gorseinon
Llangyfelach
Ystradgynlais
Loughor
Gowerton
Waunarlwydd
Penclawdd
Crofty
Llanmorlais
Blue Anchor
Three Crosses
Dunvant
Killay
Upper Killay
Cilfrew
Forest-fach
Cadle
Cwmdu
Landore
Swansea
(Abertawe)
Sketty
Brynmill
Glynn Vivian
Clyne Valley
Swansea Museum
National Waterfront Museum
Mayals
Black Pill
West Cross
Lovespoon Gallery
Oystermouth Castle
The Mumbles
(Y Mwmbwls)
Newton
Mumbles Hd.
Trwyn yr Mwmbwls
Swansea Bay
Bae Abertawe
Cork 10:00
Ilfracombe 0:50
Whiteford Pt.
Trwyn Whiteford
Whiteford
Llanrhidian Sands
Traeth Llanrhidian
Wernffrwd
Cheriton
Landimore
Weobley Castle
Llanmadoc
Burry Green
Llangennith
Llanrhidian
Burry Holms
Rhossili Bay
Bae Rhossili
Burry
Reynoldston
Gower
The Beacon
Llanddewi
Knelston
Rhossili
Worms Head
Penrhyn-Gŵyr
Middleton
Scurlage
Penrice
Nicholaston
Penmaen
Parkmill
Gower Heritage Centre
Pennard
Kittle
Bishopston
Mansefield
Southgate
Oldway
Ilston
Lunnon
Llethrid
Oxwich
Oxwich Castle
Oxwich Bay
Bae Oxwich
Pilton Green
Horton
Overton
Port-Eynon
Port Eynon Pt.
Port Eynon Bay
Bae Port Eynon
Pwlldu Hd.
Pen Pwlldu
Gower Coast
Pant-lasau
Clydach
Ynystawe
Glais
Morriston
Llansamlet
Birchgrove
Skewen
Trebanos
Alltwen
Pontardawe
Glantawe Riverside Park
Rhyd-y-fro
Ynysmeudwy
Craig-cefn-parc
Rhyd-y-gwin
Rhyd-y-pandy
Felindre
Cwm-Dulais
Pentrebach
Graig Fawr
Garnswllt
Mynydd y Gwair
Felindre
Ammanford
(Rhydaman)
Betws
Pantyffynnon
Tycroes
Pontamman
Glanaman
Garnant
Gwaun-Cae-Gurwen
Gwaun-Leision
Tairgwaith
Cwmgors
Brynamman
Twynmynydd
Tir-y-dail
Llandybie
Pentre-Gwenlais
Caer-bryn
Dre-fach
Llandyfan
Trapp
Carreg Cennen Castle & Farm
Y Mynydd Du
Black Mountain
Neuadd
Trichrug
Capel Gwynfe
Pontbren Araeth
Bethlehem
Pont-ar-llechau
Dyffryn Ceidrych
Manordeilo
Cwmifor
Rhosmaen
Pen-y-banc
Felindre
Llangadog
Hermon
Ashfield
Halfway
Llansadwrn
Waunclunda
Cwmdwr
Llanwrda
Porthyrhyd
Crugybar
Caio
Dolaucothi Gold Mines
Pumsaint
Caeo Forest
Esgair Ferchon
Llandre
Cwrt-y-cadno
Harford
Ffaldybrenin
Ffarmers
Llanycrwys
Mynydd Mallaen
Pentrefelin
Llanfair Clydogau
Bryn Brawd
Llanddewi-Brefi
Pentre-rhew
Olmarch
Commins Capel Betws
Capel Betws Lleucu
Llwyn-y-groes
Llangeitho
Welsh Gold Centre
Tregaron
Y Drum
Bwlch-Llan
Llundain-fach
Trefilan
Tal-sarn
Gartheli
Abermeurig
Felindre
Crynfryn
Afon Cothi
Afon Amman
Afon Cywyn
Afon Tywi
Lliedi Resrs.

Ceredigion
(Sir Ceredigion)
Carmarthenshire
(Sir Gaerfyrddin)
Powys
SN
Aberaeron
Aberarth
Llanrhystud
Llansantffraed
Llanon
Monachty
Cilcennin
Pennant
Cross Inn
Bethania
Nebo
Rhyd-Rosser
Rhydfudr
Trefenter
Llangwyryfon
Llanddeiniol
Blaenplwyf
Chancery
Rhydyfelin
Moriah
Capel Seion
Llanfarian
Gors
New Cross
Pisgah
Llanfihangel-y-Creuddyn
Aberffrwd
Ystumtuen
Ysbyty Cynfyn
Devil's Bridge
Mynydd Bach
Trisant
Cnwch-coch
Llanilar
Pentre-llyn
Rhos-y-garth
Abermagwr
Crosswood
Wenallt
Llanafan
Lledrod
Tynygraig
Ysbyty Ystwyth
Pont-rhyd-y-groes
Cwmystwyth
Blaenycwm
New Row
Tanyrhydiau
Ystradmeurig
Ffair-Rhos
Pontrhydfendigaid
Strata Florida Abbey
Swyddffynnon
Bronnant
Bontnewydd
Blaenpennal
Tyncelyn
Penuwch
Tyn-yr-eithin
Cors Caron
Crynfryn
Llangeitho
Tregaron
Welsh Gold Centre
Bwlch-Llan
Capel Betws Lleucu
Commins Capel Betws
Llundain-fach
Trefilan
Gartheli
Tal-sarn
Llwyn-y-groes
Abermeurig
Olmarch
Llanddewi-Brefi
Pentre-rhew
Ystrad Aeron
Felinfach
Felindre
Temple Bar
Ffynnon-oer
Llangybi
Dihewyd
Ciliau Aeron
Cribyn
Silian
Betws Bledrws
Llanfair Clydogau
Gorsgoch
Maestir
Lampeter (Llanbedr Pont Steffan)
Olwen
Cellan
Pentrefelin
Cwmann
Pentre-bach
Llanwnnen
Cwrt-newydd
Aber
Cwmsychpant
Alltyblaca
Dre-fach
Llanwenog
Pencarreg
Llanybydder
Parc-y-rhôs
Ram
Llanycrwys
Ffarmers
Ffaldybrenin
Cwrt-y-cadno
Mynydd Mallaen
Harford
Mynydd Pencarreg
Brynteg
Rhuddlan
Glan-Duar
Ty Mawr
Esgairdawe
Pumsaint
Dolaucothi Gold Mines
Caio
Llandre
Caeo Forest
Aber-Giâr
Llanllwni
Rhydcymerau
Crugybar
Porthyrhyd
Siloh
Cilycwm
Divlyn
Llanfair-ar-y-bryn
Cynghordy
New Inn
Llidiad Nenog
Llansawel
Edwinsford
Talley Abbey
Talley
Cynros
Cwm-byr
Gwernogle
Abergorlech
Brechfa Forest
Nant-y-ffin
Pen-y-garn
Waunclunda
Llansadwrn
Cwmdwr
Llanwrda
Cwmdu
Halfway
Felindre
Brechfa
Llandovery (Llanymddyfri)
Myrtle Hill
Cilgwyn
Myddfai
Llangadog
Ashfield
Hermon
Soar
Llanfynydd
Capel Isaac
Horeb
Pant-glas
Salem
Cwmifor
Manordeilo
Pantgwyn
Pen-y-banc
Rhosmaen
Bethlehem
Dyffryn Ceidrych
Pont-ar-llechau
Capel Gwynfe
Pontbren Araeth
Trichrug
Neuadd
Twynllanan
Llanddeusant
Talsarn
Usk Reservoir
Vale of Tywi (Dyffryn Tywi)
Llandeilo
Ffairfach
Dinefwr Park
Broad Oak
Llangathen
Court Henry
Cilsan
Pentrefelin
Felindre
Dryslwyn
Aberglasney
Llanegwad
Llanarthne
Nantgaredig
Felingwm isaf
Felingwm uchaf
Llanfihangel-uwch-Gwili
Pont-ar-gothi
Capel Dewi
Golden Grove
Carreg Cennen Castle & Farm
Trapp
Foel Fraith
Black Mountain (Y Mynydd Du)
Fan Brycheiniog
Pont Aber
Nantycaws
The National Botanic Garden of Wales
Penrhiwgoch
Temple Bar
Milo
Maesybont
Carmel
Llandyfan
Dre-fach
Llandybie
Pentre-Gwenlais
Llanddarog
Porthyrhyd
Cwmisfael
Foel-gastell
Cefneithin
Gorslas
Caer-bryn
Pen-y-groes
Tir-y-dail
Twynmynydd
Brynamman
Rhosaman
Glanaman
Garnant
Gwaun-Leision
Tairgwaith
Gwaun-Cae-Gurwen
Ammanford
Betws (Rhydaman)
Pantyffynnon
Saron
Penybanc
Cwm-y-glo
Morfa
Cross Hands
Tumble
Cwm-mawr
Drefach
Bancffosfelen
Crwbin
Pontyberem
Capel Hendre
Cwmgwili
Tycroes
Cwmgors
Meinciau
Pentre
Pont-Henri
Pontyates
Carway
Greynor
Garnswllt
Mynydd y Gwair
Llannon
Llwyn-teg
Cynheidre
Sylen
Llanedi
Sardis
Pentrebach
Graig Fawr
Horeb
Five Roads
Fforest
Pontarddulais
Hendy
Cwm-Dulais
Felindre
Rhyd-y-pandy
Rhyd-y-gwin
Craig-cefn-parc
Pontardawe
Trebanos
Alltwen
Rhyd-y-fro
Ynysmeudwy
Cilybebyll
Gellinudd
Rhôs
Faerdre
Clydach
Ystalyfera
Godre'r-graig
Gurnos
Lower Cwm-twrch
Upper Cwm-twrch
Cwmllynfell
Ystradowen
Cwmgiedd
Ystradgynlais
Abercraf
Penrhos
Craig-y-nos
Glyntawe
The National Showcaves for Wales
Dan-yr-Ogof
Pen-y-cae
Penwyllt
Caehopkin
Coelbren
Onllwyn
Dyffryn Cellwen
Seven Sisters
Nant-y-cafn
Swansea Valley (Cwm Abertawe)
Vale of Neath (Cwm Nedd)
Rheola Forest
Crynant
Resolven
Melincourt
Glyn-neath (Glynedd)
Pontneddfechan
Morfa Glas
Blaengwrach
Cwmgwrach
Fforest Fawr
Fan Gihirych
Fan Fawr
Ystradfellte
Ystradfellte Res.
Beacons Res.
Cantref Res.
Heol Senni
Crai
Felin-Crai
Cray Res.
Glas Fynydd Forest
Cwmwysg
Pont ar Hydfer
Trecastle
Llywel
Sennybridge (Pont Senni)
Defynnog
Penpont
Pentre'r-felin
Trallong
Mynydd Illtyd
Mountain Centre
Libanus
Tai'r Bull
Glyn Tarell
Llwyn y Celyn
Craig Cerrig Gleisiad a Fan Frynych
Penderyn
Pontbren Llwyd
Hirwaun
Rhigos
Cwm-hwnt
Tre-Gibbon
Penywaun
Cwmdare
Aberdare
Halfway
Llandeilo'r Fan
Pentre-bach
Mynydd Bwlch-y-groes
Llanfihangel Nant Bran
Pont-faen
Blaendyryn
Merthyr Cynog
Tirabad
Crychan Forest
Mynydd Epynt
Cefn-gorwydd
Pentre-ty-gwyn
Babel
Rhandirmwyn
Nant-y-Bai
Ystradffin
Mynydd Trawsnant
Llyn Brianne Res.
Soar-y-Mynydd
Tywi Forest
Dolgoch
Bryn Crwn
Drygarn Fawr
Abergwesyn
Cwm Irfon
Cambrian Woollen Mill
Llanwrtyd
Llanwrtyd Wells (Llanwrtud)
Beulah
Llangammarch Wells
Llanfechan
Garth
Troed-rhiwdalar
Pentre-llwyn-llwyd
Llanafan-fawr
Pentre Dolau-Honddu
Claerwen Reservoir
Caban-coch Res.
Garreg-ddu Res.
Penygarreg Res.
Craig-goch Res.
Elan Village
Rhayader (Rhaeadr Gwy)
Llansantffraed Cwmdeuddwr
The Gigrin Farm Red Kite Feeding Centre
Gaufron
Nant-glas
Llanwrthwl
Argoed Mill
St Harmon
Pant-y-dwr
Nantgwyn
Trawsallt
Geifas
Pen y Garn
Dibyn Du
Y Drum
Esgair Cerrig
Tyncornel
Bryn Brawd
Esgair Ferchon
Mynydd Rhos-wen
Fantasy Farm Park
Llanerchaeron
Hafod Estate
Coed Rheidol
0 1 2 3 4 5 6 miles
0 1 2 3 4 5 6 7 8 9 10 km

David's Well
Llanbadarn Fynydd
Black Mountain
Dutlas
Upper Treverward
Llanfair Waterdine
Purlogue
Hobarris
Chapel Lawn
New Invention
Clungunford
Onibury
Bromfield
Hopton Castle
Hoptonheath
Abcott
Twitchen
Rhydmoeddu
Red Lion Hill
Beacon Hill
Skyborry Green
Bedstone
Marlow
Shelderton
Bucknell
Leintwardine
Kinton
Ludlow
Bwlch-y-sarnau
Llanbister
Crug
Knucklas
Stowe
Knighton (Tref-y-Clawdd)
Milebrook
Buckton
Brampton Bryan
Teme
Walford
Downton on the Rock
Burrington
Aston
Overton
Ludford
Moel Hywel
Abbey-cwm-hir
Llangunllo
Adforton
Elton
Ashford Bowdler
Llandewi Ystradenny
Bleddfa
Monaughty
Pilleth
Rhos-y-meirch
Letton
Leinthall Starkes
Richards Castle
Birtley
Wigmore
Woofferton
Ongar Street
Lower Lye
Leinthall Earls
Brimfield
Comberton
Orleton
Nantmel
Dolau
Cascob
Whitton
Norton
Lingen
Limebrook
Yatton
Llanfihangel Rhydithon
Dolley Green
Croft Castle
Bircher
Fron
Gwystre
Crossgates
Radnor Forest
Maes-Treylow
Discoed
Stapleton
Judges Lodging
Kinsham
Aymestrey
Yarpole
Middleton on the Hill
Penybont
Beggar's Bush
Presteigne (Llanandras)
Byton
Mortimer's Cross
Lucton
Ashton
Eye
Berrington Hall
The Hundred
Llanyre
Llandegley
Kinnerton
Evenjobb
Combe
Combe Moor
Water Mill and Battle Centre
Luston
Llandrindod Wells (Llandrindod)
Radnorshire Museum
Ridgebourne
Rodd
Ledicot
Lugg Green
New Radnor
Nash
Shobdon
Kingsland
Eyton
Stansbatch
Staunton on Arrow
Cobnash
The Broad
Kimbolton
Newbridge on Wye
Howey
National Cycle Collection
Knill
Titley
Stockton
Walton
Old Radnor
Yardro
Shirl Heath
Cholstrey
Leominster
Disserth
Crossway
Dolyhir
Burlingjobb
Flintsham
Offa's Dyke Path
Pembridge
Eardisland
Burton Court
Monkland
Lawton
Barons Cross
Llanfihangel-nant-Melan
Hergest Croft Gdns
Kington
Headbrook
Marston
Dunkertons Cider
Ivington Green
Ivington
Stoke Prior
Frank's Bridge
Hergest Ridge
Upper Hergest
Lower Hergest
Bearwood
Luntley
Brierley
Cors y Llyn
Gladestry
Oaklands Small Breeds Farm
Kingswood
Lyonshall
Holme Marsh
Haven
Sollers Dilwyn
Dilwyn
Aulden
Marlbrook
Newton
Llansantffraed-in-Elvel
Gwaunceste Hill
Hundred House
Glascwm
Colva
Huntington
Broxwood
Hopley's Green
Upper Hill
Birley
Hope under Dinmore
Cwmbach
Builth Road
Hengoed
Wootton
Woonton
Knapton Green
Cilmery
Llanelwedd
Cregrina
Michaelchurch-on-Arrow
Almeley
Sarnesfield
Weobley
Weobley Marsh
Bush Bank
Bodenham
Oaklands
Llanfaredd
Builth Wells (Llanfair-ym-Muallt)
Newchurch
Lower Welson
Upcott
King's Pyon
Westhope
Queenswood
Tyn-y-graig
Rhulen
Red Hill
Bryngwyn
Brilley
Eardisley
Kinnersley
Calver Hill
Ledgemoor
Canon Pyon
Urdimarsh
Maesmynis
Llanddewi'r Cwm
Llanbadarn-y-Garreg
Rhos-goch
Dol-y-cannau
Millhalf
Herefordshire
Ailey
Wormsley
Wellington
Alltmawr
Aberedw
Rhydspence
Whitney-on-Wye
Willersley
Norton Canon
Moorhampton
Yarsop
Tillington Common
Walker's Green
Marden
Llanbedr
Painscastle
Clifford
Winforton
Wye
Letton
Yazor
Mansel Lacy
Mansell Gamage
Staunton on Wye
Tillington
Moreton on Lugg
Llandeilo Graban
Bronydd
Priory Wood
Merbach
Bredwardine
Gardens & Gallery
Brinsop
Burghill
Pipe and Lyde
Kenchester Water Gardens
Credenhill
The Begwns
Clyro
Hardwicke
The Bage
Brobury
Monnington on Wye
Byford
Bishopstone
Kenchester
Stretton Sugwas
Shelwick
Gwenddwr
Erwood
Crickadarn
Hay-on-Wye (Y Gelli Gandryll)
Arthur's Stone
Moccas
Preston on Wye
Bridge Sollers
Canon Bridge
King's Acre
Holmer
Llanstephan
Llowes
Cusop
Dorstone
Blakemere
Ploughfield
The Weir
Swainshill
Lugwardine
Upper Chapel
Rhydness
Snodhill
The Flits
Lulham
Breinton
Breinton Common
Upper Breinton
Cider Museum
Hereford
Llaneglwys
Boughrood
Cwmbach
Llanigon
Peterchurch
Tyberton
Madley
Eaton Bishop
Ruckhall
Glasbury
Pipton
Tregoyd
Llyswen
Hinton
Llanrosser
Shenmore
Cublington
Lower Bullingham
Three Cocks
Velindre
Golden Valley
Vowchurch
Brampton
Clehonger
Grafton
Dinedor
Lower Chapel
Urishay Common
Turnastone
Kingstone
Portway
Twyford Common
Hay Bluff
Craswall
Upper Maes-coed
Thruxton
Allensmore
Callow
Llandefalle
Bronllys
Bronllys Castle
The Tumpa
Michaelchurch Escley
St Margaret's
Cockyard
Winnal
Dewshall Court
Aconbury
Pwllgloyw
Garthbrengy
Talachddu
Llanfilo
Talgarth
Llanelieu
Middle Maes-coed
Kerry's Gate
Sarnau
Felinfach
Tredustan
Trefecca
Newton
Dinedor
Didley
Kivernoll
King's Thorn
Little Birch
Much Birch
Llandefaelog Fach
Tredomen
Howell House
Bacton
St Devereux
Much Dewchurch
Llanddew
Llandefaelog-tre'r-graig
Trefeinon Open Farm
Pengenffordd
Llanveynoe
Lower Maes-coed
Wormbridge
Abbey Dore Court
Kilpeck
Wormelow Tump
Black Mountains
Abbey Dore
Howton
Kilpeck Castle (Rems) & Church
Hoarwithy
Llandinabo
Brecon (Aberhonddu)
Llanywern
Llanfihangel Tal-y-llyn
Mynydd Troed
Y Mynyddoedd Duon
Longtown
Ewyas Harold
Orcop Hill
Llanwarne
Harewood End
Llanfaes
Llanspyddid
Brecknock Museum
Llechfaen
Llangors
Llanthony
Priory
Clodock
Pontrilas
Bagwy Llydiart
Talyllyn
Llanhamlach
Llangorse Lake
Llangasty Talyllyn
Cathedine
Rowlestone
Monmouth Cap
Orcop
Garway Hill
Pencoyd
Llanfrynach
Pencelli
Scethrog
Trebinshwn House
Cwmrhos
Hatterrall Hill
Walterstone
Llangua
Kentchurch
Grosmont
Grosmont Castle
White Rocks
Michaelchurch
St Owen's Cross
St Weonards
Tretire
Cross Oak
Llansantffraed
Cwmdu
Oldcastle
Cwmyoy
Hoaldalbert
Talybont-on-Usk
Tretower Castle & Court
Tretower
Pen Cerig-calch
Tre-wyn
Pandy
Garway
Three Ashes
Aber-Village
Bwlch
Gaer
Stanton
Broad Oak
Llangarron
Brecon Beacons
Danywenallt
Talybont Res.
Coed-yr-ynys
Llanbedr
Llanfihangel-Crucorney
Llanfihangel Court
Llangattock Lingoed
Skenfrith Castle
Skenfrith
Norton
Llancloudy
Neuadd Reservoirs
Llangynidr
Bettws
Bont
Cross Ash
Llanrothal
Welsh Newton
Abercynafon
Crickhowell
Ffawyddog
Llangenny
Llangattock
Upper Green
Crossway
St Maughans
Llangrove
Whitchurch
Cwrt-y-gollen
Glangrwyney
Llantilio Pertholey
Wayne Green
Newcastle
Garn Caws
Craig y Cilau
Mynydd Llangynidr
Mynydd Llangattock
Llwyn-du
Mardy
Bryn-y-gwenin
Llanvetherine
White Castle
Llanfaenor
Llangattock Vibon-Avel
Maypole
Buckholt
Ganarew
Gilwern
Govilon
Abergavenny (Y Fenni)
Llantilio Crossenny
Hen Gwrt
Onen
Rockfield
Garwnant Visitor Centre
Pontsticill Reservoir
Llanelly
Clydach
Llanfoist
Llanvapley
Llanvihangel Ystern-Llewern
Dixton
Trefil
Rassau
Garnlydan
Blackrock
Cwm Clydach
Llanddewi Rhydderch
Wernyrheolydd
Penrhôs
Monmouth (Trefynwy)
Wyesham
Brecon Mountain Railway
Bryn Bach
Tafarnau-bach
Beaufort
Brynmawr
Llanelly Hill
Blorenge
Llanellen
Llangattock nigh Usk
Coed Morgan
Llanarth
Pen-yr-heol
Wonastow
Over Monnow
Pontsticill
Vaynor
Princetown
Dukestown
Sirhowy
Ebbw Vale (Glyn Ebwy)
Nantyglo
Garn-yr-erw
Bryngwyn
Dingestow
Mitchel Troy
Penallt
Tredegar
Georgetown
Coalbrookvale
Pontypool & Blaenavon Big Pit Mining Museum
Forge Side
Blaenavon
Llanover
Llanvihangel Gobion
Tregare
Raglan
Monmouth Services
Mitchel Troy Common
Pen-twyn
Dowlais
Castle Mus.
Rhymney (Rhymni)
Pontlottyn
Briery Hill
Blaina
Coity Mountain
Blaenavon Ironworks
Rhyd-y-meirch
Pen-groes-oped
Llanfair Kilgheddin
Pen-y-clawdd
Cwmcarvan
Caer Llan
Gellideg
Pen-yr-Heolgerrig
Waunlwyd
Varteg
Cwmavon
Nant-y-derry
Raglan
Hoop
Merthyr Tydfil (Merthyr Tudful)
Abertysswg
Fochriw
Ynysfach Engine House Heritage Cen.
Festival Park
Cwm
East Bank
Cwmtillery
Abertillery (Abertyleri)
Goetre
Bettws Newydd
Twyn-y-Sheriff
Kingcoed
Llangovan
Monmouthshire (Sir Fynwy)
Trellech
Whitebrook
New Tredegar (Tredegar Newydd)
Pentrebach
Tirphil
Man-moel
Garndiffaith
Penperlleni
Kemeys Commander
Llandenny
Llandogo
Abercanaid
Troedyrhiw
Hollybush
Talywain
Abersychan
Little Mill
Llanishen
Parkhouse
Aber-nant
Cwmbach
Bedlinog
Cwmfelin
Deri
Aberbeeg
Torfaen (Tor-faen)
Trevethin
Valley Inheritance
Glascoed
Monkswood
Llancayo
Llansoy
Catbrook
Trelleck Grange
Gwernesney
St Illtyd
Pen Ffrwd
Brynithel
Markham
Llanhilleth
Usk

26
Worcestershire
Herefordshire
Gloucestershire
Ludlow
Kidderminster
Bewdley
Stourport on Severn
Bromsgrove
Tenbury Wells
Leominster
Bromyard
Droitwich Spa
Worcester
Great Malvern
Malvern Link
West Malvern
Pershore
Upton upon Severn
Ledbury
Hereford
Tewkesbury
Newent
Ross-on-Wye
Cheltenham
Charlton Kings
Bishop's Cleeve
Gloucester
Churchdown
Hucclecote
Monmouth (Trefynwy)
Coleford
Cinderford
Lydney
Stonehouse
Stroud
Chalford
Frampton on Severn
Forest of Dean
Wyre Forest
The Noose
River Severn
Malvern Hills
34
25
16
0 1 2 3 4 5 6 miles
0 1 2 3 4 5 6 7 8 9 10km

27
Coventry
Kenilworth
Royal Leamington Spa
Warwick
Stratford-upon-Avon
Redditch
Studley
Alcester
Evesham
Broadway
Henley-in-Arden
Southam
Banbury
Middleton Cheney
Rugby
Shipston-on-Stour
Moreton-in-Marsh
Stow-on-the-Wold
Chipping Norton
Charlbury
Woodstock
Kidlington
Witney
Burford
Carterton
Oxford
Winchcombe
Chipping Campden
Warwick
Oxford
ter
VALE OF EVESHAM
COTSWOLDS
Edge Hill
SP
Longbridge
Shirley
Dorridge
Knowle
Balsall Common
Hampton Lucy
Wellesbourne
Kineton
Gaydon
Fenny Compton
Cropredy
Hook Norton
Bloxham
Adderbury
Deddington
Enstone
Bicester
Eynsham
Northleach
Bibury
Fairford
Lechlade
Bourton-on-the-Water
35
28
17

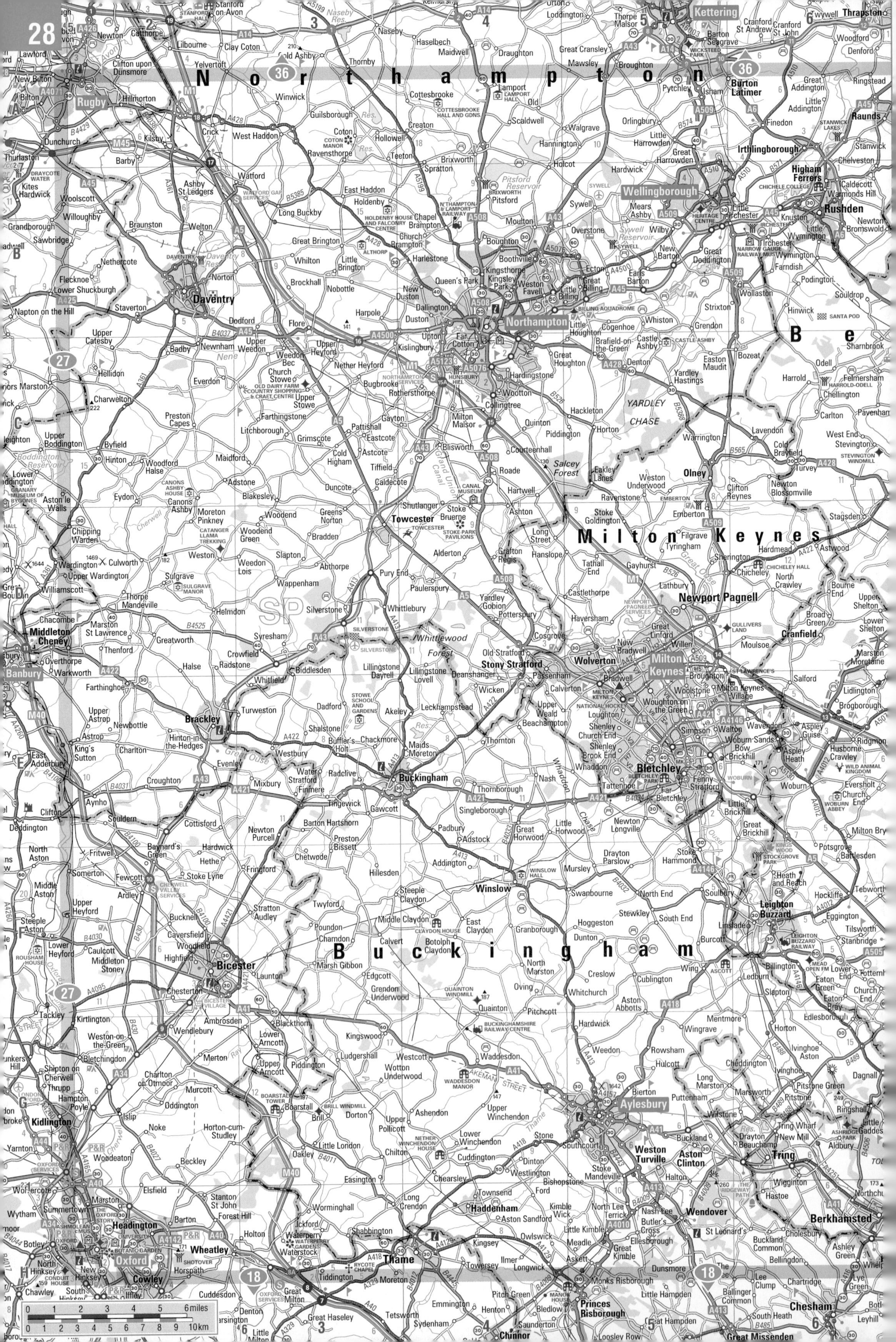
Northampton
Milton Keynes
Buckingham
Be
36
27
18
Rugby
Daventry
Northampton
Kettering
Wellingborough
Rushden
Higham Ferrers
Burton Latimer
Irthlingborough
Raunds
Thrapston
Towcester
Brackley
Banbury
Bicester
Oxford
Kidlington
Headington
Cowley
Wheatley
Thame
Aylesbury
Princes Risborough
Wendover
Tring
Berkhamsted
Chesham
Great Missenden
Leighton Buzzard
Bletchley
Newport Pagnell
Olney
Stony Stratford
Wolverton
Winslow
Haddenham
Chinnor
Middleton Cheney
Cranfield
YARDLEY CHASE
Salcey Forest
Whittlewood Forest
SP
0 1 2 3 4 5 6 miles
0 1 2 3 4 5 6 7 8 9 10 km

7
8
9
10
11
37
Cambridge
Bedford
Central
Bedfordshire
Hertford
Huntingdon
St Ives
Godmanchester
Brampton
St Neots
Eynesbury
Eaton Socon
Sandy
Biggleswade
Potton
Cambourne
Cambridge
30
Histon
Cottenham
Great Shelford
Sawston
Royston
Baldock
LETCHWORTH
HITCHIN
Stotfold
Shefford
Ampthill
Flitwick
Clophill
Luton
Dunstable
Houghton Regis
Stevenage
Buntingford
Bishop's Stortford
Stansted Mountfitchet
Sawbridgeworth
Harlow
Ware
Hertford
HODDESDON
Broxbourne
CHESHUNT
Welwyn
WELWYN GARDEN CITY
Hatfield
HARPENDEN
Wheathampstead
Redbourn
St Albans
Hemel Hempstead
London Colney
Welham Green
Brookmans Park
Epping
Kings Langley
Bricket Wood
Abbots Langley
Markyate
Kempston
Grafham Water
Great Ouse
TL
19
A
B
C
D
E
F
G
H
1
2
3
4
5
6
12

Mildenhall
Isleham
Soham
Burwell
Newmarket
Bury St Edmunds
Haverhill
Sudbury
Saffron Walden
Halstead
Braintree
Great Dunmow
Stansted Mountfitchet
Stansted Airport
Bishop's Stortford
Coggeshall
Kelvedon
Tiptree
Witham
Maldon
Chelmsford
Great Baddow
Danbury
Harlow
Lavenham
Long Melford
Clare
Cavendish
Thetford
The King's Forest
Cambridge
Sawston
Great Shelford
Linton
Thaxted
Finchingfield
Wethersfield
Castle Hedingham
Sible Hedingham
Great Yeldham
Kedington
Stoke by Clare
Glemsford
Chelmer and Blackwater Navigation
Blackwater
Osea I.
Northey I.
Heybridge Basin
Colne
Stour
Dedham
S u f f
E s s e x
TL
A11
A14
A134
A143
A1307
A120
A12
A130
A131
A414
M11
0 1 2 3 4 5 6 miles
0 1 2 3 4 5 6 7 8 9 10 km

31
7
8
9
10
11
12
A
B
C
D
E
F
G
H
TM
39
21
Thelnetham
Redgrave
Hinderclay
Wortham
Palgrave
Scole
Brockdish
Billingford Windmill
Stuston
Oakley
Hoxne
Syleham
Fressingfield
Wingfield Old College
Wingfield
Little Whittingham Green
Wissett
Linstead Parva
Chediston
Halesworth
Broadway
Holton
Blyford
Wangford
Southwold
Hen Reedbed Nature Reserve
Thrandeston
Brome
Brome Street
Cross Street
Heckfield Green
Battlesea Green
Chippenhall Green
Silverley's Green
Cratfield
Cookley
Wenhaston
Blackheath
Blythburgh
Walberswick
Botesdale
Rickinghall
Burgate
Mellis
Yaxley
Eye
Langton Green
Denham
Stradbroke
Pixey Green
Swan Green
Ashfield Green
Huntingfield
Walpole
Thorington
Bramfield
Wattisfield
Allwood Green
Thornham Parva
Cranley
Denham Street
Horham
Wootten Green
Wilby
Russel's Green
Banyard's Green
Laxfield
Heveningham
Sibton Green
Suffolk Coast
Dunwich
Dunwich Forest
Dunwich Underwater Exploration Exhibition
Cranmer Green
Gislingham
Thornham Magna
Braiseworth
Redlingfield
Athelington
Foals Green
Brundish Street
Crown Corner
Ubbeston Green
High Street
Hemp Green
Darsham
Four Ashes
Wickham Street
Stoke Ash
Occold
Thorndon
Fingal Street
Stanway Green
Brundish
Owl's Green
Sibton
Peasenhall
Yoxford
Middleton Moor
Westleton
Westleton Heath
Minsmere RSPB Nature Reserve
Crownland
Long Thurlow
Westhorpe
Finningham
Wickham Skeith
Rishangles
Southolt
Bedingfield
Worlingworth
Tannington
Badingham
Rotten End
Middleton
Wyverstone
Wyverstone Street
Bacton
Cotton
Thwaite
Brockford Street
Wetheringsett
Bedfield
Maypole Green
Dennington
Bruisyard
North Green
Theberton
Earl's Green
Ford's Green
Blacksmith's Green
Kenton
Curlew Green
Kelsale
Eastbridge
Bacton Green
Canham's Green
Mendlesham
Monk Soham
Saxtead
Saxtead Green Post Mill
Brabling Green
Cransford
Rendham
Carlton
Leiston Abbey
Haughley Green
Ward Green
Mendlesham Green
Wetherup Street
Saxtead Green
Framlingham
Swefffling
Saxmundham
Leiston
Sizewell
Wetherden
Haughley Park
Gipping
Debenham
Ashfield
Earl Soham
Great Glemham
Knodishall
Haughley
Saxham Street
Middlewood Green
Mickfield
Winston
Lampardbrook
Cole's Green
Benhall Street
Sternfield
Aldringham
Harleston
Thorney Green
Stowupland
Little Stonham
Winston Green
Brandeston
Stratford St Andrew
Benhall Green
Coldfair Green
Thorpeness
Buxhall Fen Street
Museum of East Anglian Life
Stowmarket
Forward Green
Stonham Aspal
Peats Corner
Framsden
Cretingham
Kettleburgh
Parham
Hacheston
Farnham
Friston
Buxhall
Earl Stonham
Pettaugh
Gromford
Great Finborough
Combs Ford
Combs
Creeting St Mary
Creeting Bottoms
Helmingham Hall Gardens
Helmingham
Monewden
Easton
Easton Farm Park
Letheringham
Marlesford
Little Glemham
Snape Maltings
Snape
North Warren RSPB Nature Reserve
Aldeburgh
High Street Green
Moats Tye
Crowfield
Akenfield
Charsfield
Lower Hacheston
Blaxhall
Iken
Little Finborough
Battisford
Needham Market
Beacon Hill Services
Gosbeck
Coddenham
Ashbocking
Otley
Clopton Corner
Dallinghoo
Debach
Wickham Market
Pettistree
Campsey Ash
Tunstall
Tunstall Forest
High Street
Aldeburgh Bay
Battisford Tye
Charles Tye
Ringshall
Needham Lake
Barking
Hemingstone
Swilland
Clopton
Bredfield
Rendlesham
Sudbourne
Wattisham Airfield Museum
Barking Tye
Baylham
Barham
Witnesham
Grundisburgh
Burgh
Hasketon
Ufford
Eyke
Bromeswell
Chillesford
Wattisham
Ringshall Stocks
Great Blakenham
Claydon
Henley
Melton
Butley
Great Bricett
Willisham Tye
Nedging Tye
Offton
Little Blakenham
Akenham
Tuddenham St Martin
Culpho
Boot Street
Great Bealings
Woodbridge
Rendlesham Forest
Orford Castle
Orford
Orford Ness
Orfordness-Havergate
Naughton
Somersham
Westerfield
Playford
Maidensgrave
Sutton Hoo
Capel St Andrew
Butley High Corner
Whitton
Flowton
Rushmere St Andrew
Little Bealings
Ash Street
Elmsett
Whatfield
Bramford
Westbourne
Christchurch Mansion
Martlesham
Waldringfield Heath
Sutton
Boyton
Aldham
Sproughton
Ipswich
Ipswich Mus
Martlesham Heath
Kesgrave
Rose Hill
Martlesham Heath Control Tower
Waldringfield
Shottisham
Duck Corner
Stores Corner
Hollesley
Hollesley Bay
Wolves Wood RSPB Reserve
Burstall
Hintlesham
Chantry
Stoke
Brightwell
Newbourne
Hadleigh
Chattisham
Copdock
Maidenhall
Gainsborough
Warren Heath
Bucklesham
Hemley
Alderton
Shingle Street
Layham
Coles Green
Mace Green
Belstead
Wherstead
Orwell
Nacton
Kirton
Bawdsey
Falkenham
Deben
Raydon
Capel St Mary
Great Wenham
Freston
Woolverstone
Levington
Thorpe Common
Trimley St Martin
Shelley
Holton St Mary
Pin Mill
Chelmondiston
Trimley Lower Street
Felixstowe Ferry
Vale
Bentley
Tattingstone
Alton Water Reservoir
Holbrook
Trimley St Mary
Trimley Marshes Nature Reserve
Walton
Old Felixstowe
Higham
East Bergholt
The Heath
Stutton
Lower Holbrook
Erwarton
Shotley
Felixstowe
Charles Manning's Amusement Park
Stratford St Mary
East Bergholt Place
Brantham
Stour Valley
Upper Street
Harkstead
Holbrook Bay
Shop Corner
Shotley Gate
Boxted Cross
Dedham
Bridge Cottage
Cattawade
Stour
Harwich
Harwich Redoubt Fort
Boxted Heath
Dedham Heath
Sir Alfred Munnings Art Museum
Langham
Lawford
Mistley Towers
Mistley
Bradfield
Wrabness
Parkeston
Upper Dovercourt
Dovercourt
Manningtree
Ramsey
Ardleigh
Bradfield Heath
Little Oakley
Little Bromley
Horsleycross Street
Horsley Cross
Wix
Great Oakley
Fox Street
Crockleford Heath
Great Bromley
Little Bentley
Tendring Green
Stone's Green
Esbjerg 18:00
Hoek van Holland 6:15
Colchester
Elmstead Market
Hare Green
Balls Green
Beaumont
Horsey Island
The Naze
Old Heath
Wivenhoe Cross
Beth Chatto Gdns
Tendring
Thorpe Green
Hamford Water
Wivenhoe
Frating Green
Great Bentley
Thorpe-le-Soken
Kirby-le-Soken
Maritime Museum
Rowhedge
Alresford
Weeley
Weeley Heath
Aingers Green
Walton-on-the-Naze
Fingringhoe
Thorrington
Row Heath
Kirby Cross
Frinton-on-Sea
Abberton
Little Clacton
Clacton Village
Great Holland
Langenhoe
Holland Haven
River Colne
Brightlingsea
St Osyth Heath
St Osyth Priory
St Osyth
Holland-on-Sea
Great Clacton
Mersea Island
East Mersea
Cudmore Grove
Point Clear
Clacton-on-Sea
Blue Row
Colne Estuary
Jaywick
West Mersea
Mersea Island Museum
Colne Pt.
Virley Channel
Sales Pt.
St Peters on the Wall
Dengie
Suffolk
A143
A140
A14
A12
A120
A133
A137
A1120
A1071
A1214
A1156
A1152
A1094
A144
A145
A1095
A134
A131
B1113
B1117
B1118
B1116
B1119
B1120
B1121
B1122
B1123
B1125
B1126
B1069
B1078
B1079
B1077
B1084
B1083
B1438
B1080
B1456
B1068
B1070
B1029
B1035
B1352
B1414
B1033
B1032
B1027
B1028
B1336
B1353
B1387

Gwynedd
Powys
Blaenau Ffestiniog
Llan-Ffestiniog
Beddgelert
Porthmadog
Penrhyndeudraeth
Tremadog
Penmorfa
Minffordd
Portmeirion
Maentwrog
Gellilydan
Trawsfynydd
Harlech
Llanbedr
Barmouth (Abermaw)
Dolgellau
Llanelltyd
Fairbourne
Friog
Llwyngwril
Tywyn
Aberdovey
Machynlleth
Corris
Dinas-Mawddwy
Mallwyd
Llanuwchllyn
Bala (Y Bala)
Llanfor
Frongoch
Cerrigydrudion
Pen-y-gop
Llanwddyn
Llangadfan
Llanbrynmair
Carno
Llanidloes
Llangurig
Staylittle
Dylife
Borth
Ynyslas
Talybont
Aberystwyth
Llanbadarn Fawr
Penparcau
Capel Bangor
Goginan
Ponterwyd
Devil's Bridge
Ysbyty Ystwyth
Cwmystwyth
Pontrhydygroes
Llanilar
Bow Street
Clarach
St Harmon
Rhayader
Traeth Bach
Tremadog Bay
Bae Tremadog
Barmouth Bay
Bae Bermo
Aberdovey Bar
Bae Aberdyfi
Afon Mawddach
Dovey
Dyfi
Cadair Idris
Aran Fawddwy
Arenig Fawr
Rhinog Fawr
Coed y Brenin
Dyfi Forest
Hafren Forest
Aberhirnant Forest
Migneint
Mynydd Bach
Plynlimon Pumlumon Fawr
Nant-y-Moch Reservoir
Llyn Clywedog
Lake Vyrnwy
Llyn Celyn
Source of R. Severn Blaen Hafren
Source of R. Wye Blaen Gwy
Valley Dyfi
Talyllyn Railway
Vale of Rheidol Railway
Bala Lake Railway
Centre for Alternative Technology
Maritime Museum
41
42
24
A5
A470
A487
A494
A458
A44
A493
A496
A489
A4212
SH
SN
0 1 2 3 4 5 6 miles
0 1 2 3 4 5 6 7 8 9 10km

Wrexham
(Wrecsam)
Shropshire
Marchog
Gwyddelwern
Bryneglwys
Llantysilio Mountain
Maesyrychen Mtn.
Eglwyseg Mountain
Ruabon Mountain
Pentredwr
Tai-nant
Rhosllanerchrugog
Johnstown
Rhostyllen
Marchwiel
Sontley
Stryt-issa
Penycae
Gyfelia
Eyton
Bersham
Talwrn
Cross Lanes
Industrial Estate
Bowling Bank
Bangor-is-y-coed
Cock Bank
Worthenbury
Shocklach
Chorlton Lane
Ebnal
No Man's Heath
Malpas
Bickley Moss
Cuddington Heath
Threapwood
Bell o' th' Hill
Marbury
Higher Wych
Wirswall
Tallarn Green
Corwen
Cynwyd Forest
Carrog
Llidiart-y-parc
Glyndyfrdwy
Cynwyd
Llandynan
Rhewl
Llangollen
Valle Crucis Abbey
Llangollen Steam Railway
Eliseg's Pillar
Llangollen Motor Mus
Canal Exhibition Centre
Llangollen Exhibition Centre
Plas Newydd
Acrefair
Garth
Cefn-mawr
Ruabon (Rhiwabon)
Rhos-y-Madoc
New Bridge
Cysyllte
Froncysyllte
Pentre
Halton
Erbistock
Overton Bridge
Overton (Owrtyn)
Cloy
Lightwood Green
Horseman's Green
Eglwys Cross
Grindley Brook
Brooklands
Chemistry
Whitchurch
Redbrook
Waymills
Broughall
The Chequer
Hanmer
Arowry
Bronington
Alkington
Ash Magna
Moel Fferna
Plas Nantyr
Chwarel Wynne Mine & Museum
Glyn-Ceiriog
Pontfadog
Chirk (Y Waun)
Chirk Castle
Chirk Bank
Bronygarth
Preesgweene
Weston Rhyn
Dudleston
Street Dinas
Ifton Heath
St Martin's
Dudleston Heath
Knolton Bryn
Knolton
Sandy Lane
Penley
Street Lydan
Fenn's, Whixall and Bettisfield Mosses
Tilstock
Prees Heath
Hollinwood
Welsh End
Prees Higher Heath
Tyn-y-celyn
Pandy
Bryn Du
Pentre
Tregeiriog
Llwynmawr
Craignant
Selattyn
Hengoed
Gobowen
New Marton
Ellesmere
Elson
Welshampton
The Mere
Breaden Heath
Bettisfield
Llangollen Canal
Balmer Heath
Lyneal
Colemere
Wem Moss
Northwood
Whixall
Waterloo
Quina Brook
Prees
Prees Lower Heath
Edstaston
Llechrydau
Llanarmon Dyffryn Ceiriog
Rhiwlas
Tyn-y-fedwen
Tyn-y-ffridd
Moel Sych
Cefn Canol
Llangadwaladr
Pant-glas
Llawnt
Old Oswestry Hill Fort
Hindford
Whittington Castle
Whittington
Perthy
Welsh Frankton
Lower Frankton
Tetchill
Lee
Hordley
Wolverley
Newtown
English Frankton
Prees Green
Pistyll Rhaeadr
Tan-y-pistyll
Tai-bach
Rhydycroesau
Offa's Dyke Path
Oswestry
Babbinswood
Kenwick
Horton
Lowe
Wem
Weston
Hawkstone Park
Llansilin
Moelfre
Tyn-y-coed
Middleton
Wootton
Lower Hordley
Rednal
Stanwardine in the Wood
Cockshutt
Loppington
Tilley
Aston
Wixhill
Cefn Coch
Llangynog
Llanrhaeadr-ym-Mochnant
Trefonen
Morda
Ball
Queen's Head
Haughton
Grimpo
Bagley
Petton
Noneley
Lee Brockhurst
Moston
Maesbury
Treflach
Nantmawr
Maesbury Marsh
West Felton
Westoncommon
Weston Lullingfields
Burlton
Preston Brockhurst
Llangedwyn
Pen-y-bont
Morton
Woolston
Eardiston
Wykey
Stanwardine in the Fields
Marton
Myddle
Alderton
Clive
Stanton Hine Heath
Penybontfawr
Penygarnedd
Afon Tanat
Rhos-y-brithdir
Porth-y-waen
Llynclys
Crickheath
Osbaston
Shotatton
Brownhill
Yorton
Grinshill
Moreton Corbet
Abernant
Bwlchyddar
Llanyblodwel
Pant
Cambrian Heritage Railway
Maesbrook
Knockin
Ruyton-XI-Towns
Baschurch
Prescott
Harmer Hill
Shawbury
Edgebolt
Blaen-y-cwm
Llanfechain
Llansantffraid-ym-Mechain
Llanymynech
Kinnerley
Dovaston
Hopton
Little Ness
Walford
Walford Heath
Merrington
Preston Gubbals
Muckleton
Llanfyllin
Kynaston
Nesscliffe
Yeaton
Bomere Heath
Hadnall
Tycrwyn
Llandysilio
Crosslanes
Kinton
Great Ness
Grafton
Leaton
Astley
Poynton Green
Llanfihangel-yng-Ngwynfa
Bwlch-y-cibau
Waen Fach
Deuddwr
Four Crosses
Melverley Green
Wilcott
Felton Butler
Albrighton
Bings Heath
Pentre
Forton Heath
Fitz
Mytton
High Ercall
Main
Sarnau
Arddleen
Llandrinio
Melverley
Forton
Montford Bridge
Battlefield
Haughton
Roden
Trefnanney
Geuffordd
Criggion
Shrawardine
Ensdon
Bicton
Harlescott
Haughmond Abbey
Meifod
Pentrebeirdd
Wern
Crewgreen
Coedway
Alberbury
Montford
Ford
Ditherington
Uffington
Rodington
Dolanog
Pontrobert
Glascoed
Maesgwyn-Isaf
Middletown
Wollaston
Shelton
Coton Hill
Shrewsbury
Upton Magna
Withington
Groes-lwyd
Guilsfield
Pool Quay
Trewern
Cardeston
Rowton
Shoot Hill
Hortonlane
Copthorne
Porthill
Preston
Walcot
Glyndŵr's Way
Halfway House
Wattlesborough Heath
Yockleton
Nox
Cruckton
Meole Brace
Emstrey
Attingham Park
Norton
Four Crosses
Heniarth
Clodd iau
Welshpool (Y Trallwng)
Nelly Andrews' Green
Buttington
Vennington
Westbury
Stoney Stretton
Edge
Cruckmeole
Hanwood
Atcham
Wroxeter Roman City
Melin-y-grug
Melin-y-ddôl
Cyfronydd
Welshpool & Llanfair Light Railway
Powysland
Hope
Aston Rogers
Westley
Farley
Hinton
Lea
Annscroft
Bayston Hill
Great Lyth
Lyth Hill
Cross Houses
Wroxeter
Llanfair Caereinion
Castle Caereinion
Powis Castle
Offa's Dyke
Leighton
Rowley
Asterley
Pontesbury
Plealey
Longden
Berrington
Condover
Cantlop
Bryn-penarth
Binweston
Worthen
Brockton
Minsterley
Wrentnall
Oaks
Stapleton
Cound
Golding
Cressage
Llwynderw
Mid-Wales
Fron
Trelystan
Leigh
Ploxgreen
Habberley
Church Pulverbatch
Pulverbatch
Great Ryton
Pitchford
Dorrington
Acton Pigott
Llanllugan
Manafon
Pant-y-ffridd
Berriew
Forden
Kingswood
Stockton
Marton
Betton
Meadowtown
Bentlawnt
Hope
Snailbeach
Frodesley
Acton Burnell
Langley Chapel and Gatehouse
Harley
Llanwyddelan
Adfa
New Mills
Rorrington
Wotherton
Crowsnest
Gravels
Longnor
Ruckley
Kenley
Tregynon
Brooks
Garthmyl
Middleton
Mitchell's Fold Stone Circle
Black Marsh
Pennerley
Stiperstones
Picklescott
Woolstaston
Leebotwood
Church Preen
Stretton Westwood
Hughley
Fron
Chirbury
The Marsh
Priest Weston
Shelve
The Bog
Ratlinghope
Presthope
Montgomery (Trefaldwyn)
Corndon Hill
Bridges
All Stretton
Enchmarsh
Plaish
Bourton
Bettws Cedewain
Dolforwyn Castle
Green Lane
Llandyssil
Abermule
Churchstoke
Hyssington
Roundton Hill
West Onny
Coldyeld
Bridges Long Mynd
Church Stretton
Cardington
Gretton
Easthope
Bwlch-y-ffridd
Llanllwchaiarn
Llanmerewig
Pentreheyling
Linley
Norbury
Wentnor
Little Stretton
Wall Bank
Longville in the Dale
East Wall
Brockton
Milford
Newtown (Y Drenewydd)
Hodley
Pentre
Snead
More
Hope Bowdler
Wall under Heywood
Rushbury
Wilderhope Manor
Shipton
Glanmule
Sarn
Kerry
City
Owlbury
Lydham
Asterton
Minton
Ticklerton
Hatton
Stanton Long
Eaton
Acton Scott
Working Farm
Broadstone
Myndtown
Marshbrook
The Long Mynd
Wenlock Edge
Corve Dale
Dolfor
Mainstone
Bishop's Castle
House on Crutches
Lea
Eaton
Choulton
Eyton
Plowden
Whittingslow
Holdgate
Harton
Middlehope
Munslow
Aston Munslow
Tugford
Colebatch
Lydbury North
Horderley
Woolston
Upper Affcot
Wistanstow
Alcaston
Abdon
Clun Forest
Cefn Einion
Brockton
Edgton
Westhope
Corfton
Diddlebury
Upper Heath
Boulden
Clee St Margaret
Cilfaesty Hill
Anchor
Hall of the Forest
Bryn
Acton
Lower Down
Walcot
Cheney Longville
Strefford
Lower Dinchope
Peaton
Whitcott Keysett
Hopesay
Sibdon Carwood
Newington
Halford
Craven Arms
Great Sutton
Black Mt
Newcastle
Bicton
Kempton
Aston on Clun
Seifton
Culmington
Stoke St Milborough
Felindre
Bettws-y-crwyn
Clun
Clun Mill
Clunton
Little Brampton
Stokesay
Stokesay Castle
Norton
Hayton's Bent
Cleedownton
Quabbs
Llwyn
Purslow
Broome
Clunbury
Vernolds Common
Hopton Cangeford
Beguildy
Churchbank
Twitchen
Brandhill
The Wernlas Collection
Onibury
Stanton Lacy
Upper Treverward
Hobarris
Hopton Castle
Hoptonheath
Abcott
Clungunford
Wootton
Bitterley
Middleton
David's Well
Llanbadarn Fynydd
Black Mountain
Dutlas
Glyndŵr's Way
Llanfair Waterdine
Purlogue
Chapel Lawn
Shelderton
Marlow
Bromfield
Henley
Rhydmoelddu
Beacon Hill
Skyborry Green
New Invention
Bedstone
Todding
Kinton
Leintwardine
Ludlow
Snitton
Farden
Knowbury
Bucknell
Downton on the Rock
Llanbister
Knucklas
Stowe
Buckton
Hope Bagot
Crug
Knighton (Tref-y-Clawdd)
Llangunllo
Milebrook
Brampton Bryan
Teme
Walford
Burrington
Aston
Overton
Caynham
Whitton
Abbey-cwm-hir
Adforton
Ashford Carbonell
Greete
Severn (Hafren)
Dee (Dyfrdwy)
Clun
Cymru
Powys
Wrexham
Wales
Whittington
Ruyton-XI-Towns
Stiperstones
Dee
SJ
SO
A483
A5
A49
A41
A458
A488
A489
A490
A495
A525
A528
A539
A4113
B4385
B4368
B4393
B4396
42
43
34
25

34
Stoke-on-Trent
Newcastle-under-Lyme
Hanley
Fenton
Longton
Cheadle
Madeley
Audlem
Whitchurch
Market Drayton
Stone
Eccleshall
Staffor
Stafford
Newport
Telford and Wrekin
Telford
Wellington
Hadley
Oakengates
Donnington
Dawley
Shrewsbury
Shawbury
Penkridge
Rugeley
Cannock Chase
Cannock
Hednesford
Shifnal
Albrighton
Codsall
Tettenhall
Wolverhampton
Wednesfield
Willenhall
Walsall
Bilston
Darlaston
Wednesbury
Sedgley
Coseley
Tipton
Dudley
West Bromwich
Oldbury
Smethwick
Rowley Regis
Brierley Hill
Kingswinford
Wordsley
Stourbridge
Halesowen
West M
Kidderminster
Bewdley
Stourport on Severn
Bromsgrove
Much Wenlock
Madeley
Ironbridge
Broseley
Bridgnorth
Shropshire
Cleobury Mortimer
Kinver
Wombourne
Brewood
Gnosall
Hodnet
Wem
Wyre Forest
0 1 2 3 4 5 6 miles
0 1 2 3 4 5 6 7 8 9 10 km
33
26
43
44

Ashbourne
Belper
HEANOR
Eastwood
Kimberley
ILKESTON
Nottingham
City
Duffield
Allestree
Chaddesden
Derby
City
Mickleover
Normanton
Uttoxeter
Tutbury
Willington
Repton
Melbourne
Castle Donington
Kegworth
Stapleford
BEESTON
LONG EATON
Sandiacre
Ruddington
Loughborough
Shepshed
Burton upon Trent
Horninglow
Swadlincote
Newhall
Woodville
Ashby-de-la-Zouch
COALVILLE
Whitwick
Mountsorrel
Barton-under-Needwood
Abbots Bromley
NEEDWOOD FOREST
Lichfield
Measham
Leicester
Ibstock
Birstall
Anstey
Tamworth
Market Bosworth
Atherstone
Earl Shilton
Hinckley
Burbage
Nuneaton
Bedworth
SUTTON COLDFIELD
Kingstanding
Erdington
Castle Bromwich
Coleshill
BIRMINGHAM
Solihull
Shirley
Dorridge
Coventry
Kenilworth
Rugby
Lutterworth
Aldridge
Midlands
NATIONAL FOREST
CHARNWOOD FOREST
Melton Mowbray
Ashbourne 44
45
36
27

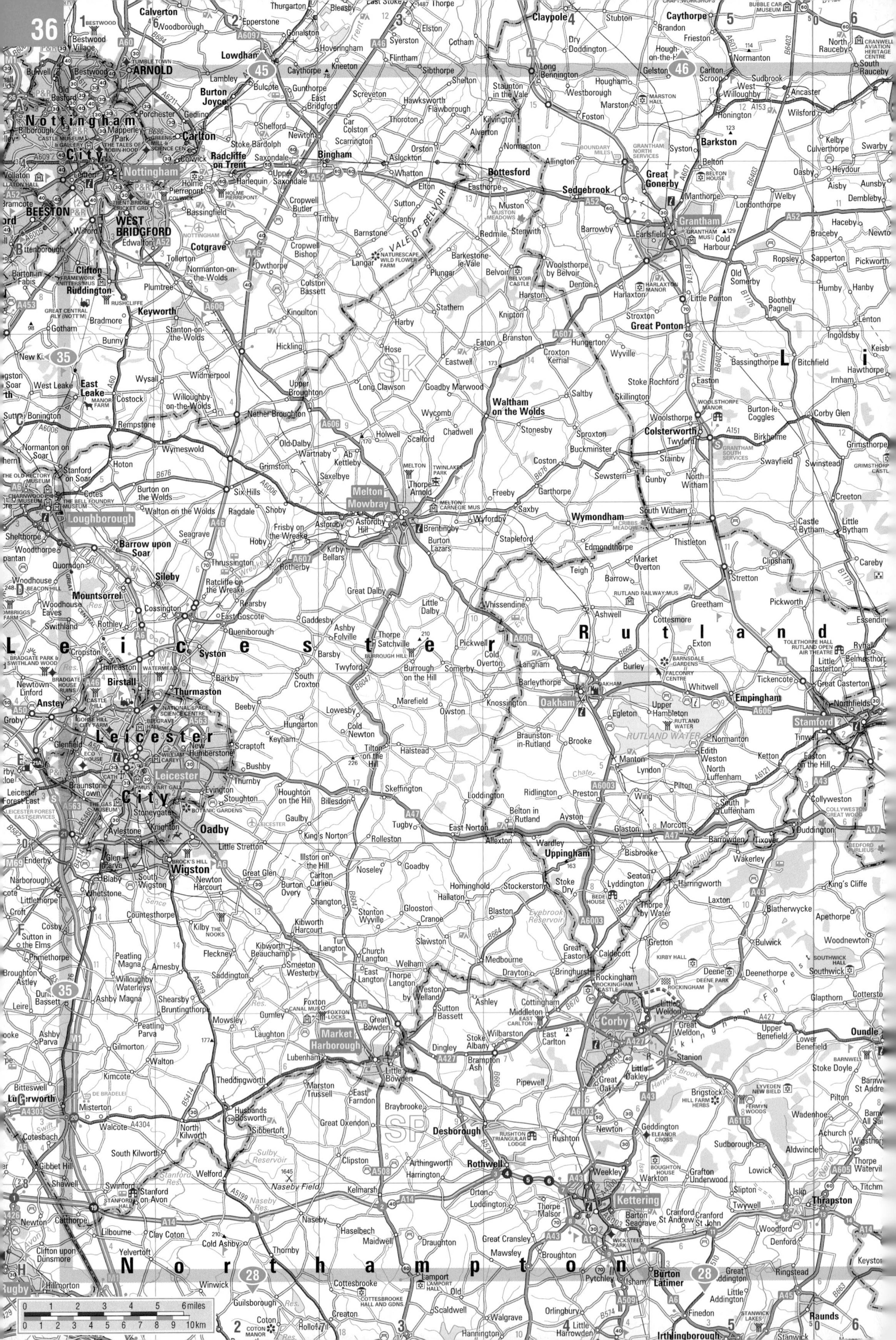

Nottingham
City
Nottingham
ARNOLD
BEESTON
WEST BRIDGFORD
Loughborough
Leicester
City
Leicester
Oadby
Wigston
Melton Mowbray
Oakham
Rutland
Rutland Water
Stamford
Grantham
Bingham
Bottesford
Uppingham
Market Harborough
Corby
Kettering
Desborough
Rothwell
Burton Latimer
Oundle
Thrapston
Lutterworth
Leicester
Northampton
Vale of Belvoir
SK
SP
45
46
35
28
0 1 2 3 4 5 6 miles
0 1 2 3 4 5 6 7 8 9 10 km

Sleaford
Heckington
Helpringham
Swineshead
Boston
Donington
Kirton
Gosberton
Pinchbeck
Spalding
Bourne
Market Deeping
Deeping St James
Crowland
Whaplode
Holbeach
Long Sutton
Sutton Bridge
Wisbech
March
Whittlesey
Peterborough
Yaxley
Ramsey
Chatteris
Sawtry
Huntingdon
St Ives
Ely
Littleport
Upwell
Morton
Rippingale
Billingborough
Horbling
Moulton
Eye
Terrington St Clement
Clenchwarton
Soham
HOLLAND FEN
HOLBEACH MARSH
BEDFORD LEVEL (MIDDLE)
BEDFORD LEVEL (SOUTH)
Deeping Fen
North Fen
Morris Fen
Farcet Fen
Whittlesey Mere
Ramsey Hollow
Tick Fen
Pidley Fen
Chatteris Fen
Marshland Fen
Upwell Fen
Euximoor Fen
Laddus Fens
Tydd St Giles Fen
Terrington Marsh
Gedney Marsh
THE WASH
BOSTON DEEPS
LYNN DEEPS
Lynn Channel
Forty Foot Drain
New Bedford River
Old Bedford River
Sixteen Foot Drain
Twenty Foot River
Great Ouse
ISLE OF ELY
Lincolnshire
Peterborough
Cambridgeshire
TF
TL
A15
A16
A17
A52
A47
A141
A142
A1101
A1
A1(M)
A14
A605
A1139
A10
A151
A1122
A1123
46
47
38
29

BRANCASTER ROADS
NORFOLK COAST
LYNN DEEPS
THE WASH
Lynn Channel
Holkham Bay
Blakeney Point
Brancaster Bay
Holme next the Sea
Titchwell
Brancaster Staithe
Burnham Deepdale
Brancaster
Burnham Norton
Burnham Overy Staithe
Holkham
Wells-Next-The-Sea
Stiffkey
Morston
Blakeney
Wiveton
Cley next the Sea
Old Hunstanton
Thornham
Burnham Westgate
Burnham Overy Town
Burnham Market
Burnham Thorpe
Cockthorpe
Langham
Glandford
Warham
Hunstanton
Ringstead
New Holkham
Wighton
Westgate
Binham
Saxlingham
Summerfield
North Creake
Copy's Green
Field Dalling
Heacham
Docking
Stanhoe
South Creake
Waterden
Great Walsingham
Little Walsingham
Lower Green
Bale
Sharrington
Sedgeford
Fring
Bircham Newton
North Barsham
Houghton St Giles
Hindringham
Brinton
Snettisham
Great Bircham
Barmer
West Barsham
East Barsham
Great Snoring
Thursford
Gunthorpe
Ingoldisthorpe
Shepherd's Port
Shernborne
Bircham Tofts
Bagthorpe
Syderstone
Blenheim Park
Sculthorpe
Little Snoring
Barney
Swanton Novers
Melton Constable
Dersingham
Wicken Green Village
Kettlestone
Fulmodestone
Anmer
Tattersett
Coxford
Dunton
Shereford
Tatterford
Hempton
Fakenham
Little Ryburgh
Stibbard
Hindolveston
Wolferton
Sandringham
West Newton
Flitcham
New Houghton
West Rudham
East Rudham
Toftrees
Great Ryburgh
Wood Norton
Hillington
Harpley
Helhoughton
Colkirk
Guist
Castle Rising
North Wootton
South Wootton
Little Massingham
West Raynham
East Raynham
Oxwick
Twyford
Foulsham
Terrington Marsh
Ongar Hill
Roydon
Congham
Great Massingham
South Raynham
Hamrow
Horningtoft
Gateley
Broom Green
Bintree
Weasenham St Peter
Whissonsett
King's Lynn
Grimston
Pott Row
Weasenham All Saints
Wellingham
Tittleshall
Stanfield
Brisley
North Elmham
Orange Row
Clenchwarton
Gaywood
Massingham Heath
Rougham
East Bilney
Billingford
Bawdeswell
Walpole Cross Keys
Terrington St Clement
West Lynn
Fairstead
Gayton
Leziate
Ashwicken
Mileham
Worthing
Hardwick
Tilney All Saints
Tilney High End
Hay Green
Fair Green
Tower End
Gayton Thorpe
West Lexham
Litcham
Bittering
Beetley
Swanton Morley
Middleton
East Walton
East Lexham
Gressenhall
Hoe
West Winch
North Runcton
East Winch
Terrington St John
Saddle Bow
Wiggenhall St Germans
West Bilney
Pentney
West Acre
Castle Acre
Newton
Beeston
Longham
Woodgate
Tilney St Lawrence
Walpole Highway
Wiggenhall St Mary the Virgin
Setchey
Blackborough End
South Acre
Great Dunham
Drury Square
Sparrow Green
Crane's Corner
Dereham
Etling Green
North Tuddenham
Marshland
Tottenhill Row
Narborough
Little Dunham
Great Fransham
Wendling
Wiggenhall St Mary Magdalen
Watlington
Wormegay
Great Palgrave
Sporle
Little Fransham
Scarning
Toftwood
Clint Green
Tottenhill
Yaxham
Marham
Shouldham
Runcton Holme
Necton
West End
Daffy Green
Westfield
Whinburgh
Marshland St James
Marshland Fen
South Runcton
Shouldham Thorpe
Beachamwell Warren
Swaffham
North Pickenham
Holme Hale
Bradenham
Garvestone
Thuxton
Emneth Hungate
Stowbridge
Stow Bardolph
Barton Bendish
Fincham
Crowshill
Shipdham
Letton Green
Reymerston
West Head
Wimbotsham
Beachamwell
Shingham
Cranworth
Southburgh
Outwell
Downham Market
Stradsett
Crimplesham
Cockley Cley
South Pickenham
Ashill
Saham Hills
Hardingham
Stow Bardolph Fen
Barroway Drove
Bexwell
Broomhill
Eastmoor
Saham Toney
Ovington
Woodrising
Carbrooke
Nordelph
Denver
Boughton
Wereham
Oxborough
Gooderstone
Great Cressingham
Caudlesprings
Hingham
Three Holes
West Dereham
Hilborough
Watton
Scoulton
Upwell Fen
Fordham
Wretton
Stoke Ferry
Whittington
Foulden
Bodney
Little Cressingham
Griston
Little Ellingham
Deopham Green
South District
Hilgay
Northwold
The Arms
Merton
Northacre
Rockland St Peter
Ten Mile Bank
Caston
Great Ellingham
Lakesend
Brookville
Thompson
Stow Bedon
Rockland All Saints
Old Bedford River
Hilgay Fen
Southery
Methwold Hythe
Methwold
Cranwich
Ickburgh
Mundford
Lower Stow Bedon
Shropham
Welney
Methwold Fens
Southery Fens
Queen's Ground
West Tofts
THETFORD FOREST PARK
BRECKLAND
Gold Hill
Brandon Creek
Apes Hall
Great Hockham
Eccles Road
Brandon Bank
Feltwell
Feltwell Fens
Wretham
Mare Fen
Hockwold cum Wilton
Weeting
Larling
Fodder Fen
Burnt Fen
Hockwold Fens
Quidenham
Littleport
Brandon
Santon Downham
Croxton
Bridgham
Kenninghall
Little Ouse
East Harling
BEDFORD LEVEL (SOUTH)
Kenninghall Heath
Little Downham
Shippea Hill Sta.
Thetford
Brettenham
Shadwell
North Lopham
Chettisham
West Fen
Prickwillow
Lakenheath
Wangford Warren
Thetford Warren
Rushford
Gasthorpe
Garboldisham
Ely
Queen Adelaide
Kenny Hill
Lakenheath Warren
Knettishall
Blo' Norton
Middle Fen
Great Fen
Mildenhall Fen
Eriswell
Elveden
Barnham
Euston
Coney Weston
Hopton
Market Weston
Thelnetham
Stuntney
Redgrave
Little Thetford
Broad Hill
Holywell Row
Beck Row
Barningham
Hinderclay
Isleham Fen
Thistley Green
West Row
Fakenham Magna
Botesdale
Rickinghall
Barway
Soham Cotes
Stretham
Isleham
Mildenhall
The King's Forest
Honington
Sapiston
Hepworth
Soham
Worlington
Barton Mills
Icklingham
Bardwell
Wattisfield
Freckenham
Tuddenham
Ixworth Thorpe
Troston
Stanton
Upthorpe
Walsham le Willows
Cranmer Green
West Stow
Ingham
Ampton
Great Livermere
Fordham
0 1 2 3 4 5 6 miles
0 1 2 3 4 5 6 7 8 9 10 km

6
7
8
9
10
11
A
B
C
D
E
F
G
H
PEDDARS WAY AND NORFOLK COAST PATH
Salthouse
MUCKLEBURGH COLLECTION
Weybourne
NORTH NORFOLK RAILWAY
Sheringham
PRIORY MAZE & GARDENS
NORFOLK SHIRE HORSE CENTRE
West Runton
CROMER MUSEUM
Cromer
Newgate
Kelling
SHERINGHAM PARK
Upper Sheringham
Beeston Regis
East Runton
Overstrand
High Kelling
Bodham
East Beckham
Aylmerton
Felbrigg
Letheringsett
West Beckham
FELBRIGG HALL
Crossdale Street
Northrepps
Sidestrand
Trimingham
Holt
PICTURECRAFT GALLERY
Gresham
BACONSTHORPE CASTLE
THERINGSETT WATERMILL
HOLT
Frogshall
Hempstead
Baconsthorpe
Sustead
Roughton
Southrepps
Gimingham
Mundesley
Hunworth
Bessingham
Hanworth
Thorpe Market
Lower Street
STOW WINDMILL
Stody
Edgefield
Plumstead
Matlaske
Thurgarton
Alby Hill
Trunch
Paston
Aldborough
Knapton
Bacton
Bradfield
Broomholm
Keswick
Edgefield Street
Little Barningham
Wickmere
ALBY CRAFTS
ALBY GARDENS
Antingham
Edingthorpe
Walcot
Briston
MANNINGTON GARDENS
Calthorpe
Erpingham
Suffield
Swafield
Colby
STRAW MUSEUM
WOLTERTON PARK
Itteringham
Edingthorpe Green
Witton Bridge
Ridlington
Happisburgh
Saxthorpe
North Walsham
Spa Common
Crostwight
Whimpwell Green
Corpusty
BLICKLING HALL
Ingworth
Banningham
Happisburgh Common
Eccles on Sea
Thurning
Blickling
Felmingham
EAST RUSTON OLD VICARAGE GARDEN
Oulton
Hempstead
Norton Corner
Silvergate
Dunkirk
Honing
Lessingham
Sea Palling
Guestwick
Heydon
Oulton Street
Tuttington
Westwick
Ingham Corner
WAXHAM GREAT BARN
Waxham
Guestwick Green
Wood Dalling
Aylsham
Bengate
East Ruston
Burgh next Aylsham
Skeyton
Worstead
Ingham
Salle
Southgate
Swanton Abbott
Sloley
Dilham
Stalham
Stalham Green
Fengate
Smallburgh
Hickling
NORFOLK COAST
Themelthorpe
Marsham
Brampton
Scottow
MUSEUM OF THE BROADS
Sutton
Hickling Green
Cawston
Little London
BURE VALLEY RAILWAY
Reepham
Booton
Eastgate
Lamas
Pennygate
Barton Turf
Hickling Heath
Horsey
Whitwell Street
Brandiston
The Heath
Buxton
Little Hautbois
Tunstead
Sco Ruston
ANT BROADS AND MARSHES
Wood Street
Catfield
Hickling Broad
HORSEY WINDMILL
WINTERTON DUNES
Haveringland
Hevingham
Stratton Strawless
WROXHAM BARNS
Neatishead
Barton Broad
HICKLING BROAD
MARTHAM BROAD
Sparham
ANIMAL ARK
Coltishall
Ashmanhaugh
RA BOAT TRIP
Irstead
Sharp Street
Potter Heigham
East Somerton
West Somerton
Winterton-on-Sea
Swannington
Waterloo
Horstead
Alderford
Upgate
New Hainford
Hainford
Belaugh
Hoveton
Threehammer Common
Thurne
Bastwick
Martham
Lenwade
DINOSAUR ADVENTURE PARK
Frettenham
HILLSIDE ANIMAL SANCTUARY
Wroxham
Upper Street
Lower Street
Ludham
LUDHAM MARSHES
Hemsby
Newport
Felthorpe
Attlebridge
Morton
Newton St Faith
Horning
Wroxham Broad
Upper Street
Repps
Rollesby
Ormesby St Michael
Scratby
California
Weston Longville
Horsford
Crostwick
BURE MARSHES
Woodbastwick
Primrose Green
Thorpe Marriot
Horsham St Faith
Spixworth
Rackheath
Ranworth
Clippesby
Filby Broad
Ormesby St Margaret
Weston Green
Ringland
Taverham
Drayton
NORWICH INTERNATIONAL
Salhouse
FAIRHAVEN WOODLAND & WATER GARDEN
Hockering
Panxworth
South Walsham
Billockby
Burgh St Margaret
Filby
CAISTER ROMAN TOWN
Caister-on-Sea
Mattishall Burgh
Honingham
Costessey
Hellesdon
Old Catton
New Rackheath
Little Plumstead
Hemblington
Upton
THE CANDLEMAKER WORKSHOP
Thrigby
THRIGBY HALL WILDLIFE GARDENS
Mautby
West Caister
Mattishall
East Tuddenham
Easton
Mile Cross
New Costessey
Upper Hellesdon
Sprowston
Thorpe End
Blofield Heath
North Burlingham
Acle
Runham
Stokesby
West End
GREAT YARMOUTH GREAT DENES
YARMOUTH
Welborne
Colton
Marlingford
Bowthorpe
Earlham
THE FORUM
New Catton
CATHEDRAL
Thorpe St Andrew
Great Plumstead
Blofield
Damgate
Brundall
Lingwood
NORWICH
Beighton
Tunstall
Runham
Great Yarmouth
SEA LIFE GREAT YARMOUTH
Brandon Parva
Barford
Bawburgh
SAINSBURY CENTRE FOR VISUAL ARTS
Colney
WHITLINGHAM
Lakenham
Postwick
Strumpshaw
South Burlingham
Moulton St Mary
THE Halvergate Marshes
Barnham Broom
Great Melton
Little Melton
Cringleford
Trowse Newton
Surlingham
Buckenham
Halvergate
Cobholm Island
ELIZABETHAN HOUSE, MAXIMUM NELSON/TOLHOUSE MUSEUMS
Wramplingham
High Green
Eaton
Kirby Bedon
Hassingham
Freethorpe
BROADS
Burgh Castle
Southtown
EXHIBITION GALLERIES
AMAZONIA-WORLD OF REPTILES
Carleton Forehoe
Hethersett
Keswick
Arminghall
Bramerton
MID YARE
Southwood
Wickhampton
BERNEY ARMS WINDMILL
PLEASURE BEACH
Kimberley
Crownthorpe
Ketteringham
Caistor St Edmund
Framingham Pigot
Rockland St Mary
Claxton
Cantley
Limpenhoe
Bradwell
Gorleston-on-Sea
Framingham Earl
Hellington
Ashby St Mary
PETTITTS ANIMAL ADVENTURE PARK
Belton
Wymondham
East Carleton
Swardeston
Dunston
Poringland
Stoke Holy Cross
Yelverton
Langley Street
Reedham
REDWINGS HORSE SANCTUARY
Morley St Botolph
Swainsthorpe
Mulbarton
Bergh Apton
Hardley Street
Silfield
Howe
Thurton
ST OLAVES PRIORY
Fritton
Hopton on Sea
Suton
Bracon Ash
Hawes' Green
Shotesham
Brooke
Chedgrave
Lower Thurlton
The Dell
Lound
Wreningham
Newton Flotman
Stubb's Green
Sisland
Loddon
Thurlton
Thorpe
SOMERLEYTON HALL
Blundeston
Ashwellthorpe
Flordon
Saxlingham Thorpe
Seething
Spooner Row
Fundenhall
Hapton
Saxlingham Nethergate
Kirstead Green
Mundham
Stubbs Green
Hales
Herringfleet
Corton
Besthorpe
Fundenhall Street
Tasburgh
Saxlingham Green
HALES HALL BARN & GARDENS
Raveningham
RAVENINGHAM GARDENS
Haddiscoe
Somerleyton
PLEASUREWOOD HILLS LEISURE PARK
Attleborough
Tacolneston
Forncett St Mary
Tharston
Hempnall
Thwaite St Mary
Toft Monks
Maypole Green
LOWESTOFT AND EAST SUFFOLK MARITIME MUSEUM
Oulton
Bunwell
Forncett End
INDUSTRIAL STEAM MUSEUM
Stratton St Michael
Road Green
Woodton
Hedenham
Kirby Cane
Stockton
Wheatacre
Normanstone
Puddledock
Carleton Rode
Forncett St Peter
Long Stratton
Hempnall Green
Fritton
Morningthorpe
Topcroft
Cobbler's Green
Ellingham
Kirby Row
Aldeby
Burgh St Peter
Oulton Broad
HERITAGE/VISITOR CENTRE
Old Buckenham
Hargate
Wacton
Topcroft Street
Ditchingham
Broome
Geldeston
Gillingham
LOWESTOFT MUSEUM
CARLTON MARSHES NATURE RESERVE
Lowestoft
Kirkley
Aslacton
Shelton
Shelton Green
Waveney
Beccles
New Buckenham
Tibenham
Great Moulton
Hardwick
Earsham
Bungay
Mettingham
Shipmeadow
Worlingham
Barnby
Carlton Colville
Pakefield
Pristow Green
Sneath Common
Great Green
Denton
Barsham
North Cove
Mutford
Banham
Goose Green
Tivetshall St Margaret
North Green
Bush Green
NORFOLK AND SUFFOLK AVIATION MUSEUM
Flixton
Ringsfield
Ilketshall St Andrew
Ringsfield Corner
Hulver Street
Rushmere
Gisleham
Kessingland
Kessingland Beach
Winfarthing
Tivetshall St Mary
Pulham Market
Alburgh
Ilketshall St Margaret
Ellough
AFRICA ALIVE
Gissing
Pulham St Mary
Homersfield
Henstead
Benacre
Mill Green
Starston
St Cross South Elmham
St Michael South Elmham
Ilketshall St Lawrence
Redisham
Sotterley
Shelfanger
Burston
Garlic Street
Harleston
Wortwell
Redenhall
Mendham
St Margaret South Elmham
SOUTH ELMHAM HALL
All Saints South Elmham
Stone Street
Shadingfield
West End
Wrentham
Fersfield
Shimpling
Rushall
Dickleburgh
Cox Common
Brampton
Stoven
Clay Common
BENACRE
Bressingham
Walcot Green
Needham
100TH BOMB GROUP MEMORIAL MUS
Withersdale Street
Rumburgh
Mill Common
Frostenden
Covehithe
Roydon
Diss
Thelveton
Weybread
Metfield
St James South Elmham
Spexhall
South Cove
BRESSINGHAM MUSEUM GARDENS
Thorpe Abbotts
Uggeshall
Magpie Green
Palgrave
Scole
Brockdish
Wissett
Westhall
Broadway
Cove Bottom
BILLINGFORD WINDMILL
Wangford
Reydon Smear
Wortham
Stuston
Oakley
Hoxne
Syleham
WINGFIELD OLD COLLEGE
Fressingfield
Little Whittingham Green
Linstead Parva
Chediston
Halesworth
Holton
Blyford
Reydon
Thrandeston
Brome
Brome Street
Cross Street
Wingfield
HEN REEDBED NATURE RESERVE
SOUTHWOLD MUSEUM
Southwold
Burgate
Langton Green
Heckfield Green
Chippenhall Green
Silverley's Green
Cratfield
Cookley
Wenhaston
Blythburgh
Mellis
Yaxley
Eye
Battlesea Green
Denham
Pixey Green
Swan Green
Huntingfield
Blackheath
Walberswick
Stradbroke
Ashfield Green
Walpole
Thorington
Thornham Parva
Cranley
Wootten Green
Russel's Green
Banyard's Green
Bramfield
SUFFOLK COAST
Denham Street
Horham
Wilby
Laxfield
Heveningham
Sibton Green
Dunwich
Thornham Magna
Braiseworth
Redlingfield
Athelington
Foals Green
Brundish Street
Ubbeston Green
High Street
Dunwich Forest
DUNWICH UNDERWATER EXPLORATION EXHIBITION
TG
TM
A149
A148
A140
A1151
A1062
A149
A1064
A47
A1074
A11
A146
A143
A144
A145
A12
A1117
A1095
B1436
B1145
B1149
B1354
B1150
B1159
B1152
B1140
B1135
B1172
B1108
B1113
B1332
B1527
B1136
B1074
B1077
B1134
B1062
B1123
B1124
B1126
B1127
B1387
B1116
B1118
B1117
B1125
B1437
31

Isle of Anglesey
(Sir Ynys Môn)
ANGLESEY / YNYS MÔN
Wilfa Head
Pen Wilfa
Cemaes Bay
Bae Cemaes
Cemlyn Bay
Bae Cemlyn
WYLFA POWER STATION AND OBSERVATION TOWER
The Skerries
Ynysoedd y Moelrhoniaid
Carmel Head
Pen Carmel
Llanbadrig
Porthllechog
Bull Bay
Porth Llechog
Amlwch Port
Amlwch
Burwen
Cemaes
Tregele
Llanfechell
Rhosbeirio
Bodewryd
Point Lynas
Trwyn Eilian
Llaneilian
Pengorffwysfa
Penysarn
Nebo
Dulas
Llanfairynghornwy
Llanfflewyn
Rhosgoch
Carreglefn
Llanrhyddlad
Rhydwyn
Church Bay
Porth Swtan
Rhosybol
Tyn-y-pwll
City Dulas
Brynrefail
Ty-mawr
Llanallgo
Llanbabo
Alaw Res.
Gwredog
Llanfaethlu
LLYNON WINDMILL
Llanddeusant
Llandyfrydog
Mynydd Bodafon
HOLYHEAD BAY
BAE CAERGYBI
DUBLIN 1:49
DUN LAOGHAIRE 1:59
DUBLIN 3:15
Elim
Llanerchymedd
Hebron
Maenaddwyn
Llanfwrog
Llantrisant
Bachau
North Stack
BREAKWATER
HOLYHEAD MOUNTAIN 220
Llaingoch
Holyhead
(Caergybi)
Llanfachraeth
Carmel
Capel Coch
Brynteg
Goferydd
South Stack
ELLINS TOWER RSPB RESERVE
PENRHOS FEILW STANDING STONES
Kingsland
Newlands Park
Pen-llyn
Llechcynfarwy
CORS ERDDREINIOG
Penrhosfeilw
ANGLESEY
Llanynghenedl
Valley
Bodedern
Trefor
Tregaian
Penrhyn Mawr
Trearddur
Glan-traeth
Four Mile Bridge
Caergeiliog
Bryngwran
Llynfaes
Llangwyllog
Glan Gors
Rhosmeirch
Llanfihangel yn Nhowyn
Gwalchmai
Bodffordd
ORIEL YNYS MÔN
Talwrn
Holy Island
Ynys Gybi
Llanfairyneubwll
Heneglwys
Llangefni
Rhoscolyn
Capel-gwyn
Ddrydwy
Cymyran Bay
Bae Cymyran
Llanfaelog
Pencarnisiog
Cerrigceinwen
Llangristiolus
HENBLAS COUNTRY PARK
Rhosneigr
Bryn Du
Soar
Capel Mawr
Pentre Berw
Gaerwen
Afon Cefni
Bethel
Trefdraeth
Llanddaniel Fab
Llangwyfan-isaf
Llangadwaladr
Aberffraw
Hermon
Malltraeth
Llangaffo
Brynsiencyn
Bodorgan
Newborough
Dwyran
SEA ZOO
NEWBOROUGH WARREN AND YNYS LLANDDWYN
Pen-lon
MODEL VILLAGE
BIRD WORLD
FOEL FARM PARK
Malltraeth Bay
Bae Malltraeth
Newborough Forest
MENAI STRAIT
SEIONT II MARITIME MUSEUM
CASTLE & REGIMENTAL MUS
Llanddwyn I.
Ynys Llanddwyn
Caernarfon
The Bar
Abermenai Pt.
Trwyn Abermenai
WELSH HIGHLAND RAILWAY
Llanfaglan
Bontnewydd
CAERNARFON AIR MUSEUM
Saron
Glan-rhyd
Morfa Dinlle
Llanwnda
Rhostryfan
Dinas Dinlle
Ffrwd
Llandwrog
GLYNLLIFON
Groeslon
Carmel
Cilgwyn
Talysarn
Penygroes
SH
CAERNARFON BAY
BAE CAERNARFON
Pontllyfni
Tan-yr-allt
Llanllyfni
Nebo
Aberdesach
WELSH LIFE
Tainlon
Clynnog-fawr
Nasareth
Capel Uchaf
Gyrn-goch
Pant-glas
Bryn-yr-eryr
509 BWLCH MAWR
522 GYRN DDU
Upper Clynnog
Dafarn Faig
Trefor
564 YR EIFL
Llanaelhaearn
Pen-sarn
Cenin
Garndolbenmaen
Llecheiddior
Llithfaen
Carreg Ddu
Porth Dinllaen
Pistyll
Morfa Nefyn
Nefyn
Llwyndyrys
Pencaenewydd
Llangybi
LLEYN HISTORICAL MARITIME MUSEUM
Edern
Tan-y-graig
Fron
Llanarmon
Llanystumdwy
Porth Ysgadan
Glanrhyd
Rhos-fawr
Y Ffôr
PENARTH FAWR MEDIEVAL HOUSE
Chwilog
LLOYD GEORGE MEMORIAL MUSEUM
Rhos-y-llan
CORS GEIRCH
Boduan
Llannor
Abererch
HAVEN
Tudweiliog
BODVEL HALL ADVENTURE PARK
Efailnewydd
Dinas
Rhyd-y-clafdy
Denio
Pwllheli
Carreg yr Imbill
South Beach
Porth Golmon
Garnfadryn
Penrhos
Bryn-mawr
Llaniestyn
PENRHYN LLYN
Pen-y-graig
Llangwnnadl
Rhedyn
Sarn Meyllteyrn
Llanbedrog
Penrhyn Mawr
Ty-hen
Pen-y-groeslon
Bryncroes
Botwnnog
Nanhoron
Mynytho
Trwyn Llanbedrog
Methlem
Rhydlios
Llandegwning
St Tudwal's Road
Angorfa St Tudwal
Capel Carmel
Rhoshirwaun
304 MYNYDD RHIW
PLAS-YN-RHIW
Llawrdref Bellaf
Llangian
Abersoch
Rhiw
191
Porth Neigwl or Hell's Mouth
Llanengan
St Tudwal's Island East
Ynys St Tudwal Dwyrain
Uwchmynydd
Aberdaron
Llanfaelrhys
Sarn Bach
Bwlchtocyn
Marchroes
St Tudwal's Island West
Ynys St Tudwal Gorllewin
Bodermid
Bardsey Sound
Swnt Enlli
Pen-y-cil
Cilan Uchaf
LLEYN / LLŶN
Trwyn Cilan
YNYS ENLLI
167
Bardsey Island
Ynys Enlli
0 1 2 3 4 5 6 miles
0 1 2 3 4 5 6 7 8 9 10 km

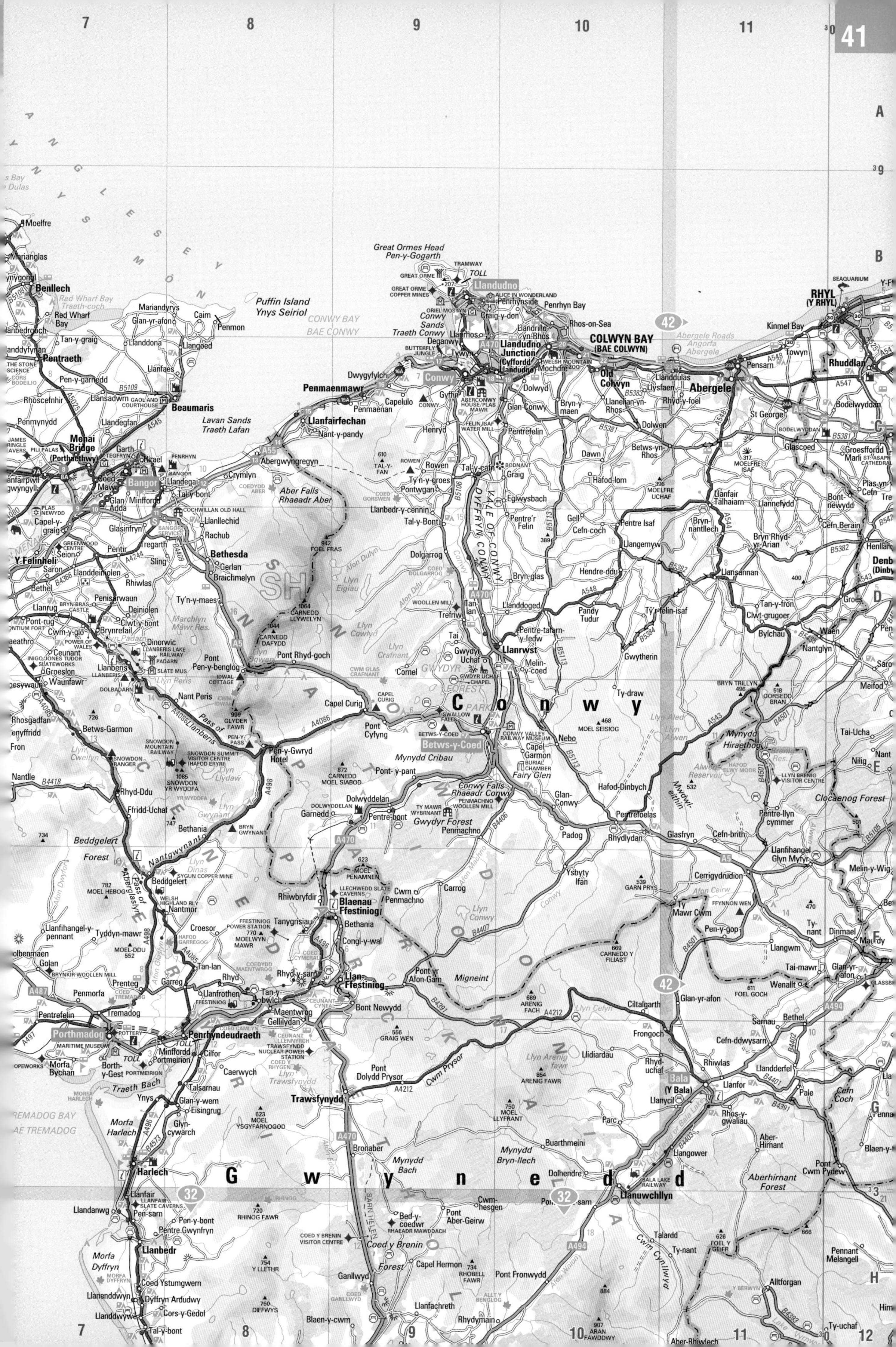

41
7
8
9
10
11
12
A
B
C
D
E
F
G
H
ANGLESEY
YNYS MÔN
Moelfre
Marianglas
Benllech
Red Wharf Bay
Traeth-coch
Pentraeth
Puffin Island
Ynys Seiriol
CONWY BAY
BAE CONWY
Great Ormes Head
Pen-y-Gogarth
Llandudno
Penrhynside
Craig-y-don
Penrhyn Bay
Rhos-on-Sea
COLWYN BAY
(BAE COLWYN)
Old Colwyn
Llanddulas
Abergele
Abergele Roads
Angorfa Abergele
RHYL
(Y RHYL)
Kinmel Bay
Towyn
Pensarn
Rhuddlan
Llandudno Junction
(Cyffordd Llandudno)
Deganwy
Conwy
Conwy Sands
Traeth Conwy
Mochdre
Penmaenmawr
Penmaenan
Capelulo
Llanfairfechan
Nant-y-pandy
Lavan Sands
Traeth Lafan
Beaumaris
Llansadwrn
Llandegfan
Menai Bridge
(Porthaethwy)
Bangor
Llandegai
Tal-y-bont
Abergwyngregyn
Aber Falls
Rhaeadr Aber
Bethesda
Gerlan
Rachub
Llanllechid
Y Felinheli
Llanrug
Llanberis
Deiniolen
Dinorwic
Nant Peris
Pass of Llanberis
Pont Pen-y-benglog
Pont Rhyd-goch
Capel Curig
Pen-y-Gwryd Hotel
Betws-Garmon
Rhyd-Ddu
Beddgelert
Forest
Nantgwynant
Beddgelert
Nantmor
Tremadog
Porthmadog
Penrhyndeudraeth
Minffordd
Portmeirion
Harlech
Morfa Harlech
TREMADOG BAY
BAE TREMADOG
Llanbedr
Llanfair
Talsarnau
Blaenau Ffestiniog
Llan Ffestiniog
Maentwrog
Gellilydan
Trawsfynydd
Tanygrisiau
Dolwyddelan
Pont-y-pant
Betws-y-Coed
Llanrwst
Trefriw
Dolgarrog
Tal-y-Bont
Rowen
Henryd
Glan-Conwy
Eglwysbach
VALE OF CONWY
DYFFRYN CONWY
Llanddoged
Pandy Tudur
Llangernyw
Gwytherin
Nebo
Pentrefoelas
Rhydlydan
Ysbyty Ifan
Cerrigydrudion
Llanfair Talhaiarn
Llansannan
Bylchau
Nantglyn
Groes
Clocaenog Forest
Llyn Brenig
Llyn Alwen
Mynydd Hiraethog
Frongoch
Bala
(Y Bala)
Llanycil
Llanuwchllyn
Llangower
Rhos-y-gwaliau
Llandderfel
Llanfor
Aberhirnant Forest
Bronaber
Mynydd Bach
Coed y Brenin
Forest
Ganllwyd
Llanfachreth
Migneint
Snowdonia
SNOWDONIA NATIONAL PARK
GWYDYR FOREST
Gwydyr Forest
Conwy
Gwynedd
32
42

SC
SH
I R I S H
S E A
LIVERPOOL
BAY
BELFAST 8:00
DOUGLAS 4:15
(Winter only)
DUBLIN 7:00
DOUGLAS 2:30
(March-Nov)
Crosby Channel
Southport
Marshside
Churchtown
Blowick
Birkdale
Hillside
Ainsdale-on-Sea
Ainsdale
Shirdley Hill
Woodvale
Halsall
Formby Hills
Freshfield
Formby
Formby Pt.
Little Altcar
Great Altcar
Downholland Cross
Barton
Haskayne
Hightown
Ince Blundell
Lydiate
Little Crosby
Lunt
Sefton
Thornton
Netherton
Great Crosby
LITHERLAND
Waterloo
Seaforth
Orrell
Bootle
New Brighton
Walton
Kirkdale
Mockbeggar Wharf
Liscard
Egremont
Wallasey
Leasowe
Meols
Moreton
Seacombe
Poulton
Bidston
HOYLAKE
West Hoyle Bank
Hilbre I.
Claughton
Birkenhead
Upton
Greasby
Grange
West Kirby
Woodchurch
Frankby
Tranmere
Rock Ferry
Prenton
New Ferry
Port Sunlight
BEBINGTON
Storeton
Caldy
Thurstaston
Irby
Thingwall
Barnston
Brimstage
Pensby
Heswall
Bromborough
Eastham
Thornton Hough
Dawpool Bank
Gayton
Raby
Parkgate
Neston
Hinderton
Willaston
Hooton
Childer Thornton
Little Neston
Ness
Burton
Gayton Sands
Holywell Bank
Welsh Channel
Point of Ayr
Yr Parlwr Du
River Dee
Afon Dyfrdwy
Talacre
Gwespyr
Gronant
Ffynnongroyw
Picton
Prestatyn
Gwaenysgor
Llanasa
Mostyn
Mostyn Quay
SEAQUARIUM
RHYL
(Y RHYL)
Y-Ffrith
Meliden
Kinmel Bay
Abergele Roads
Angorfa
Abergele
Rhos-on-Sea
COLWYN BAY
(BAE COLWYN)
Old Colwyn
Llanddulas
Llysfaen
Abergele
Towyn
Pensarn
Rhuddlan
Dyserth
Trelawnyd
Trelogan
Axton
Glan-y-don
Whitford
Greenfield
Carmel
Walwen
Gorsedd
Pant-y-Wacco
Cwm
Holywell
(Treffynnon)
Bagillt
Rhyd-y-foel
Llanelian-yn-Rhos
Bryn-y-maen
Dolwen
St George
Bodelwyddan
Rhuallt
Pen-y-cefn
Brynford
Dolphin
Betws-yn-Rhos
Glascoed
Groesffordd Marli
St Asaph
(Llanelwy)
Waen
Tremeirchion
Babell
Caerwys
Pentre Halkyn
Flint (Y Fflint)
Mount Pleasant
Oakenholt
Dawn
Hafod-lom
Moelfre Uchaf
Llanfair Talhaiarn
Llannefydd
Plas-yn-Cefn
Trefnant
Bont-newydd
Bodfari
Afon-wen
Ysceifiog
Lixwm
Rhes-y-cae
Halkyn
Flint Mountain
Connah's Quay
Shotton
Gell
Cefn-coch
Pentre Isaf
Bryn-nantllech
Llangernyw
Bryn Rhyd-yr-Arian
Cefn Berain
Green
Henllan
Denbigh
(Dinbych)
Nannerch
Rhosesmor
Northop
Northop Hall
Hendre
Rhydymwyn
C o n w y
Hendre-ddu
Llansannan
Llandyrnog
Waen
Llangwyfan
Flintshire
(Sir Y Fflint)
Soughton
New Brighton
Buckley
(Bwcle)
Hawarden
(Penarlâg)
Queensferry
Sealand
Pandy Tudur
Tan-y-fron
Clwt-grugoer
Tŷ'n-y-felin-isaf
Bylchau
Groes
Peniel
Llanrhaeadr
Prion
Pentre Llanrhaeadr
Llangynhafal
Llanynys
Gellifor
Cilcain
Pantymwyn
Gwernaffield
Mold
(Yr Wyddgrug)
Tafarn-y-gelyn
Cadole
Mynydd Isa
Llong
Spon Green
Broughton
Nantglyn
Saron
Hirwaen
Gwernymynydd
Maeshafn
Nercwys
Pontblyddyn
Penyffordd
Higher Kinnerton
Ty-draw
Meifod
Rhewl
Llanbedr-Dyffryn-Clwyd
Llanferres
Leeswood
Coed-Talon
Hope
(Yr Hôb)
MOEL SEISIOG
Llyn Aled
Llyn Alwen
Mynydd Hiraethog
Cyffylliog
Bontuchel
Llanfwrog
Ruthin
(Rhuthun)
Eryrys
Treuddyn
Caergwrle
Nebo
Tai-Ucha
Denbighshire
Llanarmon-yn-Ial
Graianrhyd
Cefn-y-bedd
Llay
Alwen Reservoir
Nant Uchaf
Efenechtyd
Llanfair-Dyffryn-Clwyd
Nilig
Pwll-glas
Graig-fechan
Rhydtalog
Ffrith
Brymbo
Bwlchgwyn
Gwersyllt
Gresford
Hafod-Dinbych
Pennant
Clocaenog
(Sir Ddinbych)
Pentre-celyn
Four Crosses
Moss
Glan-Conwy
Mwdwl-eithin
Clocaenog Forest
Clawdd-newydd
Llandegla
Gwynfryn
Minera
Rhosrobin
Pentrefoelas
Pentre-llyn-cymmer
Pen-y-stryt
Coedpoeth
New Broughton
Padog
Rhydlydan
Glasfryn
Cefn-brith
Derwen
Rhyd-y-meudwy
Bersham
Wrexham
Llanfihangel Glyn Myfyr
Llanelidan
CYRN Y BRAIN
ESCLUSHAM MOUNTAIN
Rhostyllen
Ysbyty Ifan
GARN PRYS
Cerrigydrudion
Bryn Saith Marchog
Melin-y-Wig
Maesyr Cefn Mtn
Pentredwr
Eglwyseg Mountain
Tai-nant
Johnstown
Marchwiel
Sontley
Rhosllanerchrugog
Ty Mawr
Cwm
Bettws Gwerfil Goch
Gwyddelwern
Bryneglwys
Pen-y-gop
Ty-nant
Dinmael
Morfydd
Llantysilio Mountain
Llandynan
Rhewl
Ruabon Mountain
Penycae
Stryt-issa
Gyfelia
Cock Bank
Eyton
CARNEDD Y FILIAST
Llangwm
Maerdy
Carrog
LLANGOLLEN STEAM RAILWAY
VALLE CRUCIS ABBEY
Acrefair
Tai-mawr
Glan-yr-afon
Druid
Corwen
Llidiart-y-parc
Glyndyfrdwy
Llangollen
Cefn-mawr
Ruabon
(Rhiwabon)
New Bridge
Rhos-y-Madoc
Erbistock
Wenallt
Cynwyd Forest
Cynwyd
Garth
Froncysyllte
0 1 2 3 4 5 6 miles
0 1 2 3 4 5 6 7 8 9 10km

CHORLEY
Ramsbottom
Edgworth
Rochdale
HEYWOOD
Bury
Bolton
Horwich
Standish
Wigan
WESTHOUGHTON
FARNWORTH
Radcliffe
Middleton
Skelmersdale
ORMSKIRK
Burscough
Rainford
Kirkby
Knowsley
St Helens
Prescot
Huyton
Haydock
Newton-le-Willows
ASHTON-IN-MAKERFIELD
Leigh
ATHERTON
Tyldesley
Worsley
Swinton
PRESTWICH
SALFORD
Eccles
MANCHESTER
Trafford Park
URMSTON
Stretford
Irlam
Cadishead
Partington
SALE
Altrincham
GATLEY
Cheadle
Warrington
Widnes
Runcorn
Speke
Liverpool Airport
Garston
Lymm
Manchester Airport
WILMSLOW
Knutsford
Alderley Edge
Macclesfield
Ellesmere Port
Frodsham
Helsby
Northwich
Weaverham
Hartford
Winsford
Middlewich
Holmes Chapel
Sandbach
Congleton
Elworth
Tarporley
Crewe
Nantwich
Alsager
Kidsgrove
Tunstall
Burslem
Stoke-on-Trent
Hanley
Newcastle-under-Lyme
Audlem
Whitchurch
Malpas
Farndon
Holt
Biddulph
Greater Manchester
Merseyside
Halton
Cheshire
Cheshire East
Cheshire West and Chester

Greater Manchester
West Yorkshire
South Yorkshire
Peak District National Park
High Peak
Hope Forest
Cheshire East
Staffordshire
Derbyshire Dales
Rochdale
Littleborough
Heywood
Bury
Radcliffe
Middleton
Royton
Shaw
Milnrow
Oldham
Chadderton
Prestwich
Whitefield
Salford
Eccles
Manchester
Trafford Park
Stretford
Sale
Altrincham
Hale
Gatley
Cheadle
Stockport
Denton
Hyde
Ashton-under-Lyne
Stalybridge
Dukinfield
Mossley
Droylsden
Bredbury
Romiley
Marple
Hazel Grove
Bramhall
Manchester Airport
Wilmslow
Alderley Edge
Knutsford
Poynton
Bollington
Prestbury
Macclesfield
Congleton
Holmes Chapel
Biddulph
Kidsgrove
Alsager
Tunstall
Burslem
Stoke-on-Trent
Hanley
Newcastle-under-Lyme
Fenton
Leek
Cheddleton
Cheadle
Glossop
Hadfield
New Mills
Low Leighton
Whaley Bridge
Chapel-en-le-Frith
Buxton
Burbage
Edale
Castleton
Hope
Hathersage
Bamford
Tideswell
Bakewell
Ashford in the Water
Baslow
Youlgrave
Matlock
Cromford
Wirksworth
Ashbourne
Hartington
Huddersfield
Marsden
Meltham
Slaithwaite
Holmfirth
Penistone
Stocksbridge
Denby Dale
Skelmanthorpe
Clayton West
Kirkburton
Mirfield
Horbury
Saddleworth Moor
Dove Stone Res.
Crowden
Kinder Scout
Ladybower Res.
Howden Moors
Midhope Moors
Axe Edge
Dove Dale
Alton
Scale: 0 1 2 3 4 5 6 miles; 0 1 2 3 4 5 6 7 8 9 10 km

Goole Fields
Goole Moors
Crigglestone
Hemsworth
South Elmsall
South Kirkby
Adwick le Street
Thorne
Crowle
Royston
Darton
Barnsley
Cudworth
Thurnscoe
Bentley
Armthorpe
Doncaster
Hatfield
Stainforth
Hatfield Moors
Thorne Waste or Moors
ISLE OF AXHOLME
Epworth
Darfield
Wombwell
Goldthorpe
Bolton upon Dearne
Worsbrough
Hoyland
Wath upon Dearne
Mexborough
Warmsworth
Bessacarr
Swinton
Conisbrough
New Edlington
New Rossington
Chapeltown
Rawmarsh
Thrybergh
Dalton
Rotherham
Maltby
Tickhill
Harworth
Bawtry
Gainsborough
Beckingham
Sheffield
Whiston
Thurcroft
Dinnington
Langold
Blyth
Aston
Handsworth
Beighton
Carlton in Lindrick
RETFORD
ECKINGTON
Dronfield
Worksop
Staveley
Clowne
Whitwell
Creswell
Chesterfield
Brimington
Bolsover
Market Warsop
Shirebrook
Edwinstowe
Ollerton
Boughton
Tuxford
East Markham
North Wingfield
Clay Cross
MANSFIELD WOODHOUSE
Mansfield
Clipstone
SHERWOOD FOREST
SHERWOOD PINES FOREST PARK
Bilsthorpe
Rainworth
SUTTON IN ASHFIELD
KIRKBY IN ASHFIELD
ALFRETON
Somercotes
Southwell
Newark-on-Trent
Sutton on Trent
Annesley Woodhouse
RIPLEY
HUCKNALL
Calverton
HEANOR
Eastwood
ARNOLD
Belper
Kimberley
Burton Joyce
ILKESTON
Nottingham City
Carlton
Lowdham
N o t t i n g h a m

North Lincolnshire
North East Lincolnshire
Lincolnshire
Scunthorpe
Grimsby
Immingham
Brigg
Gainsborough
Lincoln
Sleaford
Newark-on-Trent
Market Rasen
Horncastle
Caistor
Winterton
Barton
Burton upon Stather
Flixborough
Crosby
Frodingham
Ashby
Bottesford
Messingham
Broughton
Appleby
Santon
Wressle
Hibaldstow
Scawby
Kirton in Lindsey
Scotter
Laughton Forest
Laughton
Blyton
Epworth
Isle of Axholme
Haxey
Owston Ferry
Keadby
Gunness
Althorpe
Belton
Burringham
Yaddlethorpe
Barnetby le Wold
Elsham
Melton Ross
Kirmington
Habrough
Ulceby
Thornton Curtis
Wootton
Keelby
Stallingborough
Healing
Laceby
Waltham
Binbrook
Tealby
Walesby
Nettleton
Moortown
Waddingham
Snitterby
Atterby
Bishop Norton
Glentham
Spital in the Street
Hemswell
Harpswell
Corringham
Springthorpe
Heapham
Upton
Kexby
Willingham by Stow
Stow
Sturton by Stow
Saxilby
Torksey
Marton
Knaith
Lea
West Stockwith
East Stockwith
Walkerith
Morton
Faldingworth
Friesthorpe
Wickenby
Snelland
Wragby
Langworth
Nettleham
Welton
Dunholme
Scothern
Sudbrooke
Reepham
Cherry Willingham
Fiskerton
Washingborough
Heighington
Branston
Canwick
Bracebridge Heath
Waddington
North Hykeham
South Hykeham
Skellingthorpe
Doddington
Birchwood
Boultham
Whisby
Eagle
Thorpe on the Hill
Bassingham
Navenby
Wellingore
Leadenham
Fulbeck
Caythorpe
Brant Broughton
Welbourn
Cranwell
Ruskington
Leasingham
Metheringham
Martin
Timberland
Billinghay
Woodhall Spa
Tattershall
Coningsby
Kirkstead
Bardney
Southrey
Stixwould
Heckington
Helpringham
Ancaster
Wilsford
Barkston
Claypole
Balderton
Collingham
Sutton on Trent
Dunham
North Clifton
South Clifton
Swinderby
Norton Disney
Stapleford
Winthorpe
Coddington
Beckingham
Barnby in the Willows
Westborough
Long Bennington
Dry Doddington
Hougham
Marston
Sudbrook
Honington
Holland Fen
Wildmore Fen
South Kyme Fen
Swineshead
Hubbert's Bridge

Skeffling
Kilnsea
53
TA
SPURN
SPURN HEAD
ROTTERDAM 10:25
ZEEBRUGGE 10:25
CLEETHORPES
MOUTH OF THE HUMBER
CLEETHORPES COAST LIGHT RAILWAY
PLEASURE ISLAND THEME PARK
Humberston
Tetney Lock
North Cotes
Tetney
N O R T H
Donna Nook
Marshchapel
Eskham
Wragholme
Grainthorpe
Fulstow
LINCOLNSHIRE WOLDS RLY
North Somercotes
DONNA NOOK
Skidbrooke North End
S E A
Covenham St Bartholomew
Conisholme
South Somercotes
Saltfleet
Covenham St Mary
Utterby
Yarburgh
Skidbrooke
ALVINGHAM MILL
Alvingham
Fotherby
Little Grimsby
Saltfleetby St Clements
SALTFLEETBY THEDDLETHORPE
North Cockerington
RUSHMOOR
Saltfleetby All Saints
Theddlethorpe St Helen
South Cockerington
Saltfleetby St Peter
Louth
Keddington
Grimoldby
Theddlethorpe All Saints
SEAL SANCTUARY & NATURE CENTRE
Stewton
ST JAMES
Manby
Hallington
Little Carlton
Great Carlton
Meers Bridge
Mablethorpe
Legbourne
South Reston
Gayton le Marsh
Trusthorpe
Little Cawthorpe
North Reston
Strubby
Tathwell
Withern
Thorpe
Sutton on Sea
Haugham
Muckton
Tothill
Maltby le Marsh
Sandilands
Authorpe
Beesby
Maidenwell
Burwell
Woodthorpe
WOODY'S TOP
Hannah
Farforth
Ruckland
Belleau
CLAYTHORPE WATER MILL AND WILDFOWL GARDENS
Saleby
Markby
White Pit
Swaby
Aby
Asserby
Ketsby
South Thoresby
ALFORD WINDMILL
ALFORD MANOR HOUSE
Bilsby
Huttoft
South Ormsby
Rigsby
Alford
Haugh
Tetford
Calceby
Anderby
ON YOUR MARQUES
Well
Farlesthorpe
Mumby
Authorpe Row
Brinkhill
Driby
Cumberworth
Salmonby
Somersby
Ulceby
Helsey
Chapel St Leonards
TF
Sutterby
Bonthorpe
Hogsthorpe
Ashby Puerorum
Bag Enderby
Harrington
Langton
Claxby
Willoughby
Greetham
Aswardby
Sloothby
HARDY'S ANIMAL FARM
Skendleby
Hagworthingham
Sausthorpe
Ingoldmells
FANTASY ISLAND CHILDREN'S PLAYDROME & THE MILLENNIUM ROLLERCOASTER
SNIPE DALES
Partney
Addlethorpe
Lusby
Welton le Marsh
FUNCOAST WORLD
Hameringham
Mavis Enderby
Raithby
Scremby
Asgarby
Candlesby
Orby
Orby Marsh
Spilsby
Ashby by Partney
GUNBY HALL
Hareby
Old Bolingbroke
Hundleby
Burgh le Marsh
Winthorpe
Seathorne
NORTHCOTE HEAVY HORSE CENTRE
Bratoft
BOLINGBROKE
Halton Holegate
Great Steeping
NATURELAND SEAL SANCTUARY
BURGH LE MARSH WINDMILL
West Keal
Toynton All Saints
Irby in the Marsh
CHURCH FARM MUS
Skegness
East Keal
THE LIFEBOAT STATION
East Kirkby
Toynton St Peter
Firsby
Toynton Fen Side
Little Steeping
LINCOLNSHIRE AVIATION HERITAGE CENTRE
Keal Cotes
Thorpe Culvert
Thorpe St Peter
Croft
Revesby Bridge
Thorpe Fendykes
Wainfleet All Saints
Seacroft
Croft Marsh
Stickford
New Bolingbroke
Wainfleet Bank
MAGDALEN MUSEUM
GIBRALTAR POINT
Fen Side
Midville
New Leake
Wainfleet Tofts
Wainfleet St Mary
Stickney
Eastville
Friskney Eaudike
Wainfleet Sand
Medlam
East Fen
Friskney
Carrington
Lade Bank
Wrangle Bank
Fen
Northlands
Friskney Tofts
Leake Commonside
SIBSEY TRADER MILL
Sibsey
Old Leake
Wrangle Lowgate
Friskney Flats
Frithville
Wrangle
Hurn's End
38
BRANCASTER ROADS
Hill Dyke
Boston Long Hedges
Leverton Outgate
Frith Bank
Leverton Highgate
BOSTON DEEPS
Cowbridge
Leverton
Leverton Lucasgate
Benington
LYNN DEEPS
Haltoft End
Brancaster Bay
SCOLT HEAD ISLAND
HOLME DUNES
GUILDHALL
Butterwick
37
HOLME BIRD OBSERVATORY
Holme next the Sea
Titchwell
Brancaster Staithe
Burnham Deepdale
Freiston
Skirbeck
T H E W A S H
Thornham
Brancaster
Burnham Norton
Fishtoft
Old Hunstanton
Westgate
Wyberton
Scrane End
Hunstanton
Burnham Market
A
B
C
D
E
F
G
H
7
8
9
10
11

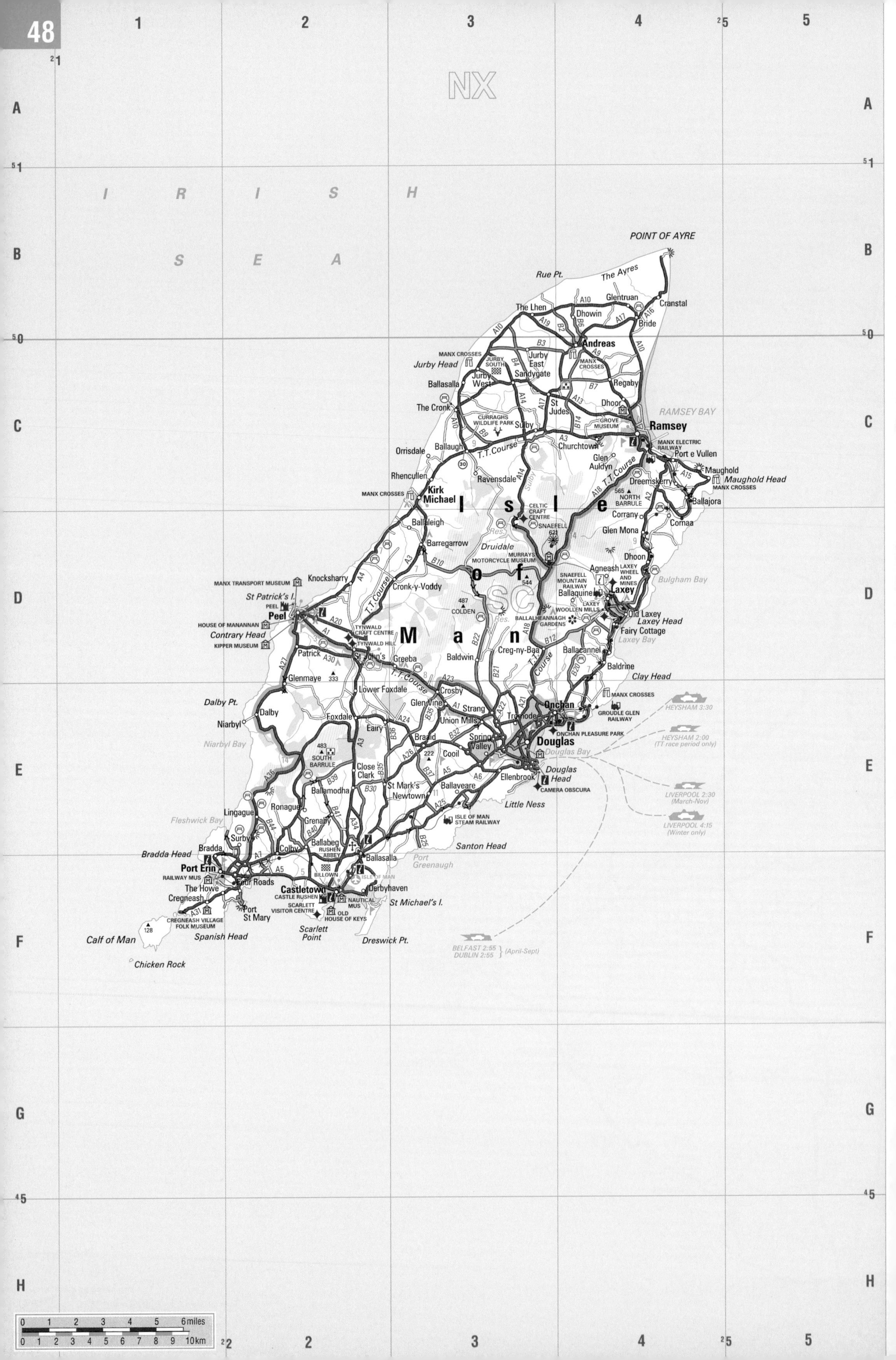

NX

IRISH

S E A

POINT OF AYRE

Rue Pt.

The Ayres

The Lhen   Glentruan   Cranstal
A10
B6   Dhowin   A17   Bride
A19   B2   A16
MANX CROSSES   JURBY   Andreas   A9   A10
Jurby Head   SOUTH   Jurby   MANX CROSSES
Ballasalla   B3   East   A9   Regaby
Jurby   Sandygate   B7
West   A14   St   A13   Dhoor   RAMSEY BAY
The Cronk   Judes   GROVE   Ramsey
CURRAGHS   Suby   MUSEUM   Manx Electric
WILDLIFE PARK   A3   Churchtown   Railway   Port e Vullen
Orrisdale   Ballaugh   Glen   A15   Maughold
T.T.Course   Auldyn   A18   Dreemskerry   Maughold Head
Rhencullen   30   Ravensdale   A14   T.T. Course   565   MANX CROSSES
MANX CROSSES   Kirk   Isle   NORTH   A2   Ballajora
Michael   CELTIC   BARRULE   Corrany
Ballaleigh   CRAFT CENTRE   SNAEFELL   Cornaa
Barregarrow   B10   621   Glen Mona   9
Druidale   MURRAYS   Dhoon
MANX TRANSPORT MUSEUM   MOTORCYCLE MUSEUM   Agneash   LAXEY   Bulgham Bay
Knocksharry   A4   of   SNAEFELL MOUNTAIN   WHEEL AND MINES
St Patrick's I.   Cronk-y-Voddy   544   RAILWAY   Ballaquine   Laxey
PEEL   T.T.Course   487   Ballalheannagh   LAXEY   Old Laxey
HOUSE OF MANANNAN   Peel   COLDEN   GARDENS   WOOLLEN MILLS   Laxey Head
Contrary Head   A20   Man   B22   A18   Fairy Cottage
KIPPER MUSEUM   A1   Baldwin   Creg-ny-Baa   B12   Ballacannel   Laxey Bay
Patrick   TYNWALD CRAFT CENTRE   B21   Baldrine
A30   Tynwald Hill   St John's   Greeba   A23   Clay Head
Glenmaye   333   Crosby   B20
T.T. Course   Glen Vine   Strang   MANX CROSSES
Dalby Pt.   Lower Foxdale   A1   Union Mills   Onchan   GROUDLE GLEN
Dalby   A24   A22   Tromode   RAILWAY   HEYSHAM 3:30
Niarbyl   Foxdale   B35   Braaid   B32   Spring   ONCHAN PLEASURE PARK
Niarbyl Bay   Eairy   Valley   Douglas   HEYSHAM 2:00
483   A26   222   Cooil   A6   Douglas Bay   (TT race period only)
SOUTH   Close   Ellenbrook   CAMERA OBSCURA
BARRULE   Clark   St Mark's   Douglas   LIVERPOOL 2:30
Lingague   Ronague   Newtown   Ballaveare   Head   (March-Nov)
Fleshwick Bay   B44   Grenaby   A25   Little Ness   LIVERPOOL 4:15
Surby   B40   A24   ISLE OF MAN   (Winter only)
Bradda Head   Bradda   Ballabeg   STEAM RAILWAY
Port Erin   Colby   RUSHEN   Ballasalla   Santon Head
RAILWAY MUS   A5   ABBEY   Billown   Port
The Howe   Four Roads   Castletown   Greenaugh
Cregneash   A3   CASTLE RUSHEN   Derbyhaven
CREGNEASH VILLAGE   Port   SCARLETT   NAUTICAL MUS   St Michael's I.
128   FOLK MUSEUM   St Mary   VISITOR CENTRE   OLD
Calf of Man   Spanish Head   Scarlett   HOUSE OF KEYS
Point   Dreswick Pt.   BELFAST 2:55
Chicken Rock   DUBLIN 2:55   (April-Sept)

0 1 2 3 4 5 6 miles
0 1 2 3 4 5 6 7 8 9 10km

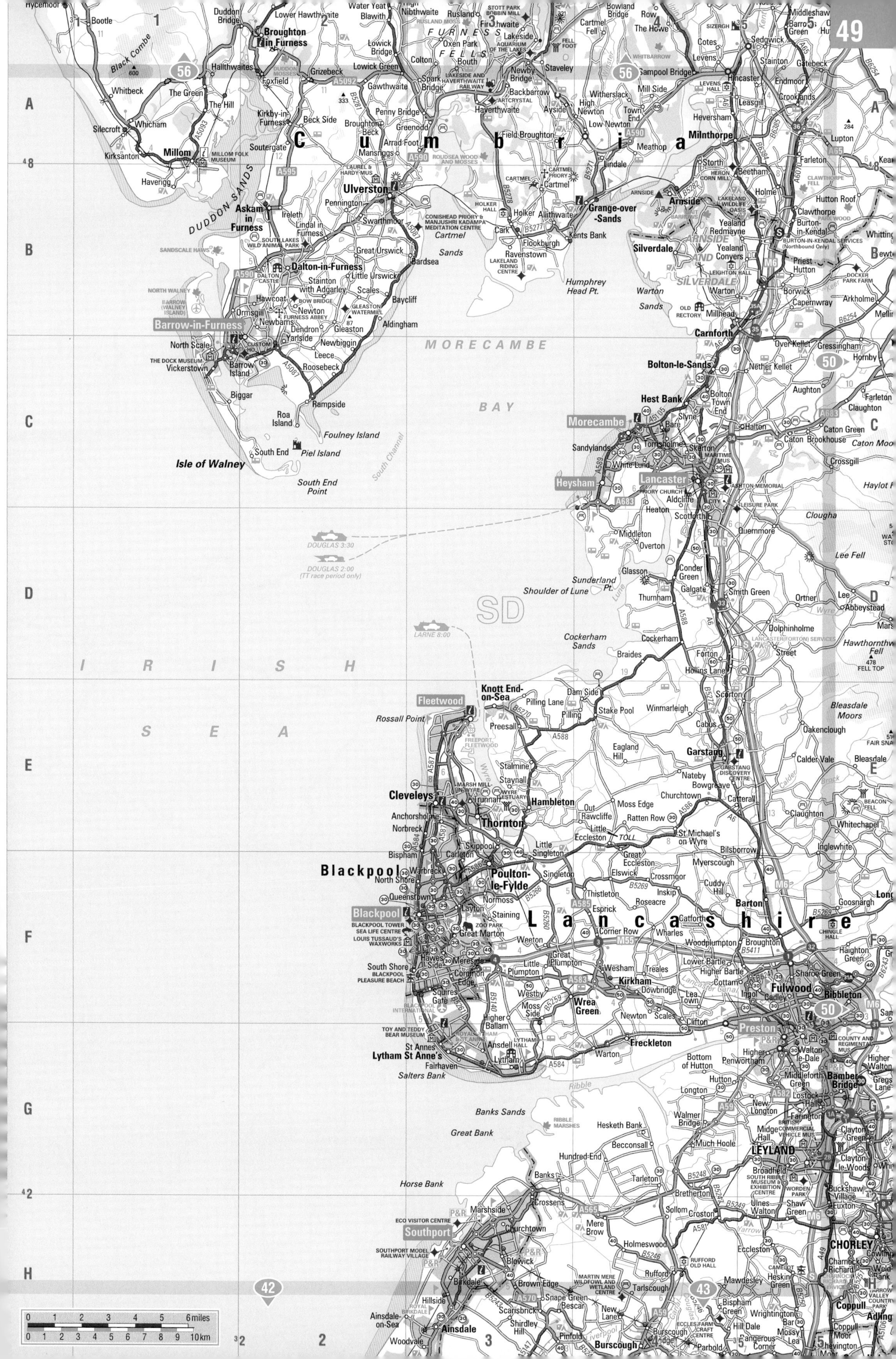
Cumbria
Lancashire
MORECAMBE
BAY
IRISH
SEA
SD
FURNESS
FELLS
DUDDON SANDS
Bootle
Black Combe
Whitbeck
Silecroft
Whicham
Kirksanton
Millom
Haverigg
Duddon Bridge
Broughton in Furness
Hallthwaites
The Green
The Hill
Foxfield
Grizebeck
Kirkby-in-Furness
Soutergate
Askam in Furness
Ireleth
Lindal in Furness
Dalton-in-Furness
Barrow-in-Furness
North Scale
Vickerstown
Barrow Island
Biggar
Isle of Walney
South End
Piel Island
Roa Island
Rampside
Foulney Island
South End Point
South Channel
Hawcoat
Ormsgill
Newbarns
Dendron
Yarlside
Leece
Roosebeck
Newbiggin
Gleaston
Scales
Stainton with Adgarley
Little Urswick
Great Urswick
Baycliff
Aldingham
Bardsea
Swarthmoor
Pennington
Ulverston
Lowick Bridge
Lowick Green
Gawthwaite
Penny Bridge
Greenodd
Arrad Foot
Mansriggs
Spark Bridge
Colton
Oxen Park
Rusland
Finsthwaite
Lakeside
Newby Bridge
Backbarrow
Haverthwaite
Nibthwaite
Water Yeat
Blawith
Lower Hawthwaite
Field Broughton
Cartmel
Cartmel Sands
Holker
Allithwaite
Cark
Flookburgh
Ravenstown
Kents Bank
Humphrey Head Pt.
Grange-over-Sands
Lindale
Meathop
Ayside
High Newton
Low Newton
Witherslack
Town End
Staveley
Cartmel Fell
Bowland Bridge
Row
The Howe
Sampool Bridge
Mill Side
Levens
Cotes
Sedgwick
Hincaster
Leasgill
Heversham
Milnthorpe
Storth
Beetham
Arnside
Silverdale
Yealand Redmayne
Yealand Conyers
Warton
Warton Sands
Millhead
Carnforth
Bolton-le-Sands
Hest Bank
Slyne
Bolton Town End
Bare
Morecambe
Torrisholme
Skerton
Sandylands
White Lund
Heysham
Lancaster
Aldcliffe
Heaton
Scotforth
Middleton
Overton
Sunderland Pt.
Shoulder of Lune
Glasson
Thurnham
Conder Green
Galgate
Cockerham
Cockerham Sands
Braides
Forton
Hollins Lane
Knott End-on-Sea
Pilling Lane
Pilling
Dam Side
Stake Pool
Preesall
Winmarleigh
Eagland Hill
Garstang
Nateby
Bowgreave
Catterall
Churchtown
Scorton
Cabus
Fleetwood
Rossall Point
Stalmine
Staynall
Cleveleys
Hambleton
Thornton
Anchorsholme
Norbreck
Bispham
Blackpool
North Shore
Queenstown
Layton
Carleton
Skippool
Poulton-le-Fylde
Normoss
Staining
Little Singleton
Singleton
Out Rawcliffe
Little Eccleston
Moss Edge
Ratten Row
St Michael's on Wyre
Great Eccleston
Elswick
Bilsborrow
Myerscough
Great Marton
Marton
Weeton
Hawes Side
South Shore
Squires Gate
St Annes
Lytham St Anne's
Lytham
Ansdell
Fairhaven
Salters Bank
Westby
Moss Side
Wrea Green
Kirkham
Wesham
Treales
Esprick
Thistleton
Roseacre
Wharles
Catforth
Woodplumpton
Broughton
Barton
Freckleton
Warton
Newton
Clifton
Preston
Fulwood
Ribbleton
Penwortham
Hutton
Longton
Walmer Bridge
Much Hoole
Hesketh Bank
Becconsall
Tarleton
Hundred End
Banks Sands
Great Bank
Horse Bank
Banks
Crossens
Marshside
Churchtown
Southport
Birkdale
Hillside
Ainsdale-on-Sea
Ainsdale
Woodvale
Scarisbrick
Shirdley Hill
Burscough
Rufford
Holmeswood
Mere Brow
Sollom
Croston
Bretherton
Leyland
Chorley
Eccleston
Mawdesley
Bispham Green
Parbold
Heskin Green
Coppull
Lupton
Farleton
Holme
Hutton Roof
Clawthorpe
Burton-in-Kendal
Priest Hutton
Borwick
Capernwray
Over Kellet
Nether Kellet
Gressingham
Hornby
Aughton
Halton
Caton Green
Caton
Brookhouse
Crossgill
Quernmore
Clougha
Lee Fell
Ortner
Abbeystead
Dolphinholme
Street
Oakenclough
Calder Vale
Bleasdale
Claughton
Whitechapel
Inglewhite
Goosnargh
Haighton Green
Bamber Bridge
DOUGLAS 3:30
DOUGLAS 2:00 (TT race period only)
LARNE 8:00
0 1 2 3 4 5 6 miles
0 1 2 3 4 5 6 7 8 9 10 km

Y O R K S H I R E
D A L E S
N A T I O N A L
P A R K
L a n c a s h i r e
F O R E S T
O F
B O W L A N D
SD
LANGSTROTHDALE CHASE
W E N S L E Y D A L E
Kirkby Lonsdale
Clitheroe
Skipton
Burnley
Blackburn
Preston
Keighley
Rochdale
Bury
Settle
Ingleton
High Bentham
Low Bentham
Grassington
Malham
Gisburn
Barnoldswick
Earby
COLNE
NELSON
Brierfield
Padiham
ACCRINGTON
Oswaldtwistle
Great Harwood
Whalley
Longridge
Ribchester
Chatburn
Haslingden
RAWTENSTALL
Bacup
Todmorden
Hebden Bridge
Mytholmroyd
Littleborough
Whitworth
Ramsbottom
Edgworth
Tottington
Horwich
Chorley
LEYLAND
Bamber Bridge
Fulwood
Ribbleton
HEYWOOD
Milnrow
Slaidburn
Newton
Dunsop Bridge
Whitewell
Chipping
Waddington
West Bradford
Grindleton
Sawley
Bolton-by-Bowland
Hellifield
Long Preston
Gargrave
Earby
Foulridge
Trawden
Wycoller
Barrowford
Barley
Sabden
Pendleton
Downham
Rimington
Twiston
Horton in Ribblesdale
Stainforth
Giggleswick
Langcliffe
Austwick
Clapham
Kettlewell
Starbotton
Buckden
Arncliffe
Litton
Kilnsey
Conistone
Threshfield
Linton
Hetton
Rylstone
Cracoe
Burton in Lonsdale
Wennington
Hornby
Caton
Gressingham
Wray
Bentham
Dent
Dentdale
Gawthrop
Cowgill
Deepdale
Ribblehead
Hawes
Gayle
Buckden Pike
Pen-y-Ghent
Ingleborough
Whernside
Pendle Hill
Forest of Rossendale
THE FOREST OF PENDLE
THE FOREST OF TRAWDEN
KEIGHLEY MOOR
Longridge Fell
Trough of Bowland
Gisburn Forest
Stocks Reservoir
Darwen
Rishton
Clayton-le-Moors
Church
Belthorn
Hoddlesden
Edenfield
Helmshore
Stubbins
Turton Bottoms
Chapeltown
Egerton
Rivington
Adlington
Coppull
Whittle-le-Woods
Higher Walton
Samlesbury
Mellor
Wilpshire
Clayton-le-Woods
Euxton
Buckshaw Village
Anglezarke Moor
Walton-le-Dale
M6
M61
M65
M66
M62
A65
A59
A56
A682
A666
A671
A6068
A629
A646
A680
A675
A677
A687
A683
B6479
B6480
B6478
B6255
B6160
B6265
B6243
B6245
57
49
43
44
0 1 2 3 4 5 6 miles
0 1 2 3 4 5 6 7 8 9 10 km

Middleham
Coverham
Bedale
Aiskew
Leeming
Londonderry
Thornton-le-Moor
Borrowby
Knayton
Upsall
Kirby Knowle
Old Byland
Rievaulx
HAMBLETON HILLS
Thirsk
Old Thirsk
Sowerby
Sutton-under-Whitestonecliffe
Masham
West Tanfield
Kirby Wiske
Newsham
Pickhill
Ainderby Quernhow
Baldersby
Topcliffe
Dalton
Ripon
RIPON CATHEDRAL
Sharow
Copt Hewick
Bishopton
Studley Roger
STUDLEY ROYAL WATER GARDEN
FOUNTAINS ABBEY
NIDDERDALE
Pateley Bridge
Dishforth
Norton-le-Clay
Kirby Hill
Boroughbridge
Aldborough
Easingwold
Stillington
Crayke
Brafferton
Helperby
Myton-on-Swale
Tholthorpe
Alne
Huby
Tollerton
Markington
Bishop Monkton
Ripley
RIPLEY CASTLE
Knaresborough
Harrogate
Starbeck
Pannal
Spofforth
Wetherby
Boston Spa
Collingham
Tadcaster
Bramham
MARSTON MOOR
Upper Poppleton
York
Copmanthorpe
Bishopthorpe
ILKLEY
Ilkley Moor
Burley in Wharfedale
Otley
Menston
Guiseley
Yeadon
Bramhope
Horsforth
Baildon
BINGLEY
SHIPLEY
Bradford
PUDSEY
LEEDS
Morley
Rothwell
GARFORTH
Kippax
Sherburn in Elmet
CASTLEFORD
Ferrybridge
Knottingley
Pontefract
Featherstone
Normanton
Wakefield
OSSETT
Horbury
Dewsbury
BATLEY
Heckmondwike
Cleckheaton
BRIGHOUSE
Halifax
Elland
Mirfield
Huddersfield
Sowerby Bridge
Queensbury
Hemsworth
South Elmsall
Crigglestone
Selby
Sutton
Hensall

North Yorkshire
City of York
The East Riding of Yorkshire
North Lincolnshire
THE CARRS
THE WOLDS
HOWARDIAN HILLS
NORTH RIDING FOREST PARK
Rievaulx Moor
Helmsley
Kirkbymoorside
Pickering
Thornton-le-Dale
Malton
Norton-on-Derwent
Old Malton
Hovingham
Easingwold
Strensall
Haxby
York
Bishopthorpe
Copmanthorpe
Upper Poppleton
Stamford Bridge
Pocklington
Market Weighton
Holme-on-Spalding-Moor
Driffield
Beverley
Cottingham
Hessle
Barton-upon-Humber
Humber Bridge
Selby
Barlby
Howden
Goole
Snaith
Carlton
Thorne
Crowle
Scunthorpe
Winterton
Gilberdyke
North Cave
South Cave
North Ferriby
Sledmere
Fridaythorpe
Wetwang
Seamer
Sherburn
Rillington
Castle Howard
Eden Camp Modern History Theme Museum
Flamingo Land
Yorkshire Air Museum
Wharram Percy Medieval Village
Yorkshire Wolds Way
Goole Fields
Goole Moors
Thorne Waste or Moors
Redcliff Channel
Read's Island
Southfield Reservoir
Dutch River
0 1 2 3 4 5 6 miles
0 1 2 3 4 5 6 7 8 9 10 km
59
51
45
46

53
6
7
8
9
10
11
A
B
C
D
E
F
G
H
SCARBOROUGH CASTLE
Scarborough
South Bay
Osgodby
Cayton Bay
Yons Nab
CLEVELAND WAY
A165
Cayton
Lebberston
Gristhorpe
A1039
Filey Brigg
Filey
Folkton
Muston
Filey Bay
Primrose Valley
Hunmanby
Hunmanby Moor
Reighton Sands
Reighton Gap
Reighton
Speeton
Burton Fleming
B1229
Buckton
Bempton
B1255
Grindale
A165
Flamborough
FLAMBOROUGH HEAD
B1259
Boynton
B1253
SEWERBY HALL AND GARDENS
Sewerby
BONDVILLE MODEL VILLAGE
PRIORY
Rudston
BAYLE MUSEUM
Bridlington
Bessingby
West Hill
OLD PENNY MEMORIES
Carnaby
Haisthorpe
A614
Hilderthorpe
BURTON AGNES HALL
Thornholme
Kilham
PARK ROSE BIRD OF PREY CENTRE
BRIDLINGTON BAY
BURTON AGNES MANOR HOUSE
Burton Agnes
N O R T H
Harpham
Fraisthorpe
Lowthorpe
Nafferton
Gransmoor
Barmston
Great Kelk
Lissett
Gembling
Ulrome
A165
Wansford
B1249
Foston on the Wolds
SKIPSEA CASTLE
CRUCKLEY ANIMAL FARM
B1249
Church End
Skipsea
Skipsea Brough
Beeford
TA
S E A
Brigham
North Frodingham
B1242
Dunnington
Rotsea
Hempholme
Bewholme
Atwick
North Cliff
Burshill
Hornsea Mere
Hornsea
HORNSEA MUSEUM
Brandesburton
Baswick Steer
Seaton
B1244
FREEPORT HORNSEA
Hornsea Bridge
Leven
Leven Canal
Catwick
Sigglesthorne
Goxhill
Rolston
Mappleton
Little Hatfield
A165
Routh
A1035
B1243
Rise
Great Hatfield
Great Cowden
Long Riston
Tickton
Arnold
Withernwick
New Ellerby
B1242
Meaux
Skirlaugh
Weel
Marton
West Newton
Aldbrough
East Newton
FRIARY
Woodmansey
Wawne
Old Ellerby
BURTON CONSTABLE HALL
Flinton
Thearne
Garton
Dunswell
Swine
Coniston
Grimston
Bransholme
Thirtleby
Sproatley
Humbleton
Fitling
Sutton on Hull
Ganstead
Hilston
Kingston-upon-Hull
A1033
B1238
Bilton
B1240
Lelley
Owstwick
Tunstall
Sutton Ings
B1239
Elstronwick
Newland
Stoneferry
Preston
Burton Pidsea
North End
Roos
Sculcoates
Summergangs
B1242
Waxholme
WILBERFORCE HOUSE
West End
A165
Owthorne
Withernsea
P&R
Marfleet
A1033
Salt End
Rimswell
THE DEEP
STREETLIFE
Hedon
Haven Side
Burstwick
B1362
Halsham
East End
FERENS ART GALLERY
KINGSTON UPON HULL
A1033
Camerton
Paull
Thorngumbald
Ryehill
Keyingham
FORT PAULL
Hollym
Ottringham
Goxhill Haven
Winestead
A1033
Little Humber
New Holland
Holmpton
Thorney Crofts
Patrington
Goxhill
Cherry Cob Sands
B1445
Out Newton
Barrow upon Humber
South End
Welwick
Weeton
East Halton
Sunk Island
Skeffling
Easington
THORNTON ABBEY
A1077
Thornton Curtis
North Killingholme
Wootton
A160
South Killingholme
Immingham
Kilnsea
Ulceby
Ulceby Skitter
46
47
MUSEUM
B1211
Habrough
A180
B1211
Croxton
SPURN
Kirmington
Brocklesby
Stallingborough
A180
Keelby Ross
Pyewipe
ROTTERDAM 10:25
ZEEBRUGGE 10:25

19
2
20
3
4
5
6
Pinmore Mains
Carleton Castle
260
Bennane Hd.
Poundland
B734
Pinwherry
335
Pindonnan
Bellamore
Colmonell
66
66
Knockdolian
265
Ballochmorrie
Black Clauchrie
Loch Moan
Water of Minnoch
Palgowan
G A L
F O
Forest
Ballantrae Bay
Heronsford
Glen Tig
Water of Tig
Ballantrae
B7044
Balkissock
Barrhill
Laggan
Eldrick
A714
Glentrool
Downan Pt.
Auchencrosh
Arecleoch Forest
Glentrool Village
Glentrool Visitor Centre
B7027
Drumlamford Loch
Dornal
LARNE 1:00 (Mar-Oct)
LARNE 1:45
BELFAST 3:15
BELFAST 2:20
439
Benerairi
Chirmorrie
Bargrennan
A77
Loch Dornal
Loch Ochiltree
Du
Loch Maberry
Clachaneasy
Loch Middle
Milleur Pt.
Mark
Glen App
Miltonise
Craig Airie Fell
Kirroughtree Forest
Corsewall Pt.
17
287
Loch Derry
Polbae
Portencalzie
257
Laggangairn Standing Stones
Barnhills
Knowe
Ga
North Cairn
South Cairn
B738
Corsewall
Cairnryan
Penwhirn Res.
Main Water of Luce
Cross Water of Luce
Dounan Bay
Loch Connell
Kirkcolm
Artfield Fell
244
B7027
Penninghame Forest
Carseriggan
Mains of Airies
Ervie
Braid Fell
Challoch
Low Salchrie
B798
The Wig
Black Loch
Loch Ryan
New Luce
213
Knocknain
B738
Loch Heron
Benfield
Slouchnawen Bay
Leswalt
Craigencross
A77
Innermessan
Auchmantle
Southern Upland Way
Loch Ronald
Shennanton
A75
B7043
Black Loch
Drumphail
205
Tarf Water
14
B735
123
A718
A751
Castle Kennedy Gardens
B733
Kirkcowan
Glenstockadale
Stranraer
White Loch
Whitecairn
Aird
Castle Kennedy
Craighlaw Mains
Broadsea Bay
T H E R H I N S
Castle of St John Visitor Centre
Carscreugh
Knockglass
Wigtown District Museum
Soulseat Loch
A75
Glenwhan Gardens
Glenluce Abbey
Dernaglar Loch
High Mindork
Spittal
Mark
Dunragit
Glenluce
Knock Moss
Torhou
Lochans
Castle of Park
Bladnoch
Black Hd.
182
B7077
Whitefield Loch
131
Dunskey Ho.
B7084
Torrs Warren
A747
B7052
NW
A77
Luce Sands
Milton
Fell Loch
T H E
Little Wheels
Portpatrick
Awhirk
Stairhaven
Castle Loch
Culmazie
Stoneykirk
Auchenmalg
Mochrum Loch
M A C
B7005
A716
Port of Spittal Bay
B7042
Auchenmalg Bay
Culshabbin
Alticry
B7005
197
Barrachan
Cairngarroch
Sandhead
Loch Head
Kirkmadrine Stones
Sandhead Bay
Chapel Finian
Cairngarroch Bay
Money Hd.
Elrig
Mote of Druchtag
Clachanmore
A747
Mochrum
Airyhass
Hole Stone Bay
Ardwell Gdns
Ardwell
Milton Pt.
Drumtroddan
Drummod
Ardwell Mains
Chapel Rossan Bay
Ardwell Pt.
Logan Mains
Port William
Monreith Mains
Logan Botanic Garden
Balgowan Pt.
L U C E B A Y
Moor Ravenstone
Mull of Logan
Logan Fish Pond Marine Life Centre
Barsalloch Fort
Barsalloch Pt.
Monreith
Port Nessock or Port Logan Bay
Monreith Animal World, Shore Centre and Museum
Port Logan
Monreith Bay
Cairnywellan Hd.
B7065
A716
Clanyard Bay
Low Clanyard
Laggantalluch Hd.
Kirkmaiden
Drummore
164
Cailliness Pt.
Damnaglaur
B7041
Crammag Hd.
Maryport
Cairngaan
Port Kemin
Mull of Galloway
52
A
B
C
D
E
F
G
H
0 1 2 3 4 5 6 miles
0 1 2 3 4 5 6 7 8 9 10 km

55
7
8
9
10
11
12
A
B
C
D
E
F
G
H
Dumfries and Galloway
Castlemaddy
Dundeugh
Kendoon
Glenhoul
Glencrosh
Castlefairn
Holmhead
Dalmacallan Forest
Stairh
Wallaceton
Glenmidge
Auldgirth
MULLWHARCHAR
MERRICK
Loch Enoch
Loch Neldricken
Loch Valley
SILVER FLOWE
RHINNS OF KELLS
CORSERINE
Forrest Lodge
Loch Harrow
Loch Dungeon
GLENKENS
Carsfad Loch
Earlstoun Loch
Millquarter
St John's Town of Dalry
Bogue
Corriedoo Forest
Lochinvar
WETHER HILL
Lochurr
BOGRIE HILL
Loch Urr
Sundaywell
Dunscore
Milton
Cairn Water
ELLISLAND FARM
Newtonairds
Drumpark
Glenkiln Res.
Irongray
Newbridge
Terregles Banks
Glenkiln
Glen
Shawhead
BRUCE'S STONE
Glen Trool
Loch Trool
Drumbuie
Garroch
Glenlee
Clatteringshaws Forest
Clatteringshaws Loch
Loch Dee
New Galloway
Balmaclellan
Blackcraig
Knocklearn
Gibbshill
BLOWPLAIN OPEN FARM
Ironmacannie
Craig
Corsock
LAMACHAN HILL
CLATTERINGSHAWS FOREST WILDLIFE CENTRE
RAIDERS ROAD FOREST DRIVE
Bennan Forest
Cairn Edward Hill
Loch Ken
Merkland
Urr Water
Brooklands
Brae
Lochfoot
Lochrutton Loch
Crocketford or Ninemile Bar
Milton Loch
Milton
Auchenreoch Loch
Kirkpatrick Durham
Springholm
Beeswing
Lochaber Loch
Loch Arthur
Mabie Forest
WILD GOAT PARK
Loch Grannoch
FELL OF FLEET
Stroan Loch
Mossdale
Drumrash
Parton
Penkiln Burn
Palnure Burn
Minnigaff
Creebridge
Newton Stewart
CAIRNSMORE OF FLEET
Loch Skerrow
Woodhall Loch
Craig
Crossmichael
Old Bridge of Urr
Clarebrand
Haugh of Urr
Kirkgunzeon
DRUMCOLTRAN TOWER
SHAMBELLIE COSTUME
Fleet Forest
Clints of Dromore
Lochenbreck Loch
Laurieston
Laurieston Forest
Townhead of Greenlaw
MOTE OF URR
Palnure
Big Water of Fleet
LONG FELL
Loch Whinyeon
Loch Mannoch
Loch Glentoo
Loch Bargatton
THREAVE CASTLE
Castle Douglas
Carlingwark Loch
OLD BUITTLE TOWER
Barhill
Dalbeattie
Balteršan
Causeway End
Carsegowan
GEM ROCK MUSEUM
Creetown
Glengap Forest
BENGRAY
Glengap
KELTON MAINS OPEN FARM
THREAVE GARDENS
Bridge of Dee
Rhonehouse or Kelton Hill
Gelston
Dalbeattie Forest
Drumstinchall
Caulkerbush
Wigtown Sands
Wigtown
SCOTLAND'S BOOK TOWN
NX
FLEET VALLEY
Glen
Anwoth
CARDONESS CASTLE
MILL ON THE FLEET
Gatehouse of Fleet
Valleyfield
Ringford
Airieland
Palnackie
ORCHARDTON TOWER
Barnbarroch
Sandyhills
Mainsriddle
CAIRNHARROW
Carsluith
CARSLUITH CASTLE
CAIRNHOLY CAIRNS
Girthon
GALLOWAY HYDRO VISITOR CENTRE
Twynholm
Tongland
BROUGHTON HOUSE AND GARDEN
BENGAIRN
Kippford or Scaur
MOTE OF MARK
Rockcliffe
ROUGH ISLAND
Rough I.
Colvend
Portling
Mersehead Sands
VISITOR CENTRE
Braehead
Kirkinner
Baldoon Sands
Ravenshall Pt.
Ringdoo Pt.
Fleet Bay
Sandgreen
Barharrow
MACLELLAN'S CASTLE
STEWARTRY MUSEUM
Kirkcudbright
Whinnieliggate
EAST STEWARTRY COAST
Castlehill Pt.
Auchencairn
Auchencairn Bay
Hestan I.
Islands of Fleet
Knockbrex
Kirkandrews
Borgue
St Mary's Isle
Mutehill
Kirkcarswell
Dundrennan
Rascarrel
Balcary Pt.
Rascarrel Bay
Orroland
Sorbie
Garlieston
WIGTOWN BAY
Eggerness Pt.
GALLOWAY HOUSE GARDENS
Borness
Borness Pt.
Ross
Kirkcudbright Bay
Townhead
Balmae
Netherlaw
DUNDRENNAN ABBEY
Port Mary
Abbey Hd.
Little Ross
Cults
CRUGGLETON CHURCH AND CASTLE
Bishopton
Whithorn
PRIORY AND MUSEUM
Port Allen
Portyerrock Bay
Cairn Hd.
ST NINIAN'S CHAPEL
Isle of Whithorn
Cutcloy
BURROW HEAD
SOLWAY FIRTH
ST BEES HEAD
A712
A762
A713
A702
A75
A711
A745
A746
A714
A755
A710
A76
B729
B7000
B7075
B794
B795
B796
B727
B736
B793
B7004
B7005
B7052
B7063
B727
60
67
56

Kirkbean
ARBIGLAND GARDENS
JOHN PAUL JONES COTTAGE MUSEUM
Southerness
Southerness Pt.
60
SOLWAY FIRTH COAST
Cardurnock
Anthorn
Easton
Boustead Hill
Drumburgh Moss
Kirkandrews upon Eden
Kingstown
Houghton
Linstock
Low Crosby
Grinsdale
Edentown
Stanwix
Carlisle
Warwick on Eden
Whitrigg
Kirkbride
Fingland
Finglandrigg Woods
Thurstonfield
Moorhouse
Tullie House Mus & Gall
Botcherby
Scotby
Skinburness
Newton Arlosh
Wedholme Flow
South Solway Mosses
Little Bampton
Little Orton
Great Orton
Newby West
Harraby
Wetheral
61
Silloth
Greenrow
Calvo
Seaville
Causewayhead
Kingside Hill
Aikton
Wiggonby
Baldwinholme
Upperby
Cummersdale
Carleton
Brisco
Cumwhinton
Blitterlees
Abbey Town
Kelsick
Lessonhall
Oulton
Durdar
Beckfoot
Highlaws
Pelutho
Dundraw
Waverbridge
Thursby
Dalston
Cotehill
Wreay
Newtown
Blencogo
Wigton
West Curthwaite
East Curthwaite
Buckabank
Bromfield
Waverton
Brackenthwaite
Gaitsgill
Low Hesket
Holme St Cuthbert
Mawbray
Langrigg
Waterside
Red Dial
Westward
Rosley
Raughton Head
Stockdalewath
Southwaite
Dubmill Pt.
Edderside
New Cowper
Westnewton
Bolton Low Houses
Welton
High Head Sculpture Valley
Allonby
Watchhill
Fletchertown
Brocklebank
Sebergham
Ivegill
Low Braithwaite
Allonby Bay
Aspatria
Hayton
Ellen
Blennerhasset
Mealsgate
Boltongate
Thomas Close
Calthwaite
Prospect
Oughterside
Sandale
Caldbeck
Sowerby Row
Allerby
Threapland
Torpenhow
Hesket Newmarket
Crosscanonby
Crosby Villa
Parsonby
Plumbland
Bothel
Whitrigg
Ireby
Hutton End
Crosby
Bullgill
Gilcrux
Uldale
Fell Side
Branthwaite
Millhouse
Maryport Maritime Museum
Maryport
High Ireby
Binsey
Low Row
Lamonby
Unthank
Skelton
Dearham
Tallentire
Blindcrake
Sunderland
High Pike
High Row
Ellonby
Bewaldeth
Orthwaite
Hutton Roof
Flimby
Dovenby
Bridekirk
Broughton Moor
Standingstone
Knott
Mosedale
Johnby
Little Blencow
Great Blencow
Siddick
Great Broughton
Little Broughton
Papcastle
Wordsworth Ho
Cockermouth
Castlegate Ho
Embleton
Bassenthwaite
Great Calva
Mungrisdale
Greystoke
Camerton
Seaton
Great Clifton
Brigham
Bassenthwaite Lake
Skiddaw Forest
North Side
Workington
Helena Thompson Mus
Stainburn
Bridgefoot
Little Clifton
Greysouthen
Wythop Mill
Mirehouse
Skiddaw
Skiddaw House
Saddleback or Blencathra
Berrier
Motherby
Beckstones Art Gallery
Penruddock
Westfield
Mossbay
Eaglesfield
Deanscales
Sandybeck Meadow
Thornthwaite Forest
Lorton Vale
Scales
Troutbeck
Hutton
Dacre
Harrington
Winscales
Dean
Low Lorton
Thornthwaite
Thornthwaite Galleries
Millbeck
Applethwaite
Cars of the Stars Motor Mus
Threlkeld
High Harrington
Branthwaite
Mosser
High Lorton
Whinlatter Pass
Cumberland Pencil Museum
Distington
Pardshaw
Heritage/Visitor Centre
Braithwaite
Keswick
Castlerigg Stone Circle
Matterdale End
Wreay
Ullock
Mockerkin
Thackthwaite
Whinlatter Forest Park
Grisedale Pike
Portinscale
Longthwaite
Watermillock
Lowca
Pica
Loweswater
Brackenthwaite Fell
Derwent Water
Dockray
Aira Force
Knotts
Moresby
Asby
Lamplugh
Stair
Derwentwater
St John's Beck
Dowthwaitehead
Parton
Arlecdon
Moresby Parks
Loweswater Fell
Little Town
Stanah
Sandwich
Howtown
Loadpot Hill
Bransty
Walk Mill
The Rum Story
Rowrah
High Leys
Kirkland
Croasdale
Rannerdale
Crummock Water
Derwent Fells
Grange
Fisher Place
Helvellyn
Glenridding
Martindale Common
Whitehaven
Haig Colliery Mining Museum
Frizington
Hensingham
Great Borne
Buttermere
Buttermere Fell
High Seat
Thirlmere
Watendlath
Patterdale
Dale Head
Saltom Bay
Sandwith
Mirehouse
Cleator Moor
Moor Row
Ennerdale Bridge
Ennerdale Forest
High Stile
Ennerdale
Borrowdale
Rosthwaite
Bridgend
Grisedale Beck
Angle Tarn
Haweswater Reservoir
Wath Brow
Ennerdale Water
Ennerdale Fell
Seatoller
Honister Hause
Stonethwaite
Wythburn
Hartsop
Brothers Water
Rottington
Cleator
Longlands Lake
Black Sail
Pillar
Seathwaite
Ullscarf
Wythburn Fells
Grisedale Tarn
St Bees
Egremont
Wilton
Lake District National Park
Cumbrian Mountains
High Street
Great Gable
Harter
High White Stones
Easedale Tarn
Grasmere
Thorney How
Butharlyp Howe
Couldertoni
Thornhill
Middletown
Nethertown
Haile
Seatallan
Wasdale Head
Stickle Tarn
Dove Cottage and Wordsworth Museum
Kirkstone Pass
Inn
Beckermet
Copeland Forest
Scafell Pike
Bow Fell
Langdale Pikes
Chapel Stile
Rydal
Rydal Mount
Homes of Football
Braystones
Calder Bridge
Wastwater
Burnmoor Tarn
Elterwater
Langdale
Ambleside
Kentmere
High Sellafield
Sellafield Visitors Centre
Calder Hall
Wellington
The Screes
Nether Wasdale
Little Langdale
Clappersgate
Waterhead
Troutbeck
Gosforth
Hardknott Fort
Hard Knott Pass
Wrynose Pass
Skelwith Bridge
Roman Fort
Windermere Submarine
Seascale
Santon Bridge
Eskdale Green
Beckfoot
Boot
Eskdale
Cockley Beck
Furness Fells
Brockhole - Nat Pk Visitor Centre
Holehird Gardens
Troutbeck Bridge
Elfhow
Holmrook
Harter Fell
Seathwaite Tarn
Coniston Coppermines
Outgate
Hawkshead Courthouse
High Wray
Low Wray
Colthouse
Windermere Steamboats & Mus
Ings
Staveley
Drigg
Coniston Holly How
Coniston
Hawkshead
Windermere
The Old Man of Coniston
Ruskin Mus
Bowmanstead
Birker Fell
Saltcoats
Ravenglass and Eskdale Railway & Mus
Ravenglass
Muncaster Castle & World Owl Centre
Devoke Water
Woodend
Hall Dunnerdale
Seathwaite
Gondola
Brantwood
Hawkshead Grizedale Forest Park Visitor Centre
Near Sawrey
Far Sawrey
The World of Beatrix Potter
Bowness-on-Windermere
Ferney Green
Ulpha Fell
Grizedale Forest
Grizedale
Grizedale Forest Park
Broad Oak
Caw
Torver
Storrs
Winster
Newbiggin
Whitfell
Ulpha
Hoses
Lane End
Corney Fell
Satterthwaite
Force Mills
Underbarrow
Crosthwaite
Stub Place
Corney
Broughton Mills
Forest Spinners
Selker Bay
Hycemoor
Water Yeat
Blawith
High Nibthwaite
Furness Fells
Rusland
Rusland Moss
Stott Park Bobbin Mill
Finsthwaite
Bowland Bridge
Bootle
Lower Hawthwaite
Duddon Bridge
Broughton in Furness
Oxen Park
Lakeside
Aquarium of the Lakes
Fell Foot
Cartmel Fell
Row
The Howe
Black Combe
Lowick Bridge
Lowick Green
Colton
Bouth
Whitbarrow
Sampool Br
Hallthwaites
Foxfield
Duddon Mosses
Grizebeck
Gawthwaite
Spark Bridge
Lakeside and Haverthwaite Railway
Newby Bridge
Backbarrow
Mill Side
Witherslack
High Newton
Town End
Whitbeck
The Green
The Hill
Penny Bridge
Greenodd
Artcrystal
Haverthwaite
Ayside
Low Newton
49
Kirkby-in-Furness
Beck Side
Broughton Beck
Arrad Foot
Field Broughton
Meathop
Silecroft
Whicham
Soutergate
NX
SC
0 1 2 3 4 5 6 miles
0 1 2 3 4 5 6 7 8 9 10 km

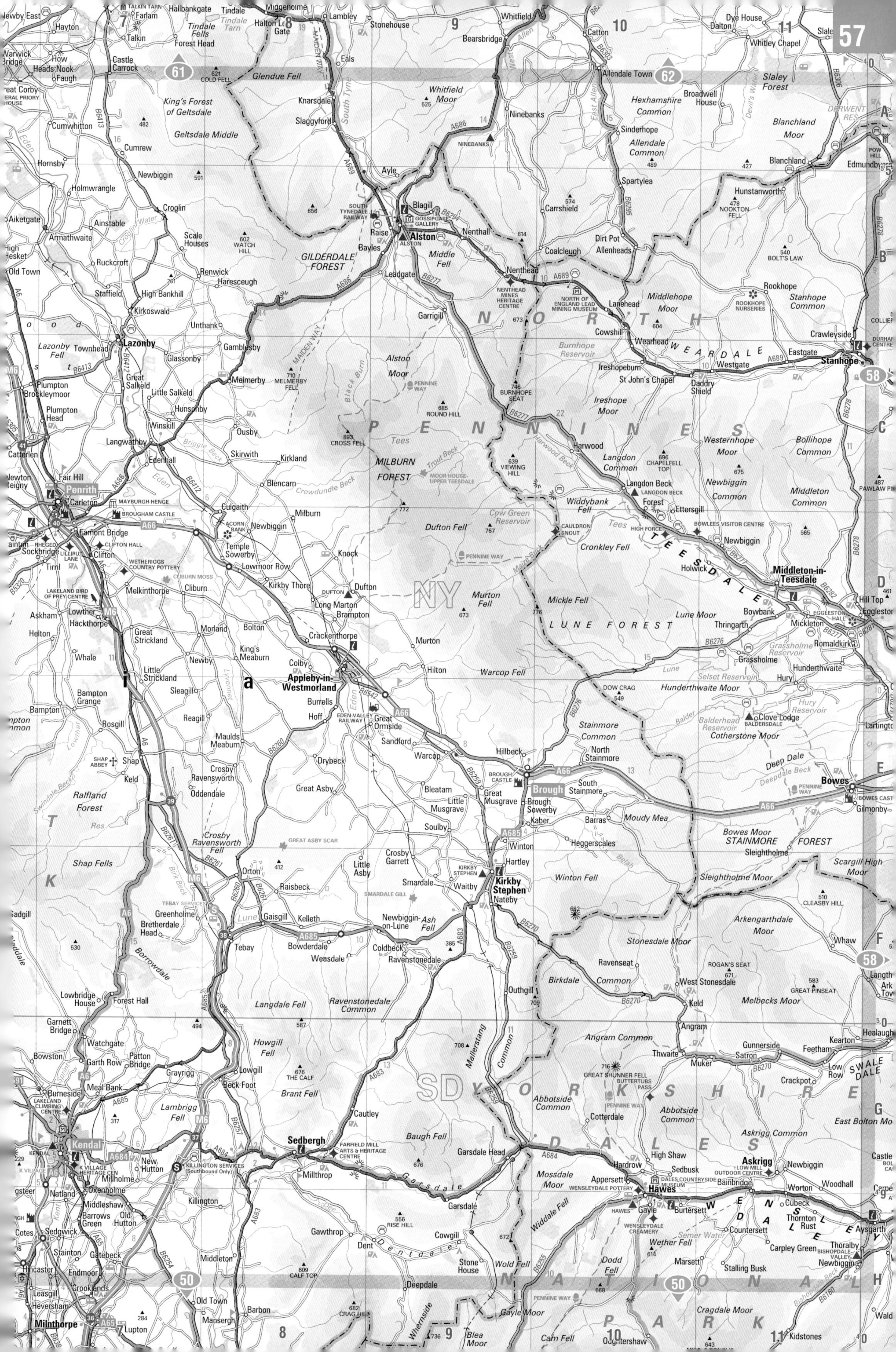
Farlam
Hallbankgate
Tindale
Midgeholme
Lambley
Stonehouse
Whitfield
Catton
Dalton
Dye House
Slaley
Hayton
Tindale Fells
Tindale Tarn
Halton Lea Gate
Forest Head
Talkin
Bearsbridge
Whitley Chapel
How
Heads Nook
Faugh
Castle Carrock
61
621 COLD FELL
Glendue Fell
Eals
Allendale Town
62
Slaley Forest
Great Corby
Whitfield Moor
Broadwell House
King's Forest of Geltsdale
Knarsdale
Hexhamshire Common
525
Ninebanks
Cumwhitton
Slaggyford
South Tyne
Blanchland Moor
482
Geltsdale Middle
Sinderhope
Allendale Common
Cumrew
NINEBANKS
489
Blanchland
Edmundbyers
Hornsby
Newbiggin
Ayle
427
591
Spartylea
Hunstanworth
Holmwrangle
Carrshield
574
478 NOOKTON FELL
Croglin
Blagill
Aiketgate
Ainstable
SOUTH TYNEDALE RAILWAY
656
GOSSIPGATE GALLERY
Armathwaite
Scale Houses
Raise
Alston
Nenthall
Dirt Pot
614
602 WATCH HILL
Bayles
Middle Fell
Allenheads
Coalcleugh
540 BOLT'S LAW
Old Town
Ruckcroft
GILDERDALE FOREST
Renwick
Leadgate
Nenthead
Hareseugh
261
Staffield
High Bankhill
NENTHEAD MINES HERITAGE CENTRE
NORTH OF ENGLAND LEAD MINING MUSEUM
Rookhope
Lanehead
Middlehope Moor
Stanhope Common
Kirkoswald
Garrigill
ROOKHOPE NURSERIES
Unthank
673
604
Cowshill
Lazonby Fell
Townhead
Lazonby
Crawleyside
Gamblesby
Wearhead
Burnhope Reservoir
WEARDALE
Eastgate
Stanhope
Glassonby
Alston Moor
Ireshopeburn
Westgate
St John's Chapel
Daddry Shield
58
Plumpton
Brockleymoor
Great Salkeld
Melmerby
710 MELMERBY FELL
PENNINE WAY
746 BURNHOPE SEAT
Little Salkeld
685 ROUND HILL
Plumpton Head
Hunsonby
Ireshope Moor
Winskill
893 CROSS FELL
Ousby
Langwathby
Tees
PENNINES
Westernhope Moor
Bollihope Common
Harwood
Skirwith
Kirkland
Catterlen
MILBURN FOREST
639 VIEWING HILL
Langdon Common
696 CHAPELFELL TOP
675
Edenhall
Trout Beck
MOOR HOUSE-UPPER TEESDALE
Newton Reigny
Fair Hill
Penrith
Blencarn
Crowdundle Beck
Langdon Beck
Newbiggin Common
Middleton Common
487 PAWLAW PIKE
Carleton
MAYBURGH HENGE
Widdybank Fell
Forest
Ettersgill
Culgaith
772
BROUGHAM CASTLE
Milburn
Dufton Fell
Cow Green Reservoir
767
HIGH FORCE
BOWLEES VISITOR CENTRE
Eamont Bridge
Newbiggin
ACORN BANK
CAULDRON SNOUT
Newbiggin
565
RHEGED
CLIFTON HALL
Temple Sowerby
Cronkley Fell
TEESDALE
Sockbridge
Clifton
LILLIPUT LANE
Knock
PENNINE WAY
Holwick
Middleton-in-Teesdale
Tirril
WETHERIGGS COUNTRY POTTERY
Lowmoor Row
CLIBURN MOSS
Kirkby Thore
Dufton
NY
Murton Fell
Mickle Fell
Melkinthorpe
Cliburn
DUFTON
LAKELAND BIRD OF PREY CENTRE
Long Marton
Hill Top
Eggleston
Askham
Lowther
Brampton
673
776
Lune Moor
Bowbank
Mickleton
EGGLESTON HALL
Hackthorpe
Morland
Bolton
LUNE FOREST
Thringarth
Helton
Great Strickland
Crackenthorpe
Romaldkirk
King's Meaburn
Murton
Grassholme Reservoir
Whale
Newby
Grassholme
Colby
Hilton
Hunderthwaite
Little Strickland
Appleby-in-Westmorland
Warcop Fell
Lune
Selset Reservoir
Hury
Sleagill
DOW CRAG
549
Hunderthwaite Moor
Bampton Grange
Burrells
Hury Reservoir
Bampton
Reagill
Hoff
EDEN VALLEY RAILWAY
Great Ormside
Balderhead Reservoir
Clove Lodge
BALDERSDALE
Lartington
Rosgill
Maulds Meaburn
Sandford
Stainmore Common
Cotherstone Moor
SHAP ABBEY
Shap
Drybeck
Hillbeck
North Stainmore
Deep Dale
Warcop
Deepdale Beck
Keld
Crosby Ravensworth
BROUGH CASTLE
Brough
South Stainmore
Bowes
Ralfland Forest
Oddendale
Great Asby
Bleatarn
Great Musgrave
Brough Sowerby
PENNINE WAY
BOWES CASTLE
Little Musgrave
Kaber
Barras
Moudy Mea
Gilmonby
Res.
Soulby
Winton
Bowes Moor
STAINMORE FOREST
Crosby Ravensworth Fell
GREAT ASBY SCAR
Crosby Garrett
Heggerscales
Sleightholme
Hartley
Shap Fells
412
Little Asby
KIRKBY STEPHEN
Kirkby Stephen
Winton Fell
Scargill High Moor
Orton
Raisbeck
Smardale
Waitby
Sleightholme Moor
SMARDALE GILL
Nateby
510 CLEASBY HILL
TEBAY SERVICES
Greenholme
Gaisgill
Kelleth
Newbiggin-on-Lune
Ash Fell
662
Arkengarthdale Moor
Bretherdale Head
Tebay
Bowderdale
Coldbeck
385
Stonesdale Moor
Whaw
530
Weasdale
Ravenstonedale
Ravenseat
ROGAN'S SEAT
671
58
Borrowdale
Birkdale
Common
West Stonesdale
583 GREAT PINSEAT
Length
Outhgill
Lowbridge House
Forest Hall
Langdale Fell
Ravenstonedale Common
709
Keld
Melbecks Moor
587
Angram
Garnett Bridge
494
Howgill Fell
708
Mallerstang
Angram Common
Gunnerside
Kearton
Healaugh
Watchgate
Satron
Feetham
Bowston
Patton Bridge
Common
Thwaite
Muker
Low Row
SWALE DALE
Garth Row
Lowgill
676 THE CALF
716 GREAT SHUNNER FELL
BUTTERTUBS PASS
Crackpot
Meal Bank
Grayrigg
Beck Foot
SD
YORKSHIRE
Burneside
LAKELAND CLIMBING CENTRE
Brant Fell
Abbotside Common
PENNINE WAY
Abbotside Common
Lambrigg Fell
Cotterdale
Askrigg Common
East Bolton Moor
317
Cautley
Kendal
Baugh Fell
DALES
Castle Bolton
Sedbergh
FARFIELD MILL ARTS & HERITAGE CENTRE
Garsdale Head
High Shaw
Askrigg
K VILLAGE HERITAGE CEN
New Hutton
KILLINGTON SERVICES (Southbound Only)
676
Hardrow
Sedbusk
LOW MILL OUTDOOR CENTRE
Newbiggin
Millholme
Millthrop
Mossdale Moor
Appersett
DALES COUNTRYSIDE MUSEUM
Bainbridge
Woodhall
Oxenholme
Garsdale
WENSLEYDALE POTTERY
Hawes
Worton
Natland
Killington
HAWES
Gayle
Burtersett
WENSLEYDALE
Middleshaw
Garsdale
Widdale Fell
Thornton Rust
Barrows Green
Old Hutton
556 RISE HILL
Cowgill
WENSLEYDALE CREAMERY
Countersett
Aysgarth
Sedgwick
Gawthrop
Dent
Dentdale
672
Semer Water
Carpley Green
Thoralby
Stainton
Gatebeck
Middleton
Wether Fell
614
BISHOPDALE VALLEY
Newbiggin
Stone House
Wold Fell
Dodd Fell
Marsett
Stalling Busk
Endmoor
609 CALF TOP
50
NATIONAL
Crooklands
Deepdale
668
50
PARK
Leasgill
PENNINE WAY
Heversham
Old Town
Barbon
Gayle Moor
Cragdale Moor
Milnthorpe
284
Mansergh
682 CRAG HILL
Whernside
736
Blea Moor
Cam Fell
Oughtershaw
643
Kidstones
Lupton

58
Durham
Hartlepool
Stockton-on-Tees
Middlesbrough
Darlington
North York
SUNDERLAND
WASHINGTON
STANLEY
CHESTER-LE-STREET
HOUGHTON-LE-SPRING
SEAHAM
PETERLEE
NEWTON AYCLIFFE
BILLINGHAM
Consett
Bishop Auckland
Barnard Castle
Richmond
Catterick Garrison
Northallerton
Bedale
Leyburn
Thirsk
Yarm
Sedgefield
Spennymoor
Crook
Wolsingham
Stanhope
Scotch Corner
WENSLEYDALE
SWALE DALE
Hamsterley Forest
Beacon Pt.
0 1 2 3 4 5 6 miles
0 1 2 3 4 5 6 7 8 9 10 km

NZ
SE
ST HILDA'S PARISH CHURCH
Seaton Carew
Tees Bay
REDCAR
Salt Scar
Coatham
Dormanstown
Marske-by-the-Sea
Saltburn-by-the-Sea
MINIATURE RAILWAY
SALTBURN SMUGGLERS HERITAGE CENTRE
CHRIS BIRKBECK INTERNATIONAL RALLY SCHOOL
KIRKLEATHAM OLD HALL MUSEUM
Kirkleatham
Grangetown
South Bank
Yearby
New Marske
Lazenby
Wilton
Upleatham
Dunsdale
TOCKETTS WATER MILL
Skelton
Brotton
Carlin How
Skinningrove
Loftus
Boulby
Staithes
Easington
North Skelton
Kilton Thorpe
Eston
Ormesby
FLATTS LANE WOODLAND
Redcar and Cleveland
GUISBOROUGH PRIORY
Guisborough
Boosbeck
Margrove Park
Charltons
Lingdale
Stanghow
Liverton
Roxby
Hinderwell
Port Mulgrave
Runswick Bay
Kettleness
Goldsborough
Newton Mulgrave
Ellerby
Nunthorpe
Hutton Gate
Hutton Village
Gisborough Moor
Moorsholm
Scaling
Scaling Dam Res.
Newton under Roseberry
Commondale Moor
Mickleby
East Barnby
West Barnby
Lythe
Sandsend
Sandsend Wyke
THE DRACULA EXPERIENCE
SUTCLIFFE GALLERY
Whitby
Saltwick Bay
WHITBY ABBEY
CAPTAIN COOK MEMORIAL MUSEUM
East Row
Dunsley
Great Ayton
Little Ayton
New Row
Commondale
Danby Low Moor
Lealholm Moor
Ugthorpe
Newholm
Ruswarp
Stokesley
Easby
Kildale
Kildale Moor
Danby
THE MOORS CENTRE
Stonegate
Castleton
Ainthorpe
Houlsyke
Lealholm
Aislaby
Sleights
Stainsacre
Briggswath
High Hawsker
Sneaton
Great Broughton
Battersby
Ingleby Greenhow
Westerdale
Low Garth
Street
Glaisdale
MUSEUM OF VICTORIAN SCIENCE
Egton
Egton Bridge
Grosmont
GROSMONT GALLERY
Esk Valley
Ugglebarnby
Sneatonthorpe
Raw
Ness Pt.
CLEVELAND WAY
Robin Hood's Bay
OLD COASTGUARD STATION
BOGGLE HOLE
Fylingthorpe
Littlebeck
Westerdale Moor
Glaisdale Moor
Egton High Moor
Beck Hole
Goathland
Old Peak
Ravenscar
Urra
Seave Green
Farndale Moor
Chop Gate
COCKAYNE RIDGE
Wake Lady Green
Cockayne
Rosedale Moor
WHEELDALE MOOR ROMAN ROAD
Flask Inn
Fylingdales Moor
Staintondale
STAINTONDALE SHIRE HORSE FARM
NORTH YORK MOORS NATIONAL PARK
Bilsdale West Moor
Bilsdale East Moor
Church Houses
Blakey Ridge
Thorgill
Rosedale Abbey
Wheeldale Moor
Goathland Moor
Harwood Dale Forest
Harwood Dale
Cloughton Newlands
Cloughton Wyke
Cloughton
Fangdale Beck
Bransdale
Rudland Rigg
Low Mill
ROSEDALE
PICKERING MOOR
Pickering Forest
Saltergate
Langdale Forest
Broxa Forest
Burniston
East Moors
Spaunton Moor
Cropton
Hartoft End
Forest
Stape
Newton Dale
MOORLAND EXPERIENCE
TOLL
Cromer Pt.
Scalby Ness Rocks
Helmsley Moor
Skiplam Moor
RYEDALE FOLK MUSEUM
Lastingham
Levisham
Langdale End
Broxa
Silpho
Hackness
Suffield
Scalby
SEA LIFE CENTRE
KINDERLAND
North Bay
Gillamoor
Hutton-le-Hole
Spaunton
Newton-on-Rawcliffe
Lockton
Staindale Forest
NORTH RIDING FOREST PARK
Troutsdale
Wrench Green
Wykeham Forest
Everley
Barrowcliff
Newby
Scarborough
SCARBOROUGH CASTLE
ROTUNDA MUS.
Rievaulx Moor
Fadmoor
Appleton-le-Moors
NORTH YORKSHIRE MOORS RAILWAY
Low Dalby
DALBY FOREST VISITOR CENTRE
Dalby Forest
FORGE VALLEY WOODLANDS
Falsgrave
Carlton
Kirkbymoorside
Keldholme
Sinnington
Wrelton
Aislaby
East Ayton
West Ayton
THE HONEY FARM
Byland
Rievaulx
RIEVAULX ABBEY
HELMSLEY
Pockley
Beadlam
Kirkby Mills
Welburn
Middleton
ST PETER AND ST PAUL CHURCH
PICKERING CASTLE
Sawdon
Hutton Buscel
WORDSWORTH GALLERY
Irton
Osgodby
Old Kirby
Helmsley
Rye Dale
Scawton
DUNCOMBE PARK
Wombleton
Great Edstone
Marton
Pickering
Ellerburn
Thornton-le-Dale
Wilton
Allerston
Ebberston
Snainton
Ruston
Wykeham
Seamer
Eastfield
Cayton
Lebberston
Sproxton
Nawton
Normanby
Brompton
Harome

East Ayrshire
Dumfries and
NS
NX
Muirkirk
Smallburn
Kames
Glespin
Robertson Law
Roberton
Cowgill Upper Reservoir
Culter Waterhead Reservoir
CULTER FELL
Airds Moss
Cronberry
Lugar
Logan
Holmhead
Cumnock
Netherthird
Craigens
Glenmuir
Glenmuirshaw
WARDLAW HILL
CAIRN TABLE
Glentaggart
Middle Muir
AUCHENSAUGH HILL
Crawfordjohn
Abington
ABINGTON SERVICES
TEWSGILL HILL
Camps Water
Camps Reservoir
GLENWHAPPEN RIG
Tweedsmuir
Glenbreck
DRAKE LAW
Duneaton Water
Kirkton
Crawford
Dalblair
MOUNT STUART
Fingland
RAKE LAW
WELLGRAIN DOD
Elvanfoot
CRAIGMAID
CLYDE LAW
Source of River Tweed
KIRKLAND HILL
Kirkland
Pathhead
Mansfield
Connel Park
Bankglen
New Cumnock
Kirkconnel
Kelloholm
Leadhills
LEADHILLS & WANLOCKHEAD RLY
MUSEUM OF LEAD MINING
WANLOCKHEAD BEAM ENGINE
Wanlockhead
LOTUS LODGE
GREEN LOWTHER
LOWTHER HILL
Mennock Pass
March
Watermeetings
Nether Howecleuch
DEVIL'S BEEF TUB
Ericstane
Granton
Howslad
Burnside
Dalleagles
THE KNIPE
CONRIG HILL
Crawick
Sanquhar
TOLBOOTH MUSEUM
SANQUHAR POST OFFICE
Mennock
SOUTHERN UPLAND WAY
Daer Reservoir
Potrail Water
Kello Water
Afton Water
Euchan Water
BLACKCRAIG HILL
Afton Reservoir
CAIRN HILL
Moffat
Coatsgate
Durisdeermill
DURISDEER PARISH CHURCH
Durisdeer
BALLENCLEUCH LAW
Easter Earshaig
Garpol Water
Beattock
Kinnelhead
Enterkinfoot
Carsphairn Forest
Scar Water
CAIRNKINNA HILL
Enoch
GANA HILL
Holestane
MORTON CASTLE
QUEENSBERRY
DRUMLANRIG CASTLE
Carronbridge
Locherben
CAIRNSMORE OF CARSPHAIRN
Corlae
BENBRACK
Benbuie
Auchenbrack
Shinnel Water
Auchenbainzie
Burnhead
Thornhill
Gatelawbridge
Lochwood
Water of Ken
Penpont
Loch Ettrick
Dalwhat Water
Tynron
Keir Mill
Closeburn
Forest of Ae
St Ann's
Carsphairn
Knowehead
Kendoon Loch
Craigdarroch
Moniaive
JAMES PATERSON MUSEUM
Kirkland
MAXWELTON HOUSE
Park
Blackacre
Johnstonebridge
Chapelhill
Glencrosh
Ae Village
Courance
Black Water
Dalmacallan Forest
Straith
Wallaceton
Glenmidge
Nethermill
Parkgate
Templand
Dundeugh
Kendoon
Glenhoul
KENDOON
WETHER HILL
Castlefairn
Holmhead
Carsfad Loch
Auldgirth
Dalswinton
Auchencairn
Shieldhill
Lochurr
BOGRIE HILL
Loch Urr
Lochinvar
ELLISLAND FARM
Duncow
Sundaywell
Dunscore
Milton
Marjoriebanks
Lochmaben
Earlstoun Loch
Millquarter
Cairn Water
Gallaberry
Amisfield
St John's Town of Dalry
Bogue
Corriedoo Forest
Newtonairds
Kirkton
Tinwald
LOCHMABEN CASTLE
Garroch
Glenlee
Blackcraig
Holywood
Locharbriggs
Heathhall
Knocklearn
Drumpark
Irongray
DUMFRIES AND GALLOWAY AVIATION MUS
Gibbshill
Glenkiln Res.
Newbridge
LINCLUDEN COLLEGE
The Grove
Torthorwald
Hightae
New Galloway
Balmaclellan
BLOWPLAIN OPEN FARM
Glenkiln
Terregles Banks
Lincluden
OLD BRIDGE HOUSE MUS
RAMMERSCALES HOUSE
Dumfries
Maxwelltown
Greystone
Collin
CLATTERINGSHAWS FOREST WILDLIFE CENTRE
Ironmacannie
Craig
Corsock
Glen
Shawhead
BURNS HOUSE
ROBERT BURNS CENTRE
Greenlea
Cargenbridge
DUMFRIES MUSEUM & CAMERA OBSCURA
Racks
Cleughbrae
RAIDERS ROAD FOREST DRIVE
Merkland
Urr Water
Brooklands
Brae
Lochfoot
Lochrutton Loch
Bennan Forest
Cairn Edward Hill
Loch Ken
Drumrash
Auchenreoch Loch
Crocketford or Ninemile Bar
Milton Loch
Islesteps
Kingholm Quay
Mouswald
Lochar Moss
Mossdale
Parton
Kirkpatrick Durham
Mabie Forest
Mabie
Kelton
Stroan Loch
Springholm
Milton
Lochaber Loch
Loch Arthur
KIRKCONNELL FLOW
Beeswing
MCOLTRAN TOWER
Glencaple
Bankend
Clarencefield
Loch Skerrow
Old Bridge of Urr
Kirkconnell
Woodhall Loch
Crossmichael
Kirkgunzeon
SHAMBELLIE HOUSE COSTUME MUSEUM
New Abbey
SWEETHEART ABBEY
New Abbey Pow
Shearington
Blackshaw
CAERLAVEROCK CASTLE
Eastpark
Bowhouse
Fleet Forest
Craig
Clarebrand
Haugh of Urr
Lochenbreck Loch
Townhead of Greenlaw
NEW ABBEY CORN MILL
NITH ESTUARY
Overton
WILDFOWL AND WETLAND CENTRE
CAERLAVEROCK
Blackshaw Bank
Laurieston
MOTE OF URR
Laurieston Forest
Loch Glentoo
THREAVE CASTLE
LONG FELL
Loch Kindar
Loch Whinyeon
KELTON MAINS OPEN FARM
Castle Douglas
OLD BUITTLE TOWER
Drumburn
Loch Bargatton
Carlingwark Loch
Bar Hill
CRIFFELL
Glengap Forest
Glengap
THREAVE GARDENS
Dalbeattie
Bridge of Dee
Rhonehouse or Kelton Hill
BENGRAY
Carsethorn
Kirkbean
ARBIGLAND GARDENS
Gelston
Dalbeattie Forest
Drumstinchall
Prestonmill
FLEET
Ringford
Airieland
Palnackie
Caulkerbush
Anworth
MILL ON THE FLEET
Gatehouse of Fleet
CARDONESS CASTLE
Valleyfield
Barnbarroch
Mainsriddle
JOHN PAUL JONES COTTAGE MUSEUM
ORCHARDTON TOWER
Sandyhills
Colvend
Southerness
Southerness Pt.
Girthon
GALLOWAY HYDRO VISITOR CENTRE
Twynholm
Kippford or Scaur
MOTE OF MARK
Rockcliffe
Portling
Mersehead Sands
Tongland
BROUGHTON HOUSE AND GARDEN
BENGAIRN
ROUGH ISLAND
Rough I.
EAST STEWARTRY COAST
Castlehill Pt.
Whinnieliggate
STEWARTRY
Kirkcudbright
Auchencairn
Auchencairn Bay
Fleet Bay
GLENKENS
LOWTHER HILLS
NITHSDALE
0 1 2 3 4 5 6 miles
0 1 2 3 4 5 6 7 8 9 10km
68
69
67
55
56

Scottish Borders
Galloway
Cumbria
NT
NY
Ettrick Forest
Eskdalemuir Forest
Craik Forest
Wauchope Forest
Kielder Forest Park
Newcastleton Forest
Kershope Forest
Tinnisburn Forest
Castle O'er Forest
Spadeadam Forest
King's Forest of Geltsdale
Solway Coast
Teviotdale
Eskdale
Liddesdale
Selkirk
Philiphaugh
Bowhill
Yarrow
Yarrow Feus
Mountbenger
Dryhope
Cappercleuch
Meggethead
Talla Linnfoots
Crookhaugh
Hearthstane
Stanhope
Birkhill
Ettrickhill
Ettrick
Ramseycleuch
Tushielaw
Wardlaw
Crosslee
Newburgh
Gilmanscleuch
Ettrickbridge
Kirkhope
Sundhope
Buccleuch
Redfordgreen
Glenkerry
Nether Dalgliesh
Craik
Howpasley
Capplegill
Roundstonefoot
Davington
Eskdalemuir
Laverhay
Waterhead
Sandyford
Castle O'er
Boreland
Dinwoodie Mains
Georgefield
Bentpath
Jamestown
Ewes
Arkleton
Potholm
Langholm
Sibbaldbie
Corrie Common
Paddockhole
Lockerbie
Bankshill
Kirtleton
Burnswark
Castlemilk
Kettleholm
Middleshaw
Waterbeck
Middlebie
Springkell
Ecclefechan
Eaglesfield
Hoddomcross
Hoddom Mains
Dalton
Kirtlebridge
Brydekirk
Creca
Newton
Hollee
Charlesfield
Annan
Welldale
Shawhill
Powfoot
Cummertrees
Dornock
Eastriggs
Browhouses
Rigg
Gretna Green
Gretna
Springfield
Kirkpatrick-Fleming
Chapelknowe
Evertown
Milltown
Woodhouselees
Canonbie
Riddings
Rowanburn
Claygate
Moat
Netherby
Easton
Longtown
Woll
Ashkirk
Clerklands
Lilliesleaf
Midlem
Longnewton
Belses
Bloomfield
Ancrum
Greenhouse
Chesters
Lanton
Hassendean
Minto
Newton
Horsleyhill
Clarilaw
Appletreehall
Denholm
Bedrule
Ashybank
Burnfoot
Cauldmill
Kirkton
Hallrule
Hawick
Wilton
Borthwickshiels
Roberton
Borthwickbrae
Burnfoot
Deanburnhaugh
Branxholm Park
Branxholme
Newmill
Broadhaugh
Northhouse
Dodburn
Teviothead
Castleweary
Priesthaugh
Langburnshiels
Singdean
Bonchester Bridge
Hobkirk
Cleuch Head
Southdean
Todrig
Gorrenberry
Hermitage
Newlands
Steele Road
Larriston
Dinlabyre
Saughtree
Deadwater
Kielder
Old Castleton
Newcastleton or Copshaw Holm
Kershopefoot
Caulside
Baileyhead
Crossings
Catlowdy
Blackpool Gate
Roughsike
Roadhead
Haggbeck
Bewcastle
The Flatt
Stapleton
Spadeadam Farm
Kirkcambeck
Boltonfellend
Hethersgill
Kirklinton
Smithfield
Sandysike
Westlinton
Scaleby Hill
Scaleby
Todhills
Blackford
Rockcliffe
Harker
Laversdale
Irthington
Newtown
Walton
Banks
Lanercost
Low Row
Brampton
Milton
Gilsland Spa
West Hall
Bowness-on-Solway
Port Carlisle
Glasson
Drumburgh
Cardurnock
Anthorn
Easton
Whitrigg
Kirkbride
Fingland
Newton Arlosh
Silloth
Calvo
Seaville
Causewayhead
Kingside Hill
Burgh by Sands
Boustead Hill
Beaumont
Cargo
Kingstown
Houghton
Linstock
Low Crosby
Newby East
Kirkandrews upon Eden
Grinsdale
Stanwix
Carlisle
Thurstonfield
Moorhouse
Kirkbampton
Oughterby
Little Bampton
Aikton
Wiggonby
Great Orton
Little Orton
Newby West
Morton
Upperby
Botcherby
Harraby
Scotby
Wetheral
Great Corby
Warwick on Eden
Warwick Bridge
How
Heads Nook
Faugh
Hayton
Castle Carrock
Talkin
Farlam
Hallbankgate
Tindale
Forest Head
Cummersdale
Carleton
Cumwhinton
Cumwhitton
Baldwinholme
Durdar
Brisco
Halton
Glendue Fell
Denton Fell
Tindale Fells
Geltsdale Middle
St. Mary's Loch
Megget Reservoir
Loch of the Lowes
Loch Skeen
Fruid Reservoir
Black Esk Reservoir
Akermoor Loch
Shaws Under Loch
Hellmoor Loch
69
70
62
56
57
A7
A708
A74(M)
A75
A6071
A69
M6
A595
B709
B711
B6399
B6357
B6318

THE CHEVIOT HILLS
NORTHUMBERLAND NATIONAL PARK
Northumberland
KIELDER FOREST PARK
Kielder Forest
Redesdale Forest
Wark Forest
Kielder Water
Jedburgh
Wooler
Rothbury
Bellingham
Otterburn
Haltwhistle
Haydon Bridge
Hexham
Corbridge
Prudhoe
Allendale Town
Gilsland
Greenhead
Kielder
Falstone
Byrness
Catcleugh
Elsdon
Alwinton
Harbottle
Holystone
Thropton
Chollerford
Humshaugh
Wark
Simonburn
Kirk Yetholm
Town Yetholm
Morebattle
Crailing
Nisbet
Ancrum
Bonjedward
Camptown
Oxnam
Hownam
Chatto
Cessford
Linton
Crookhouse
Frogden
Kalemouth
Chesters
Southdean
Bonchester Bridge
Hobkirk
Denholm
Bedrule
Hundalee
Deadwater
Saughtree
Redesdale Camp
Rochester
Horsley
Elishaw
Otterburn Camp
West Woodburn
East Woodburn
Ridsdale
Knowesgate
Kirkwhelpington
Cambo
Hartburn
Scots' Gap
Middleton
Capheaton
Kirkharle
Great Bavington
Little Bavington
Thockrington
Kirkheaton
Hallington
Ryal
Ingoe
Black Heddon
Matfen
Fenwick
Stamfordham
Ouston
Great Whittington
Bingfield
Colwell
Great Swinburne
Gunnerton
Barrasford
Chollerton
Walwick
Low Brunton
Wall
Hill Head
Acomb
Fourstones
Warden
Newbrough
Sandhoe
Aydon
Halton
Dilston
Riding Mill
Broomhaugh
Stocksfield
Bywell
Slaley
Whitley Chapel
Dye House
Dalton
Langley
Catton
Whitfield
Ninebanks
Sinderhope
Broadwell House
Lambley
Eals
Knarsdale
Midgeholme
Halton Lea Gate
Tindale
Hallbankgate
Rowfoot
Plenmeller
Melkridge
Redburn
Henshaw
Bardon Mill
Chesterwood
Low Gate
Whiteside
Upper Denton
West Hall
Wiley Sike
Spadeadam Farm
Butterburn
Churnsike Lodge
Whygate
Stonehaugh
Park End
Birtley
Redesmouth
Hesleyside
Charlton
Lanehead
Greenhaugh
Gatehouse
The Eals
Bower
Hareshaw Head
Sills
Featherwood
Blindburn
Barrowburn
Shillmoor
Linshiels
Netherton
Burradon
Biddlestone
Scrainwood
Alnham
Sharperton
Flotterton
Hepple
Caistron
Great Tosson
Newtown
Whitton
Warton
Snitter
Cartington
Lorbottle
Callaly
Yetlington
Whittingham
Thrunton
Glanton
Powburn
Branton
Ingram
Brandon
Greensidehill
Langleeford
Ilderton
Roseden
Roddam
Wooperton
North Middleton
South Middleton
Earle
Humbleton
Akeld
Chatton
Chillingham
Newtown
Lilburn Tower
East Lilburn
Hepburn
Old Bewick
New Bewick
Hethpool
Cliftoncote
Mowhaugh
Sourhope
Hownam Mains
Swinside Hall
Mossburnford
Bairnkine
Falla
Mervinslaw
Howden
Lanton
Newton
Crailinghall
Whitton
Nether Hindhope
The Cheviot 815
Windy Gyle 619
Mounthooley
Auchope Cairn 726
Cushat Law 616
Kidland Forest
Shill Moor
Harwood Forest
Thrunton Wood
Leithope Forest
Kielderhead Moor
Emblehope Moor
Wainhope Moor
Blackburn Common
Blakehope Fell
Troughend Common
Hopehouse
Paddaburn Moor
Spadeadam Forest
Black Fell
Haughton Common
Thirlwall Common
Denton Fell
Plenmellar Common
Glendue Fell
Whitfield Moor
Hexhamshire Common
Blanchland Moor
Slaley Forest
Allendale Common
Craik Moor
Whitelyne Common
Tindale Fells
COURSE OF HADRIAN'S WALL
HOUSESTEADS ROMAN FORT
CHESTERS ROMAN FORT
BIRDOSWALD ROMAN FORT
ROMAN ARMY MUSEUM
CHESTERHOLM MUSEUM (VINDOLANDA)
KIELDER CASTLE VISITOR CENTRE
TOWER KNOWE VISITOR CENTRE
KIELDER WATER BIRDS OF PREY CENTRE
BLACK MIDDENS BASTLE HOUSE
JEDBURGH ABBEY
MARY QUEEN OF SCOTS' HOUSE
JEDBURGH CASTLE JAIL & MUSEUM
FERNIEHIRST CASTLE
JEDFOREST DEER & FARM PARK
HARESTANES COUNTRYSIDE VISITOR CENTRE
WATERLOO MONUMENT
TEVIOT WATER GARDENS
CHILLINGHAM CASTLE
WILD CATTLE OF CHILLINGHAM
INGRAM NATIONAL PARK CENTRE
LADY'S WELL
CRAGSIDE HOUSE
HERTERTON HOUSE GARDEN
WALLINGTON
BELSAY HALL
AYDON CASTLE
BORDER HISTORY MUS
DILSTON PHYSIC GDN
HEXHAM ABBEY
HIGHLAND CATTLE CENTRE
PENNINE WAY
DERE STREET
A68
A69
A696
A697
A6088
A6079
A686
B6320
B6318
B6342
B6341
70
71
61
57
0 1 2 3 4 5 6 miles
0 1 2 3 4 5 6 7 8 9 10 km
NT
NY

NORTHUMBERLAND COAST
NU
NZ
Warenford
Newham
Newstead
Rosebrough
Fleetham
Chathill
Ellingham
Preston
PRESTON TOWER
Swinhoe
Benthall
Beadnell Bay
High Newton-by-the-Sea
Low Newton-by-the-Sea
Embleton Bay
Brunton
Christon Bank
Embleton
Dunstan Steads
Castle Point
DUNSTANBURGH CASTLE
Brownyside
North Charlton
West Ditchburn
South Charlton
Eglingham
Rock
Craster
Dunstan
Rennington
Littlemill
Howick
Littlehoughton
Howick Haven
Shipley
HULNE PRIORY
Longhoughton
Boulmer
Boulmer Haven
Bolton
ALNWICK ABBEY
Alnwick
Denwick
Abberwick
Broome Park
Hawkhill
Lesbury
Lemmington Hall
EDLINGHAM CASTLE
Bilton
Alnmouth
Alnmouth Bay
High Buston
Shilbottle
Low Buston
Birling
Eastfield Hall
Warkworth
Newton-on-the-Moor
Gloster Hill
Amble
Coquet I.
Hauxley
Hazon
Swarland Estate
Guyzance
North Togston
Brainshaugh
Swarland
Acklington
Radcliffe
Togston
Broomhill
South Broomhill
Felton
LONGFRAMLINGTON GARDENS
West Thirston
East Thirston
Red Row
DRURIDGE BAY
Weldon
Eshott
West Chevington
Druridge Bay
Helm
Widdrington
Longhorsley
Causey Park Bridge
Stobswood
Widdrington Station
Cresswell
The Scars
Fenrother
Tritlington
Ulgham
Ellington
Linton
Lynemouth
THE SANCTUARY WILDLIFE CENTRE
Stanton
COLLIERY MUSEUM
Beacon Pt.
Hebron
Longhirst
QUEEN ELIZABETH II
Woodhorn
Pigdon
Pegswood
Ashington
Newbiggin-by-the-Sea
NORTHUMBRIA CRAFT CENTRE
Bothal
WANSBECK
Hirst
Mitford
Throphill
Morpeth
Stakeford
North Seaton
Guide Post
Scotland Gate
West Sleekburn
Molesden
Choppington
Hepscott
Cambois
Tranwell
Bedlington Station
East Sleekburn
Clifton
Whalton
Bedlington
Cowpen
BLYTH
Netherton
Bebside
Shilvington
Saltwick
BEDLINGTON
Newsham
East Hartford
New Delaval
Stannington
PLESSEY WOODS
Ogle
Shankhouse
KIRKLEY HALL
Nelson Village
New Hartley
Seaton Sluice
Seaton
SEATON DELAVAL HALL
Higham Dykes
Berwick Hill
NORTHUMBERLAND CHEESE FARM
Cramlington
Southfield
East Cramlington
Seaton Delaval
Hartley
ST MARY'S LIGHTHOUSE
St Mary's or Bait I.
Brenkley
Seaton Burn
Holywell
Seghill
Ponteland
Dinnington
Annitsford
Earsdon
WHITLEY BAY
Brunswick Village
Dudley
Wide Open
Burradon
Backworth
Prestwick
Darras Hall
Hazlerigg
Camperdown
Monkseaton
AMSTERDAM 15:30
NEWCASTLE INTERNATIONAL
Killingworth
Shiremoor
Cullercoats
Medburn
High Callerton
Woolsington
Marden
BLUE REEF AQUARIUM
TYNEMOUTH CASTLE & PRIORY
Black Callerton
Kenton Bankfoot
Longbenton
STEPHENSON RAILWAY MUSEUM
Tynemouth
North Walbottle
Gosforth
THE RISING SUN
North Shields
ARBEIA ROMAN FORT AND MUSEUM
Westerhope
Kenton
Jesmond
WALLSEND
Willington
South Shields
Heddon-on-the-Wall
Throckley
Heaton
Tyne Tunnel
SOUTH SHIELDS MUSEUM
Walbottle
NEWCASTLE UPON TYNE
Byker
Jarrow
BEDE'S WORLD
ST PAUL'S MONASTERY
Westoe
THE LEAS AND MARSDEN ROCK
Marsden Bay
Newburn
Clara Vale
Scotswood
CASTLE KEEP
Walker
Harton
Marsden
Wylam
Ryton
Crawcrook
Gateshead
Hebburn
SOUTER LIGHTHOUSE
BLAYDON
METROLAND
Dunston
INTERNATIONAL STADIUM
Hedworth
Boldon Colliery
Whiteleas
Cleadon
Whitburn Colliery
Greenside
Winlaton
Bensham
Felling
Pelaw
Coalburns
Whitburn
Whickham
Carr Hill
Boldon
Barlow
FULWELL WINDMILL
Fulwell
High Spen
Highfield
Low Fell
Downhill
Hylton Castle
Southwick
Roker
Rowlands Gill
Sunniside
Street Gate
Chowdene
Wrekenton
Monkwearmouth
NATIONAL GLASS CENTRE
ST PETER'S CHURCH
SUNDERLAND MINSTER
GIBSIDE
Byermoor
Lamesley
Springwell
Usworth
Castletown
STATION MUS
Blackhall Mill
DERWENTCOTE STEEL FURNACE
Marley Hill
ANGEL OF THE NORTH
Blackfell
South Hylton
Pallion
Burnopfield
Kibblesworth
Leazes
TANFIELD RAILWAY
Birtley
WASHINGTON
High Barnes
Sunderland
Hobson
High Westwood
Medomsley
Tanfield
Lambton
THE WILDFOWL & WETLANDS TRUST
Pennywell
Hendon
Tantobie
BEAMISH
Ouston
Beamish
Urpeth
Perkinsville
Barley Mow
PENSHAW MON
Fatfield
Penshaw
East Herrington
New Silksworth
Dipton
Tanfield Lea
STANLEY
Rickleton
Shiney Row
Tunstall
Ryhope
Catchgate
West Pelton
Pelton
New Herrington
Doxford Park
RYHOPE ENGINES MUS
Leadgate
Annfield
The Middles
Grange Villa
CHESTER-LE-STREET
Bournmoor
Newbottle
Burdon
71
58
A
B
C
D
E
F
G
H
7
8
9
10
11
12

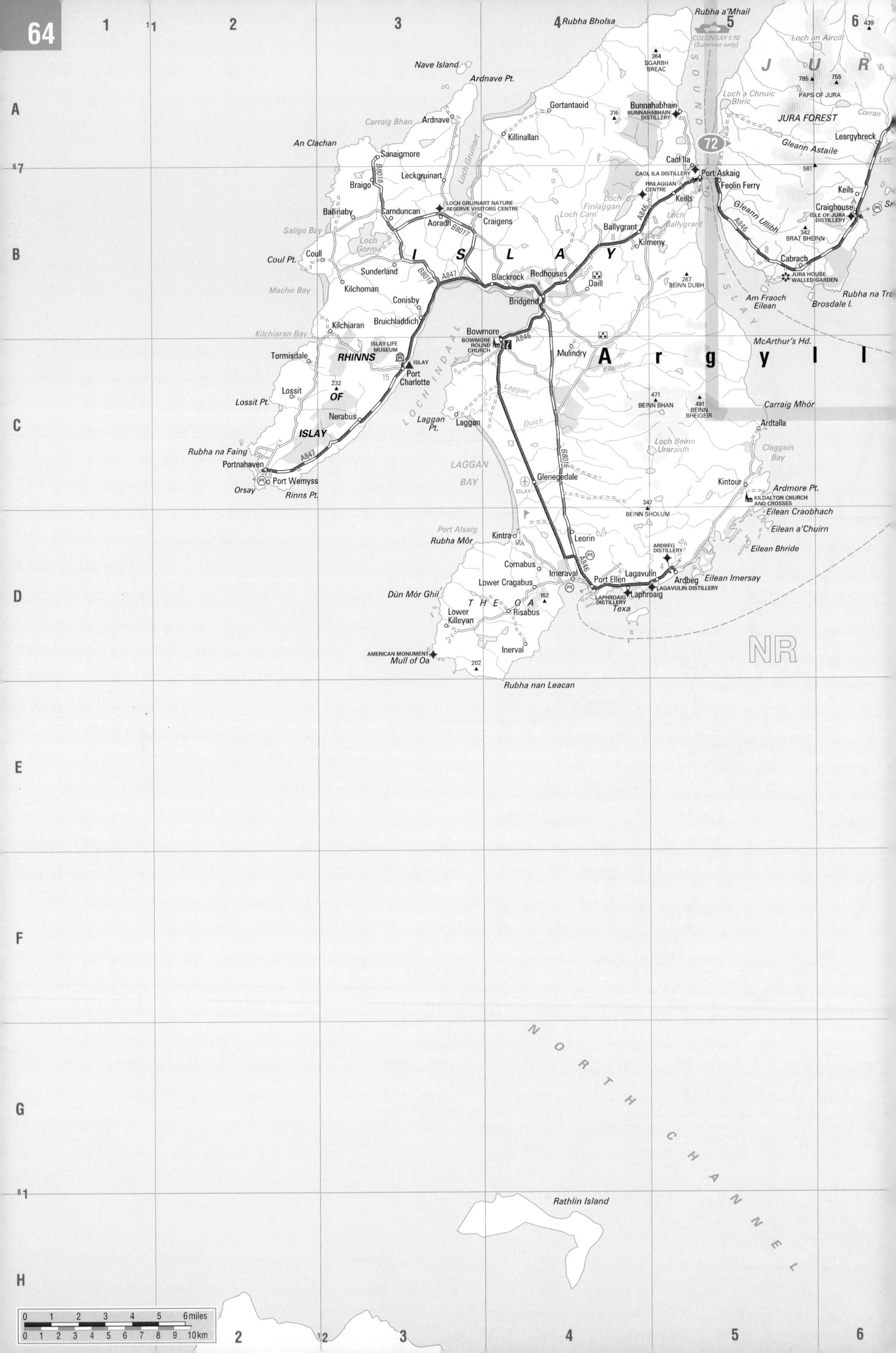

Rubha a'Mhail
Rubha Bholsa
COLONSAY 1:10 (Summer only)
SOUND OF ISLAY
Nave Island
Ardnave Pt.
Loch an Aircill
JURA
PAPS OF JURA
Loch a Chnuic Bhric
JURA FOREST
Corran
Gortantaoid
Bunnahabhain
BUNNAHABHAIN DISTILLERY
SGARBH BREAC
Carraig Bhan
Ardnave
An Clachan
Killinallan
Loch Gruinart
72
Leargybreck
Gleann Astaile
Sanaigmore
Caol Ila
CAOL ILA DISTILLERY
Port Askaig
Feolin Ferry
Braigo
Leckgruinart
FINLAGGAN CENTRE
Keills
Loch Finlaggan
Gleann Ullibh
Craighouse
ISLE OF JURA DISTILLERY
Ballinaby
Carnduncan
LOCH GRUINART NATURE RESERVE VISITORS CENTRE
Aoradh
Craigens
Loch Cam
Loch Ballygrant
Ballygrant
Saligo Bay
BRAT BHEINN
Loch Gorm
ISLAY
Kilmeny
Coull
Coul Pt.
Sunderland
Blackrock
Redhouses
Daill
Sorn
Cabrach
Machir Bay
Kilchoman
JURA HOUSE WALLED GARDEN
BEINN DUBH
Rubha na Traille
Bridgend
Conisby
Am Fraoch Eilean
Brosdale I.
Bruichladdich
Kilchiaran
Kilchiaran Bay
Bowmore
BOWMORE ROUND CHURCH
McArthur's Hd.
ISLAY LIFE MUSEUM
Tormisdale
RHINNS OF ISLAY
Port Charlotte
Mulindry
Argyll
Kilennan
LOCH INDAAL
Laggan
Lossit
Lossit Pt.
BEINN BHAN
BEINN BHEIGEIR
Carraig Mhór
Nerabus
Laggan Pt.
Duich
Ardtalla
Loch Beinn Uraraidh
Claggain Bay
Rubha na Faing
Portnahaven
Port Wemyss
Orsay
Rinns Pt.
LAGGAN BAY
Glenegedale
Kintour
Ardmore Pt.
KILDALTON CHURCH AND CROSSES
BEINN SHOLUM
Eilean Craobhach
Port Alsaig
Rubha Mór
Kintra
Leorin
Eilean a'Chuirn
ARDBEG DISTILLERY
Eilean Bhride
Cornabus
Imeraval
Lagavulin
Port Ellen
Ardbeg
Eilean Imersay
Lower Cragabus
LAGAVULIN DISTILLERY
Dùn Mór Ghil
THE OA
LAPHROAIG DISTILLERY
Laphroaig
Texa
Lower Killeyan
Risabus
Inerval
AMERICAN MONUMENT
Mull of Oa
Rubha nan Leacan
NR
NORTH CHANNEL
Rathlin Island
A846
A847
B8016
B8017
B8018
0 1 2 3 4 5 6 miles
0 1 2 3 4 5 6 7 8 9 10 km

Lagg
Loch Lesgamaill
Island of Danna
CASTLE SWEEN
Lochead
ST COLUMBA'S CAVE
Achahoish
Eilean Mòr
ST CORMAC'S CHAPEL
CHAPEL
Kilmory
Kilmory Bay
Ellary
Clachbreck
Erines
STOB ODHAR
Baile Boidheach
Loch Caolisport
An Dùnan
Knockrome
Lowlandman's Bay
Ormsary
Pt. of Knap
Druimdrishaig
Loch Chaorain
Loch nan Torran
Barfad
Tarbert
East Loch Tarbert
West Tarbert
Miller's Bay
Cretshengan
CRUACH LAGAIN
Coulaghailtro
Kilberry Hd.
SCULPTURED STONES
Kilberry
Torinturk
DUN
Rhu
Corranbuie
Kennacraig
Redhouse
CNOC A'BHAILESHIOS
Carse Ho.
Dunmore
WEST LOCH TARBERT
Loch Stornoway
Ardpatrick
Kilchamaig
Whitehouse
Rubha Leathan
Ardpatrick Ho.
Gartnagrenach
Portachoillan
Glenreasdell Mains
Skipness
SKIPNESS CASTLE
Skipness Pt.
Skipness Bay
and Bute
Ardpatrick Pt.
Eilean Tràighe
Claonaig
Ronachan Pt.
Clachan
CRUACH NAM FIADH
Claonaig Bay
Loch Ciaran
Eilean Garbh
West Tarbert Bay
East Tarbert Bay
Tarbert
Gigha Island
Druimyeon More
Ardminish
Ardminish Bay
ACHAMORE GARDENS
Gigalum Island
Cara Island
SOUND OF GIGHA
Balochroy
Crossaig Glen
Crossaig
Loch Garasdale
CRUACH MHIC GOUGAN
Rhunahaorine
Cour Bay
Cour
BEINN BHREAC
Tayinloan
CNOC NAN CRAOBH
Carradale Water
Killean
Beacharr
CRUACH MHIC-AN T-SAOIR
CRUACH NAN GABHAR
Grogport
Brackley
Muasdale
Clachaig Water
Amod
Carradale
Port Righ
Glenacardoch Pt.
Belloch
Barr Water
Glenbarr
CLAN MACALISTER CENTRE
BEINN BHREAC
Bridgend
Torrisdale-Square
BEINN AN TUIRC
Carradale Pt.
Carradale Bay
Cleongart
Saddell Glen
Bellochantuy Bay
Bellochantuy
Saddell
SADDELL ABBEY
A'CHRUACH
Saddell Bay
Killocraw
Lussa Loch
Tangy Loch
SGREADAN HILL
Ugadale
Skeroblingarry
Black Bay
Westport
Kilchenzie
Glenlussa Water
Peninver
Ardnacross Bay
KINTYRE
West Darlochan
CAMPBELTOWN
Machrihanish Bay
Kilmichael
Low Smerby
Machrihanish
Trodigal
Campbeltown
CAMPBELTOWN HERITAGE CENTRE
Campbeltown Loch
Island Davaar
DAVAAR ISLAND CAVE PAINTING
Drumlemble
Stewarton
Kilkerran
Kildalloig
Knocknaha
Earadale Pt.
BEINN GHUILEAN
Achinhoan Hd.
Woodbank
THE SLATE
CNOC MOY
Feochaig
Rubh'a' Mharaiche
Glen Breackerie
CNOC ODHAR
Conie Glen
Johnston's Pt.
North Carrine
Keprigan
Strone Glen
Machariock
Polliwilline Bay
Carskiey
Southend
Cove Pt.
Brunerican Bay
MULL OF KINTYRE
Port Mean
Rubha Chlachan
Sheep I.
Sanda Island
Kilfinan Bay
Kilfinan
BEINN BHREAC
KYLES OF BUTE
Drum
Melldalloch
Auchalick Bay
Port Driseach
Tighnabruaich
Auchenlochan
Kames
Ardmarnock Bay
Barmore I.
Asgog Loch
Portavadie
Millhouse
Glenan Bay
Blair's Ferry
Kyles of Bute
Asgog Bay
Kilbride Bay
Ardlamont Ho.
Ardlamont Pt.
Ardentraive
Colintraive
Algaltraig
LOCH STRIVEN
ISLAND OF BUTE
Glen More
WINDY HILL
Kames B.
St Colmac
ROTHESAY CASTLE
Rothesay
Ettrick Bay
Straad
Loch Fad
Loch Quien
Inchmarnock
Scalpsie
Ardscalpsie Pt.
Scalpsie Bay
Stravanan Bay
SOUND OF BUTE
Cock of Arran
LOCHRANZA CASTLE
Lochranza
Loch Ranza
Millstone Pt.
Catacol Bay
Catacol
ISLE OF ARRAN DISTILLERY
KILBRANNAN SOUND
MEALL NAN DAMH
Thundergay
NORTH SANNOX FARM PARK
Sannox
Sannox Bay
NORTH
Glen Sannox
Pirnmill
Loch Tanna
Whitefarland
CÌR MHÒR
BEINN BHARRAIN
BEINN TARSUINN
GOAT FELL
Corrie
NS
Imachar
ISLE OF ARRAN
Glen Iorsa
Glen Rosa
BRODICK CASTLE
ARRAN AROMATICS VISITOR CENTRE
Brodick Bay
ARDROSSAN
Dougarie
ISLE OF ARRAN HERITAGE MUSEUM
Brodick
Strathwhillan
Machrie Water
Auchagallon
Glenloig
A'CHRUACH
Glen Cloy
Machrie Bay
Tormore
MACHRIE MOOR STANDING STONES
Claughlands Pt.
Margnaheglish
KING'S CAVE
BALMICHAEL VISITOR CENTRE
Balmichael
Blairbeg
Lamlash
Lamlash Bay
Holy Island
Cordon
Torbeg
Shiskine
Drumadoon Pt.
Kingscross Pt.
Blackwaterfoot
Drumadoon Bay
Kilpatrick
KILPATRICK DUN
TIGHVEIN
Auchencairn
Kingscross
Knockenkelly
Whiting Bay
North Kiscadale
South Kiscadale
Glenree
Sliddery Water
Largymore
GLENASHDALE FALLS
Brown Hd.
CARN BAN
Corriecravie
Kilmory Water
Largybeg
Sliddery
Lagg
Levencorroch
Dippin
Dippin Head
TORRYLINN CAIRN
Kilmory
SOUTH BANK FARM PARK
Bennan
Kildonan
Bennan Hd.
Sound of Pladda
Pladda

Inchmarnock
Scalpsie
Skipness
SKIPNESS CASTLE
Skipness Pt.
Skipness Bay
Claonaig
269
CRUACH
NAM FIADH
Claonaig Bay
Ardscalpsie Pt.
Scalpsie Bay
Stravanan Bay
Kingarth
Kilchattan Bay
157
ST BLANE'S CHAPEL
Great Cumbrae Island
Downcraig Ferry
CHRISTIAN HERITAGE MUSEUM
MUSEUM OF THE CUMBRAES
Millport
Fairlie
484
RISH LAW
Ladyland
Moor
Muirhead Reservoir
Camphill Reservoir
Kilbirnie
Beith
Glengarnock
Longbar
The Den
73
SOUND OF BUTE
0:30
Cock of Arran
Garroch Hd.
The Tan
Little Cumbrae Island
HUNTERSTON POWER STATION VISITOR CENTRE
387
KAIM HILL
Knockendon Reservoir
Rye Water
Drakemyre
Highfield
Blairland
aig Glen
Crossaig
Loch Ranza
LOCHRANZA CASTLE
Lochranza
Millstone Pt.
Thirdpart
Portencross
Giffordland
Dalry
Catacol Bay
Catacol
LOCHRANZA
ISLE OF ARRAN DISTILLERY
444
Farland Hd.
West Kilbride
BLACKSHAW FARM PARK
Cour Bay
Cour
570
MEALL NAN DAMH
Thundergay
573
NORTH SANNOX FARM PARK
Sannox
Sannox Bay
North Ayrshire
Seamill
Dalgarven
AYRSHIRE MUSEUM OF COUNTRY LIFE & COSTUME
Pirnmill
NORTH
Loch Tanna
859
Glen Sannox
ABBEY
Kilwinning
Grogport
65
Whitefarland
798
CIR MHÒR
721
BEINN BHARRAIN
Corrie
Horse Isle
Chapelhill
Dykesmains
EGLINTON
BEINN TARSUINN
825
874
GOAT FELL
Ardrossan
NORTH AYRSHIRE MUSEUM
Stevenston
Saltcoats
Imachar
ISLE
ARRAN
0:55
Irvine
Carradale
Port Righ
BRODICK
Glen Rosa
BRODICK CASTLE
ARRAN AROMATICS VISITOR CENTRE
SCOTTISH MARITIME MUSEUM
Fullarton
Dougarie
228
Glen Iorsa
OF
Brodick Bay
Irvine Bay
Carradale Pt.
ISLE OF ARRAN HERITAGE MUSEUM
Brodick
Strathwhillan
Machrie Water
Auchagallon
Machrie Bay
Glenloig
A'CHRUACH
512
Glen Cloy
ARRAN
Clauchlands Pt.
Barassie
Tormore
MACHRIE MOOR STANDING STONES
503
Blairbeg
Margnaheglish
North Bay
Muirhead
KING'S CAVE
BALMICHAEL VISITOR CENTRE
Balmichael
Lamlash
Lamlash Bay
Holy Island
Troon
Torbeg
Shiskine
Cordon
314
South Bay
ROYAL TROON
Drumadoon Pt.
Lady Isle
Blackwaterfoot
Drumadoon Bay
Kilpatrick
KILPATRICK DUN
458
TIGHVEIN
Auchencairn
Kingscross Pt.
Kingscross
LARNE 1:50 (March-Oct)
Knockenkelly
Whiting Bay
Sliddery Water
North Kiscadale
South Kiscadale
Prestwi
Glenree
GLENASHDALE FALLS
Largymore
NR
Brown Hd.
CARN BAN
Corriecravie
Kilmory Water
Largybeg
Woodfie
Newton on Ayr
Wallacetown
Sliddery
Dippin
Lagg
Levencorroch
Dippin Head
Ayr
Kilmory
SOUTH BANK FARM PARK
Kildonan
Seafield
TORRYLINN CAIRN
Bennan
Bennan Hd.
Sound of Pladda
BURNS COTTAGE
Pladda
Heads of Ayr
HEADS OF AYR FARM PARK
Doonfoot
Alloway
BURNS NATIONAL HERITAGE PARK
Fisherton
Dunure
287
Culroy
Minish
ELECTRIC BRAE
Culzean Bay
270
CULZEAN CASTLE
Whitefaulds
Maybole
COLLEGIATE CHURCH
Kirkmichael
Aitkenhe
Maidenhead Bay
CULZEAN
Maidens
Kirkoswald
CROSSRAGUEL ABBEY
TURNBERRY
Turnberry Bay
SOUTER JOHNNIE'S COTTAGE
Crossh
Turnberry
Brest Rocks
252
Ruglen
Townhead
Water of Girvan
Wallacetown
Dipple
Burnhead
Dailly
BARGANY GARDENS
Old Dailly
Ailsa Craig
338
Ayrs
Girvan
Penkill
Houdston
Penwhapple Res.
Glendoune
355
MULL OF MILJOAN
Dalwyne
Woodland Bay
Tormitchell
South Balloch
NW
Pinminnoch
Auchensoul
Barr
Changue Forest
Kennedy's Pass
297
GREY HILL
Pinmore
Stinchar
Currarie
Merkland
565
CRAIGENRI
Lendalfoot
Straid
Pinmore Mains
CARLETON CASTLE
260
Poundland
Pinwherry
335
PINDONNAN
Bennane Hd.
Bellamore
Colmonell
265
Knockdolian
Ballochmorrie
Black Clauchrie
54
Ballantrae Bay
Heronsford
Glen Tig
Water of Tig
Duisk
Ballantrae
Barrhill
Balkissock
Laggan
Eldrick
Gle
0 1 2 3 4 5 6 miles
0 1 2 3 4 5 6 7 8 9 10 km

Barrhead
Neilston
Newton Mearns
Clarkston
Busby
Carmunnock
Bothwell
MOTHERWELL
HAMILTON
WISHAW
Newmains
East Kilbride
Eaglesham
Larkhall
Carluke
Stonehouse
Strathaven
Lanark
Blackwood
Kirkmuirhill
Lesmahagow
Coalburn
Douglas
Stewarton
Kilmaurs
Kilmarnock
Riccarton
Galston
Newmilns
Darvel
Greenholm
Mauchline
Catrine
Tarbolton
Auchinleck
Cumnock
Netherthird
Drongan
Ochiltree
Muirkirk
New Cumnock
Kirkconnel
Sanquhar
Wanlockhead
Patna
Dalmellington
Dalrymple
Carsphairn
Moniaive
St John's Town of Dalry
Renfrewshire
East
South Lanarkshire
East Ayrshire
Dumfries and Galloway
LOWTHER HILLS
NITHSDALE
CLYDESDALE
THE GLENKENS
RHINNS OF KELLS
Flow Moss
Airds Moss
Carsphairn Forest
Dundeugh Forest
Tairlaw Forest
CARRICK FOREST
Dalmacallan Forest
Corriedoo Forest
68
60
55

LOCH LOMOND
AND THE TROSSACHS
NATIONAL PARK
West
Dunbartonshire
East
Dunbartonshire
Inverclyde
Renfrewshire
East
Renfrewshire
CUNNINGHAME
CLYDE MUIRSHIEL REGIONAL PARK
CAMPSIE FELLS
KILPATRICK HILLS
Glasgow
GLASGOW
Helensburgh
ALEXANDRIA
DUMBARTON
PORT GLASGOW
Greenock
CLYDEBANK
BEARSDEN
Milngavie
KIRKINTILLOCH
Kilsyth
CUMBERNAULD
COATBRIDGE
AIRDRIE
RENFREW
Paisley
JOHNSTONE
Barrhead
Newton Mearns
Rutherglen
Cambuslang
Uddingston
Bellshill
MOTHERWELL
HAMILTON
East Kilbride
Larkhall
Strathaven
Stonehouse
Lochwinnoch
Kilbirnie
Beith
Dalry
Kilwinning
Stevenston
Irvine
Kilmarnock
Stewarton
Kilmaurs
Galston
Newmilns
Darvel
Troon
Prestwick
Mauchline
Catrine
Muirkirk
Auchinleck
Killearn
Balfron
Drymen
Buchlyvie
Fintry
Kippen
Gargunnock
Erskine Bridge
Glasgow Prestwick International
Irvine Bay
Lady Isle
Flow Moss
Kype Muir
Rough Moss
Airds Moss
East Ayrshire
Lanarkshire
NS
KILCREGGAN 0:25
LARNE 1:50 (March-Oct)
0 1 2 3 4 5 6 miles
0 1 2 3 4 5 6 7 8 9 10 km

Clackmannanshire
Menstrie
Tillicoultry
Dollar
Alva
Tullibody
Devonside
Coalsnaughton
Cambuskenneth
Stirling
Cambus
Sauchie
Forest Mill
ALLOA
Clackmannan
Kennet
Kilbagie
Bannockburn
South Alloa
Cowie
Dunmore
Throsk
Fallin
Kincardine
Devilla Forest
Airth
Plean
Letham
Kincardine Bridge
Torwood
Dunipace
DENNY
Stenhousemuir
Larbert
Carron
Carronshore
Skinflats
GRANGEMOUTH
Bonnybridge
FALKIRK
Laurieston
Dennyloanhead
High Bonnybridge
Glen Village
Redding
Reddingmuirhead
Polmont
Brightons
Grangepans
Carriden
Bo'ness
Muirhouses
Blackness
Mannerston
Linlithgow
Linlithgow Bridge
Philpstoun
Old Philpstoun
Whitecross
Maddiston
Shieldhill
California
Falkirk
West
Lothian
Standburn
Avonbridge
Westfield
Torphichen
Slamannan
Crossburn
Binniehill
Limerigg
Longriggend
Caldercruix
Armadale
Bathgate
Boghall
Whiteside
Windyknowe
Westrigg
Blackridge
Bathville
Mayfield
Forrestfield
Blackburn
Harthill
Whitburn
East Whitburn
Eastfield
West Benhar
Salsburgh
Kirk of Shotts
Hirst
Longridge
Stoneybury
Fauldhouse
Greenburn
Breich
Shotts
Dykehead
Stane
Hareshaw
Hartwood
Allanton
Bonkle
Newmains
Morningside
Bogside
Kingshill Plantation
Waterloo
Carluke
Yieldshields
Roadmeetings
Kilncadzow
Braidwood
Cartland
Carstairs
Carstairs Junction
West End
Carnwath
Kaimend
Newbigging
Nemphlar
Ravenstruther
Hazelbank
Kirkfieldbank
Lanark
New Lanark
Hyndford Bridge
Pettinain
Libberton
Auchenheath
Dillarburn
Hawksland
Brocketsbrae
Sandilands
Harleyholm
Covington
Thankerton
Quothquan
Biggar
Wolfclyde
Causewayend
Symington
Coulter
Douglas Water
Rigside
Coalburn
Braehead
Happendon
Uddington
Tinto Hills
Tinto
Wiston
Newton
Lamington
Roberton Law
Roberton
Douglas
Douglas West
Middle Muir
Glentaggart
Crawfordjohn
Abington
Crawford
Kirkton
Drake Law
Fife
Saline
Comrie
Oakley
Carnock
Blairhall
Gowkhall
Cowstrandburn
Wellwood
Milesmark
DUNFERMLINE
Crossford
Cairneyhill
High Valleyfield
Low Torry
Torryburn
Culross
Charlestown
Limekilns
Rosyth
Inverkeithing
North Queensferry
Forth Road Bridge
Queensferry
Dalmeny
Newton
Kirkliston
Winchburgh
Threemiletown
Bridgend
Ecclesmachan
Broxburn
Uphall
Dechmont
Wester Dechmont
Uphall Station
Pumpherston
Deans
LIVINGSTON
Mid Calder
East Calder
Oakbank
Seafield
Bellsquarry
Polbeth
West Calder
Addiewell
Loganlea
Woolfords Cottages
Tarbrax
Auchengray
Wilsontown
Rootpark
Forth
Climpy
Braehead
Dunsyre
Dolphinton
Walston
Elsrickle
Melbourne
Candy Mill
Skirling
Broughton
Kelty
Lochgelly
Lassodie
Cowdenbeath
Hill of Beath
Crossgates
Fordell
Halbeath
Kingseat
Townhill
Bowershall
Aberdour
Dalgety Bay
Hillend
Burntisland
Kinghorn
Pettycur
Kirkcaldy
Linktown
Auchtertool
Balmule
Cardenden
Auchterderran
Chapel
Templehall
Dysart
Pathhead
Gallatown
Kinglassie
Lochore
Ballingry
Crosshill
Glencraig
Lumphinnans
Blairingone
Pownill
Cleish
Cleish Hills
Hill End
Balgonar
Knock Hill
Rumbling Bridge
Inchkeith
Inchcolm
Inchmickery
Cramond I.
Firth of Forth
Drum Sands
Cramond
Cramond Bridge
Davidson's Mains
Barnton
Turnhouse
Ingliston
Gogar
Ratho Station
Ratho
Newbridge
Burnside
Bonnington
Wilkieston
Hermiston
Sighthill
Murrayfield
Corstorphine
Gorgie
Craiglockhart
Colinton
Juniper Green
Currie
Balerno
Malleny Mills
Kirknewton
Edinburgh
EDINBURGH
Granton
Newhaven
Leith
Drylaw
Morningside
Braid
Liberton
Fairmilehead
Straiton
Loanhead
Bilston
Roslin
Penicuik
Kirkhill
Milton Bridge
Auchendinny
Silverburn
Bonnyrigg and Lasswade
Polton
Rosewell
Eskbank
Dalkeith
Gilmerton
Danderhall
Newcraighall
Craigmillar
Duddingston
Portobello
Joppa
Musselburgh
Pentland Hills
Regional Park
Carlops
Nine Mile Burn
Leadburn
Howgate
Easter Howgate
Midlothian
Temple
Carrington
Whim Farm
Cowdenburn
Waterheads
West Linton
Halmyre Mains
Romannobridge
Damside
Mountain Cross
Blyth Bridge
Drochil
Kirkurd
Eddleston
Scottish Borders
Peebles
Kings Muir
Hallyne
Stobo
Kirkton Manor
Glentress
Glentress Forest
Cardrona
Cardrona Forest
Kirkburn
Dreva Forest
Upper Tweeddale
Castlehill
Bellspool
Drumelzier
Rachan Mill
Stanhope
Langhaugh
Glen Ho
Blake Muir
Kirkhouse
Traquair
Crookhaugh
Hearthstane
Tweedsmuir
Dryhope
Cappercleuch
Mountbenger
Glenbreck
Talla Reservoir
Megget Reservoir
Gilmanscleuch
Culter Fell
Broad Law
Dollar Law
Black Law
Moorfoot Hills
Blackhope Scar
Dewar
Whitehope Law
Bleak Law
Mendick Hill
White Craig
Byrehope Mount
Black Mount
Cobbinshaw Reservoir
Crosswood Reservoir
Baddinsgill Reservoir
West Water Reservoir
Woodmuir Plantation
Hare Hill
Harlaw Reservoir
Threipmuir Reservoir
Harperrig Reservoir
Glencorse Res.
Gladhouse Reservoir
Rosebery Reservoir
Portmore Loch
Camps Reservoir
Cowgill Upper Reservoir
Culter Waterhead Reservoir
Broken Cross Muir
Tewsgill Hill
Glenwhappen Rig
Blakehope Head
Pykestone Hill
Dun Rig
Stob Law
Black Meldon
White Meldon
Broughton Heights
Loch Glow
Loch Fitty
Loch Gelly
Torry Bay
St. Margaret's Hope
Inverkeithing Bay
Kirkcaldy
Coaltown
Thornton
Stenton
West Wemyss

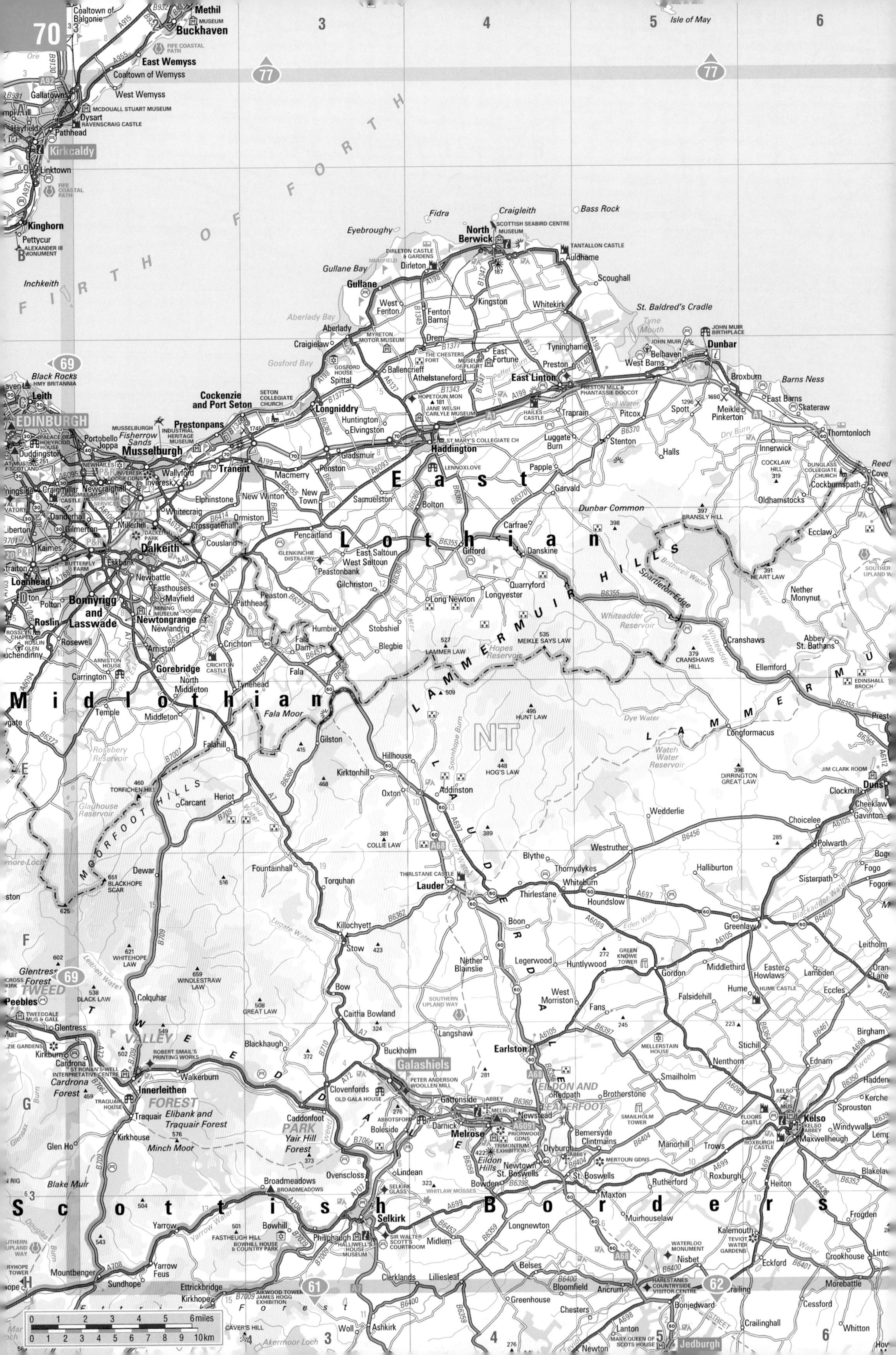

FIRTH OF FORTH
East Lothian
Midlothian
Scottish Borders
LAMMERMUIR HILLS
LAMMERMUIR
LAUDERDALE
TWEEDDALE
MOORFOOT HILLS
Ettrick Forest
NT
EDINBURGH
Kirkcaldy
Galashiels
Jedburgh
Methil
Buckhaven
Coaltown of Balgonie
East Wemyss
Coaltown of Wemyss
West Wemyss
Gallatown
Dysart
Pathhead
Linktown
Kinghorn
Pettycur
Inchkeith
Isle of May
Fidra
Craigleith
Bass Rock
Eyebroughy
North Berwick
Dirleton
Gullane Bay
Gullane
West Fenton
Fenton Barns
Kingston
Whitekirk
Auldhame
Scoughall
Aberlady Bay
Aberlady
Craigielaw
Gosford Bay
Drem
Ballencrieff
Athelstaneford
East Fortune
Tyninghame
St. Baldred's Cradle
Tyne Mouth
Dunbar
Belhaven
West Barns
Preston
East Linton
Broxburn
Barns Ness
East Barns
Skateraw
Black Rocks
Leith
Cockenzie and Port Seton
Prestonpans
Longniddry
Spittal
Huntington
Elvingston
Haddington
Traprain
Pitcox
Stenton
Spott
Meikle Pinkerton
Thorntonloch
Portobello
Joppa
Musselburgh
Fisherrow Sands
Duddingston
Tranent
Wallyford
Inveresk
Gladsmuir
Macmerry
Penston
Craigmillar
Newcraighall
Danderhall
Gilmerton
Millerhill
Whitecraig
Elphinstone
New Winton
Crossgatehall
Ormiston
New Town
Samuelston
Bolton
Papple
Garvald
Luggate Burn
Halls
Innerwick
Oldhamstocks
Cockburnspath
Reed Cove
Dunbar Common
Kaimes
Dalkeith
Eskbank
Cousland
Pencaitland
East Saltoun
West Saltoun
Peastonbank
Gilchriston
Gifford
Carfrae
Danskine
Quarryford
Longyester
Long Newton
Loanhead
Bonnyrigg and Lasswade
Newtongrange
Newlandrig
Mayfield
Easthouses
Newbattle
Polton
Roslin
Rosewell
Pathhead
Peaston
Humbie
Stobshiel
Blegbie
Fala Dam
Fala
Crichton
Arniston
Gorebridge
Carrington
North Middleton
Tynehead
Temple
Middleton
Fala Moor
Gilston
Hillhouse
Kirktonhill
Oxton
Addinston
Falahill
Heriot
Carcant
Ecclaw
Nether Monynut
Cranshaws
Abbey St. Bathans
Ellemford
Longformacus
Whiteadder Reservoir
Hopes Reservoir
Watch Water Reservoir
Rosebery Reservoir
Gladhouse Reservoir
Wedderlie
Choicelee
Polwarth
Cheeklaw
Gavinton
Clockmill
Duns
Westruther
Blythe
Thornydykes
Whiteburn
Halliburton
Sisterpath
Fogo
Lauder
Thirlestane
Houndslow
Boon
Greenlaw
Fountainhall
Torquhan
Dewar
Killochyett
Stow
Nether Blainslie
Legerwood
Huntlywood
Gordon
Middlethird
Easter Howlaws
Lambden
Leitholm
Glentress Forest
Peebles
Colquhar
Bow
Caitha Bowland
West Morriston
Fans
Hume
Falsidehill
Eccles
Birgham
Langshaw
Blackhaugh
Buckholm
Earlston
Stichill
Ednam
Nenthorn
Smailholm
Glentress
Kirkburn
Cardrona
Cardrona Forest
Innerleithen
Walkerburn
Traquair
Elibank and Traquair Forest
Clovenfords
Caddonfoot
Gattonside
Darnick
Melrose
Newstead
Redpath
Brotherstone
Bemersyde
Clintmains
Manorhill
Trows
Kelso
Maxwellheugh
Sprouston
Hadden
Kerchesters
Windywalls
Kirkhouse
Glen Ho
Minch Moor
Boleside
Yair Hill Forest
Eildon Hills
Dryburgh
Newtown St. Boswells
St. Boswells
Bowden
Rutherford
Roxburgh
Heiton
Blake Muir
Broadmeadows
Ovenscloss
Lindean
Maxton
Muirhouselaw
Yarrow
Bowhill
Selkirk
Philiphaugh
Longnewton
Midlem
Kalemouth
Frogden
Crookhouse
Linton
Mountbenger
Yarrow Feus
Sundhope
Ettrickbridge
Kirkhope
Clerklands
Lilliesleaf
Belses
Bloomfield
Ancrum
Nisbet
Eckford
Morebattle
Greenhouse
Chesters
Bonjedward
Crailing
Cessford
Crailinghall
Whitton
Woll
Ashkirk
Lanton
Newton
Akermoor Loch
Hopetoun Mon
Hailes Castle
Tantallon Castle
Dirleton Castle & Gardens
Scottish Seabird Centre Museum
Myreton Motor Museum
Museum of Flight
John Muir Birthplace
Preston Mill & Phantassie Doocot
Lennoxlove
Glenkinchie Distillery
Crichton Castle
Dalkeith Park
Butterfly Farm
Mining Museum
Arniston House
Thirlestane Castle
Hume Castle
Mellerstain House
Greenknowe Tower
Smailholm Tower
Floors Castle
Roxburgh Castle
Kelso Abbey
Abbotsford
Melrose Abbey
Priorwood Gdns
Trimontium Exhibition
Dryburgh Abbey
Mertoun Gdns
Peter Anderson Woollen Mill
Old Gala House
Robert Smail's Printing Works
Traquair House
Tweeddale Mus & Gall
Kailzie Gardens
St Ronan's Well Interpretative Centre
Bowhill House & Country Park
Halliwell's House Museum
Sir Walter Scott's Courtroom
Selkirk Glass
Fastheugh Hill
Aikwood Tower James Hogg Exhibition
Harestanes Countryside Visitor Centre
Waterloo Monument
Teviot Water Gardens
Mary Queen of Scots House
Jim Clark Room
Edinshall Broch
Dunglass Collegiate Church
Whitlaw Mosses
Southern Upland Way
Fife Coastal Path
McDouall Stuart Museum
Ravenscraig Castle
Alexander III Monument
HMY Britannia
Seton Collegiate Church
Musselburgh Industrial Heritage Museum
Bransly Hill
Heart Law
Cocklaw Hill
Crenshaws Hill
Lammer Law
Meikle Says Law
Hunt Law
Hog's Law
Collie Law
Dirrington Great Law
Torfichen Hill
Blackhope Scar
Whitehope Law
Windlestraw Law
Great Law
Black Law
Dye Water
Eden Water
Leader Water
Gala Water
Lugate Water
Leithen Water
Yarrow Water
Kale Water
Blackadder Water
Bothwell Water
Monynut Water
Spartleton Edge
Whiteadder Water
Biel Water
Peffer Burn
Dry Burn
Birns Water
Soonhope Burn
Tweed
0 1 2 3 4 5 6 miles
0 1 2 3 4 5 6 7 8 9 10 km
69
77
61
62

NORTH SEA
NU
NORTHUMBERLAND COAST
Siccar Pt.
Wheat Stack
FAST CASTLE
ST ABB'S HEAD
St. Abb's Head
KITTIWAKE GALLERY
Lumsdaine
Coldingham Moor
Northfield
St Abbs
Coldingham Bay
St. Abb's Haven
Grantshouse
Huxton
Coldingham
COLDINGHAM PRIORY
Houndwood
Eye Water
Ale Water
Cairncross
EYEMOUTH MUSEUM
Eyemouth
Reston
AYTON CASTLE
Auchencrow
Ayton
Burnmouth
Prenderguest
Lamberton Beach
Lintlaw
Chirnside
Lamberton
Chirnsidebridge
Edrom
Foulden
Clappers
Whiteadder Water
FOULDEN TITHE BARN
Buxley
MANDERSTON
CRUMSTANE FARM PARK
Allanton
Hutton
Highfields
Berwick-upon-Tweed
BARRACKS MUSEUM & RAMPARTS
Blackadder West
Paxton
East Ord
Tweedmouth
TOWER HOUSE POTTERY
Spittal
PAXTON HOUSE
Tweed
Sinclair's Hill
Whitsome
Fishwick
UNION SUSPENSION BRIDGE
Loanend
Prior Park
Redshin Cove
Horncliffe
Horndean
Thornton Park
Murton
Scremerston
Ladykirk
Leet Water
NORHAM CASTLE
Thornton
Swinton
SWINTON KIRK
Norham
West Allerdean
Cheswick
Simprim
Shoreswood
Shoresdean
Goswick
Grindon
Ancroft
DEVIL'S CAUSEWAY
North Low
Haggerston
LINDISFARNE
Emmanuel Hd.
Felkington
Berrington
South Low
Beal
Holy Island (Lindisfarne)
Shellacres
Causeway
Holy Island Sands
Holy Island
LINDISFARNE CASTLE
Castle Pt.
Castle Heaton
Duddo
Bowsden
LINDISFARNE PRIORY
HERITAGE CENTRE
Lennel
Coldstream
HIRSEL
Cornhill-on-Tweed
HEATHERSLAW LIGHT RAILWAY
ERROL HUT SMITHY AND WOOD WORKSHOP
Barmoor Castle
Barmoor Lane End
West Kyloe
Fenwick
Fenham
Guile Pt.
Etal
HEATHERSLAW CORNMILL
Lowick
East Kyloe
Kyloe Hills
LADY WATERFORD HALL
Wark
East Learmouth
Crookham
Buckton
Farne Islands
West Learmouth
ST CUTHBERT'S WAY
Branxton
Ford
Elwick
Ross
Staple Sound
Budle Bay
Pressen
Holburn
Detchant
BAMBURGH CASTLE
FARNE ISLANDS
Inner Sound
Flodden
Middleton
Budle
Bamburgh
Coldfield
Downham
Howtel
Kimmerston
Hetton Steads
Easington
Waren Mill
Mindrum
Milfield
Fenton Town
Nesbit
North Hazelrigg
Belford
Spindlestone
Glororum
Burton
Pawston
Kilham
Doddington
South Hazelrigg
Mousen
Bradford
Seahouses
Lanton
West Horton
East Horton
Bellshill
Elford
North Sunderland
Shotton
Westnewton
Coupland
Newtown
Warenton
Adderstone
Lucker
Kirknewton
Akeld
Wooler
Wetwood Hall
Newham Hall
Beadnell
KIRK YETHOLM
Kirk Yetholm
Hethpool
Humbleton
Chatton
Greendikes
Warenford
Swinhoe
Benthall
Earle
Newham
Fleetham
Beadnell Bay
Middleton Hall
Haugh Head
Newstead
Chathill
College Burn
Rosebrough
Ellingham
Preston
High Newton-by-the-Sea
CHILLINGHAM CASTLE
Chillingham
WILD CATTLE OF CHILLINGHAM
Newtown
PRESTON TOWER
Brunton
Low Newton-by-the-Sea
PENNINE WAY
COLD LAW
North Middleton
Lilburn Tower
East Lilburn
Hepburn
Brownyside
North Charlton
Christon Bank
Embleton Bay
Cliftoncote
South Middleton
Embleton
Dunstan Steads
Castle Point
DUNSTANBURGH CASTLE
THE SCHIL
MOUNTHOOLEY
Ilderton
Old Bewick
West Ditchburn
Mowhaugh
Langleeford
Roseden
Roddam
Bowmont Water
62
63

ROSS OF MULL
Iona
Fionnphort
Bunessan
LOCH SCRIDAIN
BROLASS
Pennycross
Lochbuie
Carsaig
Seil
Luing
Scarba
SCARBA, LUNGA AND THE GARVELLACHS
Garvellachs
Gulf of Corryvreckan
COLONSAY
Scalasaig
Kiloran
Oronsay
JURA
Craighouse
Tarbert
Lagg
PAPS OF JURA
JURA FOREST
Feolin Ferry
Port Askaig
ISLAY
Bridgend
Bowmore
SOUND OF JURA
SOUND OF ISLAY
FIRTH OF LORN
KNAPDALE
Kilberry
Tayvallich
Crinan
Gigha Island
NM
NR
78
79
64
65

Oban
Glenamachrie
Glen Lonan
Pass of Brander
Falls of Cruachan
Kilchurn Castle
Lochawe
Strath of Orchy
Achnafalnich
Inverlochy
Dalmally
McIntyre Monument
Gallanach
Kilbride
Kilmore
Barran
Glen Feochan
Glenfeochan House Gardens
515 Beinn Ghlas
Cruachan Dam Visitor Centre
Ardanaiseig Gardens
Ardanaiseig
Innis Chonain
Inishail Chapel
Inishail
Am Buth
Loch Feochan
Kilchrenan
Annat
North Port
Cladich
Kilninver
Barochreal
Glen Euchar
Musdale
368 A'Chruach
Bragleenmore
South Port
Portsonachan
Loch Scamadale
Argyll and Bute
515 Beinn Chapull
438 Carn Dearg
Braes of Lorn
Blaran
Loch Tralaig
267 Uach Rarey
Inverinan
Ballimeanoch
Tullich
Glen Aray
Lochavich Ho
Drissaig
Kilmun
Melfort
Kilmelford
Glenmore
Loch Avich
Dalavich
Blarghour
589 Cruach Mhor
Kames
Lagalochan
Ardchonnell Castle
Portinnisherrich
Inveraray Castle
Bell Tower
Combined Operations Museum Inveraray
Inveraray Jail
Inveraray
Newtown
Maritime Museum
491 Carn Duchara
Inverliever Forest
Kilmaha
Eredine
365
Garraron
Barravullin
Durran
514 An Suidhe
Arichamish
350 Cruach an Eachlaich
Torran
Kintraw
Eredine Forest
Dalchenna
462 Beinn Dearg
Auchindrain
Auchindrain Open Air Museum
Loch Leacann
Ardfern
Ford
Ederline
Finchairn
Finchairn Castle
458 Cruach Mhic Fhionnlaich
227 Creag Mhor
Carnassarie Castle
Loch Gaineamhach
Furnace
Creggans
Clachan Strachur
Strachur Bay
Kilmartin
Kilmartin House Trust
319
420
Crarae
Crarae Glen Gardens
Newton
Glen Sluain
Slockavullin
Minard
Garbhallt
Lachlan Castle
Glenbranter
Glenbranter Forest
231 Dun Dubh
Gleann Airigh
Tullochgorm
Lachlan Bay
Cup and Ring Marks
Dunadd Fort
Moine Mhor
Kilmichael Glassary
Bridgend
Lephinmore
Strathlachlan Forest
493
Caol Ghleann
Loch Glashan
Asknish
Lochgair
Lephinchapel
Dunans
Rock Markings
Cairnbaan
Lochgilphead
Kilmory Castle Gardens
Kilmory Woodland Park
Carrick
Port Ann
Conchra
Glendaruel Forest
Cruach Chuilceachan
435
Largiemore
Achnaba
Otter Ferry
Ardrishaig
Castleton
Loch Gilp
Clachan of Glendaruel
Kilmodan Sculptured Stones
432 Cruach nan Cuilean
Balliemore
Craigendive
Eilean Mòr
Ballimore
Achabraid
Inverneill
Auchnaha
Auchenbreck
405
458 Cruach nan Caorach
Loch Riddon
Glen Lean
Clachaig
Sandbank
Kilfinan Bay
Kilfinan
454 Beinn Bhreac
Kyles of Bute
506 Beinn Bhreac
Drum
Erines
Melldalloch
Auchalick Bay
Ardentraive
Colintraive
Algaltraig
562 Sob Odhar
266
Ardmarnock Bay
Port Driseach
Tighnabruaich
Barmore I.
Auchenlochan
Kames
Loch Chaorain
Asgog Loch
Island of Bute
Glen More
Windy Hill 278
227
Millhouse
Portavadie
Blair's Ferry
Glenan Bay
Barfad
329
Tarbert
East Loch Tarbert
West Tarbert
Asgog Bay
Kilbride Bay
Ardlamont Ho.
St Colmac
Ettrick Bay
Port Bannatyne
Kames B.
Ardyne Pt.
Rothesay Castle
Rothesay
Rothesay Bay
Craigmore
Ardencraig Gardens
Montford
Victorian Fernery
Ascog
Loch Fad
Corranbuie
Rhu
422 Cnoc A'Bhaileshios
Kennacraig
Redhouse
Ardlamont Pt.
Straad
Kerrycroy
Rubha Leathan
Whitehouse
254
Scoulag
Mount Stuart House and Garden
Loch Quien
Scalpsie
Inchmarnock
60
Glenreasdell Mains
Skipness
Skipness Castle
Skipness Pt.
Skipness Bay
Claonaig
Claonaig Bay
269 Cruach Am Fiadh
Sound of Bute
Ardscalpsie Pt.
Scalpsie Bay
Stravanan Bay
Kingarth
Kilchattan Bay
157
St Blane's Chapel
Cock of Arran
Crossaig
Lochranza
Lochranza Castle
Garroch Hd.
Little Cumbrae Island
66
74
Cruachan
Loch Nant
277
Sior Loch
Teatle Water
Allt Fearna
Eas a' Ghaill
Ben Lui
1130
978 Beinn Dubhchraig
739 Meall nan Tighearn
Lochan Shira
Lochan Stron Mor
948 Beinn Bhuidhe
550 Beinn Ghlas
Brannie Burn
Glen Shira
Glen Fyne
Allt na Lairige
733 Troisgeach
Inverarnan
Ardlui
645 Maol Breac
Glenfyne Lodge
Clachan
Dubh Loch
Kiblaan Burn
Drishaig
Cairndow
811
Loch Sloy
941 Ben Vorlich
Loch Lomond
Ardkinglas Woodland Garden
Ardno
Glen Kinglas
916
Inveruglas
St Catherine's
901 Beinn an Lochain
Rest and Be Thankful
1011 Beinn Ime
849
Hell's Glen
565 Cruach nan Capull
Monevechadan
Glen Croe
881
Succoth
Tarbet
Arrochar
847 Ben Donich
Ardgartan
Stuckgowan
Ardmay
Drimsynie
Lochgoilhead
Trossachs
Corrow
703 Beinn Lochain
Cnoc Coinnich
Blairlomond
Glen Douglas
Inverbeg
Inverbeg Gallery
Doune Hill 734
779 Beinn Bheula
Invernoaden
Ardgoil Forest
519 The Saddle
Glenmallan
National
Argyll
Loch Goil
Loch Eck
Carrick Castle
Beinn Eich 702
Edentaggart
Glen Luss
618 Beinn Bheag
Portincaple
Whistlefield
713 Beinn Chaorach
Garelochhead
659 Creachan Mor
593 Beinn Ruisg
741 Beinn Mhor
Bernice
Forest
Beinn Ruadh 664
Glenfinart Deer Farm
Glenfinart Forest
Ardentinny
Glen Finart
Strone House Gardens
Faslane Port
Glen Fruin
Park
Glenmassan
Glen Massan
Coulport
Rahane
Gare Loch
Shandon
601 Sgorach Mor
Loch Tarsan
Benmore Botanic Garden
Benmore
Uig
Ardpeaton
Glenarn Garden
The Hill House
Clynder
202
Rhu
Rosneath
Cove
Helensburgh
Craigendoran
Inverecka
Ardbeg
Dalinlongart
Kilmun Arboretum
Blairmore
Kilmun
Linn Botanic Gardens
Cove Bay
Strone
Strone Pt.
Holy Loch
Portkil
Rosneath Pt.
Kilcreggan
Ardnadam
Hunter's Quay
611 Cruach nan Capull
Glenstriven
Glen Kin
St John's Church
Kirn
Dunoon
Gourock
Ashton
Greenock
Greenock West
Midton
McLean Mus & Art Gall
HM Customs & Excise Museum & Exhibition
Newark Castle
Port Glasgow
Central
Levan
Larkfield
Braeside
Ravenscraig
Strone
Highland Mary's Statue
Cloch Pt.
Bullwood
Lunderston Bay
522 Black Craig
Inverchaolain
Loch Striven
418 Corlarach Hill
Corlarach Forest
Glen Fyne
Loch Thom
Inverclyde
303
Gryfe Resrs.
Devol
Mid Auchinleck
Inverkip
Shielhill
Garvock
Strathgryfe
Innellan
Wave Whisper Gallery
Newton Park
Port Lamont
Wemyss Bay
Upper Skelmorlie
441 Creuch Hill
Duchal Moor
Toward
Toward Pt.
Skelmorlie
Clyde
Meigle
Muirshiel
Queenside Muir
Muirshiel
Hill of Stake
522
Routenburn
Noddsdale Water
Waterhead Moor
Regional
Mistylaw Muir
Largs Bay
Largs
Vikingar!
Old Kirk
Tomont End
Christian Heritage Museum
Great Cumbrae Island
Downcraig Ferry
484 Irish Law
Ladyland Moor
Lochwinnoch
Muirhead Reservoir
Kelburn Country Centre
Camphill Reservoir
Park
Museum of the Cumbraes
Millport
Fairlie
Fairlie Roads
Kilbirnie
387 Kaim Hill
Knockendon Reservoir
Rye Water
Kilbirnie Loch
Glengarnock
Longbar
Beith
The Tan
Hunterston Power Station Visitor Centre
68
Bannachra Muir
Colgrain
Duchlage
Blairglas
Aldochlay
Luss
This Bagpipe Wor
A
B
C
D
E
F
G
H
7
8
9
10
11
12
NN
NS
0:25
0:20
0:35
0:30
0:12
A85
A819
A83
A815
A816
A886
A8003
A844
A78
A760
A770
A761
A82
A814
A817
A818
A761
B840
B845
B828
B839
B833
B8000
B836
B875
B878
B881
B8001
B842
B8024
B8025
B896
B899
B883
B788
B784
B780
B8038

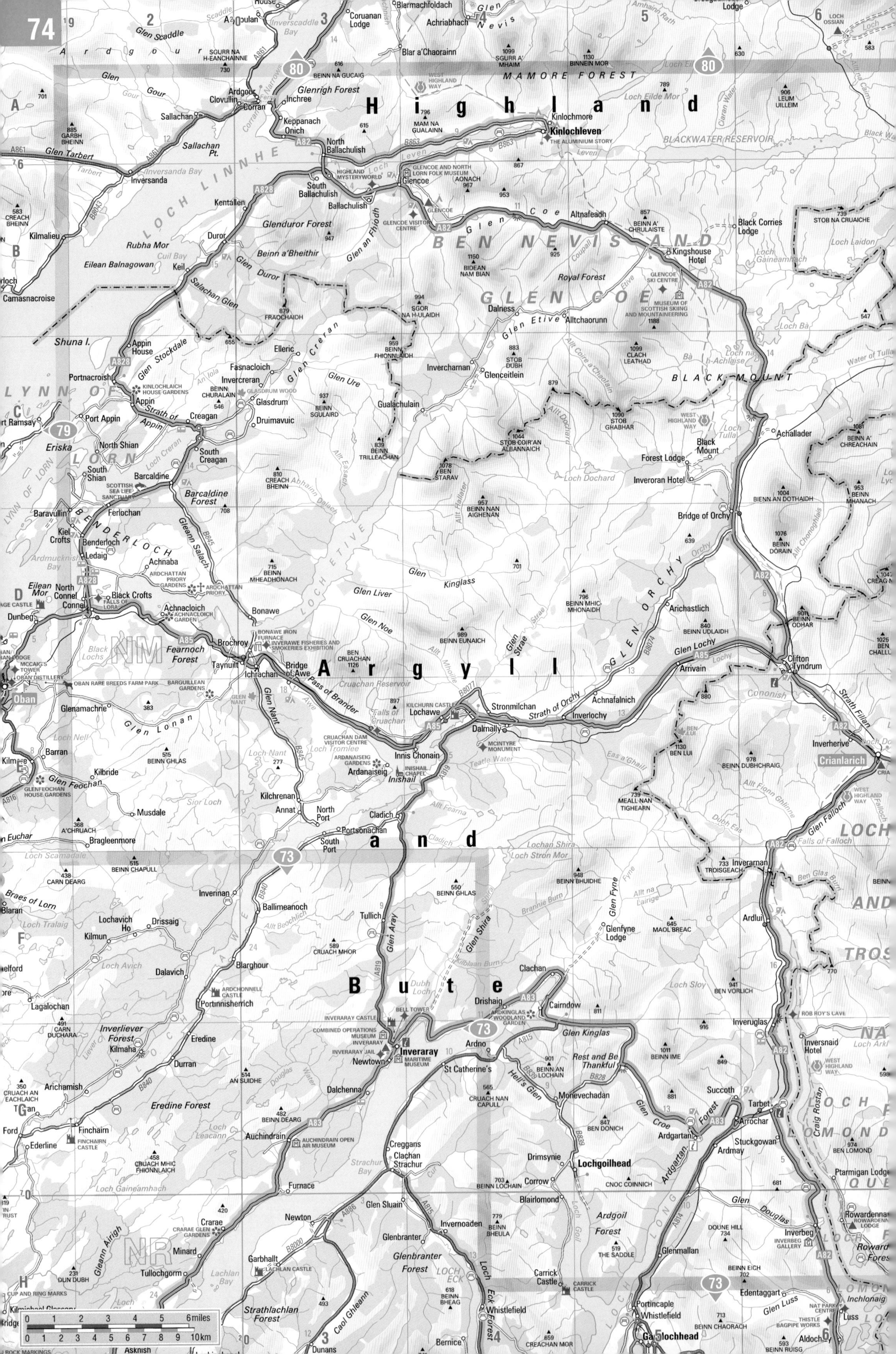
Glen Scaddle
Ardgour
SGURR NA H-EANCHAINNE 730
Inverscaddle Bay
Coruanan Lodge
Blarmachfoldach
Achriabhach
Glen Nevis
Amhainn Rath
Lodge
LOCH OSSIAN
80
BEINN NA GUCAIG 616
Blar a'Chaorainn
1099 SGURR A' MHAIM
1130 BINNEIN MOR
630
583
Glen Gour
Ardgour
Clovullin
Corran
Corran Narrows
Inchree
Glenrigh Forest
WEST HIGHLAND WAY
MAMORE FOREST
Loch Eilde Mor
789
906 LEUM UILLEIM
701
Highland
796 MAM NA GUALAINN
615
Kinlochmore
Kinlochleven
THE ALUMINIUM STORY
Sallachan
Keppanach
Onich
885 GARBH BHEINN
A82
North Ballachulish
B863
BLACKWATER RESERVOIR
Leven
Glen Tarbert
A861
Sallachan Pt.
LOCH LINNHE
Inversanda Bay
Inversanda
Tarbert
HIGHLAND MYSTERYWORLD
GLENCOE AND NORTH LORN FOLK MUSEUM
Glencoe
AONACH 967
867
953
South Ballachulish
Ballachulish
A828
Kentallen
583 CREACH BHEINN
GLENCOE
GLENCOE VISITOR CENTRE
Glen an Fhiodh
Glen Coe
Altnafeadh
857 BEINN A' CHRULAISTE
Black Corries Lodge
STOB NA CRUAICHE 739
Loch Laidon
Kilmalieu
Duror
Glenduror Forest
947
BEN NEVIS AND
Kingshouse Hotel
Rubha Mor
Beinn a'Bheithir
1150 BIDEAN NAM BIAN
925
Coupall
Loch Gaineamhach
Eilean Balnagowan
Cuil Bay
Keil
Glen Duror
Royal Forest
GLENCOE SKI CENTRE
Camasnacroise
Salachan Glen
GLEN COE
MUSEUM OF SCOTTISH SKIING AND MOUNTAINEERING
879 FRAOCHAIDH
994 SGOR NA H-ULAIDH
Dalness
Glen Etive
Alltchaorunn
1188
547
Loch Bà
Shuna I.
655
Appin House
Elleric
Glen Creran
959 BEINN FHIONNLAIDH
883 STOB DUBH
1099 CLACH LEATHAD
Water of Tulla
Glen Stockdale
Inverchamian
Glenceitlein
Allt Coire a'Chaorainn
Loch na h-Achlaise
LYNN OF
Portnacroish
Fasnacloich
Glen Ure
879
BLACK MOUNT
KINLOCHLAICH HOUSE GARDENS
An Iola
Invercreran
BEINN CHURALAIN
GLASDRUM WOOD
Appin
546
Glasdrum
937 BEINN SGULAIRD
Gualachulain
1090 STOB GHABHAR
WEST HIGHLAND WAY
Achallader
1081 BEINN A' CHREACHAIN
Port Ramsay
79
Port Appin
Strath of Appin
Creagan
Druimavuic
Allt Dochard
Loch Tulla
Eriska
North Shian
LORN
Loch Creran
South Creagan
839 BEINN TRILLEACHAN
1044 STOB COIR'AN ALBANNAICH
Black Mount
Forest Lodge
South Shian
Barcaldine
1078 BEN STARAV
Loch Dochard
Inveroran Hotel
LYNN OF LORN
SCOTTISH SEA LIFE SANCTUARY
Barcaldine Forest
810 CREACH BHEINN
Abhainn Dalach
Allt Easach
957 BEINN NAN AIGHENAN
1004 BIENN AN DOTHAIDH
953 BEINN MHANACH
Baravullin
BENDERLOCH
Ferlochan
708
Allt Hallater
Bridge of Orchy
Kiel Crofts
Benderloch
Gleann Salach
1076 BEINN DORAIN
Allt Chonoghlais
Ledaig
Ardmucknish Bay
LOCH ETIVE
639
Achnaba
715 BEINN MHEADHONACH
Glen Kinglass
701
GLEN ORCHY
1042 CREAG M
ARDCHATTAN PRIORY GARDENS
ARDCHATTAN PRIORY
A828
Eilean Mor
North Connel
Connel
Black Crofts
FALLS OF LORA
Glen Liver
796 BEINN MHIC-MHONAIDH
Arichastlich
901 BEINN ODHAR
Dunbeg
Achnacloich
ACHNACLOICH GARDEN
Bonawe
Glen Noe
840 BEINN UDLAIDH
1025 BEN CHALLU
NM
Fearnoch Forest
BONAWE IRON FURNACE
INVERAWE FISHERIES AND SMOKERIES EXHIBITION
Brochroy
BEN CRUACHAN 1126
989 BEINN EUNAICH
Glen Strae
Strae
B8074
Glen Lochy
Clifton
Tyndrum
Black Lochs
Taynuilt
Bridge of Awe
Argyll
Arrivain
MCCAIG'S TOWER
OBAN DISTILLERY
Oban
OBAN RARE BREEDS FARM PARK
BARGUILLEAN GARDENS
Ichrachan
Pass of Brander
Cruachan Reservoir
Allt Mhoille
B8077
Stronmilchan
Achnafalnich
880
Cononish
Strath Fillan
Glenamachrie
383
GLEN NANT
Glen Nant
897
Falls of Cruachan
KILCHURN CASTLE
Lochawe
Strath of Orchy
Inverlochy
Glen Lonan
A85
Dalmally
MCINTYRE MONUMENT
BEN LUI
1130 BEN LUI
Inverherive
Loch Nell
CRUACHAN DAM VISITOR CENTRE
Loch Tromlee
Innis Chonain
Teatle Water
Eas a'Ghaill
978 BEINN DUBHCHRAIG
Crianlarich
Barran
515 BEINN GHLAS
Loch Nant 277
B845
ARDANAISEIG GARDENS
Ardanaiseig
INISHAIL CHAPEL
Inishail
A819
Allt Fionn Ghlinne
Kilmore
Kilbride
Glen Feochan
GLENFEOCHAN HOUSE GARDENS
Kilchrenan
739 MEALL NAN TIGHEARN
WEST HIGHLAND WAY
Dubh Eas
Glen Falloch
Sior Loch
Musdale
Annat
North Port
Allt Fearna
368 A'CHRUACH
Cladich
Loch Euchar
Bragleenmore
Portsonachan
South Port
and
Cladich
Lochan Shira
Loch Stron Mor
Falls of Falloch
LOCH
Loch Scamadale
73
515 BEINN CHAPULL
733 TROISGEACH
Inverarnan
438 CARN DEARG
550 BEINN GHLAS
948 BEINN BHUIDHE
Ben Glas Burn
Inverinan
B840
Braes of Lorn
Ballimeanoch
Glen Shira
Brannie Burn
Glen Fyne
Allt na Lairige
Ardlui
Loch Tralaig
Allt Beochlich
Tullich
Glenfyne Lodge
645 MAOL BREAC
Lochavich Ho
Drissaig
Kilmun
589 CRUACH MHOR
Glen Aray
TROS
Loch Avich
Blarghour
Kilblaan Burn
770
Dalavich
Dubh Loch
Clachan
Loch Sloy
941 BEN VORLICH
Bute
ARDCHONNELL CASTLE
Drishaig
Cairndow
ARDKINGLAS WOODLAND GARDEN
Portinnisherrich
BELL TOWER
A83
811
Lagalochan
INVERARAY CASTLE
ROB ROY'S CAVE
Inveruglas
491 CARN DUCHARA
COMBINED OPERATIONS MUSEUM
73
916
Inverliever Forest
INVERARAY JAIL
Glen Kinglas
Inversnaid Hotel
Eredine
Inveraray
Ardno
1011 BEINN IME
Kilmaha
Newtown
MARITIME MUSEUM
901 BEINN AN LOCHAIN
Rest and Be Thankful
849
WEST HIGHLAND WAY
Durran
514 AN SUIDHE
St Catherine's
Hell's Glen
B828
350 CRUACH AN EACHLAICH
Arichamish
Douglas Water
Dalchenna
565 CRUACH NAN CAPULL
Monevechadan
881
Succoth
B840
Eredine Forest
Glen Croe
Tarbet
Arrochar
LOCH LOMOND
Craig Rostan
Ford
Finchairn
482 BEINN DEARG
847 BEN DONICH
Ardgartan
Forest
974 BEN LOMOND
Ederline
FINCHAIRN CASTLE
Auchindrain
AUCHINDRAIN OPEN AIR MUSEUM
Loch Leacann
Creggans
Stuckgowan
Ardmay
458 CRUACH MHIC FHIONNLAICH
Clachan Strachur
Drimsynie
Lochgoilhead
Ardgartan
Ptarmigan Lodge
Strachur Bay
703 BEINN LOCHAIN
Corrow
CNOC COINNICH
681
Loch Gaineamhach
Furnace
Cur
Blairlomond
Glen Douglas
Rowardennan
ROWARDENNAN LODGE
420
Newton
A886
Glen Sluain
A815
Ardgoil Forest
DOUNE HILL 734
Inverbeg
INVERBEG GALLERY
Crarae
CRARAE GLEN GARDENS
Invernoaden
779 BEINN BHEULA
LOCH LONG
A814
Roward Forest
NR
Minard
Glenbranter
519 THE SADDLE
Glenmallan
Garbhallt
B8000
Glenbranter Forest
Loch Goil
Gleann Airigh
231 DUN DUBH
Tullochgorm
LACHLAN CASTLE
Lachlan Bay
LOCH ECK
Carrick Castle
CARRICK CASTLE
BEINN EICH 702
CUP AND RING MARKS
618 BEINN BHEAG
Edentaggart
Inchlonaig
493
Caol Ghleann
Strathlachlan Forest
Whistlefield
Portincaple
Whistlefield
713 BEINN CHAORACH
Glen Luss
NAT PARK CENTRE
THISTLE BAGPIPE WORKS
Luss
Eck Forest
Bernice
659 CREACHAN MOR
Garelochhead
593 BEINN RUISG
Aldochlay
Dunans
Asknish
ROCK MARKINGS
0 1 2 3 4 5 6 miles
0 1 2 3 4 5 6 7 8 9 10 km

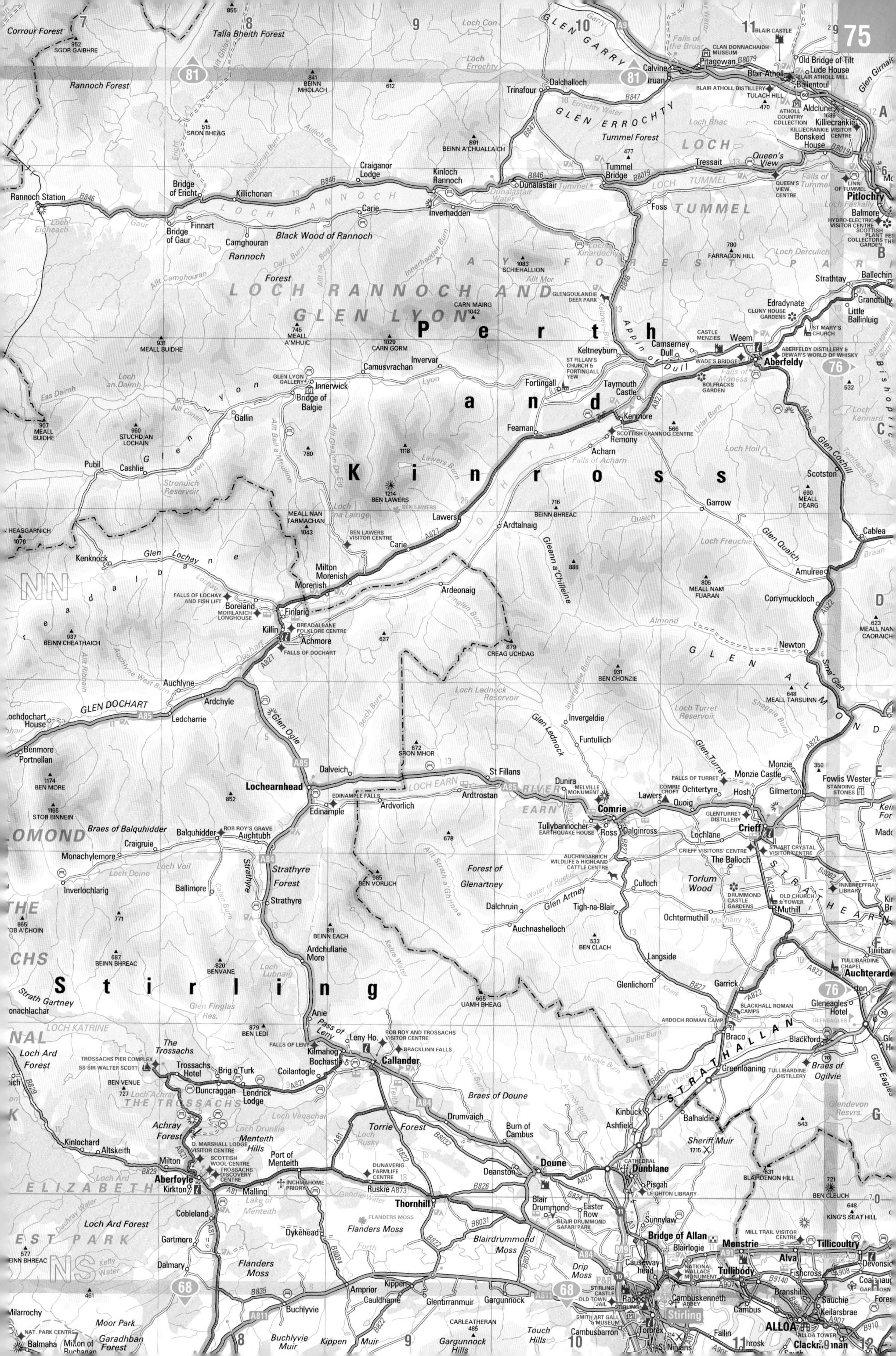

Corrour Forest
952 SGOR GAIBHRE
Talla Bheith Forest
Rannoch Forest
841 BEINN MHOLACH
612
515 SRON BHEAG
891 BEINN A'CHUALLAICH
Loch Con
Loch Errochty
GLEN GARRY
Falls of the Bruar
CLAN DONNACHAIDH MUSEUM
BLAIR CASTLE
Pitagowan
Calvine
Struan
Blair Atholl
Old Bridge of Tilt
Lude House
BLAIR ATHOLL MILL
Bridge of Tilt
Ballentoul
BLAIR ATHOLL DISTILLERY
TULACH HILL
470
ATHOLL COUNTRY COLLECTION
Aldclune
1689
Killiecrankie
KILLIECRANKIE VISITOR CENTRE
Bonskeid House
Glen Girnaig
Dalchalloch
Trinafour
GLEN ERROCHTY
Errochty Water
Tummel Forest
477
Loch Bhac
LOCH TUMMEL
Tressait
Queen's View
QUEEN'S VIEW CENTRE
Falls of Tummel
LINN OF TUMMEL
Pitlochry
Loch Faskally
Balmore
HYDRO-ELECTRIC VISITOR CENTRE
SCOTTISH PLANT COLLECTORS GARDEN
Tummel Bridge
Dunalastair
Dunalastair Water
Craiganor Lodge
Kinloch Rannoch
Rannoch Station
Loch Eigheach
Bridge of Ericht
Killichonan
LOCH RANNOCH
Carie
Inverhadden
Finnart
Bridge of Gaur
Camghouran
Black Wood of Rannoch
Rannoch Forest
Foss
TUMMEL
780 FARRAGON HILL
Loch Derculich
Loch Kinardochy
TAY FOREST PARK
1083 SCHIEHALLION
LOCH RANNOCH AND GLEN LYON
GLENGOULANDIE DEER PARK
Strathtay
Ballechin
Grandtully
Edradynate
CLUNY HOUSE GARDENS
Little Ballinluig
CASTLE MENZIES
Weem
ST MARY'S CHURCH
ABERFELDY DISTILLERY & DEWAR'S WORLD OF WHISKY
Aberfeldy
Camserney
Dull
WADE'S BRIDGE
Appin of Dull
Keltneyburn
ST FILLAN'S CHURCH & FORTINGALL YEW
Fortingall
Taymouth Castle
Falls of Moness
BOLFRACKS GARDEN
532
Loch Kennard
CARN MAIRG 1042
931 MEALL BUIDHE
745 MEALL A'MHUIC
1029 CARN GORM
Perth and Kinross
Camusvrachan
Invervar
GLEN LYON GALLERY
Innerwick
Bridge of Balgie
Loch an Daimh
Eas Daimh
Glen Lyon
Gallin
907 MEALL BUIDHE
960 STUCHD AN LOCHAIN
Pubil
Cashlie
Stronuich Reservoir
780
1118
Lawers Burn
1214 BEN LAWERS
BEN LAWERS
Fearnan
Kenmore
SCOTTISH CRANNOG CENTRE
Remony
566
Acharn
Falls of Acharn
LOCH TAY
Loch Hoil
Glen Cochill
Scotston
690 MEALL DEARG
Garrow
Kinross
716 BEINN BHREAC
Quaich
Loch Freuchie
Glen Quaich
Cablea
Braan
Amulree
MEALL NAN TARMACHAN 1043
Loch na Lairige
BEN LAWERS VISITOR CENTRE
Lawers
Carie
Ardtalnaig
Gleann a'Chilleine
888
805 MEALL NAM FUARAN
Corrymuckloch
BEN HEASGARNICH 1076
Kenknock
Glen Lochay
Breadalbane
NN
Milton Morenish
Morenish
Ardeonaig
Fingien Burn
FALLS OF LOCHAY AND FISH LIFT
Boreland
MOIRLANICH LONGHOUSE
Finlarig
BREADALBANE FOLKLORE CENTRE
Killin
Achmore
FALLS OF DOCHART
637
879 CREAG UCHDAG
Almond
Newton
623 MEALL NAN CAORAICH
937 BEINN CHEATHAICH
Allt Ribbain
GLEN ALMOND
931 BEN CHONZIE
Sma' Glen
648 MEALL TARSUINN
Auchlyne
Ardchyle
GLEN DOCHART
Lochdochart House
Ledcharrie
Glen Ogle
Loch Lednock Reservoir
Invergeldie
Loch Turret Reservoir
Glen Lednock
Funtullich
Glen Turret
Benmore
Portnellan
1174 BEN MORE
1165 STOB BINNEIN
672 SRON MHOR
Dalveich
St Fillans
LOCH EARN
Lochearnhead
EDINAMPLE FALLS
Edinample
Ardvorlich
Ardtrostan
RIVER EARN
Dunira
MELVILLE MONUMENT
Comrie
Lawers
COMRIE CROFT
FALLS OF TURRET
Ochtertyre
Monzie Castle
Monzie
350
Fowlis Wester
STANDING STONES
Hosh
Gilmerton
Quoig
852
Braes of Balquhidder
LOMOND
ROB ROY'S GRAVE
Balquhidder
Auchtubh
Craigruie
Monachylemore
Loch Doine
Loch Voil
Inverlochlarig
678
Tullybannocher
EARTHQUAKE HOUSE
Ross
Dalginross
GLENTURRET DISTILLERY
Crieff
Lochlane
CRIEFF VISITORS' CENTRE
STUART CRYSTAL VISITOR CENTRE
The Balloch
STRATHEARN
Strathyre Forest
Strathyre
Ballimore
985 BEN VORLICH
Forest of Glenartney
AUCHINGARRICH WILDLIFE & HIGHLAND CATTLE CENTRE
Culloch
Torlum Wood
DRUMMOND CASTLE GARDENS
INNERPEFFRAY LIBRARY
OLD CHURCH & TOWER
Muthill
865 STOB A'CHOIN
771
811 BEINN EACH
Dalchruin
Glen Artney
Tigh-na-Blair
Auchnashelloch
Ochtermuthill
Machany Water
533 BEN CLACH
687 BEINN BHREAC
820 BENVANE
Ardchullarie More
Loch Lubnaig
Langside
TULLIBARDINE CHAPEL
Auchterarder
Stirling
Strath Gartney
Glen Finglas Res.
665 UAMH BHEAG
Glenlichorn
Garrick
Knaik
Gleneagles Hotel
GLENEAGLES
BLACKHALL ROMAN CAMPS
ARDOCH ROMAN CAMP
LOCH KATRINE
Loch Ard Forest
879 BEN LEDI
Anie
Pass of Leny
ROB ROY AND TROSSACHS VISITOR CENTRE
BRACKLINN FALLS
FALLS OF LENY
Leny Ho.
Kilmahog
Bochastle
Callander
Bullie Burn
Braco
STRATHALLAN
Blackford
Greenloaning
TULLIBARDINE DISTILLERY
Braes of Ogilvie
Glen Eagles
TROSSACHS PIER COMPLEX
SS SIR WALTER SCOTT
The Trossachs
Trossachs Hotel
Brig o'Turk
Coilantogle
BEN VENUE 727
Loch Achray
Duncraggan
Lendrick Lodge
THE TROSSACHS
Braes of Doune
Muckle Burn
Glendevon Resvrs.
Achray Forest
Loch Drunkie
Loch Venachar
Torrie Forest
Drumvaich
Burn of Cambus
Kinbuck
Ashfield
Balhaldie
543
Kinlochard
Altskeith
D. MARSHALL LODGE VISITOR CENTRE
Menteith Hills
Loch Rusky
Sheriff Muir
1715
Milton
SCOTTISH WOOL CENTRE
TROSSACHS DISCOVERY CENTRE
Port of Menteith
DUNAVERIG FARMLIFE CENTRE
Deanston
Doune
CATHEDRAL
Dunblane
631 BLAIRDENON HILL
721 BEN CLEUCH
Aberfoyle
Kirkton
QUEEN ELIZABETH FOREST PARK
INCHMAHOME PRIORY
Malling
Ruskie
Thornhill
Blair Drummond
Easter Row
Pisgah
LEIGHTON LIBRARY
648 KING'S SEAT HILL
Lake of Menteith
Cobleland
Loch Ard Forest
FLANDERS MOSS
Flanders Moss
BLAIR DRUMMOND SAFARI PARK
Sunnylaw
Duchray Water
Gartmore
Dykehead
Blairdrummond Moss
Bridge of Allan
Blairlogie
MILL TRAIL VISITOR CENTRE
Menstrie
Tillicoultry
577 BEINN BHREAC
Dalmary
Kelty Water
Flanders Moss
Drip Moss
Causewayhead
NATIONAL WALLACE MONUMENT
Tullibody
Alva
Fishcross
Devonside
461
B835
Arnprior
Kippen
Cauldhame
Glentirranmuir
Gargunnock
STIRLING CASTLE
OLD TOWN JAIL
Raploch
Cambuskenneth
ABBEY
Cambus
Branshill
Sauchie
Keilarsbrae
Coalsnaughton
Milarrochy
Buchlyvie
Moor Park
CARLEATHERAN 485
SMITH ART GALLERY & MUSEUM
Stirling
ALLOA
ALLOA TOWER
NAT. PARK CENTRE
Balmaha
Milton of Buchanan
Garadhban Forest
Buchlyvie Muir
Kippen Muir
Gargunnock Hills
Touch Hills
Cambusbarron
Torbrex
St Ninians
1314
Fallin
Throsk
Clackmannan
81
76
68

82
75
69
Perth and Kinross
Clackmannanshire
Pitlochry
Blair Atholl
Killiecrankie
Moulin
Edradour Distillery
Milton of Edradour
Glen Brerachan
Strathardle
Kirkmichael
Ashintully Castle
Enochdhu
Straloch
Tarvie
Dalnavaid
Ben Vrackie
Glen Shee
Dalnaglar Castle
Cray
Meikle Forter
Folda
Glenisla Forest
Brewlands Bridge
Kirkton of Glenisla
Forest of Alyth
Blacklunans
Glen Prosen
Glen Clova
Glenprosen Village
Dykehead
Cortachy
Balintore
Kirriemuir
Kinnordy
Northmuir
Westmuir
Kirkton of Kingoldrum
Bridgend of Lintrathen
Loch of Lintrathen
Bridge of Craigisla
Dykends
Bellaty
Ballintuim
Netherton
Bridge of Cally
Blackcraig Forest
Forest of Clunie
Cochrage Muir
Tullymurdoch
Bamff
Alyth
New Alyth
Ruthven
Meigle
Kirkinch
Eassie
Glamis
Charleston
Castleton
Blairgowrie
Rattray
Rosemount
Kinloch
Coupar Angus
Newtyle
Ardler
Sidlaw Hills
Lundie
Auchterhouse
Muirhead
Birkhill
Dundee
Invergowrie
Longforgan
Kingoodie
Tay Rail Bridge
Newport
Firth of Tay
Balmerino
Kilmany
Rathillet
Creich
Brunton
Luthrie
Moonzie
Cupar
Kilmaron Castle
Lindifferon
Newburgh
Mugdrum I.
Errol
Carse of Gowrie
Braes of the Carse
Inchture
Castle Huntly
Grange
Kinnaird
Rait
Kilspindie
Kinfauns
Glencarse
St Madoes
Chapelhill
Glendoick
Kinfauns Forest
Scone
Perth
Luncarty
Stanley
Moneydie
Redgorton
Pitcairngreen
Almondbank
Methven
Tibbermore
Huntingtower Castle
Cherrybank
Craigie
Friarton
Tarsappie
Rhynd
Elcho
Bridge of Earn
Forgandenny
Forteviot
Dunning
Aberargie
Abernethy
Dron
Kintillo
Glenfoot
Pitmedden Forest
Auchtermuchty
Strathmiglo
Dunshalt
Ladybank
Pitlessie
Falkland
Freuchie
Lomond Hills
Kettlebridge
Kingskettle
Springfield
Glenrothes
Leslie
Markinch
Kennoway
Windygates
Methil
Buckhaven
East Wemyss
West Wemyss
Dysart
Kirkcaldy
Thornton
Cardenden
Auchterderran
Lochgelly
Lochore
Ballingry
Kelty
Cowdenbeath
Lumphinnans
Kinross
Milnathort
Loch Leven
St Serf's Island
Scotlandwell
Kinnesswood
Cleish
Cleish Hills
Crook of Devon
Drum
Powmill
Rumbling Bridge
Dollar
Tillicoultry
Alva
Devonside
Coalsnaughton
Forest Mill
Saline
Blairingone
Yetts o' Muckhart
Pool o' Muckhart
Glendevon
Glen Devon
Glen Eagles
Gleneagles
Auchterarder
Aberuthven
Tullibardine
Kinkell Bridge
Strathearn
Muthill
Crieff
Madderty
Findo Gask
Clathy
Gilmerton
Fowlis Wester
Keillour Forest
Buchanty
Glen Almond
Harrietfield
Chapelhill
Logiealmond
Little Glenshee
Amulree
Corrymuckloch
Newton
Sma' Glen
Glen Quaich
Strathbraan
Cablea
Trochry
Ballinlick
Inver
Dunkeld
Birnam
Little Dunkeld
Caputh
Spittalfield
Murthly
Meikleour
Kinclaven
Cargill
Burrelton
Woodside
Balbeggie
Guildtown
Wolfhill
St Martins
Collace
Kinrossie
Saucher
Dunsinane Hill
Obney Hills
Bankfoot
Waterloo
Tullybelton
Loch of Lowes
Butterstone
Clunie
Craigie
Concraigie
Riemore
Craigvinean Forest
Dalguise
Guay
Dowally
Kindallachan
Ballinluig
Logierait
Tulliemet
Grandtully
Strathtay
Ballechin
Balnaguard
Aberfeldy
Glen Cochill
Scotston
Milton of Dalcapon
Tummel
Balmore
Loch Faskally
Falls of Tummel
Bonskeid House
Aldclune
Old Bridge of Tilt
Lude House
Glen Girnaig

Brechin
Montrose
Forfar
Letham
Arbroath
Carnoustie
Monifieth
Tayport
Tay Bridge
Leuchars
St Andrews
ST ANDREWS BAY
Crail
Anstruther Easter
Anstruther Wester
Pittenweem
St Monans
Elie
Earlsferry
Isle of May
NO
NT
Edzell
Dunlappie
North Water Bridge
Marykirk
Johnshaven
St Cyrus
Milton Ness
Kirriemuir
Inverkeilor
Lunan Bay
Lang Craig
Ethie Mains
Red Head
Auchmithie
The Deil's Heid
Elliot
East Haven
Barry Links
Buddon Ness
Broughty Ferry
Tentsmuir Forest
Eden Mouth
Guardbridge
Kingsbarns
Cambo Ness
Fife Ness
Largo Bay
Chapel Ness
Sauchar Pt.

NF
NL
Canna
A'Chill
Garrisdale Pt.
Sanday
Canna Harbour
Sound of Canna
Guirdil Bay
Rubha Shamhnan Insir
Kilmory
Kilmory Glen
Kinloch Glen
Rubha na Roinne
MALLAIG 2:30
0:55
84
85
388
A'Bhrideanach
Kinloch
Loch Scresort
KINLOCH CASTLE
571 ORVAL
R Ù M
Rubha Port na Caranean
Schooner Pt.
Oigh-sgeir
Harris
Glen Harris
812 ASKIVAL
781 AINSHVAL
Rubha Sgorr an t-Snidhe
THE SMALL ISLES
1:00
1:10
Rubha nam Meirleach
SOUND OF RÙM
Bay of Laig
Cleadale
Rubha an Fhasaidh
Eigg
Kildonnan
393 AN SGURR
Galmisdale
SOUND OF EIGG
0:35
Eilean nan Each
137
Port Mor
Muck
Bhatarsaigh (Vatersay)
Uidh
Bagh Bhatarsaigh
Bhatarsaigh
Flodaigh (Flodday)
Caolas Shanndraigh
207
Sanndraigh (Sandray)
Lingeigh (Lingay)
Greanamul
Caolas Phabaigh
Theisgeir (Heiskers)
171
Pabaidh (Pabbay)
Caolas Mhiui Laigh
273
Miùgh Laigh (Mingulay)
Bearnaraigh (Berneray)
Caolas Bhearnaraigh
Barra Hd.
Sanna Point
Sanna Bay
Sanna
Achnaha
Portuairk
Point of Ardnamurchan
ARDNAMURCHAN LIGHTHOUSE
Achosnich
B8007
Ormsaigmore
Ormsaigbeg
An Acairseid
Kilchoan Bay
Cairns of Coll
Eilean Mor
Rubha Mor
Bousd
Sorisdale
Cliad Bay
Arnabost
Gallanach
B8072
Grishipoll
B8071
73
COLL
OBAN 2:40
Ballyhaugh
104
Loch Cliad
Hogh Bay
B8070
Arinagour
Totronald
Feall Bay
Arileod
Acha
Loch Eatharna
Eilean Ornsay
Breachacha Castle
Friesland
Calgary Pt.
Gunna
Crossapol Bay
Soa
Loch Breachacha
TIREE
Vaul Bay
Salum
Caolas
Rubha Dubh
Vaul
B8069
Ruaig
Hough Skerries
Balephetrish Bay
Balevullin
B8068
Gott Bay
0:55
Soa
R. Chraiginis
Kenovay
Scarinish
Kilkenneth
Moss
B8065
Heanish
Middleton
Heylipol
Crossapol
Rubha Traigh an Duin
Port Mor
Barrapol
Hynish Bay
Loch a'Phuill
B8067
Balemartine
Rinn Thorbhais
Balephuil
141
Mannal
Balephuil Bay
Port Snoig
Hynish
Ardmore Bay
Ardmore Pt.
Quinish Pt.
Glengorm Castle
MULL MUSEUM
Rubha an Aird
Caliach Pt.
Sunipol
Mornish
Quinish
Mishnish
'S AIRDE BEINN
292
MULL LITTLE THEATRE
Penmore Mill
B8073
Dervaig
Achnadrish
Calgary
Calgary Bay
THE OLD BYRE HERITAGE CENTRE
Lettermore
Treshnish Pt.
Ensay
342 CARN MOR
Haunn
Achnacraig
Rubh a'Chaoil
Burg
Kilninian
Achleck
Fanmore
390
Treshnish Isles
Fladda
LOCH TUATH
Ballygown
EAS FORS WATERFALL
424 BEINN NA DRISE
Eilean Dioghlum
Lunga
Gometra
Lagganulva
Laggan Bay
Bearnus
313
Oskamull
Ulva
Ulva House
Killiemor
LOCH NA KEAL
Bac Mor
Little Colonsay
Eorsa
ISLE OF
INCH KENNETH CHAPEL
Inch Kenneth
Derryguaig
Staffa
STAFFA
FINGAL'S CAVE
Balnahard
MACKINNON'S CAVE
Erisgeir
(April-Oct) 0:45
519 BEINN NA SREINE
561
Glen Seilisdeir
ARDMEANACH
Killiemor House
THE BURG
Eilean Annraidh
MACLEAN'S CROSS
IONA ABBEY AND CATHEDRAL
Rubha nan Cearc
100
IONA HERITAGE CENTRE
Kintra
LOCH SCRIDAIN
Iona
Baile Mor
ST COLUMBA EXHIBITION & WELCOME CENTRE
Aridhglas
Loch Lathaich
Tor
Stac an Aoineidh
Fionnphort
A849
Eorabus
Sound of Iona
Fidden
Tiraghoil
Bunessan
Lee
376 CRUACHAN MIN
Loch Assapol
Erraid
ROSS OF MULL
Soa I.
Ardalanish
Uisken
Scoor
Ardchiavaig
Malcolm's
125
Eilean a'Chalmain
Rubha nam Braithrean
Rubh Ardalanish
72
Torran Rocks
Scale : 1:332 000
(approx 5 miles to 1 inch)
0 1 2 3 4 5 6 miles
0 1 2 3 4 5 6 7 8 9 10km

NG
NH
NM
NN
Highland
Argyll and Bute
KNOYDART
SOUND OF SLEAT
SOUND OF ARISAIG
ORAR, MOIDART AND ARDNAMURCHAN
ARDNAMURCHAN
MOIDART
SUNART
MORVERN
KINGAIRLOCH
LOCH SHIEL
LOCH SUNART
LOCH LINNHE
LOCH ARKAIG
LOCH QUOICH
LOCH EIL
LOCH MORAR
LOCH NEVIS
LOCH ETIVE
SOUND OF MULL
FIRTH OF LORN
LYNN OF LORN
BENDERLOCH
ISLAND OF MULL
Ardgour
Mallaig
Fort William
Oban
Kerrera
Lismore
Seil
Luing
Armadale
Ardvasar
Aird of Sleat
Point of Sleat
Inverie
Glasnacardoch
Morar
Arisaig
Lochailort
Glenfinnan
Kinlocheil
Corpach
Banavie
Caol
Inverlochy
Claggan
Strontian
Salen
Acharacle
Glenborrodale
Kilchoan
Lochaline
Corran
Ardgour
Onich
North Ballachulish
South Ballachulish
Ballachulish
Glencoe
Kentallen
Duror
Appin
Portnacroish
Port Appin
Creagan
Barcaldine
Benderloch
Connel
North Connel
Dunbeg
Taynuilt
Bridge of Awe
Lochawe
Dalmally
Innis Chonain
Kilninver
Kilmelford
Arduaine
Craignure
Lochdon
Pennyghael
Tobermory
Dervaig
Salen
Dalnabreck
Kinlochmoidart
Glenuig
Kilmory
Pennygown
Kilbride
Kilmore
Glen Coe
Glen Nevis
Glen Etive
Glen Tarbert
Glen Scaddle
Glen Loy
Glen Mallie
Glen Dessarry
Glen Pean
Glen Kingie
Glen Lonan
Glen Euchar
Glen More
Pass of Brander
Braes of Lorn
Glenfinnan Monument
Dunstaffnage Castle
Castle Tioram
Duart Castle
Ardtornish Castle
Kilchurn Castle
Easdale
Garvellachs
Eilean Shona
Eilean Musdile
Shuna I.
Insh I.

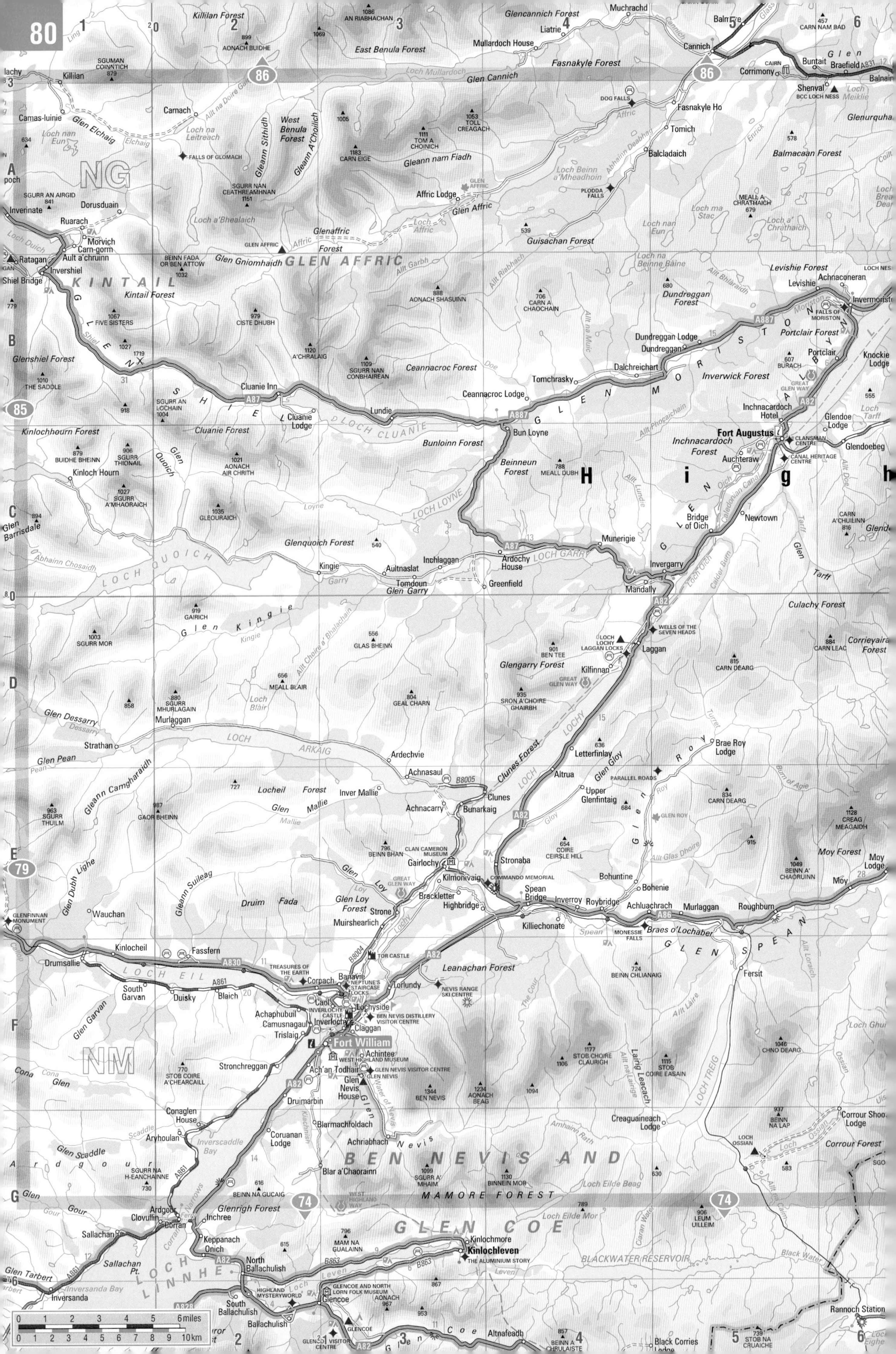
Killilan Forest
AN RIABHACHAN
AONACH BUIDHE
East Benula Forest
Glencannich Forest
Muchrachd
Liatrie
Mullardoch House
Fasnakyle Forest
Balnain
Cannich
CARN NAM BAD
Buntait
Braefield
Corrimony
Shenval
BCC LOCH NESS
Loch Meiklie
Glenurquhart
SGUMAN COINNTICH
Killilan
Loch Mullardoch
Glen Cannich
DOG FALLS
Fasnakyle Ho
Tomich
Camas-luinie
Glen Elchaig
Carnach
Loch na Leitreach
West Benula Forest
Gleann A'Chòilich
TOLL CREAGACH
TOM A CHOINICH
CARN EIGE
Gleann nam Fiadh
Balcladaich
Balmacaan Forest
FALLS OF GLOMACH
Gleann Sithidh
SGURR NAN CEATHREAMHNAN
Loch Beinn a'Mheadhoin
PLODDA FALLS
NG
SGURR AN AIRGID
Inverinate
Dorusduain
Affric Lodge
GLEN AFFRIC
Glen Affric
MEALL A' CHRATHAICH
Ruarach
Morvich
Carn-gorm
Loch a'Bhealaich
Loch Affric
Loch ma Stac
Loch nan Eun
Loch a' Chrathaich
Glenaffric Forest
Guisachan Forest
Ault a'chruinn
Ratagan
Inversheil
Shiel Bridge
BEINN FADA OR BEN ATTOW
Glen Gniomhaidh
GLEN AFFRIC
Allt Garbh
Loch na Beinne Baine
Levishie Forest
Levishie
Achnaconeran
Invermoriston
KINTAIL
Kintail Forest
AONACH SHASUINN
CARN A CHAOCHAIN
Dundreggan Forest
FALLS OF MORISTON
Portclair Forest
FIVE SISTERS
CISTE DHUBH
A887
Dundreggan Lodge
Dundreggan
Glenshiel Forest
A'CHRALAIG
SGURR NAN CONBHAIREAN
Ceannacroc Forest
Dalchreichart
Portclair
Knockie Lodge
BURACH
Tomchrasky
Inverwick Forest
THE SADDLE
Cluanie Inn
Ceannacroc Lodge
GLEN MORISTON
GREAT GLEN WAY
SGURR AN LOCHAIN
A87
Lundie
Inchnacardoch Hotel
A82
Glendoe Lodge
Cluanie Lodge
LOCH CLUANIE
Bun Loyne
Fort Augustus
Kinlochhourn Forest
Cluanie Forest
Bunloinn Forest
Inchnacardoch Forest
CLANSMAN CENTRE
Glendoebeg
BUIDHE BHEINN
SGURR THIONAIL
AONACH AIR CHRITH
Glen Quoich
Beinneun Forest
MEALL DUBH
Auchteraw
CANAL HERITAGE CENTRE
Kinloch Hourn
Highland
SGURR A'MHAORAICH
LOCH LOYNE
Loyne
Caledonian Canal
Glen Barrisdale
GLEOURAICH
Bridge of Oich
Newtown
CARN A'CHUILINN
Glenquoich Forest
Munerigie
Abhainn Chosaidh
LOCH QUOICH
Kingie
Aultnaslat
Inchlaggan
Ardochy House
LOCH GARRY
Invergarry
Glen Tarff
Tomdoun
Glen Garry
Greenfield
Mandally
Culachy Forest
GAIRICH
Glen Kingie
SGURR MOR
GLAS BHEINN
LOCH LOCHY
WELLS OF THE SEVEN HEADS
LAGGAN LOCKS
BEN TEE
Laggan
CARN LEAC
Corrieyairack Forest
CARN DEARG
Glengarry Forest
Kilfinnan
MEALL BLAIR
SRON A'CHOIRE GHAIRBH
GEAL CHARN
SGURR MHURLAGAIN
Loch Blair
Glen Dessarry
Murlaggan
Strathan
LOCH ARKAIG
Ardechvie
Letterfinlay
Brae Roy Lodge
Glen Roy
Glen Pean
Gleann Camgharaidh
Achnasaul
B8005
Clunes Forest
Altrua
Glen Gloy
PARALLEL ROADS
Locheil Forest
Inver Mallie
Clunes
Upper Glenfintaig
CARN DEARG
SGURR THUILM
GAOR BHEINN
Glen Mallie
Achnacarry
Bunarkaig
GLEN ROY
CREAG MEAGAIDH
BEINN BHAN
CLAN CAMERON MUSEUM
Gairlochy
Stronaba
COIRE CEIRSLE HILL
Allt Glas Dhoire
Moy Forest
BEINN A' CHAORUINN
Moy Lodge
Glen Dubh Lighe
Gleann Suileag
Glen Loy
Kilmonivaig
COMMANDO MEMORIAL
Bohuntine
Bohenie
Moy
Wauchan
Druim Fada
Glen Loy Forest
Brackletter
Highbridge
Spean Bridge
Inverroy
Roybridge
Achluachrach
Murlaggan
Roughburn
GLENFINNAN MONUMENT
Strone
Muirshearlich
Killiechonate
A86
Braes o'Lochaber
MONESSIE FALLS
GLEN SPEAN
Kinlocheil
Fassfern
TOR CASTLE
Drumsallie
LOCH EIL
A830
TREASURES OF THE EARTH
Corpach
Banavie
NEPTUNE'S STAIRCASE LOCKS
Leanachan Forest
BEINN CHLIANAIG
Fersit
South Garvan
Duisky
Blaich
A861
Caol
Lochyside
Torlundy
NEVIS RANGE SKI CENTRE
Glen Garvan
Achaphubuil
INVERLOCHY CASTLE
Inverlochy
BEN NEVIS DISTILLERY VISITOR CENTRE
Camusnagaul
Claggan
Trislaig
Fort William
Achintee
WEST HIGHLAND MUSEUM
CHNO DEARG
NM
STOB CHOIRE CLAURIGH
STOB COIRE EASAIN
Loch Ghuilbinn
Glen Cona
STOB COIRE A'CHEARCAILL
Stronchreggan
Ach'an Todhair
GLEN NEVIS VISITOR CENTRE
GLEN NEVIS
Nevis House
Water of Nevis
BEN NEVIS
AONACH BEAG
Laírig Leacach
LOCH TREIG
Druimarbin
Conaglen House
Blarmachfoldach
Creaguaineach Lodge
BEINN NA LAP
Corrour Shooting Lodge
Aryhoulan
Coruanan Lodge
Achriabhach
Amhainn Rath
Glen Scaddle
Inverscaddle Bay
LOCH OSSIAN
Corrour Forest
Ardgour
BEN NEVIS AND
SGURR NA H-EANCHAINNE
Blar a'Chaorainn
SGURR A' MHAIM
BINNEIN MOR
Loch Eilde Beag
BEINN NA GUCAIG
WEST HIGHLAND WAY
MAMORE FOREST
Glen Gour
Glenrigh Forest
Loch Eilde Mor
LEUM UILLEIM
Ardgour
Clovullin
Corran
Inchree
GLEN COE
Sallachan
Corran Narrows
Keppanach
Onich
MAM NA GUALAINN
Kinlochmore
Kinlochleven
THE ALUMINIUM STORY
BLACKWATER RESERVOIR
Black Water
Sallachan Pt.
LOCH LINNHE
North Ballachulish
B863
Leven
Glen Tarbert
Inversanda Bay
Inversanda
HIGHLAND MYSTERYWORLD
GLENCOE AND NORTH LORN FOLK MUSEUM
AONACH EAGACH
South Ballachulish
Ballachulish
Glencoe
GLENCOE VISITOR CENTRE
Glen Coe
Altnafeadh
BEINN A CHRULAISTE
Black Corries Lodge
STOB NA CRUAICHE
Rannoch Station
A82
0 1 2 3 4 5 6 miles
0 1 2 3 4 5 6 7 8 9 10 km
86
85
79
74

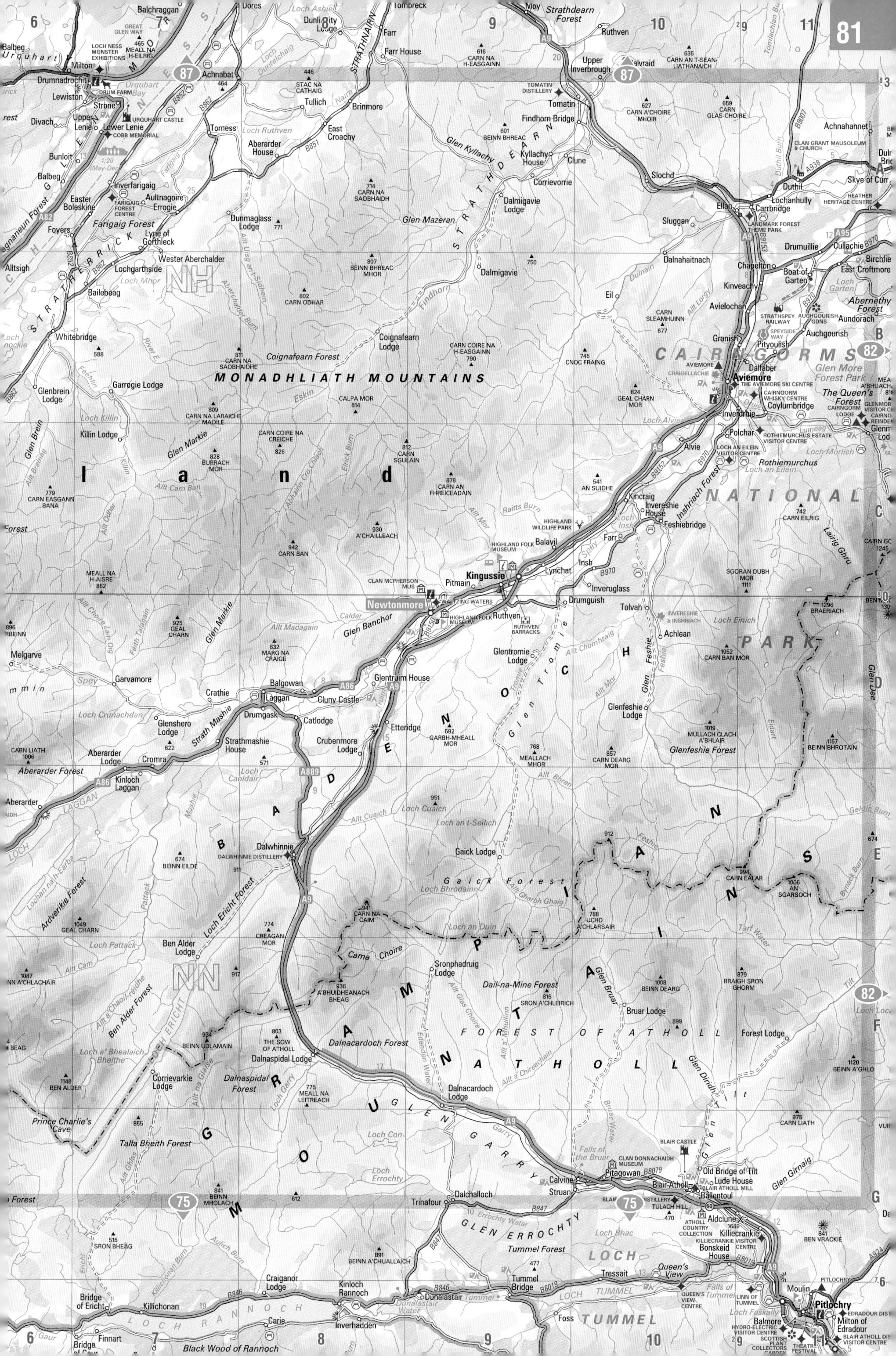
Balchraggan
Dores
Loch Ashie
Dunlichity Lodge
Tombreck
Moy
Strathdearn Forest
Ruthven
Balbeg
Urquhart
Milton
Drumnadrochit
LOCH NESS MONSTER EXHIBITIONS
GREAT GLEN WAY
465 MEALL NA H-EILRIG
Lewiston
DRUM FARM
Urquhart Bay
Strone
Divach
Upper Lenie
Lower Lenie
URQUHART CASTLE
COBB MEMORIAL
Achnabat
464
Loch Duntelchaig
446 STAC NA CATHAIG
STRATHNAIRN
Farr
Farr House
Tullich
Brinmore
Nairn
East Croachy
Torness
Loch Ruthven
Aberarder House
B851
B852
B862
Bunloit
Balbeg
Inverfarigaig
Easter Boleskine
FARIGAIG FOREST CENTRE
Aultnagoire
Errogie
Farigaig Forest
Foyers
Lyne of Gorthleck
Wester Aberchalder
Lochgarthside
Loch Mhor
Bailebeag
Alltsigh
STRATHERRICK
A82
Dunmaglass Lodge
771
616 CARN NA H-EASGAINN
714 CARN NA SAOBHAIDH
Glen Mazeran
Glen Kyllachy
601 BEINN BHREAC
STRATHDEARN
Kyllachy House
Clune
Corrievorrie
Dalmigavie Lodge
Dalmigavie
750
807 BEINN BHREAC MHOR
802 CARN ODHAR
Findhorn
Upper Inverbrough
Calvraid
TOMATIN DISTILLERY
Tomatin
Findhorn Bridge
635 CARN AN T-SEAN-LIATHANAICH
627 CARN A'CHOIRE MHOIR
659 CARN GLAS-CHOIRE
Slochd
Achnahannet
CLAN GRANT MAUSOLEUM & CHURCH
Duthil
Lochanhully
Skye of Curr
HEATHER HERITAGE CENTRE
Carrbridge
LANDMARK FOREST THEME PARK
Ellan
Sluggan
Dalnahaitnach
Dulnain
Drumuillie
Cullachie
Birchfield
Chapelton
Boat of Garten
East Croftmore
Loch Garten
Abernethy Forest
Kinveachy
Avielochan
STRATHSPEY RAILWAY
AUCHGOURISH GDNS
Aundorach
Auchgourish
SPEYSIDE WAY
Granish
Pityoulish
Eil
CARN SLEAMHUINN 677
745 CNOC FRAING
CAIRNGORMS
NATIONAL
PARK
AVIEMORE
CRAIGELLACHIE
Aviemore
THE AVIEMORE SKI CENTRE
Dalfaber
CAIRNGORM WHISKY CENTRE
Coylumbridge
Glen More Forest Park
The Queen's Forest
CAIRNGORM LODGE
Glenmore
Inverdruie
Polchar
ROTHIEMURCHUS ESTATE VISITOR CENTRE
Loch Alvie
Alvie
LOCH AN EILEIN VISITOR CENTRE
Rothiemurchus
Loch an Eilein
Loch Morlich
824 GEAL CHARN MOR
Whitebridge
588
811 CARN NA SAOBHAIDHE
Coignafearn Forest
Coignafearn Lodge
CARN COIRE NA H-EASGAINN 790
MONADHLIATH MOUNTAINS
Garrogie Lodge
Glenbrein Lodge
Eskin
CALPA MOR 814
Loch Killin
Killin Lodge
809 CARN NA LARAICHE MAOILE
CARN COIRE NA CREICHE 826
812 CARN SGULAIN
Glen Markie
828 BURRACH MOR
Glen Brein
Allt Cam Ban
779 CARN EASGANN BANA
878 CARN AN FHREICEADAIN
541 AN SUIDHE
Kincraig
Insh
Inveresiie House
Feshiebridge
Inshriach Forest
742 CARN EILRIG
Lairig Ghru
HIGHLAND WILDLIFE PARK
Raitts Burn
930 A'CHAILLEACH
942 CARN BAN
HIGHLAND FOLK MUSEUM
Balavil
Farr
Loch Insh
Spey
Lynchat
Insh
B970
Inveruglass
MEALL NA H-AISRE 862
CLAN MCPHERSON MUS
Pitmain
Kingussie
Newtonmore
WALTZING WATERS
HIGHLAND FOLK MUSEUM
Ruthven
RUTHVEN BARRACKS
Drumguish
Tolvah
SGORAN DUBH MOR 1111
1296 BRAERIACH
INVERESHIE & INSHRIACH
Loch Einich
Achlean
896
925 GEAL CHARN
Glen Markie
Allt Madagain
Glen Banchor
Calder
832 MARG NA CRAIGE
Glentromie Lodge
Glen Tromie
Allt Chomhraig
1052 CARN BAN MOR
Glen Feshie
Glen Dee
Melgarve
Spey
Garvamore
Crathie
Balgowan
A86
Glentruim House
Laggan
Cluny Castle
Drumgask
Catlodge
Loch Crunachdan
Glenshero Lodge
Strath Mashie
Strathmashie House
622
Etteridge
592 GARBH-MHEALL MOR
Glenfeshie Lodge
1019 MULLACH CLACH A'BHLAIR
Glenfeshie Forest
Eidart
1157 BEINN BHROTAIN
CARN LIATH 1006
Aberarder Lodge
Cromra
571
Crubenmore Lodge
768 MEALLACH MHOR
857 CARN DEARG MOR
Aberarder Forest
Kinloch Laggan
Loch Caoldair
A889
Allt Bhran
Aberarder
LAGGAN
951
Allt Cuaich
Loch Cuaich
Loch an t-Seilich
Geldie Burn
LOCH
674 BEINN EILDE
Dalwhinnie
DALWHINNIE DISTILLERY
911
Gaick Lodge
912
Feshie
994 CARN EALAR
1006 AN SGARSOCH
Bynack Burn
674
Ardverikie Forest
Pattack
Loch Ericht Forest
A9
Gaick Forest
Loch Bhrodainn
941 CARN NA CAIM
788 UCHD A'CHLARSAIR
1049 GEAL CHARN
774 CREAGAN MOR
Loch an Duin
Tarf Water
Loch Pattack
Ben Alder Lodge
Cama' Choire
Sronphadruig Lodge
1087
917
936 A'BHUIDHEANACH BHEAG
Dail-na-Mine Forest
Glen Bruar
1008 BEINN DEARG
879 BRAIGH SRON GHORM
816 SRON A'CHLEIRICH
Bruar Lodge
899
Ben Alder Forest
934 BEINN UDLAMAIN
803 THE SOW OF ATHOLL
Dalnacardoch Forest
FOREST OF ATHOLL
Forest Lodge
Loch a' Bhealaich Bheithe
Dalnaspidal Lodge
1120 BEINN A'GHLO
1148 BEN ALDER
Corrievarkie Lodge
Dalnaspidal Forest
775 MEALL NA LEITREACH
Dalnacardoch Lodge
Glen Tilt
Glen Dirridh
975 CARN LIATH
Prince Charlie's Cave
855
Talla Bheith Forest
Loch Con
GLEN GARRY
BLAIR CASTLE
Falls of the Bruar
CLAN DONNACHAIDH MUSEUM
Old Bridge of Tilt
Lude House
Glen Girnaig
Loch Errochty
Calvine
Pitagowan
Blair Atholl
Struan
Bridge of Tilt
Forest
841 BEINN MHOLACH
612
Dalchalloch
Trinafour
B847
BLAIR ATHOLL DISTILLERY
TULACH HILL
470
Ballentoul
Aldclune
ATHOLL COUNTRY COLLECTION
Killiecrankie
KILLIECRANKIE VISITOR CENTRE
841 BEN VRACKIE
Errochty Water
GLEN ERROCHTY
Loch Bhac
Tummel Forest
LOCH TUMMEL
515 SRON BHEAG
891 BEINN A'CHUALLAICH
477
Bonskeid House
B8019
Aulich Burn
Craiganor Lodge
Kinloch Rannoch
Tummel Bridge
Tressait
Queen's View
QUEEN'S VIEW CENTRE
Falls of Tummel
LINN OF TUMMEL
Moulin
Bridge of Ericht
Killichonan
B846
LOCH RANNOCH
Dunalastair
Dunalastair Water
Carie
Inverhadden
Foss
Loch Faskally
Pitlochry
EDRADOUR DISTILLERY
Milton of Edradour
Balmore
HYDRO-ELECTRIC VISITOR CENTRE
SCOTTISH PLANT COLLECTORS
THEATRE FESTIVAL
BLAIR ATHOLL DISTILLERY VISITOR CENTRE
Finnart
Black Wood of Rannoch
Gaur
NH
NN
87
75
82
A
B
C
D
E
F
G
6
7
8
9
10
11

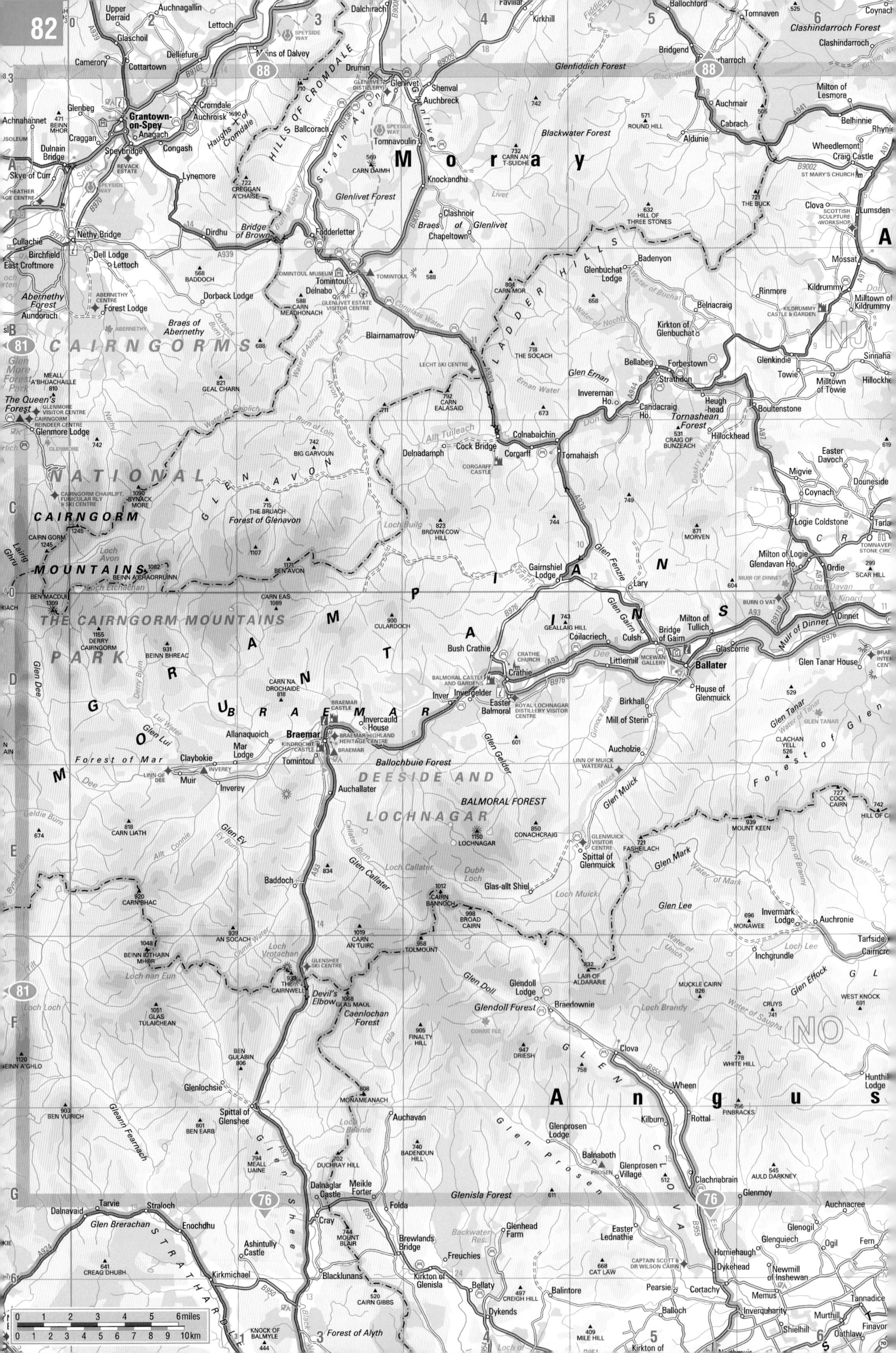
Moray
Angus
GRAMPIAN MOUNTAINS
CAIRNGORMS NATIONAL PARK
CAIRNGORM MOUNTAINS
THE CAIRNGORM MOUNTAINS
DEESIDE AND LOCHNAGAR
BRAEMAR
LADDER HILLS
HILLS OF CROMDALE
Glen Clova
Strathardle
Upper Derraid
Auchnagallin
Lettoch
Glaschoil
Mains of Dalvey
Dellefure
Camerory
Cottartown
Dalchirach
Favillar
Kirkhill
Ballochford
Tomnaven
Coynach
Clashindarroch Forest
Clashindarroch
Bridgend
Glenfiddich Forest
Drumin
Glenlivet
Shenval
Auchbreck
Cromdale
Auchroisk
Glenbeg
Grantown-on-Spey
Achnahannet
Anagach
Craggan
Haughs of Cromdale
Ballcorach
Tomnavoulin
Dulnain Bridge
Speybridge
Congash
Skye of Curr
Lynemore
Revack Estate
Carn Daimh
Glenlivet Forest
Knockandhu
Blackwater Forest
Round Hill
Auchmair
Cabrach
Aldunie
Milton of Lesmore
Belhinnie
Rhynie
Wheedlemont
Craig Castle
St Mary's Church
The Buck
Clova
Lumsden
Scottish Sculpture Workshop
Creggan A'Chaise
Clashnoir
Braes of Glenlivet
Chapeltown
Hill of Three Stones
Cullachie
Nethy Bridge
Dirdhu
Bridge of Brown
Fodderletter
Birchfield
Dell Lodge
Lettoch
East Croftmore
Tomintoul Museum
Tomintoul
Delnabo
Glenlivet Estate Visitor Centre
Badenyon
Glenbuchat Lodge
Mossat
Kildrummy
Milltown of Kildrummy
Kildrummy Castle & Garden
Rinmore
Belnacraig
Kirkton of Glenbuchat
Abernethy Forest
Aundorach
Forest Lodge
Baddoch
Dorback Lodge
Carn Meadhonach
Carn Mor
Conglass Water
Blairnamarrow
Braes of Abernethy
The Socach
Lecht Ski Centre
Glen More Forest Park
Meall A'Bhuachaille
Geal Charn
Carn Ealasaid
Glen Ernan
Bellabeg
Forbestown
Strathdon
Glenkindie
Towie
Milltown of Towie
Sinnahard
Hillockhead
The Queen's Forest
Glenmore Visitor Centre
Cairngorm Reindeer Centre
Glenmore Lodge
Inverernan Ho.
Candacraig Ho.
Heugh-head
Tornashean Forest
Boultenstone
Colnabaichin
Allt Tuileach
Big Garvoun
Delnadamph
Cock Bridge
Corgarff
Corgarff Castle
Tornahaish
Craig of Bunzeach
Hillockhead
Easter Davoch
Migvie
Douneside
Coynach
Cairngorm Chairlift, Funicular Rly & Ski Centre
Bynack More
The Bruach
Forest of Glenavon
Glen Avon
Cairngorm
Loch Builg
Brown Cow Hill
Morven
Logie Coldstone
Tarland
Tomnaverie Stone Circle
Cairn Gorm
Loch Avon
Ben Avon
Beinn A'Chaorruinn
Gairnshiel Lodge
Glen Fenzie
Lary
Milton of Logie
Glendavan Ho.
Ordie
Scar Hill
Muir of Dinnet
Burn o Vat
Loch Davan
Loch Kinord
Dinnet
Loch Etchachan
Ben Macdui
Carn Eas
Culardoch
Geallaig Hill
Glen Gairn
Milton of Tullich
Bridge of Gairn
Coilacriech
Culsh
Derry Cairngorm
Beinn Bhreac
Bush Crathie
Crathie Church
Crathie
Littlemill
McEwan Gallery
Ballater
Glascorrie
Glen Tanar House
Balmoral Castle and Gardens
House of Glenmuick
Birkhall
Glen Dee
Carn na Drochaide
Braemar Castle
Inver
Invergelder
Easter Balmoral
Royal Lochnagar Distillery Visitor Centre
Mill of Sterin
Glen Tanar
Invercauld House
Braemar Highland Heritage Centre
Allanaquoich
Glen Lui
Kindrochit Castle
Mar Lodge
Glen Gelder
Aucholzie
Clachan Yell
Forest of Glen Tanar
Forest of Mar
Claybokie
Tomintoul
Ballochbuie Forest
Linn of Muick Waterfall
Linn of Dee
Muir
Inverey
Auchallater
Glen Muick
Balmoral Forest
Cock Cairn
Hill of Cat
Mount Keen
Carn Liath
Glen Ey
Lochnagar
Conachcraig
Glenmuick Visitor Centre
Spittal of Glenmuick
Fasheilach
Glen Mark
Loch Callater
Glen Callater
Dubh Loch
Baddoch
Glas-allt Shiel
Loch Muick
Carn Bhac
Cairn Bannoch
Broad Cairn
Glen Lee
Monawee
Invermark Lodge
Auchronie
Tarfside
An Socach
Carn an Tuirc
Tolmount
Loch Lee
Inchgrundle
Beinn Iutharn Mhor
Loch Vrotachan
Glenshee Ski Centre
Lair of Aldararie
Loch nan Eun
The Cairnwell
Devil's Elbow
Glas Maol
Glen Doll
Glendoll Lodge
Braedownie
Muckle Cairn
Glen Effock
West Knock
Loch Loch
Glas Tulaichean
Caenlochan Forest
Glendoll Forest
Corrie Fee
Loch Brandy
Cruys
Water of Saughs
Finalty Hill
Driesh
Clova
White Hill
Beinn A'Ghlo
Ben Gulabin
Hunthill Lodge
Glenlochsie
Monamenach
Wheen
Ben Vuirich
Spittal of Glenshee
Auchavan
Finbracks
Kilburn
Rottal
Gleann Fearnach
Ben Earb
Glenprosen Lodge
Glen Shee
Badendun Hill
Balnaboth
Glenprosen Village
Glen Prosen
Meall Uaine
Duchray Hill
Auld Darkney
Dalnaglar Castle
Meikle Forter
Clachnabrain
Glenmoy
Glenisla Forest
Dalnavaid
Tarvie
Straloch
Folda
Auchnacree
Glen Brerachan
Enochdhu
Cray
Mount Blair
Glenhead Farm
Backwater Res.
Easter Lednathie
Glenogil
Glenquiech
Ogil
Fern
Ashintully Castle
Brewlands Bridge
Freuchies
Hornieshaugh
Creag Dhubh
Cat Law
Captain Scott & Dr Wilson Cairn
Dykehead
Newmill of Inshewan
Kirkmichael
Blacklunans
Kirkton of Glenisla
Bellaty
Balintore
Pearsie
Cortachy
Memus
Tannadice
Cairn Gibbs
Creigh Hill
Balloch
Dykends
Inverquharity
Murthill
Shielhill
Oathlaw
Finavon
Knock of Balmyle
Forest of Alyth
Mile Hill
Kirkton of
0 1 2 3 4 5 6 miles
0 1 2 3 4 5 6 7 8 9 10 km
NJ
NO

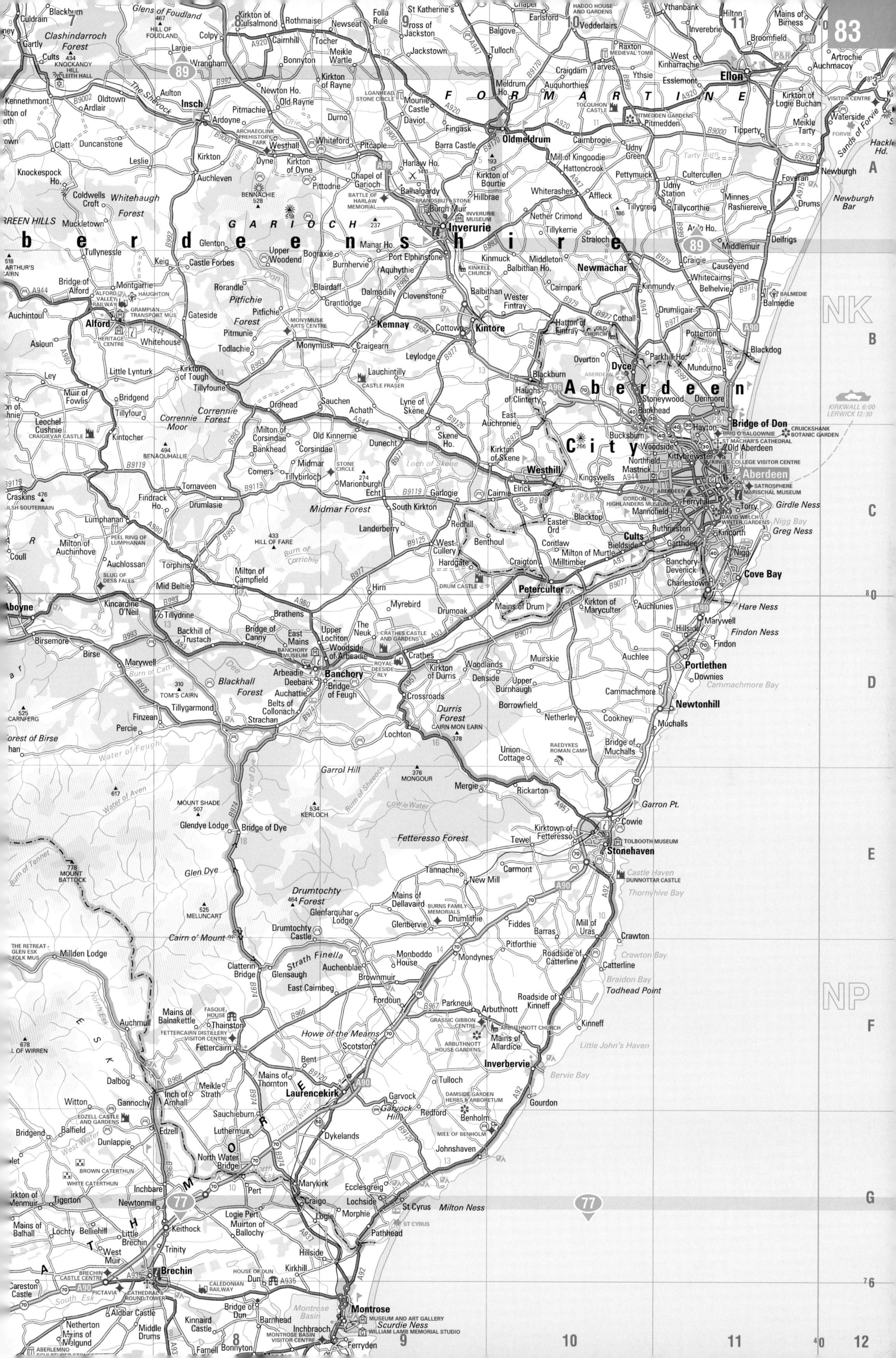
Aberdeenshire
Aberdeen City
FORMARTINE
GARIOCH
MEARNS
ANGUS
Glens of Foudland
Clashindarroch Forest
Blackburn
Culdrain
Gartly
Cults
Knockandy Hill
Leith Hall
Kennethmont
Kirkton of Culsalmond
Rothmaise
Newseat
Folla Rule
St Katherine's
Cross of Jackston
Jackstown
Hill of Foudland
Largie
Colpy
Wrangham
Cairnhill
Tocher
Meikle Wartle
Bonnyton
Kirkton of Rayne
Insch
Aulton
Oldtown
Ardlair
The Shevock
Newton Ho.
Old Rayne
Pitmachie
Ardoyne
Durno
Mounie Castle
Daviot
Loanhead Stone Circle
Archaeolink Prehistory Park
Westhall
Whiteford
Pitcaple
Clatt
Duncanstone
Leslie
Kirkton
Oyne
Kirkton of Oyne
Knockespock Ho.
Auchleven
Pittodrie
Chapel of Garioch
Harlaw Ho.
Battle of Harlaw Memorial
Balhalgardy
Coldwells Croft
Whitehaugh Forest
Bennachie
Muckletown
Inverurie
Inverurie Museum
Brandsbutt Stone
Burgh Muir
Glenton
Tullynessle
Keig
Castle Forbes
Upper Woodend
Bograxie
Manar Ho.
Port Elphinstone
Burnhervie
Aquhythie
Bridge of Alford
Montgarrie
Alford Valley Railway
Haughton
Grampian Transport Mus
Heritage Centre
Alford
Rorandle
Pitfichie Forest
Pitfichie
Blairdaff
Dalmadilly
Grantlodge
Clovenstone
Auchintoul
Gateside
Monymusk Arts Centre
Kemnay
Cottown
Kintore
Asloun
Pitmunie
Whitehouse
Todlachie
Monymusk
Craigearn
Leylodge
Kirkton of Tough
Tillyfourie
Little Lynturk
Lauchintilly
Castle Fraser
Ley
Muir of Fowlis
Bridgend
Tillyfour
Leochel-Cushnie
Craigievar Castle
Kintocher
Correnie Moor
Corrennie Forest
Ordhead
Sauchen
Achath
Lyne of Skene
Milton of Corsindae
Old Kinnernie
Corsindae
Bankhead
Midmar
Stone Circle
Dunecht
Skene Ho.
Loch of Skene
Benaquhallie
Comers
Tillybirloch
Marionburgh
Echt
Craskins
Tornaveen
Findrack Ho.
Drumlasie
Midmar Forest
South Kirkton
Lumphanan
Peel Ring of Lumphanan
Hill of Fare
Landerberry
Milton of Auchinhove
Coull
Auchlossan
Torphins
Slug of Dess Falls
Mid Beltie
Milton of Campfield
Burn of Corrichie
Aboyne
Kincardine O'Neil
Tillydrine
Backhill of Trustach
Bridge of Canny
Brathens
East Mains
Upper Lochton
The Neuk
Birsemore
Birse
Marywell
Burn of Cattie
Banchory Museum
Woodside of Arbeadie
Arbeadie
Deebank
Banchory
Bridge of Feugh
Auchattie
Belts of Collonach
Strachan
Royal Deeside Rly
Crathes Castle and Gardens
Crathes
Blackhall Forest
Tom's Cairn
Carnferg
Tillygarmond
Finzean
Percie
Forest of Birse
Water of Feugh
Water of Aven
Mount Shade
Glendye Lodge
Bridge of Dye
Water of Dye
Kerloch
Garrol Hill
Burn of Sheeoch
Mongour
Lochton
Crossroads
Durris Forest
Cairn Mon Earn
Kirkton of Durris
Woodlands
Denside
Upper Burnhaugh
Borrowfield
Mount Battock
Burn of Tennet
Glen Dye
Drumtochty Forest
Meluncart
Glenfarquhar Lodge
Drumtochty Castle
Cairn o' Mount
Fetteresso Forest
Cowie Water
The Retreat - Glen Esk Folk Mus
Millden Lodge
Clatterin Bridge
Glensaugh
Strath Finella
Auchenblae
East Cairnbeg
Monboddo House
Brownmuir
Fordoun
Mains of Balnakettle
Fasque House
Thainston
Fettercairn Distillery Visitor Centre
Fettercairn
Auchmull
North Esk
Hill of Wirren
Howe of the Mearns
Scotston
Bent
Dalbog
Inch of Arnhall
Meikle Strath
Mains of Thornton
Laurencekirk
Witton
Gannochy
Edzell Castle and Gardens
Sauchieburn
Bridgend
Balfield
Edzell
Luthermuir
Luther Water
Dunlappie
West Water
Brown Caterthun
White Caterthun
North Water Bridge
Dykelands
Inchbare
Newtonmill
Tigerton
Kirkton of Menmuir
Pert
Marykirk
Craigo
Logie
Logie Pert
Muirton of Ballochy
Mains of Balhall
Lochty
Bellehill
Little Brechin
Keithock
Trinity
West Muir
Brechin
Brechin Castle Centre
Careston Castle
Pictavia
Caledonian Railway
Cathedral & Round Tower
South Esk
Aldbar Castle
Middle Drums
Kinnaird Castle
Bridge of Dun
House of Dun
Dun
Barnhead
Netherton
Mains of Melgund
Aberlemno
Farnell
Bonnyton
Kirkhill
Hillside
Montrose Basin
Montrose
Inchbraoch
Montrose Basin Visitor Centre
Museum and Art Gallery
Scurdie Ness
William Lamb Memorial Studio
Ferryden
Pathhead
St Cyrus
Milton Ness
Ecclesgreig
Lochside
Morphie
Garvock
Garvock Hill
Redford
Damside Garden Herbs & Arboretum
Benholm
Mill of Benholm
Johnshaven
Tulloch
Gourdon
Inverbervie
Bervie Bay
Arbuthnott
Arbuthnott Church
Arbuthnott House Gardens
Grassic Gibbon Centre
Mains of Allardice
Parkneuk
Kinneff
Roadside of Kinneff
Little John's Haven
Todhead Point
Braidon Bay
Catterline
Roadside of Catterline
Crawton Bay
Crawton
Mondynes
Pitforthie
Barras
Mill of Uras
Fiddes
Glenbervie
Drumlithie
Burns Family Memorials
Mains of Dellavaird
Tannachie
New Mill
Carmont
Thornyhive Bay
Castle Haven
Dunnottar Castle
Stonehaven
Tolbooth Museum
Tewel
Kirktown of Fetteresso
Cowie
Garron Pt.
Mergie
Rickarton
Union Cottage
Raedykes Roman Camp
Bridge of Muchalls
Muchalls
Netherley
Cookney
Newtonhill
Cammachmore
Cammachmore Bay
Portlethen
Downies
Auchlee
Muirskie
Hillside
Findon
Findon Ness
Marywell
Hare Ness
Auchlunies
Kirkton of Maryculter
Charlestown
Cove Bay
Banchory-Devenick
Nigg
Nigg Bay
Greg Ness
Kincorth
Garthdee
Bieldside
Cults
Milltimber
Milton of Murtle
Contlaw
Craigton
Peterculter
Mains of Drum
Drumoak
Drum Castle
Hardgate
West Cullery
Benthoul
Myrebird
Hirn
Redhill
Garlogie
Cairnie
Elrick
Easter Ord
Blacktop
Westhill
Kirkton of Skene
Kingswells
Mastrick
Northfield
Woodside
Bucksburn
Kittybrewster
Aberdeen
Ferryhill
Torry
Mannofield
Ruthrieston
Gordon Highlanders Museum
David Welch Winter Gardens
Satrosphere
Marischal Museum
King's College Visitor Centre
St Machar's Cathedral
Old Aberdeen
Brig o' Balgownie
Bridge of Don
Cruickshank Botanic Garden
Hayton
Bankhead
Stoneywood
Denmore
Dyce
Overton
Parkhill Ho.
Mundurno
Haughs of Clinterty
Blackburn
East Auchronie
Hatton of Fintray
Old Church
Cothall
Cairnpark
Balbithan
Wester Fintray
Kinkell Church
Kinmuck
Balbithan Ho.
Middleton
Newmachar
Kinmundy
Drumligair
Potterton
Corby Loch
Blackdog
Belhelvie
Whitecairns
Balmedie
Causeyend
Craigie
Middlemuir
Delfrigs
Straloch
Tillykerrie
Nether Crimond
Whiterashes
Affleck
Tillygreig
Hattoncrook
Pettymuick
Udny Station
Tillycorthie
Rashiereive
Minnes
Drums
Newburgh Bar
Newburgh
Foveran
Foveran Burn
Cultercullen
Mill of Kingoodie
Udny Green
Tarty Burn
Cairnbrogie
Oldmeldrum
Barra Castle
Kirkton of Bourtie
Hillbrae
Fingask
Meldrum Ho.
Tulloch
Balgove
Craigdam
Tarves
Auquhorthies
Tolquhon Castle
Pitmedden Gardens
Pitmedden
Ythsie
Raxton
Medieval Tomb
Haddo House and Gardens
Chapel
Earlsford
Vedderlairs
Ythanbank
Inverebrie
West Kinharrachie
Esslemont
Ellon
Hilton
Broomfield
Mains of Birness
Artrochie
Auchmacoy
Kirkton of Logie Buchan
Visitor Centre
Waterside
Forvie
Sands of Forvie
Meikle Tarty
Tipperty
Hackley Hd.
Kirkwall 6:00
Lerwick 12:30
NK
NP
89
77

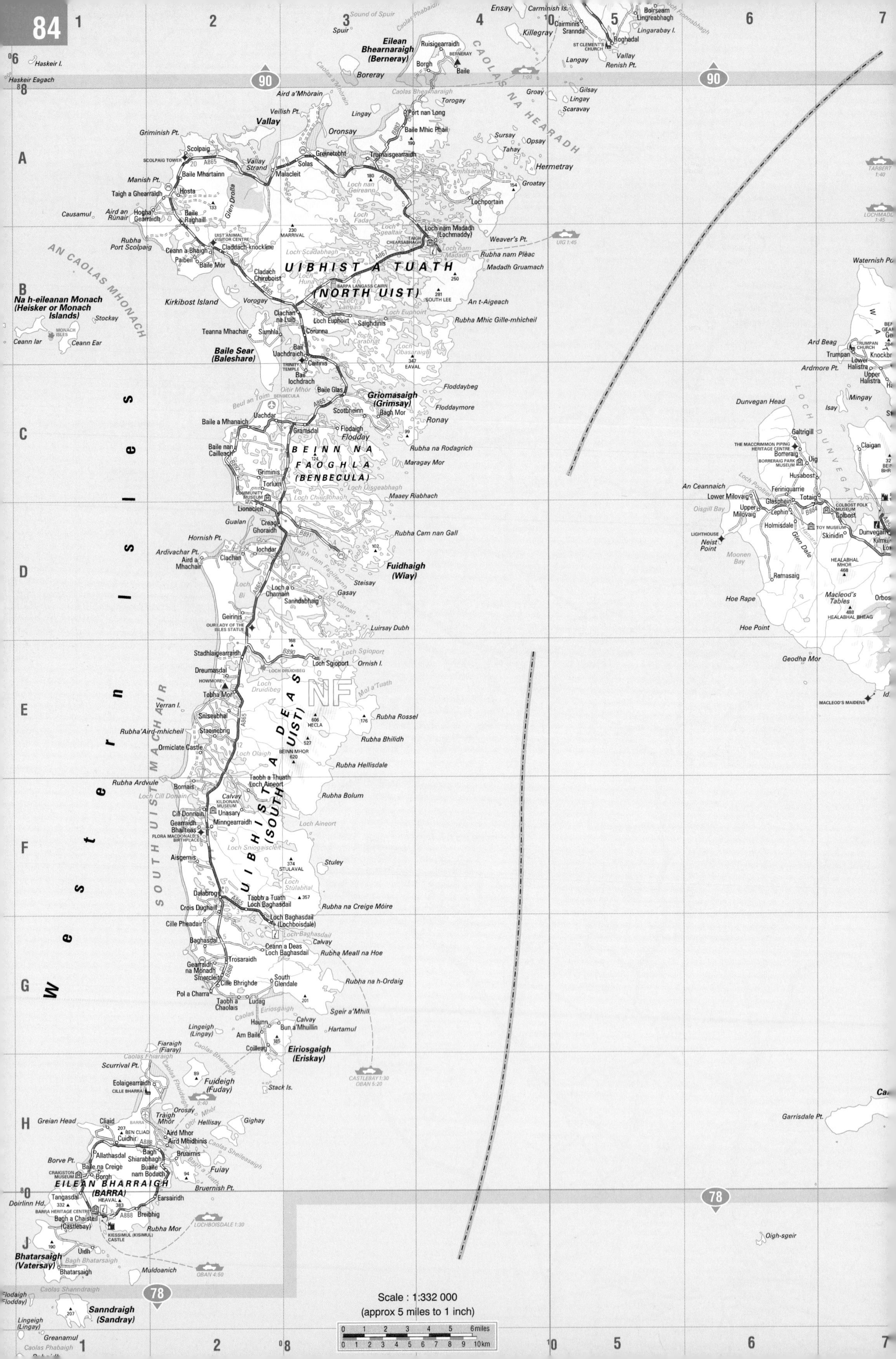
Western Isles
UIBHIST A TUATH (NORTH UIST)
BEINN NA FAOGHLA (BENBECULA)
UIBHIST A DEAS (SOUTH UIST)
EILEAN BHARRAIGH (BARRA)
Scale : 1:332 000
(approx 5 miles to 1 inch)

8
9
10
11
12
13
91
Fladda-chùain
Eilean Trodday
Rubha Hunish
Rubha na h-Aiseig
Duntulm Castle
Duntulm
Balmacqueen
Kilmaluag
Lub Score
Hungladder
Museum of Island Life
Borneskeitaig
Eilean Flodigarry
Flodigarry
Kilmuir
Flora MacDonald's Memorial
Meall na Suiramach 543
Kilvaxter
Balgown
Digg
Glashvin
The Quiraing
Staffin Bay
Staffin I.
Brogaig
Stenscholl
Staffin
Trotternish
Linicro
Totscore
Kilbride Point
Kilt Rock
Kilt Rock & Mealt Falls
466 Biod Buidhe
Elishader
Maligar
Loch Mealt
Valtos
Ascrib Islands
Idrigill
Uig
Uig Bay
Marishader
Garros
Rubha nam Brathairean
Balnaknock
611 Beinn Edra
Culnaknock
Breckrey
Ru Chorachan
Earlish
Lealt
Lealt Falls
Loch Snizort
Lower Tote
Upper Tote
A87
Peinlich
607 Creag a'Lain
Island of Rona
125
Greshornish Pt.
Lyndale Pt.
Eilean Garbh
Lyndale Ho.
Kingsburgh
719 The Storr
Old Man of Storr
Greshornish
Treaslane
Suladale
Flashader
Trotternish
Bearreraig Bay
Eilean Tigh
Garbh Eilean
An Caol
Holm I.
The Aird
Kensaleyre
Bernisdale
Edinbane
Blackhill
Loch Leathan
Eilean Fladday
254
Tote
Borve
Glen Bernisdale
Skeabost
Carbost
Loch Fada
Manish Pt.
Torran
Arnish
Prince Charles's Cave
Angus Skill Museum
Cruachan Beinn a'Chearcaill 266
Uigshader
Drumuie
Achachork
392
Rubha na h Airde Glaise
Brochel Castle
Brochel
Glengrasco
An Tuireann Arts Centre
Torvaig
Portree
Loch Connan
Shulishadermor
The Aros Experience
Glame
385
Island of Raasay
Vatten
Ose
B885
417
Heatherfield
Penifiler
413 Ben Tianavaig
Balmeanach
Balachuirn
Glenmore
Mugeary
Loch Duagrich
Holoman Bay
443 Dun Caan
Camastianavaig
Tianavaig Bay
Rubha na'Leac
Bracadale
Tarner I.
Ullinish
Struan
Coillore
Conordan
Oskaig
Lower Ollach
B883
Raasay
Raasay Ho.
Clachan
Raasay Outdoor Centre
Inverarish
Upper Ollach
Gedintailor
Battle of the Braes Monument
The Braes
Narrows of Raasay
East Suisnish
North Fearns
Eyre Point
Eyre
Oronsay
Portnalong
Rubha an Clach
Fiskavaig
Fernilea
Arnaval 369
Talisker Distillery
Carbost
439 Roineval
444 Ben Lee
Peinchorran
Caol Mòr
Drynoch
Crossal
A863
Loch Harport
Loch Sligachan
Sconser
Gleann Oraid
Talisker Bay
Talisker
Merkadale
Glamaig 775
Moll
Scalpay
Sligachan Hotel
Loch Ainort
Scalpay Ho.
Luib
Dunan
Old Skye Crofter's House
Caolas Scalpay
Eynort
445 Beinn Bhreac
Glen Brittle Forest
459
Sgurr nan Gillean 964
Glen Sligachan
570 Glas Bheinn Mhor
736 Marsco
Red Hills
A87
Skye Serpentarium
Broadford Bay
Corry
Waterloo
Lower Breakish
Upper Breakish
Eynort
Grula
Loch Eynort
Sgurr a'Ghreadaidh 973
The Cuillin Hills
Bla Bheinn 928
Broadford
732
Harrapool
World of Wood
Skye Environmental Centre
Skulamus
Glenbrittle
Cuillin Hills
Glenbrittle House
Loch Coruisk
Loch na Creitheach
Torrin
Kilbride
B8083
Strath Suardal
A851
Bualintur
992 Sgurr Alasdair
924 Sgurr nan Eag
Camasunary
Strathaird
Kirkibost
301
Heast
Loch Slapin
Rubh an Dunain
Ben Meabost 346
Kilmarie
Soay
Soay Sound
Loch Scavaig
Rubha Suisnish
Kinloch
Drumfearn
Loch Eishort
Mol-chlach
Elgol
Boat Trips
Glasnakille
B8083
Prince Charles's Cave
Eilean na h-Airde
Rubha na h-Easgainne
Ord
Dunsgiath Castle
Tokavaig
Duisdalemore
Camuscross
Isleornsay
Ornsay
Tarskavaig
Tarskavaig Pt.
Achnacloich
Sleat
Teangue
Knock Castle
Knock Bay
Ferindonald
Kilbeg
Kilmore
Rubha Shamhnan Insir
Glen Meadhonach
Armadale Castle
Armadale Gardens
Clan Donald Centre
Armadale Bay
Canna Harbour
Sound of Canna
Guirdil Bay
Kilmory
Kilmory Glen
0:55
Mallaig 2:30
Rubha Charn nan Cearc
280
Calligarry
Ardvasar
Aird of Sleat
Ard Thurinish
388
Kinloch Glen
Rubha na Roinne
0:30
78
571 Orval
Kinloch
Loch Scresort
Kinloch Castle
Rùm
Rubha Port na Caranean
Point of Sleat
Sound of Rùm
Harris
Glen Harris
812 Askival
781 Ainshval
Rubha Sgorr an t-Snidhe
1:15
Eigg 1:00
Muck 1:10
Eigg 1:20
Small Isles
Rubha nam Meirleach
Sound of Sleat
Bay of Laig
Cleadale
Seana Chamas
Aultgrishan
Midtown
Brae
Rubha 'Ard na Bà
Tournaig
Aird Dubh
Peterburn
Naast
Loch Bad a'Chreamh
Inverewe Garden
Londubh
Port Erradale
North Erradale
Poolewe
Fionn Loch
Rubha Bàn
Big Sand
Loch Tollaidh
Longa Island
Caolas Beag
Carn Dearg
Strath
Gairloch Heritage Museum
Smithstown
Gairloch
Loch Gairloch
Meall an Doirean 420
791 Beinn Airigh Charr
Charlestown
A832
Port Henderson
Aird
B8056
Badachro
Kerrysdale
Eilean Subhainn
Loch Maree Islands
Opinan
Shieldaig
Kerry
Loch Bad an Sgalaig
Victoria Falls
Talladale
South Erradale
Loch Clàir
Redpoint
Dubh Loch
Loch Gaineamhach
Wester Ross
Flowerdale Forest
875 Baosbheinn
Shieldaig Forest
Loch na h-Oidhche
624 Beinn Bhreac
Loch a'Bhealaich
Rubha na Fearn
Fearnmore
Beinn Eighe National Nature Reserve
985 Beinn Alligin
Fearnbeg
Lower Diabaig
Torridon Forest
1054 Liathach
Arinacrinachd
Alligin Shuas
Rechullin
Cuaig
Kenmore
Loch a'Chracaich
Ardheslaig
Inveralligin
Torridon Ho.
Upper Loch Torridon
Fasag
Torridon
Torridon Visitor Centre
Glen Torridon
Loch Shieldaig
Callakille
Lonbain
Shieldaig
Balgy
A896
Annat
Abhainn Thrail
Loch Gaineamhach
493 Croic-bheinn
Ben-damph Forest
Loch an Eoin
Ben Shieldaig 439
Glenshieldaig Forest
902 Beinn Damh
993 Maol Chean-dearg
626 Beinn a'Chlachain
Loch Lundie
Applecross Forest
513
Chapel of St Maelrubha
Applecross Ho.
Applecross Bay
Loch Coultrie
Applecross
896 Beinn Bhan
Rassal Ashwood
Highland
Camusteel
Camusterrach
Bealach na Ba
Ard-dhubh
Culduie
710 Meall Gorm
Kirkton
A896
Sanachan
Toscaig
Eilean na Bà
Ardarroch
Achintraid
Slumbay
Lochcarron
Attadale
Inner Sound
Kishorn I.
Strome Castle
395
Crowlin Islands
Uags
Ardaneaskan
Stromemore
Ardnarff
An Dubh-aird
Eilean Mòr
Loch Carron
Stromeferry
486 Carn nan Iomairean
Plockton
Craig Highland Farm
Achmore
Longay
Port Cam
Duirinish
Drumbuie
Gleann Udalain
Allt-nan-sùgh
Sallachy
Black Is.
Erbusaig
Badicaul
Balmacara Square
Auchertyre
Loch Long
Guillamon I.
Pabay
Kyle of Lochalsh
Castle Moil
Lochalsh Woodland Garden
Balmacara
Reraig
Kirkton
Nostie
Ardelve
Dornie
Bundalloch
Camas-luinie
Kyleakin
Brightwater Visitor Centre
Loch Alsh
Glas Eilean
Totaig
Eilean Donan Castle
Keppoch
Ardintoul Pt.
Sgurr na Coinnich 739
Kylerhea Otter Haven
Letterfearn
Invershiel
Glen Arroch
Kylerhea
Bernera
Galltair
603 Beinn a'Chuirn
Loch Duich
Ratagan
610 Ben Aslak
Glenelg
Glenelg Bay
Bernera Barracks
Shiel Bridge
Eilanreach
Glenelg Brochs
Balvraid
Glen More
779
Sandaig Is.
Upper Sandaig
874 Beinn a'Chapaill
Glenshiel Forest
80
974 Beinn Sgritheall
1010 The Saddle
Beinn nan Caorach 774
Arnisdale
Glen Arnisdale
Corran
Loch Hourn
Kinlochhourn Forest
Rubha Ard Slisneach
Inverguseran
713 Druim Fada
785 Beinn na Caillich
Knoydart
Barrisdale Bay
Airor
1020 Ladhar Bheinn
Glen Barrisdale
Gleann na Guiserein
Sandaig
Sandaig Bay
Luinne Bheinn 939
Scottas
Inverie
Inverie Bay
Gleann an Dubh-Lochain
79
Rubha Raonuill
Mallaig Heritage Centre
0:45
946 Meall Buidhe
Mallaig
522
Loch Nevis
Beinn Bhuidhe 855
Glasnacardoch
Camusrory
1040 Sgurr na Ciche
Stoul
Kylesknoydart
Beoraidbeg
Bracara
Bracorina
Tarbet
Kylesmorar
Morar
North Morar
Brinacory
Swordland
Kinlochmorar
Loch Morar
829 Carn Mor
Scamadale
Bunacaimb
Portnaluchaig
Back of Keppoch
Eilean Ighe
Letterm
South Morar
Oban
718 An Stac
Glen Dessarry
86
A
B
C
D
E
F
G
H
J

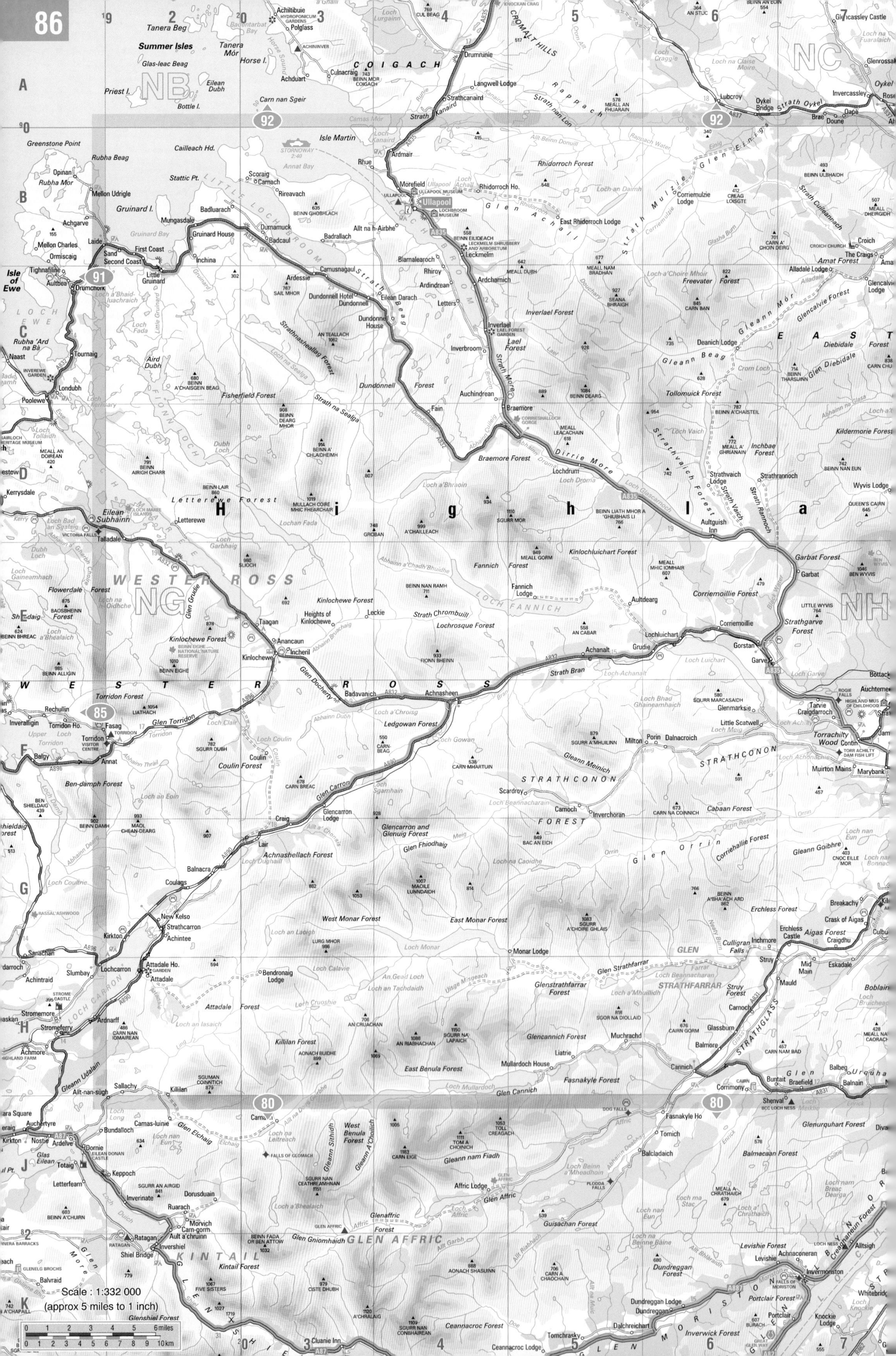
86
Scale : 1:332 000
(approx 5 miles to 1 inch)
0 1 2 3 4 5 6 miles
0 1 2 3 4 5 6 7 8 9 10 km
NB
NC
NG
NH
92
91
85
80
Summer Isles
Tanera Beg
Tanera Mòr
Horse I.
Glas-leac Beag
Priest I.
Eilean Dubh
Bottle I.
Achiltibuie
Hydroponicum Gardens
Polglass
Badentarbat Bay
Achduart
Culnacraig
COIGACH
Beinn Mor Coigach
Carn nan Sgeir
Isle Martin
Stornoway 2:40
Annat Bay
Cul Beag
Loch Lurgainn
Knockan Crag
CROMALT HILLS
Drumrunie
Langwell Lodge
Strathcanaird
Strath Kanaird
Rappach
Strath nan Lon
Meall an Fhuarain
An Stuc
Loch Craggie
Loch na Claise Moire
Lubcroy
Oykel Bridge
Strath Oykel
Invercassley
Glencassley Castle
Glenrossal
Brae
Doune
Greenstone Point
Rubha Beag
Cailleach Hd.
Opinan
Rubha Mor
Mellon Udrigle
Stattic Pt.
Scoraig
Carnach
Rireavach
LITTLE LOCH BROOM
Gruinard I.
Badluarach
Mungasdale
Gruinard Bay
Gruinard House
Achgarve
Mellon Charles
Ormiscaig
Laide
Sand
First Coast
Second Coast
Little Gruinard
Inchina
Isle of Ewe
Tighnafiline
Aultbea
Drumchork
LOCH EWE
Rubha 'Ard na Bà
Tournaig
Naast
Inverewe Garden
Londubh
Poolewe
Loch Kernsary
Aird Dubh
Loch Fada
Dundonnell Hotel
Dundonnell
Ardessie
Sail Mhor
Camusnagaul
Dundonnell House
An Teallach
Strathnasheallag Forest
Beinn a' Chaisgein Beag
Fisherfield Forest
Strath na Sealga
Beinn Dearg Mhor
Dubh Loch
Fionn Loch
Beinn Airigh Charr
Meall an Doirean
Gairloch Heritage Museum
Kerrysdale
Eilean Subhainn
Loch Maree Islands
Letterewe
Letterewe Forest
Beinn Lair
Mullach Coire Mhic Fhearchair
Lochan Fada
Victoria Falls
Talladale
Loch Garbhaig
Slioch
WESTER ROSS
Flowerdale Forest
Baosbheinn
Shieldaig
Beinn Bhreac
Beinn Alligin
Beinn Eighe
Beinn Eighe National Nature Reserve
Kinlochewe Forest
Glen Grudie
Taagan
Anancaun
Incheril
Kinlochewe
Heights of Kinlochewe
Leckie
Kinlochewe Forest
Morefield
Ullapool Museum
Ullapool
Lochbroom Museum
Rhue
Ardmair
Rhidorroch Forest
Rhidorroch Ho.
Loch Achall
Glen Achall
East Rhidorroch Lodge
Loch an Daimh
Beinn Ghobhlach
Allt na h-Airbhe
Badrallach
Badcaul
Dumamuck
LOCH BROOM
Beinn Eilideach
Leckmelm Shrubbery and Arboretum
Leckmelm
Blarnalearoch
Rhiroy
Ardindrean
Letters
Ardcharnich
Meall Dubh
Eilean Darach
Strath Beag
Inverlael
Lael Forest Garden
Lael Forest
Inverbroom
Inverlael Forest
Strath More
Auchindrean
Dundonnell Forest
Fain
Braemore
Corrieshalloch Gorge
Braemore Forest
Meall Leacachain
Dirrie More
Lochdrum
Loch Droma
Loch a' Bhraoin
Beinn Dearg
Meall nam Bradhan
Seana Bhraigh
Douchary
Strath Mulzie
Corriemulzie Lodge
Creag Loisgte
Glen Einig
Beinn Ulbhaidh
Strath Cuileannach
Meall Dheirgidh
Carn a' Choin Deirg
Croich Church
Croich
The Craigs
Amat Forest
Alladale Lodge
Glencalvie Lodge
Glencalvie Forest
Loch a'Choire Mhoir
Freevater Forest
Carn Ban
Gleann Mòr
Deanich Lodge
Gleann Beag
Diebidale
Glen Diebidale
Beinn Tharsuinn
Crom Loch
Tollomuick Forest
Beinn a' Chaisteil
Loch Vaich
Strathvaich Forest
Meall a' Ghrianain
Inchbae Forest
Kildermorie Forest
Beinn nan Eun
Strathvaich Lodge
Strath Vaich
Strathrannoch
Strath Rannoch
Wyvis Lodge
Queen's Cairn
EAST
Beinn Liath Mhor a' Ghiubhais Li
Sgurr Mor
Loch Glascarnoch
Aultguish Inn
Highland
A' Chailleach
Groban
Meall Gorm
Fannich Forest
Kinlochluichart Forest
Meall Mhic Iomhair
Garbat Forest
Garbat
Ben Wyvis
Little Wyvis
Strathgarve Forest
Corriemoillie Forest
Beinn nan Ramh
Loch Fannich
Fannich Lodge
Aultdearg
Strath Chrombuill
Lochrosque Forest
Fionn Bheinn
An Cabar
Lochluichart
Corriemoillie
Gorstan
Garve
Loch Garve
Loch Luichart
Grudie
Achanalt
Strath Bran
Loch Achanalt
Glen Docherty
Badavanich
Achnasheen
Loch a' Chroisg
Ledgowan Forest
Carn Beag
Loch Gowan
Carn Mhartuin
Loch Bhad Ghainneamhaich
Sgurr Marcasaidh
Glenmarksie
Little Scatwell
Loch Meig
Sgurr a' Mhuilinn
Milton
Porin
Dalnacroich
Gleann Meinich
STRATHCONON
Scardroy
Camoch
Inverchoran
Loch Beannacharain
FOREST
Bac an Eich
Carn na Coinnich
Cabaan Forest
Rogie Falls
Auchterneed
Highland Mus of Childhood
Tarvie
Craigdarroch
Torrachilty Wood
Torr Achilty Dam Fish Lift
Contin
Muirton Mains
Marybank
Orrin Reservoir
Glen Orrin
Corriehallie Forest
Gleann Goibhre
Cnoc Eille Mor
Beinn a' Bha'ach Ard
Erchless Forest
Breakachy
Crask of Aigas
Aigas Forest
Erchless Castle
Inchmore
Culligran Falls
GLEN
Craigdhu
Struy
Mid Main
Eskadale
Glen Strathfarrar
STRATHFARRAR
Struy Forest
Mauld
Boblainy
Glenstrathfarrar Forest
Loch a'Mhuillidh
Sgor na Diollaid
Cairn Gorm
Carnoch
Glassburn
Balmore
STRATHGLASS
Meall na Caorach
Carn nam Bad
Rechullin
Inveralligin
Torridon Ho.
Fasag
Torridon
Torridon Visitor Centre
Upper Loch Torridon
Torridon Forest
Liathach
Glen Torridon
Balgy
Annat
Abhainn Thràil
Sgurr Dubh
Loch Clair
Loch Coulin
Coulin
Coulin Forest
Ben-damph Forest
Loch an Eoin
Carn Breac
Glen Carron
Loch Sgamhain
Glencarron Lodge
Craig
Lair
Ben Shieldaig
Beinn Damh
Maol Chean-dearg
Shieldaig Forest
Achnashellach Forest
Loch Dughaill
Glencarron and Glenuig Forest
Glen Fhiodhaig
Loch na Caoidhe
Balnacra
Coulags
Loch Coultrie
Rassal Ashwood
Maoile Lunndaidh
West Monar Forest
East Monar Forest
Sgurr a' Choire Ghlais
New Kelso
Strathcarron
Achintee
Kirkton
Loch an Laoigh
Lurg Mhor
Loch Monar
Monar Lodge
Sanachan
Slumbay
Lochcarron
Attadale Ho.
Garden
Attadale
Achintraid
Strome Castle
LOCH CARRON
Bendronaig Lodge
Loch Calavie
An Gead Loch
Loch an Tachdaidh
Uisge Misgeach
Attadale Forest
Loch Cruoshie
Loch an Iasaich
Stromemore
Ardnarff
Carn nan Iomairean
Stromeferry
An Cruachan
An Riabhachan
Sgurr na Lapaich
Glencannich Forest
Muchrachd
Achmore
Highland Farm
Killilan Forest
Aonach Buidhe
East Benula Forest
Liatrie
Mullardoch House
Cannich
Fasnakyle Forest
Gleann Udalain
Sallachy
Killilan
Allt-nan-sùgh
Sguman Coinntich
Loch Mullardoch
Glen Cannich
Cairn
Corrimony
Buntait
Glen Urquhart
Braefield
Balbeg
Balnain
Shenval
BCC Loch Ness
Glenurquhart Forest
Auchertyre
Camas-luinie
Bundalloch
Glen Elchaig
Carnach
Loch na Leitreach
West Benula Forest
Gleann Sithidh
Gleann A'Choilich
Tom a' Choinich
Toll Creagach
Dog Falls
Fasnakyle Ho
Tomich
Nostie
Ardelve
Dornie
Eilean Donan Castle
Glas Eilean
Totaig
Falls of Glomach
Carn Eige
Gleann nam Fiadh
Balcladaich
Balmacaan Forest
Keppoch
Sgurr an Airgid
Sgurr nan Ceathreamhnan
Affric Lodge
Glen Affric
Loch Beinn a'Mheadhoin
Plodda Falls
Meall a' Chrathaich
Letterfearn
Inverinate
Dorusduain
Loch a'Bhealaich
Loch ma Stac
Loch nan Eun
Loch a' Chrathaich
Beinn a' Chuirn
Ruarach
Morvich
Carn-gorm
Glenaffric
Glen Affric Forest
GLEN AFFRIC
Guisachan Forest
Ratagan
Aultachruinn
Inversheil
Shiel Bridge
KINTAIL
Kintail Forest
Beinn Fada or Ben Attow
Glen Gniomhaidh
Allt Garbh
Aonach Shasuinn
Carn a' Chaochain
Loch na Beinne Baine
Levishie Forest
Levishie
Achnaconeran
Invermoriston
Dundreggan Forest
Loch Ness
Glenelg Brochs
Balvraid
Glen More
Five Sisters
Ciste Dhubh
A'Chralaig
Sgurr nan Conbhairean
Ceannacroc Forest
Ceannacroc Lodge
Glenshiel Forest
Cluanie Inn
GLEN SHIEL
Tomchrasky
Dundreggan Lodge
Dundreggan
Dalchreichart
GLEN MORISTON
Inverwick Forest
Portclair Forest
Portclair
Burach
Knockie Lodge
Whitebridge
Alltsigh
Falls of Moriston
Creag nan Eun Forest

ND
NJ
93
81
88
Sallachy
Lairg Lodge
Lairg Muir
Lairg
Saval
Claonel
Gruids
Torroble
Achany
Shin Forest
Achinduich
Linsidemore
Achnahanat
Inveran
Invershin
Craigton
Culrain
Balblair
Airdens
Clashcoig
Migdale
Bonar Bridge
Ardgay
Lower Gledfield
Soyal
Dounie
Kincardine
Upper Ardchronie
Fearn Lodge
Easter Fearn
Strathcarron
Spinningdale
Ospisdale
Whiteface
Clashmore
Skibo Castle
Muie
Ardachu
Strath Fleet
Pittentrail
Rogart
Rogart Station
Morvich
Dalreavoch
Rhilochan
East Langwell
Farlary
Loch Brora
Achrimsdale
East Clyne
West Clyne
Clynelish
Dalchalm
Brora
Doll
Backies
Golspie
Culmaily
Kirkton
Torboll Farm
Little Torboll
Cambusmore Lodge
Loch Fleet
Cambusavie Farm
Skelbo
Littleferry
Fourpenny
Embo
Embo Street
Pitgrudy
Dornoch
Dornoch Sands
Achvaich
Badninish
Rearquhar
Poles
Proncy
Gablon
Evelix
Camore
Lonemore
Meikle Ferry
Ardmore
Edderton
Ferry Point
DORNOCH FIRTH
Whiteness Sands
Tarbat Ness
Wilkhaven
Bindal
Portmahomack
Rockfield
Inver
Arbol
Tarrel
Balnagall
Lochslin
Rhynie
Fearn Station
Geanies House
Hill of Fearn
Fearn
Hilton of Cadboll
Balintore
Shandwick
Loans of Tulloch
Arabella
Tain
Morangie
Tarlogie
Aldie
Hilton
Quarryhill
Morangie Forest
Balleigh
Meikle Gluich
Aultnamain Inn
ROSS
Strath Rory
Ardross Forest
Ardross
Ardross Castle
Stittenham
Easter Ardross
Dalnavie
Western Lealty
Achandunie
Nonikiln
Mossfield
Alness
Dalmore
Achnagarron
Rosskeen
Invergordon
Saltburn
Balintraid
Barbaraville
Tomich
Kilmuir
Rhicullen
Stonyfield
Milton
Tarbat Ho.
Tullich Muir
Kildary
Scotsburn
Torran
Logie Hill
Newfield
Lamington
East Lamington
Braeantra
Strath Rusdale
Inchlumpie
Boath
Ankerville
Chapelhill
Pitcalnie
Nigg
Nigg Bay
Sands of Nigg
Mount Canisp
Balnabruaich
Castlecraig
Balnapaling
Nigg Ferry
King's Cave
Port an Righ
Cromarty
Sutors of Cromarty
Newton
Eileanach Lodge
Glen Glass
Novar House
Assynt Ho.
Evanton
Redburn
Culcairn
Swordale
Drummond
Foulis Castle
Ardullie
Clach Liath Forest
Woodlands
Mountgerald
Tulloch Castle
Dingwall
Fodderty
Maryburgh
Conon Bridge
Conon House
Balblair
Newhall Point
Resolis
Newhall House
Cullicudden
Jemimaville
Shore Mill
Muirton
Glenurquhart
Millbuie Forest
BLACK ISLE
Upper Eathie
Findon Mains
Shoreton
Culbo
Urquhart
Culbokie
Raddery
Balmungie
Killen
Rosemarkie
Fortrose
Chanonry Pt.
Fort George
Kirkton
Ardersier
Baddock
Whiteness Head
MORAY FIRTH
Nairn
Tradespark
Auldearn
Moss-side
Culbin Forest
Kintessack
Moy Ho.
Dyke
Kincorth Ho.
Findhorn
Findhorn Bay
Forres
Kinloss
Grange Hall
Burghead
Burghead Bay
Hopeman
Cummingston
Roseisle
Roseisle Forest
Lower Hempriggs
Coltfield
Alves
Miltonhill
Newton
Springfield
Mains of Burgie
Monaughty Forest
Barnhill
Blervie Castle
Califer
Rafford
Altyre Ho.
Moor of Granary
Moray
Altyre Woods
Dallas Forest
Dallas
Branchill
Newtyle Forest
Craigroy
Drumine Forest
Logie
Relugas
Dunphail
Glenernie
Beachans
Mount
Ferness
Darnaway Forest
Whitemire
Conicavel
Easter Milton
Wester Milton
Earlsmill
Blackhills
Laiken Forest
Geddes House
Regoul
Littlemill
Mid Urchany
Achavraat
Redburn
Newlands of Fleenas Wood
Balmore
Glenferness House
Dulsie
Cawdor
Clephanton
Rosefield
Piperhill
Culcharry
Easter Galcantray
Kirkton of Barevan
Mains of Clunas
Gollanfield
Milton of Gollanfield
Muir of the Clans
Lochside
Fisherton
Castle Stuart
Tornagrain
Croy
Cantraywood
Culloden Forest
Cantraydoune
Cantraybruich
Assich Forest
Newton
Culloden
Balloch
Smithton
Newlands
Westhill
Castletown
House of Daviot
Daviot
Craggie
Scatraig
Leys Castle
Inverness
North Kessock
Charlestown
South Kessock
Longman Pt.
Kilmuir
Drumderfit
Munlochy
Allangrange Mains
Bogallan
Tore
Arpafeelie
Redcastle
Kilcoy
Fettes
Muckernich
Belmaduthy
Knockbain
Rosehaugh Mains
Suddie
Roskill House
Avoch
Duncanston
Easter Kinkell
Leanaig
Cornton
Alcaig
Muir of Ord
Balvaird
Milton
Windhill
Tomich House
Beauly
Kirkhill
Lentran
Bunchrew
Drumchardine
Easter Moniack
Newtonhill
Leachkin
Balchraggan
Cabrich
THE AIRD
Dunain Ho.
Dochgarroch
Dochfour Ho.
Lochend
Lairgmore
Abriachan
Balchraggan
Strath Dores
Drumashie Moor
Essich
Dores
Balnafoich
Tombreck
Dunlichity Lodge
Farr
Farr House
Strathnairn
Drummossie
Achnabat
Stone
Lower Lenie
Torness
Aberarder House
Loch Ruthven
East Croachy
Tullich
Brinmore
Inverfarigaig
Aultnagoire
Errogie
Farigaig Forest
Lyne of Gorthleck
Dunmaglass Lodge
Wester Aberchalder
Lochgarthside
Glen Mazeran
Dalmigavie Lodge
Dalmigavie
Coignafearn Lodge
Coignafearn Forest
MONADHLIATH MOUNTAINS
Garrogie Lodge
Moy Hall
Moy
Strathdearn Forest
Ruthven
Upper Inverbrough
Balvraid
Tomatin
Findhorn Bridge
Glen Kyllachy
Kyllachy House
Clune
Corrievorrie
Strathdearn
Slochd
Daless
Aitnoch
Dava
Lochindorb
Lochindorb Lodge
Upper Derraid
Auchnagallin
Glaschoil
Camerory
Cottartown
Dellefure
Lettoch
Mains of Dalvey
Advie
Strathspey
Achnahannet
Glenbeg
Grantown-on-Spey
Craggan
Anagach
Dulnain Bridge
Speybridge
Congash
Cromdale
Auchroisk
Hills of Cromdale
Haughs of Cromdale
Ballcorach
Skye of Curr
Duthil
Lochanhully
Carrbridge
Ellan
Sluggan
Dalnahaitnach
Drumuillie
Cullachie
Nethy Bridge
Dell Lodge
Lettoch
Birchfield
East Croftmore
Boat of Garten
Chapelton
Kinveachy
Avielochan
Abernethy Forest
Aundorach
Forest Lodge
Braes of Abernethy
Auchgourish
Granish
Pityoulish
Dalfaber
Aviemore
Glen More Forest Park
The Queen's Forest
Eil
Lynemore
Dirdhu
Bridge of Brown
Fodderletter
Glenlivet Forest
Tomintoul
Delnabo
Dorback Lodge
CAIRNGORMS NATIONAL PARK
Loch Moy
Loch Ashie
Loch Duntelchaig
Urquhart Bay
Loch Mhor
Eskin
River E
Gurr
Upper Knockando
Carn Kitty
Larig Hill
Mill Buie
Loch Dallas
Loch Craggie
Loch Migdale
Loch Buidhe
Loch Laro
Cromarty Bay
Udale Bay
Alness Bay
Munlochy Bay
Avoch Bay
Beauly Firth
Rosemarkie Bay
The Bar

1
2
3
4
5
A
B
C
D
E
F
G
H
Halliman Skerries
Covesea Skerries
LOSSIEMOUTH FISHERIES & COMMUNITY MUSEUM
Branderburgh
Stotfield
Covesea
Lossiemouth
BURGHEAD MUSEUM
Burghead
Hopeman
Duffus
Gordonstoun
Cummingston
Roseisle
Roseisle Forest
DUFFUS CASTLE
PALACE OF SPYNIE
Loch Spynie
Lossie Forest
S P E Y   B A Y
Spynie
Leuchars Ho.
Lochhill
Kingston
TUGNET ICE HOUSE
Spey Bay
DOLPHIN CENTRE
Garmouth
Portknockie
Findochty
THE BUCKIE DRIFTER
Gordonsburgh
Portessie
Buckie
Buckpool
Rathven
Cullen
Cullen Bay
Logie Hd.
Sandend Bay
Redhythe Pt.
FINDLATER CASTLE
Sandend
Portsoy
Seatown
Lower Kempriggs
Quarrywood
Bishopmill
Elgin
ELGIN MUSEUM
CATHEDRAL
CASHMERE VISITOR CENTRE
Newton
Coltfield
Alves
Miltonhill
OLD MILLS
MORAY MOTOR MUSEUM
New Elgin
Urquhart
Lochs Crofts
Lhanbryde
Porttanachy
Nether Dallachy
Upper Dallachy
Slackhead
Portgordon
Cairnfield Ho.
Drybridge
Lintmill
JOINER'S WORKSHOP
Fordyce
Milton
Kirktown of Deskford
DESKFORD CHURCH
Ardiecow
Berryhillock
Pittendreich
Miltonduff
Moss of Barmuckity
COXTON TOWER
Bogmoor
SPEYSIDE WAY
BAXTERS HIGHLAND VILLAGE
Auchenhalrig
Newlands of Tynet
Broadley
ST. GREGORY'S CHAPEL
Clochan
Shiel Muir
Mains of Burgie
Monaughty Forest
PLUSCARDEN ABBEY
Paddockhaugh
Auchtertyre
BIRNIE CHURCH
Barnhill
Foresterseat
Longmorn
Blackhills
Mosstodloch
FOCHABERS FOLK MUSEUM
Fochabers
Dipple
Braes of Enzie
Speymouth Forest
Craibstone
Little Toux
Newmills of Boyne
Thornshill
MILLBUIES
Orbliston
Ordiequish
Teindland Forest
Inchberry
Wood of Ordiequish
MILLSTONE HILL
Deerhill
Mains of Edingight
Gordonstown
Cornhill
Grange Crossroads
Edingight Ho.
KNOCK HILL
Finnygaud
Dallas Forest
Kellas
Glenlatterach
Glen of Rothes
Forgie
Broadrashes
Aultmore
Crannoch
Sillyearn
Knowes of Elrick
Bracobrae
Davoch of Grange
Knock
Glen Barry
Branchill
Dallas
Moray
Auchinroath
Newlands
Newmill
Drumnagorrach
Farmtown
Aberchirder
Old Crombie
Knauchland
Marnoch
Craigroy
CAIRN UISH
MILL BUIE
Rothes
GLEN GRANT DISTILLERY
Mulben
Keith
STRATHISLA DISTILLERY
ISLA
Rosarie Forest
Balloch Wood
Milltown of Rothiemay
Mains of Mayen
Yonder Bognie
Bogniebrae
FOURMAN HILL
Burn of Rothes
SPEYSIDE WAY
BEN AIGAN
KEITH AND DUFFTOWN RLY
Elchies Forest
CAILLICHE
Whiteacen
Dandaleith
Towiemore
STRATH
Edintore
Glen of Coachford
Ruthven
LADYCROFT AGRICULTURAL MUSEUM
Maggieknockater
Little Pitlurg
Coachford
Cairnie
CARDHU DISTILLERY
Archiestown
Ringorm
Craigellachie
Drummuir Castle
Kininvie Ho.
Drummuir
NJ
THE BIN
The Bin Forest
Corse of Kinnoir
Upper Knockando
Cardow
SPEYSIDE WAY VISITOR CENTRE
SPEYSIDE COOPERAGE VISITOR CENTRE
Knockando Ho.
Midtown of Buchromb
Daugh of Cairnborrow
NORDIC SKI CENTRE
HUNTLY CASTLE
Lessendrum
Corse
Knockando
Carron
Speyview
Charlestown of Aberlour
SPEY
Daugh of Kinermony
Milltown of Edinvillie
BALVENIE CASTLE
GLENFIDDICH DISTILLERY
Milltown of Auchindoun
Cairnborrow
Huntly
BRANDER MUSEUM
Drumblade
Brideswell
Slioch
Dufftown
Torry
Haugh of Glass
Deveron
Kirktown of Mortlach
MEIKLE CONVAL
Marypark
Bellehiglash
GLENFARCLAS DISTILLERY
AUCHINDOUN CASTLE
S T R A T H B O G I E
Bailiesward
Bridgend
Thomastown
CRAGGANMORE DISTILLERY
Glen Rinnes
THE SCALP
Succoth
Tillathrowie
Kirkstile
Shanquhar
Hillhead
Advie
Bridge of Avon
BEN RINNES
Favillar
Dullan Water
Glen Fiddich
Ballochford
Coynachie
Blackburn
Glens of Foudland
Dalchirach
Kirkhill
Tomnaven
Clashindarroch Forest
Clashindarroch
Kirkney
Culdrain
HILL OF FOUDLAND
Lettoch
SPEYSIDE WAY
Mains of Dalvey
HILLS OF CROMDALE
Bridgend
Inverharroch
Glenfiddich Forest
Kirkney Water
Gartly
Cults
KNOCKANDY HILL
LEITH HALL
Drumin
GLENLIVET DISTILLERY
Glenlivet
Shenval
Auchbreck
Black Water
Milton of Lesmore
Kennethmont
Milton of Noth
Oldtown
Ardlair
Auchmair
Blackwater Forest
ROUND HILL
Cabrach
Aldunie
Belhinnie
Rhynie
Cottown
Clatt
Duncanstone
Haughs of Cromdale
Ballcorach
SPEYSIDE WAY
Tomnavoulin
Strath Avon
CARN DAIMH
CARN AN T-SUIDHE
Wheedlemont
Craig Castle
ST MARY'S CHURCH
Knockespock Ho.
Leslie
CREGGAN A'CHAISE
Knockandhu
Glenlivet Forest
THE BUCK
Clova
SCOTTISH SCULPTURE WORKSHOP
Lumsden
Coldwells Croft
Whitehaugh Forest
Clashnoir
Braes of Glenlivet
Chapeltown
HILL OF THREE STONES
CORREEN HILLS
Muckletown
Bridge of Brown
Fodderletter
LADDER HILLS
Aber
Tullynessle
Badenyon
Mossat
LORD ARTHUR'S CAIRN
TOMINTOUL MUSEUM
Tomintoul
TOMINTOUL
Glenbuchat Lodge
CARN MOR
Water of Buchat
Rinmore
Kildrummy
Don
Bridge of Alford
Montgarrie
Delnabo
CARN MEADHONACH
GLENLIVET ESTATE VISITOR CENTRE
Conglass Water
Water of Nochty
Belnacraig
KILDRUMMY CASTLE & GARDEN
Milltown of Kildrummy
Auchintoul
ALFORD VALLEY RAILWAY
GRAMPIAN TRANSPORT MUSEUM
Alford
HERITAGE CENTRE
Dorback Lodge
Dorback Burn
Water of Ailnack
Blairnamarrow
Kirkton of Glenbuchat
Asloun
LECHT SKI CENTRE
THE SOCACH
Bellabeg
Forbestown
Strathdon
Glenkindie
Towie
Milltown of Towie
Sinnahard
Hillockhead
Ley
Little Lynturk
CAIRNGORMS
Glen Ernan
Ernan Water
Inverernan Ho.
Candacraig Ho.
Heugh-head
Boultenstone
Milton of Cushnie
Muir of Fowlis
Bridgend
Tillyfour
CARN EALASAID
Tornashean Forest
Hillockhead
Leochel-Cushnie
CRAIGIEVAR CASTLE
Kintocher
NATIONAL
Allt Tuileach
Colnabaichin
Cock Bridge
Delnadamph
BIG GARVOUN
Corgarff
CORGARFF CASTLE
Tornahaish
CRAIG OF BUNZEACH
Deskry Water
Easter Davoch
BENAQUHALLIE
Migvie
Douneside
Craskins
CULSH SOUTERRAIN
Findrack Ho.
Lumphanan
GLEN AVON
PARK
Coynach
THE BRUACH
Forest of Glenavon
Loch Builg
BROWN COW HILL
MORVEN
Logie Coldstone
Tarland
CROMAR
PEEL RING OF LUMPHANAN
Milton of Auchinhove
Milton of Logie
Glendavan Ho.
TOMNAVERIE STONE CIRCLE
Coull
Ordie
Auchlossan
Glen Fenzie
Gairnshiel Lodge
BEN AVON
0 1 2 3 4 5 6 miles
0 1 2 3 4 5 6 7 8 9 10km
87
82
82

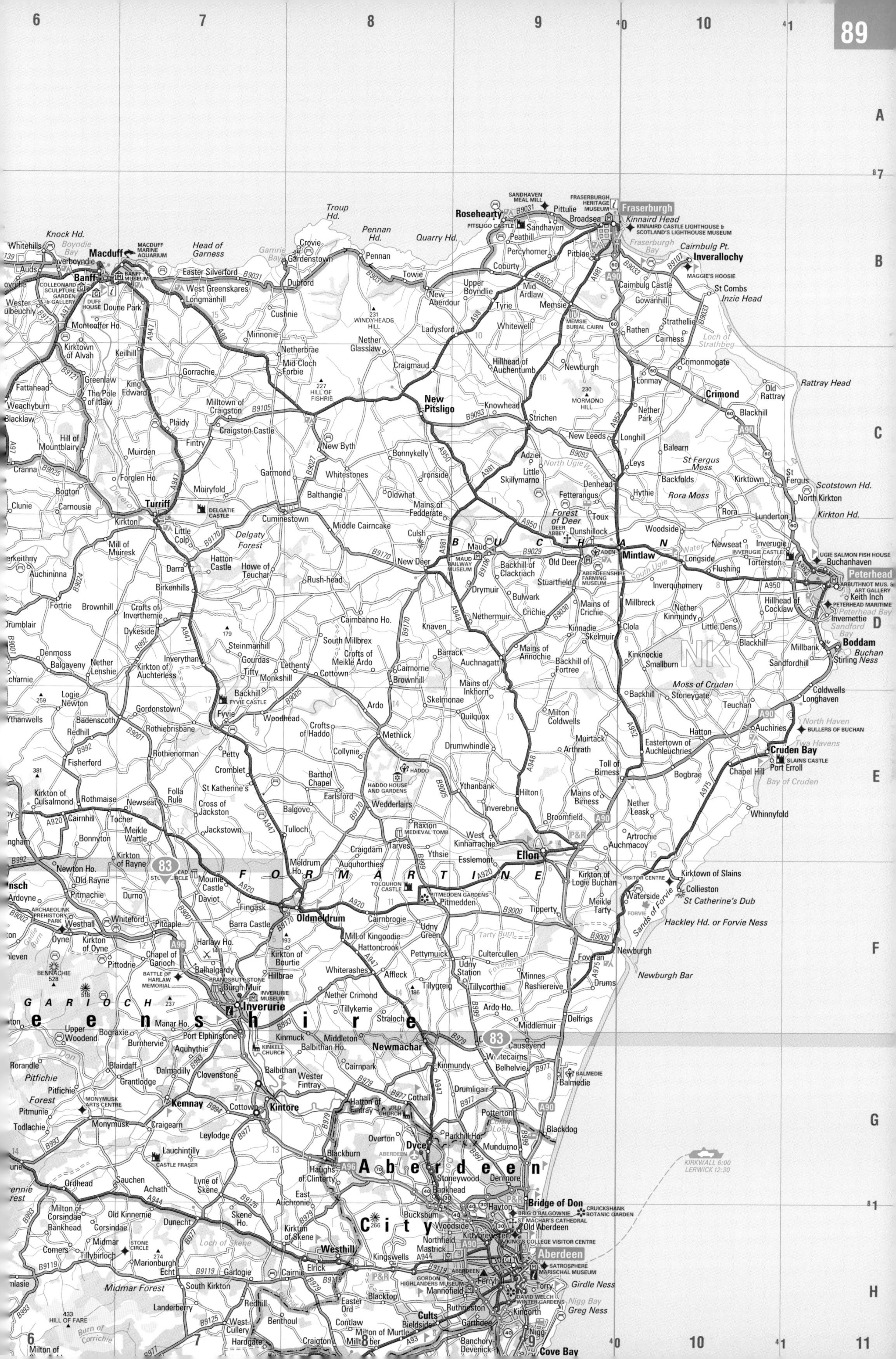
6
7
8
9
10
A
B
C
D
E
F
G
H
11
Troup Hd.
Pennan Hd.
Quarry Hd.
Knock Hd.
Head of Garness
Gamrie Bay
Boyndie Bay
Whitehills
Macduff
MACDUFF MARINE AQUARIUM
Inverboyndie
Banff
BANFF MUSEUM
DUFF HOUSE
COLLEONARD SCULPTURE GARDEN & GALLERY
Doune Park
Montcoffer Ho.
Kirktown of Alvah
Crovie
Gardenstown
Pennan
Towie
Easter Silverford
West Greenskares
Longmanhill
Dubford
Cushnie
Minnonie
Netherbrae
Mid Cloch Forbie
231 WINDYHEADS HILL
227 HILL OF FISHRIE
Nether Glasslaw
Craigmaud
New Aberdour
Upper Boyndlie
Ladysford
Rosehearty
SANDHAVEN MEAL MILL
PITSLIGO CASTLE
Sandhaven
Pittulie
Peathill
Percyhorner
Coburty
Mid Ardlaw
Tyrie
Whitewell
Memsie
MEMSIE BURIAL CAIRN
FRASERBURGH HERITAGE MUSEUM
Fraserburgh
Broadsea
Kinnaird Head
KINNAIRD CASTLE LIGHTHOUSE & SCOTLAND'S LIGHTHOUSE MUSEUM
Fraserburgh Bay
Pitblae
Cairnbulg Pt.
Inverallochy
MAGGIE'S HOOSIE
Cairnbulg Castle
Gowanhill
St Combs
Inzie Head
Rathen
Strathellie
Cairness
Loch of Strathbeg
Crimonmogate
Lonmay
Crimond
Rattray Head
Old Rattray
Blackhill
Newburgh
230 MORMOND HILL
Hillhead of Auchentumb
Knowhead
Strichen
New Pitsligo
Nether Park
New Leeds
Longhill
Balearn
St Fergus Moss
Leys
Backfolds
Rora Moss
Kirktown
St Fergus
Scotstown Hd.
North Kirkton
Kirkton Hd.
Rora
Lunderton
Fattahead
Greenlaw
The Pole of Itlaw
King Edward
Weachyburn
Blacklaw
Gorrachie
Milltown of Craigston
Plaidy
Craigston Castle
Fintry
Hill of Mountblairy
Muirden
Forglen Ho.
Cranna
Bogton
Clunie
Carnousie
Turriff
Kirkton
Muiryfold
DELGATIE CASTLE
Little Colp
Delgaty Forest
Garmond
New Byth
Whitestones
Balthangie
Bonnykelly
Ironside
Oldwhat
Mains of Fedderate
Cuminestown
Middle Cairncake
Culsh
Adziel
Little Skillymarno
North Ugie Water
Denhead
Fetterangus
Hythie
Forest of Deer
Toux
DEER ABBEY
Dunshillock
Woodside
Newseat
Inverugie
INVERUGIE CASTLE
UGIE SALMON FISH HOUSE
Buchanhaven
Peterhead
ARBUTHNOT MUS. & ART GALLERY
Keith Inch
PETERHEAD MARITIME
Peterhead Bay
Invernettie
B U C H A N
Maud
MAUD RAILWAY MUSEUM
New Deer
Backhill of Clackriach
Old Deer
ADEN
ABERDEENSHIRE FARMING MUSEUM
Mintlaw
Longside
Torterston
Flushing
South Ugie Water
Stuartfield
Inverquhomery
Mill of Muiresk
Hatton Castle
Howe of Teuchar
Rush-head
Darra
Auchininna
Birkenhills
Fortrie
Brownhill
Crofts of Inverthernie
Drymuir
Bulwark
Crichie
Mains of Crichie
Millbreck
Nether Kinmundy
Hillhead of Cocklaw
Drumblair
Dykeside
Cairnbanno Ho.
Knaven
Nethermuir
Kinnadie
Skelmuir
Clola
Little Dens
Sandford Bay
Boddam
Buchan Ness
Stirling
Millbank
Blackhill
Denmoss
Balgaveny
Nether Lenshie
Inverythan
Kirkton of Auchterless
Steinmanhill
Gourdas
Tifty
Monkshill
South Millbrex
Crofts of Meikle Ardo
Lethenty
Cottown
Cairnorie
Brownhill
Barrack
Auchnagatt
Mains of Annochie
Backhill of Fortree
Kinknockie
Smallburn
NK
Sandfordhill
Moss of Cruden
Coldwells
Longhaven
Logie Newton
Backhill
FYVIE CASTLE
Fyvie
Gordonstown
Ythanwells
Badenscoth
Redhill
Rothiebrisbane
Woodhead
Crofts of Haddo
Ardo
Mains of Inkhorn
Skelmonae
Quilquox
Milton of Coldwells
Backhill
Stoneygate
Teuchan
North Haven
BULLERS OF BUCHAN
Auchiries
Two Havens
Hatton
Muirtack
Arthrath
Eastertown of Auchleuchries
Cruden Bay
SLAINS CASTLE
Port Erroll
Bay of Cruden
Chapel Hill
Bogbrae
Fisherford
Rothienorman
Petty
Cromblet
Methlick
Collynie
Drumwhindle
HADDO
HADDO HOUSE AND GARDENS
Barthol Chapel
Earlsford
Ythanbank
Toll of Birness
Mains of Birness
Hilton
Kirkton of Culsalmond
Rothmaise
Newseat
Folla Rule
St Katherine's
Cross of Jackston
Jackstown
Balgove
Tulloch
Wedderlairs
Inverebrie
Broomfield
Nether Leask
Whinnyfold
Artrochie
Auchmacoy
Cairnhill
Tocher
Meikle Wartle
Bonnyton
Kirkton of Rayne
Raxton
MEDIEVAL TOMB
Tarves
Craigdam
Auquhorthies
Ythsie
West Kinharrachie
Esslemont
Ellon
Newton Ho.
Old Rayne
STONE CIRCLE
Mounie Castle
Meldrum Ho.
F O R M A R T I N E
Kirkton of Logie Buchan
VISITOR CENTRE
Kirktown of Slains
Collieston
St Catherine's Dub
Insch
Pitmachie
Durno
Daviot
TOLQUHON CASTLE
PITMEDDEN GARDENS
Pitmedden
Waterside
Sands of Forvie
FORVIE
Meikle Tarty
Ardoyne
ARCHAEOLINK PREHISTORY PARK
Westhall
Whiteford
Pitcaple
Fingask
Oldmeldrum
Barra Castle
Cairnbrogie
Udny Green
Tipperty
Hackley Hd. or Forvie Ness
Oyne
Kirkton of Oyne
Harlaw Ho.
Mill of Kingoodie
Hattoncrook
Kirkton of Bourtie
Tarty Burn
Culterculen
Pettymuick
Udny Station
Foveran
Newburgh
Foveran Burn
Newburgh Bar
Pittodrie
BENNACHIE 528
Chapel of Garioch
BATTLE OF HARLAW MEMORIAL
Balhalgardy
BRANDSBUTT STONE
Burgh Muir
Hillbrae
Whiterashes
Affleck
Tillygreig
Tillycorthie
Minnes
Rashiereive
Drums
G A R I O C H
INVERURIE MUSEUM
Inverurie
Nether Crimond
Tillykerrie
Straloch
Ardo Ho.
Middlemuir
Delfrigs
e e n s h i r e
Upper Woodend
Bograxie
Manar Ho.
Port Elphinstone
Burnhervie
Aquhythie
KINKELL CHURCH
Kinmuck
Balbithan Ho.
Middleton
Newmachar
Whitecairns
Causeyend
Belhelvie
BALMEDIE
Balmedie
Rorandle
Pitfichie
Blairdaff
Dalmadilly
Clovenstone
Balbithan
Wester Fintray
Cairnpark
Kinmundy
Forest
Pitmunie
Grantlodge
Kemnay
MONYMUSK ARTS CENTRE
Kintore
Cottown
Hatton of Fintray
Cothall
OLD CHURCH
Drumligair
Potterton
Todlachie
Monymusk
Craigearn
Leylodge
Overton
Dyce
Parkhill Ho.
Corby Loch
Mundurno
Blackdog
Lauchintilly
CASTLE FRASER
Blackburn
Haughs of Clinterty
ABERDEEN
Aberdeen
Stoneywood
Denmore
KIRKWALL 6:00
LERWICK 12:30
Ordhead
Sauchen
Lyne of Skene
Achath
Auchronie
East Auchronie
Bankhead
Bridge of Don
CRUICKSHANK BOTANIC GARDEN
BRIG O'BALGOWNIE
ST MACHAR'S CATHEDRAL
Old Aberdeen
Hayton
Milton of Corsindae
Old Kinnernie
Skene Ho.
Dunecht
Corsindae
Bankhead
266
City
Bucksburn
Woodside
Kittybrewster
KING'S COLLEGE VISITOR CENTRE
Midmar
STONE CIRCLE
274
Loch of Skene
Kirkton of Skene
Northfield
Mastrick
Aberdeen
Comers
Tillybirloch
Marionburgh
Echt
Westhill
Kingswells
SATROSPHERE
MARISCHAL MUSEUM
Garlogie
Cairnie
Elrick
GORDON HIGHLANDERS MUSEUM
Ferryhill
Torry
Girdle Ness
Midmar Forest
South Kirkton
Blacktop
Mannofield
DAVID WELCH WINTER GARDENS
Nigg Bay
Greg Ness
Landerberry
Redhill
Easter Ord
Ruthrieston
Kincorth
433 HILL OF FARE
Benthoul
West Cullery
Cults
Bieldside
Garthdee
Burn of Corrichie
Hardgate
Craigton
Contlaw
Milltimber
Milton of Murtle
Banchory-Devenick
Nigg
Cove Bay
Milton of
83

90
St. Kilda
NA
NF
ST KILDA
Boreray
Soay
St Kilda or Hirta (Hiort)
CONACHAIR
MULLACH BI
Loch a' Ghlinne
Bagh a Bhaile
Dun
Na h-Eileanan Flannach
Western Isles
EILEAN SIAR
An Galan Uigeach
AN CAOLAS
Harsgeir
Floday
Campay
Little Bernera
Pabay Mor
Vacsay
Great Bernera
Breacleit
Tobson
Bhaltos
Aird Uig
Cliobh
Miabhig
Timsgearraidh
Cradhlastadh
Uigen
Riof
Vuia Mor
Tacleit
Circebost
Barraglom
Tobhtarol
Crulabhig
Keava
Eilean Kearstay
Calanais
CALLANISH STANDING STONES
Linsiadar
Gearraidh na h-Aibhne
Breascleit
Tolastadh a Chaolais
Carlabhagh
Dun Charlabhaigh
DUN CARLOWAY BROCH
Borghastan
Na Gearrannan
GEARRANNAN BLACKHOUSE VILLAGE
Dail Beag
Dail Mor
Siabost bho Dheas
SHAWBOST NORSE MILL
Siabost bho Thuath
Bàgh Dhail Beag
Loch Chàrlabhaigh
IRON AGE HOUSE
Crothair
Ard More Mangersta
Càrnais
Mangurstadh
Eadar Dha Fhadhail
SUAINAVAL
Cairisiadar
Geisiadar
Floday
Vuia Beag
Loch Ròg
Aird Fenish
Aird Brenish
Islibhig
Breanais
MEALISVAL
Loch Suainabhal
Einacleite
Giosla
Loch Grunabhat
Loch Chaolartan
Loch Fuaroil
BEINN MHEADHONACH
Mealasta Island
Caolas an Eilein
Loch Morsgail
Loch Cro Criosdaig
Loch Corrigerod
Loch Tungabhat
Loch Smuaisabhat
Loch Langabhat
Morsgail Forest
Loch Reasort
Kearstay
Scarp
Bràighe Mòr
Loch Tamanabhaigh
Loch Tealasabhaigh
Loch Crabhadail
Loch a'Ghlinne
SOUTH LEWIS, HARRIS AND NORTH UIST
Huisinis
Caolas an Scarp
Gaisgeir
Hushinish Pt.
Bàgh Huisinis
TIRGA MOR
ULLAVAL
STULAVAL
UISGNAVAL MORE
CLISHAM
Forest of Harris
Abhainn Suidhe
Gobhaig
Horsanish
Arda Mòra
CEANN A TUATH NA HEARADH
Taransay Glorigs
Soay Beag
Soay Mòr
Cliasmol
Miabhag
Bun Abhainn Eadarra
OLD WHALING STATION
LOCH A SIAR
Camus an t-suithean
Tarasaigh (Taransay)
Paible
Isay
Aird Asaig
Aird a' Mhulaidh
Aline Lodge
Seaforth I.
Loch Shiphoirt
Maraig
Reinigeadal
RHENIGIDALE
Loch Trollamarig
Lochan Lacasdail
Ceann Tarabhaigh
Aird an Troim
Loch Strandabhat
BEN LUSKENTYRE
Losgaintir
LUSKENTYRE BEACH
Caolas Tharasaigh
Rubha Sgeirigin
Seilebost
South Harris Forest
Tairbeart (Tarbert)
Urgha
Carragraich
Caolas Scalpaigh
Carnach
Sgeotasaigh
Scalpay
Rudha Cr
Loch Ceann Dibig
Miabhag
NA HEARADH (HARRIS)
Toe Head
Coppay
CHAIPAVAL
Borve Lodge
Buirgh
Sgarasta Mhor
Aird Mhighe
Drinisiadar
Kennacley
Plocropol Pt.
Plocropol
Greosabhagh
Leac a Li
Liceasto
Scadabhagh
Rubha Bhocaig
Geocrab
Cluthar
Caolas Stocinis
Stockinish I.
Loch Langabhat
Beacrabhaic
BLEAVAL
Loch Greosabhagh
Rubha'an Teampuill
Shillay
Little Shillay
Sound of Shillay
Taobh Tuath
SEALLAM!
Fleoideabhagh
Manais
Loch Steiseabhat
Aird Mhighe
Loch Fleoideabhagh
Cuidhtinis
Brenish Pt.
Pabaidh (Pabbay)
Quinish
Sound of Spuir
Caolas Phabaidh
Spuir
An t-Ob (Leverburgh)
Fionnsbhagh
ROINEABHAL
Ensay
Carminish Is.
Cairminis
Srannda
Killegray
Boirseam
Lingreabhagh
Loch Fionnsbhagh
Lingarabay I.
ST CLEMENT'S CHURCH
Roghadal
Vallay
Renish Pt.
Langay
Eilean Bhearnaraigh (Berneray)
Ruisigearraidh
BERNERAY
Borgh
Baile
Boreray
CAOLAS NA HEARADH
Caolas a' Mhòrain
Haskeir I.
Haskeir Eagach
Aird a'Mhòrain
Caolas Bhearnaraigh
Torogay
Groay
Gilsay
Lingay
Scaravay
84
Scale : 1:332 000
(approx 5 miles to 1 inch)
Veilish Pt.
Vallay
Griminish Pt.
Lingay
Oronsay
Port nan Long
Baile Mhic Phail
Sursay
Tahay
Opsay
Scolpaig
Vallay Strand
Solas
Greinetobht
Trumaisgearraidh
Hermetray
A859
A858
B8011
B887
0 1 2 3 4 5 6 miles
0 1 2 3 4 5 6 7 8 9 10 km

8
9
10
11
12
13
A
B
C
D
E
F
G
H
J
RUBHA ROBHANAIS
(BUTT OF LEWIS)
CHURCH OF ST MOULAG
Eòropaidh
Coig Peighinnean
HARBOUR VIEW GALLERY
Lional
Port Nis
Cross Sands
Suainebost
Tàbost
Cros
Aird Dhail
Dail bho Dheas
Dail bho Thuath
Sgiogarstaigh
Glen Cross
Gabhsann bho Thuath
Gabhsann bho Dheas
Mealabost Bhuirgh
Bail Àrd Bhuirgh
Coig Peighinnean Bhuirgh
Cuiashader
Cellar Head
Loch Langabhat
Rubha Leathann
Siadar
Siadar Iarach
Siadar Uarach
Aird Barvas
TRUSHAL STONE
Baile an Truiseil
Loch Mòr Shanndabhat
BLACK HOUSE MUSEUM
Labost
Barabhas Iarach
Barabhas Uarach
Barabhas
Brù
Àrnol
Bragar
248 MUIRNEAG
Baill' Ur Tholastaidh
Tolastadh bho Thuath
Tolsta Head
Gleann Mòr Barvas
Gleann Bhruthadail
Glen Bragar
Loch Sgeireach Mòr
Gleann Tholàstaidh
Port Bun a' Ghlinne
Griais
Creag Fhraoch
Bac
Col
Col Uarach
Vatisker Pt.
Breibhig
Coll Sands
292 BEINN MHOLACH
BROAD BAY OR LOCH A TUATH
Aird Thunga
Port Nan Giùran
Rubha an t-Siumpain
Cnoc Amhlaigh
Port Mholair
Aird
Tunga
Sròn Ruadh
Grianan
Newmarket
An Gleann Ur
Lacasdal
MUSEUM NAN EILEAN
STORNOWAY
LEWS LODM CENTRE
Stornoway
Sanndabhaig
AN LANNTAIR GALLERY
Mealabost
Aiginis
ST COLUMBA'S
Sulaisiadar
Garrabost
EYE PENINSULA
Seisiadar
Pabail Uarach
Pabail Iarach
An Cnoc
Suardail
Bàgh Phabail
Tolm
Holm I.
A'Chearc
ULLAPOOL 2:40
LEWIS
OLD LEWIS
Loch Urabhal
223
Loch a' Ghainmhich
Acha Mor
Arnish Moor
Griomsidar
Ben Casgro
Liurbost
Raerinish Pt.
Ranais
Crosbost
Soval Lodge
Barkin Is.
Tabhaidh Mhor
Eilean Chaluim Chille
Ceos
Lacasaidh
Cromor
Eilean Orasaidh
Gearraidh Bhaird
Cabharstadh
Eilean Thoraidh
Sildinis
Cearsadair
Tàbost
KERSHADER
Marbhig
Ceann Shiphoirt
Calbost
Taobh a' Ghlinne
Grabhair
Loch Odhairn
Kebock Head
PARK OR PAIRC
Orasaigh
Eisgean
Leumrabhagh
Loch Shell or Loch Sealg
Srianach
Eilean Iubhard
470 CRIONAIG
Mol Truisg
Gob Rubh'Uisenis
Rubha Bhrollum
Rubha a'Bhaird
CAOLAS NAN EILEAN
Garbh Eilean
Eilean Mhuire
Na h-Eileanan Mòra (Shiant Islands)
Eilean an Tighe
NB
NG
92
Glas-leac Beag
Priest I.
Greenstone Point
Rubha Beag
Opinan
Rubha Mor
Mellon Udrigle
Gruinard I.
Sròn a' Gheodha Dhuibh
Eilean Furadh Mór
Rubha Reidh
Achgarve
Gruinard Bay
Mellon Charles
Laide
Ormiscaig
Sand
First Coast
Second Coast
Loch an Draing
Cove
Tighnafiline
Aultbea
296 AN CUAIDH
Isle of Ewe
86
Drumchork
Little Gruinard
Loch Sguod
Melvaig
Inverasdale
LOCH EWE
Midtown
Aultgrishan
Seana Chamas
Brae
Rubha 'Ard na Bà
Peterburn
Naast
Tournaig
INVEREWE GARDEN
Loch Bad a' Chreamh
Port Erradale
North Erradale
Poolewe
Londubh
FIONN LOCH
Rubha Bàn
Big Sand
85
CARN DEARG
Longa Island
Strath
Smithstown
GAIRLOCH HERITAGE MUSEUM
Gairloch
MEALL AN DOIREAN 420
LOCH GAIRLOCH
Charlestown
791 BEINN AIRIGH CHARR
Port Henderson
Badachro
Fladda-chùain
Eilean Trodday
Rubha Hunish
Rubha na h-Aiseig
DUNTULM CASTLE
Duntulm
Kilmaluag

NB
NG
91
86
CAPE WRATH
Kearvaig
Geodha Ruadh na Fola
Bay of Keisgaig
Loch Keisgaig
Geodha Ruadh
Am Balg
Rubh'an Fhir Léithe
Sandwood Loch
Strath Shinary
Loch na Gainimh
Sheigra
Balchrick
Droman
Oldshore Beg
Oldshoremore
Eilean Roin Mor
Loch Clash
Kinlochbervie
Badcall
Achriesgill
Bagh Loch an Roin
Achlyness
Rhiconich
Loch Dughaill
Ardmore Pt.
Rubha Ruadh
Ardmore
Ceathramh Garbh
Faraid Head
Balnakeil Bay
Balnakeil
Durness
DURNESS VISITOR CENTRE
SMOO CAVE
Eilean Hoan
Inshore
Achiemore
Keoldale
Sangomore
Leirinmore
Sangobeg
Eilean Cluimhrig
Rispond
Kyle of Durness
Loch Airigh na Beinne
Grudie
Sarsgrum
MEALL MEADHONACH
Portnancon
LOCH ERIBOLL
Heilam
Hope
Eilean Choraidh
Eriboll
Polla
Strath Beag
Strath Dionard
Gualin Ho.
FARRMHEALL
BEINN SPIONNAIDH
CRANSTACKIE
GANU MOR
Foinaven
AN LEAN-CHARN
BEN HOPE
Loch Crocach
NORTH-WEST SUTHERLAND
Loch Dionard
Handa Island
Fanagmore
Tarbet
Foindle
Loch Laxford
Laxford Bridge
Loch an Easain Uaine
ARKLE
Scourie Bay
Scourie More
Scourie
Rubh'Aird an t-Sionnaich
Gorm Loch
Lochstack Lodge
Alltnacaillich
Glen Golly
Upper Badcall
Lower Badcall
Badcall Bay
BEN STACK
Strath Stack
BEINN AUSKAIRD
Gobernuisgach Lodge
Eil. a'Bhreitheimh
Rubha a'Mhucard
Meall Mór
Achfary
Lochmore Lodge
REAY FOREST
Loch More
Calbha Mór
Calbha Beag
Eddrachillis Bay
Duartmore Forest
Aultanrynie
Loch Coire na Saidhe Duibhe
Point of Stoer
Cirean Geardail
R. nan Còsan
Eilean Chrona
Oldany Island
Culkein Drumbeg
Kylestrome
Kylesku
Glendhu
Forest
Kinloch
Loch a'Ghorm-choire
BEN HEE
Cluas Deas
Culkein
Clashnessie Bay
Oldany
Drumbeg
Nedd
Loch Glendhu
Gleann Dubh
Unapool
Achnacarnin
Clashmore
Clashnessie
Balchladich
Rienachait
Stoer
Gleann Leireag
Newton
Loch Glencoul
Glen Coul
BEINN LEOID
Loch Merkland
Merkland Lodge
Rubh'a' Mhill Dheirg
Bay of Stoer
Clachtoll
Loch Crocach
Loch Beannach
QUINAG
Lochassynt Lodge
EAS COUL AULIN WATERFALL
Loch an Eircill
Loch Dubh a'Chuail'
Highland
R. Leumair
Achmelvich Bay
Rhicarn
LOCH ASSYNT
BEINN UIDHE
Corrykinloch
Glen Fiag
Fiag Plantation
Achmelvich
Little Assynt
Skiag Bridge
ARDVRECK CASTLE
Gorm Loch Mor
Fionn Loch Mor
Overscaig Hotel
Rubha Rodha
Baddidarach
ASSYNT VISITOR CENTRE
Brackloch
Lochinver
Glencanisp Lodge
Loch Feith an Leòthaid
Inchnadamph
Inchnadamph Forest
Soyea I.
Loch Inver
Kirkaig Pt.
A'Chleit
Badnaban
Strathan
ASSYNT-
MAOVALLY
Loch Kirkaig
Inverkirkaig
Glencanisp Forest
Stronchrubie
BEN MORE ASSYNT
Rubha Coigeach
Rubha na Breige
Eilean Mór
SUILVEN
CANISP
Fionn Loch
Loch na Gainimh
BREABAG
MEALL AN AONAICH
Duchally
Strath an Lòin
ENARD BAY
Falls
COIGACH
Camas Eilean Ghlais
Rubha Mor
Reiff
Rubh'a' Choin
Inverpolly Lodge
Loch Awe
Cam Loch
Benmore Forest
Brae of Achnahaird
Loch Sionascaig
Loch Veyatie
Ledmore
Altandhu
SUMMER ISLES SMOKEHOUSE
Eilean Mullagrach
Aird of Coigach
Inverpolly Forest
CUL MOR
HIGHLAND & RARE BREEDS FARM
Elphin
Altnacealgach Hotel
Loch Ailsh
Benmore Lodge
BEINN SGEIREACH
Isle Ristol
Polbain
Loch Osgaig
STAC POLLAIDH
Drumrunie Forest
Knockan
Glas-leac Mór
Loch Bad a'Ghaill
Loch an Doire Dhuibh
Loch Urigill
KNOCKAN CRAG
Glen Oykel
BEINN AN EOIN
Glencassley Castle
Achiltibuie
HYDROPONICUM GARDENS
Badentarbat Bay
Loch Lurgainn
CUL BEAG
AN STUC
Glen Cassley
Tanera Beg
Polglass
CROMALT HILLS
Summer Isles
Tanera Mór
Horse Sound
ACHININVER
Drumrunie
Loch Craggie
Glas-leac Beag
Horse I.
COIGACH
Loch na Claise Moire
Glenross
Achduart
Culnacraig
BEINN MOR COIGACH
Eilean Dubh
Priest I.
Bottle I.
Carn nan Sgeir
Langwell Lodge
Strathcanaird
Rappach
Strath nan Lon
MEALL AN FHUARAIN
Lubcroy
Oykel Bridge
Strath Oykel
Invercassley
Brae
Doune
Camas Mór
Strath Kanaird
Isle Martin
STORNOWAY 2:40
Allt-Beinn Donuill
Rappach Water
Glen Einig
Greenstone Point
Rubha Beag
Cailleach Hd.
Annat Bay
Ardmair
Rhue
Rhidorroch Forest
Opinan
Static Pt.
Scoraig
Camach
Morefield
Ullapool
ULLAPOOL MUSEUM
Loch Achall
Rhidorroch Ho.
Loch an Daimh
Strath Mulzie
Corriemulzie Lodge
CREAG LOISGTE
BEINN ULBHAIDH
Strath Cuileannach
MEALL DHEIRGIDH
LITTLE LOCH BROOM
Rireavach
BEINN GHOBHLACH
LOCHBROOM MUSEUM
Glen Achall
East Rhidorroch Lodge
Badluarach
Dumamuck
Badcaul
Gruinard House
Badrallach
Allt na h-Airbhe
BEINN EILIDEACH
LECKMELM SHRUBBERY AND ARBORETUM
CARN A' CHOIN DEIRG
Croich
CROICK CHURCH
Scale 1:332 000
(approx 5 miles to 1 inch)
0 1 2 3 4 5 6 miles
0 1 2 3 4 5 6 7 8 9 10km

8
9
10
11
12
13
14
A
B
C
D
E
G
H
J
K
NC
ND
NH
NJ
94
87
Strathy Point
Totegan
Rubha Thormaid
Eilean nan Ron
Ardmore Pt.
Kirtomy Pt.
Farr Pt.
Brawl
Aultiphurst
Baligill
Portskerra
Melvich
Bighouse
Red Pt.
Fresgoe
Sandside Ho.
Isauld
Reay
Dounreay
Buldoo
Achreamie
Crosskirk
Bridge of Forss
Brims Ness
Spear Hd.
Holborn Hd.
Scrabster
Thurso
Thurso East
Clardon Hd.
Clardon
Haimer
Millbank
Newlands of Geise
Geise
Weydale
Westfield
Achvarasdal
Shebster
Lieurary
Buckies
Sordale
Braal Castle
Halkirk
Calder Mains
Broubster
Shurrery
Shurrery Lodge
Brawlbin
Scotscalder Station
Olgrinmore
Harpsdale
Dorrery
Spittal
Westerdale
Strathmore Lodge
Lochmore Cottage
Altnabreac Station
Lochdhu
Dalnawillan Lodge
Glutt Lodge
Strathan
Midfield
West Strathan
Talmine
Skinnet
Midtown
Skerray
Achtoty
Airdtorrisdale
Torrisdale
Skullomie
Coldbackie
Borgie
Rabbit Is.
Farr
Swordly
Kirtomy
Armadale
Lednagullin
Strathy
Bettyhill
Achina
Invernaver
Leckfurin
Skelpick
Achvuoldrach
Tongue
Kirkiboll
Ribigill
Kinloch Lodge
KYLE OF TONGUE
Borgie Forest
Strathy Forest
Bowside Lodge
Golval
Achiemore
Upper Bighouse
Craigtown
Dalhalvaig
Trantlemore
Trantlebeg
STRATH HALLADALE
Forsinain
Forsinard
Forsinard Station
Achagary
Carnachy
Rhifail
Skail
Langdale
Syre
Dalvina Lo.
STRATHNAVER
Loch Loyal Lodge
Inchkinloch
Garvault Hotel
Achentoul Forest
Badanloch Forest
Badanloch Lodge
Kinbrace
Achentoul
Lochside
Knockfin Heights
Naver Forest
Mudale
Altnaharra
Clebrig
Loch Choire Lodge
Loch Choire Forest
Strath Vagastie
Crask Inn
Borrobol Forest
Borrobol Lodge
Altanduin
Kildonan Lodge
STRATH OF KILDONAN
BEN ARMINE FOREST
Ben Armine Lodge
Strath na Seilge
Strath Skinsdale
Craggie
Torrish
Kilphedir
Langwell Forest
Wag
Auultibea
Braemore
Balnabruich
Dunbeath
Knockally
Ramscraigs
Borgue
Newport
Berriedale
Langwell Ho.
Ousdale
Ord Point
Navidale
Helmsdale
West Helmsdale
Marrel
Gartymore
Portgower
Lothmore
Lothbeg
Lothbeg Pt.
Rhian
Shinness
Achnairn
Dalchork
Dalchork Wood
Dalnessie
Achnaluachrach
West Langwell
Strath Brora
Balnacoil
Gordonbush
Dalreavoch
Rhilochan
Colaboll
Sallachy
Saval
Lairg Lodge
Lairg Muir
Lairg
East Langwell
Farlary
Achrimsdale
East Clyne
West Clyne
Clynelish
Dalchalm
Brora
Doll
Backies
Golspie
Muie
Ardachu
Strath Fleet
Rogart
Pittentrail
Rogart Station
Morvich
Torroble
Claonel
Gruids
Achany
Shin Forest
Achinduich
Lairg
Invershin
Inveran
Culrain
Balblair
Craigton
Airdens
Clashcoig
Migdale
Bonar Bridge
Torboll Farm
Little Torboll
Cambusmore Lodge
Culmaily
Kirkton
Cambusavie Farm
Skelbo
Littleferry
Fourpenny
Embo
Badninish
Achvaich
Rearquhar
Poles
Proncy
Embo Street
Gablon
Soyal
Lower
Linsidemore
Ardchu

HOY
Flotta
Burray
SOUTH RONALDSAY
SOUTH WALLS
Swona
PENTLAND FIRTH
95
Island of Stroma
Langaton Point
Nethertown
Uppertown
Muckle Skerry
Pentland Skerries
DUNNET HEAD
DUNCANSBY HEAD
Stacks of Duncansby
John o' Groats
Canisbay
Gills
Mey
Castle of Mey
Dunnet
Dunnet Bay
Brough
Thurso
Scrabster
Holborn Hd.
Clardon Hd.
Brims Ness
Crosskirk
Dounreay
Reay
Isauld
Achvarasdal
Bridge of Forss
Castletown
Halkirk
Georgemas
Mybster
Watten
Wick
Keiss
Keiss Castle
Auckengill
Northlands Viking Centre
Freswick
Skirza Head
Nybster
Sinclair's Bay
Noss Head
Castle Sinclair
Castle Girnigoe
Staxigoe
Papigoe
Broadhaven
Wick Heritage Centre
Old Wick
Castle of Old Wick
South Hd.
Hempriggs House
Thrumster
Sarclet
Sarclet Hd.
Ulbster
Whaligoe
Bruan
Mid Clyth
West Clyth
Lybster
Lybster Art Gallery
Forse
Latheron
Latheronwheel
Clan Gunn Heritage Centre
Laidhay Croft Museum
Dunbeath
Dunbeath Heritage Centre
Dunbeath Castle
Dunbeath Bay
Berriedale
Badbea Clearance Village
Ousdale
Navidale
Helmsdale
Timespan Heritage Centre
Portgower
Lothmore
Lothbeg Pt.
Ord Point
Langwell Forest
Morven
Scaraben
Ben Alisky
Cnoc Loch Mhadaidh
Grey Cairns of Camster
Camster
Hill of Oliclett
Rangag
Achavanich
Stemster Hill
Altnabreac Station
Lochdhu
Dalnawillan Lodge
Glutt Lodge
Strathmore Lodge
Lochmore Cottage
Westerdale
Spittal
Scotscalder Station
Olgrinmore
Shurrery
Shurrery Lodge
Dorrery
Broubster
Loch Watten
Loch of Wester
Mains of Watten
Killimster
Reiss
Winless
Bilbster
Strath
Achairn Burn
Badlipster
Tannach
Newton
Whiterow
Milton
Stirkoke Ho.
H i g h l a n d
NC
ND
93
A9
A99
A836
A882
A895
A897
B870
B874
B876
B855
Scale : 1:332 000
(approx 5 miles to 1 inch)
0 1 2 3 4 5 6 miles
0 1 2 3 4 5 6 7 8 9 10 km

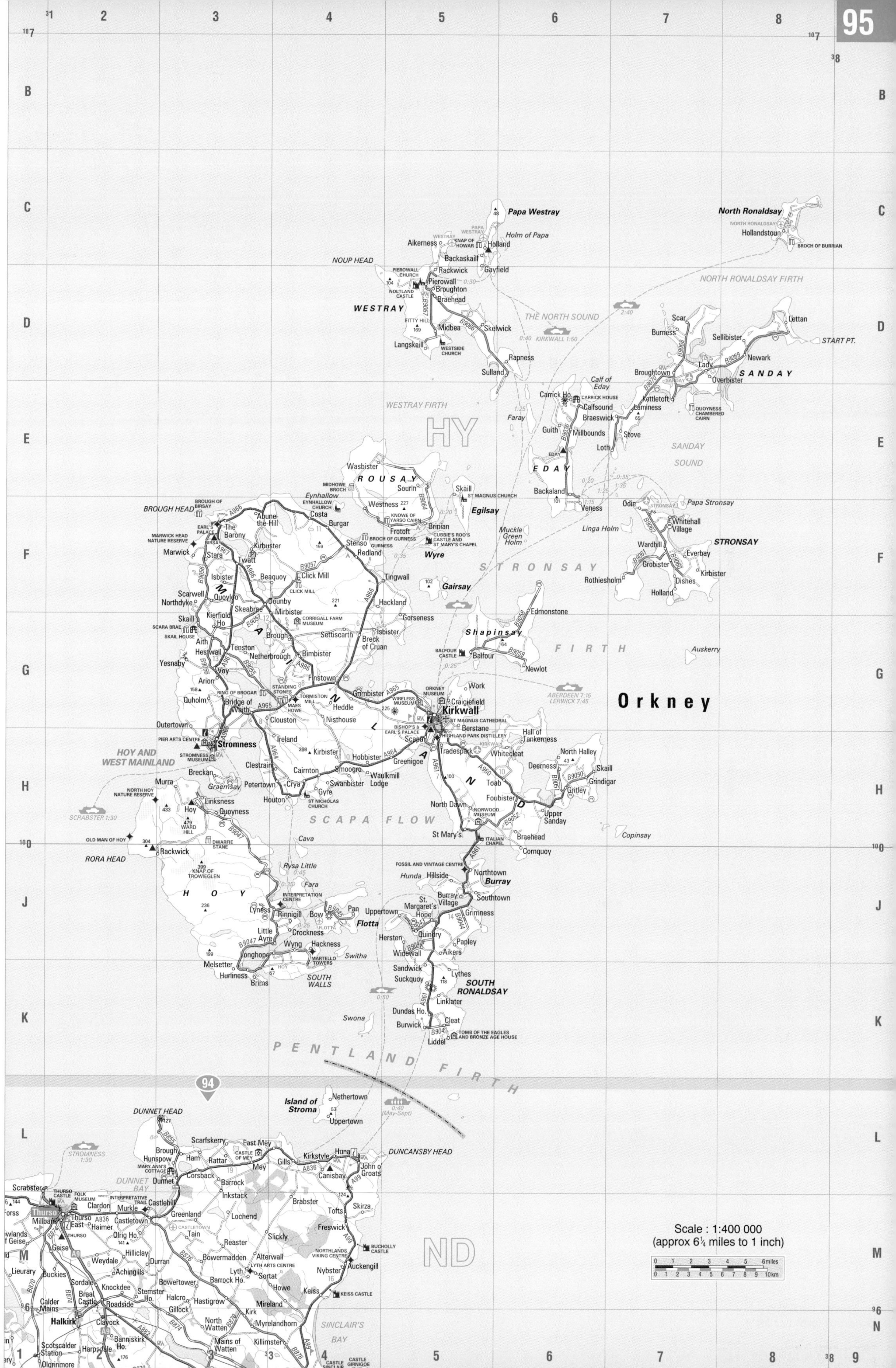
Orkney
Papa Westray
Holm of Papa
North Ronaldsay
Hollandstoun
BROCH OF BURRIAN
NORTH RONALDSAY FIRTH
Aikerness
Holland
Backaskaill
Gayfield
NOUP HEAD
Rackwick
Pierowall
Broughton
Braehead
WESTRAY
Midbea
Skelwick
Langskaill
Rapness
Sulland
THE NORTH SOUND
KIRKWALL 1:50
Scar
Burness
Lettan
Sellibister
START PT.
Newark
Lady
Broughtown
Overbister
SANDAY
Calf of Eday
Carrick Ho.
Calfsound
Kettletoft
Laminess
QUOYNESS CHAMBERED CAIRN
Braeswick
Millbounds
Stove
Guith
Loth
SANDAY SOUND
WESTRAY FIRTH
Faray
HY
EDAY
Backaland
Veness
Odie
Papa Stronsay
Whitehall Village
Linga Holm
STRONSAY
Wardhill
Everbay
Grobister
Kirbister
Rothiesholm
Dishes
Holland
Wasbister
ROUSAY
Sourin
MIDHOWE BROCH
Eynhallow
Westness
Skaill
Egilsay
Costa
Burgar
Brinian
Frotoft
BROUGH HEAD
BROUGH OF BIRSAY
Abune-the-Hill
The Barony
Kirbuster
MARWICK HEAD NATURE RESERVE
Marwick
Stara
Twatt
Stenso
Redland
Wyre
Muckle Green Holm
STRONSAY
Isbister
Click Mill
Beaquoy
Tingwall
Gairsay
Scarwell
Northdyke
Quoyloo
Dounby
Hackland
Edmonstone
Skaill
SCARA BRAE
Kierfiold Ho
Mirbister
CORRIGALL FARM MUSEUM
Gorseness
Aith
Brough
Settiscarth
Isbister
Breck of Cruan
Shapinsay
Balfour
Yesnaby
Hestwall
Tenston
Netherbrough
Bimbister
FIRTH
Auskerry
Voy
Newlot
Arion
Finstown
Work
Quholm
RING OF BRODGAR
STANDING STONES
Grimbister
Bridge of Waith
TORMISTON MILL
MAES HOWE
Heddle
Craigiefield
Kirkwall
ST MAGNUS CATHEDRAL
Outertown
Clouston
Nisthouse
Berstane
Hall of Tankerness
PIER ARTS CENTRE
Stromness
Ireland
Scapa
HIGHLAND PARK DISTILLERY
Tradespark
Whitecleat
North Halley
HOY AND WEST MAINLAND
Kirbister
Hobbister
Greenigoe
Deerness
Skaill
Clestrain
Cairnton
Smoogro
Waulkmill Lodge
Toab
Grindigar
Breckan
Graemsay
Murra
Petertown
Crya
Swanbister
Gyre
Gritley
Foubister
Houton
Linksness
Quoyness
Hoy
North Dawn
Upper Sanday
SCRABSTER 1:30
SCAPA FLOW
NORWOOD MUSEUM
WARD HILL
OLD MAN OF HOY
St Mary's
ITALIAN CHAPEL
Braehead
Copinsay
DWARFIE STANE
Cornquoy
Cava
Rackwick
RORA HEAD
Rysa Little
FOSSIL AND VINTAGE CENTRE
Northtown
KNAP OF TROWIEGLEN
Fara
Hunda
Hillside
Burray
HOY
INTERPRETATION CENTRE
Burray Village
Southtown
Lyness
Rinnigill
Bow
Pan
St. Margaret's Hope
Grimness
Uppertown
Flotta
Little Ayre
Crockness
Herston
Quindry
Wyng
Hackness
Papley
Widewall
Aikers
Longhope
MARTELLO TOWERS
Switha
Melsetter
Sandwick
Lythes
Hurliness
Brims
SOUTH WALLS
Suckquoy
SOUTH RONALDSAY
Dundas Ho.
Linklater
Swona
Burwick
Cleat
Liddel
TOMB OF THE EAGLES AND BRONZE AGE HOUSE
PENTLAND FIRTH
94
Island of Stroma
Nethertown
Uppertown
DUNNET HEAD
(May-Sept)
Scarfskerry
East Mey
Brough
Hunspow
Ham
Rattar
CASTLE OF MEY
Kirkstyle
Huna
DUNCANSBY HEAD
STROMNESS 1:30
MARY ANN'S COTTAGE
Gills
Mey
Canisbay
John o' Groats
Corsback
Dunnet
DUNNET BAY
Barrock
Scrabster
THURSO CASTLE
FOLK MUSEUM
INTERPRETATIVE TRAIL
Inkstack
Brabster
Clardon
Murkle
Castlehill
Skirza
Forss
Thurso
Thurso East
Castletown
Greenland
Lochend
Tofts
Millbank
Haimer
Tain
Freswick
Olrig Ho.
Slickly
Geise
Reaster
Hilliclay
Weydale
Durran
Bowermadden
Alterwall
NORTHLANDS VIKING CENTRE
BUCHOLLY CASTLE
ND
Achingills
Auckengill
Lieurary
Buckies
Lyth
LYTH ARTS CENTRE
Nybster
Sordale
Bowertower
Barrock Ho.
Sortat
Knockdee
Stemster Ho.
Howe
Keiss
KEISS CASTLE
Calder Mains
Braal Castle
Roadside
Halcro
Hastigrow
Mireland
Halkirk
Clayock
Gillock
Kirk
North Watten
Myrelandhorn
SINCLAIR'S BAY
Scotscalder Station
Harpsdale
Bannskirk Ho.
Mains of Watten
Killimster
Olgrinmore
CASTLE SINCLAIR
CASTLE GIRNIGOE
Scale : 1:400 000
(approx 6¼ miles to 1 inch)
6miles
10km

Shetland
HO
HP
HT
HU
Hermaness
Hermaness Visitor Centre
Saxa Vord
The Garths
Norwick
Burrafirth
Valsgarth
Quoys
Haroldswick
Unst Heritage Centre
Unst Boat Haven
Baliasta
Keen of Hamer
Buness
Baltasound
Balta
Unst
Westing
Caldback
Gloup
Cullivoe
Greenbank
Underhoull
Lund
Stonganess
Belmont
Uyeasound
Muness
Muness Castle
Clivocast
Ramnageo
South Garth
Uyea
Gutcher
Linga
The Hall
Sellafirth
North Sandwick
Colvister
Cunnister
Basta
Grimister
Camb
Brough Lodge
Vord Hill
Fetlar
Windhouse
Houbie
Mid Yell
Hascosay
Tresta
Funzie
Aith
Interpretative Centre
Harkland
West Sandwick
Colgrave Sound
Yell
Aywick
Otterswick
Swarister
West Yell
Gossabrough
Setter
Hamnavoe
Ulsta
Burravoe
Houlland
Brough
Old Haa
Copister
Bigga
Uyea
Isbister
North Roe
South-haa
Yell Sound
Housetter
Ronas Hill
North Collafirth
Heylor
Voe
Ollaberry
Hamnavoe
Scarff
Ure
Braehoulland
Eastwick
Esha Ness
Burnside
Urafirth
Tangwick Haa Museum
Tangwick
Hillswick
Bardister
Stenness
North Gluss
Burraland
Brough
Sullom Voe Oil Terminal
Samphrey
Mossbank
Sullom
Graven
Laxobigging
Scatsta
Nibon
Mangaster
Haggrister
Trondavoe
Hamnavoe
Housay
Bruray
Out Skerries
Voxter
St. Magnus Bay
Islesburgh
Brae
Lunna
Collafirth
Busta
Burravoe
Swining
Lunning
Skaw
Whalsay
Roesound
Wethersta
Vidlin
Gardin
Brough
Nisthouse
Isbister
Hillside
Laxo
Marrister
Hanseatic Booth
Little-ayre
Voe
Levaneap
Huxter
Symbister
Clate
Papa Little
Gonfirth
Biggings
Vementry
Dury
Quoys
Papa Stour
Laxfirth
Neap
Garth
Brindister
Melby
Engamoor
Noonsbrough
Braewick
East Burrafirth
Sandness
Clousta
Brettabister
West Burrafirth
Sandness Hill
Unifirth
Aith
Setter
Skellister
Catfirth
Brough
Textile Working Mus
Dale of Walls
Twatt
Houlland
Freester
Eswick
Bixter
Westerfield
Bridge of Walls
Effirth
Stanydale
Heglibister
Mid Walls
Temple
Tresta
Huxter
Girlsta
Gletness
Sembister
Annifirth
Burraland
Browland
West Houlland
Sound
Hellister
Wadbister
Walls
Gruting
Garderhouse
Leeans
Sand
Sandsound
Breiwick
Laxfirth
Vaila
Culswick
Easter Skeld
Lerwick
Gott
Agricultural Mus
White Ness
Veensgarth
Gremista
Heogan
Gunnista
Wester Skeld
Reawick
Fort Charlotte
Westerwick
Silwick
South Whiteness
Holmsgarth
Setter
Lerwick
Shetland Museum
Brough
Up Helly Aa
Isle of Noss
Hildasay
Scalloway
Uppersound
Sound
Noss
Harrier
Foula
Ham
The Sneug
Hametoun
Foula
Port Arthur
Wick
Grindiscol
Cutts
Gulberwick
Kirkabister
Uradale
Cave of the Bard
Hamnavoe
Croft Trail
Wester Quarff
Brindister
Easter Quarff
West Burra
Grunasound
Fladdabister
Papil
Houss
Okraquoy
Aithsetter
Bremirehoull
Gord
Greenmow
South Havra
Royl Field
Mail
Leebotten
Maywick
Hoswick
Stove
Sandwick
Channerwick
Mousa Broch
Ireland
Northpunds
Cumliewick
Bigton
Levenwick
Southpunds
Scousburgh
Noss
Skelberry
Longfield
Boddam
Croft House Museum
Ringasta
Hillwell
Quendale
Quendale Mill
Fitful Head
Exnaboe
Toab
Scatness
Sumburgh
Grutness
Jarlshof
Ness of Burgi
Sumburgh Head
Fetlar
Mainland
Shetland
Foula 2:15
Walls 2:15
Scalloway 3:30
(Summer only)
Foula 3:30
(Summer only)
Aberdeen 12:00
Kirkwall 5:30
Fair Isle 4:30
(Summer only)
Fair Isle 2:40
Fair Isle
HZ
Sumburgh 2:40
Lerwick 4:30
(Summer only)
Fair Isle Lodge & Bird Observatory
Stoneybreck
Fair Isle
George Waterston Museum
Scale : 1:400 000
(approx 6¼ miles to 1 inch)
6 miles
10 km

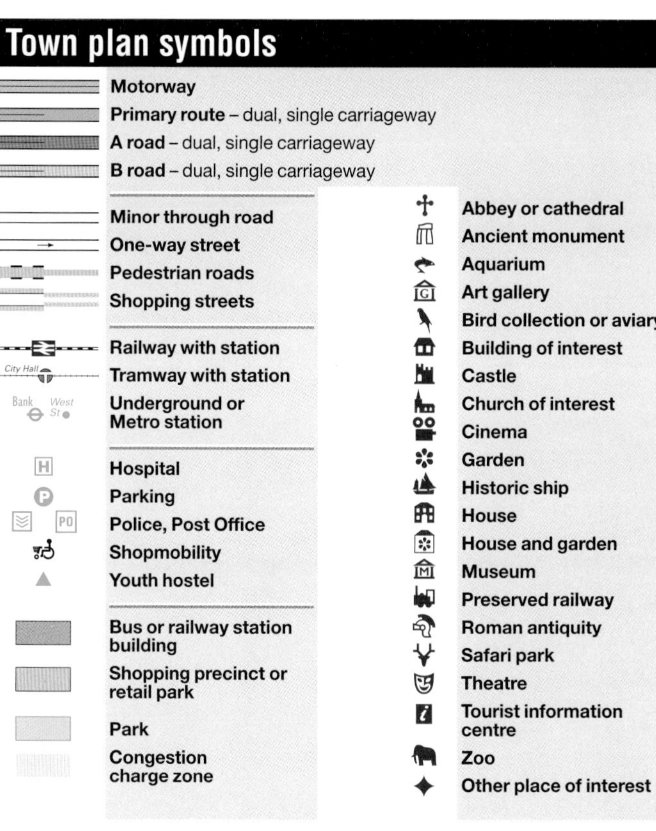

Town plan symbols

Motorway

Primary route – dual, single carriageway

A road – dual, single carriageway

B road – dual, single carriageway

Minor through road

One-way street

Pedestrian roads

Shopping streets

Railway with station

Tramway with station

Underground or Metro station

Hospital

Parking

Police, Post Office

Shopmobility

Youth hostel

Bus or railway station building

Shopping precinct or retail park

Park

Congestion charge zone

✝ Abbey or cathedral

Ancient monument

Aquarium

Art gallery

Bird collection or aviary

Building of interest

Castle

Church of interest

Cinema

Garden

Historic ship

House

House and garden

Museum

Preserved railway

Roman antiquity

Safari park

Theatre

Tourist information centre

Zoo

Other place of interest

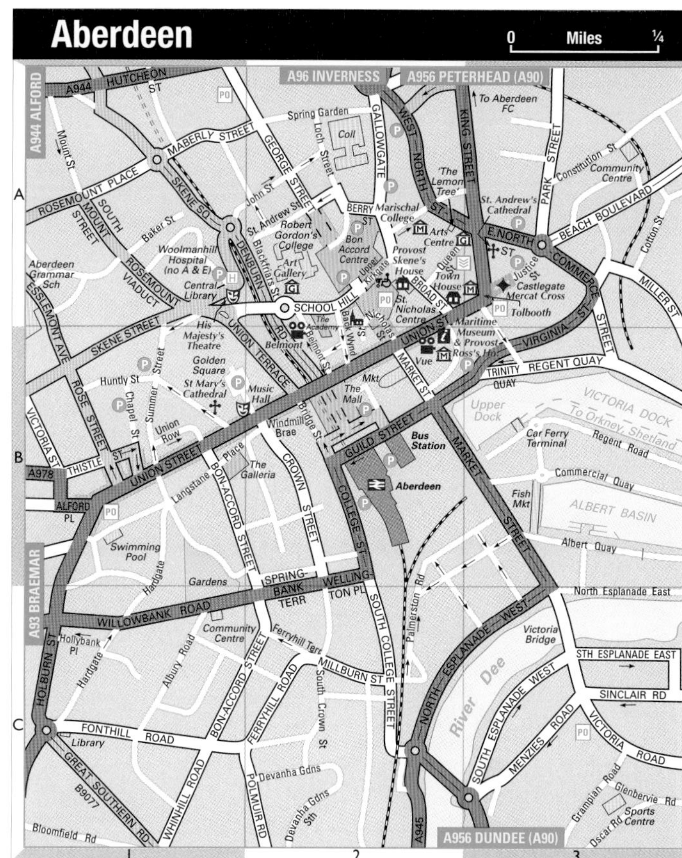

Aberdeen

Bath

Blackpool

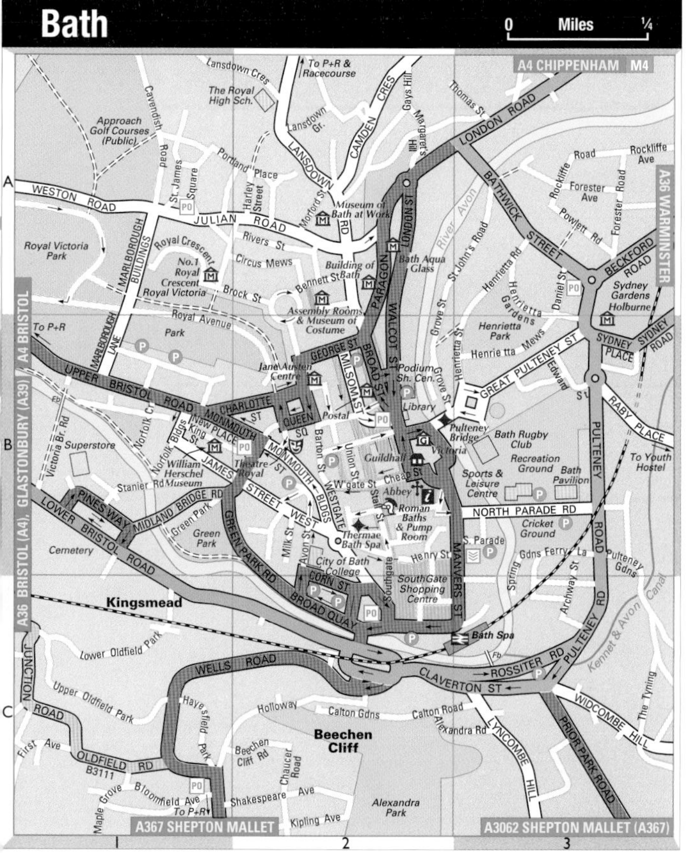

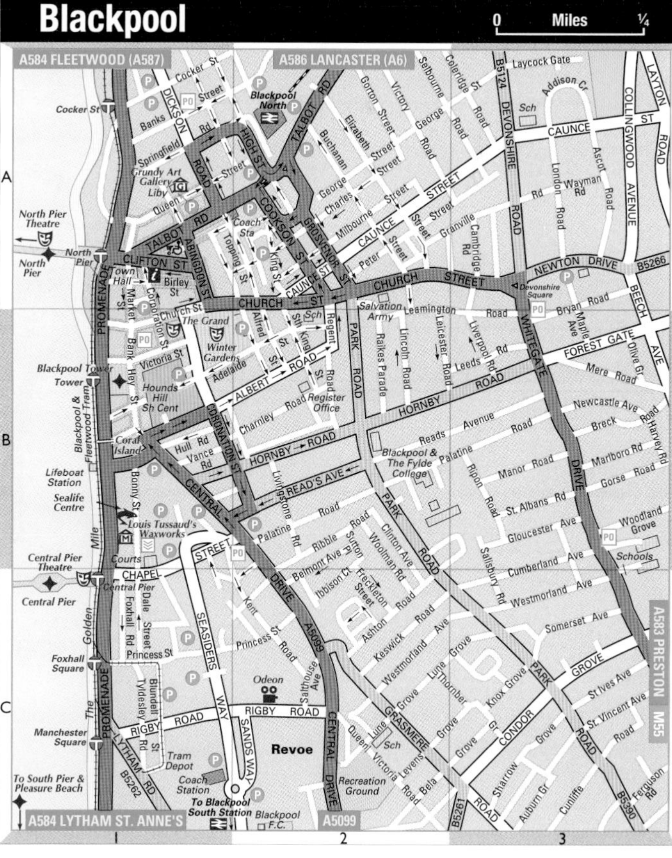

Birmingham

0 Miles ¼

A4040 OUTER RING ROAD
A41 WOLVERHAMPTON M5
A34 WALSALL M6
A38(M) TO M6
A5127 SUTTON COLDFIELD
A47 CASTLE BROMWICH M6
A457 DUDLEY
A456 KIDDERMINSTER M5
A4540 RING ROAD
A38 BROMSGROVE
A441 REDDITCH
A41 STRATFORD-UPON-AVON (A34, A3400) M42
A45 COVENTRY, AIRPORT & NEC M42
GIB HEATH
WINSON GREEN
NEW TOWN
ASTON
BROOKFIELDS
DUDDESTON
LADYWOOD
BORDESLEY
Birmingham City Hospital (A & E)
HM Prison
Edgbaston Reservoir
Jewellery Quarter
Aston University
Snow Hill
Pallasades Centre
New Street
Moor Street
Bullring
Millennium Point
Thinktank (Science & Discovery)
Birmingham City F.C.
National Indoor Arena
The ICC
Symphony Hall
Town Hall
Council Ho.
Coach Station
St. Thomas' Peace Garden
Broadway Plaza
Edgbaston Shopping Centre

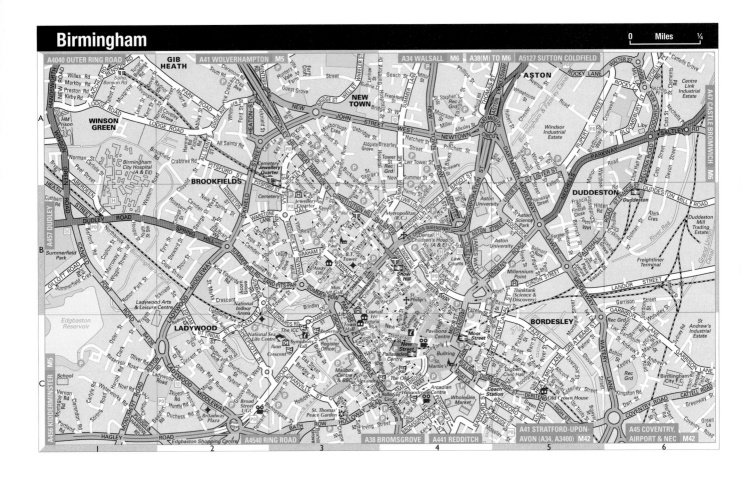

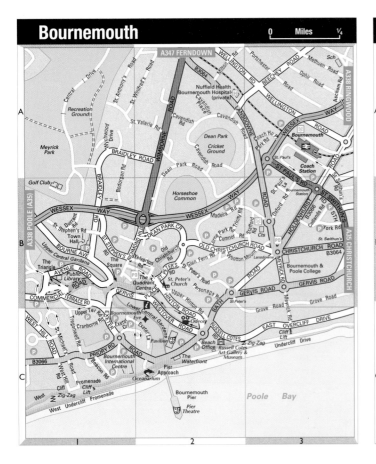

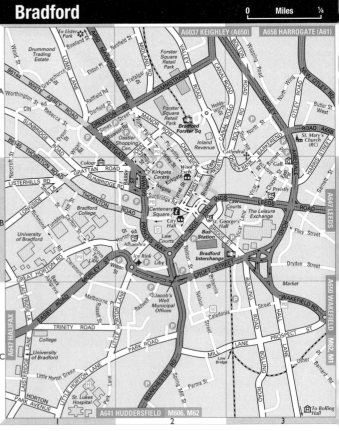

Bristol

0 Miles ¼

A4018 TO M5
A38 TO M5
A4032 TO M32 & M4
A432 MANGOTSFIELD
A420 CHIPPENHAM
A4 AVONMOUTH & M5
A370 WESTON-SUPER-MARE
A38 TAUNTON
A37 SHEPTON MALLET
A4 BATH
CLIFTON
Bristol Temple Meads
Bristol Cathedral
Cabot Tower
Queen Elizabeth Hospital School
University of Bristol
Bristol Royal Infirmary (A & E)
Bristol Royal Children's Hospital (A & E)
Bristol Eye Hosp (A & E)
The Mall
Castle Park
SS Great Britain & The Matthew
Maritime Heritage Centre
Floating Harbour
River Avon (New Cut)
Queen Square
Redcliffe Bridge
St. Mary Redcliffe
Millennium Square
Prince St Bridge
Amphitheatre
Baltic Wharf Leisure Centre & Caravan Park
Spike Island Artspace
The Create Centre
Plimsoll Bridge
Avon Bridge
Bath Bridge
Bedminster Bridge
To Clifton Suspension Bridge
To Camp Bristol Zoo Gardens
A B C
1 2 3 4 5 6

Brighton

0 Miles ¼

Cambridge

0 Miles ¼

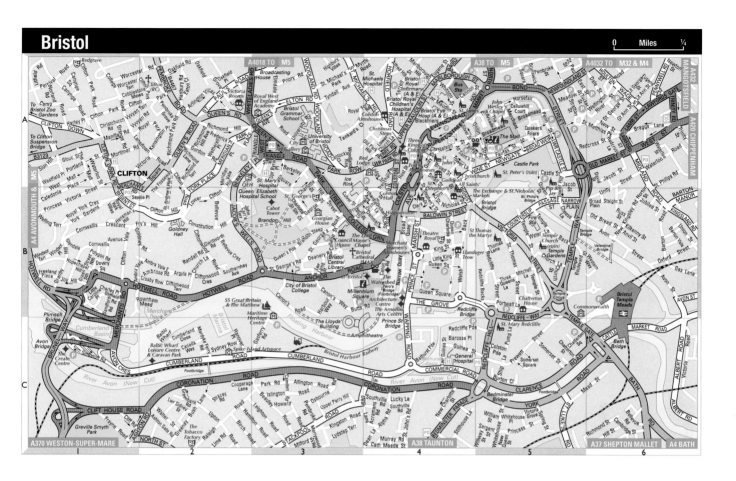

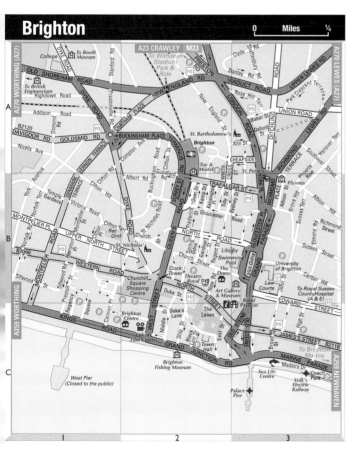

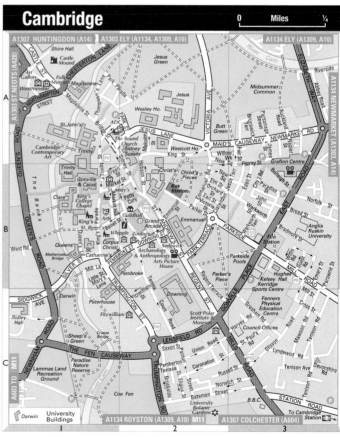

Canterbury

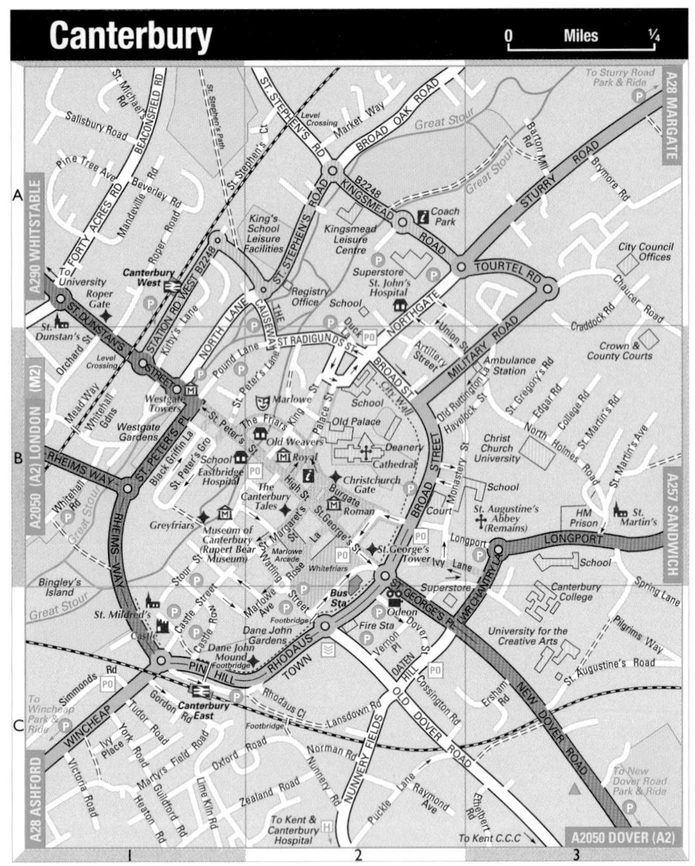

Cardiff / Caerdydd

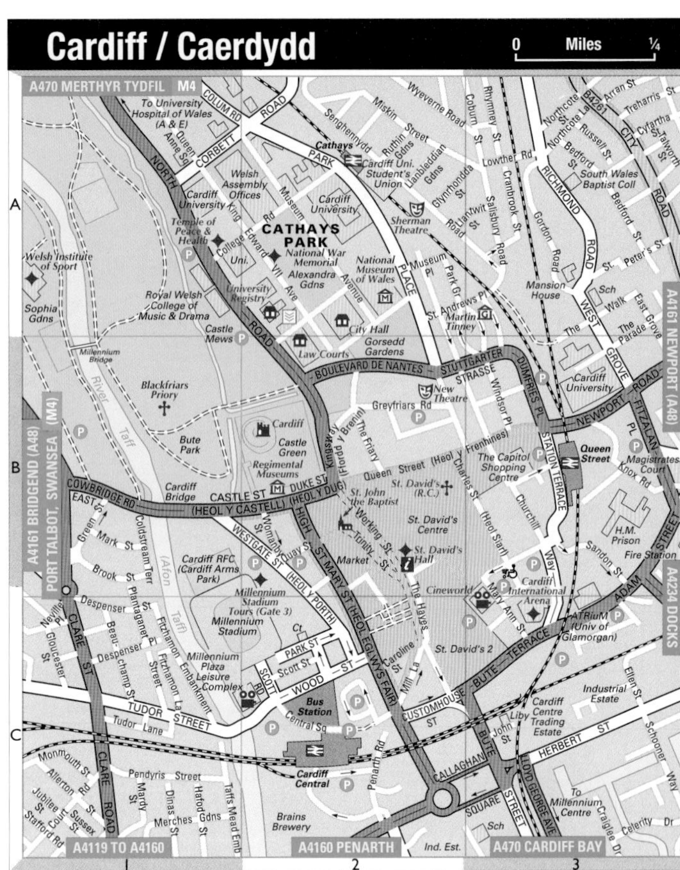

Cheltenham

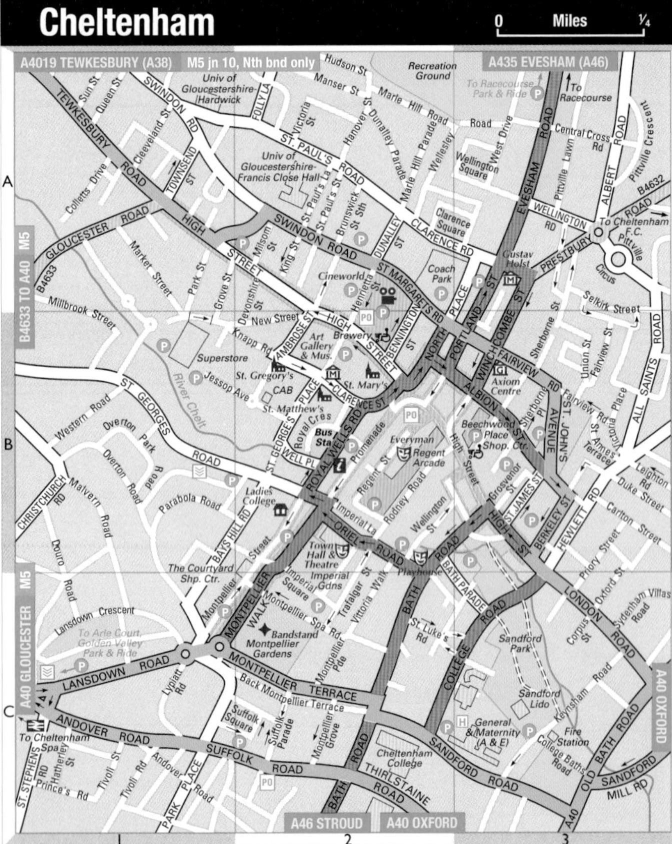

Chester

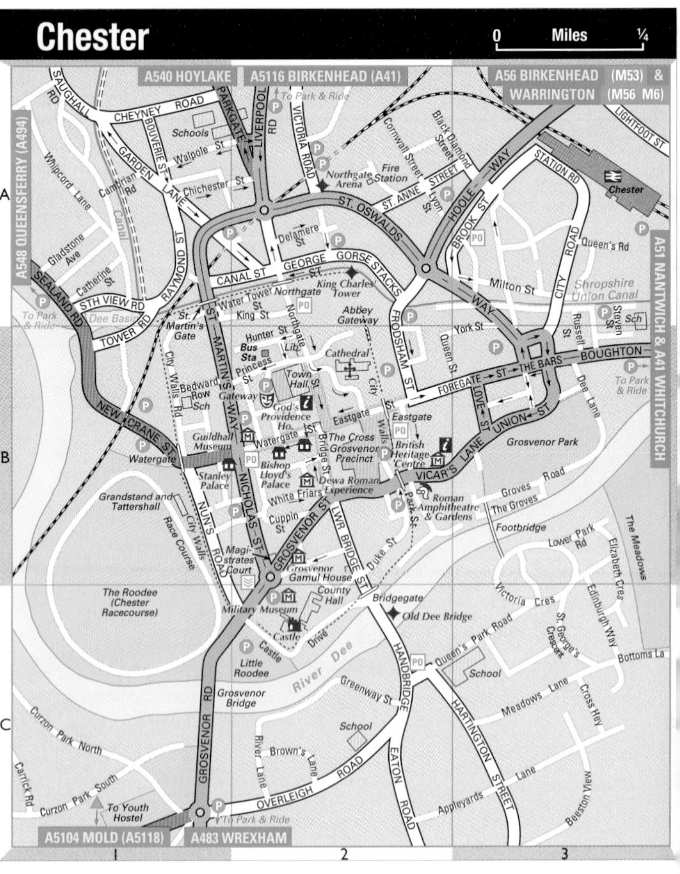

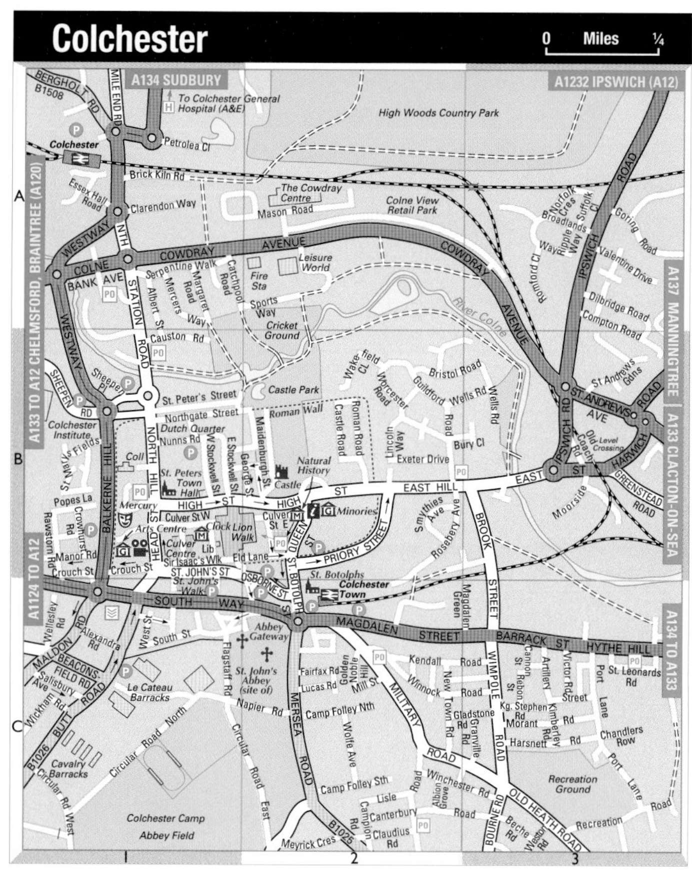

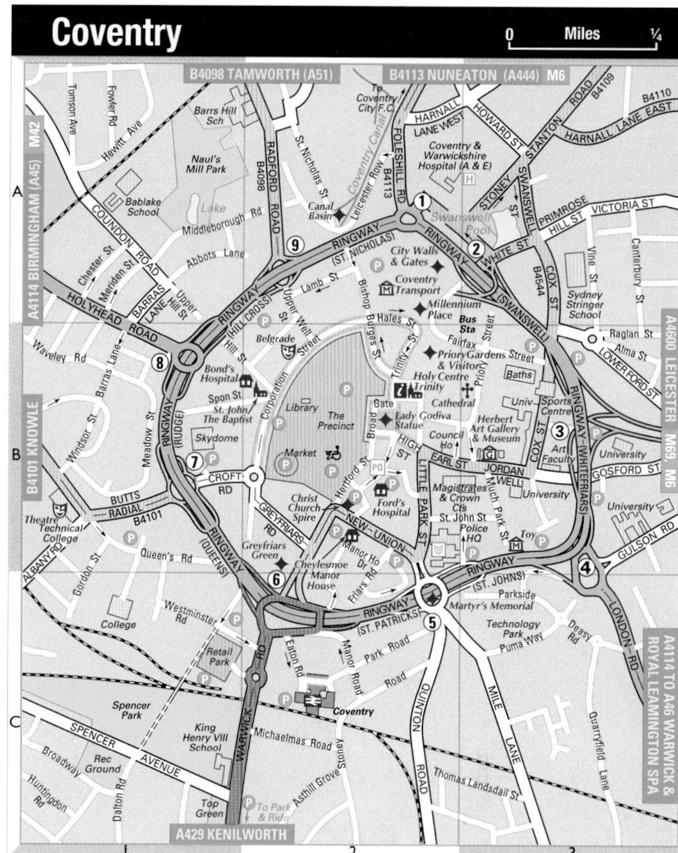

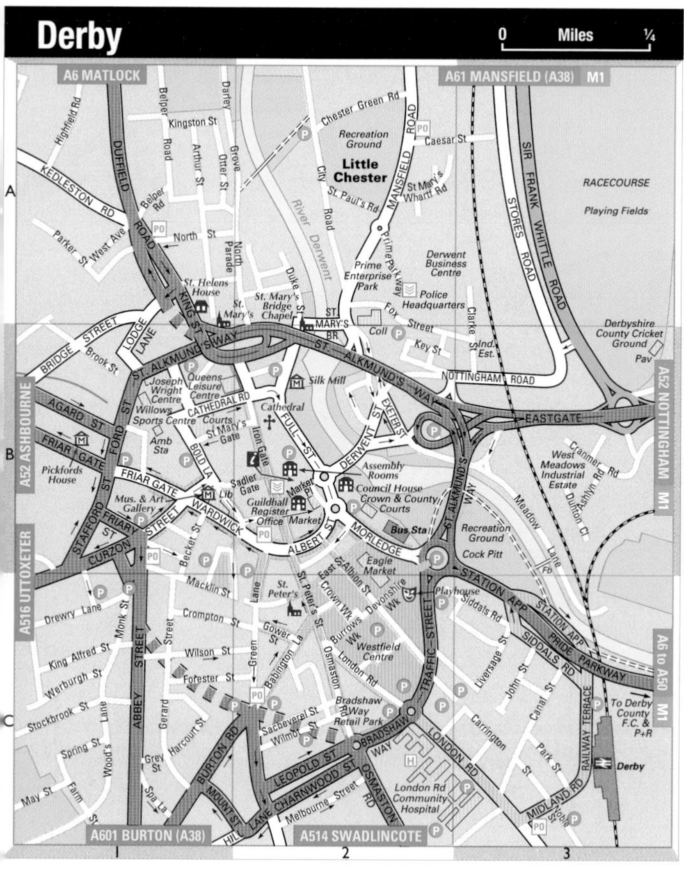

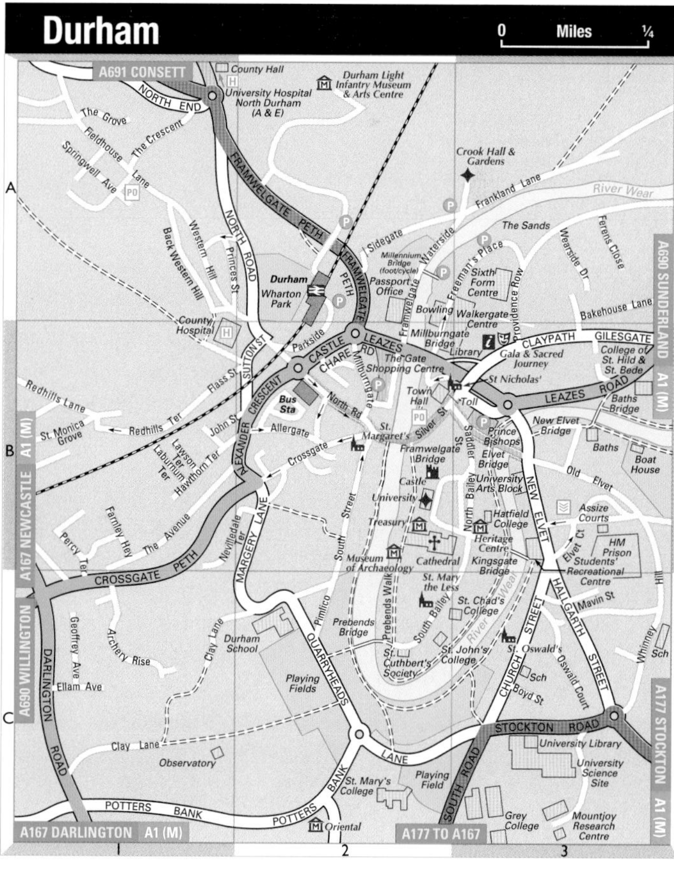

Edinburgh

0 ___ Miles ___ ¼

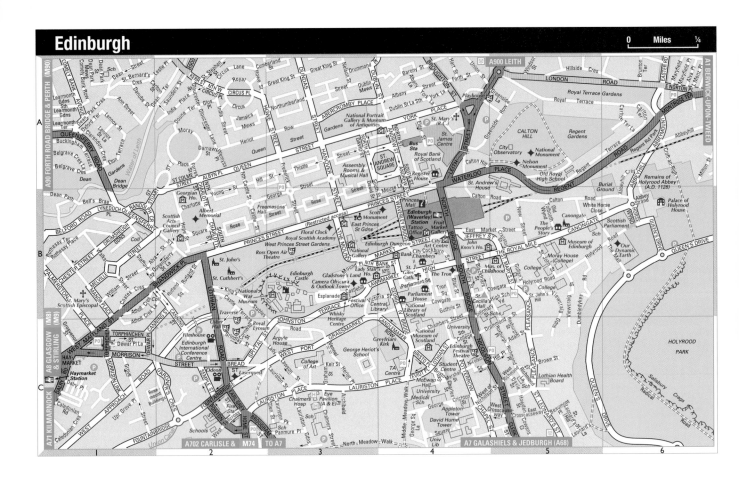

Exeter

0 ___ Miles ___ ¼

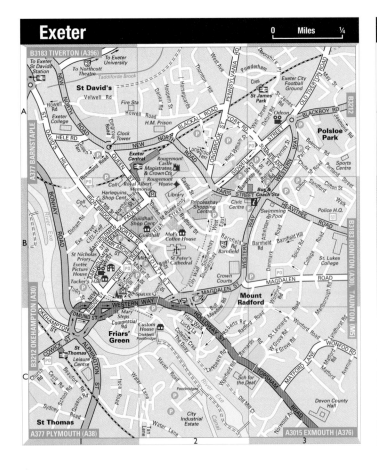

Gloucester

0 ___ Miles ___ ¼

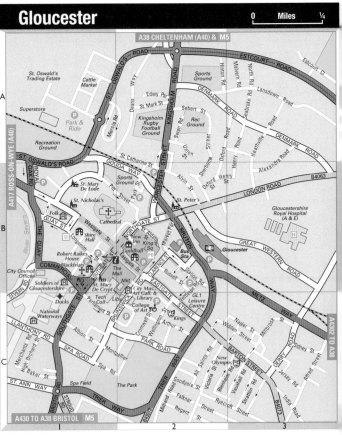

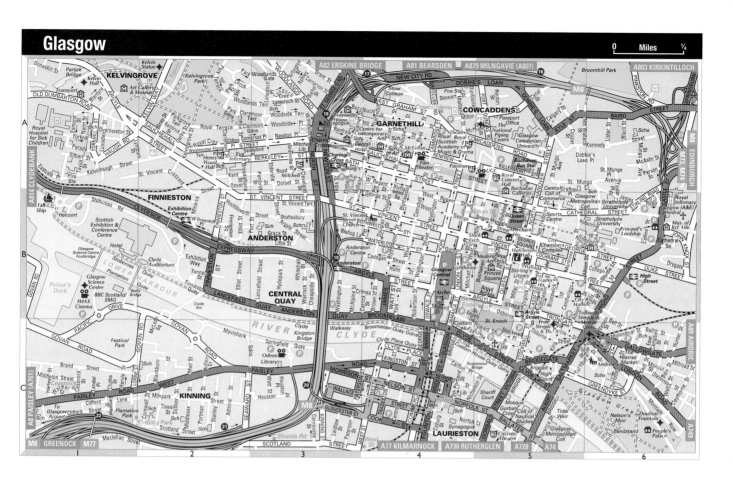

Glasgow

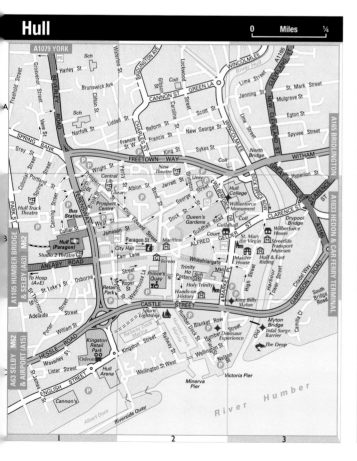

Hull

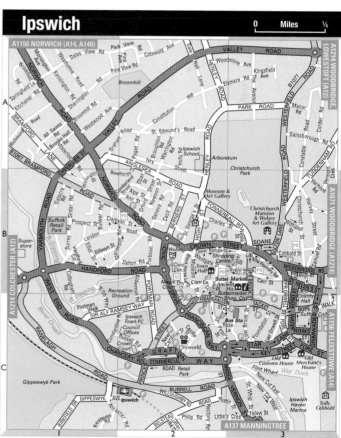

Ipswich

104
REGENT'S PARK
REGENT'S PARK
SOMERS TOWN
Euston
St. Pancras International
King's Cross
British Library
BLOOMSBURY
FITZROVIA
University of London
British Museum
University College
SOHO
MAYFAIR
ST. JAMES'S
GREEN PARK
HYDE PARK
ST. JAMES'S PARK
WESTMINSTER
Victoria
Charing Cross
Houses of Parliament
Westminster Abbey
Buckingham Palace
Buckingham Palace Gardens
Trafalgar Square
Piccadilly Circus
Oxford Circus
Marble Arch
Hyde Park Corner
Wellington Arch
Belgrave Square
Grosvenor Square
Regents College
Queen Mary's Gardens
Open Air Theatre
Madame Tussaud's
Wallace Collection
Royal Academy of Arts
Covent Garden
Royal Opera Ho
National Gall
Westminster Cathedral (RC)
Westminster Bridge
Lambeth Bridge
EUSTON ROAD
MARYLEBONE ROAD
OXFORD STREET
PICCADILLY
REGENT STREET
PARK LANE
WHITEHALL
VICTORIA STREET
STRAND
KINGSWAY
CHARING CROSS ROAD
TOTTENHAM COURT ROAD
SHAFTESBURY AVENUE
Miles
0
1/2

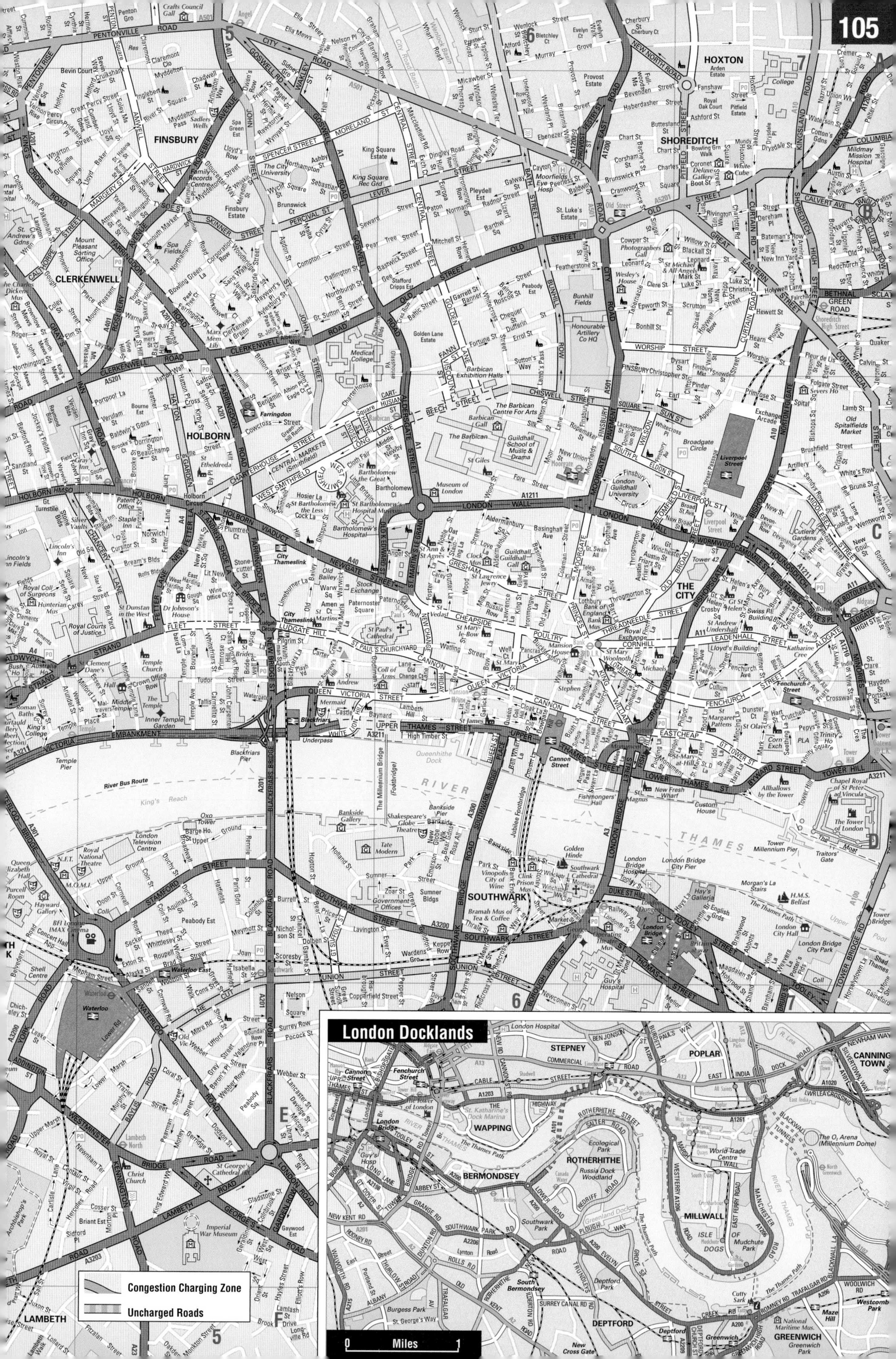
FINSBURY
HOXTON
SHOREDITCH
CLERKENWELL
HOLBORN
THE CITY
SOUTHWARK
LAMBETH
PENTONVILLE ROAD
CITY ROAD
GOSWELL ROAD
OLD STREET
CLERKENWELL ROAD
FARRINGDON ROAD
HOLBORN
LONDON WALL
CHEAPSIDE
FLEET STREET
STRAND
VICTORIA EMBANKMENT
UPPER THAMES STREET
LOWER THAMES STREET
CANNON STREET
QUEEN VICTORIA STREET
SOUTHWARK STREET
STAMFORD STREET
BLACKFRIARS BRIDGE
SOUTHWARK BRIDGE
LONDON BRIDGE
TOWER BRIDGE ROAD
BOROUGH HIGH ST
WATERLOO ROAD
WESTMINSTER BRIDGE ROAD
KENNINGTON ROAD
BISHOPSGATE
COMMERCIAL STREET
GREAT EASTERN STREET
KINGSLAND ROAD
HACKNEY ROAD
MOORGATE
ALDERSGATE STREET
NEWGATE STREET
Farringdon
Barbican
Moorgate
Liverpool Street
Fenchurch Street
Cannon Street
Blackfriars
Waterloo
Waterloo East
London Bridge
Southwark
St Paul's Cathedral
The Barbican
Museum of London
Bank of England
Tower 42
Monument
Tate Modern
Shakespeare's Globe Theatre
The Millennium Bridge (footbridge)
Southwark Cathedral
The Tower of London
H.M.S. Belfast
London City Hall
Imperial War Museum
Royal Courts of Justice
Temple
Honourable Artillery Co HQ
Bunhill Fields
Mount Pleasant Sorting Office
RIVER THAMES
River Bus Route
5
6
7
A
B
C
D
E
F
London Docklands
STEPNEY
POPLAR
CANNING TOWN
WAPPING
ROTHERHITHE
BERMONDSEY
MILLWALL
ISLE OF DOGS
DEPTFORD
GREENWICH
The O2 Arena (Millennium Dome)
Cutty Sark
National Maritime Mus.
Greenwich Park
Mudchute Park
Southwark Park
Burgess Park
0 Miles 1
Congestion Charging Zone
Uncharged Roads

Leeds

0 Miles ¼

A660 SKIPTON (A65)
A58 WETHERBY
A61 HARROGATE
A65 SKIPTON
A647 BRADFORD
A64 YORK
A62 HUDDERSFIELD & M62
A643 DEWSBURY (A653) & M621
A653 DEWSBURY & (M621, M1, M62)
A639 to M621, (M1)
City Centre Loop Road
A61 CASTLEFORD & M1

LITTLE WOODHOUSE
MABGATE
QUARRY HILL
RICHMOND HILL
NEW WORTLEY
GRANARY WHARF
STEANDER
WAREHOUSE HILL
CROWN POINT
CAMP FIELD
CAVALIER HILL

Leicester

0 Miles ¼

Lincoln

0 Miles ¼

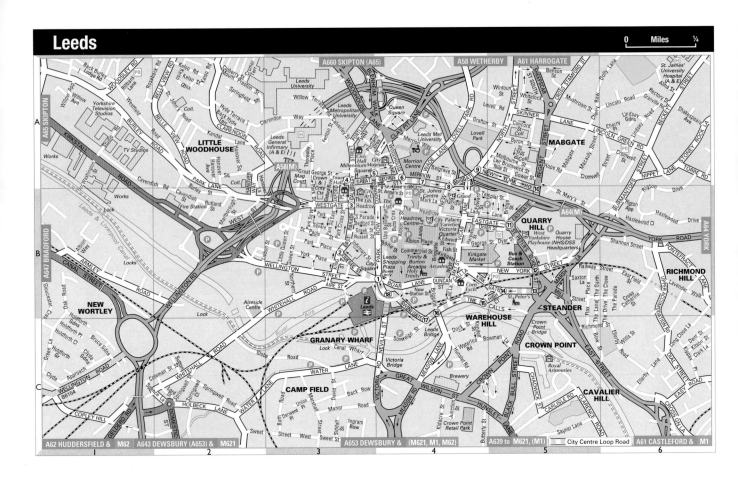

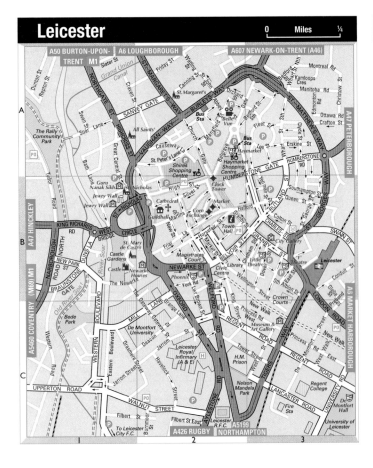

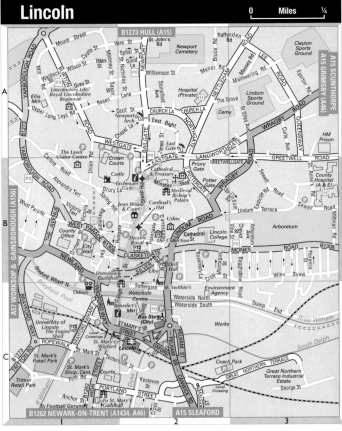

Liverpool

0 Miles ¼

A5036 TO A565 | A565 SOUTHPORT | A5038 KIRKDALE | A59 PRESTON M57 & M58 & KINGSWAY TUNNEL | A580 TO A59 | A5049 WEST DERBY

A57 WARRINGTON | A5047 TO M62 & MANCHESTER

A5036 TO A562 | A561 GARSTON | A5038 TO A561

RIVER MERSEY

Manchester

0 Miles ¼

A6042 TO A56 | A56 BURY | A665 TO A56 | A664 ROCHDALE | A62 OLDHAM

A6 PRESTON M6 | M602 | A57 WARRINGTON | M60 | A5065 TO A56

A662 DROYLSDEN | A635 ASHTON-u-Lyne

A56 ALTRINCHAM | A6144 STRETFORD | A5103 MANCHESTER AIRPORT (M56) | A34 CONGLETON | A6 STOCKPORT | A57 DENTON

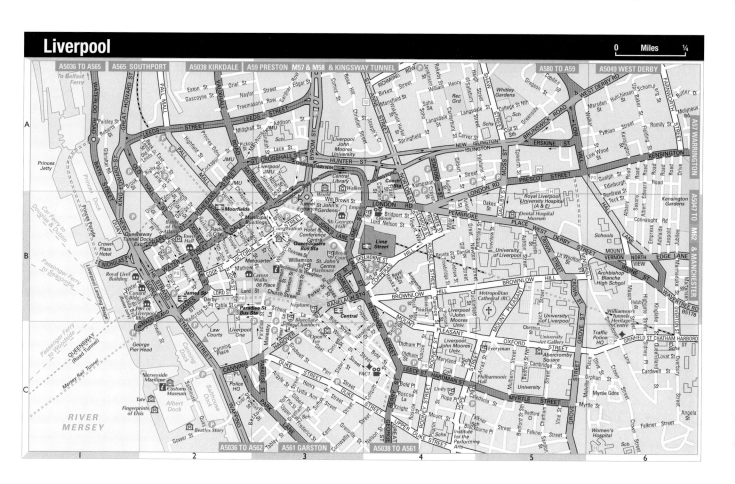

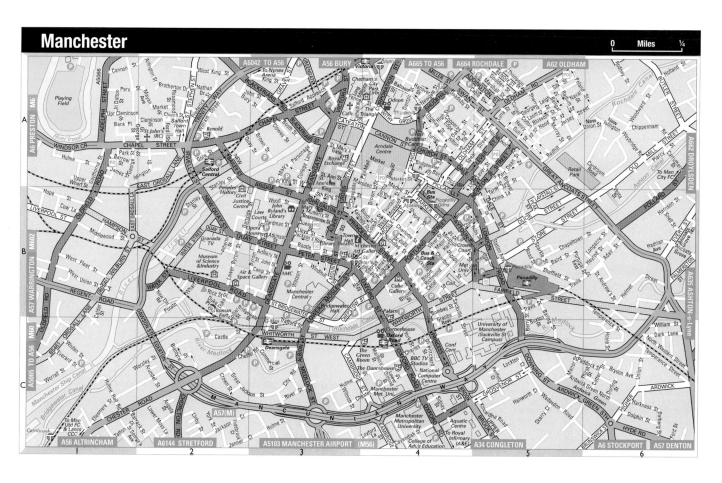

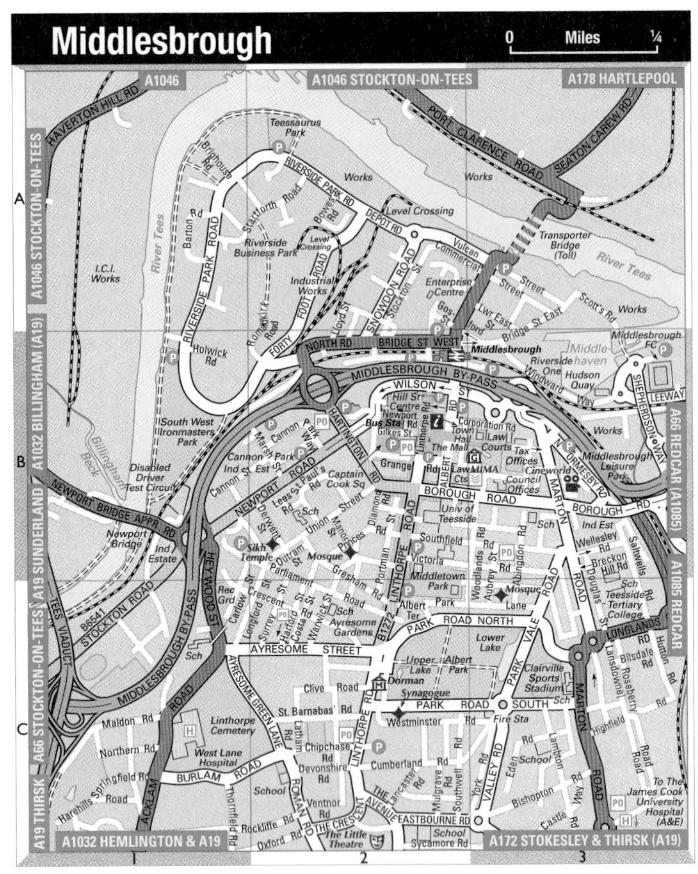
Middlesbrough
0 Miles ¼
A1046
A1046 STOCKTON-ON-TEES
A178 HARTLEPOOL
A1046 STOCKTON-ON-TEES
A1032 BILLINGHAM (A19)
A19 SUNDERLAND
A66 REDCAR (A1085)
A1085 REDCAR
A19 THIRSK - A66 STOCKTON-ON-TEES
A1032 HEMLINGTON & A19
A172 STOKESLEY & THIRSK (A19)
Teessaurus Park
Works
Level Crossing
Transporter Bridge (Toll)
River Tees
I.C.I. Works
Riverside Business Park
Industrial Works
Enterprise Centre
Middlesbrough
Middlehaven
Riverside One
Hudson Quay
Middlesbrough FC
MIDDLESBROUGH BY-PASS
South West Ironmasters Park
Disabled Driver Test Circuit
Bus Sta
Corporation Rd
Town Hall
Law Courts
Tax Offices
Council Offices
Cineworld
Middlesbrough Leisure Park
BOROUGH ROAD
Univ of Teesside
Captain Cook Sq
Newport Bridge
Ind Estate
Sikh Temple
Mosque
Middletown Park
Albert Park
Teesside Tertiary College
Ayresome Gardens
AYRESOME STREET
PARK ROAD NORTH
Lower Lake
Upper Lake
Clairville Sports Stadium
Dorman Museum
Synagogue
PARK ROAD SOUTH
Westminster
Fire Sta
Linthorpe Cemetery
West Lane Hospital
BURLAM ROAD
Cumberland Rd
The Little Theatre
EASTBOURNE RD
To The James Cook University Hospital (A&E)
MARTON ROAD
ACKLAM ROAD
1
2
3
A
B
C

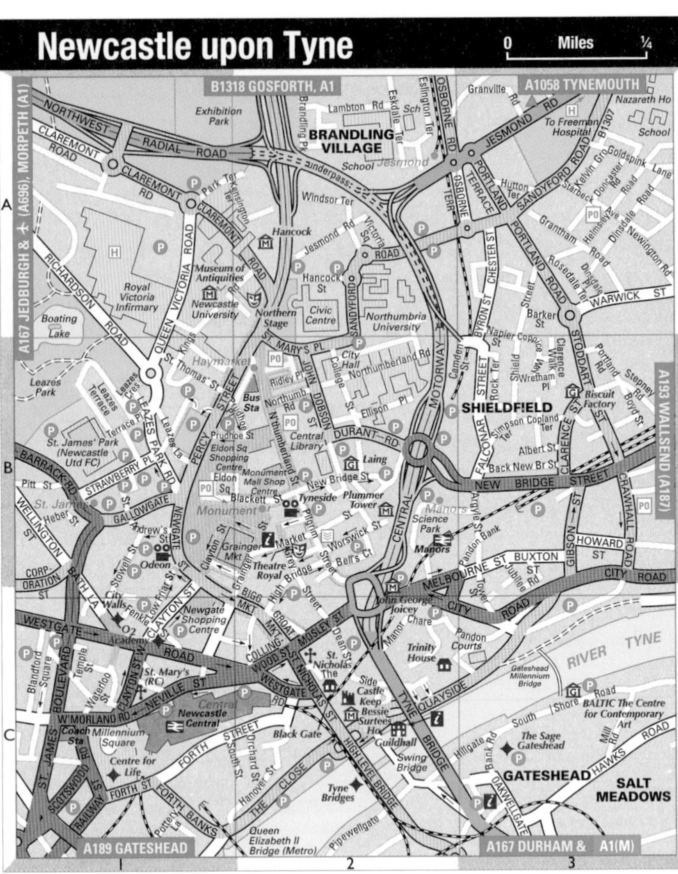
Newcastle upon Tyne
0 Miles ¼
B1318 GOSFORTH, A1
A1058 TYNEMOUTH
A167 JEDBURGH & (A696), MORPETH (A1)
A193 WALLSEND (A187)
A189 GATESHEAD
A167 DURHAM & A1(M)
Exhibition Park
BRANDLING VILLAGE
Jesmond
NORTHWEST RADIAL ROAD
CLAREMONT ROAD
Royal Victoria Infirmary
Hancock
Museum of Antiquities
Newcastle University
Northern Stage
Civic Centre
Northumbria University
Boating Lake
Leazes Park
St. James' Park (Newcastle Utd FC)
Haymarket
Bus Sta
Central Library
Eldon Sq Shopping Centre
Monument
Laing
Plummer Tower
Tyneside
SHIELDFIELD
Biscuit Factory
NEW BRIDGE STREET
Manors
Science Park
Grainger Mkt
Theatre Royal
Odeon
Newgate Shopping Centre
O2 Academy
St. Mary's (RC)
St. Nicholas
Castle Keep
Bessie Surtees Ho.
Guildhall
Newcastle Central
Centre for Life
Millennium Square
Black Gate
Swing Bridge
Tyne Bridges
RIVER TYNE
Gateshead Millennium Bridge
BALTIC The Centre for Contemporary Art
The Sage Gateshead
GATESHEAD
SALT MEADOWS
Queen Elizabeth II Bridge (Metro)
MELBOURNE ST
CITY ROAD
WESTGATE ROAD
1
2
3
A
B
C

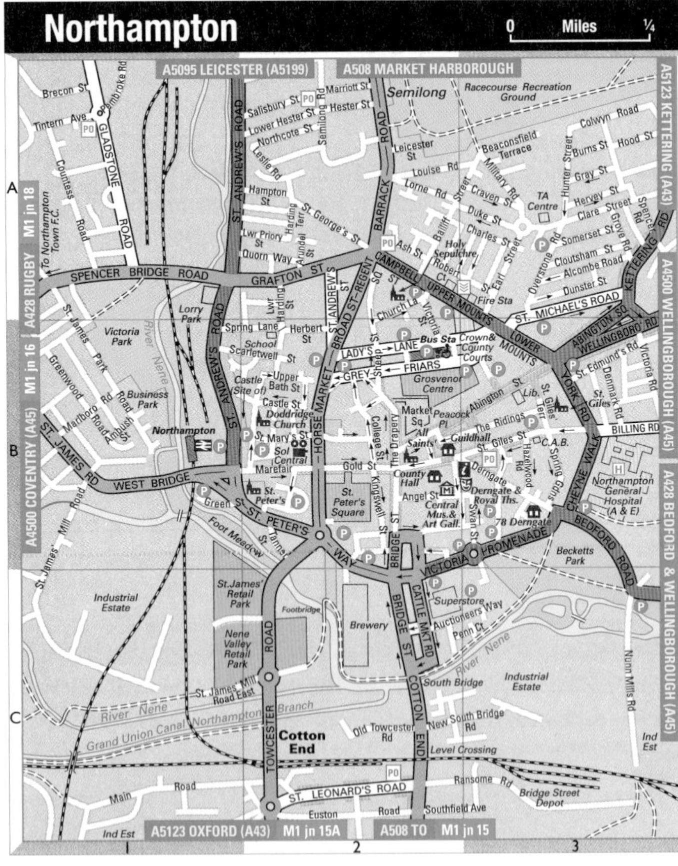
Northampton
0 Miles ¼
A5095 LEICESTER (A5199)
A508 MARKET HARBOROUGH
A5123 KETTERING (A43)
A4500 WELLINGBOROUGH
A428 BEDFORD & WELLINGBOROUGH (A45)
A428 RUGBY M1 jn 18
M1 jn 16
A4500 COVENTRY (A45)
A5123 OXFORD (A43)
M1 jn 15A
A508 TO M1 jn 15
Ind Est
Semilong
Racecourse Recreation Ground
To Northampton Town F.C.
SPENCER BRIDGE ROAD
GRAFTON ST
Victoria Park
Lorry Park
Business Park
Northampton
WEST BRIDGE
Castle Site of
Doddridge Church
St. Mary
Sol Central
St. Peter's
St. Peter's Square
Grosvenor Centre
Bus Sta
Crown & County Courts
Holy Sepulchre
Fire Sta
County Hall
Guildhall
Central Mus. & Art Gall.
Derngate & Royal Ths.
78 Derngate
Northampton General Hospital (A & E)
Beckets Park
ST. MICHAEL'S ROAD
VICTORIA PROMENADE
St. James' Retail Park
Nene Valley Retail Park
Industrial Estate
Brewery
Superstore
River Nene
Grand Union Canal (Northampton Branch)
Cotton End
Level Crossing
Bridge Street Depot
ST. LEONARD'S ROAD
South Bridge
1
2
3
A
B
C

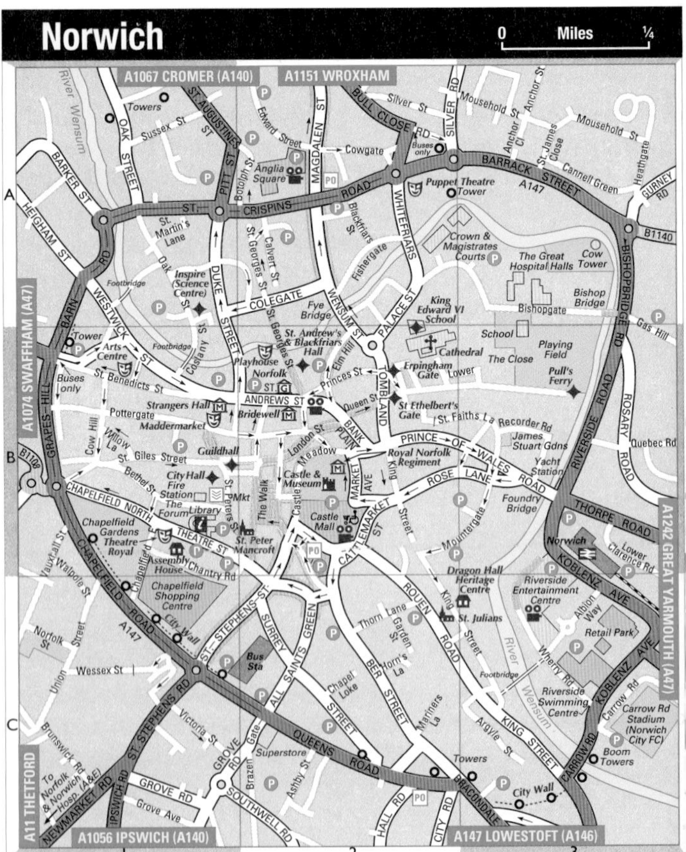
Norwich
0 Miles ¼
A1067 CROMER (A140)
A1151 WROXHAM
A1074 SWAFFHAM (A47)
A1242 GREAT YARMOUTH (A47)
A11 THETFORD
A1056 IPSWICH (A140)
A147 LOWESTOFT (A146)
River Wensum
Towers
Anglia Square
Puppet Theatre
BARRACK STREET
Crown & Magistrates Courts
The Great Hospital Halls
Cow Tower
Bishop Bridge
Inspire (Science Centre)
Fye Bridge
King Edward VI School
St. Andrew's & Blackfriars Hall
Cathedral
The Close
Playing Field
Pull's Ferry
Arts Centre
Playhouse
Norfolk
Erpingham Gate
Strangers Hall
Bridewell
St Ethelbert's Gate
Maddermarket
Guildhall
City Hall
Fire Station
The Forum
Library
Castle & Museum
Castle Mall
Royal Norfolk Regiment
Chapelfield Gardens
Theatre Royal
Assembly House
St. Peter Mancroft
Chapelfield Shopping Centre
Bus Sta
Dragon Hall Heritage Centre
St. Julians
Riverside Entertainment Centre
Retail Park
Riverside Swimming Centre
Norwich
Carrow Rd Stadium (Norwich City FC)
Boom Towers
City Wall
Superstore
Wessex St
To Norfolk & Norwich Hosp (A&E)
1
2
3
A
B
C

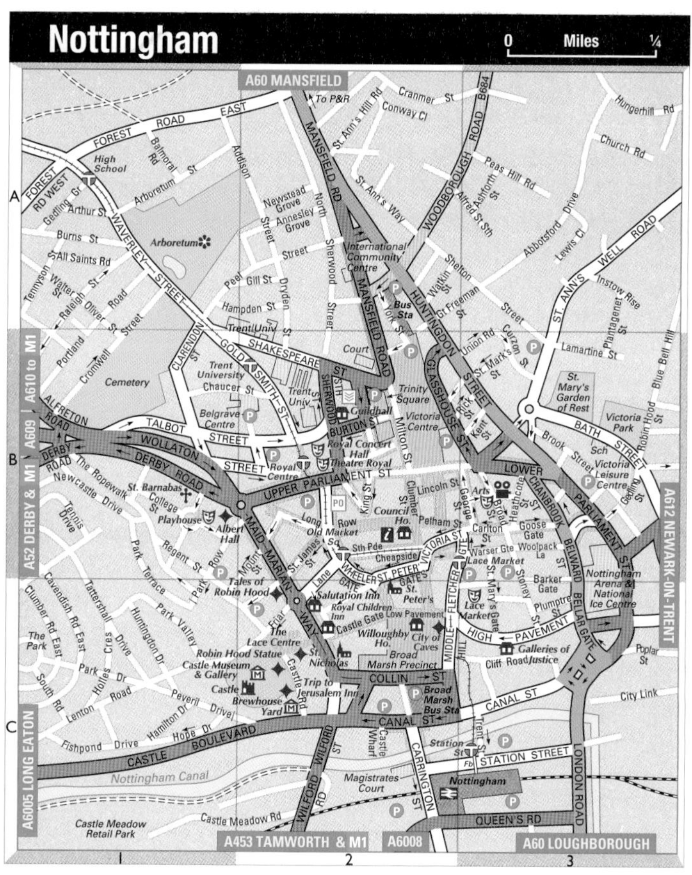
Nottingham
0 Miles ¼
A60 MANSFIELD
A52 DERBY & M1
A610 to M1
A609
A612 NEWARK-ON-TRENT
A6005 LONG EATON
A453 TAMWORTH & M1
A6008
A60 LOUGHBOROUGH
Forest Road East
High School
Arboretum
Cemetery
Trent University
Belgrave Centre
Talbot Street
Wollaton Street
Derby Road
Upper Parliament St
Playhouse
Albert Hall
Tales of Robin Hood
Salutation Inn
Robin Hood Statue
Castle Museum & Gallery
Castle
Brewhouse Yard
Trip to Jerusalem Inn
Castle Boulevard
Nottingham Canal
Castle Meadow Retail Park
Castle Meadow Rd
Maid Marian Way
Council Ho.
Old Market Square
Royal Concert Hall
Theatre Royal
Guildhall
Victoria Centre
Bus Sta
International Community Centre
Mansfield Road
Huntingdon Street
Glasshouse St
Lace Market
Lace Centre
Galleries of Justice
Broad Marsh Precinct
Broad Marsh Bus Sta
Collin St
Canal St
Station Street
Nottingham
Queen's Rd
London Road
Magistrates Court
Lower Parliament St
Victoria Park
Victoria Leisure Centre
Nottingham Arena & National Ice Centre
St. Mary's Garden of Rest
Lamartine St
City Link
Fishpond Drive
The Park
Tattershall Drive
Park Valley
Willoughby Ho.
City of Caves
High Pavement
Hockley
Woolpack La
Barker Gate
Plumptre St
Carlton St
Goose Gate
Woodborough Road
Alfreton Road

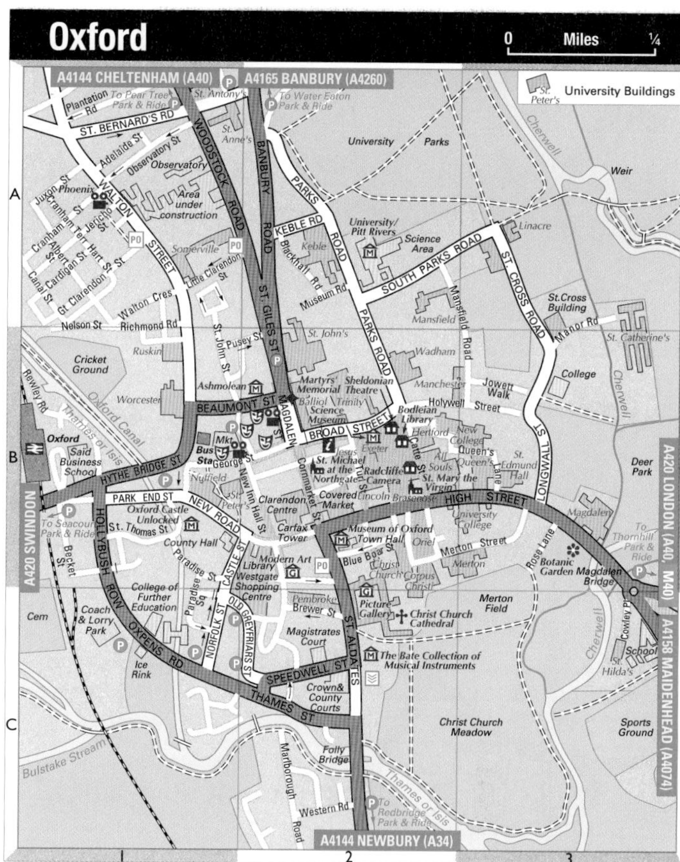
Oxford
0 Miles ¼
University Buildings
St. Peter's
A4144 CHELTENHAM (A40)
A4165 BANBURY (A4260)
A420 SWINDON
A420 LONDON (A40) M40
A4158 MAIDENHEAD (A4074)
A4144 NEWBURY (A34)
University Parks
Weir
Linacre
University/Pitt Rivers
Science Area
South Parks Road
St. Cross Building
Manor Rd
St. Catherine's
College
Deer Park
Keble
Keble Rd
Museum Rd
St. John's
Ruskin
Worcester
Cricket Ground
Ashmolean
Beaumont St
Broad Street
Martyrs' Memorial
Sheldonian Theatre
Bodleian Library
Hertford
New College
Queen's
St. Edmund Hall
Holywell Street
Oxford
Said Business School
Hythe Bridge St
Park End St
Oxford Castle Unlocked
County Hall
Clarendon Centre
Covered Market
Carfax Tower
Radcliffe Camera
St. Mary the Virgin
All Souls
High Street
Museum of Oxford
Town Hall
Oriel
Merton Street
Merton
Botanic Garden
Magdalen Bridge
Christ Church Cathedral
Picture Gallery
Merton Field
Christ Church Meadow
Christ Church
The Bate Collection of Musical Instruments
Magistrates Court
Crown & County Courts
Westgate Shopping Centre
Modern Art
Speedwell St
Thames St
Folly Bridge
Ice Rink
College of Further Education
Coach & Lorry Park
Cem
Sports Ground
Cherwell
Bulstake Stream
Thames or Isis
Oxford Canal
Walton Street
Woodstock Road
Banbury Road
St. Giles St
Parks Road
St. Bernard's Rd
Observatory
Somerville
Jowett Walk
Longwall St
Rose Lane
Wadham
Mansfield
Manchester
Plantation Rd
To Water Eaton Park & Ride
To Pear Tree Park & Ride
To Seacourt Park & Ride
To Redbridge Park & Ride
To Thornhill Park & Ride

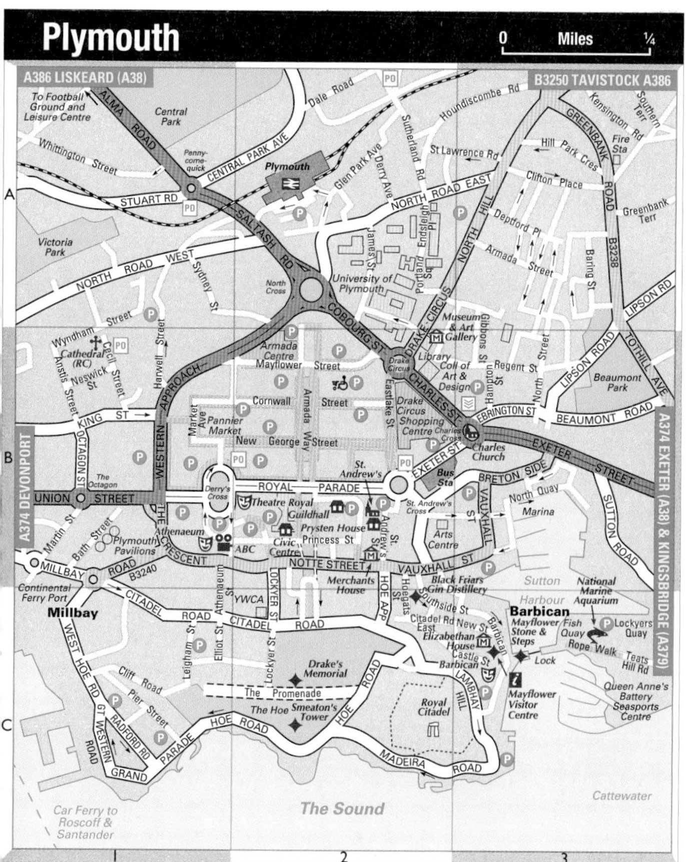
Plymouth
0 Miles ¼
A386 LISKEARD (A38)
B3250 TAVISTOCK A386
A374 DEVONPORT
A374 EXETER (A38) & KINGSBRIDGE (A379)
To Football Ground and Leisure Centre
Central Park
Plymouth
Victoria Park
North Road West
North Road East
University of Plymouth
North Cross
Armada Centre
Mayflower Street
Cornwall Street
Pannier Market
New George Street
Royal Parade
Union Street
Theatre Royal
Guildhall
St. Andrew's
Prysten House
Drake Circus Shopping Centre
Museum & Art Gallery
Charles Church
Exeter Street
Beaumont Park
Beaumont Road
Bretonside
Bus Sta
Marina
North Quay
Sutton Harbour
National Marine Aquarium
Barbican
Mayflower Stone & Steps
Mayflower Visitor Centre
Elizabethan House
Black Friars Gin Distillery
Merchants House
Royal Citadel
Drake's Memorial
Smeaton's Tower
The Hoe
The Promenade
Hoe Road
Madeira Road
The Sound
Cattewater
Car Ferry to Roscoff & Santander
Continental Ferry Port
Millbay
Cathedral (RC)
Citadel Road
Notte Street
Vauxhall St
Lockyers Quay
Queen Anne's Battery Seasports Centre
Fish Quay
Western Approach
Athenaeum
ABC
Civic Centre
YWCA
Plymouth Pavilions
Grand Parade
Stuart Rd
Saltash Rd
Cobourg St
Tavistock Place

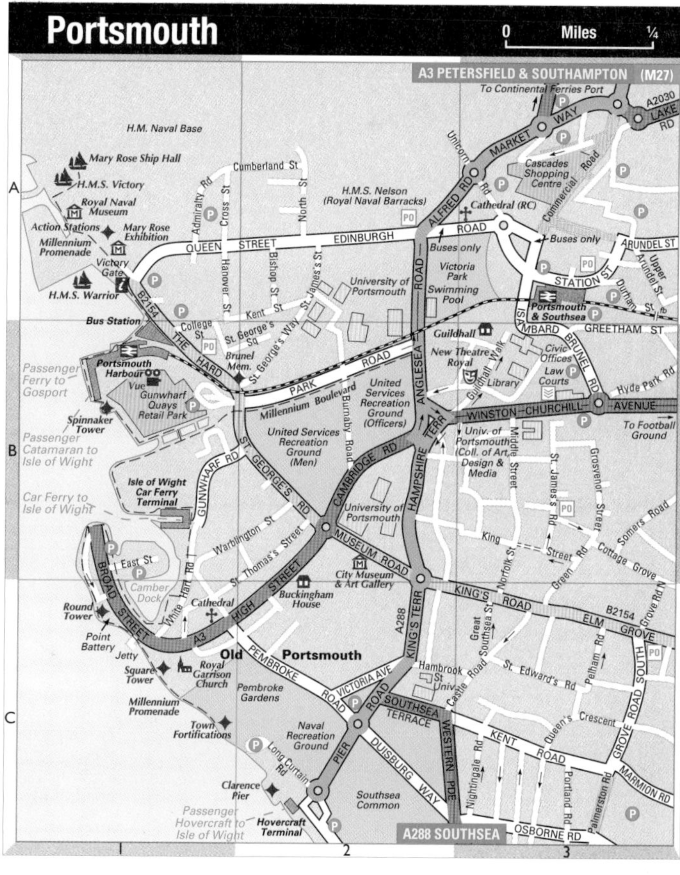
Portsmouth
0 Miles ¼
A3 PETERSFIELD & SOUTHAMPTON (M27)
To Continental Ferries Port
A2030 Lake Rd
A288 SOUTHSEA
H.M. Naval Base
Mary Rose Ship Hall
H.M.S. Victory
Royal Naval Museum
Action Stations
Mary Rose Exhibition
Millennium Promenade
Victory Gate
H.M.S. Warrior
H.M.S. Nelson (Royal Naval Barracks)
Bus Station
Portsmouth Harbour
Gunwharf Quays Retail Park
Spinnaker Tower
Passenger Ferry to Gosport
Passenger Catamaran to Isle of Wight
Car Ferry to Isle of Wight
Isle of Wight Car Ferry Terminal
University of Portsmouth
Victoria Park
Swimming Pool
Cathedral (RC)
Cascades Shopping Centre
Portsmouth & Southsea
Guildhall
New Theatre Royal
Library
Civic Offices
Law Courts
Winston Churchill Avenue
United Services Recreation Ground (Officers)
United Services Recreation Ground (Men)
Millennium Boulevard
Museum Road
City Museum & Art Gallery
Buckingham House
Cathedral
Old Portsmouth
Royal Garrison Church
Square Tower
Round Tower
Point Battery
Pembroke Gardens
Town Fortifications
Naval Recreation Ground
Clarence Pier
Passenger Hovercraft to Isle of Wight
Hovercraft Terminal
Southsea Common
Southsea Terrace
Kings Road
Elm Grove
Queen Street
Edinburgh Road
Commercial Road
Hampshire Terr
Cambridge Rd
High Street
Broad Street
King's Terr
To Football Ground
Greetham St
Hyde Park Rd
Kent Road
Osborne Rd

Reading

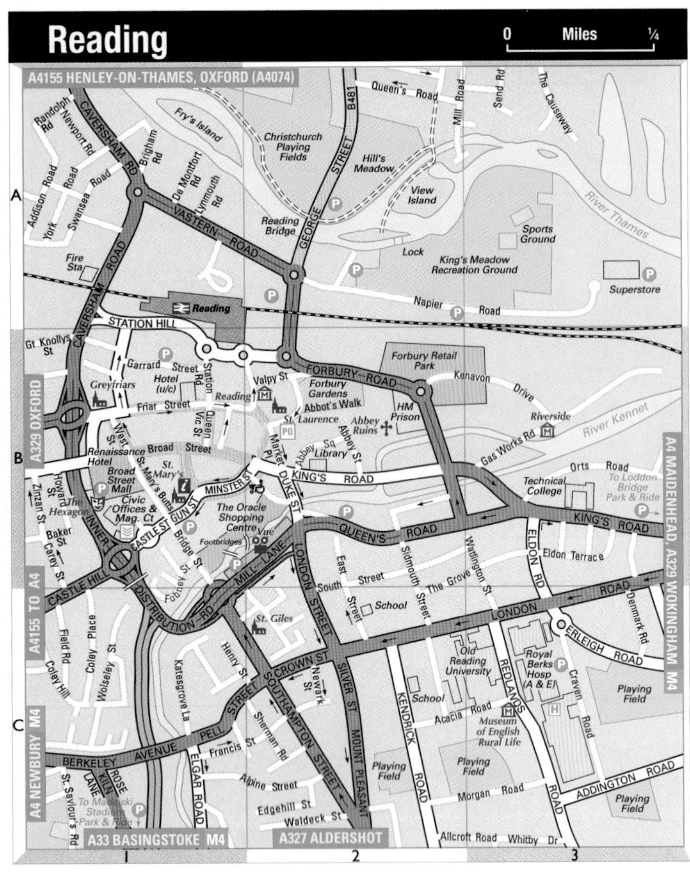
0 Miles ¼
A4155 HENLEY-ON-THAMES, OXFORD (A4074)
A329 OXFORD
A4155 TO A4
A4 NEWBURY M4
A33 BASINGSTOKE M4
A327 ALDERSHOT
A4 MAIDENHEAD, A329 WOKINGHAM, M4
Fry's Island
Christchurch Playing Fields
Hill's Meadow
View Island
Reading Bridge
Sports Ground
King's Meadow Recreation Ground
Lock
River Thames
Superstore
Napier Road
Reading
STATION HILL
Forbury Retail Park
Kenavon Drive
Forbury Gardens
Abbot's Walk
Abbey Ruins
HM Prison
Riverside
River Kennet
Gas Works Rd
Orts Road
Technical College
To Loddon Bridge Park & Ride
Greyfriars
Friar Street
Broad Street
St. Laurence
Library
Renaissance Hotel
Broad Street Mall
Civic Offices & Mag. Ct
The Hexagon
The Oracle Shopping Centre
KING'S ROAD
QUEEN'S ROAD
Eldon Terrace
St. Giles
LONDON ROAD
Old Reading University
School
Royal Berks Hosp (A & E)
ERLEIGH ROAD
Playing Field
Museum of English Rural Life
Acacia Road
BERKELEY AVENUE
Francis St
Alpine Street
Edgehill St
Waldeck St
Morgan Road
ADDINGTON ROAD
Allcroft Road
Whitby Dr
To Madejski Stadium Park & Ride
A
B
C
1
2
3

Salisbury

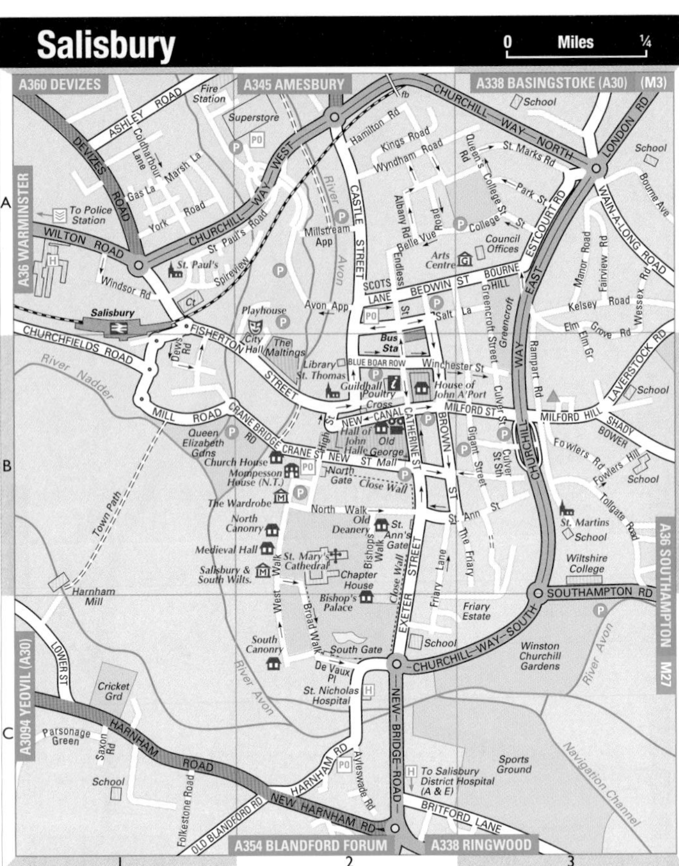
0 Miles ¼
A360 DEVIZES
A345 AMESBURY
A338 BASINGSTOKE (A30) (M3)
A36 WARMINSTER
A3094 YEOVIL (A30)
A354 BLANDFORD FORUM
A338 RINGWOOD
A36 SOUTHAMPTON M27
Fire Station
Superstore
CHURCHILL WAY NORTH
School
To Police Station
WILTON ROAD
St. Paul's
Windsor Rd
Salisbury
Millstream App
Playhouse
City Hall
The Maltings
Library
St. Thomas
Guildhall
Poultry Cross
House of John A'Port
Council Offices
Arts Centre
BOURNE HILL
Kelsey Road
MILFORD HILL
St. Martins
School
Wiltshire College
Hall of John Halle
Old George Mall
Church House
Mompesson House (N.T.)
The Wardrobe
North Canonry
Medieval Hall
Salisbury & South Wilts.
St. Mary's Cathedral
Chapter House
Bishop's Palace
South Canonry
South Gate
St. Nicholas Hospital
Friary Estate
Winston Churchill Gardens
SOUTHAMPTON RD
CHURCHILL WAY SOUTH
Harnham Mill
Cricket Grd
Parsonage Green
School
HARNHAM ROAD
NEW HARNHAM RD
To Salisbury District Hospital (A & E)
Sports Ground
BRITFORD LANE
Navigation Channel
River Avon
River Nadder
Town Path
A
B
C
1
2
3

Scarborough

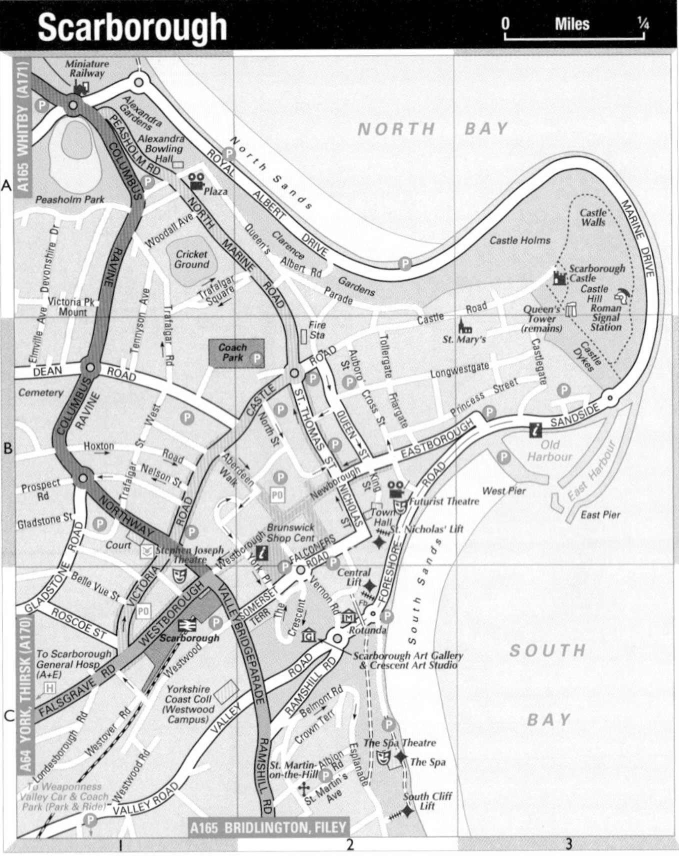
0 Miles ¼
A165 WHITBY (A171)
A64 YORK, THIRSK (A170)
A165 BRIDLINGTON, FILEY
Miniature Railway
NORTH BAY
North Sands
Peasholm Park
Alexandra Bowling Hall
Plaza
Cricket Ground
Castle Holms
Castle Walls
Scarborough Castle
Castle Hill Roman Signal Station
Queen's Tower (remains)
St. Mary's
Coach Park
Victoria Pk Mount
Cemetery
Fire Sta
Longwestgate
Old Harbour
East Harbour
East Pier
West Pier
Futurist Theatre
St. Nicholas' Lift
Town Hall
Brunswick Shop Cent
Stephen Joseph Theatre
Central Lift
Rotunda
Scarborough
Scarborough Art Gallery & Crescent Art Studio
SOUTH BAY
South Sands
To Scarborough General Hosp (A+E)
Yorkshire Coast Coll (Westwood Campus)
The Spa Theatre
The Spa
South Cliff Lift
St. Martin-on-the-Hill
To Weaponness Valley Car & Coach Park (Park & Ride)
VALLEY ROAD
A
B
C
1
2
3

Southampton

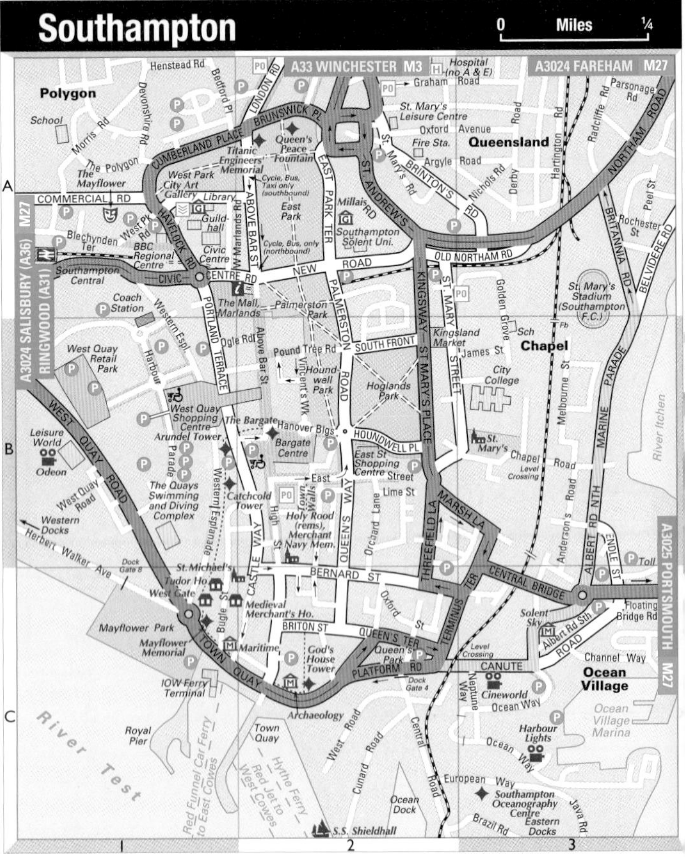
0 Miles ¼
A33 WINCHESTER M3
A3024 FAREHAM M27
A3024 SALISBURY (A36) RINGWOOD (A31) M27
A3025 PORTSMOUTH M27
Polygon
Hospital (no A & E)
St. Mary's Leisure Centre
Queensland
Titanic Engineers' Memorial
Queen's Peace Fountain
West Park City Art Gallery
Library
Guildhall
Civic Centre
BBC Regional Centre
East Park
Southampton Solent Uni.
Southampton Central
Coach Station
The Mall Marlands
West Quay Retail Park
West Quay Shopping Centre
The Bargate
Bargate Centre
Hoglands Park
St. Mary's Stadium (Southampton F.C.)
Chapel
City College
Leisure World
Odeon
The Quays Swimming and Diving Complex
Catchcold Tower
Holy Rood (rems), Merchant Navy Mem.
Western Docks
Tudor Ho
West Gate
Medieval Merchant's Ho.
Mayflower Park
Mayflower Memorial
Maritime
God's House Tower
Archaeology
IOW Ferry Terminal
Royal Pier
River Test
Town Quay
Red Funnel Car Ferry to East Cowes
Red Jet to West Cowes
Hythe Ferry
Ocean Dock
S.S. Shieldhall
Cineworld
Ocean Village
Harbour Lights
Southampton Oceanography Centre
Eastern Docks
Floating Bridge Rd
Canute
A
B
C
1
2
3

Sheffield

0 Miles ¼

A61 BARNSLEY M1
A6135 BARNSLEY
A6109 ROTHERHAM M1
A6178 ROTHERHAM M1
A57 WORKSOP M1, M18
A6135 ECKINGTON M1
A61 CHESTERFIELD
A621 TO A61
B6388
A625 HATHERSAGE
A57 GLOSSOP

BIRKENDALE
PORT MAHON
CROOKESMOOR
NETHER-THORPE
BROOMFIELD
PARK HILL

Sheff Wed FC
Infirmary Road
Foundry Climbing Centre
Kelham Island Industrial Museum
To Northern General Hosp (A & E)
Recreation Ground
Crookes Valley Park
Weston Park Museum
Mappin Art Gallery
University of Sheffield
Children's Hosp (A&E)
Royal Hallamshire Hospital
University Drama Studio
Octagon
Univ of Sheffield
University Turner Mus. of Glass
Portobello
West One
Devonshire Green
Fire & Police Museum
Crown Court
Castle Market
Victoria Quays
Fitzalan Sq. Ponds Forge
Ponds Forge Sports Centre
Bus/Coach Station
Cathedral
St. Peter & St. Paul
Cutler's Hall
City Hall
Cathedral (RC)
Crucible
Lyceum
Montgomery
Town Hall
Winter Garden
Millennium Galleries
Sheffield Hallam Univ
The Showroom
Sheffield Station / Sheffield Hallam University
Furnival Square
Site Gallery
The Leadmill
Yorkshire Artspace
Dept. for Education & Employment
Tax Office
Sheff Utd FC
Skate Central
Granville Rd / Sheffield College
Monument Gdns
Playing Field
Sports Ground
University
Botanical Gardens
Hallam Univ
Holberry Gdns
Sunny Bank
Hyde Park
Manor Oaks Road
Shalesmoor
Netherthorpe Road
Sheffield/Tinsley Canal
River Don

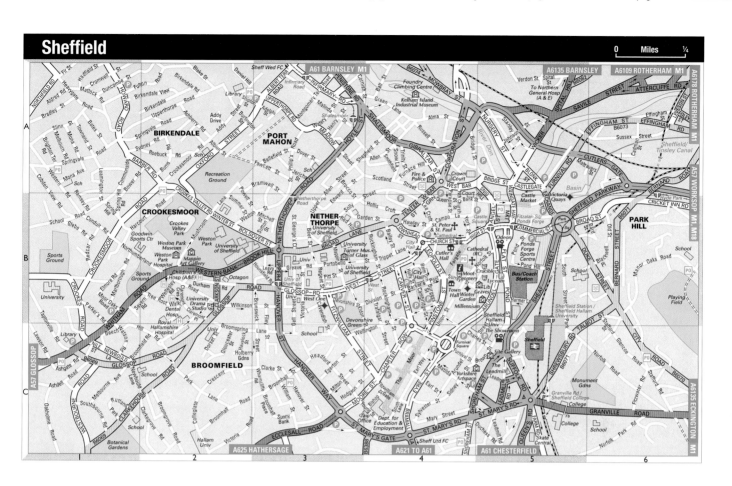

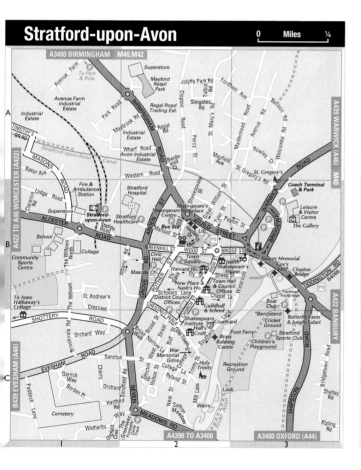

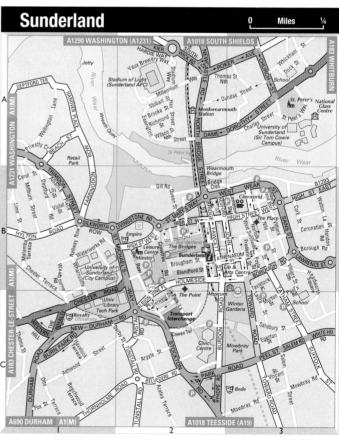

Swansea / Abertawe

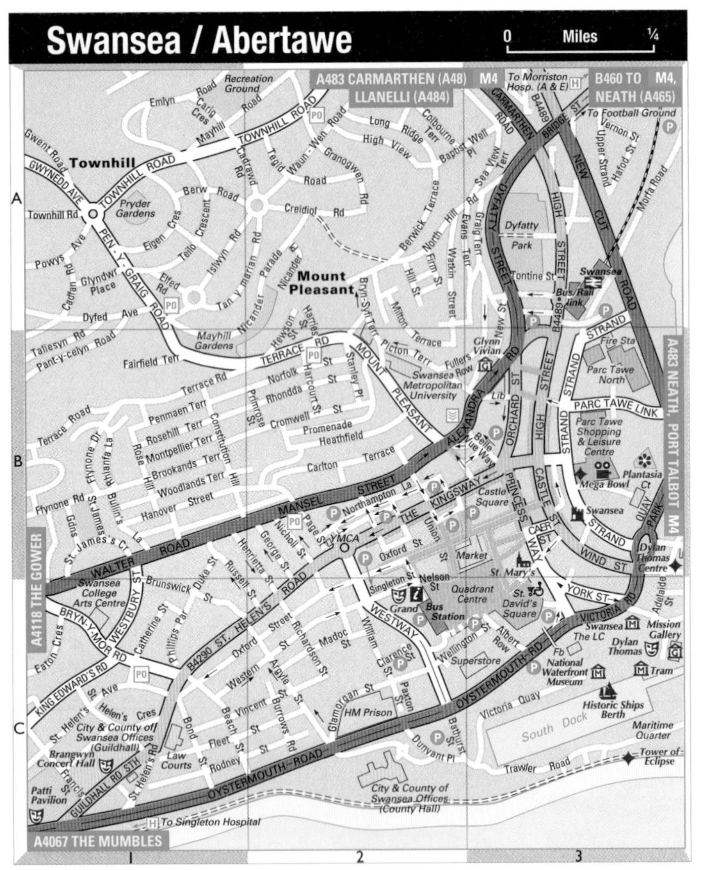
0 Miles ¼
A483 CARMARTHEN (A48) M4 LLANELLI (A484)
B460 TO M4, NEATH (A465)
To Morriston Hosp. (A & E)
To Football Ground
Townhill
Mount Pleasant
Dyfatty Park
Swansea
Bus/Rail link
Swansea Metropolitan University
Parc Tawe North
Parc Tawe Shopping & Leisure Centre
Plantasia
Mega Bowl
Castle Square
Market
Quadrant Centre
Bus Station
St. David's Square
Swansea College Arts Centre
YMCA
Grand
HM Prison
Superstore
The LC
Dylan Thomas
National Waterfront Museum
Swansea Museum
Mission Gallery
Tram
Historic Ships Berth
Maritime Quarter
South Dock
Tower of Eclipse
City & County of Swansea Offices (Guildhall)
Brangwyn Concert Hall
Patti Pavilion
Law Courts
City & County of Swansea Offices (County Hall)
To Singleton Hospital
A4067 THE MUMBLES
A4118 THE GOWER
A483 NEATH, PORT TALBOT M4
MANSEL STREET
WALTER ROAD
ST. HELEN'S ROAD
OYSTERMOUTH ROAD
KINGSWAY
WESTWAY
ALEXANDRA RD
STRAND
HIGH STREET
NEW CUT ROAD
A
B
C
1
2
3

Winchester

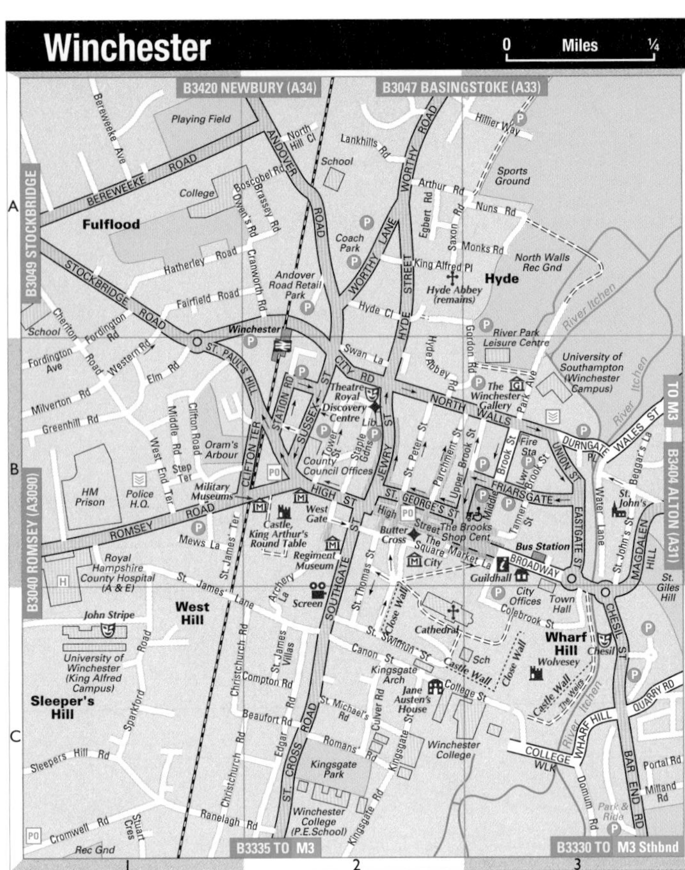
0 Miles ¼
B3420 NEWBURY (A34)
B3047 BASINGSTOKE (A33)
B3049 STOCKBRIDGE
B3040 ROMSEY (A3090)
TO M3
B3404 ALTON (A31)
Fulflood
Hyde
Hyde Abbey (remains)
Playing Field
College
School
Sports Ground
North Walls Rec Gnd
Coach Park
Andover Road Retail Park
Winchester
River Park Leisure Centre
University of Southampton (Winchester Campus)
Theatre Royal
Discovery Centre
The Winchester Gallery
Oram's Arbour
HM Prison
Police H.Q.
Military Museums
County Council Offices
Castle, King Arthur's Round Table
West Gate
Regiment Museum
Butter Cross
The Brooks Shop Cent
City Museum
Guildhall
Bus Station
City Offices
Town Hall
Royal Hampshire County Hospital (A & E)
John Stripe
University of Winchester (King Alfred Campus)
West Hill
Sleeper's Hill
Screen
Cathedral
Kingsgate Arch
Jane Austen's House
Wharf Hill
Wolvesey
Winchester College
Kingsgate Park
Winchester College (P.E.School)
Rec Gnd
Park & Ride
B3335 TO M3
B3330 TO M3 Sthbnd
River Itchen
A
B
C
1
2
3

Worcester

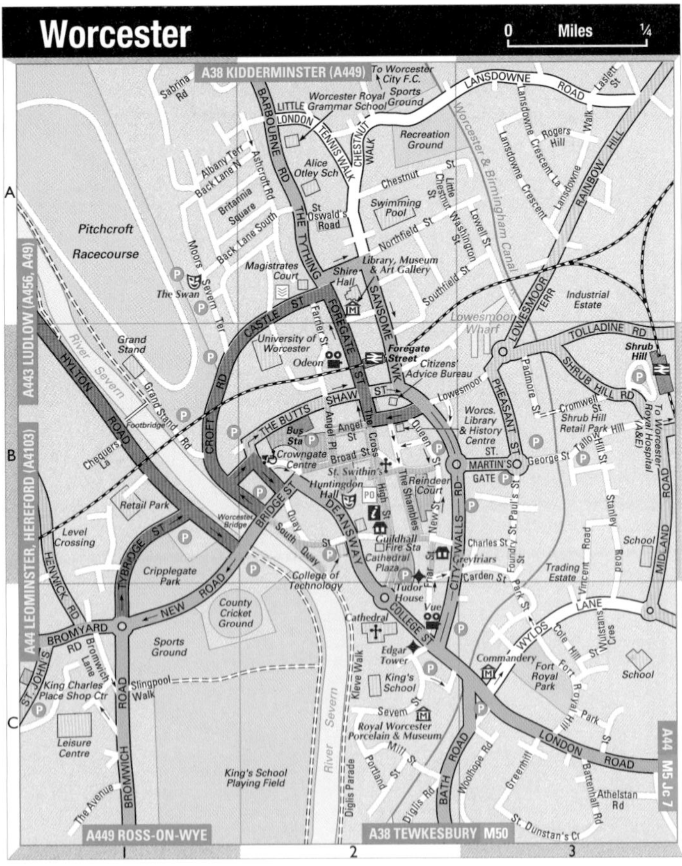
0 Miles ¼
A38 KIDDERMINSTER (A449)
To Worcester City F.C.
Worcester Royal Grammar School
Sports Ground
Recreation Ground
Alice Otley Sch
Pitchcroft Racecourse
Swimming Pool
Magistrates Court
Shire Hall
Library, Museum & Art Gallery
The Swan
Grand Stand
University of Worcester
Odeon
Foregate Street
Citizens' Advice Bureau
Industrial Estate
Lowesmoor Wharf
Shrub Hill
Worcs. Library & History Centre
Cromwell Shrub Hill Retail Park
To Worcester Royal Hospital (A&E)
Crowngate Centre
St. Swithin's
Huntingdon Hall
Reindeer Court
The Shambles
Guildhall
Fire Sta
Cathedral Plaza
Greyfriars
Retail Park
Level Crossing
Cripplegate Park
College of Technology
County Cricket Ground
Tudor House
Cathedral
Edgar Tower
King's School
Commandery
Fort Royal Park
Trading Estate
School
Sports Ground
King Charles Place Shop Ctr
Leisure Centre
King's School Playing Field
Royal Worcester Porcelain & Museum
River Severn
Worcester & Birmingham Canal
A443 LUDLOW (A456, A49)
A44 LEOMINSTER, HEREFORD (A4103)
A449 ROSS-ON-WYE
A38 TEWKESBURY M50
A44 M5-Jc 7
A
B
C
1
2
3

York

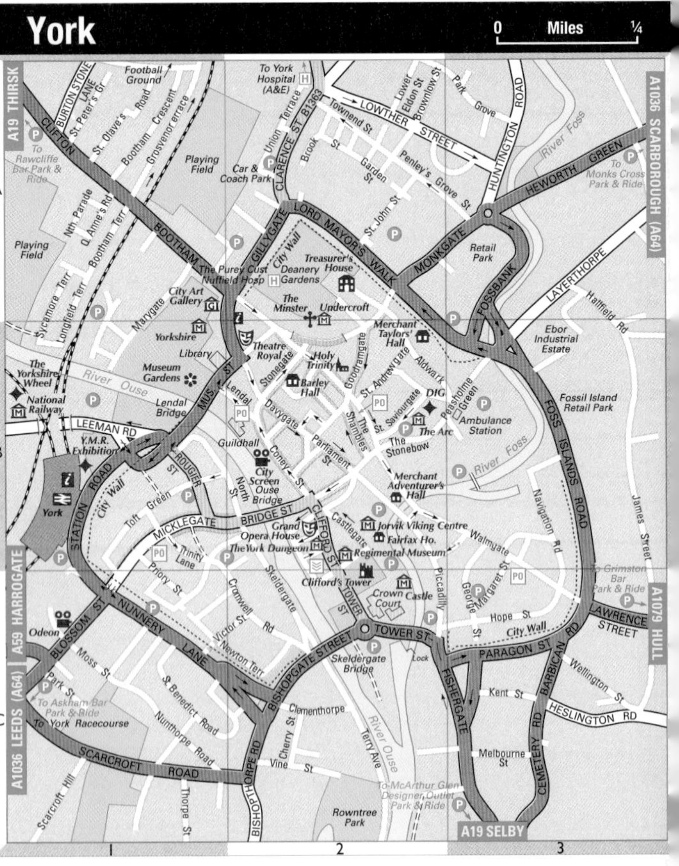
0 Miles ¼
A19 THIRSK
A1036 SCARBOROUGH (A64)
Football Ground
To York Hospital (A&E)
To Rawcliffe Bar Park & Ride
To Monks Cross Park & Ride
Playing Field
Car & Coach Park
Retail Park
The Purey Cust Nuffield Hosp
Treasurer's House
Deanery Gardens
The Minster
Undercroft
City Art Gallery
Yorkshire Museum Gardens
Library
Theatre Royal
Holy Trinity
Merchant Taylors' Hall
Ebor Industrial Estate
The Yorkshire Wheel
National Railway Museum
Lendal Bridge
Barley Hall
DIG
The Arc
Ambulance Station
Fossil Island Retail Park
Y.M.R. Exhibition
York
Guildhall
City Screen
Ouse Bridge
The Stonebow
Merchant Adventurer's Hall
Jorvik Viking Centre
Fairfax Ho.
Grand Opera House
The York Dungeon
Regimental Museum
Clifford's Tower
Crown Court
Castle
Odeon
Skeldergate Bridge
To Askham Bar Park & Ride
To York Racecourse
Clementhorpe
To McArthur Glen Designer Outlet Park & Ride
Rowntree Park
To Grimston Bar Park & Ride
River Ouse
River Foss
A59 HARROGATE
A1036 LEEDS (A64)
A1079 HULL
A19 SELBY
A
B
C
1
2
3

Index to road maps of Britain

Abbreviations used in the index

Abbreviation	Name
Aberdeen	Aberdeen City
Aberds	Aberdeenshire
Ald	Alderney
Anglesey	Isle of Anglesey
Angus	Angus
Argyll	Argyll and Bute
Bath	Bath and North East Somerset
Bedford	Bedford
Bl Gwent	Blaenau Gwent
Blackburn	Blackburn with Darwen
Blackpool	Blackpool
Bmouth	Bournemouth
Borders	Scottish Borders
Brack	Bracknell
Bridgend	Bridgend
Brighton	City of Brighton and Hove
Bristol	City and County of Bristol
Bucks	Buckinghamshire
C Beds	Central Bedfordshire
Caerph	Caerphilly
Cambs	Cambridgeshire
Cardiff	Cardiff
Carms	Carmarthenshire
Ceredig	Ceredigion
Ches E	Cheshire East
Ches W	Cheshire West and Chester
Clack	Clackmannanshire
Conwy	Conwy
Corn	Cornwall
Cumb	Cumbria
Darl	Darlington
Denb	Denbighshire
Derby	City of Derby
Derbys	Derbyshire
Devon	Devon
Dorset	Dorset
Dumfries	Dumfries and Galloway
Dundee	Dundee City
Durham	Durham
E Ayrs	East Ayrshire
E Dunb	East Dunbartonshire
E Loth	East Lothian
E Renf	East Renfrewshire
E Sus	East Sussex
E Yorks	East Riding of Yorkshire
Edin	City of Edinburgh
Essex	Essex
Falk	Falkirk
Fife	Fife
Flint	Flintshire
Glasgow	City of Glasgow
Glos	Gloucestershire
Gtr Man	Greater Manchester
Guern	Guernsey
Gwyn	Gwynedd
Halton	Halton
Hants	Hampshire
Hereford	Herefordshire
Herts	Hertfordshire
Highld	Highland
Hrtlpl	Hartlepool
Hull	Hull
IoM	Isle of Man
IoW	Isle of Wight
Invclyd	Inverclyde
Jersey	Jersey
Kent	Kent
Lancs	Lancashire
Leicester	City of Leicester
Leics	Leicestershire
Lincs	Lincolnshire
London	Greater London
Luton	Luton
M Keynes	Milton Keynes
M Tydf	Merthyr Tydfil
Mbro	Middlesbrough
Medway	Medway
Mers	Merseyside
Midloth	Midlothian
Mon	Monmouthshire
Moray	Moray
N Ayrs	North Ayrshire
N Lincs	North Lincolnshire
N Lanark	North Lanarkshire
N Som	North Somerset
N Yorks	North Yorkshire
NE Lincs	North East Lincolnshire
Neath	Neath Port Talbot
Newport	City and County of Newport
Norf	Norfolk
Northants	Northamptonshire
Northumb	Northumberland
Nottingham	City of Nottingham
Notts	Nottinghamshire
Orkney	Orkney
Oxon	Oxfordshire
Pboro	Peterborough
Pembs	Pembrokeshire
Perth	Perth and Kinross
Plym	Plymouth
Poole	Poole
Powys	Powys
Ptsmth	Portsmouth
Reading	Reading
Redcar	Redcar and Cleveland
Renfs	Renfrewshire
Rhondda	Rhondda Cynon Taff
Rutland	Rutland
S Ayrs	South Ayrshire
S Glos	South Gloucestershire
S Lanark	South Lanarkshire
S Yorks	South Yorkshire
Scilly	Scilly
Shetland	Shetland
Shrops	Shropshire
Slough	Slough
Som	Somerset
Soton	Southampton
Staffs	Staffordshire
Southend	Southend-on-Sea
Stirling	Stirling
Stockton	Stockton-on-Tees
Stoke	Stoke-on-Trent
Suff	Suffolk
Sur	Surrey
Swansea	Swansea
Swindon	Swindon
T&W	Tyne and Wear
Telford	Telford and Wrekin
Thurrock	Thurrock
Torbay	Torbay
Torf	Torfaen
V Glam	The Vale of Glamorgan
W Berks	West Berkshire
W Dunb	West Dunbartonshire
W Isles	Western Isles
W Loth	West Lothian
W Mid	West Midlands
W Sus	West Sussex
W Yorks	West Yorkshire
Warks	Warwickshire
Warr	Warrington
Wilts	Wiltshire
Windsor	Windsor and Maidenhead
Wokingham	Wokingham
Worcs	Worcestershire
Wrex	Wrexham
York	City of York

How to use the index

Example

Trudoxhill Som **16** G4

- grid square
- page number
- county or unitary authority

A

b Kettleby Leics 36 C3
b Lench Worcs 27 C7
bbas Combe Som 8 B6
bberley Worcs 26 B4
bberton Essex 31 G7
bberton Worcs 26 C6
bberwick Northumb 63 B7
bbess Roding Essex 30 G2
bbey Devon 7 E10
bbey-cwm-hir Powys 25 A7
bbey Dore Hereford 25 E10
bbey Field Essex 30 F6
bbey Hulton Stoke 44 H3
bbey St Bathans Borders 70 D6
bbey Town Cumb 56 A3
bbey Village Lancs 50 G2
bbey Wood London 19 D11
bbeydale S Yorks 45 D7
bbeystead Lancs 50 D1
bbots Bickington Devon 6 E2
bbots Bromley Staffs 35 C6
bbots Langley Herts 19 A7
bbots Leigh N Som 15 D11
bbots Morton Worcs 27 C7
bbots Ripton Cambs 37 H8
bbots Salford Warks 27 C7
bbotsbury Dorset 8 F4
bbotsham Devon 6 D3
bbotskerswell Devon 5 E9
bbotsley Cambs 29 C9
bbotswood Hants 10 B2
bbotts Ann Hants 17 G10
bcott Shrops 33 H9
bdon Shrops 34 G1
ber Ceredig 23 B9
ber-Arad Carms 23 C8
ber-banc Ceredig 23 B8
ber Cowarch Gwyn 32 D4
ber-Giâr Carms 23 B10
ber-gwynfi Neath 14 B4
ber-Hirnant Gwyn 32 B5
ber-nant Rhondda 14 A6
ber-Rhiwlech Gwyn 32 C5
ber-Village Powys 25 F8
beraeron Ceredig 24 B1
beraman Rhondda 14 A6
berangell Gwyn 32 D4
berarder Highld 81 E6
berarder House Highld 81 A8
berarder Lodge Highld 81 E7
berargie Perth 76 F4
berarth Ceredig 24 B1
beravon Neath 14 B3
berbeeg Bl Gwent 15 A8
bercanaid M Tydf 14 A6
bercarn Caerph 15 B8
bercastle Pembs 22 C3
bercegir Powys 32 E4
berchirder Aberds 88 C6
bercraf Powys 24 G5
bercrombie Fife 77 G8
bercych Pembs 23 B7
bercynafon Powys 25 G7
bercynon Rhondda 14 B6
berdâr = Aberdare Rhondda 14 A5
Aberdalgie Perth 76 E3
Aberdare = Aberdâr Rhondda 14 A5
Aberdaron Gwyn 40 H3
Aberdaugleddau = Milford Haven Pembs 22 F4
Aberdeen Aberdeen 83 C11
Aberdesach Gwyn 40 E6
Aberdour Fife 69 B10
Aberdovey Gwyn 32 F2
Aberdulais Neath 14 A3
Aberedw Powys 25 D7
Abereiddy Pembs 22 C2
Abererch Gwyn 40 G5
Aberfan M Tydf 14 A6
Aberfeldy Perth 75 C11
Aberffraw Anglesey 40 D5
Aberffrwd Ceredig 32 H2
Aberford W Yorks 51 F10
Aberfoyle Stirling 75 G8
Abergavenny = Y Fenni Mon 25 G9
Abergele Conwy 42 E2
Abergorlech Carms 23 C10
Abergwaun = Fishguard Pembs 22 C4
Abergwesyn Powys 24 C5
Abergwili Carms 23 D9
Abergwynant Gwyn 32 D2
Abergwyngregyn Gwyn 41 C8
Abergynolwyn Gwyn 32 E2
Aberhonddu = Brecon Powys 25 F7
Aberhosan Powys 32 F4
Aberkenfig Bridgend 14 C4
Aberlady E Loth 70 B3
Aberlemno Angus 77 B8
Aberllefenni Gwyn 32 E3
Abermagwr Ceredig 24 A3
Abermaw = Barmouth Gwyn 32 D2
Abermeurig Ceredig 23 A10
Abermule Powys 33 F7
Abernaint Powys 33 C7
Abernant Carms 23 D8
Abernethy Perth 76 F4
Abernyte Perth 76 D5
Aberpennar = Mountain Ash Rhondda 14 B6
Aberporth Ceredig 23 A7
Abersoch Gwyn 40 H5
Abersychan Torf 15 A8
Abertawe = Swansea Swansea 14 B2
Aberteifi = Cardigan Ceredig 22 B6
Aberthin V Glam 14 D6
Abertillery = Abertyleri Bl Gwent 15 A8
Abertridwr Caerph 15 C7
Abertridwr Powys 32 D6
Abertyleri = Abertillery Bl Gwent 15 A8
Abertysswg Caerph 25 H8
Aberuthven Perth 76 F2
Aberyscir Powys 24 F6
Aberystwyth Ceredig 32 G1
Abhainn Suidhe W Isles 90 G5
Abingdon Oxon 17 B11
Abinger Common Sur 19 G8
Abinger Hammer Sur 19 G7
Abington S Lanark 60 A5
Abington Pigotts Cambs 29 D10
Ablington Glos 27 H8
Ablington Wilts 17 G8
Abney Derbys 44 E5
Aboyne Aberds 83 D7
Abram Gtr Man 43 B9
Abriachan Highld 87 H8
Abridge Essex 19 B11
Abronhill N Lanark 68 C6
Abson S Glos 16 D4
Abthorpe Northants 28 D3
Abune-the-Hill Orkney 95 F3
Aby Lincs 47 E8
Acaster Malbis York 52 E1
Acaster Selby N Yorks 52 E1
Accrington Lancs 50 G3
Acha Argyll 78 F4
Acha Mor W Isles 91 E8
Achabraid Argyll 73 E7
Achachork Highld 85 D9
Achafolla Argyll 72 B6
Achagary Highld 93 D10
Achahoish Argyll 72 F6
Achalader Perth 76 C4
Achallader Argyll 74 C6
Ach'an Todhair Highld 80 F2
Achanalt Highld 86 E5
Achanamara Argyll 72 E6
Achandunie Highld 87 D9
Achany Highld 93 J8
Achaphubuil Highld 80 F2
Acharacle Highld 79 E9
Acharn Highld 79 F10
Acharn Perth 75 C10
Acharole Highld 94 E4
Achath Aberds 83 B9
Achavanich Highld 94 F3
Achavraat Highld 87 G12
Achddu Carms 23 F9
Achduart Highld 92 J3
Achentoul Highld 93 F11
Achfary Highld 92 F5
Achgarve Highld 91 H13
Achiemore Highld 92 C6
Achiemore Highld 93 D11
A'Chill Highld 84 H7
Achiltibuie Highld 92 J3
Achina Highld 93 C10
Achinduich Highld 93 J8
Achinduin Argyll 79 H11
Achingills Highld 94 D3
Achintee Highld 80 F3
Achintee Highld 86 G2
Achintraid Highld 85 E13
Achlean Highld 81 D10
Achleck Argyll 78 G7
Achluachrach Highld 80 E4
Achlyness Highld 92 D5
Achmelvich Highld 92 G3
Achmore Highld 85 E13
Achmore Stirling 75 D8
Achnaba Argyll 73 E8
Achnaba Argyll 74 D2
Achnabat Highld 87 H8
Achnacarnin Highld 92 F3
Achnacarry Highld 80 E3
Achnacloich Argyll 74 D2
Achnacloich Highld 85 H10
Achnaconeran Highld 80 B6
Achnacraig Argyll 78 G7
Achnacroish Argyll 79 G11
Achnadrish Argyll 78 F7
Achnafalnich Argyll 74 E5
Achnagarron Highld 87 E9
Achnaha Highld 78 E7
Achnahanat Highld 87 B8
Achnahannet Highld 82 A1
Achnairn Highld 93 H8
Achnaluachrach Highld 93 J9
Achnasaul Highld 80 E3
Achnasheen Highld 86 F4
Achosnich Highld 78 E7
Achranich Highld 79 G10
Achreamie Highld 93 C13
Achriabhach Highld 80 G3
Achriesgill Highld 92 D5
Achrimsdale Highld 93 J12
Achtoty Highld 93 C9
Achurch Northants 36 G6
Achuvoldrach Highld 93 D8
Achvaich Highld 87 B10
Achvarasdal Highld 93 C12
Ackergill Highld 94 E5
Acklam Mbro 58 E5
Acklam N Yorks 52 C3
Ackleton Shrops 34 F3
Acklington Northumb 63 C8
Ackton W Yorks 51 G10
Ackworth Moor Top W Yorks 51 H10
Acle Norf 39 D10
Acock's Green W Mid 35 G7
Acol Kent 21 E10
Acomb Northumb 62 G5
Acomb York 52 D1
Aconbury Hereford 26 E2
Acre Lancs 50 G3
Acre Street W Sus 11 E6
Acrefair Wrex 33 A8
Acton Ches E 43 G9
Acton Dorset 9 G8
Acton London 19 C9
Acton Shrops 33 G9
Acton Suff 30 D5
Acton Wrex 42 G6
Acton Beauchamp Hereford 26 C3
Acton Bridge Ches W 43 E8
Acton Burnell Shrops 33 E11
Acton Green Hereford 26 C3
Acton Pigott Shrops 33 E11
Acton Round Shrops 34 F2
Acton Scott Shrops 33 G10
Acton Trussell Staffs 34 D5
Acton Turville S Glos 16 C5
Adbaston Staffs 34 C3
Adber Dorset 8 B4
Adderley Shrops 34 A2
Adderstone Northumb 71 G10
Addiewell W Loth 69 D8
Addingham W Yorks 51 E6
Addington Bucks 28 F4
Addington Kent 20 F3
Addington London 19 E10
Addinston Borders 70 E4
Addiscombe London 19 E10
Addlestone Sur 19 E7
Addlethorpe Lincs 47 F9
Adel W Yorks 51 F8
Adeney Telford 34 D3
Adfa Powys 33 E6
Adforton Hereford 25 A11
Adisham Kent 21 F9
Adlestrop Glos 27 F9
Adlingfleet E Yorks 52 G4
Adlington Lancs 43 A9
Admaston Staffs 34 C6
Admaston Telford 34 D2
Admington Warks 27 D9
Adstock Bucks 28 E4
Adstone Northants 28 C2
Adversane W Sus 11 B9
Advie Highld 88 E1
Adwalton W Yorks 51 G8
Adwell Oxon 18 B3
Adwick le Street S Yorks 45 B9
Adwick upon Dearne S Yorks 45 B8
Adziel Aberds 89 C9
Ae Village Dumfries 60 E5
Affleck Aberds 89 F8
Affpuddle Dorset 9 E7
Affric Lodge Highld 80 A3
Afon-wen Flint 42 E4
Afton IoW 10 F2
Agglethorpe N Yorks 58 H1
Agneash IoM 48 D4
Aigburth Mers 43 D6
Aiginis W Isles 91 D9
Aike E Yorks 52 E6
Aikerness Orkney 95 C5
Aikers Orkney 95 J5
Aiketgate Cumb 57 B6
Aikton Cumb 56 A4
Ailey Hereford 25 D10
Ailstone Warks 27 C9
Ailsworth Pboro 37 F7
Ainderby Quernhow N Yorks 51 A9
Ainderby Steeple N Yorks 58 G4
Aingers Green Essex 31 F8
Ainsdale Mers 42 A6
Ainsdale-on-Sea Mers 42 A6
Ainstable Cumb 57 B7
Ainsworth Gtr Man 43 A10
Ainthorpe N Yorks 59 F8
Aintree Mers 43 C6
Aird Argyll 72 C6
Aird Dumfries 54 C3
Aird Highld 85 A12
Aird W Isles 91 D10
Aird a Mhachair W Isles 84 D2
Aird a' Mhulaidh W Isles 90 F6
Aird Asaig W Isles 90 G6
Aird Dhail W Isles 91 A9
Aird Mhidhinis W Isles 84 H2
Aird Mhighe W Isles 90 H6
Aird Mhighe W Isles 90 J5
Aird Mhor W Isles 84 H2
Aird of Sleat Highld 85 H10
Aird Thunga W Isles 91 D9
Aird Uig W Isles 90 D5
Airdens Highld 87 B9
Airdrie N Lanark 68 D6
Airdtorrisdale Highld 93 C9
Airidh a Bhruaich W Isles 90 F7
Airieland Dumfries 55 D10
Airmyn E Yorks 52 G2
Airntully Perth 76 D3
Airor Highld 85 H12
Airth Falk 69 B7
Airton N Yorks 50 D5
Airyhassen Dumfries 54 E6
Aisby Lincs 36 B6
Aisby Lincs 46 C2
Aisgernis W Isles 84 F2
Aiskew N Yorks 58 H3
Aislaby N Yorks 59 F9
Aislaby N Yorks 59 H8
Aislaby Stockton 58 E5
Aisthorpe Lincs 46 D3
Aith Orkney 95 G3
Aith Shetland 96 D8
Aith Shetland 96 H5
Aithsetter Shetland 96 K6
Aitkenhead S Ayrs 66 F6
Aitnoch Highld 87 H12
Akeld Northumb 71 H8
Akeley Bucks 28 E4
Akenham Suff 31 D8
Albaston Corn 4 D5
Alberbury Shrops 33 D9
Albourne W Sus 12 E1
Albrighton Shrops 33 D10
Albrighton Shrops 34 E4
Alburgh Norf 39 G8
Albury Herts 29 F11
Albury Sur 19 G7
Albury End Herts 29 F11
Alby Hill Norf 39 B7
Alcaig Highld 87 F8
Alcaston Shrops 33 G10
Alcester Warks 27 C7
Alciston E Sus 12 F4
Alcombe Som 7 B8
Alcombe Wilts 16 E5
Alconbury Cambs 37 H7
Alconbury Weston Cambs 37 H7
Aldbar Castle Angus 77 B8
Aldborough N Yorks 51 C10
Aldborough Norf 39 B7
Aldbourne Wilts 17 D9
Aldbrough E Yorks 53 F8
Aldbrough St John N Yorks 58 E3
Aldbury Herts 28 G6
Aldcliffe Lancs 49 C4
Aldclune Perth 76 A2
Aldeburgh Suff 31 C11
Aldeby Norf 39 F10
Aldenham Herts 19 B8
Alderbury Wilts 9 B10
Aldercar Derbys 45 H8
Alderford Norf 39 D7
Alderholt Dorset 9 C10
Alderley Glos 16 B4
Alderley Edge Ches E 44 E2
Aldermaston W Berks 18 E2
Aldermaston Wharf W Berks 18 E3
Alderminster Warks 27 D9
Alder's End Hereford 26 D3
Aldersey Green Ches W 43 G7
Aldershot Hants 18 F5
Alderton Glos 27 E7
Alderton Northants 28 D4
Alderton Shrops 33 C10
Alderton Suff 31 D10
Alderton Wilts 16 C5
Alderwasley Derbys 45 G7
Aldfield N Yorks 51 C8
Aldford Ches W 43 G7
Aldham Essex 30 F6
Aldham Suff 31 D7
Aldie Highld 87 C10
Aldingbourne W Sus 11 D8
Aldingham Cumb 49 B2
Aldington Kent 13 C9
Aldington Worcs 27 D7
Aldington Frith Kent 13 C9
Aldochlay Argyll 68 A2
Aldreth Cambs 29 A11
Aldridge W Mid 35 E6
Aldringham Suff 31 B11
Aldsworth Glos 27 G8
Aldunie Moray 82 A5
Aldwark Derbys 44 G6
Aldwark N Yorks 51 C10
Aldwick W Sus 11 E8
Aldwincle Northants 36 G6
Aldworth W Berks 18 D2
Alexandria W Dunb 68 C2
Alfardisworthy Devon 6 E1
Alfington Devon 7 G10
Alfold Sur 11 A9
Alfold Bars W Sus 11 A9
Alfold Crossways Sur 19 H7
Alford Aberds 83 B7
Alford Lincs 47 E8
Alford Som 8 A5
Alfreton Derbys 45 G8
Alfrick Worcs 26 C4
Alfrick Pound Worcs 26 C4
Alfriston E Sus 12 F4
Algaltraig Argyll 73 F9
Algarkirk Lincs 37 B8
Alhampton Som 8 A5
Aline Lodge W Isles 90 F6
Alisary Highld 79 D10
Alkborough N Lincs 52 G4
Alkerton Oxon 27 D10
Alkham Kent 21 G9
Alkington Shrops 33 B11
Alkmonton Derbys 35 B7
All Cannings Wilts 17 E7
All Saints South Elmham Suff 39 G9
All Stretton Shrops 33 F10
Alladale Lodge Highld 86 C7
Allaleigh Devon 5 F9
Allanaquoich Aberds 82 D3
Allangrange Mains Highld 87 F9
Allanton Borders 71 E7
Allanton N Lanark 69 E7
Allathasdal W Isles 84 H1
Allendale Town Northumb 62 H4
Allenheads Northumb 57 B10
Allens Green Herts 29 G11
Allensford Durham 58 A1
Allensmore Hereford 25 E11
Allenton Derby 35 B9
Aller Som 8 B3
Allerby Cumb 56 C2
Allerford Som 7 B8
Allerston N Yorks 52 A4
Allerthorpe E Yorks 52 E3
Allerton Mers 43 D7
Allerton W Yorks 51 F7
Allerton Bywater W Yorks 51 G10
Allerton Mauleverer N Yorks 51 D10
Allesley W Mid 35 G9
Allestree Derby 35 B9
Allet Corn 3 E6
Allexton Leics 36 E4
Allgreave Ches E 44 F3
Allhallows Medway 20 D5
Allhallows-on-Sea Medway 20 D5
Alligin Shuas Highld 85 C13
Allimore Green Staffs 34 D4
Allington Lincs 36 A4
Allington Wilts 17 E7
Allington Wilts 17 H9
Allithwaite Cumb 49 B3
Alloa Clack 69 A7
Allonby Cumb 56 B2
Alloway S Ayrs 66 E6
Allt Carms 23 F10
Allt na h-Airbhe Highld 86 B4
Allt-nan-sùgh Highld 85 F14
Alltchaorunn Highld 74 B4
Alltforgan Powys 32 C5
Alltmawr Powys 25 D7
Alltnacaillich Highld 92 E7
Alltsigh Highld 81 B6
Alltwalis Carms 23 C9
Alltwen Neath 14 A3
Alltyblaca Ceredig 23 B10
Allwood Green Suff 31 A7
Almeley Hereford 25 C10
Almer Dorset 9 E8
Almholme S Yorks 45 B9
Almington Staffs 34 B3
Alminstone Cross Devon 6 D2
Almondbank Perth 76 E3
Almondbury W Yorks 51 H7
Almondsbury S Glos 16 C3
Alne N Yorks 51 C10
Alness Highld 87 E9
Alnham Northumb 62 B5
Alnmouth Northumb 63 B8
Alnwick Northumb 63 B7
Alperton London 19 C8
Alphamstone Essex 30 E5
Alpheton Suff 30 C5
Alphington Devon 7 G8
Alport Derbys 44 F6
Alpraham Ches E 43 G8
Alresford Essex 31 F7
Alrewas Staffs 35 D7
Alsager Ches E 43 G10
Alsagers Bank Staffs 44 H2
Alsop en le Dale Derbys 44 G5
Alston Cumb 57 B9
Alston Devon 8 D2
Alstone Glos 26 E6
Alstonefield Staffs 44 G5
Alswear Devon 7 D6
Altandhu Highld 92 H2
Altanduin Highld 93 G11
Altarnun Corn 4 C3
Altass Highld 92 J7
Alterwall Highld 94 D4
Altham Lancs 50 F3
Althorne Essex 20 B6
Althorpe N Lincs 46 B2
Alticry Dumfries 54 D5
Altnabreac Station Highld 93 E13
Altnacealgach Hotel Highld 92 H5
Altnacraig Argyll 79 J11
Altnafeadh Highld 74 B5
Altnaharra Highld 93 F8
Altofts W Yorks 51 G9
Alton Derbys 45 F7
Alton Hants 18 H4
Alton Staffs 35 A6
Alton Pancras Dorset 8 D6
Alton Priors Wilts 17 E8
Altrincham Gtr Man 43 D10
Altrua Highld 80 E4
Altskeith Stirling 75 G7
Altyre Ho. Moray 87 F13
Alva Clack 75 H11
Alvanley Ches W 43 E7
Alvaston Derby 35 B9
Alvechurch Worcs 27 A7
Alvecote Warks 35 E8
Alvediston Wilts 9 B8
Alveley Shrops 34 G3
Alverdiscott Devon 6 D4
Alverstoke Hants 10 E5
Alverstone IoW 10 F4
Alverton Notts 36 A3
Alves Moray 88 B1
Alvescot Oxon 17 A9
Alveston S Glos 16 C3
Alveston Warks 27 C9
Alvie Highld 81 C10
Alvingham Lincs 47 C7
Alvington Glos 16 A3
Alwalton Cambs 37 F7
Alweston Dorset 8 C5
Alwinton Northumb 62 C5
Alwoodley W Yorks 51 E8
Alyth Perth 76 C5
Am Baile W Isles 84 G2
Am Buth Argyll 79 J11
Amatnatua Highld 86 B7
Amber Hill Lincs 46 H6
Ambergate Derbys 45 G7
Amberley Glos 16 A5
Amberley W Sus 11 C9
Amble Northumb 63 C8
Amblecote W Mid 34 G4
Ambler Thorn W Yorks 51 G6
Ambleside Cumb 56 F5
Ambleston Pembs 22 D5
Ambrosden Oxon 28 G3
Amcotts N Lincs 46 A2
Amersham Bucks 18 B6
Amesbury Wilts 17 G8
Amington Staffs 35 E8
Amisfield Dumfries 60 E5
Amlwch Anglesey 40 A6
Amlwch Port Anglesey 40 A6
Ammanford = Rhydaman Carms 24 G3
Amod Argyll 65 E8
Amotherby N Yorks 52 B3
Ampfield Hants 10 B3
Ampleforth N Yorks 52 B1
Ampney Crucis Glos 17 A7
Ampney St Mary Glos 17 A7
Ampney St Peter Glos 17 A7
Amport Hants 17 G9
Ampthill C Beds 29 E7
Ampton Suff 30 A5
Amroth Pembs 22 F6
Amulree Perth 75 D11
An Caol Highld 85 C11
An Cnoc W Isles 91 D9
An Gleann Ur W Isles 91 D9
An t-Ob = Leverburgh W Isles 90 J5
Anagach Highld 82 A2
Anaheilt Highld 79 E11
Anancaun Highld 86 E3
Ancaster Lincs 36 A5
Anchor Shrops 33 G7
Anchorsholme Blackpool 49 E3
Ancroft Northumb 71 F8
Ancrum Borders 62 A2
Anderby Lincs 47 E9
Anderson Dorset 9 E7
Anderton Ches W 43 E9
Andover Hants 17 G10
Andover Down Hants 17 G10
Andoversford Glos 27 G7
Andreas IoM 48 C4
Anfield Mers 43 C6
Angersleigh Som 7 E10
Angle Pembs 22 F3
Angmering W Sus 11 D9
Angram N Yorks 51 E11
Angram N Yorks 57 G10
Anie Stirling 75 F8
Ankerville Highld 87 D11
Anlaby E Yorks 52 G6
Anmer Norf 38 C3
Anna Valley Hants 17 G10
Annan Dumfries 61 G7
Annat Argyll 74 E3
Annat Highld 85 C13
Annbank S Ayrs 67 D7
Annesley Notts 45 G9
Annesley Woodhouse Notts 45 G8
Annfield Plain Durham 58 A2
Annifirth Shetland 96 J3
Annitsford T&W 63 F8
Annscroft Shrops 33 E10
Ansdell Lancs 49 G3
Ansford Som 8 A5
Ansley Warks 35 F8
Anslow Staffs 35 C8
Anslow Gate Staffs 35 C7
Anstey Herts 29 E11
Anstey Leics 35 E11
Anstruther Easter Fife 77 G8

Anstruther Wester Fife 77 G8
Ansty Hants 18 G4
Ansty W Sus 12 D1
Ansty Warks 35 G9
Ansty Wilts 9 B8
Anthill Common Hants 10 C5
Anthorn Cumb 61 H7
Antingham Norf 39 B8
Anton's Gowt Lincs 46 H6
Antonshill Falk 69 B7
Antony Corn 4 F4
Anwick Lincs 46 G5
Anwoth Dumfries 55 D8
Aoradh Argyll 64 B3
Apes Hall Cambs 38 F1
Apethorpe Northants 36 F6
Apeton Staffs 34 D4
Apley Lincs 46 E5
Apperknowle Derbys 45 E7
Apperley Glos 26 F5
Apperley Bridge W Yorks 51 F7
Appersett N Yorks 57 G10
Appin Argyll 74 C2
Appin House Argyll 74 C2
Appleby N Lincs 46 A3
Appleby-in-Westmorland Cumb 57 D8
Appleby Magna Leics 35 E9
Appleby Parva Leics 35 E9
Applecross Highld 85 D12
Applecross Ho. Highld 85 D12
Appledore Devon 6 C3
Appledore Devon 7 E9
Appledore Kent 13 D8
Appledore Heath Kent 13 C8
Appleford Oxon 18 B2
Applegarthtown Dumfries 61 E7
Appleshaw Hants 17 G10
Applethwaite Cumb 56 D4
Appleton Halton 43 D8
Appleton Oxon 17 A11
Appleton-le-Moors N Yorks 59 H8
Appleton-le-Street N Yorks 52 B3
Appleton Roebuck N Yorks 52 E1
Appleton Thorn Warr 43 D9
Appleton Wiske N Yorks 58 F4
Appletreehall Borders 61 B11
Appletreewick N Yorks 51 C6
Appley Som 7 D9
Appley Bridge Lancs 43 B8
Apse Heath IoW 10 F4
Apsley End C Beds 29 E8
Apuldram W Sus 11 D7
Aquhythie Aberds 83 B9
Arabella Highld 87 D11
Arbeadie Aberds 83 D8
Arberth = Narberth Pembs 22 E6
Arbirlot Angus 77 C9
Arboll Highld 87 C11
Arborfield Wokingham 18 E4
Arborfield Cross Wokingham 18 E4
Arborfield Garrison Wokingham 18 E4
Arbour-thorne S Yorks 45 D7
Arbroath Angus 77 C9
Arbuthnott Aberds 83 F9
Archiestown Moray 88 D2
Arclid Ches E 43 F10
Ard-dhubh Highld 85 D12
Ardachu Highld 93 J9
Ardalanish Argyll 78 K6
Ardanaiseig Argyll 74 E3
Ardaneaskan Highld 85 E13
Ardanstur Argyll 73 B7
Ardargie House Hotel Perth 76 F3
Ardarroch Highld 85 E13
Ardbeg Argyll 64 D5
Ardbeg Argyll 73 E10
Ardcharnich Highld 86 C4
Ardchiavaig Argyll 78 K6
Ardchullarie More Stirling 75 F8
Ardchyle Stirling 75 E8
Arddleen Powys 33 D8
Ardechvie Highld 80 D3
Ardeley Herts 29 F10
Ardelve Highld 85 F13
Arden Argyll 68 B2
Ardens Grafton Warks 27 C8
Ardentinny Argyll 73 E10
Ardentraive Argyll 73 F9
Ardeonaig Stirling 75 D9
Ardersier Highld 87 F10
Ardessie Highld 86 C3
Ardfern Argyll 73 C7
Ardgartan Argyll 74 G5
Ardgay Highld 87 B8
Ardgour Highld 74 A3
Ardheslaig Highld 85 C12
Ardiecow Moray 88 B5
Ardindrean Highld 86 C4
Ardingly W Sus 12 D2
Ardington Oxon 17 C11
Ardlair Aberds 83 A7
Ardlamont Ho. Argyll 73 G8
Ardleigh Essex 31 F7
Ardler Perth 76 C5
Ardley Oxon 28 F2
Ardlui Argyll 74 F6
Ardlussa Argyll 72 E5
Ardmair Highld 86 B4
Ardmay Argyll 74 G5
Ardminish Argyll 65 D7
Ardmolich Highld 79 D10
Ardmore Argyll 79 J10
Ardmore Highld 87 C10
Ardmore Highld 92 D5
Ardnacross Argyll 79 G8
Ardnadam Argyll 73 F10
Ardnagrask Highld 87 G8
Ardnarff Highld 85 E13
Ardnastang Highld 79 E11
Ardnave Argyll 64 A3
Ardno Argyll 73 C10
Ardo Aberds 89 E8
Ardo Ho. Aberds 89 F9
Ardoch Perth 76 D3
Ardochy House Highld 80 C4
Ardoyne Aberds 83 A8
Ardpatrick Argyll 72 G6
Ardpatrick Ho. Argyll 72 H6
Ardpeaton Argyll 73 E11
Ardrishaig Argyll 73 E7
Ardross Fife 77 G8
Ardross Highld 87 D9
Ardross Castle Highld 87 D9
Ardrossan N Ayrs 66 B5
Ardshealach Highld 79 E9
Ardsley S Yorks 45 B7
Ardslignish Highld 79 E8
Ardtalla Argyll 64 C5
Ardtalnaig Perth 75 D10
Ardtoe Highld 79 D9
Ardtrostan Perth 75 E9
Arduaine Argyll 72 B6
Ardullie Highld 87 E8
Ardvasar Highld 85 H11
Ardvorlich Perth 75 E9
Ardwell Dumfries 54 E4
Ardwell Mains Dumfries 54 E4
Ardwick Gtr Man 44 C2
Areley Kings Worcs 26 A5
Arford Hants 18 H5
Argoed Caerph 15 B7
Argoed Mill Powys 24 B6
Arichamish Argyll 73 C8
Arichastlich Argyll 74 D5
Aridhglas Argyll 78 J6
Arileod Argyll 78 F4
Arinacrinachd Highld 85 C12
Arinagour Argyll 78 F5
Arion Orkney 95 G3
Arisaig Highld 79 C9
Ariundle Highld 79 E11
Arkendale N Yorks 51 C9
Arkesden Essex 29 E11
Arkholme Lancs 50 B1
Arkle Town N Yorks 58 F1
Arkleton Dumfries 61 D9
Arkley London 19 B9
Arksey S Yorks 45 B9
Arkwright Town Derbys 45 E8
Arle Glos 26 F6
Arlecdon Cumb 56 E2
Arlesey C Beds 29 E8
Arleston Telford 34 D2
Arley Ches E 43 D9
Arlingham Glos 26 G4
Arlington Devon 6 B5
Arlington E Sus 12 F4
Arlington Glos 27 H8
Armadale Highld 93 C10
Armadale W Loth 69 D8
Armadale Castle Highld 85 H11
Armathwaite Cumb 57 B7
Arminghall Norf 39 E8
Armitage Staffs 35 D6
Armley W Yorks 51 F8
Armscote Warks 27 D9
Armthorpe S Yorks 45 B10
Arnabost Argyll 78 F5
Arncliffe N Yorks 50 B5
Arncroach Fife 77 G8
Arne Dorset 9 F8
Arnesby Leics 36 F2
Arngask Perth 76 F4
Arnisdale Highld 85 G13
Arnish Highld 85 D10
Arniston Engine Midloth 70 D2
Arnol W Isles 91 C8
Arnold E Yorks 53 E7
Arnold Notts 45 H9
Arnprior Stirling 68 A5
Arnside Cumb 49 B4
Aros Mains Argyll 79 G8
Arowry Wrex 33 B10
Arpafeelie Highld 87 F9
Arrad Foot Cumb 49 A3
Arram E Yorks 52 E6
Arrathorne N Yorks 58 G3
Arreton IoW 10 F4
Arrington Cambs 29 C10
Arrivain Argyll 74 D5
Arrochar Argyll 74 G5
Arrow Warks 27 C7
Arthington W Yorks 51 E8
Arthingworth Northants 36 G3
Arthog Gwyn 32 D2
Arthrath Aberds 89 E9
Arthurstone Perth 76 C5
Artrochie Aberds 89 E10
Arundel W Sus 11 D9
Aryhoulan Highld 80 G2
Asby Cumb 56 D2
Ascog Argyll 73 G10
Ascot Windsor 18 E6
Ascott Warks 27 E10
Ascott-under-Wychwood Oxon 27 G10
Asenby N Yorks 51 B9
Asfordby Leics 36 D3
Asfordby Hill Leics 36 D3
Asgarby Lincs 46 H5
Asgarby Lincs 47 F7
Ash Kent 20 E2
Ash Kent 21 F9
Ash Som 8 B3
Ash Sur 18 F5
Ash Bullayne Devon 7 F6
Ash Green Warks 35 G9
Ash Magna Shrops 34 B1
Ash Mill Devon 7 D6
Ash Priors Som 7 D10
Ash Street Suff 31 D7
Ash Thomas Devon 7 E9
Ash Vale Sur 18 F5
Ashampstead W Berks 18 D2
Ashbocking Suff 31 C8
Ashbourne Derbys 44 H5
Ashbrittle Som 7 D9
Ashburton Devon 5 E8
Ashbury Devon 6 G4
Ashbury Oxon 17 C9
Ashby N Lincs 46 B3
Ashby by Partney Lincs 47 F8
Ashby cum Fenby NE Lincs 46 B6
Ashby de la Launde Lincs 46 G4
Ashby-de-la-Zouch Leics 35 D9
Ashby Folville Leics 36 D3
Ashby Magna Leics 36 F1
Ashby Parva Leics 35 G11
Ashby Puerorum Lincs 47 E7
Ashby St Ledgers Northants 28 B2
Ashby St Mary Norf 39 E9
Ashchurch Glos 26 E6
Ashcombe Devon 5 D10
Ashcott Som 15 H10
Ashdon Essex 30 D2
Ashe Hants 18 G2
Asheldham Essex 20 A6
Ashen Essex 30 D4
Ashendon Bucks 28 G4
Ashfield Carms 24 F3
Ashfield Stirling 75 G10
Ashfield Suff 31 B9
Ashfield Green Suff 31 A9
Ashfold Crossways W Sus 11 B11
Ashford Devon 6 C4
Ashford Hants 9 C10
Ashford Kent 13 B9
Ashford Sur 19 D7
Ashford Bowdler Shrops 26 A2
Ashford Carbonell Shrops 26 A2
Ashford Hill Hants 18 E2
Ashford in the Water Derbys 44 F5
Ashgill S Lanark 68 F6
Ashill Devon 7 E9
Ashill Norf 38 E4
Ashill Som 8 C2
Ashingdon Essex 20 B5
Ashington Northumb 63 E8
Ashington Som 8 B4
Ashington W Sus 11 C10
Ashintully Castle Perth 76 A4
Ashkirk Borders 61 A10
Ashlett Hants 10 D3
Ashleworth Glos 26 F5
Ashley Cambs 30 B3
Ashley Ches E 43 D10
Ashley Devon 6 E5
Ashley Dorset 9 D10
Ashley Glos 16 B6
Ashley Hants 10 A2
Ashley Hants 10 E1
Ashley Northants 36 F3
Ashley Staffs 34 B3
Ashley Green Bucks 28 H6
Ashley Heath Dorset 9 D10
Ashley Heath Staffs 34 B3
Ashmanhaugh Norf 39 C9
Ashmansworth Hants 17 F11
Ashmansworthy Devon 6 E2
Ashmore Dorset 9 C8
Ashorne Warks 27 C10
Ashover Derbys 45 F7
Ashow Warks 27 A10
Ashprington Devon 5 F9
Ashreigney Devon 6 E5
Ashtead Sur 19 F8
Ashton Ches W 43 F8
Ashton Corn 2 G5
Ashton Hants 10 C4
Ashton Hereford 26 B2
Ashton Involyd 73 F11
Ashton Northants 28 D4
Ashton Northants 37 G6
Ashton Common Wilts 16 F5
Ashton-In-Makerfield Gtr Man 43 C8
Ashton Keynes Wilts 17 B7
Ashton under Hill Worcs 26 E6
Ashton-under-Lyne Gtr Man 44 C3
Ashton upon Mersey Gtr Man 43 C10
Ashurst Hants 10 C2
Ashurst Kent 12 C4
Ashurst W Sus 11 C10
Ashurstwood W Sus 12 C3
Ashwater Devon 6 G2
Ashwell Herts 29 E9
Ashwell Rutland 36 D4
Ashwell Som 8 C2
Ashwellthorpe Norf 39 F7
Ashwick Som 16 G3
Ashwicken Norf 38 D3
Ashybank Borders 61 B11
Askam in Furness Cumb 49 B2
Askern S Yorks 45 A9
Askerswell Dorset 8 E4
Askett Bucks 28 H5
Askham Cumb 57 D7
Askham Notts 45 E11
Askham Bryan York 52 E1
Askham Richard York 51 E11
Asknish Argyll 73 D8
Askrigg N Yorks 57 G11
Askwith N Yorks 51 E7
Aslackby Lincs 37 B6
Aslacton Norf 39 F7
Aslockton Notts 36 B3
Asloun Aberds 83 B7
Aspatria Cumb 56 B3
Aspenden Herts 29 F10
Asperton Lincs 37 B8
Aspley Guise C Beds 28 E6
Aspley Heath C Beds 28 E6
Aspull Gtr Man 43 B9
Asselby E Yorks 52 G3
Asserby Lincs 47 E8
Assington Suff 30 E6
Assynt Ho. Highld 87 E8
Astbury Ches E 44 F2
Astcote Northants 28 C3
Asterley Shrops 33 E9
Asterton Shrops 33 F9
Asthall Oxon 27 G9
Asthall Leigh Oxon 27 G10
Astley Shrops 33 D11
Astley Warks 35 G9
Astley Worcs 26 B4
Astley Abbotts Shrops 34 F3
Astley Bridge Gtr Man 43 A10
Astley Cross Worcs 26 B5
Astley Green Gtr Man 43 C10
Aston Ches E 43 H9
Aston Ches W 43 E8
Aston Derbys 44 D5
Aston Hereford 25 A11
Aston Herts 29 F9
Aston Oxon 17 A10
Aston S Yorks 45 D8
Aston Shrops 33 C11
Aston Staffs 34 A3
Aston Telford 34 E2
Aston W Mid 35 G6
Aston Wokingham 18 C4
Aston Abbotts Bucks 28 F5
Aston Botterell Shrops 34 G2
Aston-By-Stone Staffs 34 B5
Aston Cantlow Warks 27 C8
Aston Clinton Bucks 28 G5
Aston Crews Hereford 26 F3
Aston Cross Glos 26 E6
Aston End Herts 29 F9
Aston Eyre Shrops 34 F2
Aston Fields Worcs 26 B6
Aston Flamville Leics 35 F10
Aston Ingham Hereford 26 F3
Aston juxta Mondrum Ches E 43 G9
Aston le Walls Northants 27 C11
Aston Magna Glos 27 E8
Aston Munslow Shrops 33 G11
Aston on Clun Shrops 33 G9
Aston-on-Trent Derbys 35 C10
Aston Rogers Shrops 33 E9
Aston Rowant Oxon 18 B4
Aston Sandford Bucks 28 H4
Aston Somerville Worcs 27 E7
Aston Subedge Glos 27 D8
Aston Tirrold Oxon 18 C2
Aston Upthorpe Oxon 18 C2
Astrop Northants 28 E2
Astwick C Beds 29 E9
Astwood M Keynes 28 D6
Astwood Worcs 26 C5
Astwood Bank Worcs 27 B7
Aswarby Lincs 37 B6
Aswardby Lincs 47 E7
Atch Lench Worcs 27 C7
Atcham Shrops 33 E11
Athelhampton Dorset 9 E6
Athelington Suff 31 A9
Athelney Som 8 B2
Athelstaneford E Loth 70 C4
Atherington Devon 6 D4
Atherstone Warks 35 F9
Atherstone on Stour Warks 27 C9
Atherton Gtr Man 43 B9
Atley Hill N Yorks 58 F3
Atlow Derbys 44 H6
Attadale Highld 86 H2
Attadale Ho. Highld 86 H2
Attenborough Notts 35 B11
Atterby Lincs 46 C3
Attercliffe S Yorks 45 D7
Attleborough Norf 38 F6
Attleborough Warks 35 F9
Attlebridge Norf 39 D7
Atwick E Yorks 53 D7
Atworth Wilts 16 E5
Aubourn Lincs 46 F3
Auchagallon N Ayrs 66 C1
Auchallater Aberds 82 E3
Aucharnie Aberds 89 D6
Auchattie Aberds 83 D8
Auchavan Angus 82 G3
Auchbreck Moray 82 A4
Auchenback E Renf 68 E4
Auchenbainzie Dumfries 60 D4
Auchenblae Aberds 83 F9
Auchenbrack Dumfries 60 D3
Auchenbreck Argyll 73 E9
Auchencairn Dumfries 55 D10
Auchencairn Dumfries 60 E5
Auchencairn N Ayrs 66 D3
Auchencrosh S Ayrs 54 B4
Auchencrow Borders 71 D7
Auchendinny Midloth 69 D11
Auchengray S Lanark 69 E8
Auchenhalrig Moray 88 B3
Auchenheath S Lanark 69 F7
Auchenlochan Argyll 73 F8
Auchenmalg Dumfries 54 D5
Auchensoul S Ayrs 66 G5
Auchentiber N Ayrs 67 B6
Auchertyre Highld 85 F13
Auchgourish Highld 81 B11
Auchincarroch W Dunb 68 B3
Auchindrain Argyll 73 C9
Auchindrean Highld 86 C4
Auchininna Aberds 89 D6
Auchinleck E Ayrs 67 D8
Auchinloch N Lanark 68 C5
Auchinroath Moray 88 C2
Auchintoul Aberds 83 B7
Auchiries Aberds 89 E10
Auchlee Aberds 83 D10
Auchleven Aberds 83 A8
Auchlochan S Lanark 69 G7
Auchlossan Aberds 83 C7
Auchlunies Aberds 83 D10
Auchlyne Stirling 75 E8
Auchmacoy Aberds 89 E9
Auchmair Moray 82 A5
Auchmantle Dumfries 54 C4
Auchmillan E Ayrs 67 D8
Auchmithie Angus 77 C9
Auchmuirbridge Fife 76 G5
Auchmull Angus 83 F7
Auchnacree Angus 77 A7
Auchnagallin Highld 87 H13
Auchnagatt Aberds 89 D9
Auchnaha Argyll 73 E8
Auchnashelloch Perth 75 F10
Aucholzie Aberds 82 D5
Auchrannie Angus 76 B5
Auchroisk Highld 82 A2
Auchronie Angus 82 E6
Auchterarder Perth 76 F2
Auchteraw Highld 80 C5
Auchterderran Fife 76 H5
Auchterhouse Angus 76 D6
Auchtermuchty Fife 76 F5
Auchterneed Highld 86 F7
Auchtertool Fife 69 A11
Auchtertyre Moray 88 C1
Auchtubh Stirling 75 E8
Auckengill Highld 94 D5
Auckley S Yorks 45 B10
Audenshaw Gtr Man 44 C3
Audlem Ches E 34 A2
Audley Staffs 43 G10
Audley End Essex 30 E5
Auds Aberds 89 B6
Aughton E Yorks 52 F3
Aughton Lancs 43 B6
Aughton Lancs 50 C1
Aughton S Yorks 45 D8
Aughton Wilts 17 F9
Aughton Park Lancs 43 B7
Auldearn Highld 87 F12
Aulden Hereford 25 C11
Auldgirth Dumfries 60 E5
Auldhame E Loth 70 B4
Auldhouse S Lanark 68 E5
Ault a'chruinn Highld 80 A1
Aultanrynie Highld 92 F6
Aultbea Highld 91 J13
Aultdearg Highld 86 E5
Aultgrishan Highld 91 J12
Aultguish Inn Highld 86 D6
Aultibea Highld 93 G13
Aultiphurst Highld 93 C11
Aultmore Moray 88 C4
Aultnagoire Highld 81 A7
Aultnamain Inn Highld 87 C9
Aultnaslat Highld 80 C3
Aulton Aberds 83 A8
Aundorach Highld 82 B1
Aunsby Lincs 36 B6
Auquhorthies Aberds 89 F8
Aust S Glos 16 C2
Austendike Lincs 37 C8
Austerfield S Yorks 45 C10
Austrey Warks 35 E8
Austwick N Yorks 50 C3
Authorpe Lincs 47 D8
Authorpe Row Lincs 47 E9
Avebury Wilts 17 E8
Aveley Thurrock 20 C2
Avening Glos 16 B5
Averham Notts 45 G11
Aveton Gifford Devon 5 G7
Avielochan Highld 81 B11
Aviemore Highld 81 B10
Avington Hants 10 A4
Avington W Berks 17 E10
Avoch Highld 87 F10
Avon Hants 9 E10
Avon Dassett Warks 27 D11
Avonbridge Falk 69 C8
Avonmouth Bristol 15 D11
Avonwick Devon 5 F8
Awbridge Hants 10 B2
Awhirk Dumfries 54 D3
Awkley S Glos 16 C2
Awliscombe Devon 7 F10
Awre Glos 26 H4
Awsworth Notts 35 A10
Axbridge Som 15 F10
Axford Hants 18 G3
Axford Wilts 17 D9
Axminster Devon 8 E1
Axmouth Devon 8 E1
Axton Flint 42 D4
Aycliff Kent 21 G10
Aycliffe Durham 58 D3
Aydon Northumb 62 G6
Aylburton Glos 16 A3
Ayle Northumb 57 B9
Aylesbeare Devon 7 G9
Aylesbury Bucks 28 G5
Aylesby NE Lincs 46 B6
Aylesford Kent 20 F4
Aylesham Kent 21 F9
Aylestone Leicester 36 E1
Aylmerton Norf 39 B7
Aylsham Norf 39 C7
Aylton Hereford 26 E3
Aymestrey Hereford 25 B11
Aynho Northants 28 E2
Ayot St Lawrence Herts 29 G8
Ayot St Peter Herts 29 G9
Ayr S Ayrs 66 D6
Aysgarth N Yorks 58 H1
Ayside Cumb 49 A3
Ayston Rutland 36 E4
Aythorpe Roding Essex 30 G2
Ayton Borders 71 D8
Aywick Shetland 96 E7
Azerley N Yorks 51 B8

B

Babbacombe Torbay 5 E10
Babbinswood Shrops 33 B9
Babcary Som 8 B4
Babel Carms 24 E5
Babell Flint 42 E4
Babraham Cambs 30 C2
Babworth Notts 45 D10
Bac W Isles 91 C9
Bachau Anglesey 40 B6
Back of Keppoch Highld 79 C9
Back Rogerton E Ayrs 67 D8
Backaland Orkney 95 E6
Backaskaill Orkney 95 C5
Backbarrow Cumb 49 A3
Backe Carms 23 E7
Backfolds Aberds 89 C10
Backford Ches W 43 E7
Backford Cross Ches W 43 E6
Backhill Aberds 89 E10
Backhill Aberds 89 E7
Backhill of Clackriach Aberds 89 D9
Backhill of Fortree Aberds 89 D9
Backhill of Trustach Aberds 83 D8
Backies Highld 93 J11
Backlass Highld 94 E4
Backwell N Som 15 E10
Backworth T&W 63 F9
Bacon End Essex 30 G3
Baconsthorpe Norf 39 B7
Bacton Hereford 25 E10
Bacton Norf 39 B9
Bacton Suff 31 B7
Bacton Green Suff 31 B7
Bacup Lancs 50 G4
Badachro Highld 85 A12
Badanloch Lodge Highld 93 F10
Badavanich Highld 86 F4
Badbury Swindon 17 C8
Badby Northants 28 C2
Badcall Highld 92 D5
Badcaul Highld 86 B3
Baddeley Green Stoke 44 G3
Baddesley Clinton Warks 27 A9
Baddesley Ensor Warks 35 F8
Baddidarach Highld 92 G3
Baddoch Aberds 82 E3
Baddock Highld 87 F10
Badenscoth Aberds 89 E7
Badenyon Aberds 82 B5
Badger Shrops 34 F3
Badger's Mount Kent 19 E11
Badgeworth Glos 26 G6
Badgworth Som 15 F9
Badicaul Highld 85 F12
Badingham Suff 31 B10
Badlesmere Kent 21 F7
Badlipster Highld 94 F4
Badluarach Highld 86 B2
Badminton S Glos 16 C5
Badnaban Highld 92 G3
Badninish Highld 87 B10
Badrallach Highld 86 B3
Badsey Worcs 27 D7
Badshot Lea Sur 18 G5
Badsworth W Yorks 45 A8
Badwell Ash Suff 30 B6
Bae Colwyn = Colwyn Bay Conwy 41 C10
Bag Enderby Lincs 47 E7
Bagby N Yorks 51 A10
Bagendon Glos 27 H7
Bagh a Chaisteil = Castlebay W Isles 84 J1
Bagh Mor W Isles 84 C3
Bagh Shiarabhagh W Isles 84 H2
Baghasdal W Isles 84 G2
Bagillt Flint 42 E5
Baginton Warks 27 A10
Baglan Neath 14 B3
Bagley Shrops 33 C10
Bagnall Staffs 44 G3
Bagnor W Berks 17 E11
Bagshot Sur 18 E6
Bagshot Wilts 17 E10
Bagthorpe Norf 38 B3
Bagthorpe Notts 45 G8
Bagworth Leics 35 E10
Bagwy Llydiart Hereford 25 F11
Bail Àrd Bhuirgh W Isles 91 B9
Bail' Iochdrach W Isles 84 C3
Bail Uachdraich W Isles 84 B3
Bail' Ur Tholastaidh W Isles 91 C10
Baildon W Yorks 51 F7
Baile W Isles 90 J4
Baile a Mhanaich W Isles 84 C2
Baile Ailein W Isles 91 E7
Baile an Truiseil W Isles 91 B8
Baile Boidheach Argyll 72 F6
Baile Glas W Isles 84 C3
Baile Mhartainn W Isles 84 A2
Baile Mhic Phail W Isles 84 A3
Baile Mor Argyll 78 J5
Baile Mor W Isles 84 B2
Baile na Creige W Isles 84 H1
Baile nan Cailleach W Isles 84 C2
Baile Raghaill W Isles 84 A2
Bailebeag Highld 81 B7
Baileyhead Cumb 61 F11
Bailiesward Aberds 88 E4
Baillieston Glasgow 68 D5
Bainbridge N Yorks 57 G11
Bainsford Falk 69 B7
Bainshole Aberds 88 E6
Bainton E Yorks 52 D5
Bainton Pboro 37 E6
Bairnkine Borders 62 B2
Baker Street Thurrock 20 C3
Baker's End Herts 29 G10
Bakewell Derbys 44 F6
Bala = Y Bala Gwyn 32 B5
Balachuirn Highld 85 D10
Balavil Highld 81 C9
Balbeg Highld 81 A6
Balbeg Highld 86 H7
Balbeggie Perth 76 E4
Balbithan Aberds 83 B9
Balbithan Ho. Aberds 83 B10
Balblair Highld 87 B8
Balblair Highld 87 E10
Balby S Yorks 45 B9
Balchladich Highld 92 F3
Balchraggan Highld 87 G8
Balchraggan Highld 87 H8
Balchrick Highld 92 D4
Balchrystie Fife 77 G7
Balcladaich Highld 80 A4
Balcombe W Sus 12 C2
Balcombe Lane W Sus 12 C2
Balcomie Fife 77 F9
Balcurvie Fife 76 G6
Baldersby N Yorks 51 B9
Baldersby St James N Yorks 51 B9
Balderstone Lancs 50 F2
Balderton Ches W 42 F6
Balderton Notts 46 G2
Baldhu Corn 3 E6
Baldinnie Fife 77 F7
Baldock Herts 29 E9
Baldovie Dundee 77 D7
Baldrine IoM 48 D4
Baldslow E Sus 13 E6
Baldwin IoM 48 D3
Baldwinholme Cumb 56 A5
Baldwin's Gate Staffs 34 A3
Bale Norf 38 B6
Balearn Aberds 89 C10
Balemartine Argyll 78 G2
Balephuil Argyll 78 G2
Balerno Edin 69 D10
Balevullin Argyll 78 G2
Balfield Angus 83 G7
Balfour Orkney 95 G5
Balfron Stirling 68 B4
Balfron Station Stirling 68 B4
Balgaveny Aberds 89 D6
Balgavies Angus 77 B8
Balgonar Fife 69 A9
Balgove Aberds 89 E8
Balgowan Highld 81 D8
Balgown Highld 85 B8
Balgrochan E Dunb 68 C5
Balgy Highld 85 C13
Balhaldie Stirling 75 G11
Balhalgardy Aberds 83 A9
Balham London 19 D9
Balhary Perth 76 C5
Baliasta Shetland 96 C8
Baligill Highld 93 C11
Balintore Angus 76 B5
Balintore Highld 87 D11
Balintraid Highld 87 D10
Balk N Yorks 51 A10
Balkeerie Angus 76 C6
Balkemback Angus 76 D6
Balkholme E Yorks 52 G3
Balkissock S Ayrs 54 A4
Ball Shrops 33 C9
Ball Haye Green Staffs 44 G3
Ball Hill Hants 17 E11
Ballabeg IoM 48 E2
Ballacannel IoM 48 D4
Ballachulish Highld 74 B3
Ballajora IoM 48 C4
Ballaleigh IoM 48 D3
Ballamodha IoM 48 E2
Ballantrae S Ayrs 54 A3
Ballaquine IoM 48 D4
Ballards Gore Essex 20 B6
Ballasalla IoM 48 C3
Ballasalla IoM 48 E2
Ballater Aberds 82 D5
Ballaugh IoM 48 C3
Ballaveare IoM 48 E3
Ballcorach Moray 82 A3
Ballechin Perth 76 B2
Balleigh Highld 87 C10
Ballencrieff E Loth 70 C3
Ballentoul Perth 81 G10
Ballidon Derbys 44 G6
Balliemore Argyll 73 E9
Balliemore Argyll 79 J11
Ballikinrain Stirling 68 B4
Ballimeanoch Argyll 73 B9
Ballimore Argyll 73 E8
Ballimore Stirling 75 F8
Ballinaby Argyll 64 B3
Ballindean Perth 76 E5
Ballingdon Suff 30 D5
Ballinger Common Bucks 18 A6
Ballingham Hereford 26 E2
Ballingry Fife 76 H4
Ballinlick Perth 76 C2
Ballinluig Perth 76 B2
Ballintuim Perth 76 B4
Balloch Angus 76 B6
Balloch Highld 87 G10
Balloch N Lanark 68 C6
Balloch W Dunb 68 B2
Ballochan Aberds 83 D7
Ballochford Moray 88 E3
Ballochmorrie S Ayrs 54 A5
Balls Cross W Sus 11 B8
Balls Green Essex 31 F7
Ballygown Argyll 78 G7
Ballygrant Argyll 64 B4
Ballyhaugh Argyll 78 F4
Balmacara Highld 85 F13
Balmacara Square Highld 85 F13
Balmaclellan Dumfries 55 B9
Balmacneil Perth 76 B2
Balmacqueen Highld 85 A9
Balmae Dumfries 55 E9
Balmaha Stirling 68 A3
Balmalcolm Fife 76 G6
Balmeanach Highld 85 D10
Balmedie Aberds 83 B11
Balmer Heath Shrops 33 B10
Balmerino Fife 76 E6
Balmerlawn Hants 10 D2
Balmichael N Ayrs 66 C2
Balmirmer Angus 77 D8
Balmore Highld 85 D7
Balmore Highld 86 H6
Balmore Highld 87 G11
Balmore Perth 76 B2
Balmule Fife 69 B11
Balmullo Fife 77 E7
Balmungie Highld 87 F10
Balnaboth Angus 82 G5
Balnabruaich Highld 87 E10
Balnabruich Highld 94 H3
Balnacoil Highld 93 H11
Balnacra Highld 86 G2
Balnafoich Highld 87 H9
Balnagall Highld 87 C11
Balnaguard Perth 76 B2
Balnahard Argyll 72 D3
Balnahard Argyll 78 H7
Balnain Highld 86 H7
Balnakeil Highld 92 C6
Balnaknock Highld 85 B9
Balnapaling Highld 87 E10
Balne N Yorks 52 H1
Balochroy Argyll 65 C8
Balone Fife 77 F7
Balornock Glasgow 68 D5
Balquharn Perth 76 D3
Balquhidder Stirling 75 E8
Balsall W Mid 35 H8
Balsall Common W Mid 35 H8
Balsall Hth. W Mid 35 G6
Balscott Oxon 27 D10
Balsham Cambs 30 C2
Baltasound Shetland 96 C8
Balterley Staffs 43 G10
Baltersan Dumfries 55 C7
Balthangie Aberds 89 C8
Baltonsborough Som 8 A4
Balvaird Highld 87 F8
Balvicar Argyll 72 B6
Balvraid Highld 85 G13
Balvraid Highld 87 H11
Bamber Bridge Lancs 50 G1
Bambers Green Essex 30 F2
Bamburgh Northumb 71 G10
Bamff Perth 76 B5
Bamford Derbys 44 D6
Bamford Gtr Man 44 A2
Bampton Cumb 57 E7
Bampton Devon 7 D8
Bampton Oxon 17 A10
Bampton Grange Cumb 57 E7
Banavie Highld 80 F3
Banbury Oxon 27 D11
Bancffosfelen Carms 23 E9
Banchory Aberds 83 D8
Banchory-Devenick Aberds 83 C11
Bancycapel Carms 23 E9
Bancyfelin Carms 23 E8
Bancyffordd Carms 23 C9
Bandirran Perth 76 D5
Banff Aberds 89 B6
Bangor Gwyn 41 C7
Bangor-is-y-coed Wrex 43 H6
Banham Norf 39 G6
Bank Hants 10 D1
Bank Newton N Yorks 50 D5
Bank Street Worcs 26 B3
Bankend Dumfries 60 G6
Bankfoot Perth 76 D3
Bankglen E Ayrs 67 E9
Bankhead Aberdeen 83 B10
Bankhead Aberds 83 C8
Banknock Falk 68 C6
Banks Cumb 61 G11
Banks Lancs 49 G3
Bankshill Dumfries 61 E7
Banningham Norf 39 C8
Banniskirk Ho. Highld 94 E3
Bannister Green Essex 30 F3
Bannockburn Stirling 69 A7
Banstead Sur 19 F9
Bantham Devon 5 G7
Banton N Lanark 68 C6
Banwell N Som 15 F9
Banyard's Green Suff 31 A9
Bapchild Kent 20 E6
Bar Hill Cambs 29 B10
Barabhas W Isles 91 C8
Barabhas Iarach W Isles 91 C8
Barabhas Uarach W Isles 91 B8
Barachandroman Argyll 79 J9
Barassie S Ayrs 66 C6
Baravullin Argyll 79 H11
Barbaraville Highld 87 D10
Barber Booth Derbys 44 D5
Barbieston S Ayrs 67 E7
Barbon Cumb 50 A2
Barbridge Ches E 43 G9
Barbrook Devon 6 B6
Barby Northants 28 A2
Barcaldine Argyll 74 C2
Barcheston Warks 27 E9
Barcombe E Sus 12 E3
Barcombe Cross E Sus 12 E3
Barden N Yorks 58 G2
Barden Scale N Yorks 51 D6
Bardennoch Dumfries 67 G8
Bardfield Saling Essex 30 F3
Bardister Shetland 96 F5
Bardney Lincs 46 F5
Bardon Leics 35 D10
Bardon Mill Northumb 62 G3
Bardowie E Dunb 68 C4
Bardrainney Invclyd 68 C2
Bardsea Cumb 49 B3
Bardsey W Yorks 51 E9
Bardwell Suff 30 A6
Bare Lancs 49 C4
Barfad Argyll 73 G7
Barford Norf 39 E7
Barford Warks 27 B9
Barford St John Oxon 27 E11
Barford St Martin Wilts 9 A9
Barford St Michael Oxon 27 E11
Barfrestone Kent 21 F9
Bargod = Bargoed Caerph 15 B7
Bargoed = Bargod Caerph 15 B7
Bargrennan Dumfries 54 B6
Barham Cambs 37 H7
Barham Kent 21 F9
Barham Suff 31 C8
Barharrow Dumfries 55 D9
Barhill Dumfries 55 C11
Barholm Lincs 37 D6
Barkby Leics 36 E2
Barkestone-le-Vale Leics 36 B3
Barkham Wokingham 18 E4
Barking London 19 C11
Barking Suff 31 C7
Barking Tye Suff 31 C7
Barkingside London 19 C11
Barkisland W Yorks 51 H6
Barkston Lincs 36 A5
Barkston N Yorks 51 F10
Barkway Herts 29 E10
Barlaston Staffs 34 B4
Barlavington W Sus 11 C8
Barlborough Derbys 45 E8
Barlby N Yorks 52 F2
Barlestone Leics 35 E10
Barley Herts 29 E10
Barley Lancs 50 E4
Barley Mow T&W 58 A3
Barleythorpe Rutland 36 E4
Barling Essex 20 C6
Barlow Derbys 45 E7
Barlow N Yorks 52 G2
Barlow T&W 63 G7
Barmby Moor E Yorks 52 E3
Barmby on the Marsh E Yorks 52 G2
Barmer Norf 38 B4
Barmoor Castle Northumb 71 G8
Barmoor Lane End Northumb 71 G9
Barmouth = Abermaw Gwyn 32 D2
Barmpton Darl 58 E4
Barmston E Yorks 53 D7
Barnack Pboro 37 E6
Barnacle Warks 35 G9
Barnard Castle Durham 58 E1
Barnard Gate Oxon 27 G11
Barnardiston Suff 30 D4
Barnbarroch Dumfries 55 D11
Barnburgh S Yorks 45 B8
Barnby Suff 39 G10
Barnby Dun S Yorks 45 B10
Barnby in the Willows Notts 46 G2
Barnby Moor Notts 45 D10
Barnes Street Kent 20 G3
Barnet London 19 B9
Barnetby le Wold N Lincs 46 B4
Barney Norf 38 B5
Barnham Suff 38 H4
Barnham W Sus 11 D8
Barnham Broom Norf 39 E6
Barnhead Angus 77 B9
Barnhill Ches W 43 G7
Barnhill Dundee 77 D7
Barnhill Moray 88 C1
Barnhills Dumfries 54 B2
Barningham Durham 58 E1
Barningham Suff 38 H5
Barnoldby le Beck NE Lincs 46 B6
Barnoldswick Lancs 50 E4
Barns Green W Sus 11 B10
Barnsley Glos 27 H7
Barnsley S Yorks 45 B7
Barnstaple Devon 6 C4
Barnston Essex 30 G3
Barnston Mers 42 D5
Barnstone Notts 36 B3
Barnt Green Worcs 27 A7
Barnton Ches W 43 E9
Barnton Edin 69 C10
Barnwell All Saints Northants 36 G6
Barnwell St Andrew Northants 36 G6
Barnwood Glos 26 G5
Barochreal Argyll 79 J11
Barons Cross Hereford 25 C11
Barr S Ayrs 66 G5
Barra Castle Aberds 83 A9
Barrachan Dumfries 54 E6
Barrack Aberds 89 D8
Barraglom W Isles 90 D6
Barrahormid Argyll 72 E6
Barran Argyll 79 J11
Barrapol Argyll 78 G2
Barras Aberds 83 E10
Barras Cumb 57 E10
Barrasford Northumb 62 F5
Barravullin Argyll 73 C7
Barregarrow IoM 48 D3
Barrhead E Renf 68 E3
Barrhill S Ayrs 54 A5
Barrington Cambs 29 D10
Barrington Som 8 C2
Barripper Corn 2 F5
Barrmill N Ayrs 67 A6
Barrock Highld 94 C4
Barrock House Highld 94 D4
Barrow Lancs 50 F3
Barrow Rutland 36 D4
Barrow Suff 30 B4
Barrow Green Kent 20 E6
Barrow Gurney N Som 15 E11
Barrow Haven N Lincs 53 G6
Barrow-in-Furness Cumb 49 C2
Barrow Island Cumb 49 C1
Barrow Nook Lancs 43 B7
Barrow Street Wilts 9 A7
Barrow upon Humber N Lincs 53 G6
Barrow upon Soar Leics 36 D1
Barrow upon Trent Derbys 35 C9
Barroway Drove Norf 38 E1
Barrowburn Northumb 62 B4
Barrowby Lincs 36 B4
Barrowcliff N Yorks 59 H11
Barrowden Rutland 36 E5
Barrowford Lancs 50 F4
Barrows Green Ches E 43 G9
Barrows Green Cumb 57 H7
Barrow's Green Mers 43 D8
Barry Angus 77 D8
Barry = Y Barri V Glam 15 E7
Barry Island V Glam 15 E7
Barsby Leics 36 D3
Barsham Suff 39 G9
Barston W Mid 35 H8
Bartestree Hereford 26 D2
Barthol Chapel Aberds 89 E8
Barthomley Ches E 43 G10
Bartley Hants 10 C2
Bartley Green W Mid 34 G6
Bartlow Cambs 30 D2
Barton Cambs 29 C11
Barton Ches W 43 G7
Barton Glos 27 F8
Barton Lancs 42 B6
Barton Lancs 49 F5
Barton N Yorks 58 F3
Barton Oxon 28 H2
Barton Torbay 5 E10
Barton Warks 27 C8
Barton Bendish Norf 38 E3
Barton Hartshorn Bucks 28 E3
Barton in Fabis Notts 35 B11
Barton in the Beans Leics 35 E9
Barton-le-Clay C Beds 29 E7
Barton-le-Street N Yorks 52 B3
Barton-le-Willows N Yorks 52 C3
Barton Mills Suff 30 A4
Barton on Sea Hants 9 E11
Barton on the Heath Warks 27 E9
Barton St David Som 8 A4
Barton Seagrave Northants 36 H4
Barton Stacey Hants 17 G11
Barton Turf Norf 39 C9
Barton-under-Needwood Staffs 35 D7
Barton-upon-Humber N Lincs 52 G6
Barton Waterside N Lincs 52 G6
Barugh S Yorks 45 B7
Barway Cambs 37 H11
Barwell Leics 35 F10
Barwick Herts 29 G10
Barwick Som 8 C4
Barwick in Elmet W Yorks 51 F9
Baschurch Shrops 33 C10
Bascote Warks 27 B11
Basford Green Staffs 44 G3
Bashall Eaves Lancs 50 E2
Bashley Hants 9 E11
Basildon Essex 20 C4
Basingstoke Hants 18 F3
Baslow Derbys 44 E6
Bason Bridge Som 15 G9
Bassaleg Newport 15 C8
Bassenthwaite Cumb 56 C4
Bassett Soton 10 C3
Bassingbourn Cambs 29 D10
Bassingfield Notts 36 B2
Bassingham Lincs 46 F3
Bassingthorpe Lincs 36 C5
Basta Shetland 96 D7
Baston Lincs 37 D7
Bastwick Norf 39 D10
Baswick Steer E Yorks 52 E6
Batchworth Heath Herts 19 B7
Batcombe Dorset 8 D5
Batcombe Som 16 H3
Bate Heath Ches E 43 E9
Batford Herts 29 G8
Bath Bath 16 E4
Bathampton Bath 16 E4
Bathealton Som 7 D9
Batheaston Bath 16 E4
Bathford Bath 16 E4
Bathgate W Loth 69 D8
Bathley Notts 45 G11
Bathpool Corn 4 D3
Bathpool Som 8 B1
Bathville W Loth 69 D8
Batley W Yorks 51 G8
Batsford Glos 27 E8
Battersby N Yorks 59 F6
Battersea London 19 D9
Battisborough Cross Devon 5 G6
Battisford Suff 31 C7
Battisford Tye Suff 31 C7
Battle E Sus 12 E6
Battle Powys 25 E7
Battledown Glos 26 F6
Battlefield Shrops 33 D11
Battlesbridge Essex 20 B4
Battlesden C Beds 28 F6
Battlesea Green Suff 39 H8
Battleton Som 7 D8
Battram Leics 35 E10
Battramsley Hants 10 E2
Baughton Worcs 26 D5
Baughurst Hants 18 F2
Baulking Oxon 17 B10
Baumber Lincs 46 E6
Baunton Glos 17 A7
Baverstock Wilts 9 A9
Bawburgh Norf 39 E7
Bawdeswell Norf 38 C6
Bawdrip Som 15 H9
Bawdsey Suff 31 D10
Bawtry S Yorks 45 C10
Baxenden Lancs 50 G3
Baxterley Warks 35 F8
Baybridge Hants 10 B4

Bradda IoM 48 F1
Bradden Northants 28 D3
Braddock Corn 4 E2
Bradeley Stoke 44 G2
Bradenham Bucks 18 B5
Bradenham Norf 38 E5
Bradenstoke Wilts 17 D7
Bradfield Essex 31 E8
Bradfield Norf 39 B8
Bradfield W Berks 18 D3
Bradfield Combust Suff 30 C5
Bradfield Green Ches E 43 G9
Bradfield Heath Essex 31 F8
Bradfield St Clare Suff 30 C6
Bradfield St George Suff 30 B6
Bradford Corn 4 D2
Bradford Derbys 44 F6
Bradford Devon 6 F3
Bradford Northumb 71 G10
Bradford W Yorks 51 F7
Bradford Abbas Dorset 8 C4
Bradford Leigh Wilts 16 E5
Bradford-on-Avon Wilts 16 E5
Bradford-on-Tone Som 7 D10
Bradford Peverell Dorset 8 E5
Brading IoW 10 F5
Bradley Derbys 44 H6
Bradley Hants 18 G3
Bradley NE Lincs 46 B6
Bradley Staffs 34 D4
Bradley W Mid 34 F5
Bradley W Yorks 51 G7
Bradley Green Worcs 26 B6
Bradley in the Moors Staffs 35 A6
Bradlow Hereford 26 E4
Bradmore Notts 36 B1
Bradmore W Mid 34 F4
Bradninch Devon 7 F9
Bradnop Staffs 44 G4
Bradpole Dorset 8 E3
Bradshaw Gtr Man 43 A10
Bradshaw W Yorks 44 A4
Bradstone Devon 4 C4
Bradwall Green Ches E 43 F10
Bradway S Yorks 45 D7
Bradwell Derbys 44 D5
Bradwell Essex 30 F5
Bradwell M Keynes 28 E5
Bradwell Norf 39 E11
Bradwell Staffs 44 H2
Bradwell Grove Oxon 27 H9
Bradwell on Sea Essex 31 H7
Bradwell Waterside Essex 30 H6
Bradworthy Devon 6 E2
Bradworthy Cross Devon 6 E2
Brae Dumfries 60 F4
Brae Highld 91 J13
Brae Highld 92 J7
Brae Shetland 96 G5
Brae of Achnahaird Highld 92 H3
Brae Roy Lodge Highld 80 D5
Braeantra Highld 87 D8
Braedownie Angus 82 F4
Braefield Highld 86 H7
Braegrum Perth 76 E3
Braehead Dumfries 55 D7
Braehead Orkney 95 D5
Braehead Orkney 95 H6
Braehead S Lanark 69 E8
Braehead S Lanark 69 G7
Braehead of Lunan Angus 77 B9
Braehoulland Shetland 96 F4
Braehungie Highld 94 G3
Braelangwell Lodge Highld 87 B8
Braemar Aberds 82 D3
Braemore Highld 86 D4
Braemore Highld 94 G2
Braes of Enzie Moray 88 C3
Braeside Invclyd 73 F11
Braeswick Orkney 95 E7
Braewick Shetland 96 H5
Brafferton Darl 58 D3
Brafferton N Yorks 51 B10
Brafield-on-the-Green Northants 28 C5
Bragar W Isles 91 C7
Bragbury End Herts 29 F9
Bragleenmore Argyll 74 E2
Braichmelyn Gwyn 41 D8
Braid Edin 69 D11
Braides Lancs 49 D4
Braidley N Yorks 50 A6
Braidwood S Lanark 69 F7
Braigo Argyll 64 B3
Brailsford Derbys 35 A8
Brainshaugh Northumb 63 C8
Braintree Essex 30 F4
Braiseworth Suff 31 A8
Braishfield Hants 10 B2
Braithwaite Cumb 56 D4
Braithwaite S Yorks 45 A10
Braithwaite W Yorks 50 E6
Braithwell S Yorks 45 C9
Bramber W Sus 11 C10
Bramcote Notts 35 B11
Bramcote Warks 35 G10
Bramdean Hants 10 B5
Bramerton Norf 39 E8
Bramfield Herts 29 G9
Bramfield Suff 31 A10
Bramford Suff 31 D8
Bramhall Gtr Man 44 D2
Bramham W Yorks 51 E10
Bramhope W Yorks 51 E8
Bramley Hants 18 F3
Bramley S Yorks 45 C8
Bramley Sur 19 G7
Bramley W Yorks 51 F8
Bramling Kent 21 F9
Brampford Speke Devon 7 G8
Brampton Cambs 29 A9
Brampton Cumb 57 D8
Brampton Cumb 61 G11
Brampton Derbys 45 E7
Brampton Hereford 25 E11
Brampton Lincs 46 E2
Brampton Norf 39 C8
Brampton S Yorks 45 B8
Brampton Suff 39 G10
Brampton Abbotts Hereford 26 F3
Brampton Ash Northants 36 G3
Brampton Bryan Hereford 25 A10
Brampton en le Morthen S Yorks 45 D8
Bramshall Staffs 35 B6
Bramshaw Hants 10 C1
Bramshill Hants 18 E4
Bramshott Hants 11 A7
Bran End Essex 30 F3
Branault Highld 79 E8
Brancaster Norf 38 A3
Brancaster Staithe Norf 38 A3
Brancepeth Durham 58 C3
Branch End Northumb 62 G6
Branchill Moray 87 F13
Brand Green Glos 26 F4
Branderburgh Moray 88 A2
Brandesburton E Yorks 53 E7
Brandeston Suff 31 B9
Brandhill Shrops 33 H10
Brandis Corner Devon 6 F3
Brandiston Norf 39 C7
Brandon Durham 58 C3
Brandon Lincs 46 H3
Brandon Northumb 62 B6
Brandon Suff 38 G3
Brandon Warks 35 H10
Brandon Bank Cambs 38 G2
Brandon Creek Norf 38 F2
Brandon Parva Norf 39 E6
Brandsby N Yorks 52 B1
Brandy Wharf Lincs 46 C4
Brane Corn 2 G3
Branksome Poole 9 E9
Branksome Park Poole 9 E9
Bransby Lincs 46 E2
Branscombe Devon 7 H10
Bransford Worcs 26 C4
Bransgore Hants 9 E10
Branshill Clack 69 A7
Bransholme Hull 53 F7
Branson's Cross Worcs 27 A7
Branston Leics 36 C4
Branston Lincs 46 F4
Branston Staffs 35 C8
Branston Booths Lincs 46 F4
Branstone IoW 10 F4
Bransty Cumb 56 E1
Brant Broughton Lincs 46 G3
Brantham Suff 31 E8
Branthwaite Cumb 56 C4
Branthwaite Cumb 56 D2
Brantingham E Yorks 52 G5
Branton Northumb 62 B6
Branton S Yorks 45 B10
Branxholm Park Borders 61 B10
Branxholme Borders 61 B10
Branxton Northumb 71 G7
Brassey Green Ches W 43 F8
Brassington Derbys 44 G6
Brasted Kent 19 F11
Brasted Chart Kent 19 F11
Brathens Aberds 83 D8
Bratoft Lincs 47 F8
Brattleby Lincs 46 D3
Bratton Telford 34 D2
Bratton Wilts 16 F6
Bratton Clovelly Devon 6 G3
Bratton Fleming Devon 6 C5
Bratton Seymour Som 8 B5
Braughing Herts 29 F10
Braunston Northants 28 B2
Braunston-in-Rutland Rutland 36 E4
Braunstone Town Leicester 36 E1
Braunton Devon 6 C3
Brawby N Yorks 52 B3
Brawl Highld 93 C11
Brawlbin Highld 94 E2
Bray Windsor 18 D6
Bray Shop Corn 4 D4
Bray Wick Windsor 18 D5
Braybrooke Northants 36 G3
Braye Ald 11
Brayford Devon 6 C5
Braystones Cumb 56 F2
Braythorn N Yorks 51 E8
Brayton N Yorks 52 F2
Brazacott Corn 6 G1
Breach Kent 20 E5
Breachacha Castle Argyll 78 F4
Breachwood Green Herts 29 F8
Breacleit W Isles 90 D6
Breaden Heath Shrops 33 B10
Breadsall Derbys 35 B9
Breadstone Glos 16 A4
Breage Corn 2 G5
Breakachy Highld 86 F7
Bream Glos 26 H3
Breamore Hants 9 C10
Brean Som 15 F8
Breanais W Isles 90 E4
Brearton N Yorks 51 C9
Breascleit W Isles 90 D7
Breaston Derbys 35 B10
Brechfa Carms 23 C10
Brechin Angus 77 A8
Breck of Cruan Orkney 95 G4
Breckan Orkney 95 H3
Breckrey Highld 85 B10
Brecon = Aberhonddu Powys 25 F7
Bredbury Gtr Man 44 C3
Brede E Sus 13 E7
Bredenbury Hereford 26 C3
Bredfield Suff 31 C9
Bredgar Kent 20 E5
Bredhurst Kent 20 E4
Bredicot Worcs 26 C6
Bredon Worcs 26 E6
Bredon's Norton Worcs 26 E6
Bredwardine Hereford 25 D10
Breedon on the Hill Leics 35 C10
Breibhig W Isles 84 J1
Breibhig W Isles 91 D9
Breich W Loth 69 D8
Breightmet Gtr Man 43 B10
Breighton E Yorks 52 F3
Breinton Hereford 25 E11
Breinton Common Hereford 25 D11
Breiwick Shetland 96 J6
Bremhill Wilts 16 D6
Bremirehoull Shetland 96 L6
Brenchley Kent 12 B5
Brendon Devon 7 B6
Brenkley T&W 63 F8
Brent Eleigh Suff 30 D6
Brent Knoll Som 15 F9
Brent Pelham Herts 29 E11
Brentford London 19 D8
Brentingby Leics 36 D3
Brentwood Essex 20 B2
Brenzett Kent 13 D9
Brereton Staffs 35 D6
Brereton Green Ches E 43 F10
Brereton Heath Ches E 44 F2
Bressingham Norf 39 G6
Bretby Derbys 35 C8
Bretford Warks 35 H10
Bretforton Worcs 27 D7
Bretherdale Head Cumb 57 F7
Bretherton Lancs 49 G4
Brettabister Shetland 96 H6
Brettenham Norf 38 G5
Brettenham Suff 30 C6
Bretton Derbys 44 E6
Bretton Flint 42 F6
Brewer Street Sur 19 F10
Brewlands Bridge Angus 76 A4
Brewood Staffs 34 E4
Briach Moray 87 F13
Briants Puddle Dorset 9 E7
Brick End Essex 30 F2
Brickendon Herts 29 H10
Bricket Wood Herts 19 A8
Bricklehampton Worcs 26 D6
Bride IoM 48 B4
Bridekirk Cumb 56 C3
Bridell Pembs 22 B6
Bridestowe Devon 4 C6
Brideswell Aberds 88 E5
Bridford Devon 5 C9
Bridfordmills Devon 5 C9
Bridge Kent 21 F8
Bridge End Lincs 37 B7
Bridge Green Essex 29 E11
Bridge Hewick N Yorks 51 B9
Bridge of Alford Aberds 83 B7
Bridge of Allan Stirling 75 H10
Bridge of Avon Moray 88 E1
Bridge of Awe Argyll 74 E3
Bridge of Balgie Perth 75 C8
Bridge of Cally Perth 76 B4
Bridge of Canny Aberds 83 D8
Bridge of Craigisla Angus 76 B5
Bridge of Dee Dumfries 55 D10
Bridge of Don Aberdeen 83 B11
Bridge of Dun Angus 77 B9
Bridge of Dye Aberds 83 E8
Bridge of Earn Perth 76 F4
Bridge of Ericht Perth 75 B8
Bridge of Feugh Aberds 83 D9
Bridge of Forss Highld 93 C13
Bridge of Gairn Aberds 82 D5
Bridge of Gaur Perth 75 B8
Bridge of Muchalls Aberds 83 D10
Bridge of Oich Highld 80 C5
Bridge of Orchy Argyll 74 D5
Bridge of Waith Orkney 95 G3
Bridge of Walls Shetland 96 H4
Bridge of Weir Renfs 68 D2
Bridge Sollers Hereford 25 D11
Bridge Street Suff 30 D5
Bridge Trafford Ches W 43 E7
Bridge Yate S Glos 16 D3
Bridgefoot Angus 76 D6
Bridgefoot Cumb 56 D2
Bridgehampton Som 8 B4
Bridgehill Durham 58 A1
Bridgemary Hants 10 D4
Bridgemont Derbys 44 D4
Bridgend Aberds 83 B7
Bridgend Aberds 88 E5
Bridgend Angus 83 G7
Bridgend Argyll 64 B4
Bridgend Argyll 65 E8
Bridgend Argyll 73 D7
Bridgend = Pen-y-bont ar Ogwr Bridgend 14 D5
Bridgend Cumb 56 E5
Bridgend Fife 76 F6
Bridgend Moray 88 E3
Bridgend N Lanark 68 C5
Bridgend Pembs 22 B6
Bridgend W Loth 69 C9
Bridgend of Lintrathen Angus 76 B5
Bridgerule Devon 6 F1
Bridges Shrops 33 F9
Bridgeton Glasgow 68 D5
Bridgetown Corn 4 C4
Bridgetown Som 7 C8
Bridgham Norf 38 G5
Bridgnorth Shrops 34 F3
Bridgtown Staffs 34 E5
Bridgwater Som 15 H9
Bridlington E Yorks 53 C7
Bridport Dorset 8 E3
Bridstow Hereford 26 F2
Brierfield Lancs 50 F4
Brierley Glos 26 G3
Brierley Hereford 25 C11
Brierley S Yorks 45 A8
Brierley Hill W Mid 34 G5
Briery Hill Bl Gwent 25 H8
Brig o'Turk Stirling 75 G8
Brigg N Lincs 46 B4
Briggswath N Yorks 59 F9
Brigham Cumb 56 C2
Brigham E Yorks 53 D6
Brighouse W Yorks 51 G7
Brighstone IoW 10 F3
Brightgate Derbys 44 G6
Brighthampton Oxon 17 A10
Brightling E Sus 12 D5
Brightlingsea Essex 31 G7
Brighton Brighton 12 F2
Brighton Corn 3 D8
Brighton Hill Hants 18 G3
Brightons Falk 69 C8
Brightwalton W Berks 17 D11
Brightwell Suff 31 D9
Brightwell Baldwin Oxon 18 B3
Brightwell cum Sotwell Oxon 18 B2
Brignall Durham 58 E1
Brigsley NE Lincs 46 B6
Brigsteer Cumb 57 H6
Brigstock Northants 36 G5
Brill Bucks 28 G3
Brilley Hereford 25 D9
Brimaston Pembs 22 D4
Brimfield Hereford 26 B2
Brimington Derbys 45 E8
Brimley Devon 5 D8
Brimpsfield Glos 26 G6
Brimpton W Berks 18 E2
Brims Orkney 95 K3
Brimscombe Glos 16 A5
Brimstage Mers 42 D6
Brinacory Highld 79 B10
Brind E Yorks 52 F3
Brindister Shetland 96 H4
Brindister Shetland 96 K6
Brindle Lancs 50 G2
Brindley Ford Stoke 44 G2
Brineton Staffs 34 D4
Bringhurst Leics 36 F4
Brington Cambs 37 H6
Brinian Orkney 95 F5
Briningham Norf 38 B6
Brinkhill Lincs 47 E7
Brinkley Cambs 30 C3
Brinklow Warks 35 H10
Brinkworth Wilts 17 C7
Brinmore Highld 81 A8
Brinscall Lancs 50 G2
Brinsea N Som 15 E10
Brinsley Notts 45 H8
Brinsop Hereford 25 D11
Brinsworth S Yorks 45 D8
Brinton Norf 38 B6
Brisco Cumb 56 A6
Brisley Norf 38 C5
Brislington Bristol 16 D3
Bristol Bristol 16 D2
Briston Norf 39 B6
Britannia Lancs 50 G4
Britford Wilts 9 B10
Brithdir Gwyn 32 D3
British Legion Village Kent 20 F4
Briton Ferry Neath 14 B3
Britwell Salome Oxon 18 B3
Brixham Torbay 5 F10
Brixton Devon 5 F6
Brixton London 19 D10
Brixton Deverill Wilts 16 H5
Brixworth Northants 28 A4
Brize Norton Oxon 27 H10
Broad Blunsdon Swindon 17 B8
Broad Campden Glos 27 E8
Broad Chalke Wilts 9 B9
Broad Green C Beds 28 D6
Broad Green Essex 30 F5
Broad Green Worcs 26 C4
Broad Haven Pembs 22 E3
Broad Heath Worcs 26 B3
Broad Hill Cambs 38 H1
Broad Hinton Wilts 17 D8
Broad Laying Hants 17 E11
Broad Marston Worcs 27 D8
Broad Oak Carms 23 D10
Broad Oak Cumb 56 G3
Broad Oak Dorset 8 E3
Broad Oak Dorset 9 C6
Broad Oak E Sus 12 D5
Broad Oak E Sus 13 E7
Broad Oak Hereford 25 F11
Broad Oak Mers 43 C8
Broad Street Kent 20 F5
Broad Street Green Essex 30 H5
Broad Town Wilts 17 D7
Broadbottom Gtr Man 44 C3
Broadbridge W Sus 11 D7
Broadbridge Heath W Sus 11 A10
Broadclyst Devon 7 G8
Broadfield Gtr Man 44 A2
Broadfield Lancs 49 G5
Broadfield Pembs 22 F6
Broadfield W Sus 12 C1
Broadford Highld 85 F11
Broadford Bridge W Sus 11 B9
Broadhaugh Borders 61 C10
Broadhaven Highld 94 E5
Broadheath Gtr Man 43 D10
Broadhembury Devon 7 F10
Broadhempston Devon 5 E9
Broadholme Derbys 45 H7
Broadholme Lincs 46 E2
Broadland Row E Sus 13 E7
Broadlay Carms 23 F8
Broadley Lancs 50 H4
Broadley Moray 88 B3
Broadley Common Essex 29 H11
Broadmayne Dorset 8 F6
Broadmeadows Borders 70 G3
Broadmere Hants 18 G3
Broadmoor Pembs 22 F5
Broadoak Kent 21 E8
Broadrashes Moray 88 C4
Broadsea Aberds 89 B9
Broadstairs Kent 21 E10
Broadstone Poole 9 E9
Broadstone Shrops 33 G11
Broadtown Lane Wilts 17 D7
Broadwas Worcs 26 C4
Broadwater Herts 29 F9
Broadwater W Sus 11 D10
Broadway Carms 23 F7
Broadway Pembs 22 E3
Broadway Som 8 C2
Broadway Suff 39 H9
Broadway Worcs 27 E7
Broadwell Glos 26 G2
Broadwell Glos 27 F9
Broadwell Oxon 17 A9
Broadwell Warks 27 B11
Broadwell House Northumb 57 A11
Broadwey Dorset 8 F5
Broadwindsor Dorset 8 D3
Broadwood Kelly Devon 6 F5
Broadwoodwidger Devon 4 C5
Brobury Hereford 25 D10
Brochel Highld 85 D10
Brochloch Dumfries 67 G8
Brochroy Argyll 74 D3
Brockamin Worcs 26 C4
Brockbridge Hants 10 C5
Brockdam Northumb 63 A7
Brockdish Norf 39 H8
Brockenhurst Hants 10 D2
Brocketsbrae S Lanark 69 G7
Brockford Street Suff 31 B8
Brockhall Northants 28 B3
Brockham Sur 19 G8
Brockhampton Glos 27 F7
Brockhampton Hereford 26 E2
Brockholes W Yorks 44 A5
Brockhurst Derbys 45 F7
Brockhurst Hants 10 D5
Brocklebank Cumb 56 B5
Brocklesby Lincs 46 A5
Brockley N Som 15 E10
Brockley Green Suff 30 C5
Brockleymoor Cumb 57 C6
Brockton Shrops 33 E9
Brockton Shrops 33 G9
Brockton Shrops 34 E3
Brockton Shrops 34 F1
Brockton Telford 34 D3
Brockweir Glos 15 A11
Brockwood Hants 10 B5
Brockworth Glos 26 G5
Brocton Staffs 34 D5
Brodick N Ayrs 66 C3
Brodsworth S Yorks 45 B9
Brogaig Highld 85 B9
Brogborough C Beds 28 E6
Broken Cross Ches E 44 E2
Broken Cross Ches W 43 E9
Brokenborough Wilts 16 C6
Bromborough Mers 42 D6
Brome Suff 39 H7
Brome Street Suff 39 H7
Bromeswell Suff 31 C10
Bromfield Cumb 56 B3
Bromfield Shrops 33 H10
Bromham Bedford 29 C7
Bromham Wilts 16 E6
Bromley London 19 E11
Bromley W Mid 34 G5
Bromley Common London 19 E11
Bromley Green Kent 13 C8
Brompton Medway 20 E4
Brompton N Yorks 52 A5
Brompton N Yorks 58 G4
Brompton-on-Swale N Yorks 58 G3
Brompton Ralph Som 7 C9
Brompton Regis Som 7 C8
Bromsash Hereford 26 F3
Bromsberrow Hth. Glos 26 E4
Bromsgrove Worcs 26 A6
Bromyard Hereford 26 C3
Bromyard Downs Hereford 26 C3
Bronaber Gwyn 41 G9
Brongest Ceredig 23 B8
Bronington Wrex 33 B10
Bronllys Powys 25 E8
Bronnant Ceredig 24 B3
Bronwydd Arms Carms 23 D9
Bronydd Powys 25 D9
Bronygarth Shrops 33 B8
Brook Carms 23 F7
Brook Hants 10 B2
Brook Hants 10 C1
Brook IoW 10 F2
Brook Kent 13 B9
Brook Sur 18 H6
Brook Sur 19 G7
Brook End Bedford 29 B7
Brook Hill Hants 10 C1
Brook Street Kent 13 C8
Brook Street Kent 20 G2
Brook Street W Sus 12 D2
Brooke Norf 39 F8
Brooke Rutland 36 E4
Brookenby Lincs 46 C6
Brookend Glos 16 B2
Brookfield Renfs 68 D3
Brookhouse Lancs 49 C5
Brookhouse Green Ches E 44 F2
Brookland Kent 13 D8
Brooklands Dumfries 60 F4
Brooklands Gtr Man 43 C10
Brooklands Shrops 33 A11
Brookmans Park Herts 19 A9
Brooks Powys 33 F7
Brooks Green W Sus 11 B10
Brookthorpe Glos 26 G5
Brookville Norf 38 F3
Brookwood Sur 18 F6
Broom C Beds 29 D8
Broom S Yorks 45 C8
Broom Warks 27 C7
Broom Worcs 34 H5
Broom Green Norf 38 C5
Broom Hill Dorset 9 D9
Broome Norf 39 F9
Broome Shrops 33 G10
Broome Park Northumb 63 B7
Broomedge Warr 43 D10
Broomer's Corner W Sus 11 B10
Broomfield Aberds 89 E9
Broomfield Essex 30 G4
Broomfield Kent 20 F5
Broomfield Kent 21 E8
Broomfield Som 7 C11
Broomfleet E Yorks 52 G4
Broomhall Ches E 43 H9
Broomhall Windsor 18 E6
Broomhaugh Northumb 62 G6
Broomhill Norf 38 E2
Broomhill Northumb 63 C8
Broomhill S Yorks 45 B8
Broomholm Norf 39 B9
Broomley Northumb 62 G6
Broompark Durham 58 B3
Broom's Green Glos 26 E4
Broomy Lodge Hants 9 C11
Brora Highld 93 J12
Broseley Shrops 34 E2
Brotherhouse Bar Lincs 37 D8
Brotherstone Borders 70 G5
Brothertoft Lincs 46 H6
Brotherton N Yorks 51 G10
Brotton Redcar 59 E7
Broubster Highld 93 C13
Brough Cumb 57 E9
Brough Derbys 44 D5
Brough E Yorks 52 G5
Brough Highld 94 C4
Brough Notts 46 G2
Brough Orkney 95 G4
Brough Shetland 96 F7
Brough Shetland 96 F6
Brough Shetland 96 G7
Brough Shetland 96 H6
Brough Shetland 96 J7
Brough Lodge Shetland 96 D7
Brough Sowerby Cumb 57 E9
Broughall Shrops 34 A1
Broughton Borders 69 G10
Broughton Cambs 37 H8
Broughton Flint 42 F6
Broughton Hants 10 A2
Broughton Lancs 49 F5
Broughton M Keynes 28 D5
Broughton N Lincs 46 B3
Broughton N Yorks 50 D5
Broughton N Yorks 52 B3
Broughton Northants 36 H4
Broughton Orkney 95 D5
Broughton Oxon 27 E11
Broughton V Glam 14 D5
Broughton Astley Leics 35 F11
Broughton Beck Cumb 49 A2
Broughton Common Wilts 16 E5
Broughton Gifford Wilts 16 E5
Broughton Hackett Worcs 26 C6
Broughton in Furness Cumb 56 H4
Broughton Mills Cumb 56 G4
Broughton Moor Cumb 56 C2
Broughton Park Gtr Man 44 B2
Broughton Poggs Oxon 17 A9
Broughtown Orkney 95 D7
Broughty Ferry Dundee 77 D7
Browhouses Dumfries 61 G8
Browland Shetland 96 H4
Brown Candover Hants 18 H2
Brown Edge Lancs 42 A6
Brown Edge Staffs 44 G3
Brown Heath Ches W 43 F7
Brownhill Aberds 89 D8
Brownhill Aberds 89 D6
Brownhill Blackburn 50 F2
Brownhill Shrops 33 C10
Brownhills Fife 77 F8
Brownhills W Mid 34 E6
Brownlow Ches E 44 F2
Brownlow Heath Ches E 44 F2
Brownmuir Aberds 83 F9
Brown's End Glos 26 E4
Brownshill Glos 16 A5
Brownston Devon 5 F7
Brownyside Northumb 63 A7
Broxa N Yorks 59 G10
Broxbourne Herts 29 H10
Broxburn E Loth 70 C5
Broxburn W Loth 69 C9
Broxholme Lincs 46 E3
Broxted Essex 30 F2
Broxton Ches W 43 G7
Broxwood Hereford 25 C10
Broyle Side E Sus 12 E3
Brù W Isles 91 C8
Bruairnis W Isles 84 H2
Bruan Highld 94 G5
Bruar Lodge Perth 81 F10
Brucehill W Dunb 68 C2
Bruera Ches W 43 F7
Bruern Abbey Oxon 27 F9
Bruichladdich Argyll 64 B3
Bruisyard Suff 31 B10
Brumby N Lincs 46 B2
Brund Staffs 44 F5
Brundall Norf 39 E9
Brundish Suff 31 B9
Brundish Street Suff 31 A9
Brunery Highld 79 D10
Brunshaw Lancs 50 F4
Brunswick Village T&W 63 F8
Bruntcliffe W Yorks 51 G8
Bruntingthorpe Leics 36 F2
Brunton Fife 76 E6
Brunton Northumb 63 A8
Brunton Wilts 17 F9
Brushford Devon 6 F5
Brushford Som 7 D8
Bruton Som 8 A5
Bryanston Dorset 9 D7
Brydekirk Dumfries 61 F7
Bryher Scilly 2 C2
Brymbo Wrex 42 G5
Brympton Som 8 C4
Bryn Carms 23 F10
Bryn Gtr Man 43 B8
Bryn Neath 14 B4
Bryn Shrops 33 G8
Bryn-coch Neath 14 B3
Bryn Du Anglesey 40 C5
Bryn Gates Gtr Man 43 B8
Bryn-glas Conwy 41 D10
Bryn Golau Rhondda 14 C5
Bryn-Iwan Carms 23 C8
Bryn-mawr Gwyn 40 G4
Bryn-nantllech Conwy 42 F2
Bryn-penarth Powys 33 E7
Bryn Rhyd-yr-Arian Conwy 42 F2
Bryn Saith Marchog Denb 42 G3
Bryn Sion Gwyn 32 D4
Bryn-y-gwenin Mon 25 G10
Bryn-y-maen Conwy 41 C10
Bryn-yr-eryr Gwyn 40 F5
Brynamman Carms 24 G4
Brynberian Pembs 22 C6
Brynbryddan Neath 14 B3
Brynbuga = Usk Mon 15 A9
Bryncae Rhondda 14 C5
Bryncethin Bridgend 14 C5
Bryncir Gwyn 40 F6
Bryncroes Gwyn 40 G4
Bryncrug Gwyn 32 E2
Bryneglwys Denb 42 H4
Brynford Flint 42 E4
Bryngwran Anglesey 40 C5
Bryngwyn Ceredig 23 B7
Bryngwyn Mon 25 H10
Bryngwyn Powys 25 D8
Brynhenllan Pembs 22 C5
Brynhoffnant Ceredig 23 A8
Brynithel Bl Gwent 15 A8
Brynmawr Bl Gwent 25 G8
Brynmenyn Bridgend 14 C5
Brynmill Swansea 14 B2
Brynna Rhondda 14 C5
Brynrefail Anglesey 40 B6
Brynrefail Gwyn 41 D7
Brynsadler Rhondda 14 C6
Brynsiencyn Anglesey 40 D6
Brynteg Anglesey 40 B6
Brynteg Ceredig 23 B9
Buaile nam Bodach W Isles 84 H2
Bualintur Highld 85 F9
Buarthmeini Gwyn 41 G10
Bubbenhall Warks 27 A10
Bubwith E Yorks 52 F3
Buccleuch Borders 61 B9
Buchanhaven Aberds 89 D11
Buchanty Perth 76 E2
Buchlyvie Stirling 68 A4
Buckabank Cumb 56 B5
Buckden Cambs 29 B8
Buckden N Yorks 50 B5
Buckenham Norf 39 E9
Buckerell Devon 7 F10
Buckfast Devon 5 E8
Buckfastleigh Devon 5 E8
Buckhaven Fife 76 H6
Buckholm Borders 70 G3
Buckholt Mon 26 G2
Buckhorn Weston Dorset 9 B6
Buckhurst Hill Essex 19 B11
Buckie Moray 88 B4
Buckies Highld 94 D3
Buckingham Bucks 28 E3
Buckland Bucks 28 G5
Buckland Devon 5 G7
Buckland Glos 27 E7
Buckland Hants 10 E2
Buckland Herts 29 E10
Buckland Kent 21 G10
Buckland Oxon 17 B10
Buckland Sur 19 F9
Buckland Brewer Devon 6 D3
Buckland Common Bucks 28 H6
Buckland Dinham Som 16 F4
Buckland Filleigh Devon 6 F3
Buckland in the Moor Devon 5 D8
Buckland Monachorum Devon 4 E5
Buckland Newton Dorset 8 D5
Buckland St Mary Som 8 C1
Bucklebury W Berks 18 D2
Bucklegate Lincs 37 B9
Bucklerheads Angus 77 D7
Bucklers Hard Hants 10 E3
Bucklesham Suff 31 D9
Buckley = Bwcle Flint 42 F5
Bucklow Hill Ches E 43 D10
Buckminster Leics 36 C4
Bucknall Lincs 46 F5
Bucknall Stoke 44 H3
Bucknell Oxon 28 F2
Bucknell Shrops 25 A10
Buckpool Moray 88 B4
Buck's Cross Devon 6 D2
Bucks Green W Sus 11 A9
Bucks Horn Oak Hants 18 G5
Buck's Mills Devon 6 D2
Bucksburn Aberdeen 83 C10
Buckskin Hants 18 F3
Buckton E Yorks 53 B7
Buckton Hereford 25 A10
Buckton Northumb 71 G9
Buckworth Cambs 37 H7
Budbrooke Warks 27 B9
Budby Notts 45 F10
Budd's Titson Corn 4 A3
Bude Corn 4 A3
Budlake Devon 7 G8
Budle Northumb 71 G10
Budleigh Salterton Devon 7 H9
Budock Water Corn 3 F6
Buerton Ches E 34 A2
Buffler's Holt Bucks 28 E3
Bugbrooke Northants 28 C3
Buglawton Ches E 44 F2
Bugle Corn 3 D9
Bugley Wilts 16 G5
Bugthorpe E Yorks 52 D3
Buildwas Shrops 34 E2
Builth Road Powys 25 C7
Builth Wells = Llanfair-ym-Muallt Powys 25 C7
Buirgh W Isles 90 H5
Bulby Lincs 37 C6
Bulcote Notts 36 A2
Buldoo Highld 93 C12
Bulford Wilts 17 G8
Bulford Camp Wilts 17 G8
Bulkeley Ches E 43 G8
Bulkington Warks 35 G9
Bulkington Wilts 16 F6
Bulkworthy Devon 6 E2
Bull Hill Hants 10 E2
Bullamoor N Yorks 58 G4
Bullbridge Derbys 45 G7
Bullbrook Brack 18 E5
Bulley Glos 26 G4
Bullgill Cumb 56 C2
Bullington Hants 17 G11
Bullington Lincs 46 E4
Bull's Green Herts 29 G9
Bullwood Argyll 73 F10
Bulmer Essex 30 D5
Bulmer N Yorks 52 C2
Bulmer Tye Essex 30 E5
Bulphan Thurrock 20 C3
Bulverhythe E Sus 13 F6
Bulwark Aberds 89 D9
Bulwell Nottingham 45 H9
Bulwick Northants 36 F5
Bumble's Green Essex 29 H11
Bun Abhainn Eadarra W Isles 90 G6
Bun a'Mhuillin W Isles 84 G2
Bun Loyne Highld 80 C4
Bunacaimb Highld 79 C9
Bunarkaig Highld 80 E3
Bunbury Ches E 43 G8
Bunbury Heath Ches E 43 G8
Bunchrew Highld 87 G9
Bundalloch Highld 85 F13
Buness Shetland 96 C8
Bunessan Argyll 78 J6
Bungay Suff 39 G9
Bunker's Hill Lincs 46 E3
Bunker's Hill Lincs 46 G6
Bunkers Hill Oxon 27 G11
Bunloit Highld 81 A7
Bunnahabhain Argyll 64 A5
Bunny Notts 36 C1
Buntait Highld 86 H6
Buntingford Herts 29 F10
Bunwell Norf 39 F7
Burbage Derbys 44 E4
Burbage Leics 35 F10
Burbage Wilts 17 E9
Burchett's Green Windsor 18 C5
Burcombe Wilts 9 A9
Burcot Oxon 18 B2
Burcott Bucks 28 F5
Burdon T&W 58 A4
Bures Suff 30 E6
Bures Green Suff 30 E6
Burford Ches E 43 G9
Burford Oxon 27 G9
Burford Shrops 26 B2
Burg Argyll 78 G6
Burgar Orkney 95 F4
Burgate Hants 9 C10
Burgate Suff 39 H6
Burgess Hill W Sus 12 E2
Burgh Suff 31 C9
Burgh by Sands Cumb 61 H9
Burgh Castle Norf 39 E10
Burgh Heath Sur 19 F9
Burgh le Marsh Lincs 47 F9
Burgh Muir Aberds 83 A9
Burgh next Aylsham Norf 39 C8
Burgh on Bain Lincs 46 D6
Burgh St Margaret Norf 39 D10
Burgh St Peter Norf 39 F10
Burghclere Hants 17 E11
Burghead Moray 87 E14
Burghfield W Berks 18 E3
Burghfield Common W Berks 18 E3
Burghfield Hill W Berks 18 E3
Burghill Hereford 25 D11
Burghwallis S Yorks 45 A9
Burham Kent 20 E4
Buriton Hants 10 B6
Burland Ches E 43 G9
Burlawn Corn 3 B8
Burleigh Brack 18 E5
Burlescombe Devon 7 E9
Burleston Dorset 9 E6
Burley Hants 9 D11
Burley Rutland 36 D4
Burley W Yorks 51 F8
Burley Gate Hereford 26 D2
Burley in Wharfedale W Yorks 51 E7
Burley Lodge Hants 9 D11
Burley Street Hants 9 D11
Burleydam Ches E 34 A2
Burlingjobb Powys 25 C9
Burlow E Sus 12 E4
Burlton Shrops 33 C10
Burmarsh Kent 13 C9
Burmington Warks 27 E9
Burn N Yorks 52 G1
Burn of Cambus Stirling 75 G10
Burnaston Derbys 35 B8
Burnbank S Lanark 68 E6
Burnby E Yorks 52 E4
Burncross S Yorks 45 C7
Burneside Cumb 57 G7
Burness Orkney 95 D7
Burneston N Yorks 58 H4
Burnett Bath 16 E3
Burnfoot Borders 61 B11
Burnfoot Borders 61 B10
Burnfoot E Ayrs 67 F7
Burnfoot Perth 76 G2
Burnham Bucks 18 C6
Burnham N Lincs 53 H6
Burnham Deepdale Norf 38 A4
Burnham Green Herts 29 G9
Burnham Market Norf 38 A4
Burnham Norton Norf 38 A4
Burnham-on-Crouch Essex 20 B6
Burnham-on-Sea Som 15 G9
Burnham Overy Staithe Norf 38 A4
Burnham Overy Town Norf 38 A4
Burnham Thorpe Norf 38 A4
Burnhead Dumfries 60 D4
Burnhead S Ayrs 66 F5
Burnhervie Aberds 83 B9
Burnhill Green Staffs 34 E3
Burnhope Durham 58 B2
Burnhouse N Ayrs 67 A6
Burniston N Yorks 59 G11
Burnlee W Yorks 44 B5
Burnley Lancs 50 F4
Burnley Lane Lancs 50 F4
Burnmouth Borders 71 D8
Burnopfield Durham 63 H7
Burnsall N Yorks 50 C6
Burnside Angus 77 B8
Burnside E Ayrs 67 E8
Burnside Fife 76 G4
Burnside S Lanark 68 D5
Burnside Shetland 96 F4
Burnside W Loth 69 C9
Burnside of Duntrune Angus 77 D7
Burnswark Dumfries 61 F7
Burnt Heath Derbys 44 E6
Burnt Houses Durham 58 D2
Burnt Yates N Yorks 51 C8
Burntcommon Sur 19 F7
Burnthouse Corn 3 F6
Burntisland Fife 69 B11
Burnton E Ayrs 67 F7
Burntwood Staffs 35 E6
Burnwynd Edin 69 D10
Burpham Sur 19 F7
Burpham W Sus 11 D9
Burradon Northumb 62 C5
Burradon T&W 63 F8
Burrafirth Shetland 96 B8
Burraland Shetland 96 F5
Burraland Shetland 96 J4
Burras Corn 2 F5
Burravoe Shetland 96 F7
Burravoe Shetland 96 G5
Burray Village Orkney 95 J5
Burrells Cumb 57 E8
Burrelton Perth 76 D5
Burridge Devon 6 C4
Burridge Hants 10 C4
Burrill N Yorks 58 H3
Burringham N Lincs 46 B2
Burrington Devon 6 E5
Burrington Hereford 25 A11
Burrington N Som 15 F10
Burrough Green Cambs 30 C3
Burrough on the Hill Leics 36 D3
Burrow-bridge Som 8 B2
Burrowhill Sur 18 E6
Burry Swansea 23 G9
Burry Green Swansea 23 G9
Burry Port = Porth Tywyn Carms 23 F9
Burscough Lancs 43 A7
Burscough Bridge Lancs 43 A7
Bursea E Yorks 52 F4
Burshill E Yorks 53 E6
Bursledon Hants 10 D3
Burslem Stoke 44 H2
Burstall Suff 31 D7
Burstock Dorset 8 D3
Burston Norf 39 G
Burston Staffs 34 B5
Burstow Sur 12 B2
Burstwick E Yorks 53 G8
Burtersett N Yorks 57 H1
Burtle Som 15 G9
Burton Ches W 42 E
Burton Ches W 43 F
Burton Dorset 9 E1
Burton Lincs 46 E
Burton Northumb 71 G1
Burton Pembs 22 F
Burton Som 7 B1
Burton Wilts 16 D
Burton Agnes E Yorks 53 C
Burton Bradstock Dorset 8 F
Burton Dassett Warks 27 C1
Burton Fleming E Yorks 53 B
Burton Green W Mid 35 H
Burton Green Wrex 42 G
Burton Hastings Warks 35 F1
Burton-in-Kendal Cumb 49 B
Burton in Lonsdale N Yorks 50 B
Burton Joyce Notts 36 A
Burton Latimer Northants 28 A
Burton Lazars Leics 36 D
Burton-le-Coggles Lincs 36 C
Burton Leonard N Yorks 51
Burton on the Wolds Leics 36 C
Burton Overy Leics 36
Burton Pedwardine Lincs 37 A
Burton Pidsea E Yorks 53
Burton Salmon N Yorks 51 G1
Burton Stather N Lincs 52 H
Burton upon Stather N Lincs 52 H
Burton upon Trent Staffs 35
Burtonwood Warr 43
Burwardsley Ches W 43
Burwarton Shrops 34
Burwash E Sus 12
Burwash Common E Sus 12 D
Burwash Weald E Sus 12
Burwell Cambs 30
Burwell Lincs 47
Burwen Anglesey 40
Burwick Orkney 95
Bury Cambs 37
Bury Gtr Man 44
Bury Som 7
Bury W Sus 11
Bury Green Herts 29 F
Bury St Edmunds Suff 30
Burythorpe N Yorks 52
Busby E Renf 68
Buscot Oxon 17
Bush Bank Hereford 25 C
Bush Crathie Aberds 82
Bush Green Norf 39
Bushbury W Mid 34
Bushby Leics 36
Bushey Herts 19
Bushey Heath Herts 19
Bushley Worcs 26
Bushton Wilts 17
Buslingthorpe Lincs 46
Busta Shetland 96
Butcher's Cross E Sus 12
Butcher's Pasture Essex 30
Butcombe N Som 15 E
Butetown Cardiff 15
Butleigh Som 8
Butleigh Wootton Som 15 H
Butler's Cross Bucks 28
Butler's End Warks 35
Butlers Marston Warks 27 C
Butley Suff 31 C
Butley High Corner Suff 31 D
Butt Green Ches E 43
Butterburn Cumb 62
Buttercrambe N Yorks 52
Butterknowle Durham 58
Butterleigh Devon 7
Buttermere Cumb 56
Buttermere Wilts 17 E
Buttershaw W Yorks 51
Butterstone Perth 76
Butterton Staffs 44
Butterwick Durham 58
Butterwick Lincs 47
Butterwick N Yorks 52
Butterwick N Yorks 52
Buttington Powys 33
Buttonoak Worcs 34
Butt's Green Hants 10
Buttsash Hants 10
Buxhall Suff 31
Buxhall Fen Street Suff 31
Buxley Borders 71
Buxted E Sus 12
Buxton Derbys 44
Buxton Norf 39
Buxworth Derbys 44
Bwcle = Buckley Flint 42
Bwlch Powys 25
Bwlch-Llan Ceredig 23 A
Bwlch-y-cibau Powys 33
Bwlch-y-fadfa Ceredig 23
Bwlch-y-ffridd Powys 33
Bwlch-y-sarnau Powys 25
Bwlchgwyn Wrex 42
Bwlchnewydd Carms 23
Bwlchtocyn Gwyn 40

roes-y-mwyalch Torf 15 B9
roeserw Neath 14 B4
roesor Gwyn 41 F8
roesyceiliog Carms 23 E9
roesyceiliog Torf 15 B9
roesywaun Gwyn 41 E7
roft Leics 35 F11
roft Lincs 47 F9
roft Pembs 22 B6
roft Warr 43 C9
roft-on-Tees N Yorks 58 F3
roftamie Stirling 68 B3
roftmalloch W Loth 69 D8
rofton W Yorks 51 H9
rofton Wilts 17 E9
rofts of Benachielt Highld 94 G3
rofts of Haddo Aberds 89 E8
rofts of Inverthernie Aberds 89 D7
rofts of Meikle Ardo Aberds 89 D8
rofty Swansea 23 G10
roggan Argyll 79 J10
roglin Cumb 57 B7
roich Highld 86 B7
rois Dughaill W Isles 84 F2
romarty Highld 87 E10
romblet Aberds 89 E7
romdale Highld 82 A2
romer Herts 29 F9
romer Norf 39 A8
romford Derbys 44 G6
romhall S Glos 16 B3
romhall Common S Glos 16 C3
romor W Isles 91 E9
romra Highld 81 D7
romwell Notts 45 F11
ronberry E Ayrs 67 D9
rondall Hants 18 G4
ronk-y-Voddy IoM 48 D3
ronton Mers 43 D7
ook Cumb 56 G6
ook Durham 58 C2
ook of Devon Perth 76 G3
ookedholm E Ayrs 67 C7
ookes S Yorks 45 D7
ookham Northumb 71 G8
ookham W Berks 18 E2
ookham Village Hants 18 F4
ookhaugh Borders 69 H10
ookhouse Borders 70 H6
ooklands Cumb 49 A5
opredy Oxon 27 D11
opston Leics 36 D1
opthorne Worcs 26 D6
opton N Yorks 59 H8
opwell Bishop Notts 36 B2
opwell Butler Notts 36 B2
os W Isles 91 A10
osbost W Isles 91 E8
osby Cumb 56 C2
osby IoM 48 E3
osby N Lincs 46 A2
osby Garrett Cumb 57 F9
osby Ravensworth Cumb 57 E8
osby Villa Cumb 56 C2
oscombe Som 16 G2
oss Som 15 F10
oss Ash Mon 25 G11
oss-at-Hand Kent 20 G4
oss Green Devon 4 C4
oss Green Suff 30 C6
oss Green Suff 30 C5
oss Green Warks 27 C10
oss-hands Carms 22 D6
oss Hands Carms 23 E10
oss Hands Pembs 22 E5
oss Hill Derbys 45 H8
oss Houses Shrops 33 E11
oss in Hand E Sus 12 D4
oss in Hand Leics 35 G11
oss Inn Ceredig 23 A8
oss Inn Ceredig 24 B2
oss Inn Rhondda 14 C6
oss Keys Kent 20 F2
oss Lane Head Shrops 34 F3
oss Lanes Corn 2 G5
oss Lanes N Yorks 51 C11
oss Lanes Wrex 43 H6
oss o' th' hands Derbys 44 H6
oss Oak Powys 25 F8
oss of Jackston Aberds 89 E7
oss Street Suff 39 H7
oss Trickett's Dorset 9 D9
ossaig Argyll 65 C9
ossal Highld 85 E9
ossapol Argyll 78 G2
ossburn Falk 69 C7
ossbush W Sus 11 D9
sscanonby Cumb 56 C2
ssdale Street Norf 39 B8
ssens Mers 49 H3
ssflatts W Yorks 51 E7
ssford Fife 69 B9
ssford S Lanark 69 F7
ssgate Lincs 37 C8
ssgatehall E Loth 70 D2
ssgates Fife 69 B10
ssgates Powys 25 B7
ssgill Lancs 50 C1
sshill E Ayrs 67 D7
sshill Fife 76 H4
sshill S Ayrs 66 F6
sshouse E Ayrs 67 C6
ssings Cumb 61 F11
sskeys Caerph 15 B8
sskirk Highld 93 B13
sslanes Shrops 33 D9
sslee Borders 61 B9
sslee Renfs 68 D3
ssmichael Dumfries 55 C10
ssmoor Lancs 49 F4
ssroads Aberds 83 D9
ssroads E Ayrs 67 C7
ssway Hereford 26 E3
ssway Mon 25 G11
Crossway Powys 25 C7
Crossway Green Worcs 26 B5
Crossways Dorset 9 F6
Crosswell Pembs 22 C6
Crosswood Ceredig 24 A3
Crosthwaite Cumb 56 G6
Croston Lancs 49 H4
Crostwick Norf 39 D8
Crostwight Norf 39 C9
Crothair W Isles 90 D6
Crouch Kent 20 F3
Crouch Hill Dorset 8 C6
Crouch House Green Kent 19 G11
Croucheston Wilts 9 B9
Croughton Northants 28 E2
Crovie Aberds 89 B8
Crow Edge S Yorks 44 B5
Crow Hill Hereford 26 F3
Crowan Corn 2 F5
Crowborough E Sus 12 C4
Crowcombe Som 7 C10
Crowdecote Derbys 44 F5
Crowden Derbys 44 C4
Crowell Oxon 18 B4
Crowfield Northants 28 D3
Crowfield Suff 31 C8
Crowhurst E Sus 13 E6
Crowhurst Sur 19 G10
Crowhurst Lane End Sur 19 G10
Crowland Lincs 37 D8
Crowlas Corn 2 F4
Crowle N Lincs 45 A11
Crowle Worcs 26 C6
Crowmarsh Gifford Oxon 18 C3
Crown Corner Suff 31 A9
Crownhill Plym 4 F5
Crownland Suff 31 B7
Crownthorpe Norf 39 E6
Crowntown Corn 2 F5
Crows-an-wra Corn 2 G2
Crowshill Norf 38 E5
Crowsnest Shrops 33 E9
Crowthorne Brack 18 E5
Crowton Ches W 43 E8
Croxall Staffs 35 D7
Croxby Lincs 46 C5
Croxdale Durham 58 C3
Croxden Staffs 35 B6
Croxley Green Herts 19 B7
Croxton Cambs 29 B9
Croxton N Lincs 46 A4
Croxton Norf 38 G4
Croxton Staffs 34 B3
Croxton Kerrial Leics 36 C4
Croxtonbank Staffs 34 B3
Croy Highld 87 G10
Croy N Lanark 68 C6
Croyde Devon 6 C3
Croydon Cambs 29 D10
Croydon London 19 E10
Crubenmore Lodge Highld 81 D8
Cruckmeole Shrops 33 E10
Cruckton Shrops 33 D10
Cruden Bay Aberds 89 E10
Crudgington Telford 34 D2
Crudwell Wilts 16 B6
Crug Powys 25 A8
Crugmeer Corn 3 B8
Crugybar Carms 24 E3
Crulabhig W Isles 90 D6
Crumlin = Crymlyn Caerph 15 B8
Crumpsall Gtr Man 44 B2
Crundale Kent 21 G7
Crundale Pembs 22 E4
Cruwys Morchard Devon 7 E7
Crux Easton Hants 17 F11
Crwbin Carms 23 E9
Crya Orkney 95 H4
Cryers Hill Bucks 18 B5
Crymlyn = Crumlin Caerph 15 B8
Crymlyn Gwyn 41 C8
Crymych Pembs 22 C6
Crynant Neath 14 A3
Crynfryn Ceredig 24 B2
Cuaig Highld 85 C12
Cuan Argyll 72 B6
Cubbington Warks 27 B10
Cubeck N Yorks 57 H11
Cubert Corn 3 D6
Cubley S Yorks 44 B6
Cubley Common Derbys 35 B7
Cublington Bucks 28 F5
Cublington Hereford 25 E11
Cuckfield W Sus 12 D2
Cucklington Som 9 B6
Cuckney Notts 45 E9
Cuckoo Hill Notts 45 C11
Cuddesdon Oxon 18 A3
Cuddington Bucks 28 G4
Cuddington Ches W 43 E9
Cuddington Heath Ches W 43 H7
Cuddy Hill Lancs 49 F4
Cudham London 19 F11
Cudliptown Devon 4 D6
Cudworth S Yorks 45 B7
Cudworth Som 8 C2
Cuffley Herts 19 A10
Cuiashader W Isles 91 B10
Cuidhir W Isles 84 H1
Cuidhtinis W Isles 90 J5
Culbo Highld 87 E9
Culbokie Highld 87 F9
Culburnie Highld 86 G7
Culcabock Highld 87 G9
Culcairn Highld 87 E9
Culcharry Highld 87 F11
Culcheth Warr 43 C9
Culdrain Aberds 88 E5
Culduie Highld 85 D12
Culford Suff 30 A5
Culgaith Cumb 57 D8
Culham Oxon 18 B2
Culkein Highld 92 F3
Culkein Drumbeg Highld 92 F4
Culkerton Glos 16 B6
Cullachie Highld 81 A11
Cullen Moray 88 B5
Cullercoats T&W 63 F9
Cullicudden Highld 87 E9
Cullingworth W Yorks 51 F6
Cullipool Argyll 72 B6
Cullivoe Shetland 96 C7
Culloch Perth 75 F10
Culloden Highld 87 G10
Cullompton Devon 7 F9
Culmaily Highld 87 B11
Culmazie Dumfries 54 D6
Culmington Shrops 33 G10
Culmstock Devon 7 E10
Culnacraig Highld 92 J3
Culnaknock Highld 85 B10
Culpho Suff 31 D9
Culrain Highld 87 B8
Culross Fife 69 B8
Culroy S Ayrs 66 E6
Culsh Aberds 82 D5
Culsh Aberds 89 D8
Culshabbin Dumfries 54 D6
Culswick Shetland 96 J4
Cultercullen Aberds 89 F9
Cults Aberdeen 83 C10
Cults Aberds 88 E5
Cults Dumfries 55 E7
Culverstone Green Kent 20 E3
Culverthorpe Lincs 36 A6
Culworth Northants 28 D2
Culzie Lodge Highld 87 D8
Cumbernauld N Lanark 68 C6
Cumbernauld Village N Lanark 68 C6
Cumberworth Lincs 47 E9
Cuminestown Aberds 89 C8
Cumlewick Shetland 96 L6
Cummersdale Cumb 56 A5
Cummertrees Dumfries 61 G7
Cummingston Moray 88 B1
Cumnock E Ayrs 67 D8
Cumnor Oxon 17 A11
Cumrew Cumb 57 A7
Cumwhinton Cumb 56 A6
Cumwhitton Cumb 57 A7
Cundall N Yorks 51 B10
Cunninghamhead N Ayrs 67 B6
Cunnister Shetland 96 D7
Cupar Fife 76 F6
Cupar Muir Fife 76 F6
Cupernham Hants 10 B2
Curbar Derbys 44 E6
Curbridge Hants 10 C4
Curbridge Oxon 27 H10
Curdridge Hants 10 C4
Curdworth Warks 35 F7
Curland Som 8 C1
Curlew Green Suff 31 B10
Currarie S Ayrs 66 G4
Currie Edin 69 D10
Curridge W Berks 17 D11
Curry Mallet Som 8 B2
Curry Rivel Som 8 B2
Curtisden Green Kent 12 B6
Curtisknowle Devon 5 F8
Cury Corn 2 G5
Cushnie Aberds 89 B7
Cushuish Som 7 C10
Cusop Hereford 25 D9
Cutcloy Dumfries 55 F7
Cutcombe Som 7 C8
Cutgate Gtr Man 44 A2
Cutiau Gwyn 32 D2
Cutlers Green Essex 30 E2
Cutnall Green Worcs 26 B5
Cutsdean Glos 27 E7
Cutthorpe Derbys 45 E7
Cutts Shetland 96 K6
Cuxham Oxon 18 B3
Cuxton Medway 20 E4
Cuxwold Lincs 46 B5
Cwm Bl Gwent 25 H8
Cwm Denb 42 E3
Cwm Swansea 14 B2
Cwm-byr Carms 24 E3
Cwm-Cewydd Gwyn 32 D4
Cwm-cou Ceredig 23 B7
Cwm-Dulais Swansea 14 A2
Cwm-felin-fach Caerph 15 B7
Cwm Ffrwd-oer Torf 15 A8
Cwm-hesgen Gwyn 32 C3
Cwm-hwnt Rhondda 24 H6
Cwm Irfon Powys 24 D5
Cwm-Llinau Powys 32 E4
Cwm-mawr Carms 23 E10
Cwm-parc Rhondda 14 B5
Cwm Penmachno Conwy 41 F9
Cwm-y-glo Carms 23 E10
Cwm-y-glo Gwyn 41 D7
Cwmafan Neath 14 B3
Cwmaman Rhondda 14 B6
Cwmann Carms 23 B10
Cwmavon Torf 25 H9
Cwmbach Carms 23 D7
Cwmbach Carms 23 F9
Cwmbach Powys 25 C7
Cwmbach Powys 25 E8
Cwmbach Rhondda 14 A6
Cwmbelan Powys 32 G5
Cwmbrân = Cwmbran Torf 15 B8
Cwmbran = Cwmbrân Torf 15 B8
Cwmbrwyno Ceredig 32 G3
Cwmcarn Caerph 15 B8
Cwmcarvan Mon 25 H11
Cwmcych Carms 23 C7
Cwmdare Rhondda 14 A5
Cwmderwen Powys 32 E5
Cwmdu Carms 24 E3
Cwmdu Powys 25 F8
Cwmdu Swansea 14 B2
Cwmduad Carms 23 C8
Cwmdwr Carms 24 E4
Cwmfelin Bridgend 14 C4
Cwmfelin M Tydf 14 A6
Cwmfelin Boeth Carms 22 E6
Cwmfelin Mynach Carms 23 D7
Cwmffrwd Carms 23 E9
Cwmgiedd Powys 24 G4
Cwmgors Neath 24 G4
Cwmgwili Carms 23 E10
Cwmgwrach Neath 14 A4
Cwmhiraeth Carms 23 C8
Cwmifor Carms 24 F3
Cwmisfael Carms 23 E9
Cwmllynfell Neath 24 G4
Cwmorgan Pembs 23 C7
Cwmpengraig Carms 23 C8
Cwmrhos Powys 25 F8
Cwmsychpant Ceredig 23 B9
Cwmtillery Bl Gwent 25 H9
Cwmwysg Powys 24 F5
Cwmyoy Mon 25 F9
Cwmystwyth Ceredig 24 A4
Cwrt Gwyn 32 E2
Cwrt-newydd Ceredig 23 B9
Cwrt-y-cadno Carms 24 D3
Cwrt-y-gollen Powys 25 G9
Cydweli = Kidwelly Carms 23 F9
Cyffordd Llandudno = Llandudno Junction Conwy 41 C9
Cyffylliog Denb 42 G3
Cyfronydd Powys 33 E7
Cymer Neath 14 B4
Cyncoed Cardiff 15 C7
Cynghordy Carms 24 D5
Cynheidre Carms 23 F9
Cynwyd Denb 33 A6
Cynwyl Elfed Carms 23 D8
Cywarch Gwyn 32 D4

D

Dacre Cumb 56 D6
Dacre N Yorks 51 C7
Dacre Banks N Yorks 51 C7
Daddry Shield Durham 57 C10
Dadford Bucks 28 E3
Dadlington Leics 35 F10
Dafarn Faig Gwyn 40 F6
Dafen Carms 23 F10
Daffy Green Norf 38 E5
Dagenham London 19 C11
Daglingworth Glos 26 H6
Dagnall Bucks 28 G6
Dail Beag W Isles 90 C7
Dail bho Dheas W Isles 91 A9
Dail bho Thuath W Isles 91 A9
Dail Mor W Isles 90 C7
Daill Argyll 64 B4
Dailly S Ayrs 66 F5
Dairsie or Osnaburgh Fife 77 F7
Daisy Hill Gtr Man 43 B9
Dalabrog W Isles 84 F2
Dalavich Argyll 73 B8
Dalbeattie Dumfries 55 C11
Dalblair E Ayrs 67 E9
Dalbog Angus 83 F7
Dalbury Derbys 35 B8
Dalby IoM 48 E2
Dalby N Yorks 52 B2
Dalchalloch Perth 75 A10
Dalchalm Highld 93 J12
Dalchenna Argyll 73 C9
Dalchirach Moray 88 E1
Dalchork Highld 93 H8
Dalchreichart Highld 80 B4
Dalchruin Perth 75 F10
Dalderby Lincs 46 F6
Dale Pembs 22 F3
Dale Abbey Derbys 35 B10
Dale Head Cumb 56 E6
Dale of Walls Shetland 96 H3
Dalelia Highld 79 E10
Daless Highld 87 H11
Dalfaber Highld 81 B11
Dalgarven N Ayrs 66 B5
Dalgety Bay Fife 69 B10
Dalginross Perth 75 E10
Dalguise Perth 76 C2
Dalhalvaig Highld 93 D11
Dalham Suff 30 B4
Dalinlongart Argyll 73 E10
Dalkeith Midloth 70 D2
Dallam Warr 43 C8
Dallas Moray 87 F14
Dalleagles E Ayrs 67 E8
Dallinghoo Suff 31 C9
Dallington E Sus 12 E5
Dallington Northants 28 B4
Dallow N Yorks 51 B7
Dalmadilly Aberds 83 B9
Dalmally Argyll 74 E4
Dalmarnock Glasgow 68 D5
Dalmary Stirling 75 H8
Dalmellington E Ayrs 67 F7
Dalmeny Edin 69 C10
Dalmigavie Highld 81 B9
Dalmigavie Lodge Highld 81 A9
Dalmore Highld 87 E9
Dalmuir W Dunb 68 C3
Dalnabreck Highld 79 E9
Dalnacardoch Lodge Perth 81 F9
Dalnacroich Highld 86 F6
Dalnaglar Castle Perth 76 A4
Dalnahaitnach Highld 81 A10
Dalnaspidal Lodge Perth 81 F8
Dalnavaid Perth 76 A3
Dalnavie Highld 87 D9
Dalnawillan Lodge Highld 93 E13
Dalness Highld 74 B4
Dalnessie Highld 93 H9
Dalqueich Perth 76 G3
Dalreavoch Highld 93 J10
Dalry N Ayrs 66 B5
Dalrymple E Ayrs 67 E6
Dalserf S Lanark 69 E7
Dalston Cumb 56 A5
Dalswinton Dumfries 60 E5
Dalton Dumfries 61 F7
Dalton Lancs 43 B7
Dalton N Yorks 51 B10
Dalton N Yorks 58 F2
Dalton Northumb 62 H5
Dalton Northumb 63 F7
Dalton S Yorks 45 C8
Dalton-in-Furness Cumb 49 B2
Dalton-le-Dale Durham 58 B5
Dalton-on-Tees N Yorks 58 F3
Dalton Piercy Hrtlpl 58 C5
Dalveich Stirling 75 E9
Dalvina Lo. Highld 93 E9
Dalwhinnie Highld 81 E8
Dalwood Devon 8 D1
Dalwyne S Ayrs 66 G6
Dam Green Norf 39 G6
Dam Side Lancs 49 E4
Damerham Hants 9 C10
Damgate Norf 39 E10
Damnaglaur Dumfries 54 F4
Damside Borders 69 F10
Danbury Essex 30 H4
Danby N Yorks 59 F8
Danby Wiske N Yorks 58 G4
Dandaleith Moray 88 D2
Danderhall Midloth 70 D2
Dane End Herts 29 F10
Danebridge Ches E 44 F3
Danehill E Sus 12 D3
Danemoor Green Norf 39 E6
Danesford Shrops 34 F3
Daneshill Hants 18 F3
Dangerous Corner Lancs 43 A8
Danskine E Loth 70 D4
Darcy Lever Gtr Man 43 B10
Darenth Kent 20 D2
Daresbury Halton 43 D8
Darfield S Yorks 45 B8
Darfoulds Notts 45 E9
Dargate Kent 21 E7
Darite Corn 4 E3
Darlaston W Mid 34 F5
Darley N Yorks 51 D8
Darley Bridge Derbys 44 F6
Darley Head N Yorks 51 D7
Darlingscott Warks 27 D9
Darlington Darl 58 E3
Darliston Shrops 34 B1
Darlton Notts 45 E11
Darnall S Yorks 45 D7
Darnick Borders 70 G4
Darowen Powys 32 E4
Darra Aberds 89 D7
Darracott Devon 6 C3
Darras Hall Northumb 63 F7
Darrington W Yorks 51 G10
Darsham Suff 31 B11
Dartford Kent 20 D2
Dartford Crossing Kent 20 D2
Dartington Devon 5 E8
Dartmeet Devon 5 D7
Dartmouth Devon 5 F9
Darton S Yorks 45 A7
Darvel E Ayrs 68 G4
Darwell Hole E Sus 12 E5
Darwen Blackburn 50 G2
Datchet Windsor 18 D6
Datchworth Herts 29 G9
Datchworth Green Herts 29 G9
Daubhill Gtr Man 43 B10
Daugh of Kinermony Moray 88 D2
Dauntsey Wilts 16 C6
Dava Moray 87 H13
Davenham Ches W 43 E9
Davenport Green Ches E 44 E2
Daventry Northants 28 B2
David's Well Powys 33 H6
Davidson's Mains Edin 69 C11
Davidstow Corn 4 C2
Davington Dumfries 61 C8
Daviot Aberds 83 A9
Daviot Highld 87 H10
Davoch of Grange Moray 88 C4
Davyhulme Gtr Man 43 C10
Dawley Telford 34 E2
Dawlish Devon 5 D10
Dawlish Warren Devon 5 D10
Dawn Conwy 41 C10
Daws Heath Essex 20 C5
Daw's House Corn 4 C4
Dawsmere Lincs 37 B10
Dayhills Staffs 34 B5
Daylesford Glos 27 F9
Ddôl-Cownwy Powys 32 D6
Ddrydwy Anglesey 40 C5
Deadwater Northumb 62 D2
Deaf Hill Durham 58 C4
Deal Kent 21 F10
Deal Hall Essex 21 B7
Dean Cumb 56 D2
Dean Devon 5 E8
Dean Devon 6 B4
Dean Dorset 9 C8
Dean Hants 10 C4
Dean Som 16 G3
Dean Prior Devon 5 E8
Dean Row Ches E 44 D2
Deanburnhaugh Borders 61 B9
Deane Gtr Man 43 B9
Deane Hants 18 F2
Deanich Lodge Highld 86 C6
Deanland Dorset 9 C8
Deans W Loth 69 D9
Deanscales Cumb 56 D2
Deanshanger Northants 28 E4
Deanston Stirling 75 G10
Dearham Cumb 56 C2
Debach Suff 31 C9
Debden Essex 19 B11
Debden Essex 30 E2
Debden Cross Essex 30 E2
Debenham Suff 31 B8
Dechmont W Loth 69 C9
Deddington Oxon 27 E11
Dedham Essex 31 E7
Dedham Heath Essex 31 E7
Deebank Aberds 83 D8
Deene Northants 36 F5
Deenethorpe Northants 36 F5
Deepcar S Yorks 44 C6
Deepcut Sur 18 F6
Deepdale Cumb 50 A3
Deeping Gate Lincs 37 E7
Deeping St James Lincs 37 E7
Deeping St Nicholas Lincs 37 D8
Deerhill Moray 88 C4
Deerhurst Glos 26 F5
Deerness Orkney 95 H6
Defford Worcs 26 D6
Defynnog Powys 24 F6
Deganwy Conwy 41 C9
Deighton N Yorks 58 F4
Deighton W Yorks 51 H7
Deighton York 52 E2
Deiniolen Gwyn 41 D7
Delabole Corn 4 C1
Delamere Ches W 43 F8
Delfrigs Aberds 89 F9
Dell Lodge Highld 82 B2
Delliefure Highld 87 H13
Delnabo Moray 82 B3
Delnadamph Aberds 82 C4
Delph Gtr Man 44 B3
Delves Durham 58 B2
Delvine Perth 76 C4
Dembleby Lincs 36 B6
Denaby Main S Yorks 45 C8
Denbigh = Dinbych Denb 42 F3
Denbury Devon 5 E9
Denby Derbys 45 H7
Denby Dale W Yorks 44 B6
Denchworth Oxon 17 B10
Dendron Cumb 49 B2
Denel End C Beds 29 E7
Denend Aberds 88 E6
Denford Northants 36 H5
Dengie Essex 20 A6
Denham Bucks 19 C7
Denham Suff 30 B4
Denham Suff 31 A8
Denham Street Suff 31 A8
Denhead Aberds 89 C9
Denhead Fife 77 F7
Denhead of Arbilot Angus 77 C8
Denhead of Gray Dundee 76 D6
Denholm Borders 61 B11
Denholme W Yorks 51 F6
Denholme Clough W Yorks 51 F6
Denio Gwyn 40 G5
Denmead Hants 10 C5
Denmore Aberdeen 83 B11
Denmoss Aberds 89 D6
Dennington Suff 31 B9
Denny Falk 69 B7
Denny Lodge Hants 10 D2
Dennyloanhead Falk 69 B7
Denshaw Gtr Man 44 A3
Denside Aberds 83 D10
Densole Kent 21 G9
Denston Suff 30 C4
Denstone Staffs 35 A7
Dent Cumb 57 H9
Denton Cambs 37 G7
Denton Darl 58 E3
Denton E Sus 12 F3
Denton Gtr Man 44 C3
Denton Kent 21 G9
Denton Lincs 36 B4
Denton N Yorks 51 E7
Denton Norf 39 G8
Denton Northants 28 C5
Denton Oxon 18 A2
Denton's Green Mers 43 C7
Denver Norf 38 E2
Denwick Northumb 63 B8
Deopham Norf 39 E6
Deopham Green Norf 38 F6
Depden Suff 30 C4
Depden Green Suff 30 C4
Deptford London 19 D10
Deptford Wilts 17 H7
Derby Derby 35 B9
Derbyhaven IoM 48 F2
Dereham Norf 38 D5
Deri Caerph 15 A7
Derril Devon 6 F2
Derringstone Kent 21 G9
Derrington Staffs 34 C4
Derriton Devon 6 F2
Derry Hill Wilts 16 D6
Derryguaig Argyll 78 H7
Derrythorpe N Lincs 46 B2
Dersingham Norf 38 B2
Dervaig Argyll 78 F7
Derwen Denb 42 G3
Derwenlas Powys 32 F3
Desborough Northants 36 G4
Desford Leics 35 E10
Detchant Northumb 71 G9
Detling Kent 20 F4
Deuddwr Powys 33 D8
Devauden Mon 15 B10
Devil's Bridge Ceredig 32 H3
Devizes Wilts 17 E7
Devol Invclyd 68 C2
Devonport Plym 4 F5
Devonside Clack 76 H2
Devoran Corn 3 F6
Dewar Borders 70 F2
Dewlish Dorset 9 E6
Dewsbury W Yorks 51 G8
Dewsbury Moor W Yorks 51 G8
Dewshall Court Hereford 25 E11
Dhoon IoM 48 D4
Dhoor IoM 48 C4
Dhowin IoM 48 B4
Dial Post W Sus 11 C10
Dibden Hants 10 D3
Dibden Purlieu Hants 10 D3
Dickleburgh Norf 39 G7
Didbrook Glos 27 E7
Didcot Oxon 18 C2
Diddington Cambs 29 B8
Diddlebury Shrops 33 G11
Didley Hereford 25 E11
Didling W Sus 11 C7
Didmarton Glos 16 C5
Didsbury Gtr Man 44 C2
Didworthy Devon 5 E7
Digby Lincs 46 G4
Digg Highld 85 B9
Diggle Gtr Man 44 B4
Digmoor Lancs 43 B7
Digswell Park Herts 29 G9
Dihewyd Ceredig 23 A9
Dilham Norf 39 C9
Dilhorne Staffs 34 A5
Dillarburn S Lanark 69 F7
Dillington Cambs 29 B8
Dilston Northumb 62 G5
Dilton Marsh Wilts 16 G5
Dilwyn Hereford 25 C11
Dinas Carms 23 C7
Dinas Gwyn 40 G4
Dinas Cross Pembs 22 C5
Dinas Dinlle Gwyn 40 E6
Dinas-Mawddwy Gwyn 32 D4
Dinas Powys V Glam 15 D7
Dinbych = Denbigh Denb 42 F3
Dinbych-y-Pysgod = Tenby Pembs 22 F6
Dinder Som 16 G2
Dinedor Hereford 26 E2
Dingestow Mon 25 G11
Dingle Mers 42 D6
Dingleden Kent 13 C7
Dingley Northants 36 G3
Dingwall Highld 87 F8
Dinlabyre Borders 61 D11
Dinmael Conwy 32 A6
Dinnet Aberds 82 D6
Dinnington S Yorks 45 D9
Dinnington Som 8 C3
Dinnington T&W 63 F8
Dinorwic Gwyn 41 D7
Dinton Bucks 28 G4
Dinton Wilts 9 A9
Dinwoodie Mains Dumfries 61 D7
Dinworthy Devon 6 E2
Dippen N Ayrs 66 D3
Dippenhall Sur 18 G5
Dipple Moray 88 C3
Dipple S Ayrs 66 F5
Diptford Devon 5 F8
Dipton Durham 58 A2
Dirdhu Highld 82 A2
Dirleton E Loth 70 B4
Dirt Pot Northumb 57 B10
Discoed Powys 25 B9
Diseworth Leics 35 C10
Dishes Orkney 95 F7
Dishforth N Yorks 51 B9
Disley Ches E 44 D3
Diss Norf 39 H7
Disserth Powys 25 C7
Distington Cumb 56 D2
Ditchampton Wilts 9 A9
Ditcheat Som 16 H3
Ditchingham Norf 39 F9
Ditchling E Sus 12 E2
Ditherington Shrops 33 D11
Dittisham Devon 5 F9
Ditton Halton 43 D7
Ditton Kent 20 F4
Ditton Green Cambs 30 C3
Ditton Priors Shrops 34 G2
Divach Highld 81 A6
Divlyn Carms 24 E4
Dixton Glos 26 E6
Dixton Mon 26 G2
Dobcross Gtr Man 44 B3
Dobwalls Corn 4 E3
Doc Penfro = Pembroke Dock Pembs 22 F4
Doccombe Devon 5 C8
Dochfour Ho. Highld 87 H9
Dochgarroch Highld 87 G9
Docking Norf 38 B3
Docklow Hereford 26 C2
Dockray Cumb 56 D5
Dockroyd W Yorks 50 F6
Dodburn Borders 61 C10
Doddinghurst Essex 20 B2
Doddington Cambs 37 F9
Doddington Kent 20 F6
Doddington Lincs 46 E3
Doddington Northumb 71 G8
Doddington Shrops 34 H2
Doddiscombsleigh Devon 5 C9
Dodford Northants 28 B3
Dodford Worcs 26 A6
Dodington S Glos 16 C4
Dodleston Ches W 42 F6
Dods Leigh Staffs 34 B6
Dodworth S Yorks 45 B7
Doe Green Warr 43 D8
Doe Lea Derbys 45 F8
Dog Village Devon 7 G8
Dogdyke Lincs 46 G6
Dogmersfield Hants 18 F4
Dogridge Wilts 17 C7
Dogsthorpe Pboro 37 E7
Dol-fôr Powys 32 E4
Dôl-y-Bont Ceredig 32 G2
Dol-y-cannau Powys 25 D9
Dolanog Powys 33 D6
Dolau Powys 25 B8
Dolau Rhondda 14 C5
Dolbenmaen Gwyn 41 F7
Dolfach Powys 32 E5
Dolfor Powys 33 G7
Dolgarrog Conwy 41 D9
Dolgellau Gwyn 32 D3
Dolgran Carms 23 C9
Dolhendre Gwyn 41 G10
Doll Highld 93 J11
Dollar Clack 76 H2
Dolley Green Powys 25 B9
Dollwen Ceredig 32 G2
Dolphin Flint 42 E4
Dolphinholme Lancs 49 D5
Dolphinton S Lanark 69 F10
Dolton Devon 6 E4
Dolwen Conwy 41 C10
Dolwen Powys 32 E5
Dolwyd Conwy 41 C10
Dolwyddelan Conwy 41 E9
Dolyhir Powys 25 C9
Doncaster S Yorks 45 B9
Dones Green Ches W 43 E9
Donhead St Andrew Wilts 9 B8
Donhead St Mary Wilts 9 B8
Donibristle Fife 69 B10
Donington Lincs 37 B8
Donington on Bain Lincs 46 D6
Donington South Ing Lincs 37 B8
Donisthorpe Leics 35 D9
Donkey Town Sur 18 E6
Donnington Glos 27 F8
Donnington Hereford 26 E4
Donnington Shrops 34 E1
Donnington Telford 34 D3
Donnington W Berks 17 E11
Donnington W Sus 11 D7
Donnington Wood Telford 34 D3
Donyatt Som 8 C2
Doonfoot S Ayrs 66 E6
Dorback Lodge Highld 82 B2
Dorchester Dorset 8 E5
Dorchester Oxon 18 B2
Dordon Warks 35 E8
Dore S Yorks 45 D7
Dores Highld 87 H8
Dorking Sur 19 G8
Dormansland Sur 12 B3
Dormanstown Redcar 59 D6
Dormington Hereford 26 D2
Dormston Worcs 26 C6
Dornal S Ayrs 54 B5
Dorney Bucks 18 D6
Dornie Highld 85 F13
Dornoch Highld 87 C10
Dornock Dumfries 61 G8
Dorrery Highld 94 E2
Dorridge W Mid 35 H7
Dorrington Lincs 46 G4
Dorrington Shrops 33 E10
Dorsington Warks 27 D8
Dorstone Hereford 25 D10
Dorton Bucks 28 G3
Dorusduain Highld 80 A1
Dosthill Staffs 35 F8
Dottery Dorset 8 E3
Doublebois Corn 4 E2
Dougarie N Ayrs 66 C1
Doughton Glos 16 B5
Douglas IoM 48 E3
Douglas S Lanark 69 G7
Douglas & Angus Dundee 77 D7
Douglas Water S Lanark 69 G7
Douglas West S Lanark 69 G7
Douglastown Angus 77 C7
Doulting Som 16 G3
Dounby Orkney 95 F3
Doune Highld 92 J7
Doune Stirling 75 G10
Doune Park Aberds 89 B7
Douneside Aberds 82 C6
Dounie Highld 87 B8
Dounreay Highld 93 C12
Dousland Devon 4 E6
Dovaston Shrops 33 C9
Dove Holes Derbys 44 E4
Dovenby Cumb 56 C2
Dover Kent 21 G10
Dovercourt Essex 31 E9
Doverdale Worcs 26 B5
Doveridge Derbys 35 B7
Doversgreen Sur 19 G9
Dowally Perth 76 C3
Dowbridge Lancs 49 F4
Dowdeswell Glos 26 G6
Dowlais M Tydf 25 H7
Dowland Devon 6 E4
Dowlish Wake Som 8 C2
Down Ampney Glos 17 B8
Down Hatherley Glos 26 F5
Down St Mary Devon 7 F6
Down Thomas Devon 4 F6
Downcraig Ferry N Ayrs 73 H10
Downderry Corn 4 F4
Downe London 19 E11
Downend IoW 10 F4
Downend S Glos 16 D3
Downend W Berks 17 D11
Downfield Dundee 76 D6
Downgate Corn 4 D4
Downham Essex 20 B4
Downham Lancs 50 E3
Downham Northumb 71 G7
Downham Market Norf 38 E2
Downhead Som 16 G3
Downhill Perth 76 D3
Downhill T&W 63 H9
Downholland Cross Lancs 42 B6
Downholme N Yorks 58 G2
Downies Aberds 83 D11
Downley Bucks 18 B5
Downside Som 16 G3
Downside Sur 19 F8
Downton Hants 10 E1
Downton Wilts 9 B10
Downton on the Rock Hereford 25 A11
Dowsby Lincs 37 C7
Dowsdale Lincs 37 D8
Dowthwaitehead Cumb 56 D5
Doxey Staffs 34 C5
Doxford Northumb 63 A7
Doxford Park T&W 58 A4
Doynton S Glos 16 D4
Draffan S Lanark 68 F6
Dragonby N Lincs 46 A3
Drakeland Corner Devon 5 F6
Drakemyre N Ayrs 66 A5
Drake's Broughton Worcs 26 D6
Drakes Cross Worcs 35 H6
Drakewalls Corn 4 D5
Draughton N Yorks 50 D6
Draughton Northants 36 H3
Drax N Yorks 52 G2
Draycote Warks 27 A11
Draycott Derbys 35 B10
Draycott Glos 27 E8
Draycott Som 15 F10
Draycott in the Clay Staffs 35 C7
Draycott in the Moors Staffs 34 A5
Drayford Devon 7 E6
Drayton Leics 36 F4
Drayton Lincs 37 B8
Drayton Norf 39 D7
Drayton Oxon 17 B11
Drayton Oxon 27 D11
Drayton Ptsmth 10 D5
Drayton Som 8 B3
Drayton Worcs 34 H5
Drayton Bassett Staffs 35 E7
Drayton Beauchamp Bucks 28 G6
Drayton Parslow Bucks 28 F5
Drayton St Leonard Oxon 18 B1
Dre-fach Carms 24 G3
Dre-fach Ceredig 23 B10
Drebley N Yorks 51 D6
Dreemskerry IoM 48 C4
Dreenhill Pembs 22 E4
Drefach Carms 23 C8
Drefach Carms 23 E10
Drefelin Carms 23 C8
Dreghorn N Ayrs 67 C6
Drellingore Kent 21 G9
Drem E Loth 70 C4
Dresden Stoke 34 A5
Dreumasdal W Isles 84 E2
Drewsteignton Devon 7 G6
Driby Lincs 47 E7
Driffield E Yorks 52 D6
Driffield Glos 17 B7
Drigg Cumb 56 G2
Drighlington W Yorks 51 G8
Drimnin Highld 79 F8
Drimpton Dorset 8 D3
Drimsynie Argyll 74 G4
Drinisiadar W Isles 90 H6
Drinkstone Suff 30 B6
Drinkstone Green Suff 30 B6
Drishaig Argyll 74 F4
Drissaig Argyll 73 B8
Drochil Borders 69 F10
Drointon Staffs 34 C6
Droitwich Spa Worcs 26 B5
Droman Highld 92 D4
Dron Perth 76 F4
Dronfield Derbys 45 E7
Dronfield Woodhouse Derbys 45 E7
Drongan E Ayrs 67 E7
Dronley Angus 76 D6
Droxford Hants 10 C5
Droylsden Gtr Man 44 C3
Druid Denb 32 A6
Druidston Pembs 22 E3
Druimarbin Highld 80 F2
Druimavuic Argyll 74 C3
Druimdrishaig Argyll 72 F6
Druimindarroch Highld 79 C9
Druimyeon More Argyll 65 C7
Drum Argyll 73 F8
Drum Perth 76 G3
Drumbeg Highld 92 F4
Drumblade Aberds 88 D5
Drumblair Aberds 89 D7
Drumbuie Dumfries 55 A8
Drumbuie Highld 85 E12
Drumburgh Cumb 61 H8
Drumburn Dumfries 60 G5
Drumchapel Glasgow 68 C4
Drumchardine Highld 87 G8
Drumchork Highld 91 J13
Drumclog S Lanark 68 G5
Drumderfit Highld 87 F9
Drumeldrie Fife 77 G7
Drumelzier Borders 69 G10
Drumfearn Highld 85 G11
Drumgask Highld 81 D8
Drumgley Angus 77 B7
Drumguish Highld 81 D9
Drumin Moray 88 E1
Drumlasie Aberds 83 C8
Drumlemble Argyll 65 G7
Drumligair Aberds 83 B11
Drumlithie Aberds 83 E9
Drummoddie Dumfries 54 E6
Drummond Highld 87 E9
Drummore Dumfries 54 F4
Drummuir Moray 88 D3
Drummuir Castle Moray 88 D3
Drumnadrochit Highld 81 A7
Drumnagorrach Moray 88 C5
Drumoak Aberds 83 D9
Drumpark Dumfries 60 E4
Drumphail Dumfries 54 C5
Drumrash Dumfries 55 B9
Drumrunie Highld 92 J4
Drums Aberds 89 F9
Drumsallie Highld 80 F1
Drumstinchall Dumfries 55 D11
Drumsturdy Angus 77 D7
Drumtochty Castle Aberds 83 F8
Drumtroddan Dumfries 54 E6
Drumuie Highld 85 D9
Drumuillie Highld 81 A11
Drumvaich Stirling 75 G9
Drumwhindle Aberds 89 E9
Drunkendub Angus 77 C9
Drury Flint 42 F5
Drury Square Norf 38 D5
Dry Doddington Lincs 46 H2
Dry Drayton Cambs 29 B10
Drybeck Cumb 57 E8
Drybridge Moray 88 B4
Drybridge N Ayrs 67 C6
Drybrook Glos 26 G3
Dryburgh Borders 70 G4
Dryhope Borders 61 A8
Drylaw Edin 69 C11
Drym Corn 2 F5
Drymen Stirling 68 B3
Drymuir Aberds 89 D9
Drynoch Highld 85 E9
Dryslwyn Carms 23 D10
Dryton Shrops 34 E1
Dubford Aberds 89 B8
Dubton Angus 77 B8
Duchally Highld 92 H6
Duchlage Argyll 68 B2
Duck Corner Suff 31 D10
Duckington Ches W 43 G7
Ducklington Oxon 27 H10
Duckmanton Derbys 45 E8
Duck's Cross Bedford 29 C8
Duddenhoe End Essex 29 E11
Duddingston Edin 69 C11
Duddington Northants 36 E5
Duddleswell E Sus 12 D3
Duddo Northumb 71 F8
Duddon Ches W 43 F8
Duddon Bridge Cumb 56 H4
Dudleston Shrops 33 B9
Dudleston Heath Shrops 33 B9
Dudley T&W 63 F8
Dudley W Mid 34 F5
Dudley Port W Mid 34 F5
Duffield Derbys 35 A9
Duffryn Neath 14 B4
Duffryn Newport 15 C8
Dufftown Moray 88 E3
Duffus Moray 88 B1
Dufton Cumb 57 D8
Duggleby N Yorks 52 C4
Duirinish Highld 85 E12
Duisdalemore Highld 85 G12
Duisky Highld 80 F2
Dukestown Bl Gwent 25 G8
Dukinfield Gtr Man 44 C3
Dulas Anglesey 40 B6
Dulcote Som 16 G2
Dulford Devon 7 F9
Dull Perth 75 C11
Dullatur N Lanark 68 C6
Dullingham Cambs 30 C3
Dulnain Bridge Highld 82 A1
Duloe Bedford 29 B8
Duloe Corn 4 F3
Dulsie Highld 87 G12
Dulverton Som 7 D8
Dulwich London 19 D10
Dumbarton W Dunb 68 C2
Dumbleton Glos 27 E7
Dumcrieff Dumfries 61 C7
Dumfries Dumfries 60 F5
Dumgoyne Stirling 68 B4
Dummer Hants 18 G2
Dumpford W Sus 11 B7
Dumpton Kent 21 E10
Dun Angus 77 B9
Dun Charlabhaigh W Isles 90 C6
Dunain Ho. Highld 87 G9
Dunalastair Perth 75 B10
Dunan Highld 85 F10
Dunans Argyll 73 D9
Dunball Som 15 G9
Dunbar E Loth 70 C5
Dunbeath Highld 94 H3
Dunbeg Argyll 79 H11
Dunblane Stirling 75 G10
Dunbog Fife 76 F5
Duncanston Highld 87 F8
Duncanstone Aberds 83 A7
Dunchurch Warks 27 A11
Duncote Northants 28 C3
Duncow Dumfries 60 E5
Duncraggan Stirling 75 G8
Duncrievie Perth 76 G4
Duncton W Sus 11 C8
Dundas Ho. Orkney 95 K5
Dundee Dundee 77 D7
Dundeugh Dumfries 67 H8
Dundon Som 8 A3
Dundonald S Ayrs 67 C6

E

F

Hart Hrtlpl 58 C5
Hart Common Gtr Man 43 B9
Hart Hill Luton 29 F8
Hart Station Hrtlpl 58 C5
Hartburn Northumb 62 E6
Hartburn Stockton 58 E5
Hartest Suff 30 C5
Hartfield E Sus 12 C3
Hartford Cambs 29 A9
Hartford Ches W 43 E9
Hartford End Essex 30 G3
Hartfordbridge Hants 18 F4
Hartforth N Yorks 58 F2
Harthill Ches W 43 G8
Harthill N Lanark 69 D8
Harthill S Yorks 45 D8
Hartington Derbys 44 F5
Hartland Devon 6 D1
Hartlebury Worcs 26 A5
Hartlepool Hrtlpl 58 C6
Hartley Cumb 57 F9
Hartley Kent 13 C6
Hartley Kent 20 E3
Hartley Northumb 63 F9
Hartley Westpall Hants 18 F3
Hartley Wintney Hants 18 F4
Hartlip Kent 20 E5
Hartoft End N Yorks 59 G8
Harton N Yorks 52 C3
Harton Shrops 33 G10
Harton T&W 63 G9
Hartpury Glos 26 F4
Hartshead W Yorks 51 G7
Hartshill Warks 35 F9
Hartshorne Derbys 35 C9
Hartsop Cumb 56 E6
Hartwell Northants 28 C4
Hartwood N Lanark 69 E7
Harvieston Stirling 68 B4
Harvington Worcs 27 D7
Harvington Cross Worcs 27 D7
Harwell Oxon 17 C11
Harwich Essex 31 E9
Harwood Durham 57 C10
Harwood Gtr Man 43 A10
Harwood Dale N Yorks 59 G10
Harworth Notts 45 C10
Hasbury W Mid 34 G5
Hascombe Sur 18 G6
Haselbech Northants 36 H3
Haselbury Plucknett Som 8 C3
Haseley Warks 27 B9
Haselor Warks 27 C8
Hasfield Glos 26 F5
Hasguard Pembs 22 F3
Haskayne Lancs 42 B6
Hasketon Suff 31 C9
Hasland Derbys 45 F7
Haslemere Sur 11 A8
Haslingden Lancs 50 G3
Haslingfield Cambs 29 C11
Haslington Ches E 43 G10
Hassall Ches E 43 G10
Hassall Green Ches E 43 G10
Hassell Street Kent 21 G7
Hassendean Borders 61 A11
Hassingham Norf 39 E9
Hassocks W Sus 12 E1
Hassop Derbys 44 E6
Hastigrow Highld 94 D4
Hastingleigh Kent 13 B9
Hastings E Sus 13 F7
Hastingwood Essex 29 H11
Hastoe Herts 28 H6
Haswell Durham 58 B4
Haswell Plough Durham 58 B4
Hatch C Beds 29 D8
Hatch Hants 18 F3
Hatch Wilts 9 B8
Hatch Beauchamp Som 8 B2
Hatch End London 19 B8
Hatch Green Som 8 C2
Hatchet Gate Hants 10 D2
Hatching Green Herts 29 G8
Hatchmere Ches W 43 E8
Hatcliffe NE Lincs 46 B6
Hatfield Hereford 26 C2
Hatfield Herts 29 H9
Hatfield S Yorks 45 B10
Hatfield Worcs 26 C5
Hatfield Broad Oak Essex 30 G2
Hatfield Garden Village Herts 29 H9
Hatfield Heath Essex 30 G2
Hatfield Hyde Herts 29 G9
Hatfield Peverel Essex 30 G4
Hatfield Woodhouse S Yorks 45 B10
Hatford Oxon 17 B10
Hatherden Hants 17 F10
Hatherleigh Devon 6 F4
Hathern Leics 35 C10
Hatherop Glos 27 H8
Hathersage Derbys 44 D6
Hathershaw Gtr Man 44 B3
Hatherton Ches E 43 H9
Hatherton Staffs 34 D5
Hatley St George Cambs 29 C9
Hatt Corn 4 E4
Hattingley Hants 18 H3
Hatton Aberds 89 E10
Hatton Derbys 35 C8
Hatton Lincs 46 E5
Hatton Shrops 33 F10
Hatton Warks 27 B9
Hatton Warr 43 D8
Hatton Castle Aberds 89 D7
Hatton Heath Ches W 43 F7
Hatton of Fintray Aberds 83 B10
Hattoncrook Aberds 89 F8
Haugh E Ayrs 67 D7
Haugh Gtr Man 44 A3
Haugh Lincs 47 E8
Haugh Head Northumb 71 H9
Haugh of Glass Moray 88 E4
Haugh of Urr Dumfries 55 C11
Haugham Lincs 47 D7
Haughley Suff 31 B7
Haughley Green Suff 31 B7
Haughs of Clinterty Aberdeen 83 B10
Haughton Notts 45 E10
Haughton Shrops 33 C9
Haughton Shrops 34 D1
Haughton Shrops 34 E3
Haughton Shrops 34 F2
Haughton Staffs 34 C4
Haughton Castle Northumb 62 F5
Haughton Green Gtr Man 44 C3
Haughton Moss Ches E 43 G8
Haultwick Herts 29 F10
Haunn Argyll 78 G6
Haunn W Isles 84 G2
Haunton Staffs 35 D8
Hauxley Northumb 63 C8
Hauxton Cambs 29 C11
Havant Hants 10 D6
Haven Hereford 25 C11
Haven Bank Lincs 46 G6
Haven Side E Yorks 53 G7
Havenstreet IoW 10 E4
Havercroft W Yorks 45 A7
Haverfordwest = Hwlffordd Pembs 22 E4
Haverhill Suff 30 D3
Haverigg Cumb 49 B1
Havering-atte-Bower London 20 B2
Haveringland Norf 39 C7
Haversham M Keynes 28 D5
Haverthwaite Cumb 49 A3
Haverton Hill Stockton 58 D5
Hawarden = Penarlâg Flint 42 F6
Hawcoat Cumb 49 B2
Hawen Ceredig 23 B8
Hawes N Yorks 57 H10
Hawes' Green Norf 39 F8
Hawes Side Blackpool 49 F3
Hawford Worcs 26 B5
Hawick Borders 61 B11
Hawk Green Gtr Man 44 D3
Hawkchurch Devon 8 D2
Hawkedon Suff 30 C4
Hawkenbury Kent 12 C4
Hawkenbury Kent 13 B7
Hawkeridge Wilts 16 F5
Hawkerland Devon 7 H9
Hawkes End W Mid 35 G9
Hawkesbury S Glos 16 C4
Hawkesbury Warks 35 G9
Hawkesbury Upton S Glos 16 C4
Hawkhill Northumb 63 B8
Hawkhurst Kent 13 C6
Hawkinge Kent 21 H9
Hawkley Hants 10 B6
Hawkridge Som 7 C7
Hawkshead Cumb 56 G5
Hawkshead Hill Cumb 56 G5
Hawksland S Lanark 69 G7
Hawkswick N Yorks 50 B5
Hawksworth Notts 36 A3
Hawksworth W Yorks 51 E7
Hawksworth W Yorks 51 F8
Hawkwell Essex 20 B5
Hawley Hants 18 F5
Hawley Kent 20 D2
Hawling Glos 27 F7
Hawnby N Yorks 59 H6
Haworth W Yorks 50 F6
Hawstead Suff 30 C5
Hawthorn Durham 58 B5
Hawthorn Rhondda 15 C7
Hawthorn Wilts 16 E5
Hawthorn Hill Brack 18 D5
Hawthorn Hill Lincs 46 G6
Hawthorpe Lincs 36 C6
Hawton Notts 45 G11
Haxby York 52 D2
Haxey N Lincs 45 C11
Hay Green Norf 37 D11
Hay-on-Wye = Y Gelli Gandryll Powys 25 D9
Hay Street Herts 29 F10
Haydock Mers 43 C8
Haydon Dorset 8 C5
Haydon Bridge Northumb 62 G4
Haydon Wick Swindon 17 C8
Haye Corn 4 E4
Hayes London 19 C8
Hayes London 19 E11
Hayfield Derbys 44 D4
Hayfield Fife 69 A11
Hayhill E Ayrs 67 E7
Hayhillock Angus 77 C8
Hayle Corn 2 F4
Haynes C Beds 29 D7
Haynes Church End C Beds 29 D7
Hayscastle Pembs 22 D3
Hayscastle Cross Pembs 22 D4
Hayshead Angus 77 C9
Hayton Aberdeen 83 C11
Hayton Cumb 56 B3
Hayton Cumb 61 H11
Hayton E Yorks 52 E4
Hayton Notts 45 D11
Hayton's Bent Shrops 33 G11
Haytor Vale Devon 5 D8
Haywards Heath W Sus 12 D2
Haywood S Yorks 45 A9
Haywood Oaks Notts 45 G10
Hazel Grove Gtr Man 44 D3
Hazel Street Kent 12 C5
Hazelbank S Lanark 69 F7
Hazelbury Bryan Dorset 8 D6
Hazeley Hants 18 F4
Hazelhurst Gtr Man 44 B3
Hazelslade Staffs 34 D6
Hazelton Glos 27 G7
Hazelton Walls Fife 76 E6
Hazelwood Derbys 45 H7
Hazlemere Bucks 18 B5
Hazlerigg T&W 63 F8
Hazlewood N Yorks 51 D6
Hazon Northumb 63 C7
Heacham Norf 38 B2
Head of Muir Falk 69 B7
Headbourne Worthy Hants 10 A3
Headbrook Hereford 25 C10
Headcorn Kent 13 B7
Headingley W Yorks 51 F8
Headington Oxon 28 H2
Headlam Durham 58 E2
Headless Cross Worcs 27 B7
Headley Hants 18 E2
Headley Hants 18 H5
Headley Sur 19 F9
Headon Notts 45 E11
Heads S Lanark 68 F6
Heads Nook Cumb 61 H10
Heage Derbys 45 G7
Healaugh N Yorks 51 E10
Healaugh N Yorks 58 G1
Heald Green Gtr Man 44 D2
Heale Devon 6 B5
Heale Som 16 G3
Healey Gtr Man 50 H4
Healey N Yorks 51 A7
Healey Northumb 62 H6
Healing NE Lincs 46 A6
Heamoor Corn 2 F3
Heanish Argyll 78 G3
Heanor Derbys 45 H8
Heanton Punchardon Devon 6 C4
Heapham Lincs 46 D2
Hearthstane Borders 69 H10
Heasley Mill Devon 7 C6
Heast Highld 85 G11
Heath Cardiff 15 D7
Heath Derbys 45 F8
Heath and Reach C Beds 28 F6
Heath End Hants 18 E2
Heath End Sur 18 G5
Heath End Warks 27 B9
Heath Hayes Staffs 34 D6
Heath Hill Shrops 34 D3
Heath House Som 15 G10
Heath Town W Mid 34 F5
Heathcote Derbys 44 F5
Heather Leics 35 D9
Heatherfield Highld 85 D9
Heathfield Devon 5 D9
Heathfield E Sus 12 D4
Heathfield Som 7 D10
Heathhall Dumfries 60 F5
Heathrow Airport London 19 D7
Heathstock Devon 8 D1
Heathton Shrops 34 F4
Heatley Warr 43 D10
Heaton Lancs 49 C4
Heaton Staffs 44 F3
Heaton T&W 63 G8
Heaton W Yorks 51 F7
Heaton Moor Gtr Man 44 C2
Heaverham Kent 20 F2
Heaviley Gtr Man 44 D3
Heavitree Devon 7 G8
Hebburn T&W 63 G9
Hebden N Yorks 50 C6
Hebden Bridge W Yorks 50 G5
Hebron Anglesey 40 B6
Hebron Carms 22 D6
Hebron Northumb 63 E7
Heck Dumfries 60 E6
Heckfield Hants 18 E4
Heckfield Green Suff 39 H7
Heckfordbridge Essex 30 F6
Heckington Lincs 37 A7
Heckmondwike W Yorks 51 G8
Heddington Wilts 16 E6
Heddle Orkney 95 G4
Heddon-on-the-Wall Northumb 63 G7
Hedenham Norf 39 F9
Hedge End Hants 10 C3
Hedgerley Bucks 18 C6
Hedging Som 8 B2
Hedley on the Hill Northumb 62 H6
Hednesford Staffs 34 D6
Hedon E Yorks 53 G7
Hedsor Bucks 18 C6
Hedworth T&W 63 G9
Hegdon Hill Hereford 26 C2
Heggerscales Cumb 57 E10
Heglibister Shetland 96 H5
Heighington Darl 58 D3
Heighington Lincs 46 F4
Heights of Brae Highld 87 E8
Heights of Kinlochewe Highld 86 E3
Heilam Highld 92 C7
Heiton Borders 70 G6
Hele Devon 6 B4
Hele Devon 7 F8
Helensburgh Argyll 73 E11
Helford Corn 3 G6
Helford Passage Corn 3 G6
Helhoughton Norf 38 C4
Helions Bumpstead Essex 30 D3
Hellaby S Yorks 45 C9
Helland Corn 4 D1
Hellesdon Norf 39 D8
Hellidon Northants 28 C2
Hellifield N Yorks 50 D4
Hellingly E Sus 12 E4
Hellington Norf 39 E9
Hellister Shetland 96 J5
Helm Northumb 63 D7
Helmdon Northants 28 D2
Helmingham Suff 31 C8
Helmington Row Durham 58 C2
Helmsdale Highld 93 H13
Helmshore Lancs 50 G3
Helmsley N Yorks 52 A2
Helperby N Yorks 51 C10
Helperthorpe N Yorks 52 B5
Helpringham Lincs 37 A7
Helpston Pboro 37 E7
Helsby Ches W 43 E7
Helsey Lincs 47 E9
Helston Corn 2 G5
Helstone Corn 4 C1
Helton Cumb 57 D7
Helwith Bridge N Yorks 50 C4
Hemblington Norf 39 D9
Hemel Hempstead Herts 29 H7
Hemingbrough N Yorks 52 F2
Hemingby Lincs 46 E6
Hemingford Abbots Cambs 29 A9
Hemingford Grey Cambs 29 A9
Hemingstone Suff 31 C8
Hemington Leics 35 C10
Hemington Northants 37 G6
Hemington Som 16 F4
Hemley Suff 31 D9
Hemlington Mbro 58 E6
Hemp Green Suff 31 B10
Hempholme E Yorks 53 D6
Hempnall Norf 39 F8
Hempnall Green Norf 39 F8
Hempriggs House Highld 94 F5
Hempstead Essex 30 E3
Hempstead Medway 20 E4
Hempstead Norf 39 B7
Hempstead Norf 39 C10
Hempsted Glos 26 G5
Hempton Norf 38 C5
Hempton Oxon 27 E11
Hemsby Norf 39 D10
Hemswell Lincs 46 C3
Hemswell Cliff Lincs 46 D3
Hemsworth W Yorks 45 A8
Hemyock Devon 7 E10
Hen-feddau fawr Pembs 23 C7
Henbury Bristol 16 D2
Henbury Ches E 44 E2
Hendon London 19 C9
Hendon T&W 63 H10
Hendre Flint 42 F4
Hendre-ddu Conwy 41 D10
Hendreforgan Rhondda 14 C5
Hendy Carms 23 F10
Heneglwys Anglesey 40 C6
Henfield W Sus 11 C11
Henford Devon 6 G2
Henghurst Kent 13 C8
Hengoed Caerph 15 B7
Hengoed Powys 25 C9
Hengoed Shrops 33 B8
Hengrave Suff 30 B5
Henham Essex 30 F2
Heniarth Powys 33 E7
Henlade Som 8 B1
Henley Shrops 33 H11
Henley Som 8 A3
Henley Suff 31 C8
Henley W Sus 11 B7
Henley-in-Arden Warks 27 B8
Henley-on-Thames Oxon 18 C4
Henley's Down E Sus 12 E6
Henllan Ceredig 23 B8
Henllan Denb 42 F3
Henllan Amgoed Carms 22 D6
Henllys Torf 15 B8
Henlow C Beds 29 E8
Hennock Devon 5 C9
Henny Street Essex 30 E5
Henryd Conwy 41 C9
Henry's Moat Pembs 22 D5
Hensall N Yorks 52 G1
Henshaw Northumb 62 G3
Hensingham Cumb 56 E1
Henstead Suff 39 G10
Henstridge Som 8 C6
Henstridge Ash Som 8 B6
Henstridge Marsh Som 8 B6
Henton Oxon 18 A4
Henton Som 15 G10
Henwood Corn 4 D3
Heogan Shetland 96 J6
Heol-las Swansea 14 B2
Heol Senni Powys 24 F6
Heol-y-Cyw Bridgend 14 C5
Hepburn Northumb 62 A6
Hepple Northumb 62 C5
Hepscott Northumb 63 E8
Heptonstall W Yorks 50 G5
Hepworth Suff 30 A6
Hepworth W Yorks 44 B5
Herbrandston Pembs 22 F3
Hereford Hereford 26 D2
Heriot Borders 70 E2
Hermiston Edin 69 C10
Hermitage Borders 61 D11
Hermitage Dorset 8 D5
Hermitage W Berks 18 D2
Hermitage W Sus 11 D6
Hermon Anglesey 40 D5
Hermon Carms 23 C8
Hermon Carms 24 F3
Hermon Pembs 23 C7
Herne Kent 21 E8
Herne Bay Kent 21 E8
Herner Devon 6 D4
Hernhill Kent 21 E7
Herodsfoot Corn 4 E3
Herongate Essex 20 B3
Heronsford S Ayrs 54 A4
Herriard Hants 18 G3
Herringfleet Suff 39 F10
Herringswell Suff 30 A4
Hersden Kent 21 E9
Hersham Corn 6 F1
Hersham Sur 19 E8
Herstmonceux E Sus 12 E5
Herston Orkney 95 J5
Hertford Herts 29 G10
Hertford Heath Herts 29 G10
Hertingfordbury Herts 29 G10
Hesket Newmarket Cumb 56 C5
Hesketh Bank Lancs 49 G4
Hesketh Lane Lancs 50 E2
Heskin Green Lancs 49 H5
Hesleden Durham 58 C5
Hesleyside Northumb 62 E4
Heslington York 52 D2
Hessay York 51 D11
Hessenford Corn 4 F4
Hessett Suff 30 B6
Hessle E Yorks 52 G6
Hest Bank Lancs 49 C4
Heston London 19 D8
Hestwall Orkney 95 G3
Heswall Mers 42 D5
Hethe Oxon 28 F2
Hethersett Norf 39 E7
Hethersgill Cumb 61 G10
Hethpool Northumb 71 H7
Hett Durham 58 C3
Hetton N Yorks 50 D5
Hetton-le-Hole T&W 58 B4
Hetton Steads Northumb 71 G9
Heugh Northumb 62 F6
Heugh-head Aberds 82 B5
Heveningham Suff 31 A10
Hever Kent 12 B3
Heversham Cumb 49 A4
Hevingham Norf 39 C7
Hewas Water Corn 3 E8
Hewelsfield Glos 16 A2
Hewish N Som 15 E10
Hewish Som 8 D3
Heworth York 52 D2
Hexham Northumb 62 G5
Hextable Kent 20 D2
Hexton Herts 29 E8
Hexworthy Devon 5 D7
Hey Lancs 50 E4
Heybridge Essex 20 B3
Heybridge Essex 30 H5
Heybridge Basin Essex 30 H5
Heybrook Bay Devon 4 G6
Heydon Cambs 29 D11
Heydon Norf 39 C7
Heydour Lincs 36 B6
Heylipol Argyll 78 G2
Heylor Shetland 96 E4
Heysham Lancs 49 C4
Heyshott W Sus 11 C7
Heyside Gtr Man 44 B3
Heytesbury Wilts 16 G6
Heythrop Oxon 27 F10
Heywood Gtr Man 44 A2
Heywood Wilts 16 F5
Hibaldstow N Lincs 46 B3
Hickleton S Yorks 45 B8
Hickling Norf 39 C10
Hickling Notts 36 C2
Hickling Green Norf 39 C10
Hickling Heath Norf 39 C10
Hickstead W Sus 12 D1
Hidcote Boyce Glos 27 D8
High Ackworth W Yorks 51 H10
High Angerton Northumb 62 E6
High Bankhill Cumb 57 B7
High Barnes T&W 63 H9
High Beach Essex 19 B11
High Bentham N Yorks 50 C2
High Bickington Devon 6 D5
High Birkwith N Yorks 50 B3
High Blantyre S Lanark 68 E5
High Bonnybridge Falk 69 C7
High Bradfield S Yorks 44 C6
High Bray Devon 6 C5
High Brooms Kent 12 B4
High Bullen Devon 6 D4
High Buston Northumb 63 C8
High Callerton Northumb 63 F7
High Catton E Yorks 52 D3
High Cogges Oxon 27 H10
High Coniscliffe Darl 58 E3
High Cross Hants 10 B6
High Cross Herts 29 G10
High Easter Essex 30 G3
High Eggborough N Yorks 52 G1
High Ellington N Yorks 51 A7
High Ercall Telford 34 D1
High Etherley Durham 58 D2
High Garrett Essex 30 F4
High Grange Durham 58 C2
High Green Norf 39 E7
High Green S Yorks 45 C7
High Green Worcs 26 D5
High Halden Kent 13 C7
High Halstow Medway 20 D4
High Ham Som 8 A3
High Harrington Cumb 56 D2
High Hatton Shrops 34 C2
High Hawsker N Yorks 59 F10
High Hesket Cumb 57 B6
High Hesleden Durham 58 C5
High Hoyland S Yorks 44 A6
High Hunsley E Yorks 52 F5
High Hurstwood E Sus 12 D3
High Hutton N Yorks 52 C3
High Ireby Cumb 56 C4
High Kelling Norf 39 A7
High Kilburn N Yorks 51 B11
High Lands Durham 58 D2
High Lane Gtr Man 44 D3
High Lane Worcs 26 B3
High Laver Essex 30 H2
High Legh Ches E 43 D10
High Leven Stockton 58 E5
High Littleton Bath 16 F3
High Lorton Cumb 56 D3
High Marishes N Yorks 52 B4
High Marnham Notts 46 E2
High Melton S Yorks 45 B9
High Mickley Northumb 62 G6
High Mindork Dumfries 54 D6
High Newton Cumb 49 A4
High Newton-by-the-Sea Northumb 71 H11
High Nibthwaite Cumb 56 H4
High Offley Staffs 34 C3
High Ongar Essex 20 A2
High Onn Staffs 34 D4
High Roding Essex 30 G3
High Row Cumb 56 C5
High Salvington W Sus 11 D10
High Sellafield Cumb 56 F2
High Shaw N Yorks 57 G10
High Spen T&W 63 H7
High Stoop Durham 58 B2
High Street Corn 3 D8
High Street Kent 12 C6
High Street Suff 30 D5
High Street Suff 31 A11
High Street Suff 31 C11
High Street Green Suff 31 C7
High Throston Hrtlpl 58 C5
High Toynton Lincs 46 F6
High Trewhitt Northumb 62 C6
High Valleyfield Fife 69 B9
High Westwood Durham 63 H7
High Wray Cumb 56 F5
High Wych Herts 29 G11
High Wycombe Bucks 18 B5
Higham Derbys 45 G7
Higham Kent 20 D4
Higham Lancs 50 F4
Higham Suff 30 B4
Higham Suff 31 E7
Higham Dykes Northumb 63 F7
Higham Ferrers Northants 28 B6
Higham Gobion C Beds 29 E8
Higham on the Hill Leics 35 F9
Higham Wood Kent 20 G3
Highampton Devon 6 F3
Highbridge Highld 80 E3
Highbridge Som 15 G9
Highbrook W Sus 12 C2
Highburton W Yorks 44 A5
Highbury Som 16 G3
Highclere Hants 17 E11
Highcliffe Dorset 9 E11
Higher Ansty Dorset 9 D6
Higher Ashton Devon 5 C9
Higher Ballam Lancs 49 F3
Higher Bartle Lancs 49 F5
Higher Boscaswell Corn 2 F2
Higher Burwardsley Ches W 43 G8
Higher Clovelly Devon 6 D2
Higher End Gtr Man 43 B8
Higher Kinnerton Flint 42 F6
Higher Penwortham Lancs 49 G5
Higher Town Scilly 2 C3
Higher Walreddon Devon 4 D5
Higher Walton Lancs 50 G1
Higher Walton Warr 43 D8
Higher Wheelton Lancs 50 G2
Higher Whitley Ches W 43 D9
Higher Wincham Ches W 43 E9
Higher Wych Ches W 33 A10
Highfield E Yorks 52 F3
Highfield Gtr Man 43 B10
Highfield N Ayrs 66 A6
Highfield Oxon 28 F2
Highfield S Yorks 45 D7
Highfield T&W 63 H7
Highfields Cambs 29 C10
Highfields Northumb 71 E8
Highgate London 19 C9
Highlane Ches E 44 F2
Highlane Derbys 45 D8
Highlaws Cumb 56 B3
Highleadon Glos 26 F4
Highleigh W Sus 11 E7
Highley Shrops 34 G3
Highmoor Cross Oxon 18 C4
Highmoor Hill Mon 15 C10
Highnam Glos 26 G4
Highnam Green Glos 26 F4
Highsted Kent 20 E6
Highstreet Green Essex 30 E4
Hightae Dumfries 60 F6
Hightown Ches E 44 F2
Hightown Mers 42 B6
Hightown Green Suff 30 C6
Highway Wilts 17 D7
Highweek Devon 5 D9
Highworth Swindon 17 B9
Hilborough Norf 38 E4
Hilcote Derbys 45 G8
Hilcott Wilts 17 F8
Hilden Park Kent 20 G2
Hildenborough Kent 20 G2
Hildersham Cambs 30 D2
Hilderstone Staffs 34 B5
Hilderthorpe E Yorks 53 C7
Hilfield Dorset 8 D5
Hilgay Norf 38 F2
Hill Pembs 22 F6
Hill S Glos 16 B3
Hill W Mid 35 F7
Hill Brow W Sus 11 B6
Hill Dale Lancs 43 A7
Hill Dyke Lincs 47 H7
Hill End Durham 58 C1
Hill End Fife 76 H3
Hill End N Yorks 51 D6
Hill Head Hants 10 D4
Hill Head Northumb 62 G5
Hill Mountain Pembs 22 F4
Hill of Beath Fife 69 A10
Hill of Fearn Highld 87 D11
Hill of Mountblairy Aberds 89 C6
Hill Ridware Staffs 35 D6
Hill Top Durham 57 D11
Hill Top Hants 10 D3
Hill Top W Mid 34 F5
Hill Top W Yorks 51 H9
Hill View Dorset 9 E8
Hillam N Yorks 51 G11
Hillbeck Cumb 57 E9
Hillborough Kent 21 E9
Hillbrae Aberds 83 A9
Hillbrae Aberds 88 D6
Hillbutts Dorset 9 D8
Hillclifflane Derbys 44 H6
Hillcommon Som 7 D10
Hillend Fife 69 B10
Hillerton Devon 7 G6
Hillesden Bucks 28 F3
Hillesley Glos 16 C4
Hillfarance Som 7 D10
Hillhead Aberds 88 E5
Hillhead Devon 5 F10
Hillhead S Ayrs 67 E7
Hillhead of Auchentumb Aberds 89 C9
Hillhead of Cocklaw Aberds 89 D10
Hillhouse Borders 70 E4
Hilliclay Highld 94 D3
Hillingdon London 19 C7
Hillington Glasgow 68 D4
Hillington Norf 38 C3
Hillmorton Warks 28 A2
Hillockhead Aberds 82 B6
Hillockhead Aberds 82 C5
Hillside Aberds 83 D11
Hillside Angus 77 A10
Hillside Mers 42 A6
Hillside Orkney 95 J5
Hillside Shetland 96 G6
Hillswick Shetland 96 F4
Hillway IoW 10 F5
Hillwell Shetland 96 M5
Hilmarton Wilts 17 D7
Hilperton Wilts 16 F5
Hilsea Ptsmth 10 D5
Hilston E Yorks 53 F8
Hilton Aberds 89 E9
Hilton Cambs 29 B9
Hilton Cumb 57 D9
Hilton Derbys 35 B8
Hilton Dorset 9 D6
Hilton Durham 58 D2
Hilton Highld 87 C10
Hilton Shrops 34 F3
Hilton Stockton 58 E5
Hilton of Cadboll Highld 87 D11
Himbleton Worcs 26 C6
Himley Staffs 34 F4
Hincaster Cumb 49 A5
Hinckley Leics 35 F10
Hinderclay Suff 38 H6
Hinderton Ches W 42 E6
Hinderwell N Yorks 59 E8
Hindford Shrops 33 B9
Hindhead Sur 18 H5
Hindley Gtr Man 43 B9
Hindley Green Gtr Man 43 B9
Hindlip Worcs 26 C5
Hindolveston Norf 38 C6
Hindon Wilts 9 A8
Hindringham Norf 38 B5
Hingham Norf 38 E6
Hinstock Shrops 34 C2
Hintlesham Suff 31 D7
Hinton Hants 9 E11
Hinton Hereford 25 E10
Hinton Northants 28 C2
Hinton S Glos 16 D4
Hinton Shrops 33 E10
Hinton Ampner Hants 10 B4
Hinton Blewett Bath 16 F2
Hinton Charterhouse Bath 16 F4
Hinton-in-the-Hedges Northants 28 E2
Hinton Martell Dorset 9 D9
Hinton on the Green Worcs 27 D7
Hinton Parva Swindon 17 C9
Hinton St George Som 8 C3
Hinton St Mary Dorset 9 C6
Hinton Waldrist Oxon 17 B10
Hints Shrops 26 A3
Hints Staffs 35 E7
Hinwick Bedford 28 B6
Hinxhill Kent 13 B9
Hinxton Cambs 29 D11
Hinxworth Herts 29 D9
Hipperholme W Yorks 51 G7
Hipswell N Yorks 58 G2
Hirael Gwyn 41 C7
Hiraeth Carms 22 D6
Hirn Aberds 83 C9
Hirnant Powys 33 C6
Hirst N Lanark 69 D7
Hirst Northumb 63 E8
Hirst Courtney N Yorks 52 G2
Hirwaen Denb 42 F4
Hirwaun Rhondda 24 H6
Hiscott Devon 6 D4
Histon Cambs 29 B11
Hitcham Suff 30 C6
Hitchin Herts 29 F8
Hither Green London 19 D10
Hittisleigh Devon 7 G6
Hive E Yorks 52 F4
Hixon Staffs 34 C6
Hoaden Kent 21 F9
Hoaldalbert Mon 25 F10
Hoar Cross Staffs 35 C7
Hoarwithy Hereford 26 F2
Hoath Kent 21 E9
Hobarris Shrops 33 H8
Hobbister Orkney 95 H4
Hobkirk Borders 61 B11
Hobson Durham 63 H7
Hoby Leics 36 D2
Hockering Norf 39 D6
Hockerton Notts 45 G11
Hockley Essex 20 B5
Hockley Heath W Mid 27 A8
Hockliffe C Beds 28 F6
Hockwold cum Wilton Norf 38 G3
Hockworthy Devon 7 E9
Hoddesdon Herts 29 H10
Hoddlesden Blackburn 50 G3
Hoddom Mains Dumfries 61 F7
Hoddomcross Dumfries 61 F7
Hodgeston Pembs 22 G5
Hodley Powys 33 F7
Hodnet Shrops 34 C2
Hodthorpe Derbys 45 E9
Hoe Hants 10 C4
Hoe Norf 38 D5
Hoe Gate Hants 10 C5
Hoff Cumb 57 E8
Hog Patch Sur 18 G5
Hoggard's Green Suff 30 C5
Hoggeston Bucks 28 F5
Hogha Gearraidh W Isles 84 A2
Hoghton Lancs 50 G2
Hognaston Derbys 44 G6
Hogsthorpe Lincs 47 E9
Holbeach Lincs 37 C9
Holbeach Bank Lincs 37 C9
Holbeach Clough Lincs 37 C9
Holbeach Drove Lincs 37 D9
Holbeach Hurn Lincs 37 C9
Holbeach St Johns Lincs 37 D9
Holbeach St Marks Lincs 37 B9
Holbeach St Matthew Lincs 37 B10
Holbeck Notts 45 E9
Holbeck W Yorks 51 F8
Holbeck Woodhouse Notts 45 E9
Holberrow Green Worcs 27 C7
Holbeton Devon 5 F7
Holborn London 19 C10
Holbrook Derbys 35 A9
Holbrook S Yorks 45 D8
Holbrook Suff 31 E8
Holburn Northumb 71 G9
Holbury Hants 10 D3
Holcombe Devon 5 D10
Holcombe Som 16 G3
Holcombe Rogus Devon 7 E9
Holcot Northants 28 B4
Holden Lancs 50 E3
Holdenby Northants 28 B3
Holdenhurst Bmouth 9 E10
Holdgate Shrops 34 G1
Holdingham Lincs 46 H4
Holditch Dorset 8 D2
Hole-in-the-Wall Hereford 26 F3
Holefield Borders 71 G7
Holehouses Ches E 43 E10
Holemoor Devon 6 F3
Holestane Dumfries 60 D4
Holford Som 7 B10
Holgate York 52 D1
Holker Cumb 49 B3
Holkham Norf 38 A4
Hollacombe Devon 6 F2
Holland Orkney 95 C5
Holland Orkney 95 F7
Holland Fen Lincs 46 H6
Holland-on-Sea Essex 31 G9
Hollandstoun Orkney 95 C8
Hollee Dumfries 61 G8
Hollesley Suff 31 D10
Hollicombe Torbay 5 E9
Hollingbourne Kent 20 F5
Hollington Derbys 35 B8
Hollington E Sus 13 E6
Hollington Staffs 35 B6
Hollington Grove Derbys 35 B8
Hollingworth Gtr Man 44 C4
Hollins Gtr Man 44 B2
Hollins Green Warr 43 C9
Hollins Lane Lancs 49 D4
Hollinsclough Staffs 44 F4
Hollinwood Gtr Man 44 B3
Hollinwood Shrops 33 B11
Hollocombe Devon 6 E5
Hollow Meadows S Yorks 44 D6
Holloway Derbys 45 G7
Hollowell Northants 28 A3
Holly End Norf 37 E10
Holly Green Worcs 26 D5
Hollybush Caerph 15 A7
Hollybush E Ayrs 67 E6
Hollybush Worcs 26 E4
Hollym E Yorks 53 G9
Hollywood Worcs 35 H6
Holmbridge W Yorks 44 B5
Holmbury St Mary Sur 19 G8
Holmbush Corn 3 D9
Holmcroft Staffs 34 C5
Holme Cambs 37 G7
Holme Cumb 49 B5
Holme N Yorks 51 A9
Holme Notts 46 G2
Holme W Yorks 44 B5
Holme Chapel Lancs 50 G4
Holme Green N Yorks 52 E1
Holme Hale Norf 38 E4
Holme Lacy Hereford 26 E2
Holme Marsh Hereford 25 C10
Holme next the Sea Norf 38 A3
Holme-on-Spalding-Moor E Yorks 52 F4
Holme on the Wolds E Yorks 52 E5
Holme Pierrepont Notts 36 B2
Holme St Cuthbert Cumb 56 B3
Holme Wood W Yorks 51 F7
Holmer Hereford 26 D2
Holmer Green Bucks 18 B6
Holmes Chapel Ches E 43 F10
Holmesfield Derbys 45 E7
Holmeswood Lancs 49 H4
Holmewood Derbys 45 F8
Holmfirth W Yorks 44 B5
Holmhead Dumfries 60 E3
Holmhead E Ayrs 67 D8
Holmisdale Highld 84 D6
Holmpton E Yorks 53 G9
Holmrook Cumb 56 G2
Holmsgarth Shetland 96 J6
Holmwrangle Cumb 57 B7
Holne Devon 5 E8
Holnest Dorset 8 D5
Holsworthy Devon 6 F2
Holsworthy Beacon Devon 6 F2
Holt Dorset 9 D9
Holt Norf 39 B6
Holt Wilts 16 E5
Holt Worcs 26 B5
Holt Wrex 43 G7
Holt End Hants 18 H3
Holt End Worcs 27 B7
Holt Fleet Worcs 26 B5
Holt Heath Worcs 26 B5
Holt Park W Yorks 51 E8
Holtby York 52 D2
Holton Oxon 28 H3
Holton Som 8 B5
Holton Suff 39 H9
Holton cum Beckering Lincs 46 D5
Holton Heath Dorset 9 E8
Holton le Clay Lincs 46 B6
Holton le Moor Lincs 46 C4
Holton St Mary Suff 31 E7
Holwell Dorset 8 C6
Holwell Herts 29 E8
Holwell Leics 36 C3
Holwell Oxon 27 H9
Holwick Durham 57 D11
Holworth Dorset 9 F6
Holy Cross Worcs 34 H5
Holy Island Northumb 71 F10
Holybourne Hants 18 G4
Holyhead = Caergybi Anglesey 40 B4
Holymoorside Derbys 45 F7
Holyport Windsor 18 D5
Holystone Northumb 62 C5
Holytown N Lanark 68 D6
Holywell Cambs 29 A10
Holywell Corn 3 D6
Holywell Dorset 8 D4
Holywell E Sus 12 G4
Holywell = Treffynnon Flint 42 E4
Holywell Northumb 63 F9
Holywell Green W Yorks 51 H6
Holywell Lake Som 7 D10
Holywell Row Suff 38 H3
Holywood Dumfries 60 E5
Hom Green Hereford 26 F2
Homer Shrops 34 E2
Homersfield Suff 39 G8
Homington Wilts 9 B10
Honey Hill Kent 21 E8
Honey Street Wilts 17 E8
Honey Tye Suff 30 E6
Honeyborough Pembs 22 F4
Honeybourne Worcs 27 D8
Honeychurch Devon 6 F5
Honiley Warks 27 A9
Honing Norf 39 C9
Honingham Norf 39 D7
Honington Lincs 36 A5
Honington Suff 30 A6
Honington Warks 27 D9
Honiton Devon 7 F10
Honley W Yorks 44 A5
Hoo Green Ches E 43 D10
Hoo St Werburgh Medway 20 D4
Hood Green S Yorks 45 B7
Hooe E Sus 12 F5
Hooe Plym 4 F6
Hooe Common E Sus 12 E5
Hook E Yorks 52 G3
Hook Hants 18 F4
Hook London 19 E8
Hook Pembs 22 E4
Hook Wilts 17 C7
Hook Green Kent 12 C5
Hook Green Kent 20 E3
Hook Norton Oxon 27 E10
Hooke Dorset 8 E4
Hookgate Staffs 34 B3
Hookway Devon 7 G7
Hookwood Sur 12 B1
Hoole Ches W 43 F7
Hooley Sur 19 F9
Hoop Mon 26 H2
Hooton Ches W 42 E6
Hooton Levitt S Yorks 45 C9
Hooton Pagnell S Yorks 45 B8
Hooton Roberts S Yorks 45 C8
Hop Pole Lincs 37 D7
Hope Derbys 44 D5
Hope Devon 5 H7
Hope = Yr Hôb Flint 42 G6
Hope Highld 92 C7
Hope Powys 33 E8
Hope Shrops 33 E9
Hope Staffs 44 G5
Hope Bagot Shrops 26 A2
Hope Bowdler Shrops 33 F10
Hope End Green Essex 30 F2
Hope Green Ches E 44 D3
Hope Mansell Hereford 26 G3
Hope under Dinmore Hereford 26 C2
Hopeman Moray 88 B1
Hope's Green Essex 20 C4
Hopesay Shrops 33 G9
Hopley's Green Hereford 25 C10
Hopperton N Yorks 51 D10
Hopstone Shrops 34 F3
Hopton Shrops 33 C9
Hopton Shrops 34 C1
Hopton Staffs 34 C5
Hopton Suff 38 H5
Hopton Cangeford Shrops 33 G11
Hopton Castle Shrops 33 H9
Hopton on Sea Norf 39 E11
Hopton Wafers Shrops 34 H2
Hoptonheath Shrops 33 H9
Hopwas Staffs 35 E7
Hopwood Gtr Man 44 B2
Hopwood Worcs 34 H6
Horam E Sus 12 E4
Horbling Lincs 37 B7
Horbury W Yorks 51 H8
Horcott Glos 17 A8
Horden Durham 58 B5
Horderley Shrops 33 G10
Hordle Hants 10 E1
Hordley Shrops 33 B9
Horeb Carms 23 D10
Horeb Carms 23 F9
Horeb Ceredig 23 B8
Horfield Bristol 16 D3
Horham Suff 31 A9
Horkesley Heath Essex 30 F6
Horkstow N Lincs 52 H5
Horley Oxon 27 D11
Horley Sur 12 B1
Hornblotton Green Som 8 A4
Hornby Lancs 50 C1
Hornby N Yorks 58 F4
Hornby N Yorks 58 G3
Horncastle Lincs 46 F6
Hornchurch London 20 C2
Horncliffe Northumb 71 F8
Horndean Borders 71 F7
Horndean Hants 10 C6
Horndon Devon 4 D6
Horndon on the Hill Thurrock 20 C3
Horne Sur 12 B2
Horniehaugh Angus 77 A7
Horning Norf 39 D9
Horninghold Leics 36 F4
Horninglow Staffs 35 C8
Horningsea Cambs 29 B11
Horningsham Wilts 16 G5
Horningtoft Norf 38 C5
Horns Corner Kent 12 D6
Horns Cross Devon 6 D2
Horns Cross E Sus 13 D7
Hornsby Cumb 57 A7
Hornsea E Yorks 53 E8
Hornsea Bridge E Yorks 53 E8
Hornsey London 19 C10
Hornton Oxon 27 D10
Horrabridge Devon 4 E6
Horringer Suff 30 B5
Horringford IoW 10 F4
Horse Bridge Staffs 44 G3
Horsebridge Devon 4 D5
Horsebridge Hants 10 A2
Horsebrook Staffs 34 D4
Horsehay Telford 34 E2
Horseheath Cambs 30 D3
Horsehouse N Yorks 50 A6
Horsell Sur 18 F6
Horseman's Green Wrex 33 A10
Horseway Cambs 37 G10
Horsey Norf 39 C10
Horsford Norf 39 D7
Horsforth W Yorks 51 F8
Horsham W Sus 11 A10
Horsham Worcs 26 C4
Horsham St Faith Norf 39 D8
Horsington Lincs 46 F5
Horsington Som 8 B6
Horsley Derbys 35 A9
Horsley Glos 16 B5
Horsley Northumb 62 D4
Horsley Northumb 62 G6
Horsley Cross Essex 31 F8
Horsley Woodhouse Derbys 35 A9
Horsleycross Street Essex 31 F8
Horsleyhope Durham 58 B1
Horsmonden Kent 12 B5
Horspath Oxon 18 A2
Horstead Norf 39 D8
Horsted Keynes W Sus 12 D2
Horton Bucks 28 G6
Horton Dorset 9 D9
Horton Lancs 50 D4
Horton Northants 28 C5
Horton S Glos 16 C4
Horton Shrops 33 C10
Horton Som 8 C2
Horton Staffs 44 G3
Horton Swansea 23 H9

Horton Wilts 17 E7
Horton Windsor 19 D7
Horton-cum-Studley Oxon 28 G2
Horton Green Ches W 43 H7
Horton Heath Hants 10 C3
Horton in Ribblesdale N Yorks 50 B4
Horton Kirby Kent 20 E2
Hortonlane Shrops 33 D10
Horwich Gtr Man 43 A9
Horwich End Derbys 44 D4
Horwood Devon 6 D4
Hose Leics 36 C3
Hoselaw Borders 71 G7
Hoses Cumb 56 G4
Hosh Perth 75 E11
Hosta W Isles 84 A2
Hoswick Shetland 96 L6
Hotham E Yorks 52 F4
Hothfield Kent 20 G6
Hoton Leics 36 C1
Houbie Shetland 96 D8
Houdston S Ayrs 66 G4
Hough Ches E 43 G10
Hough Ches E 44 E2
Hough Green Halton 43 D7
Hough-on-the-Hill Lincs 46 H3
Hougham Lincs 36 A4
Houghton Cambs 29 A9
Houghton Cumb 61 H10
Houghton Hants 10 A2
Houghton Pembs 22 F4
Houghton W Sus 11 C9
Houghton Conquest C Beds 29 D7
Houghton Green E Sus 13 D8
Houghton Green Warr 43 C9
Houghton-le-Side Darl 58 D3
Houghton-Le-Spring T&W 58 B4
Houghton on the Hill Leics 36 E2
Houghton Regis C Beds 29 F7
Houghton St Giles Norf 38 B5
Houlland Shetland 96 F7
Houlland Shetland 96 H5
Houlsyke N Yorks 59 F8
Hound Hants 10 D3
Hound Green Hants 18 F4
Houndslow Borders 70 F5
Houndwood Borders 71 D7
Hounslow London 19 D8
Hounslow Green Essex 30 G3
Housay Shetland 96 F8
House of Daviot Highld 87 G10
House of Glenmuick Aberds 82 D5
Housetter Shetland 96 E5
Houss Shetland 96 K5
Houston Renfs 68 D3
Houstry Highld 94 G3
Houton Orkney 95 H4
Hove Brighton 12 F1
Hoveringham Notts 45 H10
Hoveton Norf 39 D9
Hovingham N Yorks 52 B2
How Cumb 61 H11
How Caple Hereford 26 E3
How End C Beds 29 D7
How Green Kent 19 G11
Howbrook S Yorks 45 C7
Howden Borders 62 A2
Howden E Yorks 52 G3
Howden-le-Wear Durham 58 C2
Howe Highld 94 D5
Howe N Yorks 51 A9
Howe Norf 39 E8
Howe Bridge Gtr Man 43 B9
Howe Green Essex 20 A4
Howe of Teuchar Aberds 89 D7
Howe Street Essex 30 E3
Howe Street Essex 30 G3
Howell Lincs 46 H5
Howey Powys 25 C7
Howgate Midloth 69 E11
Howick Northumb 63 B8
Howle Durham 58 D1
Howle Telford 34 C2
Howlett End Essex 30 E2
Howley Som 8 D1
Hownam Borders 62 B3
Hownam Mains Borders 62 A3
Howpasley Borders 61 C9
Howsham N Lincs 46 B4
Howsham N Yorks 52 C3
Howslack Dumfries 60 C6
Howtel Northumb 71 G7
Howton Hereford 25 F11
Howtown Cumb 56 E6
Howwood Renfs 68 D2
Hoxne Suff 39 H7
Hoy Orkney 95 H3
Hoylake Mers 42 D5
Hoyland S Yorks 45 B7
Hoylandswaine S Yorks 44 B6
Hubberholme N Yorks 50 B5
Hubbert's Bridge Lincs 37 A8
Huby N Yorks 51 E8
Huby N Yorks 52 C1
Hucclecote Glos 26 G5
Hucking Kent 20 F5
Hucknall Notts 45 H9
Huddersfield W Yorks 51 H7
Huddington Worcs 26 C6
Hudswell N Yorks 58 F2
Huggate E Yorks 52 D4
Hugglescote Leics 35 D10
Hugh Town Scilly 2 C3
Hughenden Valley Bucks 18 B5
Hughley Shrops 34 F1
Huish Devon 6 E4
Huish Wilts 17 E8
Huish Champflower Som 7 D9
Huish Episcopi Som 8 B3
Huisinis W Isles 90 F4
Hulcott Bucks 28 G5
Hulland Derbys 44 H6
Hulland Ward Derbys 44 H6
Hullavington Wilts 16 C5
Hullbridge Essex 20 B5
Hulme Gtr Man 44 C2
Hulme End Staffs 44 G5
Hulme Walfield Ches E 44 F2
Hulver Street Suff 39 G10
Hulverstone IoW 10 F2
Humber Hereford 26 C2
Humber Bridge N Lincs 52 G6
Humberston NE Lincs 47 B7
Humbie E Loth 70 D3
Humbleton E Yorks 53 F8
Humbleton Northumb 71 H8
Humby Lincs 36 B6
Hume Borders 70 F6
Humshaugh Northumb 62 F5
Huna Highld 94 C5
Huncoat Lancs 50 F3
Huncote Leics 35 F11
Hundalee Borders 62 B2
Hunderthwaite Durham 57 D11
Hundle Houses Lincs 46 G6
Hundleby Lincs 47 F7
Hundleton Pembs 22 F4
Hundon Suff 30 D4
Hundred Acres Hants 10 C4
Hundred End Lancs 49 G4
Hundred House Powys 25 C8
Hungarton Leics 36 E2
Hungerford Hants 9 C10
Hungerford W Berks 17 E10
Hungerford Newtown W Berks 17 D10
Hungerton Lincs 36 C4
Hungladder Highld 85 A8
Hunmanby N Yorks 53 B6
Hunmanby Moor N Yorks 53 B7
Hunningham Warks 27 B10
Hunny Hill IoW 10 F3
Hunsdon Herts 29 G11
Hunsingore N Yorks 51 D10
Hunslet W Yorks 51 F9
Hunsonby Cumb 57 C7
Hunspow Highld 94 C4
Hunstanton Norf 38 A2
Hunstanworth Durham 57 B11
Hunsterson Ches E 43 H9
Hunston Suff 30 B6
Hunston W Sus 11 D7
Hunstrete Bath 16 E3
Hunt End Worcs 27 B7
Hunter's Quay Argyll 73 F10
Hunthill Lodge Angus 82 F6
Hunting-tower Perth 76 E3
Huntingdon Cambs 29 A9
Huntingfield Suff 31 A10
Huntingford Dorset 9 A7
Huntington E Loth 70 C3
Huntington Hereford 25 C9
Huntington Staffs 34 D5
Huntington York 52 D2
Huntley Glos 26 G4
Huntly Aberds 88 E5
Huntlywood Borders 70 F5
Hunton Kent 20 G4
Hunton N Yorks 58 G2
Hunt's Corner Norf 39 G6
Hunt's Cross Mers 43 D7
Huntsham Devon 7 D9
Huntspill Som 15 G9
Huntworth Som 8 A2
Hunwick Durham 58 C2
Hunworth Norf 39 B6
Hurdsfield Ches E 44 E3
Hurley Warks 35 F8
Hurley Windsor 18 C5
Hurlford E Ayrs 67 C7
Hurliness Orkney 95 K3
Hurn Dorset 9 E10
Hurn's End Lincs 47 H8
Hursley Hants 10 B3
Hurst N Yorks 58 F1
Hurst Som 8 C3
Hurst Wokingham 18 D4
Hurst Green E Sus 12 D6
Hurst Green Lancs 50 F2
Hurst Wickham W Sus 12 E1
Hurstbourne Priors Hants 17 G11
Hurstbourne Tarrant Hants 17 F10
Hurstpierpoint W Sus 12 E1
Hurstwood Lancs 50 F4
Hurtmore Sur 18 G6
Hurworth Place Darl 58 F3
Hury Durham 57 E11
Husabost Highld 84 C7
Husbands Bosworth Leics 36 G2
Husborne Crawley C Beds 28 E6
Husthwaite N Yorks 51 B11
Hutchwns Bridgend 14 D4
Huthwaite Notts 45 G8
Huttoft Lincs 47 E9
Hutton Borders 71 E8
Hutton Cumb 56 D6
Hutton E Yorks 52 D6
Hutton Essex 20 B3
Hutton Lancs 49 G4
Hutton N Som 15 F9
Hutton Buscel N Yorks 52 A5
Hutton Conyers N Yorks 51 B9
Hutton Cranswick E Yorks 52 D6
Hutton End Cumb 56 C6
Hutton Gate Redcar 59 E6
Hutton Henry Durham 58 C5
Hutton-le-Hole N Yorks 59 G8
Hutton Magna Durham 58 E2
Hutton Roof Cumb 50 B1
Hutton Roof Cumb 56 C5
Hutton Rudby N Yorks 58 F5
Hutton Sessay N Yorks 51 B10
Hutton Village Redcar 59 E6
Hutton Wandesley N Yorks 51 D11
Huxley Ches W 43 F8
Huxter Shetland 96 G7
Huxter Shetland 96 H5
Huxton Borders 71 D7
Huyton Mers 43 C7
Hwlffordd = Haverfordwest Pembs 22 E4
Hycemoor Cumb 56 H2
Hyde Glos 16 A5
Hyde Gtr Man 44 C3
Hyde Hants 9 C10
Hyde Heath Bucks 18 A6
Hyde Park S Yorks 45 B9
Hydestile Sur 18 G6
Hylton Castle T&W 63 H9
Hyndford Bridge S Lanark 69 F8
Hynish Argyll 78 H2
Hyssington Powys 33 F9
Hythe Hants 10 D3
Hythe Kent 21 H8
Hythe End Windsor 19 D7
Hythie Aberds 89 C10

I

Ibberton Dorset 9 D6
Ible Derbys 44 G6
Ibsley Hants 9 D10
Ibstock Leics 35 D10
Ibstone Bucks 18 B4
Ibthorpe Hants 17 F10
Ibworth Hants 18 F2
Ichrachan Argyll 74 D3
Ickburgh Norf 38 F4
Ickenham London 19 C7
Ickford Bucks 28 H3
Ickham Kent 21 F9
Ickleford Herts 29 E8
Icklesham E Sus 13 E7
Ickleton Cambs 29 D11
Icklingham Suff 30 A4
Ickwell Green C Beds 29 D8
Icomb Glos 27 F9
Idbury Oxon 27 G9
Iddesleigh Devon 6 F4
Ide Devon 7 G7
Ide Hill Kent 19 F11
Ideford Devon 5 D9
Iden E Sus 13 D8
Iden Green Kent 12 C6
Iden Green Kent 13 C7
Idle W Yorks 51 F7
Idlicote Warks 27 D9
Idmiston Wilts 17 H8
Idole Carms 23 E9
Idridgehay Derbys 44 H6
Idrigill Highld 85 B8
Idstone Oxon 17 C9
Idvies Angus 77 C8
Iffley Oxon 18 A2
Ifield W Sus 19 H9
Ifold W Sus 11 A9
Iford E Sus 12 F3
Ifton Heath Shrops 33 B9
Ightfield Shrops 34 B1
Ightham Kent 20 F2
Iken Suff 31 C11
Ilam Staffs 44 G5
Ilchester Som 8 B4
Ilderton Northumb 62 A6
Ilford London 19 C11
Ilfracombe Devon 6 B4
Ilkeston Derbys 35 A10
Ilketshall St Andrew Suff 39 G9
Ilketshall St Lawrence Suff 39 G9
Ilketshall St Margaret Suff 39 G9
Ilkley W Yorks 51 E7
Illey W Mid 34 G5
Illingworth W Yorks 51 G6
Illogan Corn 2 E5
Illston on the Hill Leics 36 F3
Ilmer Bucks 28 H4
Ilmington Warks 27 D9
Ilminster Som 8 C2
Ilsington Devon 5 D8
Ilston Swansea 23 G10
Ilton N Yorks 51 B7
Ilton Som 8 C2
Imachar N Ayrs 66 B1
Imeraval Argyll 64 D4
Immingham NE Lincs 46 A5
Impington Cambs 29 B11
Ince Ches W 43 E7
Ince Blundell Mers 42 B6
Ince in Makerfield Gtr Man 43 B8
Inch of Arnhall Aberds 83 F8
Inchbare Angus 83 G8
Inchberry Moray 88 C3
Inchbraoch Angus 77 B10
Incheril Highld 86 E3
Inchgrundle Angus 82 F6
Inchina Highld 86 B2
Inchinnan Renfs 68 D3
Inchkinloch Highld 93 E8
Inchlaggan Highld 80 C3
Inchlumpie Highld 87 D8
Inchmore Highld 86 G6
Inchnacardoch Hotel Highld 80 B5
Inchnadamph Highld 92 G5
Inchree Highld 74 A3
Inchture Perth 76 E5
Inchyra Perth 76 E4
Indian Queens Corn 3 D8
Inerval Argyll 64 D4
Ingatestone Essex 20 B3
Ingbirchworth S Yorks 44 B6
Ingestre Staffs 34 C5
Ingham Lincs 46 D3
Ingham Norf 39 C9
Ingham Suff 30 A5
Ingham Corner Norf 39 C9
Ingleborough Norf 37 D10
Ingleby Derbys 35 C9
Ingleby Lincs 46 E2
Ingleby Arncliffe N Yorks 58 F5
Ingleby Barwick Stockton 58 E5
Ingleby Greenhow N Yorks 59 F6
Inglemire Hull 53 F6
Inglesbatch Bath 16 E4
Inglesham Swindon 17 B9
Ingleton Durham 58 D2
Ingleton N Yorks 50 B2
Inglewhite Lancs 49 E5
Ingliston Edin 69 C10
Ingoe Northumb 62 F6
Ingol Lancs 49 F5
Ingoldisthorpe Norf 38 B2
Ingoldmells Lincs 47 F9
Ingoldsby Lincs 36 B6
Ingon Warks 27 C9
Ingram Northumb 62 B6
Ingrow W Yorks 51 F6
Ings Cumb 56 G6
Ingst S Glos 16 C2
Ingworth Norf 39 C7
Inham's End Cambs 37 F8
Inkberrow Worcs 27 C7
Inkpen W Berks 17 E10
Inkstack Highld 94 C4
Inn Cumb 56 F6
Innellan Argyll 73 F10
Innerleithen Borders 70 G2
Innerleven Fife 76 G6
Innermessan Dumfries 54 C3
Innerwick E Loth 70 C6
Innerwick Perth 75 C8
Innis Chonain Argyll 74 E4
Insch Aberds 83 A8
Insh Highld 81 C10
Inshore Highld 92 C6
Inskip Lancs 49 F4
Instoneville S Yorks 45 A9
Instow Devon 6 C3
Intake S Yorks 45 B9
Inver Aberds 82 D4
Inver Highld 87 C11
Inver Perth 76 C3
Inver Mallie Highld 80 E3
Inverailort Highld 79 C10
Inveraldie Angus 77 D7
Inverallign Highld 85 C13
Inverallochy Aberds 89 B10
Inveran Highld 87 B8
Inveraray Argyll 73 C9
Inverarish Highld 85 E10
Inverarity Angus 77 C7
Inverarnan Stirling 74 F6
Inverasdale Highld 91 J13
Inverbeg Argyll 74 H6
Inverbervie Aberds 83 F10
Inverboyndie Aberds 89 B6
Inverbroom Highld 86 C4
Invercassley Highld 92 J7
Invercauld House Aberds 82 D3
Inverchaolain Argyll 73 F9
Invercharnan Highld 74 C4
Inverchoran Highld 86 F5
Invercreran Argyll 74 C3
Inverdruie Highld 81 B11
Inverebrie Aberds 89 E9
Invereck Argyll 73 E10
Inverernan Ho. Aberds 82 B5
Invereshie House Highld 81 C10
Inveresk E Loth 70 C2
Inverey Aberds 82 E2
Inverfarigaig Highld 81 A7
Invergarry Highld 80 C5
Invergelder Aberds 82 D4
Invergeldie Perth 75 E10
Invergordon Highld 87 E10
Invergowrie Perth 76 D6
Inverguseran Highld 85 H12
Inverhadden Perth 75 B9
Inverharroch Moray 88 E3
Inverherive Stirling 74 E6
Inverie Highld 79 B10
Inverinan Argyll 73 B8
Inverinate Highld 85 F14
Inverkeilor Angus 77 C9
Inverkeithing Fife 69 B10
Inverkeithny Aberds 89 D6
Inverkip Invclyd 73 F11
Inverkirkaig Highld 92 H3
Inverlael Highld 86 C4
Inverlochlarig Stirling 75 F7
Inverlochy Argyll 74 E4
Inverlochy Highld 80 F3
Inverlussa Argyll 72 E5
Invermark Lodge Angus 82 E6
Invermoidart Highld 79 D9
Invermoriston Highld 80 B6
Invernaver Highld 93 C10
Inverneill Argyll 73 E7
Inverness Highld 87 G9
Invernettie Aberds 89 D11
Invernoaden Argyll 73 D10
Inveroran Hotel Argyll 74 C5
Inverpolly Lodge Highld 92 H3
Inverquharity Angus 77 B7
Inverquhomery Aberds 89 D10
Inverroy Highld 80 E4
Inversanda Highld 74 B2
Invershiel Highld 80 B1
Invershin Highld 87 B8
Inversnaid Hotel Stirling 74 G6
Inverugie Aberds 89 D11
Inveruglas Argyll 74 G6
Inveruglass Highld 81 C10
Inverurie Aberds 83 A9
Invervar Perth 75 C9
Inverythan Aberds 89 D7
Inwardleigh Devon 6 G4
Inworth Essex 30 G5
Iochdar W Isles 84 D2
Iping W Sus 11 B7
Ipplepen Devon 5 E9
Ipsden Oxon 18 C3
Ipsley Worcs 27 B7
Ipstones Staffs 44 G4
Ipswich Suff 31 D8
Irby Mers 42 D5
Irby in the Marsh Lincs 47 F8
Irby upon Humber NE Lincs 46 B5
Irchester Northants 28 B6
Ireby Cumb 56 C4
Ireby Lancs 50 B2
Ireland Orkney 95 H4
Ireland Shetland 96 L5
Ireland's Cross Shrops 34 A3
Ireleth Cumb 49 B2
Ireshopeburn Durham 57 C10
Irlam Gtr Man 43 C10
Irnham Lincs 36 C6
Iron Acton S Glos 16 C3
Iron Cross Warks 27 C7
Ironbridge Telford 34 E2
Irongray Dumfries 60 F5
Ironmacannie Dumfries 55 B9
Ironside Aberds 89 C8
Ironville Derbys 45 G8
Irstead Norf 39 C9
Irthington Cumb 61 G10
Irthlingborough Northants 28 A6
Irton N Yorks 52 A6
Irvine N Ayrs 66 C6
Isauld Highld 93 C12
Isbister Orkney 95 F3
Isbister Orkney 95 G4
Isbister Shetland 96 D5
Isbister Shetland 96 G7
Isfield E Sus 12 E3
Isham Northants 28 A5
Isle Abbotts Som 8 B2
Isle Brewers Som 8 B2
Isle of Whithorn Dumfries 55 F7
Isleham Cambs 30 A3
Isleornsay Highld 85 G12
Islesburgh Shetland 96 G5
Islesteps Dumfries 60 F5
Isleworth London 19 D8
Isley Walton Leics 35 C10
Islibhig W Isles 90 E4
Islington London 19 C10
Islip Northants 36 H5
Islip Oxon 28 G2
Istead Rise Kent 20 E3
Isycoed Wrex 43 G7
Itchen Soton 10 C3
Itchen Abbas Hants 10 A4
Itchen Stoke Hants 10 A4
Itchingfield W Sus 11 B10
Itchington S Glos 16 C3
Itteringham Norf 39 B7
Itton Devon 6 G5
Itton Common Mon 15 B10
Ivegill Cumb 56 B6
Iver Bucks 19 C7
Iver Heath Bucks 19 C7
Iveston Durham 58 A2
Ivinghoe Bucks 28 G6
Ivinghoe Aston Bucks 28 G6
Ivington Hereford 25 C11
Ivington Green Hereford 25 C11
Ivy Chimneys Essex 19 A11
Ivy Cross Dorset 9 B7
Ivy Hatch Kent 20 F2
Ivybridge Devon 5 F7
Ivychurch Kent 13 D9
Iwade Kent 20 E6
Iwerne Courtney or Shroton Dorset 9 C7
Iwerne Minster Dorset 9 C7
Ixworth Suff 30 A6
Ixworth Thorpe Suff 30 A6

J

Jack Hill N Yorks 51 D8
Jack in the Green Devon 7 G9
Jacksdale Notts 45 G8
Jackstown Aberds 89 E7
Jacobstow Corn 4 B2
Jacobstowe Devon 6 F4
Jameston Pembs 22 G5
Jamestown Dumfries 61 D9
Jamestown Highld 86 F7
Jamestown W Dunb 68 B2
Jarrow T&W 63 G9
Jarvis Brook E Sus 12 D4
Jasper's Green Essex 30 F4
Java Argyll 79 H10
Jawcraig Falk 69 C7
Jaywick Essex 31 G8
Jealott's Hill Brack 18 D5
Jedburgh Borders 62 A2
Jeffreyston Pembs 22 F5
Jellyhill E Dunb 68 C5
Jemimaville Highld 87 E10
Jersey Farm Herts 29 H8
Jesmond T&W 63 G8
Jevington E Sus 12 F4
Jockey End Herts 29 G7
John o' Groats Highld 94 C5
Johnby Cumb 56 C6
John's Cross E Sus 12 D6
Johnshaven Aberds 83 G9
Johnston Pembs 22 E4
Johnstone Renfs 68 D3
Johnstonebridge Dumfries 60 D6
Johnstown Carms 23 E9
Johnstown Wrex 42 H6
Joppa Edin 70 C2
Joppa S Ayrs 67 E7
Jordans Bucks 18 B6
Jordanthorpe S Yorks 45 D7
Jump S Yorks 45 B7
Jumpers Green Dorset 9 E10
Juniper Green Edin 69 D10
Jurby East IoM 48 C3
Jurby West IoM 48 C3

K

Kaber Cumb 57 E9
Kaimend S Lanark 69 F8
Kaimes Edin 69 D11
Kalemouth Borders 70 H6
Kames Argyll 73 B7
Kames Argyll 73 F8
Kames E Ayrs 68 H5
Kea Corn 3 E7
Keadby N Lincs 46 A2
Keal Cotes Lincs 47 F7
Kearsley Gtr Man 43 B10
Kearstwick Cumb 50 A2
Kearton N Yorks 57 G11
Kearvaig Highld 92 B5
Keasden N Yorks 50 C3
Keckwick Halton 43 D8
Keddington Lincs 47 D7
Kedington Suff 30 D4
Kedleston Derbys 35 A9
Keelby Lincs 46 A5
Keele Staffs 44 H2
Keeley Green Bedford 29 D7
Keeston Pembs 22 E4
Keevil Wilts 16 F6
Kegworth Leics 35 C10
Kehelland Corn 2 E5
Keig Aberds 83 B8
Keighley W Yorks 51 E6
Keil Highld 74 B2
Keilarsbrae Clack 69 A7
Keilhill Aberds 89 C7
Keillmore Argyll 72 E5
Keillor Perth 76 C5
Keillour Perth 76 E2
Keills Argyll 64 B5
Keils Argyll 72 G4
Keinton Mandeville Som 8 A4
Keir Mill Dumfries 60 D4
Keisby Lincs 36 C6
Keiss Highld 94 D5
Keith Moray 88 C4
Keith Inch Aberds 89 D11
Keithock Angus 77 A9
Kelbrook Lancs 50 E5
Kelby Lincs 36 A6
Keld Cumb 57 E7
Keld N Yorks 57 F10
Keldholme N Yorks 59 H8
Kelfield N Lincs 46 B2
Kelfield N Yorks 52 F1
Kelham Notts 45 G11
Kellan Argyll 79 G8
Kellas Angus 77 D7
Kellas Moray 88 C1
Kellaton Devon 5 H9
Kelleth Cumb 57 F8
Kelleythorpe E Yorks 52 D5
Kelling Norf 39 A6
Kellingley N Yorks 51 G11
Kellington N Yorks 52 G1
Kelloe Durham 58 C4
Kelloholm Dumfries 60 B3
Kelly Devon 4 C4
Kelly Bray Corn 4 D4
Kelmarsh Northants 36 H3
Kelmscot Oxon 17 B9
Kelsale Suff 31 B10
Kelsall Ches W 43 F8
Kelsall Hill Ches W 43 F8
Kelshall Herts 29 E10
Kelsick Cumb 56 A3
Kelso Borders 70 G6
Kelstedge Derbys 45 F7
Kelstern Lincs 46 C6
Kelston Bath 16 E4
Keltneyburn Perth 75 C10
Kelton Dumfries 60 F5
Kelty Fife 69 A10
Kelvedon Essex 30 G5
Kelvedon Hatch Essex 20 B2
Kelvin S Lanark 68 E5
Kelvinside Glasgow 68 D4
Kelynack Corn 2 F2
Kemback Fife 77 F7
Kemberton Shrops 34 E3
Kemble Glos 16 B6
Kemerton Worcs 26 E6
Kemeys Commander Mon 15 A9
Kemnay Aberds 83 B9
Kemp Town Brighton 12 F2
Kempley Glos 26 F3
Kemps Green Warks 27 A8
Kempsey Worcs 26 D5
Kempsford Glos 17 B8
Kempshott Hants 18 F3
Kempston Bedford 29 D7
Kempston Hardwick Bedford 29 D7
Kempton Shrops 33 G9
Kemsing Kent 20 F2
Kemsley Kent 20 E6
Kenardington Kent 13 C8
Kenchester Hereford 25 D11
Kencot Oxon 17 A9
Kendal Cumb 57 G7
Kendoon Dumfries 67 H9
Kendray S Yorks 45 B7
Kenfig Bridgend 14 C4
Kenfig Hill Bridgend 14 C4
Kenilworth Warks 27 A9
Kenknock Stirling 75 D7
Kenley London 19 F10
Kenley Shrops 34 E1
Kenmore Highld 85 C12
Kenmore Perth 75 C10
Kenn Devon 5 C10
Kenn N Som 15 E10
Kennacley W Isles 90 H6
Kennacraig Argyll 73 G7
Kennerleigh Devon 7 F7
Kennet Clack 69 A8
Kennethmont Aberds 83 A7
Kennett Cambs 30 B3
Kennford Devon 5 C10
Kenninghall Norf 38 G6
Kenninghall Heath Norf 38 G6
Kennington Kent 13 B9
Kennington Oxon 18 A2
Kennoway Fife 76 G6
Kenny Hill Suff 38 H2
Kennythorpe N Yorks 52 C3
Kenovay Argyll 78 G2
Kensaleyre Highld 85 C9
Kensington London 19 D9
Kensworth C Beds 29 G7
Kensworth Common C Beds 29 G7
Kent Street E Sus 13 E6
Kent Street Kent 20 F3
Kent Street W Sus 11 B11
Kentallen Highld 74 B3
Kentchurch Hereford 25 F11
Kentford Suff 30 B4
Kentisbeare Devon 7 F9
Kentisbury Devon 6 B5
Kentisbury Ford Devon 6 B5
Kentmere Cumb 56 F6
Kenton Devon 5 C10
Kenton Suff 31 B8
Kenton T&W 63 G8
Kenton Bankfoot T&W 63 G8
Kentra Highld 79 E9
Kents Bank Cumb 49 B3
Kent's Green Glos 26 F4
Kent's Oak Hants 10 B2
Kenwick Shrops 33 B10
Kenwyn Corn 3 E7
Keoldale Highld 92 C6
Keppanach Highld 74 A3
Keppoch Highld 85 F14
Keprigan Argyll 65 G7
Kepwick N Yorks 58 G5
Kerchesters Borders 70 G6
Keresley W Mid 35 G9
Kernborough Devon 5 G8
Kerne Bridge Hereford 26 G2
Kerris Corn 2 G3
Kerry Powys 33 G7
Kerrycroy Argyll 73 G10
Kerry's Gate Hereford 25 E10
Kerrysdale Highld 85 A13
Kersall Notts 45 F11
Kersey Suff 31 D7
Kershopefoot Cumb 61 E10
Kersoe Worcs 26 E6
Kerswell Devon 7 F9
Kerswell Green Worcs 26 D5
Kesgrave Suff 31 D9
Kessingland Suff 39 G11
Kessingland Beach Suff 39 G11
Kessington E Dunb 68 C4
Kestle Corn 3 E8
Kestle Mill Corn 3 D7
Keston London 19 E11
Keswick Cumb 56 D4
Keswick Norf 39 B9
Keswick Norf 39 E8
Ketley Telford 34 D2
Ketley Bank Telford 34 D2
Ketsby Lincs 47 E7
Kettering Northants 36 H4
Ketteringham Norf 39 E7
Kettins Perth 76 D5
Kettlebaston Suff 30 C6
Kettlebridge Fife 76 G6
Kettleburgh Suff 31 B9
Kettlehill Fife 76 G6
Kettleholm Dumfries 61 F7
Kettleness N Yorks 59 E9
Kettleshume Ches E 44 E3
Kettlesing Bottom N Yorks 51 D8
Kettlesing Head N Yorks 51 D8
Kettlestone Norf 38 B5
Kettlethorpe Lincs 46 E2
Kettletoft Orkney 95 E7
Kettlewell N Yorks 50 B5
Ketton Rutland 36 E5
Kew London 19 D8
Kew Br. London 19 D8
Kewstoke N Som 15 E9
Kexbrough S Yorks 45 B7
Kexby Lincs 46 D2
Kexby York 52 D3
Key Green Ches E 44 F2
Keyham Leics 36 E2
Keyhaven Hants 10 E2
Keyingham E Yorks 53 G8
Keymer W Sus 12 E2
Keynsham Bath 16 E3
Keysoe Bedford 29 B7
Keysoe Row Bedford 29 B7
Keyston Cambs 36 H6
Keyworth Notts 36 B2
Kibblesworth T&W 63 H8
Kibworth Beauchamp Leics 36 F2
Kibworth Harcourt Leics 36 F2
Kidbrooke London 19 D11
Kiddemore Green Staffs 34 E4
Kidderminster Worcs 34 H4
Kiddington Oxon 27 F11
Kidlington Oxon 27 G11
Kidmore End Oxon 18 D3
Kidsgrove Staffs 44 G2
Kidstones N Yorks 50 A5
Kidwelly = Cydweli Carms 23 F9
Kiel Crofts Argyll 74 D2
Kielder Northumb 62 D2
Kierfiold Ho Orkney 95 G3
Kilbagie Fife 69 B8
Kilbarchan Renfs 68 D3
Kilbeg Highld 85 H11
Kilberry Argyll 72 G6
Kilbirnie N Ayrs 66 A6
Kilbride Argyll 74 E2
Kilbride Argyll 79 J11
Kilbride Highld 85 F10
Kilburn Angus 82 G5
Kilburn Derbys 45 H7
Kilburn London 19 C9
Kilburn N Yorks 51 B11
Kilby Leics 36 F2
Kilchamaig Argyll 73 G7
Kilchattan Argyll 72 D2
Kilchattan Bay Argyll 66 A4
Kilchenzie Argyll 65 F7
Kilcheran Argyll 79 H11
Kilchiaran Argyll 64 B3
Kilchoan Argyll 72 B6
Kilchoan Highld 78 E7
Kilchoman Argyll 64 B3
Kilchrenan Argyll 74 E3
Kilconquhar Fife 77 G7
Kilcot Glos 26 F3
Kilcoy Highld 87 F8
Kilcreggan Argyll 73 E11
Kildale N Yorks 59 F7
Kildalloig Argyll 65 G8
Kildary Highld 87 D10
Kildermorie Lodge Highld 87 D8
Kildonan N Ayrs 66 D3
Kildonan Lodge Highld 93 G12
Kildonnan Highld 78 C7
Kildrummy Aberds 82 B6
Kildwick N Yorks 50 E6
Kilfinan Argyll 73 F8
Kilfinnan Highld 80 D4
Kilgetty Pembs 22 F6
Kilgwrrwg Common Mon 15 B10
Kilham E Yorks 53 C6
Kilham Northumb 71 G7
Kilkenneth Argyll 78 G2
Kilkerran Argyll 65 G8
Kilkhampton Corn 6 E1
Killamarsh Derbys 45 D8
Killay Swansea 14 B2
Killbeg Argyll 79 G9
Killean Argyll 65 D7
Killearn Stirling 68 B4
Killen Highld 87 F9
Killerby Darl 58 E2
Killichonan Perth 75 B8
Killiechonate Highld 80 E4
Killiechronan Argyll 79 G8
Killiecrankie Perth 76 A2
Killiemor Argyll 78 H7
Killiemore House Argyll 78 J7
Killilan Highld 86 H2
Killimster Highld 94 E5
Killin Stirling 75 D8
Killin Lodge Highld 81 C7
Killinallan Argyll 64 A4
Killinghall N Yorks 51 D8
Killington Cumb 57 H8
Killingworth T&W 63 F8
Killmahumaig Argyll 72 D6
Killochyett Borders 70 F3
Killocraw Argyll 65 E7
Killundine Highld 79 G8
Kilmacolm Invclyd 68 D2
Kilmaha Argyll 73 C8
Kilmahog Stirling 75 G9
Kilmalieu Highld 79 F11
Kilmaluag Highld 85 A9
Kilmany Fife 76 E6
Kilmarie Highld 85 G10
Kilmarnock E Ayrs 67 C7
Kilmaron Castle Fife 76 F6
Kilmartin Argyll 73 D7
Kilmaurs E Ayrs 67 B7
Kilmelford Argyll 73 B7
Kilmeny Argyll 64 B4
Kilmersdon Som 16 F3
Kilmeston Hants 10 B4
Kilmichael Argyll 65 F7
Kilmichael Glassary Argyll 73 D7
Kilmichael of Inverlussa Argyll 72 E6
Kilmington Devon 8 E1
Kilmington Wilts 16 H4
Kilmonivaig Highld 80 E3
Kilmorack Highld 86 G7
Kilmore Argyll 79 J11
Kilmore Highld 85 H11
Kilmory Argyll 72 F6
Kilmory Highld 79 D8
Kilmory Highld 85 H8
Kilmory N Ayrs 66 D2
Kilmuir Highld 84 D7
Kilmuir Highld 85 A8
Kilmuir Highld 87 D10
Kilmuir Highld 87 G9
Kilmun Argyll 73 B8
Kilmun Argyll 73 E10
Kiln Pit Hill Northumb 58 A1
Kilncadzow S Lanark 69 F7
Kilndown Kent 12 C6
Kilnhurst S Yorks 45 C8
Kilninian Argyll 78 G6
Kilninver Argyll 79 J11
Kilnsea E Yorks 53 H10
Kilnsey N Yorks 50 C5
Kilnwick E Yorks 52 E5
Kilnwick Percy E Yorks 52 D4
Kiloran Argyll 72 D2
Kilpatrick N Ayrs 66 D2
Kilpeck Hereford 25 E11
Kilphedir Highld 93 H12
Kilpin E Yorks 52 G3
Kilpin Pike E Yorks 52 G3
Kilrenny Fife 77 G8
Kilsby Northants 28 A2
Kilspindie Perth 76 E5
Kilsyth N Lanark 68 C6
Kiltarlity Highld 87 G8
Kilton Notts 45 E9
Kilton Som 7 B10
Kilton Thorpe Redcar 59 E7
Kilvaxter Highld 85 B8
Kilve Som 7 B10
Kilvington Notts 36 A3
Kilwinning N Ayrs 66 B6
Kimber worth S Yorks 45 C8
Kimberley Norf 39 E6
Kimberley Notts 35 A11
Kimble Wick Bucks 28 H5
Kimblesworth Durham 58 B3
Kimbolton Cambs 29 B7
Kimbolton Hereford 26 B2
Kimcote Leics 36 G1
Kimmeridge Dorset 9 G8
Kimmerston Northumb 71 G8
Kimpton Hants 17 G9
Kimpton Herts 29 G8
Kinbrace Highld 93 F11
Kinbuck Stirling 75 G10
Kincaple Fife 77 F7
Kincardine Fife 69 B8
Kincardine Highld 87 C9
Kincardine Bridge Falk 69 B8
Kincardine O'Neil Aberds 83 D7
Kinclaven Perth 76 D4
Kincorth Aberdeen 83 C11
Kincorth Ho. Moray 87 E13
Kincraig Highld 81 C10
Kincraigie Perth 76 C2
Kindallachan Perth 76 C2
Kineton Glos 27 F7
Kineton Warks 27 C10
Kinfauns Perth 76 E4
King Edward Aberds 89 C7
King Sterndale Derbys 44 E4
Kingairloch Highld 79 F11
Kingarth Argyll 73 H9
Kingcoed Mon 25 H11
Kingerby Lincs 46 C4
Kingham Oxon 27 F9
Kingholm Quay Dumfries 60 F5
Kinghorn Fife 69 B11
Kingie Highld 80 C3
Kinglassie Fife 76 H5
Kingoodie Perth 76 E6
King's Acre Hereford 25 D11
King's Bromley Staffs 35 D7
King's Caple Hereford 26 F2
King's Cliffe Northants 36 F6
King's Coughton Warks 27 C7
King's Heath W Mid 35 G6
Kings Hedges Cambs 29 B11
King's Hill Kent 20 F3
Kings Langley Herts 19 A7
King's Lynn Norf 38 C2
King's Meaburn Cumb 57 D8
King's Mills Wrex 42 H6
Kings Muir Borders 69 G11
King's Newnham Warks 35 H10
King's Newton Derbys 35 C9
King's Norton Leics 36 E2
King's Norton W Mid 35 H6
King's Nympton Devon 6 E5
King's Pyon Hereford 25 C11
King's Ripton Cambs 37 H8
King's Somborne Hants 10 A2
King's Stag Dorset 8 C6
King's Stanley Glos 16 A5
King's Sutton Northants 27 E11
King's Thorn Hereford 26 E2
King's Walden Herts 29 F8
Kings Worthy Hants 10 A3
Kingsand Corn 4 F5
Kingsbarns Fife 77 F8
Kingsbridge Devon 5 G8
Kingsbridge Som 7 C8
Kingsburgh Highld 85 C8
Kingsbury London 19 C9
Kingsbury Warks 35 F8
Kingsbury Episcopi Som 8 B3
Kingsclere Hants 18 F2
Kingscote Glos 16 B5
Kingscott Devon 6 E4
Kingscross N Ayrs 66 D3
Kingsdon Som 8 B4
Kingsdown Kent 21 G10
Kingseat Fife 69 A10
Kingsey Bucks 28 H4
Kingsfold W Sus 19 H8
Kingsford E Ayrs 67 B7
Kingsford Worcs 34 G4
Kingsforth N Lincs 52 H6
Kingsgate Kent 21 D10
Kingsheanton Devon 6 C4
Kingshouse Hotel Highld 74 B5
Kingside Hill Cumb 56 A3
Kingskerswell Devon 5 E9
Kingskettle Fife 76 G6
Kingsland Anglesey 40 B4
Kingsland Hereford 25 B11
Kingsley Ches W 43 E8
Kingsley Hants 18 H4
Kingsley Staffs 44 H4
Kingsley Green W Sus 11 A7
Kingsley Holt Staffs 44 H4
Kingsley Park Northants 28 B4
Kingsmuir Angus 77 C7
Kingsmuir Fife 77 G8
Kingsnorth Kent 13 C9
Kingstanding W Mid 35 F6
Kingsteignton Devon 5 D9
Kingsthorpe Northants 28 B4
Kingston Cambs 29 C10
Kingston Devon 5 G7
Kingston Dorset 9 D6
Kingston Dorset 9 G8
Kingston E Loth 70 B4
Kingston Hants 9 D10
Kingston IoW 10 F3
Kingston Kent 21 F8
Kingston Moray 88 B3
Kingston Bagpuize Oxon 17 B11
Kingston Blount Oxon 18 B4
Kingston by Sea W Sus 11 D11
Kingston Deverill Wilts 16 H5
Kingston Gorse W Sus 11 D9
Kingston Lisle Oxon 17 C10
Kingston Maurward Dorset 8 E6
Kingston near Lewes E Sus 12 F2
Kingston on Soar Notts 35 C11
Kingston Russell Dorset 8 E4
Kingston St Mary Som 7 D11
Kingston Seymour N Som 15 E10
Kingston Upon Hull Hull 53 G6
Kingston upon Thames London 19 E8
Kingston Vale London 19 D9
Kingstone Hereford 25 E11
Kingstone Som 8 C2
Kingstone Staffs 35 C6
Kingstown Cumb 61 H9
Kingswear Devon 5 F9
Kingswells Aberdeen 83 C10
Kingswinford W Mid 34 G4
Kingswood Bucks 28 G3
Kingswood Glos 16 B4
Kingswood Hereford 25 C9
Kingswood Kent 20 F5
Kingswood Powys 33 E8
Kingswood S Glos 16 D3
Kingswood Sur 19 F9
Kingswood Warks 27 A8
Kingthorpe Lincs 46 E5
Kington Hereford 25 C9
Kington Worcs 26 C6
Kington Langley Wilts 16 D6
Kington Magna Dorset 9 B6
Kington St Michael Wilts 16 D6
Kingussie Highld 81 C9
Kingweston Som 8 A4
Kininvie Ho. Moray 88 D3
Kinkell Bridge Perth 76 F2
Kinknockie Aberds 89 D10
Kinlet Shrops 34 G3
Kinloch Fife 76 F5
Kinloch Highld 78 B6
Kinloch Highld 85 G11
Kinloch Highld 92 F6
Kinloch Perth 76 C5
Kinloch Perth 76 C4
Kinloch Hourn Highld 80 C1
Kinloch Laggan Highld 81 E
Kinloch Lodge Highld 93 D
Kinloch Rannoch Perth 75 B9
Kinlochan Highld 79 E1
Kinlochard Stirling 75 G
Kinlochbeoraid Highld 79 C1
Kinlochbervie Highld 92 D
Kinlocheil Highld 80 F
Kinlochewe Highld 86 E
Kinlochleven Highld 74 A
Kinlochmoidart Highld 79 D1
Kinlochmorar Highld 79 B1
Kinlochmore Highld 74 A
Kinlochspelve Argyll 79 J
Kinloid Highld 79 C
Kinloss Moray 87 E1
Kinmel Bay Conwy 42 D
Kinmuck Aberds 83 B1
Kinmundy Aberds 83 B1
Kinnadie Aberds 89 D
Kinnaird Perth 76 E
Kinnaird Castle Angus 77 B
Kinneff Aberds 83 F1
Kinnelhead Dumfries 60 C
Kinnell Angus 77 B
Kinnerley Shrops 33 C
Kinnersley Hereford 25 D1
Kinnersley Worcs 26 D
Kinnerton Powys 25 B
Kinnesswood Perth 76 G
Kinninvie Durham 58 D
Kinnordy Angus 76 B
Kinoulton Notts 36 B
Kinross Perth 76 G
Kinrossie Perth 76 D
Kinsbourne Green Herts 29 G
Kinsey Heath Ches E 34 A
Kinsham Hereford 25 B1
Kinsham Worcs 26 E
Kinsley W Yorks 45 A
Kinson Bmouth 9 E
Kintbury W Berks 17 E1
Kintessack Moray 87 E1
Kintillo Perth 76 F
Kintocher Aberds 83 C
Kinton Hereford 25 A1
Kinton Shrops 33 D
Kintore Aberds 83 B
Kintour Argyll 64 C
Kintra Argyll 64 D
Kintra Argyll 78 J
Kintraw Argyll 73 C
Kinuachdrachd Argyll 72 D
Kinveachy Highld 81 B1
Kinver Staffs 34 G
Kippax W Yorks 51 F1
Kippen Stirling 68 A
Kippford or Scaur Dumfries 55 D1
Kirbister Orkney 95
Kirbister Orkney 95 H
Kirbuster Orkney 95
Kirby Bedon Norf 39
Kirby Bellars Leics 36 D
Kirby Cane Norf 39
Kirby Cross Essex 31
Kirby Grindalythe N Yorks 52 C
Kirby Hill N Yorks 51 C
Kirby Hill N Yorks 58
Kirby Knowle N Yorks 58 H
Kirby-le-Soken Essex 31
Kirby Misperton N Yorks 52 B
Kirby Muxloe Leics 35 E
Kirby Row Norf 39
Kirby Sigston N Yorks 58 G

Kirby Underdale E Yorks 52 D4
Kirby Wiske N Yorks 51 A9
Kirdford W Sus 11 B9
Kirk Highld 94 E4
Kirk Bramwith S Yorks 45 A10
Kirk Deighton N Yorks 51 D9
Kirk Ella E Yorks 52 G6
Kirk Hallam Derbys 35 A10
Kirk Hammerton N Yorks 51 D10
Kirk Ireton Derbys 44 G6
Kirk Langley Derbys 35 B8
Kirk Merrington Durham 58 C3
Kirk Michael IoM 48 C3
Kirk of Shotts N Lanark 69 D7
Kirk Sandall S Yorks 45 B10
Kirk Smeaton N Yorks 51 H11
Kirk Yetholm Borders 71 H7
Kirkabister Shetland 96 K6
Kirkandrews Dumfries 55 E9
Kirkandrews upon Eden Cumb 61 H9
Kirkbampton Cumb 61 H9
Kirkbean Dumfries 60 H5
Kirkbride Cumb 61 H8
Kirkbuddo Angus 77 C8
Kirkburn Borders 69 G11
Kirkburn E Yorks 52 D5
Kirkburton W Yorks 44 A5
Kirkby Lincs 46 C4
Kirkby Mers 43 C7
Kirkby N Yorks 59 F6
Kirkby Fleetham N Yorks 58 G3
Kirkby Green Lincs 46 G4
Kirkby In Ashfield Notts 45 G9
Kirkby-in-Furness Cumb 49 A2
Kirkby la Thorpe Lincs 46 H5
Kirkby Lonsdale Cumb 50 B2
Kirkby Malham N Yorks 50 C4
Kirkby Mallory Leics 35 E10
Kirkby Malzeard N Yorks 51 B8
Kirkby Mills N Yorks 59 H8
Kirkby on Bain Lincs 46 F6
Kirkby Overflow N Yorks 51 E9
Kirkby Stephen Cumb 57 F9
Kirkby Thore Cumb 57 D8
Kirkby Underwood Lincs 37 C6
Kirkby Wharfe N Yorks 51 E11
Kirkbymoorside N Yorks 59 H7
Kirkcaldy Fife 69 A11
Kirkcambeck Cumb 61 G11
Kirkcarswell Dumfries 55 E10
Kirkcolm Dumfries 54 C3
Kirkconnel Dumfries 60 B3
Kirkconnell Dumfries 60 G5
Kirkcowan Dumfries 54 C6
Kirkcudbright Dumfries 55 D9
Kirkdale Mers 42 C6
Kirkfieldbank S Lanark 69 F7
Kirkgunzeon Dumfries 55 C11
Kirkham Lancs 49 F4
Kirkham N Yorks 52 C3
Kirkhamgate W Yorks 51 G8
Kirkharle Northumb 62 E6
Kirkheaton Northumb 62 F6
Kirkheaton W Yorks 51 H7
Kirkhill Angus 77 A9
Kirkhill Highld 87 G8
Kirkhill Midloth 69 D11
Kirkhill Moray 88 E2
Kirkhope Borders 61 A9
Kirkhouse Borders 70 G2
Kirkiboll Highld 93 D8
Kirkibost Highld 85 G10
Kirkinch Angus 76 C6
Kirkinner Dumfries 55 D7
Kirkintilloch E Dunb 68 C5
Kirkland Cumb 56 E2
Kirkland Cumb 57 C8
Kirkland Dumfries 60 B3
Kirkland Dumfries 60 D4
Kirkleatham Redcar 59 D6
Kirklevington Stockton 58 F5
Kirkley Suff 39 F11
Kirklington N Yorks 51 A9
Kirklington Notts 45 G10
Kirklinton Cumb 61 G10
Kirkliston Edin 69 C10
Kirkmaiden Dumfries 54 F4
Kirkmichael Perth 76 B3
Kirkmichael S Ayrs 66 F6
Kirkmuirhill S Lanark 68 F6
Kirknewton Northumb 71 G8
Kirknewton W Loth 69 D10
Kirkney Aberds 88 E5
Kirkoswald Cumb 57 B7
Kirkoswald S Ayrs 66 F5
Kirkpatrick Durham Dumfries 60 F3
Kirkpatrick-Fleming Dumfries 61 F8
Kirksanton Cumb 49 A1
Kirkstall W Yorks 51 F8
Kirkstead Lincs 46 F5
Kirkstile Aberds 88 E5
Kirkstyle Highld 94 C5
Kirkton Aberds 83 A8
Kirkton Aberds 89 D6
Kirkton Angus 77 C7
Kirkton Angus 77 D7
Kirkton Borders 61 B11
Kirkton Dumfries 60 E5
Kirkton Fife 76 E6
Kirkton Highld 85 F13
Kirkton Highld 86 G2
Kirkton Highld 87 B10
Kirkton Highld 87 F10
Kirkton Perth 76 F2
Kirkton S Lanark 60 A5
Kirkton Stirling 75 G8
Kirkton Manor Borders 69 G11
Kirkton of Airlie Angus 76 B6
Kirkton of Auchterhouse Angus 76 D6
Kirkton of Auchterless Aberds 89 D7
Kirkton of Barevan Highld 87 G11
Kirkton of Bourtie Aberds 89 F8
Kirkton of Collace Perth 76 D4
Kirkton of Craig Angus 77 B10
Kirkton of Culsalmond Aberds 89 E6
Kirkton of Durris Aberds 83 D9
Kirkton of Glenbuchat Aberds 82 B5
Kirkton of Glenisla Angus 76 A5
Kirkton of Kingoldrum Angus 76 B6
Kirkton of Largo Fife 77 G7
Kirkton of Lethendy Perth 76 C4
Kirkton of Logie Buchan Aberds 89 F9
Kirkton of Maryculter Aberds 83 D10
Kirkton of Menmuir Angus 77 A8
Kirkton of Monikie Angus 77 D8
Kirkton of Oyne Aberds 83 A8
Kirkton of Rayne Aberds 83 A8
Kirkton of Skene Aberds 83 C10
Kirkton of Tough Aberds 83 B8
Kirktonhill Borders 70 E3
Kirktown Aberds 89 C10
Kirktown of Alvah Aberds 89 B6
Kirktown of Deskford Moray 88 B5
Kirktown of Fetteresso Aberds 83 E10
Kirktown of Mortlach Moray 88 E3
Kirktown of Slains Aberds 89 F10
Kirkurd Borders 69 F10
Kirkwall Orkney 95 G5
Kirkwhelpington Northumb 62 E5
Kirmington N Lincs 46 A5
Kirmond le Mire Lincs 46 C5
Kirn Argyll 73 F10
Kirriemuir Angus 76 B6
Kirstead Green Norf 39 F8
Kirtlebridge Dumfries 61 F8
Kirtleton Dumfries 61 E8
Kirtling Cambs 30 C3
Kirtling Green Cambs 30 C3
Kirtlington Oxon 27 G11
Kirtomy Highld 93 C10
Kirton Lincs 37 B9
Kirton Notts 45 F10
Kirton Suff 31 E9
Kirton End Lincs 37 A8
Kirton Holme Lincs 37 A8
Kirton in Lindsey N Lincs 46 C3
Kislingbury Northants 28 C3
Kites Hardwick Warks 27 B11
Kittisford Som 7 D9
Kittle Swansea 23 H10
Kitt's Green W Mid 35 G7
Kitt's Moss Gtr Man 44 D2
Kittybrewster Aberdeen 83 C11
Kitwood Hants 10 A5
Kivernoll Hereford 25 E11
Kiveton Park S Yorks 45 D8
Knaith Lincs 46 D2
Knaith Park Lincs 46 D2
Knap Corner Dorset 9 B7
Knaphill Sur 18 F6
Knapp Perth 76 D5
Knapp Som 8 B2
Knapthorpe Notts 45 G11
Knapton Norf 39 B9
Knapton York 52 D1
Knapton Green Hereford 25 C11
Knapwell Cambs 29 B10
Knaresborough N Yorks 51 D9
Knarsdale Northumb 57 A8
Knauchland Moray 88 C5
Knaven Aberds 89 D8
Knayton N Yorks 58 H5
Knebworth Herts 29 F9
Knedlington E Yorks 52 G3
Kneesall Notts 45 F11
Kneesworth Cambs 29 D10
Kneeton Notts 45 H11
Knelston Swansea 23 H9
Knenhall Staffs 34 B5
Knettishall Suff 38 G5
Knightacott Devon 6 C5
Knightcote Warks 27 C10
Knightley Dale Staffs 34 C4
Knighton Devon 4 G6
Knighton Leicester 36 E1
Knighton = Tref-y-Clawdd Powys 25 A9
Knighton Staffs 34 A3
Knighton Staffs 34 C3
Knightswood Glasgow 68 D4
Knightwick Worcs 26 C4
Knill Hereford 25 B9
Knipton Leics 36 B4
Knitsley Durham 58 B2
Kniveton Derbys 44 G6
Knock Argyll 79 H8
Knock Cumb 57 D8
Knock Moray 88 C5
Knockally Highld 94 H3
Knockan Highld 92 H5
Knockandhu Moray 82 A4
Knockando Moray 88 D1
Knockando Ho. Moray 88 D2
Knockbain Highld 87 F9
Knockbreck Highld 84 B7
Knockbrex Dumfries 55 E8
Knockdee Highld 94 D3
Knockdolian S Ayrs 66 H4
Knockenkelly N Ayrs 66 D3
Knockentiber E Ayrs 67 C6
Knockespock Ho. Aberds 83 A7
Knockfarrel Highld 87 F8
Knockglass Dumfries 54 D3
Knockholt Kent 19 F11
Knockholt Pound Kent 19 F11
Knockie Lodge Highld 80 B6
Knockin Shrops 33 C9
Knockinlaw E Ayrs 67 C7
Knocklearn Dumfries 60 F3
Knocknaha Argyll 65 G7
Knocknain Dumfries 54 C2
Knockrome Argyll 72 F4
Knocksharry IoM 48 D2
Knodishall Suff 31 B11
Knolls Green Ches E 44 E2
Knolton Wrex 33 B9
Knolton Bryn Wrex 33 B9
Knook Wilts 16 G6
Knossington Leics 36 E4
Knott End-on-Sea Lancs 49 E3
Knotting Bedford 29 B7
Knotting Green Bedford 29 B7
Knottingley W Yorks 51 G11
Knotts Cumb 56 D6
Knotts Lancs 50 D3
Knotty Ash Mers 43 C7
Knotty Green Bucks 18 B6
Knowbury Shrops 26 A2
Knowe Dumfries 54 B6
Knowehead Dumfries 67 G9
Knowes of Elrick Aberds 88 C6
Knowesgate Northumb 62 E5
Knoweton N Lanark 68 E6
Knowhead Aberds 89 C9
Knowl Hill Windsor 18 D5
Knowle Bristol 16 D3
Knowle Devon 6 C3
Knowle Devon 7 F6
Knowle Devon 7 H9
Knowle Shrops 26 A2
Knowle W Mid 35 H7
Knowle Green Lancs 50 F2
Knowle Park W Yorks 51 E6
Knowlton Dorset 9 C9
Knowlton Kent 21 F9
Knowsley Mers 43 C7
Knowstone Devon 7 D7
Knox Bridge Kent 13 B6
Knucklas Powys 25 A9
Knuston Northants 28 B6
Knutsford Ches E 43 E10
Knutton Staffs 44 H2
Knypersley Staffs 44 G2
Kuggar Corn 2 H6
Kyle of Lochalsh Highld 85 F12
Kyleakin Highld 85 F12
Kylerhea Highld 85 F12
Kylesknoydart Highld 79 B11
Kylesku Highld 92 F5
Kylesmorar Highld 79 B11
Kylestrome Highld 92 F5
Kyllachy House Highld 81 A9
Kynaston Shrops 33 C9
Kynnersley Telford 34 D2
Kyre Magna Worcs 26 B3

L

La Fontenelle Guern 11
La Planque Guern 11
Labost W Isles 91 C7
Lacasaidh W Isles 91 E8
Lacasdal W Isles 91 D9
Laceby NE Lincs 46 B6
Lacey Green Bucks 18 B5
Lach Dennis Ches W 43 E10
Lackford Suff 30 A4
Lacock Wilts 16 E6
Ladbroke Warks 27 C11
Laddingford Kent 20 G3
Lade Bank Lincs 47 G7
Ladock Corn 3 D7
Lady Orkney 95 D7
Ladybank Fife 76 F6
Ladykirk Borders 71 F7
Ladysford Aberds 89 B9
Laga Highld 79 E9
Lagalochan Argyll 73 B7
Lagavulin Argyll 64 D5
Lagg Argyll 72 F4
Lagg N Ayrs 66 D2
Laggan Argyll 64 C3
Laggan Highld 79 D10
Laggan Highld 80 D4
Laggan Highld 81 D8
Laggan S Ayrs 54 A5
Lagganulva Argyll 78 G7
Laide Highld 91 H13
Laigh Fenwick E Ayrs 67 B7
Laigh Glengall S Ayrs 66 E6
Laighmuir E Ayrs 67 B7
Laindon Essex 20 C3
Lair Highld 86 G3
Lairg Highld 93 J8
Lairg Lodge Highld 93 J8
Lairg Muir Highld 93 J8
Lairgmore Highld 87 H8
Laisterdyke W Yorks 51 F7
Laithes Cumb 57 C6
Lake IoW 10 F4
Lake Wilts 17 H8
Lakenham Norf 39 E8
Lakenheath Suff 38 G3
Lakesend Norf 37 F11
Lakeside Cumb 56 H5
Laleham Sur 19 E7
Laleston Bridgend 14 D4
Lamarsh Essex 30 E5
Lamas Norf 39 C8
Lambden Borders 70 F6
Lamberhurst Kent 12 C5
Lamberhurst Quarter Kent 12 C5
Lamberton Borders 71 E8
Lambeth London 19 D10
Lambhill Glasgow 68 D4
Lambley Northumb 62 H2
Lambley Notts 45 H10
Lamborough Hill Oxon 17 A11
Lambourn W Berks 17 D10
Lambourne End Essex 19 B11
Lambs Green W Sus 19 H9
Lambston Pembs 22 E4
Lambton T&W 58 A3
Lamerton Devon 4 D5
Lamesley T&W 63 H8
Laminess Orkney 95 E7
Lamington Highld 87 D10
Lamington S Lanark 69 G8
Lamlash N Ayrs 66 C3
Lamloch Dumfries 67 G8
Lamonby Cumb 56 C6
Lamorna Corn 2 G3
Lamorran Corn 3 E7
Lampardbrook Suff 31 B9
Lampeter = Llanbedr Pont Steffan Ceredig 23 B10
Lampeter Velfrey Pembs 22 E6
Lamphey Pembs 22 F5
Lamplugh Cumb 56 D2
Lamport Northants 28 A4
Lamyatt Som 16 H3
Lana Devon 6 G2
Lanark S Lanark 69 F7
Lancaster Lancs 49 C4
Lanchester Durham 58 B2
Lancing W Sus 11 D10
Landbeach Cambs 29 B11
Landcross Devon 6 D3
Landerberry Aberds 83 C9
Landford Wilts 10 C1
Landford Manor Wilts 10 B1
Landimore Swansea 23 G9
Landkey Devon 6 C4
Landore Swansea 14 B2
Landrake Corn 4 E4
Landscove Devon 5 E8
Landshipping Pembs 22 E5
Landshipping Quay Pembs 22 E5
Landulph Corn 4 E5
Landwade Suff 30 B3
Lane Corn 3 C7
Lane End Bucks 18 B5
Lane End Cumb 56 G3
Lane End Dorset 9 E7
Lane End Hants 10 B4
Lane End IoW 10 F5
Lane End Lancs 50 E4
Lane Ends Lancs 50 D3
Lane Ends Lancs 50 F3
Lane Ends N Yorks 50 E5
Lane Head Derbys 44 E5
Lane Head Durham 58 E2
Lane Head Gtr Man 43 C9
Lane Head W Yorks 44 B5
Lane Side Lancs 50 G3
Laneast Corn 4 C3
Laneham Notts 46 E2
Lanehead Durham 57 B10
Lanehead Northumb 62 E3
Lanercost Cumb 61 G11
Laneshaw Bridge Lancs 50 E5
Lanfach Caerph 15 B8
Langar Notts 36 B3
Langbank Renfs 68 C2
Langbar N Yorks 51 D6
Langburnshiels Borders 61 C11
Langcliffe N Yorks 50 C4
Langdale Highld 93 E9
Langdale End N Yorks 59 G10
Langdon Corn 4 C4
Langdon Beck Durham 57 C10
Langdon Hills Essex 20 C3
Langdyke Fife 76 G6
Langenhoe Essex 31 G7
Langford C Beds 29 D8
Langford Devon 7 F9
Langford Essex 30 H5
Langford Notts 46 G2
Langford Oxon 17 A9
Langford Budville Som 7 D10
Langham Essex 31 E7
Langham Norf 38 A6
Langham Rutland 36 D4
Langham Suff 30 B6
Langhaugh Borders 69 G11
Langho Lancs 50 F3
Langholm Dumfries 61 E9
Langleeford Northumb 62 A5
Langley Ches E 44 E3
Langley Hants 10 D3
Langley Herts 29 F9
Langley Kent 20 F5
Langley Northumb 62 G4
Langley Slough 19 D7
Langley W Sus 11 B7
Langley Warks 27 B8
Langley Burrell Wilts 16 D6
Langley Common Derbys 35 B8
Langley Heath Kent 20 F5
Langley Lower Green Essex 29 E11
Langley Marsh Som 7 D9
Langley Park Durham 58 B3
Langley Street Norf 39 E9
Langley Upper Green Essex 29 E11
Langney E Sus 12 F5
Langold Notts 45 D9
Langore Corn 4 C4
Langport Som 8 B3
Langrick Lincs 46 H6
Langridge Bath 16 E4
Langridge Ford Devon 6 D4
Langrigg Cumb 56 B3
Langrish Hants 10 B6
Langsett S Yorks 44 B6
Langshaw Borders 70 G4
Langside Perth 75 F10
Langskaill Orkney 95 D5
Langstone Hants 10 D6
Langstone Newport 15 B9
Langthorne N Yorks 58 G3
Langthorpe N Yorks 51 C9
Langthwaite N Yorks 58 F1
Langtoft E Yorks 52 C6
Langtoft Lincs 37 D7
Langton Durham 58 E2
Langton Lincs 46 F6
Langton Lincs 47 E7
Langton N Yorks 52 C3
Langton by Wragby Lincs 46 E5
Langton Green Kent 12 C4
Langton Green Suff 31 A8
Langton Herring Dorset 8 F5
Langton Matravers Dorset 9 G9
Langtree Devon 6 E3
Langwathby Cumb 57 C7
Langwell Ho. Highld 94 H3
Langwell Lodge Highld 92 J4
Langwith Derbys 45 F9
Langwith Junction Derbys 45 F9
Langworth Lincs 46 E4
Lanivet Corn 3 C9
Lanlivery Corn 4 F1
Lanner Corn 2 F6
Lanreath Corn 4 F2
Lansallos Corn 4 F2
Lansdown Glos 26 F6
Lanteglos Highway Corn 4 F2
Lanton Borders 62 A2
Lanton Northumb 71 G8
Lapford Devon 7 F6
Laphroaig Argyll 64 D4
Lapley Staffs 34 D4
Lapworth Warks 27 A8
Larachbeg Highld 79 G9
Larbert Falk 69 B7
Larden Green Ches E 43 G8
Largie Aberds 88 E6
Largiemore Argyll 73 E8
Largoward Fife 77 G7
Largs N Ayrs 73 H11
Largybeg N Ayrs 66 D3
Largymore N Ayrs 66 D3
Larkfield Invclyd 73 F11
Larkhall S Lanark 68 E6
Larkhill Wilts 17 G8
Larling Norf 38 G5
Larriston Borders 61 D11
Lartington Durham 58 E1
Lary Aberds 82 C5
Lasham Hants 18 G3
Lashenden Kent 13 B7
Lassington Glos 26 F4
Lassodie Fife 69 A10
Lastingham N Yorks 59 G8
Latcham Som 15 G10
Latchford Herts 29 F10
Latchford Warr 43 D9
Latchingdon Essex 20 A5
Latchley Corn 4 D5
Lately Common Warr 43 C9
Lathbury M Keynes 28 D5
Latheron Highld 94 G3
Latheronwheel Highld 94 G3
Latheronwheel Ho. Highld 94 G3
Lathones Fife 77 G7
Latimer Bucks 19 B7
Latteridge S Glos 16 C3
Lattiford Som 8 B5
Latton Wilts 17 B7
Latton Bush Essex 29 H11
Lauchintilly Aberds 83 B9
Lauder Borders 70 F4
Laugharne Carms 23 E8
Laughterton Lincs 46 E2
Laughton E Sus 12 E4
Laughton Leics 36 G2
Laughton Lincs 37 B6
Laughton Lincs 46 C2
Laughton Common S Yorks 45 D9
Laughton en le Morthen S Yorks 45 D9
Launcells Corn 6 F1
Launceston Corn 4 C4
Launton Oxon 28 F3
Laurencekirk Aberds 83 F9
Laurieston Dumfries 55 C9
Laurieston Falk 69 C8
Lavendon M Keynes 28 C6
Lavenham Suff 30 D6
Laverhay Dumfries 61 D7
Laversdale Cumb 61 G10
Laverstock Wilts 9 A10
Laverstoke Hants 17 G11
Laverton Glos 27 E7
Laverton N Yorks 51 B8
Laverton Som 16 F4
Lavister Wrex 42 G6
Law S Lanark 69 E7
Lawers Perth 75 D9
Lawers Perth 75 E10
Lawford Essex 31 E7
Lawhitton Corn 4 C4
Lawkland N Yorks 50 C3
Lawley Telford 34 E2
Lawnhead Staffs 34 C4
Lawrenny Pembs 22 F5
Lawshall Suff 30 C5
Lawton Hereford 25 C11
Laxey IoM 48 D4
Laxfield Suff 31 A9
Laxfirth Shetland 96 H6
Laxfirth Shetland 96 J6
Laxford Bridge Highld 92 E5
Laxo Shetland 96 G6
Laxobigging Shetland 96 F6
Laxton E Yorks 52 G3
Laxton Northants 36 F5
Laxton Notts 45 F11
Laycock W Yorks 50 E6
Layer Breton Essex 30 G6
Layer de la Haye Essex 30 F6
Layer Marney Essex 30 G6
Layham Suff 31 D7
Laylands Green W Berks 17 E10
Laytham E Yorks 52 F3
Layton Blackpool 49 F3
Lazenby Redcar 59 D6
Lazonby Cumb 57 C7
Le Planel Guern 11
Le Skerne Haughton Darl 58 E4
Le Villocq Guern 11
Lea Derbys 45 G7
Lea Hereford 26 F3
Lea Lincs 46 D2
Lea Shrops 33 E10
Lea Shrops 33 G9
Lea Wilts 16 C6
Lea Marston Warks 35 F8
Lea Town Lancs 49 F4
Leabrooks Derbys 45 G8
Leac a Li W Isles 90 H6
Leachkin Highld 87 G9
Leadburn Midloth 69 E11
Leaden Roding Essex 30 G2
Leadenham Lincs 46 G3
Leadgate Cumb 57 B9
Leadgate Durham 58 A2
Leadgate T&W 63 H7
Leadhills S Lanark 60 B4
Leafield Oxon 27 G10
Leagrave Luton 29 F7
Leake N Yorks 58 G5
Leake Commonside Lincs 47 G7
Lealholm N Yorks 59 F8
Lealt Argyll 72 D5
Lealt Highld 85 B10
Leamington Hastings Warks 27 B11
Leamonsley Staffs 35 E7
Leamside Durham 58 B4
Leanaig Highld 87 F8
Leargybreck Argyll 72 F4
Leasgill Cumb 49 A4
Leasingham Lincs 46 H4
Leasingthorne Durham 58 D3
Leasowe Mers 42 C5
Leatherhead Sur 19 F8
Leatherhead Common Sur 19 F8
Leathley N Yorks 51 E8
Leaton Shrops 33 D10
Leaveland Kent 21 F7
Leavening N Yorks 52 C3
Leaves Green London 19 E11
Leazes Durham 63 H7
Lebberston N Yorks 53 A6
Lechlade-on-Thames Glos 17 B9
Leck Lancs 50 B2
Leckford Hants 17 H10
Leckfurin Highld 93 D10
Leckgruinart Argyll 64 B3
Leckhampstead Bucks 28 E4
Leckhampstead W Berks 17 D11
Leckhampstead Thicket W Berks 17 D11
Leckhampton Glos 26 G6
Leckie Highld 86 E3
Leckmelm Highld 86 B4
Leckwith V Glam 15 D7
Leconfield E Yorks 52 E6
Ledaig Argyll 74 D2
Ledburn Bucks 28 F6
Ledbury Hereford 26 E4
Ledcharrie Stirling 75 E8
Ledgemoor Hereford 25 C11
Ledicot Hereford 25 B11
Ledmore Highld 92 H5
Lednagullin Highld 93 C10
Ledsham Ches W 42 E6
Ledsham W Yorks 51 G10
Ledston W Yorks 51 G10
Ledston Luck W Yorks 51 F10
Ledwell Oxon 27 F11
Lee Argyll 78 J7
Lee Devon 6 B3
Lee Hants 10 C2
Lee Lancs 50 D1
Lee Shrops 33 B10
Lee Brockhurst Shrops 33 C11
Lee Clump Bucks 18 A6
Lee Mill Devon 5 F7
Lee Moor Devon 5 E6
Lee-on-the-Solent Hants 10 D4
Leeans Shetland 96 J5
Leebotten Shetland 96 L6
Leebotwood Shrops 33 F10
Leece Cumb 49 C2
Leechpool Pembs 22 E4
Leeds Kent 20 F5
Leeds W Yorks 51 F8
Leedstown Corn 2 F5
Leek Staffs 44 G3
Leek Wootton Warks 27 B9
Leekbrook Staffs 44 G3
Leeming N Yorks 58 H3
Leeming Bar N Yorks 58 G3
Lees Derbys 35 B8
Lees Gtr Man 44 B3
Lees W Yorks 50 F6
Leeswood Flint 42 G5
Legbourne Lincs 47 D7
Legerwood Borders 70 F4
Legsby Lincs 46 D5
Leicester Leicester 36 E1
Leicester Forest East Leics 35 E11
Leigh Dorset 8 D5
Leigh Glos 26 F5
Leigh Gtr Man 43 B9
Leigh Kent 20 G2
Leigh Shrops 33 E9
Leigh Sur 19 G9
Leigh Wilts 17 B7
Leigh Worcs 26 C4
Leigh Beck Essex 20 C5
Leigh Common Som 8 B6
Leigh Delamere Wilts 16 D5
Leigh Green Kent 13 C8
Leigh on Sea Southend 20 C5
Leigh Park Hants 10 D6
Leigh Sinton Worcs 26 C4
Leigh upon Mendip Som 16 G3
Leigh Woods N Som 16 D2
Leighswood W Mid 35 E6
Leighterton Glos 16 B5
Leighton N Yorks 51 B7
Leighton Powys 33 E8
Leighton Shrops 34 E2
Leighton Som 16 G4
Leighton Bromswold Cambs 37 H7
Leighton Buzzard C Beds 28 F6
Leinthall Earls Hereford 25 B11
Leinthall Starkes Hereford 25 B11
Leintwardine Hereford 25 A11
Leire Leics 35 F11
Leirinmore Highld 92 C7
Leiston Suff 31 B11
Leitfie Perth 76 C5
Leith Edin 69 C11
Leitholm Borders 70 F6
Lelant Corn 2 F4
Lelley E Yorks 53 F8
Lem Hill Worcs 26 A4
Lemmington Hall Northumb 63 B7
Lempitlaw Borders 70 G6
Lenchwick Worcs 27 D7
Lendalfoot S Ayrs 66 H4
Lendrick Lodge Stirling 75 G8
Lenham Kent 20 F5
Lenham Heath Kent 20 G6
Lennel Borders 71 F7
Lennoxtown E Dunb 68 C5
Lenton Lincs 36 B6
Lenton Nottingham 36 B1
Lentran Highld 87 G8
Lenwade Norf 39 D6
Leny Ho. Stirling 75 G9
Lenzie E Dunb 68 C5
Leoch Angus 76 D6
Leochel-Cushnie Aberds 83 B7
Leominster Hereford 25 C11
Leonard Stanley Glos 16 A5
Leorin Argyll 64 D4
Lepe Hants 10 E3
Lephin Highld 84 D6
Lephinchapel Argyll 73 D8
Lephinmore Argyll 73 D8
Leppington N Yorks 52 C3
Lepton W Yorks 51 H8
Lerryn Corn 4 F2
Lerwick Shetland 96 J6
Lesbury Northumb 63 B8
Leslie Aberds 83 A7
Leslie Fife 76 G5
Lesmahagow S Lanark 69 G7
Lesnewth Corn 4 B2
Lessendrum Aberds 88 D5
Lessingham Norf 39 C9
Lessonhall Cumb 56 A4
Leswalt Dumfries 54 C3
Letchmore Heath Herts 19 B8
Letchworth Herts 29 E9
Letcombe Bassett Oxon 17 C10
Letcombe Regis Oxon 17 C10
Letham Angus 77 C8
Letham Falk 69 B7
Letham Fife 76 F6
Letham Perth 76 E3
Letham Grange Angus 77 C9
Lethenty Aberds 89 D8
Letheringham Suff 31 C9
Letheringsett Norf 39 B6
Lettaford Devon 5 C8
Lettan Orkney 95 D8
Letterewe Highld 86 D2
Letterfearn Highld 85 F13
Letterfinlay Highld 80 D4
Lettermorar Highld 79 C10
Lettermore Argyll 78 G7
Letters Highld 86 C4
Letterston Pembs 22 D4
Lettoch Highld 82 B2
Lettoch Highld 87 H13
Letton Hereford 25 A10
Letton Hereford 25 D10
Letton Green Norf 38 E5
Letty Green Herts 29 G9
Letwell S Yorks 45 D9
Leuchars Fife 77 E7
Leuchars Ho. Moray 88 B2
Leumrabhagh W Isles 91 F8
Levan Invclyd 73 F11
Levaneap Shetland 96 G6
Levedale Staffs 34 D4
Leven E Yorks 53 E7
Leven Fife 76 G6
Levencorroch N Ayrs 66 D3
Levens Cumb 57 H6
Levens Green Herts 29 F10
Levenshulme Gtr Man 44 C2
Levenwick Shetland 96 L6
Leverburgh = An t-Ob W Isles 90 J5
Leverington Cambs 37 D10
Leverton Lincs 47 H8
Leverton Highgate Lincs 47 H8
Leverton Lucasgate Lincs 47 H8
Leverton Outgate Lincs 47 H8
Levington Suff 31 E9
Levisham N Yorks 59 G9
Levishie Highld 80 B6
Lew Oxon 27 H10
Lewannick Corn 4 C3
Lewdown Devon 4 C5
Lewes E Sus 12 E3
Leweston Pembs 22 D4
Lewisham London 19 D10
Lewiston Highld 81 A7
Lewistown Bridgend 14 C5
Lewknor Oxon 18 B4
Leworthy Devon 6 C5
Leworthy Devon 6 F2
Lewtrenchard Devon 4 C5
Lexden Essex 30 F6
Ley Aberds 83 B7
Ley Corn 4 E2
Leybourne Kent 20 F3
Leyburn N Yorks 58 G2
Leyfields Staffs 35 E8
Leyhill Bucks 18 A6
Leyland Lancs 49 G5
Leylodge Aberds 83 B9
Leymoor W Yorks 51 H7
Leys Aberds 89 C10
Leys Perth 76 D5
Leys Castle Highld 87 G9
Leys of Cossans Angus 76 C6
Leysdown-on-Sea Kent 21 D7
Leysmill Angus 77 C9
Leysters Pole Hereford 26 B2
Leyton London 19 C10
Leytonstone London 19 C10
Lezant Corn 4 D4
Leziate Norf 38 D2
Lhanbryde Moray 88 B2
Liatrie Highld 86 H5
Libanus Powys 24 F6
Libberton S Lanark 69 F8
Liberton Edin 69 D11
Liceasto W Isles 90 H6
Lichfield Staffs 35 E7
Lickey Worcs 34 H5
Lickey End Worcs 26 A6
Lickfold W Sus 11 B8
Liddel Orkney 95 K5
Liddesdale Highld 79 F10
Liddington Swindon 17 C9
Lidgate Suff 30 C4
Lidget S Yorks 45 B10
Lidget Green W Yorks 51 F7
Lidgett Notts 45 F10
Lidlington C Beds 28 E6
Lidstone Oxon 27 F10
Lieurary Highld 94 D2
Liff Angus 76 D6
Lifton Devon 4 C4
Liftondown Devon 4 C4
Lighthorne Warks 27 C10
Lightwater Sur 18 E6
Lightwood Stoke 34 A5
Lightwood Green Ches E 34 A2
Lightwood Green Wrex 33 A9
Lilbourne Northants 36 H1
Lilburn Tower Northumb 62 A6
Lilleshall Telford 34 D3
Lilley Herts 29 F8
Lilley W Berks 17 D11
Lilliesleaf Borders 61 A11
Lillingstone Dayrell Bucks 28 E4
Lillingstone Lovell Bucks 28 D4
Lillington Dorset 8 C5
Lillington Warks 27 B10
Lilliput Poole 9 E9
Lilstock Som 7 B10
Lilyhurst Shrops 34 D3
Limbury Luton 29 F7
Limebrook Hereford 25 B10
Limefield Gtr Man 44 A2
Limekilnburn S Lanark 68 E6
Limekilns Fife 69 B9
Limerigg Falk 69 C7
Limerstone IoW 10 F3
Limington Som 8 B4
Limpenhoe Norf 39 E9
Limpley Stoke Wilts 16 E4
Limpsfield Sur 19 F11
Limpsfield Chart Sur 19 F11
Linby Notts 45 G9
Linchmere W Sus 11 A7
Lincluden Dumfries 60 F5
Lincoln Lincs 46 E3
Lincomb Worcs 26 B5
Lincombe Devon 5 F8
Lindal in Furness Cumb 49 B2
Lindale Cumb 49 A4
Lindean Borders 70 G3
Lindfield W Sus 12 D2
Lindford Hants 18 H5
Lindifferon Fife 76 F6
Lindley W Yorks 51 H7
Lindley Green N Yorks 51 E8
Lindores Fife 76 F5
Lindridge Worcs 26 B3
Lindsell Essex 30 F3
Lindsey Suff 30 D6
Linford Hants 9 D10
Linford Thurrock 20 D3
Lingague IoM 48 E2
Lingards Wood W Yorks 44 A4
Lingbob W Yorks 51 F6
Lingdale Redcar 59 E7
Lingen Hereford 25 B10
Lingfield Sur 12 B2
Lingreabhagh W Isles 90 J5
Lingwood Norf 39 E9
Linicro Highld 85 B8
Linkenholt Hants 17 F10
Linkhill Kent 13 D7
Linkinhorne Corn 4 D4
Linklater Orkney 95 K5
Linksness Orkney 95 H3
Linktown Fife 69 A11
Linley Shrops 33 F9
Linley Green Hereford 26 C3
Linlithgow W Loth 69 C9
Linlithgow Bridge W Loth 69 C8
Linshiels Northumb 62 C4
Linsiadar W Isles 90 D7
Linsidemore Highld 87 B8
Linslade C Beds 28 F6
Linstead Parva Suff 39 H9
Linstock Cumb 61 H10
Linthwaite W Yorks 44 A5
Lintlaw Borders 71 E7
Lintmill Moray 88 B5
Linton Borders 70 H6
Linton Cambs 30 D2
Linton Derbys 35 D8
Linton Hereford 26 F3
Linton Kent 20 G4
Linton N Yorks 50 C5
Linton Northumb 63 D8
Linton W Yorks 51 E9
Linton-on-Ouse N Yorks 51 C10
Linwood Hants 9 D10
Linwood Lincs 46 D5
Linwood Renfs 68 D3
Lionacleit W Isles 84 D2
Lional W Isles 91 A10
Liphook Hants 11 A7
Liscard Mers 42 C6
Liscombe Som 7 C7
Liskeard Corn 4 E3
L'Islet Guern 11
Liss Hants 11 B6
Liss Forest Hants 11 B6
Lissett E Yorks 53 D7
Lissington Lincs 46 D5
Lisvane Cardiff 15 C7
Liswerry Newport 15 C9
Litcham Norf 38 D4
Litchborough Northants 28 C3
Litchfield Hants 17 F11
Litherland Mers 42 C6
Litlington Cambs 29 D10
Litlington E Sus 12 F4
Little Abington Cambs 30 D2
Little Addington Northants 28 A6
Little Alne Warks 27 B8
Little Altcar Mers 42 B6
Little Asby Cumb 57 F8
Little Assynt Highld 92 G4
Little Aston Staffs 35 E6
Little Atherfield IoW 10 F3
Little Ayre Orkney 95 J4
Little-ayre Shetland 96 G5
Little Ayton N Yorks 59 E6
Little Baddow Essex 30 H4
Little Badminton S Glos 16 C5
Little Ballinluig Perth 76 B2
Little Bampton Cumb 61 H8
Little Bardfield Essex 30 E3
Little Barford Bedford 29 C8
Little Barningham Norf 39 B7
Little Barrington Glos 27 G9
Little Barrow Ches W 43 E7
Little Barugh N Yorks 52 B3
Little Bavington Northumb 62 F5
Little Bealings Suff 31 D9
Little Bedwyn Wilts 17 E9
Little Bentley Essex 31 F8
Little Berkhamsted Herts 29 H9
Little Billing Northants 28 B5
Little Birch Hereford 26 E2
Little Blakenham Suff 31 D8
Little Blencow Cumb 56 C6
Little Bollington Ches E 43 D10
Little Bookham Sur 19 F8
Little Bowden Leics 36 G3
Little Bradley Suff 30 C3
Little Brampton Shrops 33 G9
Little Brechin Angus 77 A8
Little Brickhill M Keynes 28 E6
Little Brington Northants 28 B3
Little Bromley Essex 31 F7
Little Broughton Cumb 56 C2
Little Budworth Ches W 43 F8
Little Burstead Essex 20 B3
Little Bytham Lincs 36 D6
Little Carlton Lincs 47 D7
Little Carlton Notts 45 G11
Little Casterton Rutland 36 E6
Little Cawthorpe Lincs 47 D7
Little Chalfont Bucks 18 B6
Little Chart Kent 20 G6
Little Chesterford Essex 30 D2
Little Cheverell Wilts 16 F6
Little Chishill Cambs 29 E11
Little Clacton Essex 31 G8
Little Clifton Cumb 56 D2
Little Colp Aberds 89 D7
Little Comberton Worcs 26 D6
Little Common E Sus 12 F6
Little Compton Warks 27 E9
Little Cornard Suff 30 E5
Little Cowarne Hereford 26 C3
Little Coxwell Oxon 17 B9
Little Crakehall N Yorks 58 G3
Little Cressingham Norf 38 F4
Little Crosby Mers 42 B6
Little Dalby Leics 36 D3
Little Dawley Telford 34 E2
Little Dens Aberds 89 D10
Little Dewchurch Hereford 26 E2
Little Downham Cambs 37 G11
Little Driffield E Yorks 52 D6
Little Dunham Norf 38 D4
Little Dunkeld Perth 76 C3
Little Dunmow Essex 30 F3
Little Easton Essex 30 F3
Little Eaton Derbys 35 A9
Little Eccleston Lancs 49 E4
Little Ellingham Norf 38 F6
Little End Essex 20 A2
Little Eversden Cambs 29 C10
Little Faringdon Oxon 17 A9
Little Fencote N Yorks 58 G3
Little Fenton N Yorks 51 F11
Little Finborough Suff 31 C7
Little Fransham Norf 38 D5
Little Gaddesden Herts 28 G6
Little Gidding Cambs 37 G7
Little Glemham Suff 31 C10
Little Glenshee Perth 76 D2
Little Gransden Cambs 29 C9
Little Green Som 16 G4
Little Grimsby Lincs 47 C7
Little Gruinard Highld 86 C2
Little Habton N Yorks 52 B3
Little Hadham Herts 29 F11
Little Hale Lincs 37 A7
Little Hallingbury Essex 29 G11
Little Hampden Bucks 18 A5
Little Harrowden Northants 28 A5
Little Haseley Oxon 18 A3
Little Hatfield E Yorks 53 E7
Little Hautbois Norf 39 C8
Little Haven Pembs 22 E3
Little Hay Staffs 35 E7
Little Hayfield Derbys 44 D4
Little Haywood Staffs 34 C6
Little Heath W Mid 35 G9
Little Hereford Hereford 26 B2
Little Horkesley Essex 30 E6
Little Horsted E Sus 12 E3
Little Horton W Yorks 51 F7
Little Horwood Bucks 28 E4
Little Houghton Northants 28 C5
Little Houghton S Yorks 45 B8
Little Hucklow Derbys 44 E5
Little Hulton Gtr Man 43 B10
Little Humber E Yorks 53 G7
Little Hungerford W Berks 18 D2
Little Irchester Northants 28 B6
Little Kimble Bucks 28 H5
Little Kineton Warks 27 C10
Little Kingshill Bucks 18 B5
Little Langdale Cumb 56 F5
Little Langford Wilts 17 H7
Little Laver Essex 30 H2
Little Leigh Ches W 43 E9
Little Leighs Essex 30 G4
Little Lever Gtr Man 43 B10
Little London Bucks 28 G3
Little London E Sus 12 E4
Little London Hants 17 G10
Little London Hants 18 F3
Little London Lincs 37 C10
Little London Lincs 37 C8
Little London Norf 39 C7
Little London Powys 32 G6
Little Longstone Derbys 44 E5
Little Lynturk Aberds 83 B7
Little Malvern Worcs 26 D4
Little Maplestead Essex 30 E5
Little Marcle Hereford 26 E3
Little Marlow Bucks 18 C5
Little Marsden Lancs 50 F4
Little Massingham Norf 38 C3
Little Melton Norf 39 E7
Little Mill Mon 15 A9
Little Milton Oxon 18 A3
Little Missenden Bucks 18 B6
Little Musgrave Cumb 57 E9
Little Ness Shrops 33 D10
Little Neston Ches W 42 E5
Little Newcastle Pembs 22 D4
Little Newsham Durham 58 E2
Little Oakley Essex 31 F9
Little Oakley Northants 36 G4
Little Orton Cumb 61 H9

Little Ouseburn N Yorks 51 C10
Little Paxton Cambs 29 B8
Little Petherick Corn 3 B8
Little Pitlurg Moray 88 D4
Little Plumpton Lancs 49 F3
Little Plumstead Norf 39 D9
Little Ponton Lincs 36 B5
Little Raveley Cambs 37 H8
Little Reedness E Yorks 52 G4
Little Ribston N Yorks 51 D9
Little Rissington Glos 27 G8
Little Ryburgh Norf 38 C5
Little Ryle Northumb 62 B6
Little Salkeld Cumb 57 C7
Little Sampford Essex 30 E3
Little Sandhurst Brack 18 E5
Little Saxham Suff 30 B4
Little Scatwell Highld 86 F6
Little Sessay N Yorks 51 B10
Little Shelford Cambs 29 C11
Little Singleton Lancs 49 F3
Little Skillymarno Aberds 89 C9
Little Smeaton N Yorks 51 H11
Little Snoring Norf 38 B5
Little Sodbury S Glos 16 C4
Little Somborne Hants 10 A2
Little Somerford Wilts 16 C6
Little Stainforth N Yorks 50 C4
Little Stainton Darl 58 D4
Little Stanney Ches W 43 E7
Little Staughton Bedford 29 B8
Little Steeping Lincs 47 F8
Little Stoke Staffs 34 B5
Little Stonham Suff 31 B8
Little Stretton Leics 36 E2
Little Stretton Shrops 33 F10
Little Strickland Cumb 57 E7
Little Stukeley Cambs 37 H8
Little Sutton Ches W 42 E6
Little Tew Oxon 27 F10
Little Thetford Cambs 37 H11
Little Thirkleby N Yorks 51 B10
Little Thurlow Suff 30 C3
Little Thurrock Thurrock 20 D3
Little Torboll Highld 87 B10
Little Torrington Devon 6 E3
Little Totham Essex 30 G5
Little Toux Aberds 88 C5
Little Town Cumb 56 E4
Little Town Lancs 50 F2
Little Urswick Cumb 49 B2
Little Wakering Essex 20 C6
Little Walden Essex 30 D2
Little Waldingfield Suff 30 D6
Little Walsingham Norf 38 B5
Little Waltham Essex 30 G4
Little Warley Essex 20 B3
Little Weighton E Yorks 52 F5
Little Weldon Northants 36 G5
Little Welnetham Suff 30 B5
Little Wenlock Telford 34 E2
Little Whittingham Green Suff 39 H8
Little Wilbraham Cambs 30 C2
Little Wishford Wilts 17 H7
Little Witley Worcs 26 B4
Little Wittenham Oxon 18 B2
Little Wolford Warks 27 E9
Little Wratting Suff 30 D3
Little Wymington Bedford 28 B6
Little Wymondley Herts 29 F9
Little Wyrley Staffs 34 E6
Little Yeldham Essex 30 E4
Littlebeck N Yorks 59 F9
Littleborough Gtr Man 50 H5
Littleborough Notts 46 D2
Littlebourne Kent 21 F9
Littlebredy Dorset 8 F4
Littlebury Essex 30 E2
Littlebury Green Essex 29 E11
Littledean Glos 26 G3
Littleferry Highld 87 B11
Littleham Devon 5 C11
Littleham Devon 6 D3
Littlehampton W Sus 11 D9
Littlehempston Devon 5 E9
Littlehoughton Northumb 63 B8
Littlemill Aberds 82 D5
Littlemill E Ayrs 67 E7
Littlemill Highld 87 F12
Littlemill Northumb 63 B8
Littlemoor Dorset 8 F5
Littlemore Oxon 18 A2
Littleover Derby 35 B9
Littleport Cambs 38 G1
Littlestone on Sea Kent 13 D9
Littlethorpe Leics 35 F11
Littlethorpe N Yorks 51 C9
Littleton Ches W 43 F7
Littleton Hants 10 A3
Littleton Perth 76 D5
Littleton Som 8 A3
Littleton Sur 18 G6
Littleton Sur 19 E7
Littleton Drew Wilts 16 C5
Littleton-on-Severn S Glos 16 C2
Littleton Pannell Wilts 17 F7
Littletown Durham 58 B4
Littlewick Green Windsor 18 D5
Littleworth Bedford 29 D7
Littleworth Glos 16 A5
Littleworth Oxon 17 B10
Littleworth Staffs 34 D6
Littleworth Worcs 26 C5
Litton Derbys 44 E5
Litton N Yorks 50 B5
Litton Som 16 F2
Litton Cheney Dorset 8 E4
Liurbost W Isles 91 E8
Liverpool Mers 42 C6
Liverpool Airport Mers 43 D7
Liversedge W Yorks 51 G8
Liverton Devon 5 D9
Liverton Redcar 59 E8
Livingston W Loth 69 D9
Livingston Village W Loth 69 D9
Lixwm Flint 42 E4
Lizard Corn 2 H6
Llaingoch Anglesey 40 B4
Llaithddu Powys 33 G6
Llan Powys 32 E4
Llan Ffestiniog Gwyn 41 F9
Llan-y-pwll Wrex 42 G6
Llanaber Gwyn 32 D2
Llanaelhaearn Gwyn 40 F5
Llanafan Ceredig 24 A3
Llanafan-fawr Powys 24 C6
Llanallgo Anglesey 40 B6
Llanandras = Presteigne Powys 25 B10
Llanarmon Gwyn 40 G6
Llanarmon Dyffryn Ceiriog Wrex 33 B7
Llanarmon-yn-Ial Denb 42 G4
Llanarth Ceredig 23 A9
Llanarth Mon 25 G10
Llanarthne Carms 23 D10
Llanasa Flint 42 D4
Llanbabo Anglesey 40 B5
Llanbadarn Fawr Ceredig 32 G2
Llanbadarn Fynydd Powys 33 H7
Llanbadarn-y-Garreg Powys 25 D8
Llanbadoc Mon 15 B9
Llanbadrig Anglesey 40 A5
Llanbeder Newport 15 B9
Llanbedr Gwyn 32 C1
Llanbedr Powys 25 D8
Llanbedr Powys 25 F9
Llanbedr-Dyffryn-Clwyd Denb 42 G4
Llanbedr Pont Steffan = Lampeter Ceredig 23 B10
Llanbedr-y-cennin Conwy 41 D9
Llanbedrgoch Anglesey 41 B7
Llanbedrog Gwyn 40 G5
Llanberis Gwyn 41 D7
Llanbethêry V Glam 14 E6
Llanbister Powys 25 A8
Llanblethian V Glam 14 D5
Llanboidy Carms 23 D7
Llanbradach Caerph 15 B7
Llanbrynmair Powys 32 E4
Llancarfan V Glam 14 D6
Llancayo Mon 15 A9
Llancloudy Hereford 25 F11
Llancynfelyn Ceredig 32 F2
Llandaff Cardiff 15 D7
Llandanwg Gwyn 32 C1
Llandarcy Neath 14 B3
Llandawke Carms 23 E7
Llanddaniel Fab Anglesey 40 C6
Llanddarog Carms 23 E10
Llanddeiniol Ceredig 24 A2
Llanddeiniolen Gwyn 41 D7
Llandderfel Gwyn 32 B5
Llanddeusant Anglesey 40 B5
Llanddeusant Carms 24 F4
Llanddew Powys 25 E7
Llanddewi Swansea 23 H9
Llanddewi-Brefi Ceredig 24 C3
Llanddewi Rhydderch Mon 25 G10
Llanddewi Velfrey Pembs 22 E6
Llanddewi'r Cwm Powys 25 D7
Llanddoged Conwy 41 D10
Llanddona Anglesey 41 C7
Llanddowror Carms 23 E7
Llanddulas Conwy 42 E2
Llanddwywe Gwyn 32 C1
Llanddyfynan Anglesey 41 C7
Llandefaelog Fach Powys 25 E7
Llandefaelog-tre'r-graig Powys 25 F8
Llandefalle Powys 25 E8
Llandegai Gwyn 41 C7
Llandegfan Anglesey 41 C7
Llandegla Denb 42 G4
Llandegley Powys 25 B8
Llandegveth Mon 15 B9
Llandegwning Gwyn 40 G4
Llandeilo Carms 24 F3
Llandeilo Graban Powys 25 D7
Llandeilo'r Fan Powys 24 E5
Llandeloy Pembs 22 D3
Llandenny Mon 15 A10
Llandevenny Mon 15 C10
Llandewednock Corn 2 H6
Llandewi Ystradenny Powys 25 B8
Llandinabo Hereford 26 F2
Llandinam Powys 32 G6
Llandissilio Pembs 22 D6
Llandogo Mon 15 A11
Llandough V Glam 14 D5
Llandough V Glam 15 D7
Llandovery = Llanymddyfri Carms 24 E4
Llandow V Glam 14 D5
Llandre Carms 24 D3
Llandre Ceredig 32 G2
Llandrillo Denb 32 B6
Llandrillo-yn-Rhos Conwy 41 B10
Llandrindod = Llandrindod Wells Powys 25 B7
Llandrindod Wells = Llandrindod Powys 25 B7
Llandrinio Powys 33 D8
Llandudno Conwy 41 B9
Llandudno Junction = Cyffordd Llandudno Conwy 41 C9
Llandwrog Gwyn 40 E6
Llandybie Carms 24 G3
Llandyfaelog Carms 23 E9
Llandyfan Carms 24 G3
Llandyfriog Ceredig 23 B8
Llandyfrydog Anglesey 40 B6
Llandygwydd Ceredig 23 B7
Llandynan Denb 42 H4
Llandyrnog Denb 42 F4
Llandysilio Powys 33 D8
Llandyssil Powys 33 F7
Llandysul Ceredig 23 B9
Llanedeyrn Cardiff 15 C8
Llanedi Carms 23 F10
Llaneglwys Powys 25 E7
Llanegryn Gwyn 32 E1
Llanegwad Carms 23 D10
Llaneilian Anglesey 40 A6
Llanelian-yn-Rhos Conwy 41 C10
Llanelidan Denb 42 G4
Llanelieu Powys 25 E8
Llanellen Mon 25 G10
Llanelli Carms 23 G10
Llanelltyd Gwyn 32 D3
Llanelly Mon 25 G9
Llanelly Hill Mon 25 G9
Llanelwedd Powys 25 C7
Llanelwy = St Asaph Denb 42 E3
Llanenddwyn Gwyn 32 C1
Llanengan Gwyn 40 H4
Llanerchymedd Anglesey 40 B6
Llanerfyl Powys 32 E6
Llanfachraeth Anglesey 40 B5
Llanfachreth Gwyn 32 C3
Llanfaelog Anglesey 40 C5
Llanfaelrhys Gwyn 40 H4
Llanfaenor Mon 25 G11
Llanfaes Anglesey 41 C8
Llanfaes Powys 25 F7
Llanfaethlu Anglesey 40 B5
Llanfaglan Gwyn 40 D6
Llanfair Gwyn 32 C1
Llanfair-ar-y-bryn Carms 24 E5
Llanfair Caereinion Powys 33 E7
Llanfair Clydogau Ceredig 24 C3
Llanfair-Dyffryn-Clwyd Denb 42 G4
Llanfair Kilgheddin Mon 25 H10
Llanfair-Nant-Gwyn Pembs 22 C6
Llanfair Talhaiarn Conwy 42 E2
Llanfair Waterdine Shrops 33 H8
Llanfair-ym-Muallt = Builth Wells Powys 25 C7
Llanfairfechan Conwy 41 C8
Llanfairpwll-gwyngyll Anglesey 41 C7
Llanfairyneubwll Anglesey 40 C5
Llanfairynghornwy Anglesey 40 A5
Llanfallteg Carms 22 E6
Llanfaredd Powys 25 C7
Llanfarian Ceredig 32 H1
Llanfechain Powys 33 C7
Llanfechan Powys 24 C6
Llanfechell Anglesey 40 A5
Llanfendigaid Gwyn 32 E1
Llanferres Denb 42 F4
Llanfflewyn Anglesey 40 B5
Llanfihangel-ar-arth Carms 23 C9
Llanfihangel-Crucorney Mon 25 F10
Llanfihangel Glyn Myfyr Conwy 42 H2
Llanfihangel Nant Bran Powys 24 E6
Llanfihangel-nant-Melan Powys 25 C8
Llanfihangel Rhydithon Powys 25 B8
Llanfihangel Rogiet Mon 15 C10
Llanfihangel Tal-y-llyn Powys 25 F8
Llanfihangel-uwch-Gwili Carms 23 D9
Llanfihangel-y-Creuddyn Ceredig 32 H2
Llanfihangel-y-pennant Gwyn 32 E2
Llanfihangel-y-pennant Gwyn 41 F7
Llanfihangel-y-traethau Gwyn 41 G7
Llanfihangel-yn-Ngwynfa Powys 33 D6
Llanfihangel yn Nhowyn Anglesey 40 C5
Llanfilo Powys 25 E8
Llanfoist Mon 25 G9
Llanfor Gwyn 32 B5
Llanfrechfa Torf 15 B9
Llanfrothen Gwyn 41 F8
Llanfrynach Powys 25 F7
Llanfwrog Anglesey 40 B5
Llanfwrog Denb 42 G4
Llanfyllin Powys 33 D7
Llanfynydd Carms 23 D10
Llanfynydd Flint 42 G5
Llanfyrnach Pembs 23 C7
Llangadfan Powys 32 D6
Llangadog Carms 24 F4
Llangadwaladr Anglesey 40 D5
Llangadwaladr Powys 33 B7
Llangaffo Anglesey 40 D6
Llangain Carms 23 E8
Llangammarch Wells Powys 24 D6
Llangan V Glam 14 D5
Llangarron Hereford 26 F2
Llangasty Talyllyn Powys 25 F8
Llangathen Carms 23 D10
Llangattock Powys 25 G9
Llangattock Lingoed Mon 25 F10
Llangattock nigh Usk Mon 25 H10
Llangattock-Vibon-Avel Mon 25 G11
Llangedwyn Powys 33 C7
Llangefni Anglesey 40 C6
Llangeinor Bridgend 14 C5
Llangeitho Ceredig 24 C3
Llangeler Carms 23 C8
Llangelynin Gwyn 32 E1
Llangendeirne Carms 23 E9
Llangennech Carms 23 F10
Llangennith Swansea 23 G9
Llangenny Powys 25 G9
Llangernyw Conwy 41 D10
Llangian Gwyn 40 H4
Llanglydwen Carms 22 D6
Llangoed Anglesey 41 C8
Llangoedmor Ceredig 22 B6
Llangollen Denb 33 A8
Llangolman Pembs 22 D6
Llangors Powys 25 F8
Llangovan Mon 25 H11
Llangower Gwyn 32 B5
Llangrannog Ceredig 23 A8
Llangristiolus Anglesey 40 C6
Llangrove Hereford 26 G2
Llangua Mon 25 F10
Llangunllo Powys 25 A9
Llangunnor Carms 23 E9
Llangurig Powys 32 H5
Llangwm Conwy 32 A5
Llangwm Mon 15 A10
Llangwm Pembs 22 F4
Llangwnnadl Gwyn 40 G4
Llangwyfan Denb 42 F4
Llangwyfan-isaf Anglesey 40 D5
Llangwyllog Anglesey 40 C6
Llangwyryfon Ceredig 24 A2
Llangybi Ceredig 24 C3
Llangybi Gwyn 40 F6
Llangybi Mon 15 B9
Llangyfelach Swansea 14 B2
Llangynhafal Denb 42 F4
Llangynidr Powys 25 G8
Llangynin Carms 23 E7
Llangynog Carms 23 E8
Llangynog Powys 33 C6
Llangynwyd Bridgend 14 C4
Llanhamlach Powys 25 F7
Llanharan Rhondda 14 C6
Llanharry Rhondda 14 C6
Llanhennock Mon 15 B9
Llanhiledd = Llanhilleth Bl Gwent 15 A8
Llanhilleth = Llanhiledd Bl Gwent 15 A8
Llanidloes Powys 32 G5
Llaniestyn Gwyn 40 G4
Llanifyny Powys 32 G4
Llanigon Powys 25 E9
Llanilar Ceredig 24 A3
Llanilid Rhondda 14 C5
Llanilltud Fawr = Llantwit Major V Glam 14 E5
Llanishen Cardiff 15 C7
Llanishen Mon 15 A10
Llanllawddog Carms 23 D9
Llanllechid Gwyn 41 D8
Llanllowell Mon 15 B9
Llanllugan Powys 33 E6
Llanllwch Carms 23 E8
Llanllwchaiarn Powys 33 F7
Llanllwni Carms 23 C9
Llanllyfni Gwyn 40 E6
Llanmadoc Swansea 23 G9
Llanmaes V Glam 14 E5
Llanmartin Newport 15 C9
Llanmihangel V Glam 14 D5
Llanmorlais Swansea 23 G10
Llannefydd Conwy 42 E2
Llannon Carms 23 F10
Llannor Gwyn 40 G5
Llanon Ceredig 24 B2
Llanover Mon 25 H10
Llanpumsaint Carms 23 D9
Llanreithan Pembs 22 D3
Llanrhaeadr Denb 42 F3
Llanrhaeadr-ym-Mochnant Powys 33 C7
Llanrhian Pembs 22 C3
Llanrhidian Swansea 23 G9
Llanrhos Conwy 41 B9
Llanrhyddlad Anglesey 40 B5
Llanrhystud Ceredig 24 B2
Llanrosser Hereford 25 E9
Llanrothal Hereford 25 G11
Llanrug Gwyn 41 D7
Llanrumney Cardiff 15 C8
Llanrwst Conwy 41 D10
Llansadurnen Carms 23 E7
Llansadwrn Anglesey 41 C7
Llansadwrn Carms 24 E3
Llansaint Carms 23 F8
Llansamlet Swansea 14 B2
Llansannan Conwy 42 F2
Llansannor V Glam 14 D5
Llansantffraed Ceredig 24 B2
Llansantffraed Powys 25 F8
Llansantffraed Cwmdeuddwr Powys 24 B6
Llansantffraed-in-Elvel Powys 25 C7
Llansantffraid-ym-Mechain Powys 33 C8
Llansawel Carms 24 E3
Llansilin Powys 33 C8
Llansoy Mon 15 A10
Llanspyddid Powys 25 F7
Llanstadwell Pembs 22 F4
Llansteffan Carms 23 E8
Llanstephan Powys 25 D8
Llantarnam Torf 15 B9
Llanteg Pembs 22 E6
Llanthony Mon 25 F9
Llantilio Crossenny Mon 25 G10
Llantilio Pertholey Mon 25 G10
Llantood Pembs 22 B6
Llantrisant Anglesey 40 B5
Llantrisant Mon 15 B9
Llantrisant Rhondda 14 C6
Llantrithyd V Glam 14 D6
Llantwit Fardre Rhondda 14 C6
Llantwit Major = Llanilltud Fawr V Glam 14 E5
Llanuwchllyn Gwyn 41 G10
Llanvaches Newport 15 B10
Llanvair Discoed Mon 15 B10
Llanvapley Mon 25 G10
Llanvetherine Mon 25 G10
Llanveynoe Hereford 25 E10
Llanvihangel Gobion Mon 25 H10
Llanvihangel-Ystern-Llewern Mon 25 G11
Llanwarne Hereford 26 F2
Llanwddyn Powys 32 D6
Llanwenog Ceredig 23 B9
Llanwern Newport 15 C9
Llanwinio Carms 23 D7
Llanwnda Gwyn 40 E6
Llanwnda Pembs 22 C4
Llanwnnen Ceredig 23 B10
Llanwnog Powys 32 F6
Llanwrda Carms 24 E4
Llanwrin Powys 32 E3
Llanwrthwl Powys 24 B6
Llanwrtud = Llanwrtyd Wells Powys 24 D5
Llanwrtyd Powys 24 D5
Llanwrtyd Wells = Llanwrtud Powys 24 D5
Llanwyddelan Powys 33 E6
Llanyblodwel Shrops 33 C8
Llanybri Carms 23 E8
Llanybydder Carms 23 B10
Llanycefn Pembs 22 D5
Llanychaer Pembs 22 C4
Llanycil Gwyn 32 B5
Llanycrwys Carms 24 D3
Llanymawddwy Gwyn 32 D5
Llanymddyfri = Llandovery Carms 24 E4
Llanymynech Powys 33 C8
Llanynghenedl Anglesey 40 B5
Llanynys Denb 42 F4
Llanyre Powys 25 B7
Llanystumdwy Gwyn 40 G6
Llanywern Powys 25 F8
Llawhaden Pembs 22 E5
Llawnt Shrops 33 B8
Llawr Dref Gwyn 40 H4
Llawryglyn Powys 32 F5
Llay Wrex 42 G6
Llechcynfarwy Anglesey 40 B5
Llecheiddior Gwyn 40 F6
Llechfaen Powys 25 F7
Llechryd Caerph 25 H8
Llechryd Ceredig 23 B7
Llechrydau Powys 33 B8
Lledrod Ceredig 24 A3
Llenmerewig Powys 33 F7
Llethrid Swansea 23 G10
Llidiad Nenog Carms 23 C10
Llidiardau Gwyn 41 G10
Llidiart-y-parc Denb 33 A7
Llithfaen Gwyn 40 F5
Llong Flint 42 F5
Llowes Powys 25 D8
Llundain-fach Ceredig 23 A10
Llwydcoed Rhondda 14 A5
Llwyn Shrops 33 G8
Llwyn-du Mon 25 G9
Llwyn-hendy Carms 23 G10
Llwyn-têg Carms 23 F10
Llwyn-y-brain Carms 22 E6
Llwyn-y-groes Ceredig 23 A10
Llwyncelyn Ceredig 23 A9
Llwyndafydd Ceredig 23 A8
Llwynderw Powys 33 E8
Llwyndyrys Gwyn 40 F5
Llwyngwril Gwyn 32 E1
Llwynmawr Wrex 33 B8
Llwynypia Rhondda 14 B5
Llynclys Shrops 33 C8
Llynfaes Anglesey 40 C6
Llys-y-frân Pembs 22 D5
Llysfaen Conwy 41 C10
Llyswen Powys 25 E8
Llysworney V Glam 14 D5
Llywel Powys 24 E5
Loan Falk 69 C8
Loanend Northumb 71 E8
Loanhead Midloth 69 D11
Loans S Ayrs 66 C6
Loans of Tullich Highld 87 D11
Lobb Devon 6 C3
Loch a Charnain W Isles 84 D3
Loch a' Ghainmhich W Isles 91 E7
Loch Baghasdail = Lochboisdale W Isles 84 G2
Loch Choire Lodge Highld 93 F9
Loch Euphoirt W Isles 84 B3
Loch Head Dumfries 54 E6
Loch Loyal Lodge Highld 93 E9
Loch nam Madadh = Lochmaddy W Isles 84 B4
Loch Sgioport W Isles 84 E3
Lochailort Highld 79 C10
Lochaline Highld 79 G9
Lochanhully Highld 81 A11
Lochans Dumfries 54 D3
Locharbriggs Dumfries 60 E5
Lochassynt Lodge Highld 92 G4
Lochavich Ho Argyll 73 B8
Lochawe Argyll 74 E4
Lochboisdale = Loch Baghasdail W Isles 84 G2
Lochbuie Argyll 79 J9
Lochcarron Highld 85 E13
Lochdhu Highld 93 E13
Lochdochart House Stirling 75 E7
Lochdon Argyll 79 H10
Lochdrum Highld 86 D5
Lochead Argyll 72 F6
Lochearnhead Stirling 75 E8
Lochee Dundee 76 D6
Lochend Highld 87 H8
Lochend Highld 94 D4
Locherben Dumfries 60 D5
Lochfoot Dumfries 60 F4
Lochgair Argyll 73 D8
Lochgarthside Highld 81 B7
Lochgelly Fife 69 A10
Lochgilphead Argyll 73 E7
Lochgoilhead Argyll 74 G5
Lochhill Moray 88 B2
Lochindorb Lodge Highld 87 H12
Lochinver Highld 92 G3
Lochlane Perth 75 E11
Lochluichart Highld 86 E6
Lochmaben Dumfries 60 E6
Lochmaddy = Loch nam Madadh W Isles 84 B4
Lochmore Cottage Highld 94 F2
Lochmore Lodge Highld 92 F5
Lochore Fife 76 H4
Lochportain W Isles 84 A4
Lochranza N Ayrs 66 A2
Lochs Crofts Moray 88 B3
Lochside Aberds 77 A10
Lochside Highld 87 F11
Lochside Highld 92 D7
Lochside Highld 93 F11
Lochslin Highld 87 C11
Lochstack Lodge Highld 92 E5
Lochton Aberds 83 D9
Lochty Angus 77 A8
Lochty Fife 77 G8
Lochty Perth 76 E3
Lochuisge Highld 79 F10
Lochurr Dumfries 60 E3
Lochwinnoch Renfs 68 E2
Lochwood Dumfries 60 D6
Lochyside Highld 80 F3
Lockengate Corn 3 C9
Lockerbie Dumfries 61 E7
Lockeridge Wilts 17 E8
Lockerley Hants 10 B1
Locking N Som 15 F9
Lockinge Oxon 17 C11
Lockington E Yorks 52 E5
Lockington Leics 35 C10
Lockleywood Shrops 34 C2
Locks Heath Hants 10 D4
Lockton N Yorks 59 G9
Lockwood W Yorks 51 H7
Loddington Leics 36 E3
Loddington Northants 36 H4
Loddiswell Devon 5 G8
Loddon Norf 39 F9
Lode Cambs 30 B2
Loders Dorset 8 E3
Lodsworth W Sus 11 B8
Lofthouse N Yorks 51 B7
Lofthouse W Yorks 51 G9
Loftus Redcar 59 E8
Logan E Ayrs 67 D8
Logan Mains Dumfries 54 E3
Loganlea W Loth 69 D8
Loggerheads Staffs 34 B3
Logie Angus 77 A9
Logie Fife 77 E7
Logie Moray 87 F13
Logie Coldstone Aberds 82 C6
Logie Hill Highld 87 D10
Logie Newton Aberds 89 E6
Logie Pert Angus 77 A9
Logiealmond Lodge Perth 76 D2
Logierait Perth 76 B2
Login Carms 22 D6
Lolworth Cambs 29 B10
Lonbain Highld 85 C11
Londesborough E Yorks 52 E4
London Colney Herts 19 A8
Londonderry N Yorks 58 H4
Londonthorpe Lincs 36 B5
Londubh Highld 91 J13
Lonemore Highld 87 C10
Long Ashton N Som 15 D11
Long Bennington Lincs 36 A4
Long Bredy Dorset 8 E4
Long Buckby Northants 28 B3
Long Clawson Leics 36 C3
Long Common Hants 10 C4
Long Compton Staffs 34 C4
Long Compton Warks 27 E9
Long Crendon Bucks 28 H3
Long Crichel Dorset 9 C8
Long Ditton Sur 19 E8
Long Drax N Yorks 52 G2
Long Duckmanton Derbys 45 E8
Long Eaton Derbys 35 B10
Long Green Worcs 26 E5
Long Hanborough Oxon 27 G11
Long Itchington Warks 27 B11
Long Lawford Warks 35 H10
Long Load Som 8 B3
Long Marston Herts 28 G5
Long Marston N Yorks 51 D11
Long Marston Warks 27 D8
Long Marton Cumb 57 D8
Long Melford Suff 30 D5
Long Newnton Glos 16 B6
Long Newton E Loth 70 D4
Long Preston N Yorks 50 D4
Long Riston E Yorks 53 E7
Long Sight Gtr Man 44 B3
Long Stratton Norf 39 F7
Long Street M Keynes 28 D4
Long Sutton Hants 18 G4
Long Sutton Lincs 37 C10
Long Sutton Som 8 B3
Long Thurlow Suff 31 B7
Long Whatton Leics 35 C10
Long Wittenham Oxon 18 B2
Longbar N Ayrs 66 A6
Longbenton T&W 63 G8
Longborough Glos 27 F8
Longbridge W Mid 34 H6
Longbridge Warks 27 B9
Longbridge Deverill Wilts 16 G5
Longburton Dorset 8 C5
Longcliffe Derbys 44 G6
Longcot Oxon 17 B9
Longcroft Falk 68 C6
Longden Shrops 33 E10
Longdon Staffs 35 D6
Longdon Worcs 26 E5
Longdon Green Staffs 35 D6
Longdon on Tern Telford 34 D2
Longdown Devon 7 G7
Longdowns Corn 2 F6
Longfield Kent 20 E3
Longfield Shetland 96 M5
Longford Derbys 35 B8
Longford Glos 26 F5
Longford London 19 D7
Longford Shrops 34 B2
Longford Telford 34 D3
Longford W Mid 35 G9
Longfordlane Derbys 35 B8
Longforgan Perth 76 E6
Longformacus Borders 70 E5
Longframlington Northumb 63 C7
Longham Dorset 9 E9
Longham Norf 38 D5
Longhaven Aberds 89 E11
Longhill Aberds 89 C9
Longhirst Northumb 63 E8
Longhope Glos 26 G3
Longhope Orkney 95 J4
Longhorsley Northumb 63 D7
Longhoughton Northumb 63 B8
Longlane Derbys 35 B8
Longlane W Berks 17 D11
Longlevens Glos 26 F5
Longley W Yorks 44 B5
Longley Green Worcs 26 C4
Longmanhill Aberds 89 B7
Longmoor Camp Hants 11 A6
Longmorn Moray 88 C2
Longnewton Borders 70 H4
Longnewton Stockton 58 E4
Longney Glos 26 G4
Longniddry E Loth 70 C3
Longnor Shrops 33 E10
Longnor Staffs 44 F4
Longparish Hants 17 G11
Longport Stoke 44 H2
Longridge Lancs 50 F2
Longridge Staffs 34 D5
Longridge W Loth 69 D8
Longriggend N Lanark 69 C7
Longsdon Staffs 44 G3
Longshaw Gtr Man 43 B8
Longside Aberds 89 D10
Longstanton Cambs 29 B10
Longstock Hants 17 H10
Longstone Pembs 22 F6
Longstowe Cambs 29 C10
Longthorpe Pboro 37 F7
Longthwaite Cumb 56 D6
Longton Lancs 49 G4
Longton Stoke 34 A5
Longtown Cumb 61 G9
Longtown Hereford 25 F10
Longview Mers 43 C7
Longville in the Dale Shrops 33 F11
Longwick Bucks 28 H4
Longwitton Northumb 62 E6
Longwood Shrops 34 E2
Longworth Oxon 17 B10
Longyester E Loth 70 D4
Lonmay Aberds 89 C10
Lonmore Highld 84 D7
Looe Corn 4 F3
Loose Kent 20 F4
Loosley Row Bucks 18 A5
Lopcombe Corner Wilts 17 H9
Lopen Som 8 C3
Loppington Shrops 33 C10
Lopwell Devon 4 E5
Lorbottle Northumb 62 C6
Lorbottle Hall Northumb 62 C6
Lornty Perth 76 C4
Loscoe Derbys 45 H8
Losgaintir W Isles 90 H5
Lossiemouth Moray 88 A2
Lossit Argyll 64 C2
Lostford Shrops 34 B2
Lostock Gralam Ches W 43 E9
Lostock Green Ches W 43 E9
Lostock Hall Lancs 49 G5
Lostock Junction Gtr Man 43 B9
Lostwithiel Corn 4 F2
Loth Orkney 95 E7
Lothbeg Highld 93 H12
Lothersdale N Yorks 50 E5
Lothmore Highld 93 H12
Loudwater Bucks 18 B6
Loughborough Leics 35 D11
Loughor Swansea 23 G10
Loughton Essex 19 B11
Loughton M Keynes 28 E5
Loughton Shrops 34 G2
Lound Lincs 37 D6
Lound Notts 45 D10
Lound Suff 39 F11
Lount Leics 35 D9
Louth Lincs 47 D7
Love Clough Lancs 50 G4
Lovedean Hants 10 C5
Lover Wilts 9 B11
Loversall S Yorks 45 C9
Loves Green Essex 20 A3
Lovesome Hill N Yorks 58 G4
Loveston Pembs 22 F5
Lovington Som 8 A4
Low Ackworth W Yorks 51 H10
Low Barlings Lincs 46 E4
Low Bentham N Yorks 50 C2
Low Bradfield S Yorks 44 C6
Low Bradley N Yorks 50 E6
Low Braithwaite Cumb 56 B6
Low Brunton Northumb 62 F5
Low Burnham N Lincs 45 B11
Low Burton N Yorks 51 A8
Low Buston Northumb 63 C8
Low Catton E Yorks 52 D3
Low Clanyard Dumfries 54 F4
Low Coniscliffe Darl 58 E3
Low Crosby Cumb 61 H10
Low Dalby N Yorks 59 H9
Low Dinsdale Darl 58 E4
Low Ellington N Yorks 51 A8
Low Etherley Durham 58 D2
Low Fell T&W 63 H8
Low Fulney Lincs 37 C8
Low Garth N Yorks 59 F8
Low Gate Northumb 62 G5
Low Grantley N Yorks 51 B8
Low Habberley Worcs 34 H4
Low Ham Som 8 B3
Low Hesket Cumb 57 B6
Low Hesleyhurst Northumb 62 D6
Low Hutton N Yorks 52 C3
Low Laithe N Yorks 51 C7
Low Leighton Derbys 44 D4
Low Lorton Cumb 56 D3
Low Marishes N Yorks 52 B4
Low Marnham Notts 46 F2
Low Mill N Yorks 59 G7
Low Moor Lancs 50 E3
Low Moor W Yorks 51 G7
Low Moorsley T&W 58 B4
Low Newton Cumb 49 A4
Low Newton-by-the-Sea Northumb 63 A8
Low Row Cumb 56 C5
Low Row Cumb 61 G11
Low Row N Yorks 57 G11
Low Salchrie Dumfries 54 C3
Low Smerby Argyll 65 F8
Low Torry Fife 69 B9
Low Worsall N Yorks 58 F4
Low Wray Cumb 56 F5
Lowbridge House Cumb 57 F7
Lowca Cumb 56 D1
Lowdham Notts 45 H10
Lowe Shrops 33 B11
Lowe Hill Staffs 44 G3
Lower Aisholt Som 7 C11
Lower Arncott Oxon 28 G3
Lower Ashton Devon 5 C9
Lower Assendon Oxon 18 C4
Lower Badcall Highld 92 E4
Lower Bartle Lancs 49 F4
Lower Basildon W Berks 18 D3
Lower Beeding W Sus 11 B11
Lower Benefield Northants 36 G5
Lower Boddington Northants 27 C11
Lower Brailes Warks 27 E10
Lower Breakish Highld 85 F11
Lower Broadheath Worcs 26 C5
Lower Bullingham Hereford 26 E2
Lower Cam Glos 16 A4
Lower Chapel Powys 25 E7
Lower Chute Wilts 17 F10
Lower Cragabus Argyll 64 D4
Lower Crossings Derbys 44 D4
Lower Cumberworth W Yorks 44 B6
Lower Cwm-twrch Powys 24 G4
Lower Darwen Blackburn 50 G2
Lower Dean Bedford 29 B7
Lower Diabaig Highld 85 B12
Lower Dicker E Sus 12 E4
Lower Dinchope Shrops 33 G10
Lower Down Shrops 33 G9
Lower Drift Corn 2 G3
Lower Dunsforth N Yorks 51 C10
Lower Egleton Hereford 26 D3
Lower Elkstone Staffs 44 G4
Lower End C Beds 28 F6
Lower Everleigh Wilts 17 F8
Lower Farringdon Hants 18 H4
Lower Foxdale IoM 48 E2
Lower Frankton Shrops 33 B9
Lower Froyle Hants 18 G4
Lower Gledfield Highld 87 B8
Lower Green Norf 38 B5
Lower Hacheston Suff 31 C10
Lower Halistra Highld 84 C7
Lower Halstow Kent 20 E5
Lower Hardres Kent 21 F8
Lower Hawthwaite Cumb 56 H4
Lower Heath Ches E 44 F2
Lower Hempriggs Moray 87 E14
Lower Hergest Hereford 25 C9
Lower Heyford Oxon 27 F11
Lower Higham Kent 20 D4
Lower Holbrook Suff 31 E8
Lower Hordley Shrops 33 C9
Lower Horsebridge E Sus 12 E4
Lower Killeyan Argyll 64 D3
Lower Kingswood Sur 19 F9
Lower Kinnerton Ches W 42 F6
Lower Langford N Som 15 E10
Lower Largo Fife 77 G7
Lower Leigh Staffs 34 B6
Lower Lemington Glos 27 E9
Lower Lenie Highld 81 A7
Lower Lydbrook Glos 26 G2
Lower Lye Hereford 25 B11
Lower Machen Newport 15 C8
Lower Maes-coed Hereford 25 E10
Lower Mayland Essex 20 A6
Lower Midway Derbys 35 C9
Lower Milovaig Highld 84 C6
Lower Moor Worcs 26 D6
Lower Nazeing Essex 29 H10
Lower Netchwood Shrops 34 F2
Lower Ollach Highld 85 E10
Lower Penarth V Glam 15 D7
Lower Penn Staffs 34 F4
Lower Pennington Hants 10 E2
Lower Peover Ches W 43 E10
Lower Pexhill Ches E 44 E2
Lower Place Gtr Man 44 A3
Lower Quinton Warks 27 D8
Lower Rochford Worcs 26 B3
Lower Seagry Wilts 16 C6
Lower Shelton C Beds 28 D6
Lower Shiplake Oxon 18 D4
Lower Shuckburgh Warks 27 B11
Lower Slaughter Glos 27 F8
Lower Stanton St Quintin Wilts 16 C6
Lower Stoke Medway 20 D5
Lower Stondon C Beds 29 E8
Lower Stow Bedon Norf 38 F5
Lower Street Norf 39 B8
Lower Street Norf 39 D9
Lower Strensham Worcs 26 D6
Lower Stretton Warr 43 D9
Lower Sundon C Beds 29 F7
Lower Swanwick Hants 10 D3
Lower Swell Glos 27 F8
Lower Tean Staffs 34 B6
Lower Thurlton Norf 39 F10
Lower Tote Highld 85 B10
Lower Town Pembs 22 C4
Lower Tysoe Warks 27 D10
Lower Upham Hants 10 C4
Lower Vexford Som 7 C10
Lower Weare Som 15 F10
Lower Welson Hereford 25 C9
Lower Whitley Ches W 43 E9
Lower Wield Hants 18 G3
Lower Winchendon Bucks 28 G4
Lower Withington Ches E 44 F2
Lower Woodend Bucks 18 C5
Lower Woodford Wilts 9 A10
Lower Wyche Worcs 26 D4
Lowesby Leics 36 E3
Lowestoft Suff 39 F11
Loweswater Cumb 56 D3
Lowford Hants 10 C3
Lowgill Cumb 57 G8
Lowgill Lancs 50 C2
Lowick Northants 36 G5
Lowick Northumb 71 G9
Lowick Bridge Cumb 56 H4
Lowick Green Cumb 56 H4
Lowlands Torf 15 B8
Lowmoor Row Cumb 57 D8
Lownie Moor Angus 77 C7
Lowsonford Warks 27 B8
Lowther Cumb 57 D7
Lowthorpe E Yorks 53 C6
Lowton Gtr Man 43 C9
Lowton Common Gtr Man 43 C9
Loxbeare Devon 7 E8
Loxhill Sur 19 H7
Loxhore Devon 6 C5
Loxley Warks 27 C9
Loxton N Som 15 F9
Loxwood W Sus 11 A9
Lubcroy Highld 92 J6
Lubenham Leics 36 G3
Luccombe Som 7 B8
Luccombe Village IoW 10 G4
Lucker Northumb 71 G10
Luckett Corn 4 D4
Luckington Wilts 16 C5
Lucklawhill Fife 77 E7
Luckwell Bridge Som 7 C8
Lucton Hereford 25 B11
Ludag W Isles 84 G2
Ludborough Lincs 46 C6
Ludchurch Pembs 22 E6
Luddenden W Yorks 50 G6
Luddenden Foot W Yorks 50 G6
Luddesdown Kent 20 E3
Luddington N Lincs 52 H4
Luddington Warks 27 C8
Luddington in the Brook Northants 37 G7
Lude House Perth 81 G10
Ludford Lincs 46 D6
Ludford Shrops 26 A2
Ludgershall Bucks 28 G3
Ludgershall Wilts 17 F9
Ludgvan Corn 2 F4
Ludham Norf 39 D9
Ludlow Shrops 26 A2
Ludwell Wilts 9 B8
Ludworth Durham 58 B4
Luffincott Devon 6 G2
Lugar E Ayrs 67 D8
Lugg Green Hereford 25 B11
Luggate Burn E Loth 70 C5
Luggiebank N Lanark 68 C6
Lugton E Ayrs 67 A7
Lugwardine Hereford 26 D2
Luib Highld 85 F10
Lulham Hereford 25 D11
Lullenden Sur 12 B3
Lullington Derbys 35 D8
Lullington Som 16 F4
Lulsgate Bottom N Som 15 E11
Lulsley Worcs 26 C4
Lumb W Yorks 50 G6
Lumby N Yorks 51 F10
Lumloch E Dunb 68 D5
Lumphanan Aberds 83 C7
Lumphinnans Fife 69 A10
Lumsdaine Borders 71 D7
Lumsden Aberds 82 A6
Lunan Angus 77 B9
Lunanhead Angus 77 B7
Luncarty Perth 76 E3
Lund E Yorks 52 E5
Lund N Yorks 52 F2
Lund Shetland 96 C7
Lunderton Aberds 89 D11
Lundie Angus 76 D5
Lundie Highld 80 B3
Lundin Links Fife 77 G7
Lunga Argyll 72 C6
Lunna Shetland 96 G6
Lunning Shetland 96 G7
Lunnon Swansea 23 H10
Lunsford's Cross E Sus 12 E6
Lunt Mers 42 B6
Luntley Hereford 25 C10
Luppitt Devon 7 F10
Lupset W Yorks 51 H9
Lupton Cumb 50 A1
Lurgashall W Sus 11 B8
Lusby Lincs 47 F7
Luson Devon 5 G7
Luss Argyll 68 A2
Lussagiven Argyll 72 E5
Lusta Highld 85 C7
Lustleigh Devon 5 C8
Luston Hereford 25 B11
Luthermuir Aberds 83 G8
Luthrie Fife 76 F6
Luton Devon 5 D10
Luton Luton 29 F7
Luton Medway 20 E4

Lutterworth Leics 35 G11
Lutton Devon 5 F6
Lutton Lincs 37 C10
Lutton Northants 37 G7
Lutworthy Devon 7 E6
Luxborough Som 7 C8
Luxulyan Corn 4 F1
Lybster Highld 94 G4
Lydbury North Shrops 33 G9
Lydcott Devon 6 C5
Lydd Kent 13 D9
Lydd on Sea Kent 13 D9
Lydden Kent 21 G9
Lyddington Rutland 36 F4
Lyde Green Hants 18 F4
Lydeard St Lawrence Som 7 C10
Lydford Devon 4 C6
Lydford-on-Fosse Som 8 A4
Lydgate W Yorks 50 G5
Lydham Shrops 33 F9
Lydiard Green Wilts 17 C7
Lydiard Millicent Wilts 17 C7
Lydiate Mers 42 B6
Lydlinch Dorset 8 C6
Lydney Glos 16 A3
Lydstep Pembs 22 G5
Lye W Mid 34 G5
Lye Green Bucks 18 A6
Lye Green E Sus 12 C4
Lyford Oxon 17 B10
Lymbridge Green Kent 13 B10
Lyme Regis Dorset 8 E2
Lyminge Kent 21 G8
Lymington Hants 10 E2
Lyminster W Sus 11 D9
Lymm Warr 43 D9
Lymore Hants 10 E1
Lympne Kent 13 C10
Lympsham Som 15 F9
Lympstone Devon 5 C10
Lynchat Highld 81 C9
Lyndale Ho. Highld 85 C8
Lyndhurst Hants 10 D2
Lyndon Rutland 36 E5
Lyne Sur 19 E7
Lyne Down Hereford 26 E3
Lyne of Gorthleck Highld 81 A7
Lyne of Skene Aberds 83 B9
Lyneal Shrops 33 B10
Lyneham Oxon 27 F9
Lyneham Wilts 17 D7
Lynemore Highld 82 A2
Lynemouth Northumb 63 D8
Lyness Orkney 95 J4
Lyng Norf 39 D6
Lyng Som 8 B2
Lynmouth Devon 7 B6
Lynsted Kent 20 E6
Lynton Devon 6 B6
Lyon's Gate Dorset 8 D5
Lyonshall Hereford 25 C10
Lytchett Matravers Dorset 9 E8
Lytchett Minster Dorset 9 E8
Lyth Highld 94 D4
Lytham Lancs 49 G3
Lytham St Anne's Lancs 49 G3
Lythe N Yorks 59 E9
Lythes Orkney 95 K5

M

Mabe Burnthouse Corn 3 F6
Mabie Dumfries 60 F5
Mablethorpe Lincs 47 D9
Macclesfield Ches E 44 E3
Macclesfield Forest Ches E 44 E3
Macduff Aberds 89 B7
Mace Green Suff 31 D8
Macharioch Argyll 65 H8
Machen Caerph 15 C8
Machrihanish Argyll 65 F7
Machynlleth Powys 32 E3
Machynys Carms 23 G10
Mackerel's Common W Sus 11 B9
Mackworth Derbys 35 B9
Macmerry E Loth 70 C3
Madderty Perth 76 E2
Maddiston Falk 69 C8
Madehurst W Sus 11 C8
Madeley Staffs 34 A3
Madeley Telford 34 E2
Madeley Heath Staffs 43 H10
Madeley Park Staffs 34 A3
Madingley Cambs 29 B10
Madley Hereford 25 E11
Madresfield Worcs 26 D5
Madron Corn 2 F3
Maen-y-groes Ceredig 23 A8
Maenaddwyn Anglesey 40 B6
Maenclochog Pembs 22 D5
Maendy V Glam 14 D6
Maentwrog Gwyn 41 F8
Maer Staffs 34 B3
Maerdy Conwy 32 A6
Maerdy Rhondda 14 B5
Maes-Treylow Powys 25 B9
Maesbrook Shrops 33 C8
Maesbury Shrops 33 C9
Maesbury Marsh Shrops 33 C9
Maesgwyn-Isaf Powys 33 D7
Maesgwynne Carms 23 D7
Maeshafn Denb 42 F5
Maesllyn Ceredig 23 B8
Maesmynis Powys 25 D7
Maesteg Bridgend 14 B4
Maestir Ceredig 23 B10
Maesy cwmmer Caerph 15 B7
Maesybont Carms 23 E10
Maesycrugiau Carms 23 B9
Maesymeillion Ceredig 23 B9
Magdalen Laver Essex 30 H2
Maggieknockater Moray 88 D3
Magham Down E Sus 12 E5
Maghull Mers 43 B6
Magor Mon 15 C10
Magpie Green Suff 39 H6
Maiden Bradley Wilts 16 H5
Maiden Law Durham 58 B2
Maiden Newton Dorset 8 E4
Maiden Wells Pembs 22 G4
Maidencombe Torbay 5 E10
Maidenhall Suff 31 D8
Maidenhead Windsor 18 C5
Maidens S Ayrs 66 F5
Maiden's Green Brack 18 D5
Maidensgrave Suff 31 D9
Maidenwell Corn 4 D2
Maidenwell Lincs 47 E7
Maidford Northants 28 C3
Maids Moreton Bucks 28 E4
Maidstone Kent 20 F4
Maidwell Northants 36 H3
Mail Shetland 96 L6
Main Powys 33 D7
Maindee Newport 15 C9
Mains of Airies Dumfries 54 C2
Mains of Allardice Aberds 83 F10
Mains of Annochie Aberds 89 D9
Mains of Ardestie Angus 77 D8
Mains of Balhall Angus 77 A8
Mains of Ballindarg Angus 77 B7
Mains of Balnakettle Aberds 83 F8
Mains of Birness Aberds 89 E9
Mains of Burgie Moray 87 F13
Mains of Clunas Highld 87 G11
Mains of Crichie Aberds 89 D9
Mains of Dalvey Highld 87 H14
Mains of Dellavaird Aberds 83 E9
Mains of Drum Aberds 83 D10
Mains of Edingight Moray 88 C5
Mains of Fedderate Aberds 89 D8
Mains of Inkhorn Aberds 89 E9
Mains of Mayen Moray 88 D5
Mains of Melgund Angus 77 B8
Mains of Thornton Aberds 83 F8
Mains of Watten Highld 94 E4
Mainsforth Durham 58 C4
Mainsriddle Dumfries 60 H5
Mainstone Shrops 33 G8
Maisemore Glos 26 F5
Malacleit W Isles 84 A2
Malborough Devon 5 H8
Malcoff Derbys 44 D4
Maldon Essex 30 H5
Malham N Yorks 50 C5
Maligar Highld 85 B9
Mallaig Highld 79 B9
Malleny Mills Edin 69 D10
Malling Stirling 75 G8
Malltraeth Anglesey 40 D6
Mallwyd Gwyn 32 D4
Malmesbury Wilts 16 C6
Malmsmead Devon 7 B6
Malpas Ches W 43 H7
Malpas Corn 3 E7
Malpas Newport 15 B9
Malswick Glos 26 F4
Maltby S Yorks 45 C9
Maltby Stockton 58 E5
Maltby le Marsh Lincs 47 D8
Malting Green Essex 30 F6
Maltman's Hill Kent 13 B8
Malton N Yorks 52 B3
Malvern Link Worcs 26 D4
Malvern Wells Worcs 26 D4
Mamble Worcs 26 A3
Man-moel Caerph 15 A7
Manaccan Corn 3 G6
Manafon Powys 33 E7
Manais W Isles 90 J6
Manar Ho. Aberds 83 A9
Manaton Devon 5 C8
Manby Lincs 47 D7
Mancetter Warks 35 F9
Manchester Gtr Man 44 C2
Manchester Airport Gtr Man 44 D2
Mancot Flint 42 F6
Mandally Highld 80 C4
Manea Cambs 37 G10
Manfield N Yorks 58 E3
Mangaster Shetland 96 F5
Mangotsfield S Glos 16 D3
Mangurstadh W Isles 90 D5
Mankinholes W Yorks 50 G5
Manley Ches W 43 E8
Mannal Argyll 78 G2
Mannerston W Loth 69 C9
Manningford Bohune Wilts 17 F8
Manningford Bruce Wilts 17 F8
Manningham W Yorks 51 F7
Mannings Heath W Sus 11 B11
Mannington Dorset 9 D9
Manningtree Essex 31 E7
Mannofield Aberdeen 83 C11
Manor London 19 C11
Manor Estate S Yorks 45 D7
Manorbier Pembs 22 G5
Manordeilo Carms 24 F3
Manorhill Borders 70 G5
Manorowen Pembs 22 C4
Mansel Lacy Hereford 25 D11
Manselfield Swansea 23 H10
Mansell Gamage Hereford 25 D10
Mansergh Cumb 50 A2
Mansfield E Ayrs 67 E9
Mansfield Notts 45 F9
Mansfield Woodhouse Notts 45 F9
Mansriggs Cumb 49 A2
Manston Dorset 9 C7
Manston Kent 21 E10
Manston W Yorks 51 F9
Manswood Dorset 9 D8
Manthorpe Lincs 36 B5
Manthorpe Lincs 37 D6
Manton N Lincs 46 B3
Manton Notts 45 E9
Manton Rutland 36 E4
Manton Wilts 17 E8
Manuden Essex 29 F11
Maperton Som 8 B5
Maple Cross Herts 19 B7
Maplebeck Notts 45 F11
Mapledurham Oxon 18 D3
Mapledurwell Hants 18 F3
Maplehurst W Sus 11 B10
Maplescombe Kent 20 E2
Mapleton Derbys 44 H5
Mapperley Derbys 35 A10
Mapperley Park Nottingham 36 A1
Mapperton Dorset 8 E4
Mappleborough Green Warks 27 B7
Mappleton E Yorks 53 E8
Mappowder Dorset 8 D6
Mar Lodge Aberds 82 D2
Maraig W Isles 90 G6
Marazanvose Corn 3 D7
Marazion Corn 2 F4
Marbhig W Isles 91 F9
Marbury Ches E 43 H8
March Cambs 37 F10
March S Lanark 60 B5
Marcham Oxon 17 B11
Marchamley Shrops 34 C1
Marchington Staffs 35 B7
Marchington Woodlands Staffs 35 C7
Marchroes Gwyn 40 H5
Marchwiel Wrex 42 H6
Marchwood Hants 10 C2
Marcross V Glam 14 E5
Marden Hereford 26 D2
Marden Kent 12 B6
Marden T&W 63 F9
Marden Wilts 17 F7
Marden Beech Kent 12 B6
Marden Thorn Kent 13 B6
Mardy Mon 25 G10
Marefield Leics 36 E3
Mareham le Fen Lincs 46 F6
Mareham on the Hill Lincs 46 F6
Marehay Derbys 45 H7
Marehill W Sus 11 C9
Maresfield E Sus 12 D3
Marfleet Hull 53 G7
Marford Wrex 42 G6
Margam Neath 14 C3
Margaret Marsh Dorset 9 C7
Margaret Roding Essex 30 G2
Margaretting Essex 20 A3
Margate Kent 21 D10
Margnaheglish N Ayrs 66 C3
Margrove Park Redcar 59 E7
Marham Norf 38 D3
Marhamchurch Corn 4 A3
Marholm Pboro 37 E7
Mariandyrys Anglesey 41 B8
Marianglas Anglesey 41 B7
Mariansleigh Devon 7 D6
Marionburgh Aberds 83 C9
Marishader Highld 85 B9
Marjoriebanks Dumfries 60 E6
Mark Dumfries 54 D4
Mark S Ayrs 54 B3
Mark Som 15 G9
Mark Causeway Som 15 G9
Mark Cross E Sus 12 C4
Mark Cross E Sus 12 E3
Markbeech Kent 12 B3
Markby Lincs 47 E8
Market Bosworth Leics 35 E10
Market Deeping Lincs 37 E7
Market Drayton Shrops 34 B2
Market Harborough Leics 36 G3
Market Lavington Wilts 17 F7
Market Overton Rutland 36 D4
Market Rasen Lincs 46 D5
Market Stainton Lincs 46 E6
Market Warsop Notts 45 F9
Market Weighton E Yorks 52 E4
Market Weston Suff 38 H5
Markethill Perth 76 D5
Markfield Leics 35 D10
Markham Caerph 15 A7
Markham Moor Notts 45 E11
Markinch Fife 76 G5
Markington N Yorks 51 C8
Marks Tey Essex 30 F6
Marksbury Bath 16 E3
Markyate Herts 29 G7
Marland Gtr Man 44 A2
Marlborough Wilts 17 E8
Marlbrook Hereford 26 C2
Marlbrook Worcs 26 A6
Marlcliff Warks 27 C7
Marldon Devon 5 E9
Marlesford Suff 31 C10
Marley Green Ches E 43 H8
Marley Hill T&W 63 H8
Marley Mount Hants 10 E1
Marlingford Norf 39 E7
Marloes Pembs 22 F2
Marlow Bucks 18 C5
Marlow Hereford 33 H10
Marlow Bottom Bucks 18 C5
Marlpit Hill Kent 19 G11
Marlpool Derbys 45 H8
Marnhull Dorset 9 C6
Marnoch Aberds 88 C5
Marnock N Lanark 68 D6
Marple Gtr Man 44 D3
Marple Bridge Gtr Man 44 D3
Marr S Yorks 45 B9
Marrel Highld 93 H13
Marrick N Yorks 58 G1
Marrister Shetland 96 G7
Marros Carms 23 F7
Marsden T&W 63 G9
Marsden W Yorks 44 A4
Marsett N Yorks 57 H11
Marsh Devon 8 C1
Marsh W Yorks 50 F6
Marsh Baldon Oxon 18 B2
Marsh Gibbon Bucks 28 F3
Marsh Green Devon 7 G9
Marsh Green Kent 12 B3
Marsh Green Staffs 44 G2
Marsh Lane Derbys 45 E8
Marsh Street Som 7 B8
Marshall's Heath Herts 29 G8
Marshalsea Dorset 8 D2
Marshalswick Herts 29 H8
Marsham Norf 39 C7
Marshaw Lancs 50 D1
Marshborough Kent 21 F10
Marshbrook Shrops 33 G10
Marshchapel Lincs 47 C7
Marshfield Newport 15 C8
Marshfield S Glos 16 D4
Marshgate Corn 4 B2
Marshland St James Norf 37 E11
Marshside Mers 49 H3
Marshwood Dorset 8 E2
Marske N Yorks 58 F2
Marske-by-the-Sea Redcar 59 D7
Marston Ches W 43 E9
Marston Hereford 25 C10
Marston Lincs 36 A4
Marston Oxon 28 H2
Marston Staffs 34 C5
Marston Staffs 34 D4
Marston Warks 35 F8
Marston Wilts 16 F6
Marston Doles Warks 27 C11
Marston Green W Mid 35 G7
Marston Magna Som 8 B4
Marston Meysey Wilts 17 B8
Marston Montgomery Derbys 35 B7
Marston Moretaine C Beds 28 D6
Marston on Dove Derbys 35 C8
Marston St Lawrence Northants 28 D2
Marston Stannett Hereford 26 C2
Marston Trussell Northants 36 G2
Marstow Hereford 26 G2
Marsworth Bucks 28 G6
Marten Wilts 17 F9
Marthall Ches E 44 E2
Martham Norf 39 D10
Martin Hants 9 C9
Martin Kent 21 G10
Martin Lincs 46 F6
Martin Lincs 46 G5
Martin Dales Lincs 46 F5
Martin Drove End Hants 9 B9
Martin Hussingtree Worcs 26 B5
Martin Mill Kent 21 G10
Martinhoe Devon 6 B5
Martinhoe Cross Devon 6 B5
Martinscroft Warr 43 D9
Martinstown Dorset 8 F5
Martlesham Suff 31 D9
Martlesham Heath Suff 31 D9
Martletwy Pembs 22 E5
Martley Worcs 26 C4
Martock Som 8 C3
Marton Ches E 44 F2
Marton E Yorks 53 F7
Marton Lincs 46 D2
Marton Mbro 58 E6
Marton N Yorks 51 C10
Marton N Yorks 52 A3
Marton Shrops 33 C10
Marton Shrops 33 E8
Marton Warks 27 B11
Marton-le-Moor N Yorks 51 B9
Martyr Worthy Hants 10 A4
Martyr's Green Sur 19 F7
Marwick Orkney 95 F3
Marwood Devon 6 C4
Mary Tavy Devon 4 D6
Marybank Highld 86 F7
Maryburgh Highld 87 F8
Maryhill Glasgow 68 D4
Marykirk Aberds 83 G8
Marylebone Gtr Man 43 B8
Marypark Moray 88 E1
Maryport Cumb 56 C2
Maryport Dumfries 54 F4
Maryton Angus 77 B9
Marywell Aberds 83 D7
Marywell Aberds 83 D11
Marywell Angus 77 C9
Masham N Yorks 51 A8
Mashbury Essex 30 G3
Masongill N Yorks 50 B2
Masonhill S Ayrs 67 D6
Mastin Moor Derbys 45 E8
Mastrick Aberdeen 83 C10
Matching Essex 30 G2
Matching Green Essex 30 G2
Matching Tye Essex 30 G2
Matfen Northumb 62 F6
Matfield Kent 12 B5
Mathern Mon 15 B11
Mathon Hereford 26 D4
Mathry Pembs 22 C3
Matlaske Norf 39 B7
Matlock Derbys 44 F6
Matlock Bath Derbys 44 G6
Matson Glos 26 G5
Matterdale End Cumb 56 D5
Mattersey Notts 45 D10
Mattersey Thorpe Notts 45 D10
Mattingley Hants 18 F4
Mattishall Norf 39 D6
Mattishall Burgh Norf 39 D6
Mauchline E Ayrs 67 D7
Maud Aberds 89 D9
Maugersbury Glos 27 F9
Maughold IoM 48 C4
Mauld Highld 86 H7
Maulden C Beds 29 E7
Maulds Meaburn Cumb 57 E8
Maunby N Yorks 58 H4
Maund Bryan Hereford 26 C2
Maundown Som 7 D9
Mautby Norf 39 D10
Mavis Enderby Lincs 47 F7
Maw Green Ches E 43 G10
Mawbray Cumb 56 B2
Mawdesley Lancs 43 A7
Mawdlam Bridgend 14 C4
Mawgan Corn 2 G6
Mawla Corn 2 E6
Mawnan Corn 3 G6
Mawnan Smith Corn 3 G6
Mawsley Northants 36 H4
Maxey Pboro 37 E7
Maxstoke Warks 35 G8
Maxton Borders 70 G5
Maxton Kent 21 G10
Maxwellheugh Borders 70 G6
Maxwelltown Dumfries 60 F5
Maxworthy Corn 6 G1
May Bank Staffs 44 H2
Mayals Swansea 14 B2
Maybole S Ayrs 66 F6
Mayfield E Sus 12 D4
Mayfield Midloth 70 D2
Mayfield Staffs 44 H5
Mayfield W Loth 69 D8
Mayford Sur 18 F6
Mayland Essex 20 A6
Maynard's Green E Sus 12 E4
Maypole Mon 25 G11
Maypole Scilly 2 C3
Maypole Green Essex 30 F6
Maypole Green Norf 39 F10
Maypole Green Suff 31 B9
Maywick Shetland 96 L5
Meadle Bucks 28 H5
Meadowtown Shrops 33 E9
Meaford Staffs 34 B4
Meal Bank Cumb 57 G7
Mealabost W Isles 91 D9
Mealabost Bhuirgh W Isles 91 B9
Mealsgate Cumb 56 B4
Meanwood W Yorks 51 F8
Mearbeck N Yorks 50 C4
Meare Som 15 G10
Meare Green Som 8 B2
Mears Ashby Northants 28 B5
Measham Leics 35 D9
Meath Green Sur 12 B1
Meathop Cumb 49 A4
Meaux E Yorks 53 F6
Meavy Devon 4 E6
Medbourne Leics 36 F3
Medburn Northumb 63 F7
Meddon Devon 6 E1
Meden Vale Notts 45 F9
Medlam Lincs 47 G7
Medmenham Bucks 18 C5
Medomsley Durham 58 A2
Medstead Hants 18 H3
Meer End W Mid 27 A9
Meerbrook Staffs 44 F3
Meers Bridge Lincs 47 D8
Meesden Herts 29 E11
Meeth Devon 6 F4
Meggethead Borders 61 A7
Meidrim Carms 23 D7
Meifod Denb 42 G3
Meifod Powys 33 D7
Meigle N Ayrs 73 G10
Meigle Perth 76 C5
Meikle Earnock S Lanark 68 E6
Meikle Ferry Highld 87 C10
Meikle Forter Angus 76 A4
Meikle Gluich Highld 87 C9
Meikle Pinkerton E Loth 70 C6
Meikle Strath Aberds 83 F8
Meikle Tarty Aberds 89 F9
Meikle Wartle Aberds 89 E7
Meikleour Perth 76 D4
Meinciau Carms 23 E9
Meir Stoke 34 A5
Meir Heath Staffs 34 A5
Melbourn Cambs 29 D10
Melbourne Derbys 35 C9
Melbourne E Yorks 52 E3
Melbourne S Lanark 69 F9
Melbury Abbas Dorset 9 B7
Melbury Bubb Dorset 8 D4
Melbury Osmond Dorset 8 D4
Melbury Sampford Dorset 8 D4
Melby Shetland 96 H3
Melchbourne Bedford 29 B7
Melcombe Bingham Dorset 9 D6
Melcombe Regis Dorset 8 F5
Meldon Devon 6 G4
Meldon Northumb 63 E7
Meldreth Cambs 29 D10
Meldrum Ho. Aberds 89 F8
Melfort Argyll 73 B7
Melgarve Highld 81 D6
Meliden Denb 42 D3
Melin-y-coed Conwy 41 D10
Melin-y-ddôl Powys 33 E6
Melin-y-grug Powys 33 E6
Melin-y-Wig Denb 42 H3
Melinbyrhedyn Powys 32 F4
Melincourt Neath 14 A4
Melkinthorpe Cumb 57 D7
Melkridge Northumb 62 G3
Melksham Wilts 16 E6
Melldalloch Argyll 73 F8
Melling Lancs 50 B1
Melling Mers 43 B6
Melling Mount Mers 43 B7
Mellis Suff 31 A8
Mellon Charles Highld 91 H13
Mellon Udrigle Highld 91 H13
Mellor Gtr Man 44 D3
Mellor Lancs 50 F2
Mellor Brook Lancs 50 F2
Mells Som 16 G4
Melmerby Cumb 57 C8
Melmerby N Yorks 51 B9
Melmerby N Yorks 58 H1
Melplash Dorset 8 E3
Melrose Borders 70 G4
Melsetter Orkney 95 K3
Melsonby N Yorks 58 F2
Meltham W Yorks 44 A5
Melton Suff 31 C9
Melton Constable Norf 38 B6
Melton Mowbray Leics 36 D3
Melton Ross N Lincs 46 A4
Meltonby E Yorks 52 D3
Melvaig Highld 91 J12
Melverley Shrops 33 D9
Melverley Green Shrops 33 D9
Melvich Highld 93 C11
Membury Devon 8 D1
Memsie Aberds 89 B9
Memus Angus 77 B7
Menabilly Corn 4 F1
Menai Bridge = Porthaethwy Anglesey 41 C7
Mendham Suff 39 G8
Mendlesham Suff 31 B8
Mendlesham Green Suff 31 B7
Menheniot Corn 4 E3
Mennock Dumfries 60 C4
Menston W Yorks 51 E7
Menstrie Clack 75 H11
Menthorpe N Yorks 52 F2
Mentmore Bucks 28 G6
Meoble Highld 79 C10
Meole Brace Shrops 33 D10
Meols Mers 42 C5
Meonstoke Hants 10 C5
Meopham Kent 20 E3
Meopham Station Kent 20 E3
Mepal Cambs 37 G10
Meppershall C Beds 29 E8
Merbach Hereford 25 D10
Mere Ches E 43 D10
Mere Wilts 9 A7
Mere Brow Lancs 49 H4
Mere Green W Mid 35 F7
Mereclough Lancs 50 F4
Mereside Blackpool 49 F3
Mereworth Kent 20 F3
Mergie Aberds 83 E9
Meriden W Mid 35 G8
Merkadale Highld 85 E8
Merkland Dumfries 60 F3
Merkland S Ayrs 66 G5
Merkland Lodge Highld 92 G7
Merley Poole 9 E9
Merlin's Bridge Pembs 22 E4
Merrington Shrops 33 C10
Merrion Pembs 22 G4
Merriott Som 8 C3
Merrivale Devon 4 D6
Merrow Sur 19 F7
Merrymeet Corn 4 E3
Mersham Kent 13 C9
Merstham Sur 19 F9
Merston W Sus 11 D7
Merstone IoW 10 F4
Merther Corn 3 E7
Merthyr Carms 23 D8
Merthyr Cynog Powys 24 E6
Merthyr-Dyfan V Glam 15 E7
Merthyr Mawr Bridgend 14 D4
Merthyr Tudful = Merthyr Tydfil M Tydf 25 H7
Merthyr Tydfil = Merthyr Tudful M Tydf 25 H7
Merthyr Vale M Tydf 14 B6
Merton Devon 6 E4
Merton London 19 D9
Merton Norf 38 F5
Merton Oxon 28 G2
Mervinslaw Borders 62 B2
Meshaw Devon 7 E6
Messing Essex 30 G5
Messingham N Lincs 46 B2
Metfield Suff 39 G8
Metheringham Lincs 46 F4
Methil Fife 76 H6
Methlem Gwyn 40 G3
Methley W Yorks 51 G9
Methlick Aberds 89 E8
Methven Perth 76 E3
Methwold Norf 38 F3
Methwold Hythe Norf 38 F3
Mettingham Suff 39 G9
Mevagissey Corn 3 E9
Mewith Head N Yorks 50 C3
Mexborough S Yorks 45 B8
Mey Highld 94 C4
Meysey Hampton Glos 17 B8
Miabhag W Isles 90 G5
Miabhag W Isles 90 H6
Miabhig W Isles 90 D5
Michaelchurch Hereford 26 F2
Michaelchurch Escley Hereford 25 E10
Michaelchurch on Arrow Powys 25 C9
Michaelston-le-Pit V Glam 15 D7
Michaelston-y-Fedw Newport 15 C8
Michaelstow Corn 4 D1
Michealston-super-Ely Cardiff 15 D7
Micheldever Hants 18 H2
Michelmersh Hants 10 B2
Mickfield Suff 31 B8
Mickle Trafford Ches W 43 F7
Micklebring S Yorks 45 C9
Mickleby N Yorks 59 E9
Mickleham Sur 19 F8
Mickleover Derby 35 B9
Micklethwaite W Yorks 51 E7
Mickleton Durham 57 D11
Mickleton Glos 27 D8
Mickletown W Yorks 51 G9
Mickley N Yorks 51 B8
Mickley Square Northumb 62 G6
Mid Ardlaw Aberds 89 B9
Mid Auchinlech Invclyd 68 C2
Mid Beltie Aberds 83 C8
Mid Calder W Loth 69 D9
Mid Cloch Forbie Aberds 89 C7
Mid Clyth Highld 94 G4
Mid Lavant W Sus 11 D7
Mid Main Highld 86 H7
Mid Urchany Highld 87 G11
Mid Walls Shetland 96 H4
Mid Yell Shetland 96 D7
Midbea Orkney 95 D5
Middle Assendon Oxon 18 C4
Middle Aston Oxon 27 F11
Middle Barton Oxon 27 F11
Middle Cairncake Aberds 89 D8
Middle Claydon Bucks 28 F4
Middle Drums Angus 77 B8
Middle Handley Derbys 45 E8
Middle Littleton Worcs 27 D7
Middle Maes-coed Hereford 25 E10
Middle Mill Pembs 22 D3
Middle Rasen Lincs 46 D4
Middle Rigg Perth 76 G3
Middle Tysoe Warks 27 D10
Middle Wallop Hants 17 H9
Middle Winterslow Wilts 9 A11
Middle Woodford Wilts 17 H8
Middlebie Dumfries 61 F8
Middleforth Green Lancs 49 G5
Middleham N Yorks 58 H2
Middlehope Shrops 33 G10
Middlemarsh Dorset 8 D5
Middlemuir Aberds 89 F9
Middlesbrough Mbro 58 D5
Middleshaw Cumb 57 H7
Middleshaw Dumfries 61 F7
Middlesmoor N Yorks 51 B6
Middlestone Durham 58 C3
Middlestone Moor Durham 58 C3
Middlestown W Yorks 51 H8
Middlethird Borders 70 F5
Middleton Aberds 83 B10
Middleton Argyll 78 G2
Middleton Cumb 57 H8
Middleton Derbys 44 F5
Middleton Derbys 44 G6
Middleton Essex 30 E5
Middleton Gtr Man 44 B2
Middleton Hants 17 G11
Middleton Hereford 26 B2
Middleton Lancs 49 D4
Middleton Midloth 70 E2
Middleton N Yorks 51 E7
Middleton N Yorks 59 H8
Middleton Norf 38 D2
Middleton Northants 36 G4
Middleton Northumb 62 E6
Middleton Northumb 71 G10
Middleton Perth 76 C4
Middleton Perth 76 G4
Middleton Shrops 33 C9
Middleton Shrops 33 F10
Middleton Shrops 33 H11
Middleton Suff 31 B11
Middleton Swansea 23 H9
Middleton W Yorks 51 G8
Middleton Warks 35 F7
Middleton Cheney Northants 27 D11
Middleton Green Staffs 34 B5
Middleton Hall Northumb 71 H8
Middleton-in-Teesdale Durham 57 D11
Middleton Moor Suff 31 B11
Middleton-on-Leven N Yorks 58 F5
Middleton-on-Sea W Sus 11 D8
Middleton on the Hill Hereford 26 B2
Middleton-on-the-Wolds E Yorks 52 E5
Middleton One Row Darl 58 E4
Middleton Priors Shrops 34 F2
Middleton Quernham N Yorks 51 B9
Middleton St George Darl 58 E4
Middleton Scriven Shrops 34 G2
Middleton Stoney Oxon 28 F2
Middleton Tyas N Yorks 58 F3
Middletown Cumb 56 F1
Middletown Powys 33 D9
Middlewich Ches E 43 F9
Middlewood Green Suff 31 B7
Middlezoy Som 8 A2
Middridge Durham 58 D3
Midfield Highld 93 C8
Midge Hall Lancs 49 G5
Midgeholme Cumb 62 H2
Midgham W Berks 18 E2
Midgley W Yorks 44 A6
Midgley W Yorks 50 G6
Midhopestones S Yorks 44 C6
Midhurst W Sus 11 B7
Midlem Borders 70 H4
Midmar Aberds 83 C8
Midsomer Norton Bath 16 F3
Midton Invclyd 73 F11
Midtown Highld 91 J13
Midtown Highld 93 C8
Midtown of Buchromb Moray 88 D3
Midville Lincs 47 G7
Midway Ches E 44 D3
Migdale Highld 87 B9
Migvie Aberds 82 C6
Milarrochy Stirling 68 A3
Milborne Port Som 8 C5
Milborne St Andrew Dorset 9 E7
Milborne Wick Som 8 B5
Milbourne Northumb 63 F7
Milburn Cumb 57 D8
Milbury Heath S Glos 16 B3
Milcombe Oxon 27 E11
Milden Suff 30 D6
Mildenhall Suff 30 A4
Mildenhall Wilts 17 E9
Mile Cross Norf 39 D8
Mile Elm Wilts 16 E6
Mile End Essex 30 F6
Mile End Glos 26 G2
Mile Oak Brighton 11 D11
Milebrook Powys 25 A10
Milebush Kent 20 G4
Mileham Norf 38 D5
Milesmark Fife 69 B9
Milfield Northumb 71 G8
Milford Derbys 45 H7
Milford Devon 6 D1
Milford Powys 33 F6
Milford Staffs 34 C5
Milford Sur 18 G6
Milford Wilts 9 B10
Milford Haven = Aberdaugleddau Pembs 22 F4
Milford on Sea Hants 10 E1
Milkwall Glos 26 H2
Milkwell Wilts 9 B8
Mill Bank W Yorks 50 G6
Mill Common Suff 39 G10
Mill End Bucks 18 C4
Mill End Herts 29 E10
Mill Green Essex 20 A3
Mill Green Norf 39 G7
Mill Green Suff 30 D6
Mill Hill London 19 B9
Mill Lane Hants 18 F4
Mill of Kingoodie Aberds 89 F8
Mill of Muiresk Aberds 89 D6
Mill of Sterin Aberds 82 D5
Mill of Uras Aberds 83 E10
Mill Place N Lincs 46 B3
Mill Side Cumb 49 A4
Mill Street Norf 39 D6
Milland W Sus 11 B7
Millarston Renfs 68 D3
Millbank Aberds 89 D11
Millbank Highld 94 D3
Millbeck Cumb 56 D4
Millbounds Orkney 95 E6
Millbreck Aberds 89 D10
Millbridge Sur 18 G5
Millbrook C Beds 29 E7
Millbrook Corn 4 F5
Millbrook Soton 10 C2
Millburn S Ayrs 67 D7
Millcombe Devon 5 G9
Millcorner E Sus 13 D7
Milldale Staffs 44 G5
Millden Lodge Angus 83 F7
Milldens Angus 77 B8
Millerhill Midloth 70 D2
Miller's Dale Derbys 44 E5
Miller's Green Derbys 44 G6
Millgreen Shrops 34 C2
Millhalf Hereford 25 D9
Millhayes Devon 7 F11
Millhead Lancs 49 B4
Millheugh S Lanark 68 E6
Millholme Cumb 57 G7
Millhouse Argyll 73 F8
Millhouse Cumb 56 C5
Millhouse Green S Yorks 44 B6
Millhousebridge Dumfries 61 E7
Millhouses S Yorks 45 D7
Millikenpark Renfs 68 D3
Millin Cross Pembs 22 E4
Millington E Yorks 52 D4
Millmeece Staffs 34 B4
Millom Cumb 49 A1
Millook Corn 4 B2
Millpool Corn 4 D2
Millport N Ayrs 66 A4
Millquarter Dumfries 55 A9
Millthorpe Lincs 37 B7
Millthrop Cumb 57 G8
Milltimber Aberdeen 83 C10
Milltown Corn 4 F2
Milltown Derbys 45 F7
Milltown Devon 6 C4
Milltown Dumfries 61 F9
Milltown of Aberdalgie Perth 76 E3
Milltown of Auchindoun Moray 88 D3
Milltown of Craigston Aberds 89 C7
Milltown of Edinvillie Moray 88 D2
Milltown of Kildrummy Aberds 82 B6
Milltown of Rothiemay Moray 88 D5
Milltown of Towie Aberds 82 B6
Milnathort Perth 76 G4
Milner's Heath Ches W 43 F7
Milngavie E Dunb 68 C4
Milnrow Gtr Man 44 A3
Milnshaw Lancs 50 G3
Milnthorpe Cumb 49 A4
Milo Carms 23 E10
Milson Shrops 26 A3
Milstead Kent 20 F6
Milston Wilts 17 G8
Milton Angus 76 C6
Milton Cambs 29 B11
Milton Cumb 61 G11
Milton Derbys 35 C9
Milton Dumfries 54 D5
Milton Dumfries 60 E4
Milton Dumfries 60 F4
Milton Highld 86 F6
Milton Highld 86 H7
Milton Highld 87 D10
Milton Highld 87 G8
Milton Highld 94 E5
Milton Moray 88 B5
Milton N Som 15 E9
Milton Notts 45 E11
Milton Oxon 17 B11
Milton Oxon 27 E11
Milton Pembs 22 F5
Milton Perth 76 F2
Milton Ptsmth 10 E5
Milton Stirling 75 G8
Milton Stoke 44 G3
Milton W Dunb 68 C3
Milton Abbas Dorset 9 D7
Milton Abbot Devon 4 D5
Milton Bridge Midloth 69 D11
Milton Bryan C Beds 28 E6
Milton Clevedon Som 16 H3
Milton Coldwells Aberds 89 E9
Milton Combe Devon 4 E5
Milton Damerel Devon 6 E2
Milton End Glos 17 A8
Milton Ernest Bedford 29 C7
Milton Green Ches W 43 G7
Milton Hill Oxon 17 B11
Milton Keynes M Keynes 28 E5
Milton Keynes Village M Keynes 28 E5
Milton Lilbourne Wilts 17 E8
Milton Malsor Northants 28 C4
Milton Morenish Perth 75 D9
Milton of Auchinhove Aberds 83 C7
Milton of Balgonie Fife 76 G6
Milton of Buchanan Stirling 68 A3
Milton of Campfield Aberds 83 C8
Milton of Campsie E Dunb 68 C5
Milton of Corsindae Aberds 83 C8
Milton of Cushnie Aberds 83 B7
Milton of Dalcapon Perth 76 B2
Milton of Edradour Perth 76 B2
Milton of Gollanfield Highld 87 F10
Milton of Lesmore Aberds 82 A6
Milton of Logie Aberds 82 C6
Milton of Murtle Aberdeen 83 C10
Milton of Noth Aberds 83 A7
Milton of Tullich Aberds 82 D5
Milton on Stour Dorset 9 B6
Milton Regis Kent 20 E6
Milton under Wychwood Oxon 27 G9
Miltonduff Moray 88 B1
Miltonhill Moray 87 E13
Miltonise Dumfries 54 B4
Milverton Som 7 D10
Milverton Warks 27 B10
Milwich Staffs 34 B5
Minard Argyll 73 D8
Minchinhampton Glos 16 A5
Mindrum Northumb 71 G7
Minehead Som 7 B8
Minera Wrex 42 G5
Minety Wilts 17 B7
Minffordd Gwyn 32 D3
Minffordd Gwyn 41 C7
Minffordd Gwyn 41 G7
Miningsby Lincs 47 F7
Minions Corn 4 D3
Minishant S Ayrs 66 E6
Minllyn Gwyn 32 D4
Minnes Aberds 89 F9
Minngearraidh W Isles 84 F2
Minnigaff Dumfries 55 C7
Minnonie Aberds 89 B7
Minskip N Yorks 51 C9
Minstead Hants 10 C1
Minsted W Sus 11 B7
Minster Kent 20 D6
Minster Kent 21 E10
Minster Lovell Oxon 27 G10
Minsterley Shrops 33 E9
Minsterworth Glos 26 G4
Minterne Magna Dorset 8 D5
Minting Lincs 46 E5
Mintlaw Aberds 89 D10
Minto Borders 61 A11
Minton Shrops 33 F10
Minwear Pembs 22 E5
Minworth W Mid 35 F7
Mirbister Orkney 95 F4
Mirehouse Cumb 56 E1
Mireland Highld 94 D5
Mirfield W Yorks 51 H8
Miserden Glos 26 H6
Miskin Rhondda 14 C6
Misson Notts 45 C10
Misterton Leics 36 G1
Misterton Notts 45 C11
Misterton Som 8 D3
Mistley Essex 31 E8
Mitcham London 19 E9
Mitchel Troy Mon 25 G11
Mitcheldean Glos 26 G3
Mitchell Corn 3 D7
Mitcheltroy Common Mon 25 H11
Mitford Northumb 63 E7
Mithian Corn 2 D6
Mitton Staffs 34 D4
Mixbury Oxon 28 E3
Moat Cumb 61 F10
Moats Tye Suff 31 C7
Mobberley Ches E 43 E10
Mobberley Staffs 34 A6
Moccas Hereford 25 D10
Mochdre Conwy 41 C10
Mochdre Powys 33 G6
Mochrum Dumfries 54 E6
Mockbeggar Hants 9 D10
Mockerkin Cumb 56 D2
Modbury Devon 5 F7
Moddershall Staffs 34 B5
Moelfre Anglesey 41 B7
Moelfre Powys 33 C7
Moffat Dumfries 60 C6
Moggerhanger C Beds 29 D8
Moira Leics 35 D9
Mol-chlach Highld 85 G9
Molash Kent 21 F7
Mold = Yr Wyddgrug Flint 42 F5
Moldgreen W Yorks 51 H7
Molehill Green Essex 30 F2
Molescroft E Yorks 52 E6
Molesden Northumb 63 E7
Molesworth Cambs 37 H6
Moll Highld 85 E10
Molland Devon 7 D7
Mollington Ches W 43 E6
Mollington Oxon 27 D11
Mollinsburn N Lanark 68 C6
Monachty Ceredig 24 B2
Monachylemore Stirling 75 F7
Monar Lodge Highld 86 G5
Monaughty Powys 25 B9
Monboddo House Aberds 83 F9
Mondynes Aberds 83 F9
Monevechadan Argyll 74 G4
Monewden Suff 31 C9
Moneydie Perth 76 E3
Moniaive Dumfries 60 D3
Monifieth Angus 77 D7
Monikie Angus 77 D7
Monimail Fife 76 F5
Monington Pembs 22 B6
Monk Bretton S Yorks 45 B7
Monk Fryston N Yorks 51 G11
Monk Sherborne Hants 18 F3
Monk Soham Suff 31 B9
Monk Street Essex 30 F3
Monken Hadley London 19 B9
Monkhopton Shrops 34 F2
Monkland Hereford 25 C11
Monkleigh Devon 6 D3
Monknash V Glam 14 D5
Monkokehampton Devon 6 F4
Monks Eleigh Suff 30 D6
Monk's Gate W Sus 11 B11
Monks Heath Ches E 44 E2
Monks Kirby Warks 35 G10
Monks Risborough Bucks 18 A5
Monkseaton T&W 63 F9
Monkshill Aberds 89 D7
Monksilver Som 7 C9
Monkspath W Mid 35 H7
Monkswood Mon 15 A9
Monkton Devon 7 F10
Monkton Kent 21 E9
Monkton Pembs 22 F4
Monkton S Ayrs 67 D6
Monkton Combe Bath 16 E4
Monkton Deverill Wilts 16 H5
Monkton Farleigh Wilts 16 E5
Monkton Heathfield Som 8 B1
Monkton Up Wimborne Dorset 9 C9
Monkwearmouth T&W 63 H9
Monkwood Hants 10 A5
Monmouth = Trefynwy Mon 26 G2

128 Mon – Nor

Monmouth Cap Mon 25 F10
Monnington on Wye Hereford 25 D10
Monreith Dumfries 54 E6
Monreith Mains Dumfries 54 E6
Mont Saint Guern 11
Montacute Som 8 C3
Montcoffer Ho. Aberds 89 B6
Montford Argyll 73 G10
Montford Shrops 33 D10
Montford Bridge Shrops 33 D10
Montgarrie Aberds 83 B7
Montgomery = Trefaldwyn Powys 33 F8
Montrave Fife 76 G6
Montrose Angus 77 B10
Montsale Essex 21 B7
Monxton Hants 17 G10
Monyash Derbys 44 F5
Monymusk Aberds 83 B8
Monzie Perth 75 E11
Monzie Castle Perth 75 E11
Moodiesburn N Lanark 68 C5
Moonzie Fife 76 F6
Moor Allerton W Yorks 51 F8
Moor Crichel Dorset 9 D8
Moor End E Yorks 52 F4
Moor End York 52 D2
Moor Monkton N Yorks 51 D11
Moor of Granary Moray 87 F13
Moor of Ravenstone Dumfries 54 E6
Moor Row Cumb 56 E2
Moor Street Kent 20 E5
Moorby Lincs 46 F6
Moordown Bmouth 9 E9
Moore Halton 43 D8
Moorend Glos 16 A4
Moorends S Yorks 52 H2
Moorgate S Yorks 45 C8
Moorgreen Notts 45 H8
Moorhall Derbys 45 E7
Moorhampton Hereford 25 D10
Moorhead W Yorks 51 F7
Moorhouse Cumb 61 H9
Moorhouse Notts 45 F11
Moorlinch Som 15 H9
Moorsholm Redcar 59 E7
Moorside Gtr Man 44 B3
Moorthorpe W Yorks 45 A8
Moortown Hants 9 D10
Moortown IoW 10 F3
Moortown Lincs 46 C4
Morangie Highld 87 C10
Morar Highld 79 B9
Morborne Cambs 37 F7
Morchard Bishop Devon 7 F6
Morcombelake Dorset 8 E3
Morcott Rutland 36 E5
Morda Shrops 33 C8
Morden Dorset 9 E8
Morden London 19 E9
Mordiford Hereford 26 E2
Mordon Durham 58 D4
More Shrops 33 F9
Morebath Devon 7 D8
Morebattle Borders 62 A3
Morecambe Lancs 49 C4
Morefield Highld 86 B4
Moreleigh Devon 5 F8
Morenish Perth 75 D8
Moresby Cumb 56 D1
Moresby Parks Cumb 56 E1
Morestead Hants 10 B4
Moreton Dorset 9 F7
Moreton Essex 30 H2
Moreton Mers 42 C5
Moreton Oxon 18 A3
Moreton Staffs 34 D3
Moreton Corbet Shrops 34 C1
Moreton-in-Marsh Glos 27 E9
Moreton Jeffries Hereford 26 D3
Moreton Morrell Warks 27 C10
Moreton on Lugg Hereford 26 D2
Moreton Pinkney Northants 28 D2
Moreton Say Shrops 34 B2
Moreton Valence Glos 26 H4
Moretonhampstead Devon 5 C8
Morfa Carms 23 E10
Morfa Carms 23 G10
Morfa Bach Carms 23 E8
Morfa Bychan Gwyn 41 G7
Morfa Dinlle Gwyn 40 E6
Morfa Glas Neath 24 H5
Morfa Nefyn Gwyn 40 F4
Morfydd Denb 42 H4
Morgan's Vale Wilts 9 B10
Moriah Ceredig 32 H2
Morland Cumb 57 D7
Morley Derbys 35 A9
Morley Durham 58 D2
Morley W Yorks 51 G8
Morley Green Ches E 44 D2
Morley St Botolph Norf 39 F6
Morningside Edin 69 C11
Morningside N Lanark 69 E7
Morningthorpe Norf 39 F8
Morpeth Northumb 63 E8
Morphie Aberds 77 A10
Morrey Staffs 35 D7
Morris Green Essex 30 E4
Morriston Swansea 14 B2
Morston Norf 38 A6
Mortehoe Devon 6 B3
Mortimer W Berks 18 E3
Mortimer West End Hants 18 E3
Mortimer's Cross Hereford 25 B11
Mortlake London 19 D9
Morton Cumb 56 A5
Morton Derbys 45 F8
Morton Lincs 37 C6
Morton Lincs 46 C2
Morton Lincs 46 F2
Morton Norf 39 D7
Morton Notts 45 G11
Morton S Glos 16 B3
Morton Shrops 33 C8
Morton Bagot Warks 27 B8
Morton-on-Swale N Yorks 58 G4
Morvah Corn 2 F3
Morval Corn 4 F3
Morvich Highld 80 A1
Morvich Highld 93 J10
Morville Shrops 34 F2
Morville Heath Shrops 34 F2
Morwenstow Corn 6 E1
Mosborough S Yorks 45 D8
Moscow E Ayrs 67 B7
Mosedale Cumb 56 C5
Moseley W Mid 34 F5
Moseley W Mid 35 G6
Moseley Worcs 26 C5
Moss Argyll 78 G2
Moss Highld 79 E9
Moss S Yorks 45 A9
Moss Wrex 42 G6
Moss Bank Mers 43 C8
Moss Edge Lancs 49 E4
Moss End Brack 18 D5
Moss of Barmuckity Moray 88 B2
Moss Pit Staffs 34 C5
Moss-side Highld 87 F11
Moss Side Lancs 49 F3
Mossat Aberds 82 B6
Mossbank Shetland 96 F6
Mossbay Cumb 56 D1
Mossblown S Ayrs 67 D7
Mossbrow Gtr Man 43 D10
Mossburnford Borders 62 B2
Mossdale Dumfries 55 B9
Mossend N Lanark 68 D6
Mosser Cumb 56 D3
Mossfield Highld 87 D9
Mossgiel E Ayrs 67 D7
Mosside Angus 77 B7
Mossley Ches E 44 F2
Mossley Gtr Man 44 B3
Mossley Hill Mers 43 D6
Mosstodloch Moray 88 C3
Mosston Angus 77 C8
Mossy Lea Lancs 43 A8
Mosterton Dorset 8 D3
Moston Gtr Man 44 B2
Moston Shrops 34 C1
Moston Green Ches E 43 F10
Mostyn Flint 42 D4
Mostyn Quay Flint 42 D4
Motcombe Dorset 9 B7
Mothecombe Devon 5 G7
Motherby Cumb 56 D6
Motherwell N Lanark 68 E6
Mottingham London 19 D11
Mottisfont Hants 10 B2
Mottistone IoW 10 F3
Mottram in Longdendale Gtr Man 44 C3
Mottram St Andrew Ches E 44 E2
Mouilpied Guern 11
Mouldsworth Ches W 43 E8
Moulin Perth 76 B2
Moulsecoomb Brighton 12 F2
Moulsford Oxon 18 C2
Moulsoe M Keynes 28 D6
Moulton Ches W 43 F9
Moulton Lincs 37 C9
Moulton N Yorks 58 F3
Moulton Northants 28 B4
Moulton Suff 30 B3
Moulton V Glam 14 D6
Moulton Chapel Lincs 37 D8
Moulton Eaugate Lincs 37 D9
Moulton St Mary Norf 39 E9
Moulton Seas End Lincs 37 C9
Mounie Castle Aberds 83 A9
Mount Corn 3 D6
Mount Corn 4 E2
Mount Highld 87 G12
Mount Bures Essex 30 E6
Mount Canisp Highld 87 D10
Mount Hawke Corn 2 E6
Mount Pleasant Ches E 44 G2
Mount Pleasant Derbys 35 D8
Mount Pleasant Derbys 45 H7
Mount Pleasant Flint 42 E5
Mount Pleasant Hants 10 E1
Mount Pleasant W Yorks 51 G8
Mount Sorrel Wilts 9 B9
Mount Tabor W Yorks 51 G6
Mountain W Yorks 51 F6
Mountain Ash = Aberpennar Rhondda 14 B6
Mountain Cross Borders 69 F10
Mountain Water Pembs 22 D4
Mountbenger Borders 70 H2
Mountfield E Sus 12 D6
Mountgerald Highld 87 E8
Mountjoy Corn 3 C7
Mountnessing Essex 20 B3
Mounton Mon 15 B11
Mountsorrel Leics 36 D1
Mousehole Corn 2 G3
Mousen Northumb 71 G10
Mouswald Dumfries 60 F6
Mow Cop Ches E 44 G2
Mowhaugh Borders 62 A4
Mowsley Leics 36 G2
Moxley W Mid 34 F5
Moy Highld 80 E6
Moy Highld 87 H10
Moy Hall Highld 87 H10
Moy Ho. Moray 87 E13
Moy Lodge Highld 80 E6
Moyles Court Hants 9 D10
Moylgrove Pembs 22 B6
Muasdale Argyll 65 D7
Much Birch Hereford 26 E2
Much Cowarne Hereford 26 D3
Much Dewchurch Hereford 25 E11
Much Hadham Herts 29 G11
Much Hoole Lancs 49 G4
Much Marcle Hereford 26 E3
Much Wenlock Shrops 34 E2
Muchalls Aberds 83 D11
Muchelney Som 8 B3
Muchlarnick Corn 4 F3
Muchrachd Highld 86 H5
Muckernich Highld 87 F8
Mucking Thurrock 20 C3
Muckleford Dorset 8 E5
Mucklestone Staffs 34 B3
Muckleton Shrops 34 C1
Muckletown Aberds 83 A7
Muckley Corner Staffs 35 E6
Muckton Lincs 47 D7
Mudale Highld 93 F8
Muddiford Devon 6 C4
Mudeford Dorset 9 E10
Mudford Som 8 C4
Mudgley Som 15 G10
Mugdock Stirling 68 C4
Mugeary Highld 85 E9
Mugginton Derbys 35 A8
Muggleswick Durham 58 B1
Muie Highld 93 J9
Muir Aberds 82 E2
Muir of Fairburn Highld 86 F7
Muir of Fowlis Aberds 83 B7
Muir of Ord Highld 87 F8
Muir of Pert Angus 77 D7
Muirden Aberds 89 C7
Muirdrum Angus 77 D8
Muirhead Angus 76 D6
Muirhead Fife 76 G5
Muirhead N Lanark 68 D5
Muirhead S Ayrs 66 C6
Muirhouselaw Borders 70 H5
Muirhouses Falk 69 B9
Muirkirk E Ayrs 68 H5
Muirmill Stirling 68 B6
Muirshearlich Highld 80 E3
Muirskie Aberds 83 D10
Muirtack Aberds 89 E9
Muirton Highld 87 E10
Muirton Perth 76 E4
Muirton Perth 76 F2
Muirton Mains Highld 86 F7
Muirton of Ardblair Perth 76 C4
Muirton of Ballochy Angus 77 A9
Muiryfold Aberds 89 C7
Muker N Yorks 57 G11
Mulbarton Norf 39 E7
Mulben Moray 88 C3
Mulindry Argyll 64 C4
Mullardoch House Highld 86 H5
Mullion Corn 2 H5
Mullion Cove Corn 2 H5
Mumby Lincs 47 E9
Munderfield Row Hereford 26 C3
Munderfield Stocks Hereford 26 C3
Mundesley Norf 39 B9
Mundford Norf 38 F4
Mundham Norf 39 F9
Mundon Essex 20 A5
Mundurno Aberdeen 83 B11
Munerigie Highld 80 C4
Muness Shetland 96 C8
Mungasdale Highld 86 B2
Mungrisdale Cumb 56 C5
Munlochy Highld 87 F9
Munsley Hereford 26 D3
Munslow Shrops 33 G11
Murchington Devon 5 C7
Murcott Oxon 28 G2
Murkle Highld 94 D3
Murlaggan Highld 80 D2
Murlaggan Highld 80 E5
Murra Orkney 95 H3
Murrayfield Edin 69 C11
Murrow Cambs 37 E9
Mursley Bucks 28 F5
Murthill Angus 77 B7
Murthly Perth 76 D3
Murton Cumb 57 D9
Murton Durham 58 B4
Murton Northumb 71 F8
Murton York 52 D2
Musbury Devon 8 E1
Muscoates N Yorks 52 A2
Musdale Argyll 74 E2
Musselburgh E Loth 70 C2
Muston Leics 36 B4
Muston N Yorks 53 B6
Mustow Green Worcs 26 A5
Mutehill Dumfries 55 E9
Mutford Suff 39 G10
Muthill Perth 75 F11
Mutterton Devon 7 F9
Muxton Telford 34 D3
Mybster Highld 94 E3
Myddfai Carms 24 F4
Myddle Shrops 33 C10
Mydroilyn Ceredig 23 A9
Myerscough Lancs 49 F4
Mylor Bridge Corn 3 F7
Mynachlog-ddu Pembs 22 C6
Myndtown Shrops 33 G9
Mynydd Bach Ceredig 32 H3
Mynydd-bach Mon 15 B10
Mynydd Bodafon Anglesey 40 B6
Mynydd-isa Flint 42 F5
Mynyddygarreg Carms 23 F9
Mynytho Gwyn 40 G5
Myrebird Aberds 83 D9
Myrelandhorn Highld 94 E4
Myreside Perth 76 E5
Myrtle Hill Carms 24 E4
Mytchett Sur 18 F5
Mytholm W Yorks 50 G5
Mytholmroyd W Yorks 50 G6
Myton-on-Swale N Yorks 51 C10
Mytton Shrops 33 D10

N

Na Gearrannan W Isles 90 C6
Naast Highld 91 J13
Naburn York 52 E1
Nackington Kent 21 F8
Nacton Suff 31 D9
Nafferton E Yorks 53 D6
Nailbridge Glos 26 G3
Nailsbourne Som 7 D11
Nailsea N Som 15 D10
Nailstone Leics 35 E10
Nailsworth Glos 16 B5
Nairn Highld 87 F11
Nalderswood Sur 19 G9
Nancegollan Corn 2 F5
Nancledra Corn 2 F3
Nanhoron Gwyn 40 G4
Nannau Gwyn 32 C3
Nannerch Flint 42 F4
Nanpantan Leics 35 D11
Nanpean Corn 3 D8
Nanstallon Corn 3 C9
Nant-ddu Powys 25 G7
Nant-glas Powys 24 B6
Nant Peris Gwyn 41 E8
Nant Uchaf Denb 42 G3
Nant-y-Bai Carms 24 D4
Nant-y-cafn Neath 24 H5
Nant-y-derry Mon 25 H10
Nant-y-ffin Carms 23 C10
Nant-y-moel Bridgend 14 B5
Nant-y-pandy Conwy 41 C8
Nanternis Ceredig 23 A8
Nantgaredig Carms 23 D9
Nantgarw Rhondda 15 C7
Nantglyn Denb 42 F3
Nantgwyn Powys 32 H5
Nantlle Gwyn 41 E7
Nantmawr Shrops 33 C8
Nantmel Powys 25 B7
Nantmor Gwyn 41 F8
Nantwich Ches E 43 G9
Nantycaws Carms 23 E9
Nantyffyllon Bridgend 14 B4
Nantyglo Bl Gwent 25 G8
Naphill Bucks 18 B5
Nappa N Yorks 50 D4
Napton on the Hill Warks 27 B11
Narberth = Arberth Pembs 22 E6
Narborough Leics 35 F11
Narborough Norf 38 D3
Nasareth Gwyn 40 E6
Naseby Northants 36 H2
Nash Bucks 28 E4
Nash Hereford 25 B10
Nash Newport 15 C9
Nash Shrops 26 A3
Nash Lee Bucks 28 H5
Nassington Northants 37 F6
Nasty Herts 29 F10
Nateby Cumb 57 F9
Nateby Lancs 49 E4
Natland Cumb 57 H7
Naughton Suff 31 D7
Naunton Glos 27 F8
Naunton Worcs 26 E5
Naunton Beauchamp Worcs 26 C6
Navenby Lincs 46 G3
Navestock Heath Essex 20 B2
Navestock Side Essex 20 B2
Navidale Highld 93 H13
Nawton N Yorks 52 A2
Nayland Suff 30 E6
Nazeing Essex 29 H11
Neacroft Hants 9 E10
Neal's Green Warks 35 G9
Neap Shetland 96 H7
Near Sawrey Cumb 56 G5
Neasham Darl 58 E4
Neath = Castell-Nedd Neath 14 B3
Neath Abbey Neath 14 B3
Neatishead Norf 39 C9
Nebo Anglesey 40 A6
Nebo Ceredig 24 B2
Nebo Conwy 41 E10
Nebo Gwyn 40 E6
Necton Norf 38 E4
Nedd Highld 92 F4
Nedderton Northumb 63 E8
Nedging Tye Suff 31 D7
Needham Norf 39 G8
Needham Market Suff 31 C7
Needingworth Cambs 29 A10
Needwood Staffs 35 C7
Neen Savage Shrops 34 H2
Neen Sollars Shrops 26 A3
Neenton Shrops 34 G2
Nefyn Gwyn 40 F5
Neilston E Renf 68 E3
Neinthirion Powys 32 E5
Neithrop Oxon 27 D11
Nelly Andrews Green Powys 33 E8
Nelson Caerph 15 B7
Nelson Lancs 50 F4
Nelson Village Northumb 63 F8
Nemphlar S Lanark 69 F7
Nempnett Thrubwell N Som 15 E11
Nene Terrace Lincs 37 E8
Nenthall Cumb 57 B9
Nenthead Cumb 57 B9
Nenthorn Borders 70 G5
Nerabus Argyll 64 C3
Nercwys Flint 42 F5
Nerston S Lanark 68 E5
Nesbit Northumb 71 G8
Ness Ches W 42 E6
Nesscliffe Shrops 33 D9
Neston Ches W 42 E5
Neston Wilts 16 E5
Nether Alderley Ches E 44 E2
Nether Blainslie Borders 70 F4
Nether Booth Derbys 44 D5
Nether Broughton Leics 36 C2
Nether Burrow Lancs 50 B2
Nether Cerne Dorset 8 E5
Nether Compton Dorset 8 C4
Nether Crimond Aberds 89 F8
Nether Dalgliesh Borders 61 C8
Nether Dallachy Moray 88 B3
Nether Exe Devon 7 F8
Nether Glasslaw Aberds 89 C8
Nether Handwick Angus 76 C6
Nether Haugh S Yorks 45 C8
Nether Heage Derbys 45 G7
Nether Heyford Northants 28 C3
Nether Hindhope Borders 62 B3
Nether Howecleuch S Lanark 60 B6
Nether Kellet Lancs 49 C5
Nether Kinmundy Aberds 89 D10
Nether Langwith Notts 45 E9
Nether Leask Aberds 89 E10
Nether Lenshie Aberds 89 D6
Nether Monynut Borders 70 D6
Nether Padley Derbys 44 E6
Nether Park Aberds 89 C10
Nether Poppleton York 52 D1
Nether Silton N Yorks 58 G5
Nether Stowey Som 7 C10
Nether Urquhart Fife 76 G4
Nether Wallop Hants 17 H10
Nether Wasdale Cumb 56 F3
Nether Whitacre Warks 35 F8
Nether Worton Oxon 27 E11
Netheravon Wilts 17 G8
Netherbrae Aberds 89 C7
Netherbrough Orkney 95 G4
Netherburn S Lanark 69 F7
Netherbury Dorset 8 E3
Netherby Cumb 61 F9
Netherby N Yorks 51 E9
Nethercote Warks 28 B2
Nethercott Devon 6 C3
Netherend Glos 16 A2
Netherfield E Sus 12 E6
Netherhampton Wilts 9 B10
Netherlaw Dumfries 55 E10
Netherley Aberds 83 D10
Netherley Mers 43 D7
Nethermill Dumfries 60 E6
Nethermuir Aberds 89 D9
Netherplace E Renf 68 E4
Netherseal Derbys 35 D8
Netherthird E Ayrs 67 E8
Netherthong W Yorks 44 B5
Netherthorpe S Yorks 45 D9
Netherton Angus 77 B8
Netherton Devon 5 D9
Netherton Hants 17 F10
Netherton Mers 42 B6
Netherton Northumb 62 C5
Netherton Oxon 17 B11
Netherton Perth 76 B4
Netherton Stirling 68 C4
Netherton W Mid 34 G5
Netherton W Yorks 44 A5
Netherton W Yorks 51 H8
Netherton Worcs 26 D6
Nethertown Cumb 56 F1
Nethertown Highld 94 C5
Netherwitton Northumb 63 D7
Netherwood E Ayrs 68 H5
Nethy Bridge Highld 82 A2
Netley Hants 10 D3
Netley Marsh Hants 10 C2
Netteswell Essex 29 G11
Nettlebed Oxon 18 C4
Nettlebridge Som 16 G3
Nettlecombe Dorset 8 E4
Nettleden Herts 29 G7
Nettleham Lincs 46 E4
Nettlestead Kent 20 F3
Nettlestead Green Kent 20 F3
Nettlestone IoW 10 E5
Nettlesworth Durham 58 B3
Nettleton Lincs 46 B5
Nettleton Wilts 16 D5
Neuadd Carms 24 F3
Nevendon Essex 20 B4
Nevern Pembs 22 B5
New Abbey Dumfries 60 G5
New Aberdour Aberds 89 B8
New Addington London 19 E10
New Alresford Hants 10 A4
New Alyth Perth 76 C5
New Arley Warks 35 G8
New Ash Green Kent 20 E3
New Barn Kent 20 E3
New Barnetby N Lincs 46 A4
New Barton Northants 28 B5
New Bewick Northumb 62 A6
New-bigging Angus 76 C5
New Bilton Warks 35 H10
New Bolingbroke Lincs 47 G7
New Boultham Lincs 46 E3
New Bradwell M Keynes 28 D5
New Brancepeth Durham 58 B3
New Bridge Wrex 33 A8
New Brighton Flint 42 F5
New Brighton Mers 42 C6
New Brinsley Notts 45 G8
New Broughton Wrex 42 G6
New Buckenham Norf 39 F6
New Byth Aberds 89 C8
New Catton Norf 39 D8
New Cheriton Hants 10 B4
New Costessey Norf 39 D7
New Cowper Cumb 56 B3
New Cross Ceredig 32 H2
New Cross London 19 D10
New Cumnock E Ayrs 67 E9
New Deer Aberds 89 D8
New Delaval Northumb 63 F8
New Duston Northants 28 B4
New Earswick York 52 D2
New Edlington S Yorks 45 C9
New Elgin Moray 88 B2
New Ellerby E Yorks 53 F7
New Eltham London 19 D11
New End Worcs 27 C7
New Farnley W Yorks 51 F8
New Ferry Mers 42 D6
New Fryston W Yorks 51 G10
New Galloway Dumfries 55 B9
New Gilston Fife 77 G7
New Grimsby Scilly 2 C2
New Hainford Norf 39 D8
New Hartley Northumb 63 F9
New Haw Sur 19 E7
New Hedges Pembs 22 F6
New Herrington T&W 58 A4
New Hinksey Oxon 18 A2
New Holkham Norf 38 B4
New Holland N Lincs 53 G6
New Houghton Derbys 45 F8
New Houghton Norf 38 C3
New Houses N Yorks 50 B4
New Humberstone Leicester 36 E2
New Hutton Cumb 57 G7
New Hythe Kent 20 F4
New Inn Carms 23 C9
New Inn Mon 15 A10
New Inn Pembs 22 C5
New Inn Torf 15 B9
New Invention Shrops 33 H8
New Invention W Mid 34 E5
New Kelso Highld 86 G2
New Kingston Notts 35 C11
New Lanark S Lanark 69 F7
New Lane Lancs 43 A7
New Lane End Warr 43 C9
New Leake Lincs 47 G8
New Leeds Aberds 89 C9
New Longton Lancs 49 G5
New Luce Dumfries 54 C4
New Malden London 19 E9
New Marske Redcar 59 D7
New Marton Shrops 33 B9
New Micklefield W Yorks 51 F10
New Mill Aberds 83 E9
New Mill Herts 28 G6
New Mill W Yorks 44 B5
New Mill Wilts 17 E8
New Mills Ches E 43 D10
New Mills Corn 3 D7
New Mills Derbys 44 D3
New Mills Powys 33 E6
New Milton Hants 9 E11
New Moat Pembs 22 D5
New Ollerton Notts 45 F10
New Oscott W Mid 35 F6
New Park N Yorks 51 D8
New Pitsligo Aberds 89 C8
New Polzeath Corn 3 B8
New Quay = Ceinewydd Ceredig 23 A8
New Rackheath Norf 39 D8
New Radnor Powys 25 B9
New Rent Cumb 56 C6
New Ridley Northumb 62 H6
New Road Side N Yorks 50 E5
New Romney Kent 13 D9
New Rossington S Yorks 45 C10
New Row Ceredig 24 A4
New Row Lancs 50 F2
New Row N Yorks 59 E7
New Sarum Wilts 9 A10
New Silksworth T&W 58 A4
New Stevenston N Lanark 68 E6
New Street Staffs 44 G4
New Street Lane Shrops 34 B2
New Swanage Dorset 9 F9
New Totley S Yorks 45 E7
New Town E Loth 70 C3
New Tredegar = Tredegar Newydd Caerph 15 A7
New Trows S Lanark 69 G7
New Ulva Argyll 72 E6
New Walsoken Cambs 37 E10
New Waltham NE Lincs 46 B6
New Whittington Derbys 45 E7
New Wimpole Cambs 29 D10
New Winton E Loth 70 C3
New Yatt Oxon 27 G10
New York Lincs 46 G6
New York N Yorks 51 C7
Newall W Yorks 51 E7
Newark Orkney 95 D8
Newark Pboro 37 E8
Newark-on-Trent Notts 45 G11
Newarthill N Lanark 68 E6
Newbarns Cumb 49 B2
Newbattle Midloth 70 D2
Newbiggin Cumb 49 C2
Newbiggin Cumb 56 D6
Newbiggin Cumb 56 G2
Newbiggin Cumb 57 B7
Newbiggin Cumb 57 D8
Newbiggin Durham 57 D11
Newbiggin N Yorks 57 G11
Newbiggin N Yorks 57 H11
Newbiggin-by-the-Sea Northumb 63 E9
Newbiggin-on-Lune Cumb 57 F9
Newbigging Angus 77 D7
Newbigging Angus 77 D7
Newbigging S Lanark 69 F9
Newbold Derbys 45 E7
Newbold Leics 35 D10
Newbold on Avon Warks 35 H10
Newbold on Stour Warks 27 D9
Newbold Pacey Warks 27 C9
Newbold Verdon Leics 35 E10
Newborough Anglesey 40 D6
Newborough Pboro 37 E8
Newborough Staffs 35 C7
Newbottle Northants 28 E2
Newbottle T&W 58 A4
Newbourne Suff 31 D9
Newbridge Caerph 15 B8
Newbridge Ceredig 23 A10
Newbridge Corn 2 F3
Newbridge Corn 4 E4
Newbridge Dumfries 60 F5
Newbridge Edin 69 C10
Newbridge Hants 10 C1
Newbridge IoW 10 F3
Newbridge Pembs 22 C4
Newbridge Green Worcs 26 E5
Newbridge-on-Usk Mon 15 B9
Newbridge on Wye Powys 25 C7
Newbrough Northumb 62 G4
Newbuildings Devon 7 F6
Newburgh Aberds 89 C9
Newburgh Aberds 89 F9
Newburgh Borders 61 B9
Newburgh Fife 76 F5
Newburgh Lancs 43 A7
Newburn T&W 63 G7
Newbury W Berks 17 E11
Newbury Park London 19 C11
Newby Cumb 57 D7
Newby Lancs 50 E4
Newby N Yorks 50 B3
Newby N Yorks 58 E6
Newby N Yorks 59 G11
Newby Bridge Cumb 56 H5
Newby East Cumb 61 H10
Newby West Cumb 56 A5
Newby Wiske N Yorks 58 H4
Newcastle Mon 25 G11
Newcastle Shrops 33 G8
Newcastle Emlyn = Castell Newydd Emlyn Carms 23 B8
Newcastle-under-Lyme Staffs 44 H2
Newcastle Upon Tyne T&W 63 G8
Newcastleton or Copshaw Holm Borders 61 E10
Newchapel Pembs 23 C7
Newchapel Powys 32 G5
Newchapel Staffs 44 G2
Newchapel Sur 12 B2
Newchurch Carms 23 D8
Newchurch IoW 10 F4
Newchurch Kent 13 C9
Newchurch Lancs 50 F4
Newchurch Mon 15 B10
Newchurch Powys 25 C9
Newchurch Staffs 35 C7
Newcott Devon 7 F11
Newcraighall Edin 70 C2
Newdigate Sur 19 G8
Newell Green Brack 18 D5
Newenden Kent 13 D7
Newent Glos 26 F4
Newerne Glos 16 A3
Newfield Durham 58 C3
Newfield Highld 87 D10
Newford Scilly 2 C3
Newfound Hants 18 F2
Newgale Pembs 22 D3
Newgate Norf 39 A6
Newgate Street Herts 19 A10
Newhall Ches E 43 H9
Newhall Derbys 35 C8
Newhall House Highld 87 E9
Newhall Point Highld 87 E10
Newham Northumb 71 H10
Newham Hall Northumb 71 H10
Newhaven Derbys 44 G5
Newhaven E Sus 12 F3
Newhaven Edin 69 C11
Newhey Gtr Man 44 A3
Newholm N Yorks 59 E9
Newhouse N Lanark 68 D6
Newick E Sus 12 D3
Newingreen Kent 13 C10
Newington Kent 20 E5
Newington Kent 21 E10
Newington Kent 21 H8
Newington Notts 45 C10
Newington Oxon 18 B3
Newington Shrops 33 G10
Newland Glos 26 H2
Newland Hull 53 F6
Newland N Yorks 52 G2
Newland Worcs 26 D4
Newlandrig Midloth 70 D2
Newlands Borders 61 D11
Newlands Highld 87 G10
Newlands Moray 88 C3
Newlands Northumb 62 H6
Newland's Corner Sur 19 G7
Newlands of Geise Highld 94 D2
Newlands of Tynet Moray 88 B3
Newlands Park Anglesey 40 B4
Newlandsmuir S Lanark 68 E5
Newlot Orkney 95 G6
Newlyn Corn 2 G3
Newmachar Aberds 83 B10
Newmains N Lanark 69 E7
Newmarket Suff 30 B3
Newmarket W Isles 91 D9
Newmill Borders 61 B10
Newmill Corn 2 F3
Newmill Moray 88 C4
Newmill of Inshewan Angus 77 A7
Newmills of Boyne Aberds 88 C5
Newmiln Perth 76 D4
Newmilns E Ayrs 67 C8
Newnham Cambs 29 C11
Newnham Glos 26 G3
Newnham Hants 18 F4
Newnham Herts 29 E9
Newnham Kent 20 F6
Newnham Northants 28 C2
Newnham Bridge Worcs 26 B3
Newpark Fife 77 F7
Newport Devon 6 C4
Newport E Yorks 52 F4
Newport Essex 30 E2
Newport Highld 94 H3
Newport IoW 10 F4
Newport = Casnewydd Newport 15 C9
Newport Norf 39 D11
Newport = Trefdraeth Pembs 22 C5
Newport Telford 34 D3
Newport-on-Tay Fife 77 E7
Newport Pagnell M Keynes 28 D5
Newpound Common W Sus 11 B9
Newquay Corn 3 C7
Newsbank Ches E 44 F2
Newseat Aberds 89 D10
Newseat Aberds 89 E7
Newsham N Yorks 51 A9
Newsham N Yorks 58 E2
Newsham Northumb 63 F9
Newsholme E Yorks 52 G3
Newsholme Lancs 50 D4
Newsome W Yorks 44 A5
Newstead Borders 70 G4
Newstead Northumb 71 H10
Newstead Notts 45 G9
Newthorpe N Yorks 51 F10
Newton Argyll 73 D9
Newton Borders 62 A1
Newton Bridgend 14 D4
Newton Cambs 29 D11
Newton Cambs 37 D10
Newton Cardiff 15 D8
Newton Ches W 43 E8
Newton Ches W 43 F7
Newton Ches W 43 G8
Newton Cumb 49 B2
Newton Derbys 45 G8
Newton Dorset 9 C6
Newton Dumfries 61 D7
Newton Dumfries 61 F8
Newton Gtr Man 44 C3
Newton Hereford 25 E10
Newton Hereford 26 C2
Newton Highld 87 E10
Newton Highld 87 G10
Newton Highld 92 F5
Newton Highld 94 F5
Newton Lancs 49 F4
Newton Lancs 50 B1
Newton Lancs 50 D2
Newton Lincs 36 B6
Newton Moray 88 B1
Newton Norf 38 D4
Newton Northants 36 G4
Newton Northumb 62 G6
Newton Notts 36 A2
Newton Perth 75 D11
Newton S Lanark 68 D5
Newton S Lanark 69 G8
Newton S Yorks 45 B9
Newton Staffs 34 C6
Newton Suff 30 D6
Newton Swansea 14 C2
Newton W Loth 69 C9
Newton Warks 35 H11
Newton Wilts 9 B11
Newton Abbot Devon 5 D9
Newton Arlosh Cumb 61 H7
Newton Aycliffe Durham 58 D3
Newton Bewley Hrtlpl 58 D5
Newton Blossomville M Keynes 28 C6
Newton Bromswold Northants 28 B6
Newton Burgoland Leics 35 E9
Newton by Toft Lincs 46 D4
Newton Ferrers Devon 4 G6
Newton Flotman Norf 39 F8
Newton Hall Northumb 62 G6
Newton Harcourt Leics 36 F2
Newton Heath Gtr Man 44 B2
Newton Ho. Aberds 83 A8
Newton Kyme N Yorks 51 E10
Newton-le-Willows Mers 43 C8
Newton-le-Willows N Yorks 58 H3
Newton Longville Bucks 28 E5
Newton Mearns E Renf 68 E4
Newton Morrell N Yorks 58 F3
Newton Mulgrave N Yorks 59 E8
Newton of Ardtoe Highld 79 D9
Newton of Balcanquhal Perth 76 F4
Newton of Falkland Fife 76 G5
Newton on Ayr S Ayrs 66 D6
Newton on Ouse N Yorks 51 D11
Newton-on-Rawcliffe N Yorks 59 G9
Newton-on-the-Moor Northumb 63 C7
Newton on Trent Lincs 46 E2
Newton Park Argyll 73 G10
Newton Poppleford Devon 7 H9
Newton Purcell Oxon 28 E3
Newton Regis Warks 35 E8
Newton Reigny Cumb 57 C6
Newton St Cyres Devon 7 G7
Newton St Faith Norf 39 D8
Newton St Loe Bath 16 E4
Newton St Petrock Devon 6 E3
Newton Solney Derbys 35 C8
Newton Stacey Hants 17 G11
Newton Stewart Dumfries 55 C7
Newton Tony Wilts 17 G9
Newton Tracey Devon 6 D4
Newton under Roseberry Redcar 59 E6
Newton upon Derwent E Yorks 52 E3
Newton Valence Hants 10 A6
Newtonairds Dumfries 60 E4
Newtongrange Midloth 70 D2
Newtonhill Aberds 83 D11
Newtonhill Highld 87 G8
Newtonmill Angus 77 A9
Newtonmore Highld 81 D9
Newtown Argyll 73 C9
Newtown Ches W 43 E8
Newtown Corn 2 G6
Newtown Cumb 56 B2
Newtown Cumb 61 G11
Newtown Derbys 44 D3
Newtown Devon 7 D6
Newtown Glos 16 A3
Newtown Glos 26 E6
Newtown Hants 10 B2
Newtown Hants 10 C4
Newtown Hants 10 C1
Newtown Hants 10 C5
Newtown Hants 10 D3
Newtown Hants 17 E11
Newtown Hereford 26 D3
Newtown Highld 80 C5
Newtown IoM 48 E3
Newtown IoW 10 E3
Newtown Northumb 62 C6
Newtown Northumb 71 G8
Newtown Northumb 71 H9
Newtown Poole 9 E9
Newtown = Y Drenewydd Powys 33 F7
Newtown Shrops 33 B10
Newtown Staffs 44 F4
Newtown Staffs 44 F3
Newtown Wilts 9 B8
Newtown Linford Leics 35 E11
Newtown St Boswells Borders 70 G4
Newtown Unthank Leics 35 E10
Newtyle Angus 76 C5
Neyland Pembs 22 F4
Niarbyl IoM 48 E2
Nibley S Glos 16 C3
Nibley Green Glos 16 B4
Nibon Shetland 96 F5
Nicholashayne Devon 7 E10
Nicholaston Swansea 23 H10
Nidd N Yorks 51 C9
Nigg Aberdeen 83 C11
Nigg Highld 87 D11
Nigg Ferry Highld 87 E10
Nightcott Som 7 D7
Nilig Denb 42 G3
Nine Ashes Essex 20 A2
Nine Mile Burn Midloth 69 E10
Nine Wells Pembs 22 D2
Ninebanks Northumb 57 A9
Ninfield E Sus 12 E6
Ningwood IoW 10 F2
Nisbet Borders 70 H5
Nisthouse Orkney 95 G4
Nisthouse Shetland 96 G7
Niton IoW 10 G4
Nitshill Glasgow 68 D4
No Man's Heath Ches W 43 H8
No Man's Heath Warks 35 E8
Noak Hill London 20 B2
Noblethorpe S Yorks 44 B6
Nobottle Northants 28 B3
Nocton Lincs 46 F4
Noke Oxon 28 G2
Nolton Pembs 22 E3
Nolton Haven Pembs 22 E3
Nomansland Devon 7 E7
Nomansland Wilts 10 C1
Noneley Shrops 33 C10
Nonikiln Highld 87 D9
Nonington Kent 21 F9
Noonsbrough Shetland 96 H4
Norbreck Blackpool 49 E3
Norbridge Hereford 26 D4
Norbury Ches E 43 H8
Norbury Derbys 35 A7
Norbury Shrops 33 F9
Norbury Staffs 34 C3
Nordelph Norf 38 E1
Norden Gtr Man 44 A2
Norden Heath Dorset 9 F8
Nordley Shrops 34 F2
Norham Northumb 71 F8
Norley Ches W 43 E8
Norleywood Hants 10 E2
Norman Cross Cambs 37 F7
Normanby N Lincs 52 H4
Normanby N Yorks 52 A3
Normanby Redcar 59 E6
Normanby-by-Spital Lincs 46 D4
Normanby by Stow Lincs 46 D2
Normanby le Wold Lincs 46 C5
Normandy Sur 18 F6
Norman's Bay E Sus 12 F5
Norman's Green Devon 7 F9
Normanstone Suff 39 F11
Normanton Derby 35 B9
Normanton Leics 36 A4
Normanton Lincs 46 H3
Normanton Notts 45 G11
Normanton Rutland 36 E5
Normanton W Yorks 51 G9
Normanton le Heath Leics 35 D9
Normanton on Soar Notts 35 C11
Normanton-on-the-Wolds Notts 36 B2
Normanton on Trent Notts 45 F11
Normoss Lancs 49 F3
Norney Sur 18 G6
Norrington Common Wilts 16 E5
Norris Green Mers 43 C6
Norris Hill Leics 35 D9
North Anston S Yorks 45 D9
North Aston Oxon 27 F11
North Baddesley Hants 10 C2
North Ballachulish Highld 74 A3
North Barrow Som 8 B5
North Barsham Norf 38 B5
North Benfleet Essex 20 C4
North Bersted W Sus 11 D8
North Berwick E Loth 70 B4
North Boarhunt Hants 10 C5
North Bovey Devon 5 C8
North Bradley Wilts 16 F5
North Brentor Devon 4 C5
North Brewham Som 16 H4
North Buckland Devon 6 B3
North Burlingham Norf 39 D9
North Cadbury Som 8 B5
North Cairn Dumfries 54 B2
North Carlton Lincs 46 E3
North Carrine Argyll 65 H7
North Cave E Yorks 52 F4
North Cerney Glos 27 H7
North Charford Wilts 9 C10
North Charlton Northumb 63 A7
North Cheriton Som 8 B5
North Cliff E Yorks 53 E8
North Cliffe E Yorks 52 F4
North Clifton Notts 46 E2
North Cockerington Lincs 47 C7
North Coker Som 8 C4
North Collafirth Shetland 96 E5
North Common E Sus 12 D2
North Connel Argyll 74 D2
North Cornelly Bridgend 14 C4
North Cotes Lincs 47 B7
North Cove Suff 39 G10
North Cowton N Yorks 58 F3
North Crawley M Keynes 28 D6
North Cray London 19 D11
North Creake Norf 38 B4
North Curry Som 8 B2
North Dalton E Yorks 52 D5
North Dawn Orkney 95 H5
North Deighton N Yorks 51 D9
North Duffield N Yorks 52 F2
North Elkington Lincs 46 C6
North Elmham Norf 38 C5

Nor – Pen 129

orth Elmshall W Yorks 45 A8
orth End Bucks 28 F5
orth End E Yorks 53 F8
orth End Essex 30 G3
orth End Hants 17 E11
orth End Lincs 37 A8
orth End N Som 15 E10
orth End Ptsmth 10 D5
orth End Som 8 B1
orth End W Sus 11 D10
orth Erradale Highld 91 J12
orth Fambridge Essex 20 B5
orth Fearns Highld 85 E10
orth Featherstone W Yorks 51 G10
orth Ferriby E Yorks 52 G5
orth Frodingham E Yorks 53 D7
orth Gluss Shetland 96 F5
orth Gorley Hants 9 C10
orth Green Norf 39 G8
orth Green Suff 31 B10
orth Greetwell Lincs 46 E4
orth Grimston N Yorks 52 C4
orth Halley Orkney 95 H6
orth Halling Medway 20 E4
orth Hayling Hants 10 D6
orth Hazelrigg Northumb 71 G9
orth Heasley Devon 7 C6
orth Heath W Sus 11 B9
orth Hill Cambs 37 H10
orth Hill Corn 4 D3
orth Hinksey Oxon 27 H11
orth Holmwood Sur 19 G8
orth Howden E Yorks 52 F3
orth Huish Devon 5 F8
orth Hykeham Lincs 46 F3
orth Johnston Pembs 22 E4
orth Kelsey Lincs 46 B4
orth Kelsey Moor Lincs 46 B4
orth Kessock Highld 87 G9
orth Killingholme N Lincs 53 H7
orth Kilvington N Yorks 58 H5
orth Kilworth Leics 36 G2
orth Kirkton Aberds 89 C11
orth Kiscadale N Ayrs 66 D3
orth Kyme Lincs 46 G5
orth Lancing W Sus 11 D10
orth Lee Bucks 28 H5
orth Leigh Oxon 27 G10
orth Leverton with Habblesthorpe Notts 45 D11
orth Littleton Worcs 27 D7
orth Lopham Norf 38 G6
orth Luffenham Rutland 36 E5
orth Marden W Sus 11 C7
orth Marston Bucks 28 F4
orth Middleton Midloth 70 E2
orth Middleton Northumb 62 A6
orth Molton Devon 7 D6
orth Moreton Oxon 18 C2
orth Mundham W Sus 11 D7
orth Muskham Notts 45 G11
orth Newbald E Yorks 52 F5
orth Newington Oxon 27 E11
orth Newnton Wilts 17 F8
orth Newton Som 8 A1
orth Nibley Glos 16 B4
orth Oakley Hants 18 F2
orth Ockendon London 20 C2
orth Ormesby Mbro 58 D6
orth Ormsby Lincs 46 C6
orth Otterington N Yorks 58 H4
orth Owersby Lincs 46 C4
orth Perrott Som 8 D3
orth Petherton Som 8 A1
orth Petherwin Corn 4 C3
orth Pickenham Norf 38 E4
orth Piddle Worcs 26 C6
orth Poorton Dorset 8 E4
orth Port Argyll 74 E3
orth Queensferry Fife 69 B10
orth Radworthy Devon 7 C6
orth Rauceby Lincs 46 H4
orth Reston Lincs 47 D7
orth Rigton N Yorks 51 E8
orth Rode Ches E 44 F2
orth Roe Shetland 96 E5
orth Runcton Norf 38 D2
orth Sandwick Shetland 96 D7
orth Scale Cumb 49 C1
orth Scarle Lincs 46 F2
orth Seaton Northumb 63 E8
orth Shian Argyll 74 C2
orth Shields T&W 63 G9
orth Shoebury Southend 20 C6
orth Shore Blackpool 49 F3
orth Side Cumb 56 D2
orth Side Pboro 37 F8
orth Skelton Redcar 59 E7
orth Somercotes Lincs 47 C8
orth Stainley N Yorks 51 B8
orth Stainmore Cumb 57 E10
orth Stifford Thurrock 20 C3
orth Stoke Bath 16 E4
orth Stoke Oxon 18 C3
North Stoke W Sus 11 C9
North Street Hants 10 A5
North Street Kent 21 F7
North Street Medway 20 D5
North Street W Berks 18 D3
North Sunderland Northumb 71 G11
North Tamerton Corn 6 G2
North Tawton Devon 6 F5
North Thoresby Lincs 46 C6
North Tidworth Wilts 17 G9
North Togston Northumb 63 C8
North Tuddenham Norf 38 D6
North Walbottle T&W 63 G7
North Walsham Norf 39 B8
North Waltham Hants 18 G2
North Warnborough Hants 18 F4
North Water Bridge Angus 83 G8
North Watten Highld 94 E4
North Weald Bassett Essex 19 A11
North Wheatley Notts 45 D11
North Whilborough Devon 5 E9
North Wick Bath 16 E2
North Willingham Lincs 46 D5
North Wingfield Derbys 45 F8
North Witham Lincs 36 C5
North Woolwich London 19 D11
North Wootton Dorset 8 C5
North Wootton Norf 38 C2
North Wootton Som 16 G2
North Wraxall Wilts 16 D5
North Wroughton Swindon 17 C8
Northacre Norf 38 F5
Northallerton N Yorks 58 G4
Northam Devon 6 D3
Northam Soton 10 C3
Northampton Northants 28 B4
Northaw Herts 19 A9
Northbeck Lincs 37 A6
Northborough Pboro 37 E7
Northbourne Kent 21 F10
Northbridge Street E Sus 12 D6
Northchapel W Sus 11 B8
Northchurch Herts 28 H6
Northcott Devon 6 G2
Northdown Kent 21 D10
Northdyke Orkney 95 F3
Northend Bath 16 E4
Northend Bucks 18 B4
Northend Warks 27 C10
Northenden Gtr Man 44 C2
Northfield Aberdeen 83 C11
Northfield Borders 71 D8
Northfield E Yorks 52 G6
Northfield W Mid 34 H6
Northfields Lincs 36 E6
Northfleet Kent 20 D3
Northgate Lincs 37 C7
Northhouse Borders 61 C10
Northiam E Sus 13 D7
Northill C Beds 29 D8
Northington Hants 18 H2
Northlands Lincs 47 G7
Northlea Durham 58 A5
Northleach Glos 27 G8
Northleigh Devon 7 G10
Northlew Devon 6 G4
Northmoor Oxon 17 A11
Northmoor Green or Moorland Som 8 A2
Northmuir Angus 76 B6
Northney Hants 10 D6
Northolt London 19 C8
Northop Flint 42 F5
Northop Hall Flint 42 F5
Northorpe Lincs 37 B8
Northorpe Lincs 37 D6
Northorpe Lincs 46 C2
Northover Som 8 B3
Northover Som 15 H10
Northowram W Yorks 51 G7
Northport Dorset 9 F8
Northpunds Shetland 96 L6
Northrepps Norf 39 B8
Northtown Orkney 95 J5
Northway Glos 26 E6
Northwich Ches W 43 E9
Northwick S Glos 16 C2
Northwold Norf 38 F3
Northwood Derbys 44 F6
Northwood IoW 10 E3
Northwood Kent 21 E10
Northwood London 19 B7
Northwood Shrops 33 B10
Northwood Green Glos 26 G4
Norton E Sus 12 F3
Norton Glos 26 F5
Norton Halton 43 D8
Norton Herts 29 E9
Norton IoW 10 F2
Norton Mon 25 G11
Norton Northants 28 B3
Norton Notts 45 E9
Norton Powys 25 B10
Norton S Yorks 51 H11
Norton Shrops 33 G10
Norton Shrops 34 E1
Norton Shrops 34 E3
Norton Stockton 58 D5
Norton Suff 30 B6
Norton W Sus 11 D8
Norton W Sus 11 E7
Norton Wilts 16 C5
Norton Worcs 26 C5
Norton Worcs 27 D7
Norton Bavant Wilts 16 G6
Norton Bridge Staffs 34 B4
Norton Canes Staffs 34 E6
Norton Canon Hereford 25 D10
Norton Corner Norf 39 C6
Norton Disney Lincs 46 G2
Norton East Staffs 34 E6
Norton Ferris Wilts 16 H4
Norton Fitzwarren Som 7 D10
Norton Green IoW 10 F2
Norton Hawkfield Bath 16 E2
Norton Heath Essex 20 A3
Norton in Hales Shrops 34 B3
Norton-in-the-Moors Stoke 44 G2
Norton-Juxta-Twycross Leics 35 E9
Norton-le-Clay N Yorks 51 B10
Norton Lindsey Warks 27 B9
Norton Malreward Bath 16 E3
Norton Mandeville Essex 20 A2
Norton-on-Derwent N Yorks 52 B3
Norton St Philip Som 16 F4
Norton sub Hamdon Som 8 C3
Norton Woodseats S Yorks 45 D7
Norwell Notts 45 F11
Norwell Woodhouse Notts 45 F11
Norwich Norf 39 E8
Norwick Shetland 96 B8
Norwood Derbys 45 D8
Norwood Hill Sur 19 G9
Norwoodside Cambs 37 F10
Noseley Leics 36 F3
Noss Shetland 96 M5
Noss Mayo Devon 4 G6
Nosterfield N Yorks 51 A8
Nostie Highld 85 F13
Notgrove Glos 27 F8
Nottage Bridgend 14 D4
Nottingham Nottingham 36 B1
Nottington Dorset 8 F5
Notton W Yorks 45 A7
Notton Wilts 16 E6
Nounsley Essex 30 G4
Noutard's Green Worcs 26 B4
Novar House Highld 87 E9
Nox Shrops 33 D10
Nuffield Oxon 18 C3
Nun Hills Lancs 50 G4
Nun Monkton N Yorks 51 D11
Nunburnholme E Yorks 52 E4
Nuncargate Notts 45 G9
Nuneaton Warks 35 F9
Nuneham Courtenay Oxon 18 B2
Nunney Som 16 G4
Nunnington N Yorks 52 B2
Nunnykirk Northumb 62 D6
Nunsthorpe NE Lincs 46 B6
Nunthorpe Mbro 59 E6
Nunthorpe York 52 D2
Nunton Wilts 9 B10
Nunwick N Yorks 51 B9
Nupend Glos 26 H4
Nursling Hants 10 C2
Nursted Hants 11 B6
Nutbourne W Sus 11 C9
Nutbourne W Sus 11 D6
Nutfield Sur 19 F10
Nuthall Notts 35 A11
Nuthampstead Herts 29 E11
Nuthurst W Sus 11 B10
Nutley E Sus 12 D3
Nutley Hants 18 G3
Nutwell S Yorks 45 B10
Nybster Highld 94 D5
Nyetimber W Sus 11 E7
Nyewood W Sus 11 B7
Nymet Rowland Devon 7 F6
Nymet Tracey Devon 7 G6
Nympsfield Glos 16 A5
Nynehead Som 7 D10
Nyton W Sus 11 D8

O

Oad Street Kent 20 E5
Oadby Leics 36 E2
Oak Cross Devon 6 G4
Oakamoor Staffs 35 A6
Oakbank W Loth 69 D9
Oakdale Caerph 15 B7
Oake Som 7 D10
Oaken Staffs 34 E4
Oakenclough Lancs 49 E5
Oakengates Telford 34 D3
Oakenholt Flint 42 E5
Oakenshaw Durham 58 C3
Oakenshaw W Yorks 51 G7
Oakerthorpe Derbys 45 G7
Oakes W Yorks 51 H7
Oakfield Torf 15 B9
Oakford Ceredig 23 A9
Oakford Devon 7 D8
Oakfordbridge Devon 7 D8
Oakgrove Ches E 44 F3
Oakham Rutland 36 E4
Oakhanger Hants 18 H4
Oakhill Som 16 G3
Oakhurst Kent 20 F2
Oakington Cambs 29 B11
Oaklands Herts 29 G9
Oaklands Powys 25 C7
Oakle Street Glos 26 G4
Oakley Bedford 29 C7
Oakley Bucks 28 G3
Oakley Fife 69 B9
Oakley Hants 18 F2
Oakley Oxon 18 A4
Oakley Poole 9 E9
Oakley Suff 39 H7
Oakley Green Windsor 18 D6
Oakley Park Powys 32 G5
Oakmere Ches W 43 F8
Oakridge Glos 16 A6
Oakridge Hants 18 F3
Oaks Shrops 33 E10
Oaks Green Derbys 35 B7
Oaksey Wilts 16 B6
Oakthorpe Leics 35 D9
Oakwoodhill Sur 19 H8
Oakworth W Yorks 50 F6
Oape Highld 92 J7
Oare Kent 21 E7
Oare Som 7 B7
Oare W Berks 18 D2
Oare Wilts 17 E8
Oasby Lincs 36 B6
Oathlaw Angus 77 B7
Oatlands N Yorks 51 D9
Oban Argyll 79 J11
Oban Highld 79 C11
Oborne Dorset 8 C5
Obthorpe Lincs 37 D6
Occlestone Green Ches W 43 F9
Occold Suff 31 A8
Ochiltree E Ayrs 67 D8
Ochtermuthill Perth 75 F11
Ochtertyre Perth 75 E11
Ockbrook Derbys 35 B10
Ockham Sur 19 F7
Ockle Highld 79 D8
Ockley Sur 19 H8
Ocle Pychard Hereford 26 D2
Octon E Yorks 52 C6
Octon Cross E Yorks 52 C6
Odcombe Som 8 C4
Odd Down Bath 16 E4
Oddendale Cumb 57 E7
Odder Lincs 46 E3
Oddingley Worcs 26 C6
Oddington Glos 27 F9
Oddington Oxon 28 G2
Odell Bedford 28 C6
Odie Orkney 95 F7
Odiham Hants 18 F4
Odstock Wilts 9 B10
Odstone Leics 35 E9
Offchurch Warks 27 B10
Offenham Worcs 27 D7
Offham E Sus 12 E2
Offham Kent 20 F3
Offham W Sus 11 D9
Offord Cluny Cambs 29 B9
Offord Darcy Cambs 29 B9
Offton Suff 31 D7
Offwell Devon 7 G10
Ogbourne Maizey Wilts 17 D8
Ogbourne St Andrew Wilts 17 D8
Ogbourne St George Wilts 17 D9
Ogil Angus 77 A7
Ogle Northumb 63 F7
Ogmore V Glam 14 D4
Ogmore-by-Sea V Glam 14 D4
Ogmore Vale Bridgend 14 B5
Okeford Fitzpaine Dorset 9 C7
Okehampton Devon 6 G4
Okehampton Camp Devon 6 G4
Okraquoy Shetland 96 K6
Old Northants 28 A4
Old Aberdeen Aberdeen 83 C11
Old Alresford Hants 10 A4
Old Arley Warks 35 F8
Old Basford Nottingham 35 A11
Old Basing Hants 18 F3
Old Bewick Northumb 62 A6
Old Bolingbroke Lincs 47 F7
Old Bramhope W Yorks 51 E8
Old Brampton Derbys 45 E7
Old Bridge of Tilt Perth 81 G10
Old Bridge of Urr Dumfries 55 C10
Old Buckenham Norf 39 F6
Old Burghclere Hants 17 F11
Old Byland N Yorks 59 H6
Old Cassop Durham 58 C4
Old Castleton Borders 61 D11
Old Catton Norf 39 D8
Old Clee NE Lincs 46 B6
Old Cleeve Som 7 B9
Old Clipstone Notts 45 F10
Old Colwyn Conwy 41 C10
Old Coulsdon London 19 F10
Old Crombie Aberds 88 C5
Old Dailly S Ayrs 66 G5
Old Dalby Leics 36 C2
Old Deer Aberds 89 D9
Old Denaby S Yorks 45 C8
Old Edlington S Yorks 45 C9
Old Eldon Durham 58 D3
Old Ellerby E Yorks 53 F7
Old Felixstowe Suff 31 E10
Old Fletton Pboro 37 F7
Old Glossop Derbys 44 C4
Old Goole E Yorks 52 G3
Old Hall Powys 32 G5
Old Heath Essex 31 F7
Old Heathfield E Sus 12 D4
Old Hill W Mid 34 G5
Old Hunstanton Norf 38 A2
Old Hurst Cambs 37 H8
Old Hutton Cumb 57 H7
Old Kea Corn 3 E7
Old Kilpatrick W Dunb 68 C3
Old Kinnernie Aberds 83 C9
Old Knebworth Herts 29 F9
Old Langho Lancs 50 F3
Old Laxey IoM 48 D4
Old Leake Lincs 47 G8
Old Malton N Yorks 52 B3
Old Micklefield W Yorks 51 F10
Old Milton Hants 9 E11
Old Milverton Warks 27 B9
Old Monkland N Lanark 68 D6
Old Netley Hants 10 D3
Old Philpstoun W Loth 69 C9
Old Quarrington Durham 58 C4
Old Radnor Powys 25 C9
Old Rattray Aberds 89 C10
Old Rayne Aberds 83 A8
Old Romney Kent 13 D9
Old Sodbury S Glos 16 C4
Old Somerby Lincs 36 B5
Old Stratford Northants 28 D4
Old Thirsk N Yorks 51 A10
Old Town Cumb 50 A1
Old Town Cumb 57 B6
Old Town Northumb 62 D4
Old Town Scilly 2 C3
Old Trafford Gtr Man 44 C2
Old Tupton Derbys 45 F7
Old Warden C Beds 29 D8
Old Weston Cambs 37 H6
Old Whittington Derbys 45 E7
Old Wick Highld 94 E5
Old Windsor Windsor 18 D6
Old Wives Lees Kent 21 F7
Old Woking Sur 19 F7
Old Woodhall Lincs 46 F6
Oldany Highld 92 F4
Oldberrow Warks 27 B8
Oldborough Devon 7 F6
Oldbury Shrops 34 F3
Oldbury W Mid 34 G5
Oldbury Warks 35 F9
Oldbury-on-Severn S Glos 16 B3
Oldbury on the Hill Glos 16 C5
Oldcastle Bridgend 14 D5
Oldcastle Mon 25 F10
Oldcotes Notts 45 D9
Oldfallow Staffs 34 D5
Oldfield Worcs 26 B5
Oldford Som 16 F4
Oldham Gtr Man 44 B3
Oldhamstocks E Loth 70 C6
Oldland S Glos 16 D3
Oldmeldrum Aberds 89 F8
Oldshore Beg Highld 92 D4
Oldshoremore Highld 92 D5
Oldstead N Yorks 51 A11
Oldtown Aberds 83 A7
Oldtown of Ord Aberds 88 C6
Oldway Swansea 23 H10
Oldways End Devon 7 D7
Oldwhat Aberds 89 C8
Olgrinmore Highld 94 E2
Oliver's Battery Hants 10 B3
Ollaberry Shetland 96 E5
Ollerton Ches E 43 E10
Ollerton Notts 45 F10
Ollerton Shrops 34 C2
Olmarch Ceredig 24 C3
Olney M Keynes 28 C5
Olrig Ho. Highld 94 D3
Olton W Mid 35 G7
Olveston S Glos 16 C3
Olwen Ceredig 23 B10
Ombersley Worcs 26 B5
Ompton Notts 45 F10
Onchan IoM 48 E3
Onecote Staffs 44 G4
Onen Mon 25 G11
Ongar Hill Norf 38 C1
Ongar Street Hereford 25 B10
Onibury Shrops 33 H10
Onich Highld 74 A3
Onllwyn Neath 24 G5
Onneley Staffs 34 A3
Onslow Village Sur 18 G6
Onthank E Ayrs 67 B7
Openwoodgate Derbys 45 H7
Opinan Highld 85 A12
Opinan Highld 91 H13
Orange Lane Borders 70 F6
Orange Row Norf 37 C11
Orasaigh W Isles 91 F8
Orbliston Moray 88 C3
Orbost Highld 84 D7
Orby Lincs 47 F8
Orchard Hill Devon 6 D3
Orchard Portman Som 8 B1
Orcheston Wilts 17 G7
Orcop Hereford 25 F11
Orcop Hill Hereford 25 F11
Ord Highld 85 G11
Ordhead Aberds 83 B8
Ordie Aberds 82 C6
Ordiequish Moray 88 C3
Ordsall Notts 45 D10
Ore E Sus 13 E7
Oreton Shrops 34 G2
Orford Suff 31 D11
Orford Warr 43 C9
Orgreave Staffs 35 D7
Orlestone Kent 13 C8
Orleton Hereford 25 B11
Orleton Worcs 26 B3
Orlingbury Northants 28 A5
Ormesby Redcar 59 E6
Ormesby St Margaret Norf 39 D10
Ormesby St Michael Norf 39 D10
Ormiclate Castle W Isles 84 E2
Ormiscaig Highld 91 H13
Ormiston E Loth 70 D3
Ormsaigbeg Highld 78 E7
Ormsaigmore Highld 78 E7
Ormsary Argyll 72 F6
Ormsgill Cumb 49 B1
Ormskirk Lancs 43 B7
Orpington London 19 E11
Orrell Gtr Man 43 B8
Orrell Mers 42 C6
Orrisdale IoM 48 C3
Orroland Dumfries 55 E10
Orsett Thurrock 20 C3
Orslow Staffs 34 D4
Orston Notts 36 A3
Orthwaite Cumb 56 C4
Ortner Lancs 49 D5
Orton Cumb 57 F8
Orton Northants 36 H4
Orton Longueville Pboro 37 F7
Orton-on-the-Hill Leics 35 E9
Orton Waterville Pboro 37 F7
Orwell Cambs 29 C10
Osbaldeston Lancs 50 F2
Osbaldwick York 52 D2
Osbaston Shrops 33 C9
Osbournby Lincs 37 B6
Oscroft Ches W 43 F8
Ose Highld 85 D8
Osgathorpe Leics 35 D10
Osgodby Lincs 46 C4
Osgodby N Yorks 52 F2
Osgodby N Yorks 53 A6
Oskaig Highld 85 E10
Oskamull Argyll 78 G7
Osmaston Derby 35 B9
Osmaston Derbys 35 A8
Osmington Dorset 8 F6
Osmington Mills Dorset 8 F6
Osmotherley N Yorks 58 G5
Ospisdale Highld 87 C10
Ospringe Kent 21 E7
Ossett W Yorks 51 G8
Ossington Notts 45 F11
Ostend Essex 20 B6
Oswaldkirk N Yorks 52 B2
Oswaldtwistle Lancs 50 G3
Oswestry Shrops 33 C8
Otford Kent 20 F2
Otham Kent 20 F4
Othery Som 8 A2
Otley Suff 31 C9
Otley W Yorks 51 E8
Otter Ferry Argyll 73 E8
Otterbourne Hants 10 B3
Otterburn N Yorks 50 D4
Otterburn Northumb 62 D4
Otterburn Camp Northumb 62 D4
Otterham Corn 4 B2
Otterhampton Som 15 G8
Ottershaw Sur 19 E7
Otterswick Shetland 96 E7
Otterton Devon 7 H9
Ottery St Mary Devon 7 G10
Ottinge Kent 21 G8
Ottringham E Yorks 53 G8
Oughterby Cumb 61 H8
Oughtershaw N Yorks 50 A4
Oughterside Cumb 56 B3
Oughtibridge S Yorks 45 C7
Oughtrington Warr 43 D9
Oulston N Yorks 51 B11
Oulton Cumb 56 A4
Oulton Norf 39 C7
Oulton Staffs 34 B5
Oulton Suff 39 F11
Oulton W Yorks 51 G9
Oulton Broad Suff 39 F11
Oulton Street Norf 39 C7
Oundle Northants 36 G6
Ousby Cumb 57 C8
Ousdale Highld 94 H2
Ousden Suff 30 C4
Ousefleet E Yorks 52 G4
Ouston Durham 58 A3
Ouston Northumb 62 F6
Out Newton E Yorks 53 G9
Out Rawcliffe Lancs 49 E4
Outertown Orkney 95 G3
Outgate Cumb 56 G5
Outhgill Cumb 57 F9
Outlane W Yorks 51 H6
Outwell Norf 37 E11
Outwick Hants 9 C10
Outwood Sur 19 G10
Outwood W Yorks 51 G9
Outwoods Staffs 34 D3
Ovenden W Yorks 51 G6
Ovenscloss Borders 70 G3
Over Cambs 29 A10
Over Ches W 43 F9
Over S Glos 16 C2
Over Compton Dorset 8 C4
Over Green W Mid 35 F7
Over Haddon Derbys 44 F6
Over Hulton Gtr Man 43 B9
Over Kellet Lancs 49 B5
Over Kiddington Oxon 27 F11
Over Knutsford Ches E 43 E10
Over Monnow Mon 26 G2
Over Norton Oxon 27 F10
Over Peover Ches E 43 E10
Over Silton N Yorks 58 G5
Over Stowey Som 7 C10
Over Stratton Som 8 C3
Over Tabley Ches E 43 D10
Over Wallop Hants 17 H9
Over Whitacre Warks 35 F8
Over Worton Oxon 27 F11
Overbister Orkney 95 D7
Overbury Worcs 26 E6
Overcombe Dorset 8 F5
Overgreen Derbys 45 E7
Overleigh Som 15 H10
Overley Green Warks 27 C7
Overpool Ches W 43 E6
Overscaig Hotel Highld 92 G7
Overseal Derbys 35 D8
Oversland Kent 21 F7
Overstone Northants 28 B5
Overstrand Norf 39 A8
Overthorpe Northants 27 D11
Overton Aberdeen 83 B10
Overton Ches W 43 E8
Overton Dumfries 60 G5
Overton Hants 18 G2
Overton Lancs 49 D4
Overton N Yorks 52 D1
Overton Shrops 26 A2
Overton Swansea 23 H9
Overton W Yorks 51 H8
Overton = Owrtyn Wrex 33 A9
Overton Bridge Wrex 33 A9
Overtown N Lanark 69 E7
Oving Bucks 28 F4
Oving W Sus 11 D8
Ovingdean Brighton 12 F2
Ovingham Northumb 62 G6
Ovington Durham 58 E2
Ovington Essex 30 D4
Ovington Hants 10 A4
Ovington Norf 38 E5
Ovington Northumb 62 G6
Ower Hants 10 C2
Owermoigne Dorset 9 F6
Owlbury Shrops 33 F9
Owler Bar Derbys 44 E6
Owlerton S Yorks 45 D7
Owl's Green Suff 31 B9
Owlswick Bucks 28 H4
Owmby Lincs 46 B4
Owmby-by-Spital Lincs 46 D4
Owrtyn = Overton Wrex 33 A9
Owslebury Hants 10 B4
Owston Leics 36 E3
Owston S Yorks 45 A9
Owston Ferry N Lincs 46 B2
Owstwick E Yorks 53 F8
Owthorne E Yorks 53 G9
Owthorpe Notts 36 B2
Oxborough Norf 38 E3
Oxcombe Lincs 47 E7
Oxen Park Cumb 56 H5
Oxenholme Cumb 57 H7
Oxenhope W Yorks 50 F6
Oxenton Glos 26 E6
Oxenwood Wilts 17 F10
Oxford Oxon 28 H2
Oxhey Herts 19 B8
Oxhill Warks 27 D10
Oxley W Mid 34 E5
Oxley Green Essex 30 G6
Oxley's Green E Sus 12 D5
Oxnam Borders 62 B3
Oxshott Sur 19 E8
Oxspring S Yorks 44 B6
Oxted Sur 19 F10
Oxton Borders 70 E3
Oxton Notts 45 G10
Oxwich Swansea 23 H9
Oxwick Norf 38 C5
Oykel Bridge Highld 92 J6
Oyne Aberds 83 A8

P

Pabail Iarach W Isles 91 D10
Pabail Uarach W Isles 91 D10
Pace Gate N Yorks 51 D7
Packington Leics 35 D9
Padanaram Angus 77 B7
Padbury Bucks 28 E4
Paddington London 19 C9
Paddlesworth Kent 21 H8
Paddock Wood Kent 12 B5
Paddockhaugh Moray 88 C2
Paddockhole Dumfries 61 E8
Padfield Derbys 44 C4
Padiham Lancs 50 F3
Padog Conwy 41 E10
Padside N Yorks 51 D7
Padstow Corn 3 B8
Padworth W Berks 18 E3
Page Bank Durham 58 C3
Pagelsham Eastend Essex 20 B6
Pagham W Sus 11 E7
Paglesham Churchend Essex 20 B6
Paibeil W Isles 84 B2
Paible W Isles 90 H5
Paignton Torbay 5 E9
Pailton Warks 35 G10
Painscastle Powys 25 D8
Painshawfield Northumb 62 G6
Painsthorpe E Yorks 52 D4
Painswick Glos 26 H5
Pairc Shiaboist W Isles 90 C7
Paisley Renfs 68 D3
Pakefield Suff 39 F11
Pakenham Suff 30 B6
Pale Gwyn 32 B5
Palestine Hants 17 G9
Paley Street Windsor 18 D5
Palfrey W Mid 34 F6
Palgowan Dumfries 54 A6
Palgrave Suff 39 H7
Pallion T&W 63 H9
Palmarsh Kent 13 C10
Palnackie Dumfries 55 D11
Palnure Dumfries 55 C7
Palterton Derbys 45 F8
Pamber End Hants 18 F3
Pamber Green Hants 18 F3
Pamber Heath Hants 18 E3
Pamphill Dorset 9 D8
Pampisford Cambs 29 D11
Pan Orkney 95 J4
Panbride Angus 77 D8
Pancrasweek Devon 6 F1
Pandy Gwyn 32 E2
Pandy Mon 25 F10
Pandy Powys 32 E5
Pandy Wrex 33 B7
Pandy Tudur Conwy 41 D10
Panfield Essex 30 F4
Pangbourne W Berks 18 D3
Pannal N Yorks 51 D9
Panshanger Herts 29 G9
Pant Shrops 33 C8
Pant-glâs Powys 32 F3
Pant-glas Carms 23 D10
Pant-glas Gwyn 40 F6
Pant-glas Shrops 33 B8
Pant-lasau Swansea 14 B2
Pant Mawr Powys 32 G4
Pant-teg Carms 23 D9
Pant-y-Caws Carms 22 D6
Pant-y-dwr Powys 32 H5
Pant-y-ffridd Powys 33 E7
Pant-y-Wacco Flint 42 E4
Pant-yr-awel Bridgend 14 C5
Pantgwyn Carms 23 D10
Pantgwyn Ceredig 23 B7
Panton Lincs 46 E5
Pantperthog Gwyn 32 E3
Pantyffynnon Carms 24 G3
Pantymwyn Flint 42 F4
Panxworth Norf 39 D9
Papcastle Cumb 56 C3
Papigoe Highld 94 E5
Papil Shetland 96 K5
Papley Orkney 95 J5
Papple E Loth 70 C4
Papplewick Notts 45 G9
Papworth Everard Cambs 29 B9
Papworth St Agnes Cambs 29 B9
Par Corn 4 F1
Parbold Lancs 43 A7
Parbrook Som 16 H2
Parbrook W Sus 11 B9
Parc Gwyn 41 G10
Parc-Seymour Newport 15 B10
Parc-y-rhôs Carms 23 B10
Parcllyn Ceredig 23 A7
Pardshaw Cumb 56 D2
Parham Suff 31 B10
Park Dumfries 60 D5
Park Corner Oxon 18 C3
Park Corner Windsor 18 C5
Park End Mbro 58 E6
Park End Northumb 62 F4
Park Gate Hants 10 D4
Park Hill N Yorks 51 C9
Park Hill Notts 45 G10
Park Street W Sus 11 A10
Parkend Glos 26 H3
Parkeston Essex 31 E9
Parkgate Ches W 42 E5
Parkgate Dumfries 60 E6
Parkgate Kent 13 C7
Parkgate Sur 19 G9
Parkham Devon 6 D2
Parkham Ash Devon 6 D2
Parkhill Ho. Aberds 83 B10
Parkhouse Mon 15 A10
Parkhouse Green Derbys 45 F8
Parkhurst IoW 10 E3
Parkmill Swansea 23 H10
Parkneuk Aberds 83 F9
Parkstone Poole 9 E9
Parley Cross Dorset 9 E9
Parracombe Devon 6 B5
Parrog Pembs 22 C5
Parsley Hay Derbys 44 F5
Parson Cross S Yorks 45 C7
Parson Drove Cambs 37 E9
Parsonage Green Essex 30 H4
Parsonby Cumb 56 C3
Parson's Heath Essex 31 F7
Partick Glasgow 68 D4
Partington Gtr Man 43 C10
Partney Lincs 47 F8
Parton Cumb 56 D1
Parton Dumfries 55 B9
Parton Glos 26 F5
Partridge Green W Sus 11 C10
Parwich Derbys 44 G5
Passenham Northants 28 E4
Paston Norf 39 B9
Patchacott Devon 6 G3
Patcham Brighton 12 F2
Patching W Sus 11 D9
Patchole Devon 6 B5
Pateley Bridge N Yorks 51 C7
Paternoster Heath Essex 30 G6
Path of Condie Perth 76 F3
Pathe Som 8 A2
Pathhead Aberds 77 A10
Pathhead E Ayrs 67 E9
Pathhead Fife 69 A11
Pathhead Midloth 70 D2
Pathstruie Perth 76 F3
Patna E Ayrs 67 E7
Patney Wilts 17 F7
Patrick IoM 48 D2
Patrick Brompton N Yorks 58 G3
Patrington E Yorks 53 G9
Patrixbourne Kent 21 F8
Patterdale Cumb 56 E5
Pattingham Staffs 34 F4
Pattishall Northants 28 C3
Pattiswick Green Essex 30 F5
Patton Bridge Cumb 57 G7
Paul Corn 2 G3
Paulerspury Northants 28 D4
Paull E Yorks 53 G7
Paulton Bath 16 F3
Pavenham Bedford 28 C6
Pawlett Som 15 G9
Pawston Northumb 71 G7
Paxford Glos 27 E8
Paxton Borders 71 E8
Payhembury Devon 7 F9
Paythorne Lancs 50 D4
Peacehaven E Sus 12 F3
Peak Dale Derbys 44 E4
Peak Forest Derbys 44 E5
Peakirk Pboro 37 E7
Pearsie Angus 76 B6
Pease Pottage W Sus 12 C1
Peasedown St John Bath 16 F4
Peasemore W Berks 17 D11
Peasenhall Suff 31 B10
Peaslake Sur 19 G7
Peasley Cross Mers 43 C8
Peasmarsh E Sus 13 D7
Peaston E Loth 70 D3
Peastonbank E Loth 70 D3
Peat Inn Fife 77 G7
Peathill Aberds 89 B9
Peatling Magna Leics 36 F1
Peatling Parva Leics 36 G1
Peaton Shrops 33 G11
Peats Corner Suff 31 B8
Pebmarsh Essex 30 E5
Pebworth Worcs 27 D8
Pecket Well W Yorks 50 G5
Peckforton Ches E 43 G8
Peckham London 19 D10
Peckleton Leics 35 E10
Pedlinge Kent 13 C10
Pedmore W Mid 34 G5
Pedwell Som 15 H10
Peebles Borders 69 F11
Peel IoM 48 D2
Peel Common Hants 10 D4
Peel Park S Lanark 68 E5
Peening Quarter Kent 13 D7
Pegsdon C Beds 29 E8
Pegswood Northumb 63 E8
Pegwell Kent 21 E10
Peinchorran Highld 85 E10
Peinlich Highld 85 C9
Pelaw T&W 63 G8
Pelcomb Bridge Pembs 22 E4
Pelcomb Cross Pembs 22 E4
Peldon Essex 30 G6
Pellon W Yorks 51 G6
Pelsall W Mid 34 E6
Pelton Durham 58 A3
Pelutho Cumb 56 B3
Pelynt Corn 4 F3
Pemberton Gtr Man 43 B8
Pembrey Carms 23 F9
Pembridge Hereford 25 C10
Pembroke = Penfro Pembs 22 F4
Pembroke Dock = Doc Penfro Pembs 22 F4
Pembury Kent 12 B5
Pen-bont Rhydybeddau Ceredig 32 G2
Pen-clawdd Swansea 23 G10
Pen-ffordd Pembs 22 D5
Pen-groes-oped Mon 25 H10
Pen-llyn Anglesey 40 B5
Pen-lon Anglesey 40 D6
Pen-sarn Gwyn 32 C1
Pen-sarn Gwyn 40 F6
Pen-twyn Mon 26 H2
Pen-y-banc Carms 23 D10
Pen-y-bont Carms 23 D8
Pen-y-bont Gwyn 32 C2
Pen-y-bont Gwyn 32 E3
Pen-y-bont Powys 33 C8
Pen-y-bont ar Ogwr = Bridgend Bridgend 14 D5
Pen-y-bryn Gwyn 32 D2
Pen-y-bryn Pembs 22 B6
Pen-y-cae Powys 24 G5
Pen-y-cae-mawr Mon 15 B10
Pen-y-cefn Flint 42 E4
Pen-y-clawdd Mon 25 H11
Pen-y-coedcae Rhondda 14 C6
Pen-y-fai Bridgend 14 C4
Pen-y-garn Carms 23 C10
Pen-y-garn Ceredig 32 G2
Pen-y-garnedd Anglesey 41 C7
Pen-y-gop Conwy 32 A5
Pen-y-graig Gwyn 40 G3
Pen-y-groes Carms 23 E10
Pen-y-groeslon Gwyn 40 G4
Pen-y-Gwryd Hotel Gwyn 41 E8
Pen-y-stryt Denb 42 G4
Pen-yr-heol Mon 25 G11
Pen-yr-Heolgerrig M Tydf 25 H7
Penallt Mon 26 G2
Penally Pembs 22 G6
Penalt Hereford 26 F2
Penare Corn 3 E8
Penarlâg = Hawarden Flint 42 F6
Penarth V Glam 15 D7
Penbryn Ceredig 23 A7
Pencader Carms 23 C9
Pencaenewydd Gwyn 40 F6
Pencaitland E Loth 70 D3
Pencarnisiog Anglesey 40 C5
Pencarreg Carms 23 B10
Pencelli Powys 25 F7
Pencoed Bridgend 14 C5
Pencombe Hereford 26 C2
Pencoyd Hereford 26 F2
Pencraig Hereford 26 F2
Pencraig Powys 32 C6
Pendeen Corn 2 F2
Penderyn Rhondda 24 H6
Pendine Carms 23 F7
Pendlebury Gtr Man 43 B10
Pendleton Lancs 43 F3
Pendock Worcs 26 E4
Pendoggett Corn 3 B9
Pendomer Som 8 C4
Pendoylan V Glam 14 D6
Pendre Bridgend 14 C5
Penegoes Powys 32 E3
Penfro = Pembroke Pembs 22 F4
Pengam Caerph 15 B7
Penge London 19 D10
Pengenffordd Powys 25 E8
Pengorffwysfa Anglesey 40 A6
Pengover Green Corn 4 E3
Penhale Corn 2 H5
Penhale Corn 3 D8
Penhalvaen Corn 2 F6
Penhill Swindon 17 C8
Penhow Newport 15 B10
Penhurst E Sus 12 E5
Peniarth Gwyn 32 E2
Penicuik Midloth 69 D11
Peniel Carms 23 D9
Peniel Denb 42 F3
Penifiler Highld 85 D9
Peninver Argyll 65 F8
Penisarwaun Gwyn 41 D7
Penistone S Yorks 44 B6
Penjerrick Corn 3 F6
Penketh Warr 43 D8
Penkill S Ayrs 66 G5
Penkridge Staffs 34 D5
Penley Wrex 33 B10
Penllergaer Swansea 14 B2
Penllyn V Glam 14 D5
Penmachno Conwy 41 E9
Penmaen Swansea 23 H10
Penmaenan Conwy 41 C9
Penmaenmawr Conwy 41 C9
Penmaenpool Gwyn 32 D2
Penmark V Glam 14 E6
Penmarth Corn 2 F6
Penmon Anglesey 41 B8
Penmore Mill Argyll 78 F7
Penmorfa Ceredig 23 A8
Penmorfa Gwyn 41 F7
Penmynydd Anglesey 41 C7
Penn Bucks 18 B6
Penn W Mid 34 F4
Penn Street Bucks 18 B6
Pennal Gwyn 32 E3
Pennan Aberds 89 B8
Pennant Ceredig 24 B2
Pennant Denb 32 B6
Pennant Denb 42 G3
Pennant Powys 32 F4
Pennant Melangell Powys 32 C6
Pennar Pembs 22 F4
Pennard Swansea 23 H10
Pennerley Shrops 33 F9
Pennington Cumb 49 B2
Pennington Gtr Man 43 C9
Pennington Hants 10 E2
Penny Bridge Cumb 49 A3
Pennycross Argyll 79 J8
Pennygate Norf 39 C9
Pennygown Argyll 79 G8
Pennymoor Devon 7 E7
Pennywell T&W 63 H9
Penparc Ceredig 23 B7
Penparc Pembs 22 C3
Penparcau Ceredig 32 G1
Penperlleni Mon 15 A9
Penpillick Corn 4 F1
Penpol Corn 3 F7
Penpoll Corn 4 F2
Penpont Dumfries 60 D4
Penpont Powys 24 F6
Penrhôs Mon 25 G11
Penrherber Carms 23 C7
Penrhiw goch Carms 23 E10
Penrhiw-llan Ceredig 23 B8
Penrhiw-pâl Ceredig 23 B8
Penrhiwceiber Rhondda 14 B6
Penrhos Gwyn 40 G5
Penrhos Powys 24 G4
Penrhosfeilw Anglesey 40 B4
Penrhyn Bay Conwy 41 B10
Penrhyn-coch Ceredig 32 G2
Penrhyndeudraeth Gwyn 41 G8
Penrhynside Conwy 41 B10
Penrice Swansea 23 H9
Penrith Cumb 57 C7
Penrose Corn 3 B7
Penruddock Cumb 56 D6
Penryn Corn 3 F6
Pensarn Carms 23 E9
Pensarn Conwy 42 E2
Pensax Worcs 26 B4
Pensby Mers 42 D5
Penselwood Som 9 A6
Pensford Bath 16 E3
Penshaw T&W 58 A4
Penshurst Kent 12 B4
Pensilva Corn 4 E3
Penston E Loth 70 C3
Pentewan Corn 3 E9
Pentir Gwyn 41 D7
Pentire Corn 3 C6
Pentlow Essex 30 D5
Penton Mewsey Hants 17 G10
Pentraeth Anglesey 41 C7
Pentre Carms 23 E10
Pentre Powys 33 F8
Pentre Powys 33 G6
Pentre Rhondda 14 B5
Pentre Shrops 33 D9
Pentre Wrex 33 A8
Pentre Wrex 33 B7
Pentre-bâch Ceredig 23 B10
Pentre-bach Powys 24 E6
Pentre Berw Anglesey 40 C6
Pentre-bont Conwy 41 E9
Pentre-celyn Denb 42 G4
Pentre-Celyn Powys 32 E4
Pentre-chwyth Swansea 14 B2
Pentre-cwrt Carms 23 C8
Pentre Dolau-Honddu Powys 24 D6
Pentre-dwr Swansea 14 B2
Pentre-galar Pembs 22 C6
Pentre-Gwenlais Carms 24 G3
Pentre Gwynfryn Gwyn 32 C1
Pentre Halkyn Flint 42 E5
Pentre-Isaf Conwy 41 D10
Pentre Llanrhaeadr Denb 42 F3
Pentre-llwyn-llŵyd Powys 24 C6
Pentre-llyn Ceredig 24 A3

Sta – Thi 133

Stanton Harcourt Oxon 27 H11
Stanton Hill Notts 45 F8
Stanton in Peak Derbys 44 F6
Stanton Lacy Shrops 33 H10
Stanton Long Shrops 34 F1
Stanton-on-the-Wolds Notts 36 B2
Stanton Prior Bath 16 E3
Stanton St Bernard Wilts 17 E7
Stanton St John Oxon 28 H2
Stanton St Quintin Wilts 16 D6
Stanton Street Suff 30 B6
Stanton under Bardon Leics 35 D10
Stanton upon Hine Heath Shrops 34 C1
Stanton Wick Bath 16 E3
Stanwardine in the Fields Shrops 33 C10
Stanwardine in the Wood Shrops 33 C10
Stanway Essex 30 F6
Stanway Glos 27 E7
Stanway Green Suff 31 A9
Stanwell Sur 19 D7
Stanwell Moor Sur 19 D7
Stanwick Northants 28 A6
Stanwick-St-John N Yorks 58 E2
Stanwix Cumb 61 H10
Stanydale Shetland 96 H4
Staoinebrig W Isles 84 E2
Stape N Yorks 59 G8
Stapehill Dorset 9 D9
Stapeley Ches E 43 H9
Stapenhill Staffs 35 C8
Staple Kent 21 F9
Staple Som 7 B10
Staple Cross E Sus 13 D6
Staple Fitzpaine Som 8 C1
Staplefield W Sus 12 D1
Stapleford Cambs 29 C11
Stapleford Herts 29 G10
Stapleford Leics 36 D4
Stapleford Lincs 46 G2
Stapleford Notts 35 B10
Stapleford Wilts 17 H7
Stapleford Abbotts Essex 20 B2
Stapleford Tawney Essex 20 B2
Staplegrove Som 7 D11
Staplehay Som 7 D11
Staplehurst Kent 13 B6
Staplers IoW 10 F4
Stapleton Bristol 16 D3
Stapleton Cumb 61 F11
Stapleton Hereford 25 B10
Stapleton Leics 35 F10
Stapleton N Yorks 58 E3
Stapleton Shrops 33 E10
Stapleton Som 8 B3
Stapley Som 7 E10
Staploe Bedford 29 B8
Staplow Hereford 26 D3
Star Fife 76 G6
Star Pembs 23 C7
Star Som 15 F10
Stara Orkney 95 F3
Starbeck N Yorks 51 D9
Starbotton N Yorks 50 B5
Starcross Devon 5 C10
Stareton Warks 27 A10
Starkholmes Derbys 45 G7
Starlings Green Essex 29 E11
Starston Norf 39 G8
Startforth Durham 58 E1
Startley Wilts 16 C6
Stathe Som 8 B2
Stathern Leics 36 B3
Station Town Durham 58 C5
Staughton Green Cambs 29 B8
Staughton Highway Cambs 29 B8
Staunton Glos 26 F4
Staunton Glos 26 G2
Staunton in the Vale Notts 36 A4
Staunton on Arrow Hereford 25 B10
Staunton on Wye Hereford 25 D10
Staveley Cumb 56 G6
Staveley Cumb 56 H5
Staveley Derbys 45 E8
Staveley N Yorks 51 C9
Staverton Devon 5 E8
Staverton Glos 26 F5
Staverton Northants 28 B2
Staverton Wilts 16 E5
Staverton Bridge Glos 26 F5
Stawell Som 15 H9
Staxigoe Highld 94 E5
Staxton N Yorks 52 B6
Staylittle Powys 32 F4
Staynall Lancs 49 E3
Staythorpe Notts 45 G11
Stean N Yorks 51 B6
Stearsby N Yorks 52 B2
Steart Som 15 G8
Stebbing Essex 30 F3
Stebbing Green Essex 30 F3
Stedham W Sus 11 B7
Steele Road Borders 61 D11
Steen's Bridge Hereford 26 C2
Steep Hants 10 B6
Steep Marsh Hants 11 B6
Steeple Dorset 9 F8
Steeple Essex 20 A6
Steeple Ashton Wilts 16 F6
Steeple Aston Oxon 27 F11
Steeple Barton Oxon 27 F11
Steeple Bumpstead Essex 30 D3
Steeple Claydon Bucks 28 F3
Steeple Gidding Cambs 37 G7
Steeple Langford Wilts 17 H7
Steeple Morden Cambs 29 D9
Steeton W Yorks 50 E6
Stein Highld 84 C7
Steinmanhill Aberds 89 D7
Stelling Minnis Kent 21 G8
Stemster Highld 94 D3
Stemster Ho. Highld 94 D3
Stenalees Corn 3 D9
Stenhousemuir Falk 69 B7
Stenigot Lincs 46 D6
Stenness Shetland 96 F4
Stenscholl Highld 85 B9
Stenso Orkney 95 F4
Stenson Derbys 35 C9
Stenton E Loth 70 C5
Stenton Fife 76 H5
Stenwith Lincs 36 B4
Stepaside Pembs 22 F6
Stepping Hill Gtr Man 44 D3
Steppingley C Beds 29 E7
Stepps N Lanark 68 D5
Sterndale Moor Derbys 44 F5
Sternfield Suff 31 B10
Sterridge Devon 6 B4
Stert Wilts 17 F7
Stetchworth Cambs 30 C3
Stevenage Herts 29 F9
Stevenston N Ayrs 66 B5
Steventon Hants 18 G2
Steventon Oxon 17 B11
Stevington Bedford 28 C6
Stewartby Bedford 29 D7
Stewarton Argyll 65 G7
Stewarton E Ayrs 67 B7
Stewkley Bucks 28 F5
Stewton Lincs 47 D7
Steyne Cross IoW 10 F5
Steyning W Sus 11 C10
Steynton Pembs 22 F4
Stibb Corn 6 E1
Stibb Cross Devon 6 E3
Stibb Green Wilts 17 E9
Stibbard Norf 38 C5
Stibbington Cambs 37 F6
Stichill Borders 70 G6
Sticker Corn 3 D8
Stickford Lincs 47 G7
Sticklepath Devon 6 G5
Stickney Lincs 47 G7
Stiffkey Norf 38 A5
Stifford's Bridge Hereford 26 D4
Stillingfleet N Yorks 52 E1
Stillington N Yorks 52 C1
Stillington Stockton 58 D4
Stilton Cambs 37 G7
Stinchcombe Glos 16 B4
Stinsford Dorset 8 E6
Stirchley Telford 34 E3
Stirkoke Ho. Highld 94 E5
Stirling Aberds 89 D11
Stirling Stirling 68 A6
Stisted Essex 30 F4
Stithians Corn 2 F6
Stittenham Highld 87 D9
Stivichall W Mid 35 H9
Stixwould Lincs 46 F5
Stoak Ches W 43 E7
Stobieside S Lanark 68 G5
Stobo Borders 69 G10
Stoborough Dorset 9 F8
Stoborough Green Dorset 9 F8
Stobshiel E Loth 70 D3
Stobswood Northumb 63 D8
Stock Essex 20 B3
Stock Green Worcs 26 C6
Stock Wood Worcs 27 C7
Stockbridge Hants 10 A2
Stockbury Kent 20 E5
Stockcross W Berks 17 E11
Stockdalewath Cumb 56 B5
Stockerston Leics 36 F4
Stockheath Hants 10 D6
Stockiemuir Stirling 68 B4
Stocking Pelham Herts 29 F11
Stockingford Warks 35 F9
Stockland Devon 8 D1
Stockland Bristol Som 15 G8
Stockleigh English Devon 7 F7
Stockleigh Pomeroy Devon 7 F7
Stockley Wilts 17 E7
Stocklinch Som 8 C2
Stockport Gtr Man 44 C2
Stocksbridge S Yorks 44 C6
Stocksfield Northumb 62 G6
Stockton Hereford 26 B2
Stockton Norf 39 F9
Stockton Shrops 33 E8
Stockton Shrops 34 F3
Stockton Warks 27 B11
Stockton Wilts 16 H6
Stockton Heath Warr 43 D9
Stockton-on-Tees Stockton 58 E5
Stockton on Teme Worcs 26 B4
Stockton on the Forest York 52 D2
Stodmarsh Kent 21 E9
Stody Norf 39 B6
Stoer Highld 92 G3
Stoford Som 8 C4
Stoford Wilts 17 H7
Stogumber Som 7 C9
Stogursey Som 7 B11
Stoke Devon 6 D1
Stoke Hants 10 D6
Stoke Hants 17 F11
Stoke Medway 20 D5
Stoke Suff 31 D8
Stoke Abbott Dorset 8 D3
Stoke Albany Northants 36 G4
Stoke Ash Suff 31 A8
Stoke Bardolph Notts 36 A2
Stoke Bliss Worcs 26 B3
Stoke Bruerne Northants 28 D4
Stoke by Clare Suff 30 D4
Stoke-by-Nayland Suff 30 E6
Stoke Canon Devon 7 G8
Stoke Charity Hants 17 H11
Stoke Climsland Corn 4 D4
Stoke D'Abernon Sur 19 F8
Stoke Doyle Northants 36 G6
Stoke Dry Rutland 36 F4
Stoke Farthing Wilts 9 B9
Stoke Ferry Norf 38 F3
Stoke Fleming Devon 5 G9
Stoke Gabriel Devon 5 F9
Stoke Gifford S Glos 16 D3
Stoke Golding Leics 35 F9
Stoke Goldington M Keynes 28 D5
Stoke Green Bucks 18 C6
Stoke Hammond Bucks 28 F5
Stoke Heath Shrops 34 C2
Stoke Holy Cross Norf 39 E8
Stoke Lacy Hereford 26 D3
Stoke Lyne Oxon 28 F2
Stoke Mandeville Bucks 28 G5
Stoke Newington London 19 C10
Stoke on Tern Shrops 34 C2
Stoke-on-Trent Stoke 44 H2
Stoke Orchard Glos 26 F6
Stoke Poges Bucks 18 C6
Stoke Prior Hereford 26 C2
Stoke Prior Worcs 26 B6
Stoke Rivers Devon 6 C5
Stoke Rochford Lincs 36 C5
Stoke Row Oxon 18 C3
Stoke St Gregory Som 8 B2
Stoke St Mary Som 8 B1
Stoke St Michael Som 16 G3
Stoke St Milborough Shrops 34 G1
Stoke sub Hamdon Som 8 C3
Stoke Talmage Oxon 18 B3
Stoke Trister Som 8 B6
Stoke Wake Dorset 9 D6
Stokeford Dorset 9 F7
Stokeham Notts 45 E11
Stokeinteignhead Devon 5 D10
Stokenchurch Bucks 18 B4
Stokenham Devon 5 G9
Stokesay Shrops 33 G10
Stokesby Norf 39 D10
Stokesley N Yorks 59 F6
Stolford Som 7 B11
Ston Easton Som 16 F3
Stondon Massey Essex 20 A2
Stone Bucks 28 G4
Stone Glos 16 B3
Stone Kent 13 D8
Stone Kent 20 D2
Stone S Yorks 45 D9
Stone Staffs 34 B5
Stone Worcs 34 H4
Stone Allerton Som 15 F10
Stone Bridge Corner Pboro 37 E8
Stone Chair W Yorks 51 G7
Stone Cross E Sus 12 F5
Stone Cross Kent 21 F10
Stone-edge Batch N Som 15 D10
Stone House Cumb 57 H9
Stone Street Kent 20 F2
Stone Street Suff 30 E6
Stone Street Suff 39 G9
Stonebroom Derbys 45 G8
Stoneferry Hull 53 F7
Stonefield S Lanark 68 E5
Stonegate E Sus 12 D5
Stonegate N Yorks 59 F8
Stonegrave N Yorks 52 B2
Stonehaugh Northumb 62 F3
Stonehaven Aberds 83 E10
Stonehouse Glos 26 H5
Stonehouse Northumb 62 H2
Stonehouse S Lanark 68 F6
Stoneleigh Warks 27 A10
Stonely Cambs 29 B8
Stoner Hill Hants 10 B6
Stone's Green Essex 31 F8
Stonesby Leics 36 C4
Stonesfield Oxon 27 G10
Stonethwaite Cumb 56 E4
Stoney Cross Hants 10 C1
Stoney Middleton Derbys 44 E6
Stoney Stanton Leics 35 F10
Stoney Stoke Som 8 A6
Stoney Stratton Som 16 H3
Stoney Stretton Shrops 33 E9
Stoneybreck Shetland 96 N8
Stoneyburn W Loth 69 D8
Stoneygate Aberds 89 E10
Stoneygate Leicester 36 E2
Stoneyhills Essex 20 B6
Stoneykirk Dumfries 54 D3
Stoneywood Aberdeen 83 B10
Stoneywood Falk 68 B6
Stonganess Shetland 96 C7
Stonham Aspal Suff 31 C8
Stonnall Staffs 35 E6
Stonor Oxon 18 C4
Stonton Wyville Leics 36 F3
Stony Cross Hereford 26 D4
Stony Stratford M Keynes 28 D4
Stonyfield Highld 87 D9
Stoodleigh Devon 7 E8
Stopes S Yorks 44 D6
Stopham W Sus 11 C9
Stopsley Luton 29 F8
Stores Corner Suff 31 D10
Storeton Mers 42 D6
Stornoway W Isles 91 D9
Storridge Hereford 26 D4
Storrington W Sus 11 C9
Storrs Cumb 56 G5
Storth Cumb 49 A4
Storwood E Yorks 52 E3
Stotfield Moray 88 A2
Stotfold C Beds 29 E9
Stottesdon Shrops 34 G2
Stoughton Leics 36 E2
Stoughton Sur 18 F6
Stoughton W Sus 11 C7
Stoul Highld 79 B10
Stoulton Worcs 26 D6
Stour Provost Dorset 9 B6
Stour Row Dorset 9 B7
Stourbridge W Mid 34 G5
Stourpaine Dorset 9 D7
Stourport on Severn Worcs 26 A5
Stourton Staffs 34 G4
Stourton Warks 27 E9
Stourton Wilts 9 A6
Stourton Caundle Dorset 8 C6
Stove Orkney 95 E7
Stove Shetland 96 L6
Stoven Suff 39 G10
Stow Borders 70 F3
Stow Lincs 37 B6
Stow Lincs 46 D2
Stow Bardolph Norf 38 E2
Stow Bedon Norf 38 F5
Stow cum Quy Cambs 30 B2
Stow Longa Cambs 29 A8
Stow Maries Essex 20 B5
Stow-on-the-Wold Glos 27 F8
Stowbridge Norf 38 E2
Stowe Shrops 25 A10
Stowe-by-Chartley Staffs 34 C6
Stowe Green Glos 26 H2
Stowell Som 8 B5
Stowford Devon 4 C5
Stowlangtoft Suff 30 B6
Stowmarket Suff 31 C7
Stowting Kent 13 B10
Stowupland Suff 31 C7
Straad Argyll 73 G9
Strachan Aberds 83 D8
Stradbroke Suff 31 A9
Stradishall Suff 30 C4
Stradsett Norf 38 E2
Stragglethorpe Lincs 46 G3
Straid S Ayrs 66 G4
Straith Dumfries 60 E4
Straiton Edin 69 D11
Straiton S Ayrs 67 F6
Straloch Aberds 89 F8
Straloch Perth 76 A3
Stramshall Staffs 35 B6
Strang IoM 48 E3
Stranraer Dumfries 54 C3
Stratfield Mortimer W Berks 18 E3
Stratfield Saye Hants 18 E3
Stratfield Turgis Hants 18 F3
Stratford London 19 C10
Stratford St Andrew Suff 31 B10
Stratford St Mary Suff 31 E7
Stratford Sub Castle Wilts 9 A10
Stratford Tony Wilts 9 B9
Stratford-upon-Avon Warks 27 C8
Strath Highld 85 A12
Strath Highld 94 E4
Strathan Highld 80 D1
Strathan Highld 92 G3
Strathan Highld 93 C8
Strathaven S Lanark 68 F6
Strathblane Stirling 68 C4
Strathcanaird Highld 92 J4
Strathcarron Highld 86 G2
Strathcoil Argyll 79 H9
Strathdon Aberds 82 B5
Strathellie Aberds 89 B10
Strathkinness Fife 77 F7
Strathmashie House Highld 81 D7
Strathmiglo Fife 76 F5
Strathmore Lodge Highld 94 F3
Strathpeffer Highld 86 F7
Strathrannoch Highld 86 D6
Strathtay Perth 76 B2
Strathvaich Lodge Highld 86 D6
Strathwhillan N Ayrs 66 C3
Strathy Highld 93 C11
Strathyre Stirling 75 F8
Stratton Corn 6 F1
Stratton Dorset 8 E5
Stratton Glos 17 A7
Stratton Audley Oxon 28 F3
Stratton on the Fosse Som 16 F3
Stratton St Margaret Swindon 17 C8
Stratton St Michael Norf 39 F8
Stratton Strawless Norf 39 C8
Stravithie Fife 77 F8
Streat E Sus 12 E2
Streatham London 19 D10
Streatley C Beds 29 F7
Streatley W Berks 18 C2
Street Lancs 49 D5
Street N Yorks 59 F8
Street Som 15 H10
Street Dinas Shrops 33 B9
Street End Kent 21 F8
Street End W Sus 11 E7
Street Gate T&W 63 H8
Street Lydan Wrex 33 B10
Streethay Staffs 35 D7
Streetlam N Yorks 58 G4
Streetly W Mid 35 F6
Streetly End Cambs 30 D3
Strefford Shrops 33 G10
Strelley Notts 35 A11
Strensall York 52 C2
Stretcholt Som 15 G8
Strete Devon 5 G9
Stretford Gtr Man 44 C2
Strethall Essex 29 E11
Stretham Cambs 30 A2
Strettington W Sus 11 D7
Stretton Ches W 43 G7
Stretton Derbys 45 F7
Stretton Rutland 36 D5
Stretton Staffs 34 D4
Stretton Staffs 35 C8
Stretton Warr 43 D9
Stretton Grandison Hereford 26 D3
Stretton-on-Dunsmore Warks 27 A11
Stretton-on-Fosse Warks 27 E9
Stretton Sugwas Hereford 25 D11
Stretton under Fosse Warks 35 G10
Stretton Westwood Shrops 34 F1
Strichen Aberds 89 C9
Strines Gtr Man 44 D3
Stringston Som 7 B10
Strixton Northants 28 B6
Stroat Glos 16 B2
Stromeferry Highld 85 E13
Stromemore Highld 85 E13
Stromness Orkney 95 H3
Stronaba Highld 80 E4
Stronachlachar Stirling 75 F7
Stronchreggan Highld 80 F2
Stronchrubie Highld 92 H5
Strone Argyll 73 E10
Strone Highld 80 E3
Strone Highld 81 A7
Strone Invclyd 73 F11
Stronmilchan Argyll 74 E4
Strontian Highld 79 E11
Strood Medway 20 E4
Strood Green Sur 19 G9
Strood Green W Sus 11 A10
Strood Green W Sus 11 B9
Stroud Glos 26 H5
Stroud Hants 10 B6
Stroud Green Essex 20 B5
Stroxton Lincs 36 B5
Struan Highld 85 E8
Struan Perth 81 G10
Strubby Lincs 47 D8
Strumpshaw Norf 39 E9
Strutherhill S Lanark 68 F6
Struy Highld 86 H6
Stryt-issa Wrex 42 H5
Stuartfield Aberds 89 D9
Stub Place Cumb 56 G2
Stubbington Hants 10 D4
Stubbins Lancs 50 H3
Stubbs Cross Kent 13 C8
Stubbs Green Norf 39 F9
Stubb's Green Norf 39 F8
Stubhampton Dorset 9 C8
Stubton Lincs 46 H2
Stuckgowan Argyll 74 G6
Stuckton Hants 9 C10
Stud Green Windsor 18 D5
Studham C Beds 29 G7
Studland Dorset 9 F9
Studley Warks 27 B7
Studley Wilts 16 D6
Studley Roger N Yorks 51 B8
Stump Cross Essex 30 D2
Stuntney Cambs 38 H1
Sturbridge Staffs 34 B4
Sturmer Essex 30 D3
Sturminster Marshall Dorset 9 D8
Sturminster Newton Dorset 9 C6
Sturry Kent 21 E8
Sturton N Lincs 46 B3
Sturton by Stow Lincs 46 D2
Sturton le Steeple Notts 45 D11
Stuston Suff 39 H7
Stutton N Yorks 51 E10
Stutton Suff 31 E8
Styal Ches E 44 D2
Styrrup Notts 45 C10
Suainebost W Isles 91 A10
Suardail W Isles 91 D9
Succoth Aberds 88 E4
Succoth Argyll 74 G5
Suckley Worcs 26 C4
Suckquoy Orkney 95 K5
Sudborough Northants 36 G5
Sudbourne Suff 31 C11
Sudbrook Lincs 36 A5
Sudbrook Mon 15 C11
Sudbrooke Lincs 46 E4
Sudbury Derbys 35 B7
Sudbury London 19 C8
Sudbury Suff 30 D5
Suddie Highld 87 F9
Sudgrove Glos 26 H6
Suffield N Yorks 59 G10
Suffield Norf 39 B8
Sugnall Staffs 34 B3
Suladale Highld 85 C8
Sulaisiadar W Isles 91 D10
Sulby IoM 48 C3
Sulgrave Northants 28 D2
Sulham W Berks 18 D3
Sulhamstead W Berks 18 E3
Sulland Orkney 95 D6
Sullington W Sus 11 C9
Sullom Shetland 96 F5
Sullom Voe Oil Terminal Shetland 96 F5
Sully V Glam 15 E7
Sumburgh Shetland 96 N6
Summer Bridge N Yorks 51 C8
Summer-house Darl 58 E3
Summercourt Corn 3 D7
Summerfield Norf 38 B3
Summergangs Hull 53 F7
Summerleaze Mon 15 C10
Summersdale W Sus 11 D7
Summerseat Gtr Man 43 A10
Summertown Oxon 28 H2
Summit Gtr Man 44 B3
Sunbury-on-Thames Sur 19 E8
Sundaywell Dumfries 60 E4
Sunderland Argyll 64 B3
Sunderland Cumb 56 C3
Sunderland T&W 63 H9
Sunderland Bridge Durham 58 C3
Sundhope Borders 70 H2
Sundon Park Luton 29 F7
Sundridge Kent 19 F11
Sunipol Argyll 78 F6
Sunk Island E Yorks 53 H8
Sunningdale Windsor 18 E6
Sunninghill Windsor 18 E6
Sunningwell Oxon 17 A11
Sunniside Durham 58 C2
Sunniside T&W 63 H8
Sunnyhurst Blackburn 50 G2
Sunnylaw Stirling 75 H10
Sunnyside W Sus 12 C2
Sunton Wilts 17 F9
Surbiton London 19 E8
Surby IoM 48 E2
Surfleet Lincs 37 C8
Surfleet Seas End Lincs 37 C8
Surlingham Norf 39 E9
Sustead Norf 39 B7
Susworth Lincs 46 B2
Sutcombe Devon 6 E2
Suton Norf 39 F6
Sutors of Cromarty Highld 87 E11
Sutterby Lincs 47 E7
Sutterton Lincs 37 B8
Sutton C Beds 29 D9
Sutton Cambs 37 H10
Sutton Kent 21 G10
Sutton London 19 E9
Sutton Mers 43 C8
Sutton N Yorks 51 G10
Sutton Norf 39 C9
Sutton Notts 36 B3
Sutton Notts 45 D10
Sutton Oxon 27 H11
Sutton Pboro 37 F6
Sutton S Yorks 45 A9
Sutton Shrops 34 B2
Sutton Shrops 34 G3
Sutton Som 8 A5
Sutton Staffs 34 C3
Sutton Suff 31 D10
Sutton Sur 19 G7
Sutton W Sus 11 C8
Sutton at Hone Kent 20 D2
Sutton Bassett Northants 36 F3
Sutton Benger Wilts 16 D6
Sutton Bonington Notts 35 C11
Sutton Bridge Lincs 37 C10
Sutton Cheney Leics 35 E10
Sutton Coldfield W Mid 35 F7
Sutton Courtenay Oxon 18 B2
Sutton Crosses Lincs 37 C10
Sutton Grange N Yorks 51 B8
Sutton Green Sur 19 F7
Sutton Howgrave N Yorks 51 B9
Sutton In Ashfield Notts 45 G8
Sutton-in-Craven N Yorks 50 E6
Sutton in the Elms Leics 35 F11
Sutton Ings Hull 53 F7
Sutton Lane Ends Ches E 44 E3
Sutton Leach Mers 43 C8
Sutton Maddock Shrops 34 E3
Sutton Mallet Som 15 H9
Sutton Mandeville Wilts 9 B8
Sutton Manor Mers 43 C8
Sutton Montis Som 8 B5
Sutton on Hull Hull 53 F7
Sutton on Sea Lincs 47 D9
Sutton-on-the-Forest N Yorks 52 C1
Sutton on the Hill Derbys 35 B8
Sutton on Trent Notts 45 F11
Sutton St Edmund Lincs 37 D9
Sutton St James Lincs 37 D9
Sutton St Nicholas Hereford 26 D2
Sutton Scarsdale Derbys 45 F8
Sutton Scotney Hants 17 H11
Sutton under Brailes Warks 27 E10
Sutton-under-Whitestonecliffe N Yorks 51 A10
Sutton upon Derwent E Yorks 52 E3
Sutton Valence Kent 20 G5
Sutton Veny Wilts 16 G5
Sutton Waldron Dorset 9 C7
Sutton Weaver Ches W 43 E8
Sutton Wick Bath 16 F2
Swaby Lincs 47 E7
Swadlincote Derbys 35 D9
Swaffham Norf 38 E4
Swaffham Bulbeck Cambs 30 B2
Swaffham Prior Cambs 30 B2
Swafield Norf 39 B8
Swainby N Yorks 58 F5
Swainshill Hereford 25 D11
Swainsthorpe Norf 39 E8
Swainswick Bath 16 E4
Swalcliffe Oxon 27 E10
Swalecliffe Kent 21 E8
Swallow Lincs 46 B5
Swallowcliffe Wilts 9 B8
Swallowfield Wokingham 18 E4
Swallownest S Yorks 45 D8
Swallows Cross Essex 20 B3
Swan Green Ches W 43 E10
Swan Green Suff 31 A9
Swanage Dorset 9 G9
Swanbister Orkney 95 H4
Swanbourne Bucks 28 F5
Swanland E Yorks 52 G5
Swanley Kent 20 E2
Swanley Village Kent 20 E2
Swanmore Hants 10 C4
Swannington Leics 35 D10
Swannington Norf 39 D7
Swanscombe Kent 20 D3
Swansea = Abertawe Swansea 14 B2
Swanton Abbott Norf 39 C8
Swanton Morley Norf 38 D6
Swanton Novers Norf 38 B6
Swanton Street Kent 20 F5
Swanwick Derbys 45 G8
Swanwick Hants 10 D4
Swarby Lincs 36 A6
Swardeston Norf 39 E8
Swarister Shetland 96 E7
Swarkestone Derbys 35 C9
Swarland Northumb 63 C7
Swarland Estate Northumb 63 C7
Swarthmoor Cumb 49 B2
Swathwick Derbys 45 F7
Swaton Lincs 37 B7
Swavesey Cambs 29 B10
Sway Hants 10 E1
Swayfield Lincs 36 C5
Swaythling Soton 10 C3
Sweet Green Worcs 26 B3
Sweetham Devon 7 G7
Sweethouse Corn 4 E1
Sweffling Suff 31 B10
Swepstone Leics 35 D9
Swerford Oxon 27 E10
Swettenham Ches E 44 F2
Swetton N Yorks 51 B7
Swffryd Caerph 15 B8
Swiftsden E Sus 12 D6
Swilland Suff 31 C8
Swillington W Yorks 51 F9
Swimbridge Devon 6 D5
Swimbridge Newland Devon 6 C5
Swinbrook Oxon 27 G9
Swinderby Lincs 46 F2
Swindon Glos 26 F6
Swindon Staffs 34 F4
Swindon Swindon 17 C8
Swine E Yorks 53 F7
Swinefleet E Yorks 52 G3
Swineshead Bedford 29 B7
Swineshead Lincs 37 A8
Swineshead Bridge Lincs 37 A8
Swiney Highld 94 G4
Swinford Leics 36 H1
Swinford Oxon 27 H11
Swingate Notts 35 A11
Swingfield Minnis Kent 21 G9
Swingfield Street Kent 21 G9
Swinhoe Northumb 71 H11
Swinhope Lincs 46 C6
Swining Shetland 96 G6
Swinithwaite N Yorks 58 H1
Swinnow Moor W Yorks 51 F8
Swinscoe Staffs 44 H5
Swinside Hall Borders 62 B3
Swinstead Lincs 36 C6
Swinton Borders 71 F7
Swinton Gtr Man 43 B10
Swinton N Yorks 51 B8
Swinton N Yorks 52 B3
Swinton S Yorks 45 C8
Swintonmill Borders 71 F7
Swithland Leics 35 D11
Swordale Highld 87 E8
Swordland Highld 79 B10
Swordly Highld 93 C10
Sworton Heath Ches E 43 D9
Swydd-ffynnon Ceredig 24 B3
Swynnerton Staffs 34 B4
Swyre Dorset 8 F4
Sychtyn Powys 32 E5
Syde Glos 26 G6
Sydenham London 19 D10
Sydenham Oxon 18 A4
Sydenham Damerel Devon 4 D5
Syderstone Norf 38 B4
Sydling St Nicholas Dorset 8 E5
Sydmonton Hants 17 F11
Syerston Notts 45 H11
Syke Gtr Man 50 H4
Sykehouse S Yorks 52 H2
Sykes Lancs 50 D2
Syleham Suff 39 H8
Sylen Carms 23 F10
Symbister Shetland 96 G7
Symington S Ayrs 67 C6
Symington S Lanark 69 G8
Symonds Yat Hereford 26 G2
Symondsbury Dorset 8 E3
Synod Inn Ceredig 23 A9
Syre Highld 93 E9
Syreford Glos 27 F7
Syresham Northants 28 D3
Syston Leics 36 D2
Syston Lincs 36 A5
Sytchampton Worcs 26 B5
Sywell Northants 28 B5

T

Taagan Highld 86 E3
Tàbost W Isles 91 F8
Tabost W Isles 91 A10
Tackley Oxon 27 F11
Tacleit W Isles 90 D6
Tacolneston Norf 39 F7
Tadcaster N Yorks 51 E10
Taddington Derbys 44 E5
Taddiport Devon 6 E3
Tadley Hants 18 E3
Tadlow C Beds 29 D9
Tadmarton Oxon 27 E10
Tadworth Sur 19 F9
Tafarn-y-gelyn Denb 42 F4
Tafarnau-bach Bl Gwent 25 G8
Taff's Well Rhondda 15 C7
Tafolwern Powys 32 E4
Tai Conwy 41 D9
Tai-bach Powys 33 C7
Tai-mawr Conwy 32 A5
Tai-Ucha Denb 42 G3
Taibach Neath 14 C3
Taigh a Ghearraidh W Isles 84 A2
Tain Highld 87 C10
Tain Highld 94 D4
Tainant Wrex 42 H5
Tainlon Gwyn 40 E6
Tai'r-Bull Powys 24 F6
Tairbeart = Tarbert W Isles 90 G6
Tairgwaith Neath 24 G4
Takeley Essex 30 F2
Takeley Street Essex 30 F2
Tal-sarn Ceredig 23 A10
Tal-y-bont Ceredig 32 G2
Tal-y-Bont Conwy 41 D9
Tal-y-bont Gwyn 32 C1
Tal-y-bont Gwyn 41 C8
Tal-y-cafn Conwy 41 C9
Tal-y-llyn Gwyn 32 E3
Tal-y-wern Powys 32 E4
Talachddu Powys 25 E7
Talacre Flint 42 D4
Talardd Gwyn 32 C4
Talaton Devon 7 G9
Talbenny Pembs 22 E3
Talbot Green Rhondda 14 C6
Talbot Village Poole 9 E9
Tale Devon 7 F9
Talerddig Powys 32 E5
Talgarreg Ceredig 23 A9
Talgarth Powys 25 E8
Talisker Highld 85 E8
Talke Staffs 44 G2
Talkin Cumb 61 H11
Talla Linnfoots Borders 61 A7
Talladale Highld 86 D2
Tallarn Green Wrex 33 A10
Tallentire Cumb 56 C3
Talley Carms 24 E3
Tallington Lincs 37 E6
Talmine Highld 93 C8
Talog Carms 23 D8
Talsarn Carms 24 F4
Talsarnau Gwyn 41 G8
Talskiddy Corn 3 C8
Talwrn Anglesey 40 C6
Talwrn Wrex 42 H5
Talybont-on-Usk Powys 25 F8
Talygarn Rhondda 14 C6
Talyllyn Powys 25 F8
Talysarn Gwyn 40 E6
Talywain Torf 15 A8
Tame Bridge N Yorks 58 F6
Tamerton Foliot Plym 4 E5
Tamworth Staffs 35 E8
Tan Hinon Powys 32 G4
Tan-lan Conwy 41 D9
Tan-lan Gwyn 41 F8
Tan-y-bwlch Gwyn 41 F8
Tan-y-fron Conwy 42 F2
Tan-y-graig Anglesey 41 C7
Tan-y-graig Gwyn 40 G5
Tan-y-groes Ceredig 23 B7
Tan-y-pistyll Powys 33 C6
Tan-yr-allt Gwyn 40 E6
Tandem W Yorks 51 H7
Tanden Kent 13 C8
Tandridge Sur 19 F10
Tanerdy Carms 23 D9
Tanfield Durham 63 H7
Tanfield Lea Durham 58 A2
Tangasdal W Isles 84 J1
Tangiers Pembs 22 E4
Tangley Hants 17 F10
Tanglwst Carms 23 C8
Tangmere W Sus 11 D8
Tangwick Shetland 96 F4
Tankersley S Yorks 45 B7
Tankerton Kent 21 E8
Tannach Highld 94 F5
Tannachie Aberds 83 E9
Tannadice Angus 77 B7
Tannington Suff 31 B9
Tansley Derbys 45 G7
Tansley Knoll Derbys 45 F7
Tansor Northants 37 F6
Tantobie Durham 58 A2
Tanton N Yorks 58 E6
Tanworth-in-Arden Warks 27 A8
Tanygrisiau Gwyn 41 F8
Tanyrhydiau Ceredig 24 B4
Taobh a Chaolais W Isles 84 G2
Taobh a' Ghlinne W Isles 91 F8
Taobh a Thuath Loch Aineort W Isles 84 F2
Taobh a Tuath Loch Baghasdail W Isles 84 F2
Taobh Tuath W Isles 90 J4
Taplow Bucks 18 C6
Tapton Derbys 45 E7
Tarbat Ho. Highld 87 D10
Tarbert Argyll 65 C7
Tarbert Argyll 72 E5
Tarbert Argyll 73 G7
Tarbert = Tairbeart W Isles 90 G6
Tarbet Argyll 74 G6
Tarbet Highld 79 B10
Tarbet Highld 92 E4
Tarbock Green Mers 43 D7
Tarbolton S Ayrs 67 D7
Tarbrax S Lanark 69 E9
Tardebigge Worcs 27 B7
Tarfside Angus 82 F6
Tarland Aberds 82 C6
Tarleton Lancs 49 G4
Tarlogie Highld 87 C10
Tarlscough Lancs 43 A7
Tarlton Glos 16 B6
Tarnbrook Lancs 50 D1
Tarporley Ches W 43 F8
Tarr Som 7 C10
Tarrant Crawford Dorset 9 D8
Tarrant Gunville Dorset 9 C8
Tarrant Hinton Dorset 9 C8
Tarrant Keyneston Dorset 9 D8
Tarrant Launceston Dorset 9 D8
Tarrant Monkton Dorset 9 D8
Tarrant Rawston Dorset 9 D8
Tarrant Rushton Dorset 9 D8
Tarrel Highld 87 C11
Tarring Neville E Sus 12 F3
Tarrington Hereford 26 D3
Tarsappie Perth 76 E4
Tarskavaig Highld 85 H10
Tarves Aberds 89 E8
Tarvie Highld 86 F7
Tarvie Perth 76 A3
Tarvin Ches W 43 F7
Tasburgh Norf 39 F8
Tasley Shrops 34 F2
Taston Oxon 27 F10
Tatenhill Staffs 35 C8
Tathall End M Keynes 28 D5
Tatham Lancs 50 C2
Tathwell Lincs 47 D7
Tatling End Bucks 19 C7
Tatsfield Sur 19 F11
Tattenhall Ches W 43 G7
Tattenhoe M Keynes 28 E5
Tatterford Norf 38 C4
Tattersett Norf 38 B4
Tattershall Lincs 46 G6
Tattershall Bridge Lincs 46 G5
Tattershall Thorpe Lincs 46 G6
Tattingstone Suff 31 E8
Tatworth Som 8 D2
Taunton Som 7 D11
Taverham Norf 39 D7
Tavernspite Pembs 22 E6
Tavistock Devon 4 D5
Taw Green Devon 6 G5
Tawstock Devon 6 D4
Taxal Derbys 44 E4
Tay Bridge Dundee 77 E7
Tayinloan Argyll 65 D7
Taymouth Castle Perth 75 C10
Taynish Argyll 72 E6
Taynton Glos 26 F4
Taynton Oxon 27 G9
Taynuilt Argyll 74 D3
Tayport Fife 77 E7
Tayvallich Argyll 72 E6
Tealby Lincs 46 C5
Tealing Angus 77 D7
Teangue Highld 85 H11
Teanna Mhachair W Isles 84 B2
Tebay Cumb 57 F8
Tebworth C Beds 28 F6
Tedburn St Mary Devon 7 G7
Teddington Glos 26 E6
Teddington London 19 D8
Tedstone Delamere Hereford 26 C3
Tedstone Wafre Hereford 26 C3
Teeton Northants 28 A3
Teffont Evias Wilts 9 A8
Teffont Magna Wilts 9 A8
Tegryn Pembs 23 C7
Teigh Rutland 36 D4
Teigncombe Devon 5 C7
Teigngrace Devon 5 D9
Teignmouth Devon 5 D10
Telford Telford 34 E2
Telham E Sus 13 E6
Tellisford Som 16 F5
Telscombe E Sus 12 F3
Telscombe Cliffs E Sus 12 F2
Templand Dumfries 60 E6
Temple Corn 4 D2
Temple Glasgow 68 D4
Temple Midloth 70 E2
Temple Balsall W Mid 35 H8
Temple Bar Carms 23 E10
Temple Bar Ceredig 23 A10
Temple Cloud Bath 16 F3
Temple Combe Som 8 B6
Temple Ewell Kent 21 G9
Temple Grafton Warks 27 C8
Temple Guiting Glos 27 F7
Temple Herdewyke Warks 27 C10
Temple Hirst N Yorks 52 G2
Temple Normanton Derbys 45 F8
Temple Sowerby Cumb 57 D8
Templehall Fife 69 A11
Templeton Devon 7 E7
Templeton Pembs 22 E6
Templeton Bridge Devon 7 E7
Templetown Durham 58 A2
Tempsford C Beds 29 C8
Ten Mile Bank Norf 38 F2
Tenbury Wells Worcs 26 B2
Tenby = Dinbych-y-Pysgod Pembs 22 F6
Tendring Essex 31 F8
Tendring Green Essex 31 F8
Tenston Orkney 95 G3
Tenterden Kent 13 C7
Terling Essex 30 G4
Ternhill Shrops 34 B2
Terregles Banks Dumfries 60 F5
Terrick Bucks 28 H5
Terrington N Yorks 52 B2
Terrington St Clement Norf 37 D11
Terrington St John Norf 37 D11
Teston Kent 20 F4
Testwood Hants 10 C2
Tetbury Glos 16 B5
Tetbury Upton Glos 16 B5
Tetchill Shrops 33 B9
Tetcott Devon 6 G2
Tetford Lincs 47 E7
Tetney Lincs 47 B7
Tetney Lock Lincs 47 B7
Tetsworth Oxon 18 A3
Tettenhall W Mid 34 E4
Teuchan Aberds 89 E10
Teversal Notts 45 F8
Teversham Cambs 29 C11
Teviothead Borders 61 C10
Tewel Aberds 83 E10
Tewin Herts 29 G9
Tewkesbury Glos 26 E5
Teynham Kent 20 E6
Thackthwaite Cumb 56 D3
Thainston Aberds 83 F8
Thakeham W Sus 11 C10
Thame Oxon 28 H4
Thames Ditton Sur 19 E8
Thames Haven Thurrock 20 C4
Thamesmead London 19 C11
Thanington Kent 21 F8
Thankerton S Lanark 69 G8
Tharston Norf 39 F7
Thatcham W Berks 18 E2
Thatto Heath Mers 43 C8
Thaxted Essex 30 E3
The Aird Highld 85 C9
The Arms Norf 38 F4
The Bage Hereford 25 D9
The Balloch Perth 75 F11
The Barony Orkney 95 F3
The Bog Shrops 33 F9
The Bourne Sur 18 G5
The Braes Highld 85 E10
The Broad Hereford 25 B11
The Butts Som 16 G4
The Camp Glos 26 H6
The Camp Herts 29 H8
The Chequer Wrex 33 A10
The City Bucks 18 B4
The Common Wilts 9 A11
The Craigs Highld 86 B7
The Cronk IoM 48 C3
The Dell Suff 39 F10
The Den N Ayrs 66 A6
The Eals Northumb 62 E3
The Eaves Glos 26 H3
The Flatt Cumb 61 F11
The Four Alls Shrops 34 B2
The Garths Shetland 96 B8
The Green Cumb 49 A1
The Green Wilts 9 A7
The Grove Dumfries 60 F5
The Hall Shetland 96 D8
The Haven W Sus 11 A9
The Heath Norf 39 C7
The Heath Suff 31 E8
The Hill Cumb 49 A1
The Howe Cumb 56 H6
The Howe IoM 48 F1
The Hundred Hereford 26 B2
The Lee Bucks 18 A6
The Lhen IoM 48 B3
The Marsh Powys 33 F9
The Marsh Wilts 17 C7
The Middles Durham 58 A3
The Moor Kent 13 D6
The Mumbles = Y Mwmbwls Swansea 14 C2
The Murray S Lanark 68 E5
The Neuk Aberds 83 D9
The Oval Bath 16 E4
The Pole of Itlaw Aberds 89 C6
The Quarry Glos 16 B4
The Rhos Pembs 22 E5
The Rock Telford 34 E2
The Ryde Herts 29 H9
The Sands Sur 18 G5
The Stocks Kent 13 D8
The Throat Wokingham 18 E5
The Vauld Hereford 26 D2
The Wyke Shrops 34 E3
Theakston N Yorks 58 H4
Thealby N Lincs 52 H4
Theale Som 15 G10
Theale W Berks 18 D3
Thearne E Yorks 53 F6
Theberton Suff 31 B11
Theddingworth Leics 36 G2
Theddlethorpe All Saints Lincs 47 D8
Theddlethorpe St Helen Lincs 47 D8
Thelbridge Barton Devon 7 E6
Thelnetham Suff 38 H6
Thelveton Norf 39 G7
Thelwall Warr 43 D9
Themelthorpe Norf 39 C6
Thenford Northants 28 D2
Therfield Herts 29 E10
Thetford Lincs 37 D7
Thetford Norf 38 G4
Theydon Bois Essex 19 B11
Thickwood Wilts 16 D5
Thimbleby Lincs 46 F6
Thimbleby N Yorks 58 G5
Thingwall Mers 42 D5
Thirdpart N Ayrs 66 B4
Thirlby N Yorks 51 A10
Thirlestane Borders 70 F4
Thirn N Yorks 58 H3
Thirsk N Yorks 51 A10
Thirtleby E Yorks 53 F7
Thistleton Lancs 49 F4
Thistleton Rutland 36 D5
Thistley Green Suff 38 H2

pper Quinton Warks 27 D8
pper Ratley Hants 10 B2
pper Rissington Glos 27 G9
pper Rochford Worcs 26 B3
pper Sandaig Highld 85 G12
pper Sanday Orkney 95 H6
pper Sapey Hereford 26 B3
pper Saxondale Notts 36 B2
pper Seagry Wilts 16 C6
pper Shelton C Beds 28 D6
pper Sheringham Norf 39 A7
pper Skelmorlie N Ayrs 73 G11
pper Slaughter Glos 27 F8
pper Soudley Glos 26 G3
pper Stondon C Beds 29 E8
pper Stowe Northants 28 C3
pper Stratton Swindon 17 C8
pper Street Hants 9 C10
pper Street Norf 39 D9
pper Street Norf 39 D9
pper Street Suff 31 E8
pper Strensham Worcs 26 E6
pper Sundon C Beds 29 F7
pper Swell Glos 27 F8
pper Tean Staffs 34 B6
pper Tillyrie Perth 76 G4
pper Tooting London 19 D9
pper Tote Highld 85 C10
pper Town N Som 15 E11
pper Treverward Shrops 33 H8
pper Tysoe Warks 27 D10
pper Upham Wilts 17 D9
pper Wardington Oxon 27 D11
pper Weald M Keynes 28 E4
pper Weedon Northants 28 C3
pper Wield Hants 18 H3
pper Winchendon Bucks 28 G4
pper Witton W Mid 35 F6
pper Woodend Aberds 83 B8
pper Woodford Wilts 17 H8
pper Wootton Hants 18 F2
pper Wyche Hereford 26 D4
pperby Cumb 56 A6
ppermill Gtr Man 44 B3
ppersound Shetland 96 J6
pperthong W Yorks 44 B5
pperthorpe N Lincs 45 B11
pperton W Sus 11 B8
ppertown Derbys 45 F7
ppertown Highld 94 C5
ppertown Orkney 95 J5
ppingham Rutland 36 F4
ppington Shrops 34 E2
psall N Yorks 58 H5
pshire Essex 19 A11
pstreet Kent 21 E9
pthorpe Suff 30 A6
pton Cambs 37 H7
pton Ches W 43 F7
pton Corn 6 F1
pton Dorset 8 F6
pton Dorset 9 E8
pton Hants 10 C2
pton Hants 17 F10
pton Leics 35 F9
pton Lincs 46 D2
pton Mers 42 D5
pton Norf 39 D9
pton Northants 28 B4
pton Notts 45 E11
pton Notts 45 G11
pton Oxon 18 C2
pton Pboro 37 E7
pton Slough 18 D6
pton Som 7 D8
pton W Yorks 45 A8
pton Bishop Hereford 26 F3
pton Cheyney Glos 16 E3
pton Cressett Shrops 34 F2
pton Cross Corn 4 D3
pton Grey Hants 18 G3
pton Hellions Devon 7 F7
pton Lovell Wilts 16 G6
pton Magna Shrops 34 D1
pton Noble Som 16 H4
pton Pyne Devon 7 G8
pton St Leonard's Glos 26 G5
pton Scudamore Wilts 16 G5
pton Snodsbury Worcs 26 C6
pton upon Severn Worcs 26 D5
pton Warren Worcs 26 B6
pwaltham W Sus 11 C8
pware Cambs 30 A2
pwell Norf 37 E10
pwey Dorset 8 F5
pwood Cambs 37 G8
adale Shetland 96 K6
afirth Shetland 96 F6
chfont Wilts 17 F7
dimarsh Hereford 26 D2
e Shetland 96 F4
e Bank N Yorks 51 B9
gha W Isles 90 H6
ishay Common Hereford 25 E10
lay Nook Stockton 58 E4
lmston Gtr Man 43 C10
peth Durham 58 A3
quhart Highld 87 F8
quhart Moray 88 B2
rra N Yorks 59 F6
ray Highld 87 F8
haw Moor Durham 58 B3
k = Brynbuga Mon 15 A9
selby Lincs 46 C4
worth T&W 63 H9
kinton Ches W 43 F8
ley W Yorks 50 E6
on Devon 7 G7
terby Lincs 47 C7
Uttoxeter Staffs 35 B6
Uwchmynydd Gwyn 40 H3
Uxbridge London 19 C7
Uyeasound Shetland 96 C7
Uzmaston Pembs 22 E4

V

Valley Anglesey 40 C4
Valley Truckle Corn 4 C1
Valleyfield Dumfries 55 D9
Valsgarth Shetland 96 B8
Valtos Highld 85 B10
Van Powys 32 G5
Vange Essex 20 C4
Varteg Torf 25 H9
Vatten Highld 85 D7
Vaul Argyll 78 G3
Vaynor M Tydf 25 G7
Veensgarth Shetland 96 J6
Velindre Powys 25 E8
Vellow Som 7 C9
Veness Orkney 95 F6
Venn Green Devon 6 E2
Venn Ottery Devon 7 G9
Vennington Shrops 33 E9
Venny Tedburn Devon 7 G7
Ventnor IoW 10 G4
Vernham Dean Hants 17 F10
Vernham Street Hants 17 F10
Vernolds Common Shrops 33 G10
Verwood Dorset 9 D9
Veryan Corn 3 F8
Vicarage Devon 7 H11
Vickerstown Cumb 49 C1
Victoria Corn 3 C8
Victoria S Yorks 44 B5
Vidlin Shetland 96 G6
Viewpark N Lanark 68 D6
Vigo Village Kent 20 E3
Vinehall Street E Sus 13 D6
Vine's Cross E Sus 12 E4
Viney Hill Glos 26 H3
Virginia Water Sur 18 E6
Virginstow Devon 6 G2
Vobster Som 16 G4
Voe Shetland 96 E5
Voe Shetland 96 G6
Vowchurch Hereford 25 E10
Voxter Shetland 96 F5
Voy Orkney 95 G3

W

Wackerfield Durham 58 D2
Wacton Norf 39 F7
Wadbister Shetland 96 J6
Wadborough Worcs 26 D6
Waddesdon Bucks 28 G4
Waddingham Lincs 46 C3
Waddington Lancs 50 E3
Waddington Lincs 46 F3
Wadebridge Corn 3 B8
Wadeford Som 8 C2
Wadenhoe Northants 36 G6
Wadesmill Herts 29 G10
Wadhurst E Sus 12 C5
Wadshelf Derbys 45 E7
Wadsley S Yorks 45 C7
Wadsley Bridge S Yorks 45 C7
Wadworth S Yorks 45 C9
Waen Denb 42 F4
Waen Denb 42 F2
Waen Fach Powys 33 D8
Waen Goleugoed Denb 42 E3
Wag Highld 93 G13
Wainfleet All Saints Lincs 47 G8
Wainfleet Bank Lincs 47 G8
Wainfleet St Mary Lincs 47 G9
Wainfleet Tofts Lincs 47 G8
Wainhouse Corner Corn 4 B2
Wainscott Medway 20 D4
Wainstalls W Yorks 50 G6
Waitby Cumb 57 F9
Waithe Lincs 46 B6
Wake Lady Green N Yorks 59 G7
Wakefield W Yorks 51 G9
Wakerley Northants 36 F5
Wakes Colne Essex 30 F5
Walberswick Suff 31 A11
Walberton W Sus 11 D8
Walbottle T&W 63 G7
Walcot Lincs 37 B6
Walcot N Lincs 52 G4
Walcot Shrops 33 G9
Walcot Swindon 17 C8
Walcot Telford 34 D1
Walcot Green Norf 39 G7
Walcote Leics 36 G1
Walcote Warks 27 C8
Walcott Lincs 46 G5
Walcott Norf 39 B9
Walden N Yorks 50 A6
Walden Head N Yorks 50 A5
Walden Stubbs N Yorks 52 H1
Waldersey Cambs 37 E10
Walderslade Medway 20 E4
Walderton W Sus 11 C6
Walditch Dorset 8 E3
Waldley Derbys 35 B7
Waldridge Durham 58 A3
Waldringfield Suff 31 D9
Waldringfield Heath Suff 31 D9
Waldron E Sus 12 E4
Wales S Yorks 45 D8
Walesby Lincs 46 C5
Walesby Notts 45 E10
Walford Hereford 25 A10
Walford Hereford 26 F2
Walford Shrops 33 C10
Walford Heath Shrops 33 D10
Walgherton Ches E 43 H9
Walgrave Northants 28 A5
Walhampton Hants 10 E2
Walk Mill Lancs 50 F4
Walkden Gtr Man 43 B10
Walker T&W 63 G8
Walker Barn Ches E 44 E3
Walker Fold Lancs 50 E2
Walkerburn Borders 70 G2
Walkeringham Notts 45 C11
Walkerith Lincs 45 C11
Walkern Herts 29 F9
Walker's Green Hereford 26 D2
Walkerville N Yorks 58 G3
Walkford Dorset 9 E11
Walkhampton Devon 4 E6
Walkington E Yorks 52 F5
Walkley S Yorks 45 D7
Wall Northumb 62 G5
Wall Staffs 35 E7
Wall Bank Shrops 33 F11
Wall Heath W Mid 34 G4
Wall under Heywood Shrops 33 F11
Wallaceton Dumfries 60 E4
Wallacetown S Ayrs 66 D6
Wallacetown S Ayrs 66 F5
Wallands Park E Sus 12 E3
Wallasey Mers 42 C6
Wallcrouch E Sus 12 C5
Wallingford Oxon 18 C3
Wallington Hants 10 D4
Wallington Herts 29 E9
Wallington London 19 E9
Wallis Pembs 22 D5
Walliswood Sur 19 H8
Walls Shetland 96 J4
Wallsend T&W 63 G8
Wallston V Glam 15 D7
Wallyford E Loth 70 C2
Walmer Kent 21 F10
Walmer Bridge Lancs 49 G4
Walmersley Gtr Man 44 A2
Walmley W Mid 35 F7
Walpole Suff 31 A10
Walpole Cross Keys Norf 37 D11
Walpole Highway Norf 37 D11
Walpole Marsh Norf 37 D10
Walpole St Andrew Norf 37 D11
Walpole St Peter Norf 37 D11
Walsall W Mid 34 F6
Walsall Wood W Mid 34 E6
Walsden W Yorks 50 G5
Walsgrave on Sowe W Mid 35 G9
Walsham le Willows Suff 30 A6
Walshaw Gtr Man 43 A10
Walshford N Yorks 51 D10
Walsoken Cambs 37 D10
Walston S Lanark 69 F9
Walsworth Herts 29 E8
Walters Ash Bucks 18 B5
Walterston V Glam 14 D6
Walterstone Hereford 25 F10
Waltham Kent 21 G8
Waltham NE Lincs 46 B6
Waltham Abbey Essex 19 A10
Waltham Chase Hants 10 C4
Waltham Cross Herts 19 A10
Waltham on the Wolds Leics 36 C4
Waltham St Lawrence Windsor 18 D5
Walthamstow London 19 C10
Walton Cumb 61 G11
Walton Derbys 45 F7
Walton Leics 36 G1
Walton M Keynes 28 E5
Walton Mers 42 C6
Walton Pboro 37 E7
Walton Powys 25 C9
Walton Som 15 H10
Walton Staffs 34 B4
Walton Suff 31 E9
Walton Telford 34 D1
Walton W Yorks 51 E10
Walton W Yorks 51 H9
Walton Warks 27 C9
Walton Cardiff Glos 26 E6
Walton East Pembs 22 D5
Walton-in-Gordano N Som 15 D10
Walton-le-Dale Lancs 50 G1
Walton-on-Thames Sur 19 E8
Walton on the Hill Staffs 34 C5
Walton on the Hill Sur 19 F9
Walton-on-the-Naze Essex 31 F9
Walton on the Wolds Leics 36 D1
Walton-on-Trent Derbys 35 D8
Walton West Pembs 22 E3
Walwen Flint 42 E5
Walwick Northumb 62 F5
Walworth Darl 58 E3
Walworth Gate Darl 58 D3
Walwyn's Castle Pembs 22 E3
Wambrook Som 8 D1
Wanborough Sur 18 G6
Wanborough Swindon 17 C9
Wandsworth London 19 D9
Wangford Suff 39 H10
Wanlockhead Dumfries 60 B4
Wansford E Yorks 53 D6
Wansford Pboro 37 F6
Wanstead London 19 C11
Wanstrow Som 16 G4
Wanswell Glos 16 A3
Wantage Oxon 17 C10
Wapley S Glos 16 D4
Wappenbury Warks 27 B10
Wappenham Northants 28 D3
Warbleton E Sus 12 E5
Warblington Hants 10 D6
Warborough Oxon 18 B2
Warboys Cambs 37 G9
Warbreck Blackpool 49 F3
Warbstow Corn 4 B3
Warburton Gtr Man 43 D10
Warcop Cumb 57 E9
Ward End W Mid 35 G7
Ward Green Suff 31 B7
Warden Kent 21 D7
Warden Northumb 62 G5
Wardhill Orkney 95 F7
Wardington Oxon 27 D11
Wardlaw Borders 61 B8
Wardle Ches E 43 G9
Wardle Gtr Man 50 H5
Wardley Rutland 36 E4
Wardlow Derbys 44 E5
Wardy Hill Cambs 37 G10
Ware Herts 29 G10
Ware Kent 21 E9
Wareham Dorset 9 F8
Warehorne Kent 13 C8
Waren Mill Northumb 71 G10
Warenford Northumb 71 H10
Warenton Northumb 71 G10
Wareside Herts 29 G10
Waresley Cambs 29 C9
Waresley Worcs 26 A5
Warfield Brack 18 D5
Warfleet Devon 5 F9
Wargrave Wokingham 18 D4
Warham Norf 38 A5
Warhill Gtr Man 44 C3
Wark Northumb 62 F4
Wark Northumb 71 G7
Warkleigh Devon 6 D5
Warkton Northants 36 H4
Warkworth Northants 27 D11
Warkworth Northumb 63 C8
Warlaby N Yorks 58 G4
Warland W Yorks 50 G5
Warleggan Corn 4 E2
Warlingham Sur 19 F10
Warmfield W Yorks 51 G9
Warmingham Ches E 43 F10
Warmington Northants 37 F6
Warmington Warks 27 D11
Warminster Wilts 16 G5
Warmlake Kent 20 F5
Warmley S Glos 16 D3
Warmley Tower S Glos 16 D3
Warmonds Hill Northants 28 B6
Warmsworth S Yorks 45 B9
Warmwell Dorset 9 F6
Warndon Worcs 26 C5
Warnford Hants 10 B5
Warnham W Sus 11 A10
Warninglid W Sus 11 B11
Warren Ches E 44 E2
Warren Pembs 22 G4
Warren Heath Suff 31 D9
Warren Row Windsor 18 C5
Warren Street Kent 20 F6
Warrington M Keynes 28 C5
Warrington Warr 43 D9
Warsash Hants 10 D3
Warslow Staffs 44 G4
Warter E Yorks 52 D4
Warthermarske N Yorks 51 B8
Warthill N Yorks 52 D2
Wartling E Sus 12 F5
Wartnaby Leics 36 C3
Warton Lancs 49 B4
Warton Lancs 49 G4
Warton Northumb 62 C6
Warton Warks 35 E8
Warwick Warks 27 B9
Warwick Bridge Cumb 61 H10
Warwick on Eden Cumb 61 H10
Wasbister Orkney 95 E4
Wasdale Head Cumb 56 F3
Wash Common W Berks 17 E11
Washaway Corn 3 C9
Washbourne Devon 5 F8
Washfield Devon 7 E8
Washfold N Yorks 58 F1
Washford Som 7 B9
Washford Pyne Devon 7 E7
Washingborough Lincs 46 E4
Washington T&W 63 H9
Washington W Sus 11 C10
Wasing W Berks 18 E2
Waskerley Durham 58 B1
Wasperton Warks 27 C9
Wasps Nest Lincs 46 F4
Wass N Yorks 52 B1
Watchet Som 7 B9
Watchfield Oxon 17 B9
Watchfield Som 15 G9
Watchgate Cumb 57 G7
Watchhill Cumb 56 B3
Watcombe Torbay 5 E10
Watendlath Cumb 56 E4
Water Devon 5 C8
Water Lancs 50 G4
Water End E Yorks 52 F3
Water End Herts 19 A9
Water End Herts 29 G7
Water Newton Cambs 37 F7
Water Orton Warks 35 F7
Water Stratford Bucks 28 E3
Water Yeat Cumb 56 H4
Waterbeach Cambs 29 B11
Waterbeck Dumfries 61 F8
Waterden Norf 38 B4
Waterfall Staffs 44 G4
Waterfoot E Renf 68 E4
Waterfoot Lancs 50 G4
Waterford Hants 10 E2
Waterford Herts 29 G10
Waterhead Cumb 56 F5
Waterhead Dumfries 61 D7
Waterheads Borders 69 E11
Waterhouses Durham 58 B2
Waterhouses Staffs 44 G4
Wateringbury Kent 20 F3
Waterloo Gtr Man 44 B3
Waterloo Highld 85 F11
Waterloo Mers 42 C6
Waterloo N Lanark 69 E7
Waterloo Norf 39 D8
Waterloo Perth 76 D3
Waterloo Poole 9 E9
Waterloo Shrops 33 B11
Waterloo Port Gwyn 40 D6
Waterlooville Hants 10 D5
Watermeetings S Lanark 60 B5
Watermillock Cumb 56 D6
Waterperry Oxon 28 H3
Waterrow Som 7 D9
Water's Nook Gtr Man 43 B9
Waters Upton Telford 34 D2
Watersfield W Sus 11 C9
Waterside Aberds 89 F10
Waterside Blackburn 50 G3
Waterside Cumb 56 B4
Waterside E Ayrs 67 B7
Waterside E Ayrs 67 F7
Waterside E Dunb 68 C5
Waterside E Renf 68 E4
Waterstock Oxon 28 H3
Waterston Pembs 22 F4
Watford Herts 19 B8
Watford Northants 28 B3
Watford Gap Staffs 35 E7
Wath N Yorks 51 B7
Wath N Yorks 51 C7
Wath N Yorks 52 B2
Wath Brow Cumb 56 E2
Wath upon Dearne S Yorks 45 B8
Watley's End S Glos 16 C3
Watlington Norf 38 D2
Watlington Oxon 18 B3
Watnall Notts 45 H9
Watten Highld 94 E4
Wattisfield Suff 31 A7
Wattisham Suff 31 C7
Wattlesborough Heath Shrops 33 D9
Watton E Yorks 52 D6
Watton Norf 38 E5
Watton at Stone Herts 29 G10
Wattston N Lanark 68 C6
Wattstown Rhondda 14 B6
Wauchan Highld 80 E1
Waulkmill Lodge Orkney 95 H4
Waun Powys 32 E4
Waun-y-clyn Carms 23 F9
Waunarlwydd Swansea 14 B2
Waunclunda Carms 24 E3
Waunfawr Gwyn 41 E7
Waungron Swansea 23 F10
Waunlwyd Bl Gwent 25 H8
Wavendon M Keynes 28 E6
Waverbridge Cumb 56 B4
Waverton Ches W 43 F7
Waverton Cumb 56 B4
Wavertree Mers 43 D6
Wawne E Yorks 53 F6
Waxham Norf 39 C10
Waxholme E Yorks 53 G9
Way Kent 21 E10
Way Village Devon 7 E7
Wayfield Medway 20 E4
Wayford Som 8 D3
Waymills Shrops 34 A1
Wayne Green Mon 25 G11
Wdig = Goodwick Pembs 22 C4
Weachyburn Aberds 89 C6
Weald Oxon 17 A10
Wealdstone London 19 C8
Weardley W Yorks 51 E8
Weare Som 15 F10
Weare Giffard Devon 6 D3
Wearhead Durham 57 C10
Weasdale Cumb 57 F8
Weasenham All Saints Norf 38 C4
Weasenham St Peter Norf 38 C4
Weatherhill Sur 12 B2
Weaverham Ches W 43 E9
Weaverthorpe N Yorks 52 B5
Webheath Worcs 27 B7
Wedderlairs Aberds 89 E8
Wedderlie Borders 70 E5
Weddington Warks 35 F9
Wedhampton Wilts 17 F7
Wedmore Som 15 G10
Wednesbury W Mid 34 F5
Wednesfield W Mid 34 E5
Weedon Bucks 28 G5
Weedon Bec Northants 28 C3
Weedon Lois Northants 28 D3
Weeford Staffs 35 E7
Week Devon 7 E6
Week St Mary Corn 4 B3
Weeke Hants 10 A3
Weekley Northants 36 G4
Weel E Yorks 53 F6
Weeley Essex 31 F8
Weeley Heath Essex 31 F8
Weem Perth 75 C11
Weeping Cross Staffs 34 C5
Weethley Gate Warks 27 C7
Weeting Norf 38 G3
Weeton E Yorks 53 G9
Weeton Lancs 49 F3
Weeton N Yorks 51 E8
Weetwood Hall Northumb 71 H9
Weir Lancs 50 G4
Weir Quay Devon 4 E5
Welborne Norf 39 E6
Welbourn Lincs 46 G3
Welburn N Yorks 52 A2
Welburn N Yorks 52 C3
Welbury N Yorks 58 F4
Welby Lincs 36 B5
Welches Dam Cambs 37 G10
Welcombe Devon 6 E1
Weld Bank Lancs 50 H1
Weldon Northumb 63 D7
Welford Northants 36 G2
Welford W Berks 17 D11
Welford-on-Avon Warks 27 C8
Welham Leics 36 F3
Welham Notts 45 D11
Welham Green Herts 29 H9
Well Hants 18 G4
Well Lincs 47 E8
Well N Yorks 51 A8
Well End Bucks 18 C5
Well Heads W Yorks 51 F6
Well Hill Kent 19 E11
Well Town Devon 7 F8
Welland Worcs 26 D4
Wellbank Angus 77 D7
Welldale Dumfries 61 G7
Wellesbourne Warks 27 C9
Welling London 19 D11
Wellingborough Northants 28 B5
Wellingham Norf 38 C4
Wellingore Lincs 46 G3
Wellington Cumb 56 F2
Wellington Hereford 25 D11
Wellington Som 7 D10
Wellington Telford 34 D2
Wellington Heath Hereford 26 D4
Wellington Hill W Yorks 51 F9
Wellow Bath 16 F4
Wellow IoW 10 F2
Wellow Notts 45 F10
Wellpond Green Herts 29 F11
Wells Som 15 G11
Wells Green Ches E 43 G9
Wells-Next-The-Sea Norf 38 A5
Wellsborough Leics 35 E9
Wellswood Torbay 5 E10
Wellwood Fife 69 B9
Welney Norf 37 F11
Welsh Bicknor Hereford 26 G2
Welsh End Shrops 33 B11
Welsh Frankton Shrops 33 B9
Welsh Hook Pembs 22 D4
Welsh Newton Hereford 25 G11
Welsh St Donats V Glam 14 D6
Welshampton Shrops 33 B10
Welshpool = Y Trallwng Powys 33 E8
Welton Cumb 56 B5
Welton E Yorks 52 G5
Welton Lincs 46 E4
Welton Northants 28 B2
Welton Hill Lincs 46 D4
Welton le Marsh Lincs 47 F8
Welton le Wold Lincs 46 D6
Welwick E Yorks 53 G9
Welwyn Herts 29 G9
Welwyn Garden City Herts 29 G9
Wem Shrops 33 C11
Wembdon Som 15 H8
Wembley London 19 C8
Wembury Devon 4 G6
Wembworthy Devon 6 F5
Wemyss Bay Invclyd 73 G10
Wenallt Ceredig 24 A3
Wenallt Gwyn 32 A5
Wendens Ambo Essex 30 E2
Wendlebury Oxon 28 G2
Wendling Norf 38 D5
Wendover Bucks 28 H5
Wendron Corn 2 F5
Wendy Cambs 29 D10
Wenfordbridge Corn 4 D1
Wenhaston Suff 39 H10
Wennington Cambs 37 H8
Wennington Lancs 50 B2
Wennington London 20 C2
Wensley Derbys 44 F6
Wensley N Yorks 58 H1
Wentbridge W Yorks 51 H10
Wentnor Shrops 33 F9
Wentworth Cambs 37 H10
Wentworth S Yorks 45 C7
Wenvoe V Glam 15 D7
Weobley Hereford 25 C11
Weobley Marsh Hereford 25 C11
Wereham Norf 38 E2
Wergs W Mid 34 E4
Wern Powys 32 D5
Wern Powys 33 D8
Wernffrwd Swansea 23 G10
Wernyrheolydd Mon 25 G10
Werrington Corn 4 C4
Werrington Pboro 37 E7
Werrington Staffs 44 H3
Wervin Ches W 43 E7
Wesham Lancs 49 F4
Wessington Derbys 45 G7
West Acre Norf 38 D3
West Adderbury Oxon 27 E11
West Allerdean Northumb 71 F8
West Alvington Devon 5 G8
West Amesbury Wilts 17 G8
West Anstey Devon 7 D7
West Ashby Lincs 46 E6
West Ashling W Sus 11 D7
West Ashton Wilts 16 F5
West Auckland Durham 58 D2
West Ayton N Yorks 52 A5
West Bagborough Som 7 C10
West Barkwith Lincs 46 D5
West Barnby N Yorks 59 E9
West Barns E Loth 70 C5
West Barsham Norf 38 B5
West Bay Dorset 8 E3
West Beckham Norf 39 B7
West Bedfont Sur 19 D7
West Benhar N Lanark 69 D7
West Bergholt Essex 30 F6
West Bexington Dorset 8 F4
West Bilney Norf 38 D3
West Blatchington Brighton 12 F1
West Bowling W Yorks 51 F7
West Bradford Lancs 50 E3
West Bradley Som 16 H2
West Bretton W Yorks 44 A6
West Bridgford Notts 36 B1
West Bromwich W Mid 34 F6
West Buckland Devon 6 C5
West Buckland Som 7 D10
West Burrafirth Shetland 96 H4
West Burton N Yorks 58 H1
West Burton W Sus 11 C8
West Butterwick N Lincs 46 B2
West Byfleet Sur 19 E7
West Caister Norf 39 D11
West Calder W Loth 69 D9
West Camel Som 8 B4
West Challow Oxon 17 C10
West Chelborough Dorset 8 D4
West Chevington Northumb 63 D8
West Chiltington W Sus 11 C9
West Chiltington Common W Sus 11 C9
West Chinnock Som 8 C3
West Chisenbury Wilts 17 F8
West Clandon Sur 19 F7
West Cliffe Kent 21 G10
West Clyne Highld 93 J11
West Clyth Highld 94 G4
West Coker Som 8 C4
West Compton Dorset 8 E4
West Compton Som 16 G2
West Cowick E Yorks 52 G2
West Cranmore Som 16 G3
West Cross Swansea 14 C2
West Cullery Aberds 83 C9
West Curry Corn 6 G1
West Curthwaite Cumb 56 B5
West Darlochan Argyll 65 F7
West Dean W Sus 11 C7
West Dean Wilts 10 B1
West Deeping Lincs 37 E7
West Derby Mers 43 C6
West Dereham Norf 38 E2
West Didsbury Gtr Man 44 C2
West Ditchburn Northumb 63 A7
West Down Devon 6 B4
West Drayton London 19 D7
West Drayton Notts 45 E11
West Ella E Yorks 52 G6
West End Bedford 28 C6
West End E Yorks 52 F5
West End E Yorks 53 F7
West End Hants 10 C3
West End Lancs 50 G3
West End N Som 15 E10
West End N Yorks 51 D7
West End Norf 38 E5
West End Norf 39 D11
West End Oxon 17 A11
West End S Lanark 69 F8
West End S Yorks 45 B10
West End Suff 39 G10
West End Sur 18 E6
West End W Sus 11 C11
West End Wilts 9 B8
West End Wilts 16 D6
West End Green Hants 18 E3
West Farleigh Kent 20 F4
West Felton Shrops 33 C9
West Fenton E Loth 70 B3
West Ferry Dundee 77 D7
West Firle E Sus 12 F3
West Ginge Oxon 17 C11
West Grafton Wilts 17 E9
West Green Hants 18 F4
West Greenskares Aberds 89 B7
West Grimstead Wilts 9 B11
West Grinstead W Sus 11 B10
West Haddlesey N Yorks 52 G1
West Haddon Northants 28 A3
West Hagbourne Oxon 18 C2
West Hagley Worcs 34 G5
West Hall Cumb 61 G11
West Hallam Derbys 35 A10
West Halton N Lincs 52 G5
West Ham London 19 C11
West Handley Derbys 45 E7
West Hanney Oxon 17 B11
West Hanningfield Essex 20 B4
West Hardwick W Yorks 51 H10
West Harnham Wilts 9 B10
West Harptree Bath 16 F2
West Hatch Som 8 B1
West Head Norf 38 E1
West Heath Ches E 44 F2
West Heath Hants 18 F2
West Heath Hants 18 F5
West Helmsdale Highld 93 H13
West Hendred Oxon 17 C11
West Heslerton N Yorks 52 B5
West Hill Devon 7 G9
West Hill E Yorks 53 C7
West Hill N Som 15 D10
West Hoathly W Sus 12 C2
West Holme Dorset 9 F7
West Horndon Essex 20 C3
West Horrington Som 16 G2
West Horsley Sur 19 F7
West Horton Northumb 71 G9
West Hougham Kent 21 G9
West Houlland Shetland 96 H4
West-houses Derbys 45 G8
West Huntington York 52 D2
West Hythe Kent 13 C10
West Ilsley W Berks 17 C11
West Itchenor W Sus 11 D6
West Keal Lincs 47 F7
West Kennett Wilts 17 E8
West Kilbride N Ayrs 66 B5
West Kingsdown Kent 20 E2
West Kington Wilts 16 D5
West Kinharrachie Aberds 89 E9
West Kirby Mers 42 D5
West Knapton N Yorks 52 B4
West Knighton Dorset 8 F6
West Knoyle Wilts 9 A7
West Kyloe Northumb 71 F9
West Lambrook Som 8 C3
West Langdon Kent 21 G10
West Langwell Highld 93 J9
West Lavington W Sus 11 B7
West Lavington Wilts 17 F7
West Layton N Yorks 58 F2
West Lea Durham 58 B5
West Leake Notts 35 C11
West Learmouth Northumb 71 G7
West Leigh Devon 6 F5
West Lexham Norf 38 D4
West Lilling N Yorks 52 C2
West Linton Borders 69 E10
West Liss Hants 11 B6
West Littleton S Glos 16 D4
West Looe Corn 4 F3
West Luccombe Som 7 B7
West Lulworth Dorset 9 F7
West Lutton N Yorks 52 C5
West Lydford Som 8 A4
West Lyng Som 8 B2
West Lynn Norf 38 C2
West Malling Kent 20 F3
West Malvern Worcs 26 D4
West Marden W Sus 11 C6
West Marina E Sus 13 F6
West Markham Notts 45 E11
West Marsh NE Lincs 46 A6
West Marton N Yorks 50 D4
West Meon Hants 10 B5
West Mersea Essex 31 G7
West Milton Dorset 8 E4
West Minster Kent 20 D6
West Molesey Sur 19 E8
West Monkton Som 8 B1
West Moors Dorset 9 D9
West Morriston Borders 70 F5
West Muir Angus 77 A8
West Ness N Yorks 52 B2
West Newham Northumb 62 F6
West Newton E Yorks 53 F7
West Newton Norf 38 C2
West Norwood London 19 D10
West Ogwell Devon 5 D9
West Orchard Dorset 9 C7
West Overton Wilts 17 E8
West Park Hrtlpl 58 C5
West Parley Dorset 9 E9
West Peckham Kent 20 F3
West Pelton Durham 58 A3
West Pennard Som 15 H11
West Pentire Corn 3 C6
West Perry Cambs 29 B8
West Putford Devon 6 E2
West Quantoxhead Som 7 B10
West Rainton Durham 58 B4
West Rasen Lincs 46 D4
West Raynham Norf 38 C4
West Retford Notts 45 D10
West Rounton N Yorks 58 F5
West Row Suff 38 H2
West Rudham Norf 38 C4
West Runton Norf 39 A7
West Saltoun E Loth 70 D3
West Sandwick Shetland 96 E6
West Scrafton N Yorks 51 A6
West Sleekburn Northumb 63 E8
West Somerton Norf 39 D10
West Stafford Dorset 8 F6
West Stockwith Notts 45 C11
West Stoke W Sus 11 D7
West Stonesdale N Yorks 57 F10
West Stoughton Som 15 G10
West Stour Dorset 9 B6
West Stourmouth Kent 21 E9
West Stow Suff 30 A5
West Stowell Wilts 17 E8
West Strathan Highld 93 C8
West Stratton Hants 18 G2
West Street Kent 20 F6
West Tanfield N Yorks 51 B8
West Taphouse Corn 4 E2
West Tarbert Argyll 73 G7
West Thirston Northumb 63 D7
West Thorney W Sus 11 D6
West Thurrock Thurrock 20 D2
West Tilbury Thurrock 20 D3
West Tisted Hants 10 B5
West Tofts Norf 38 F4
West Tofts Perth 76 D4
West Torrington Lincs 46 D5
West Town Hants 10 E6
West Town N Som 15 E10
West Tytherley Hants 10 B1
West Tytherton Wilts 16 D6
West Walton Norf 37 D10
West Walton Highway Norf 37 D10
West Wellow Hants 10 C1
West Wemyss Fife 70 A2
West Wick N Som 15 E9
West Wickham Cambs 30 D3
West Wickham London 19 E10
West Williamston Pembs 22 F5
West Willoughby Lincs 36 A5
West Winch Norf 38 D2
West Winterslow Wilts 9 A11
West Wittering W Sus 11 E6
West Witton N Yorks 58 H1
West Woodburn Northumb 62 E4
West Woodhay W Berks 17 E10
West Woodlands Som 16 G4
West Worldham Hants 18 H4
West Worlington Devon 7 E6
West Worthing W Sus 11 D10
West Wratting Cambs 30 C3
West Wycombe Bucks 18 B5
West Wylam Northumb 63 G7
West Yell Shetland 96 E6
Westacott Devon 6 C4
Westbere Kent 21 E8
Westborough Lincs 36 A4
Westbourne Bmouth 9 E9
Westbourne Suff 31 D8
Westbourne W Sus 11 D6
Westbrook W Berks 17 D11
Westbury Bucks 28 E3
Westbury Shrops 33 E9
Westbury Wilts 16 F5
Westbury Leigh Wilts 16 F5
Westbury-on-Severn Glos 26 G4
Westbury on Trym Bristol 16 D2
Westbury-sub-Mendip Som 15 G11
Westby Lancs 49 F3
Westcliff-on-Sea Southend 20 C5
Westcombe Som 16 H3
Westcote Glos 27 F9
Westcott Bucks 28 G4
Westcott Devon 7 F9
Westcott Sur 19 G8
Westcott Barton Oxon 27 F11
Westdean E Sus 12 G4
Westdene Brighton 12 F1
Wester Aberchalder Highld 81 A7
Wester Balgedie Perth 76 G4
Wester Culbeuchly Aberds 89 B6
Wester Dechmont W Loth 69 D9
Wester Denoon Angus 76 C6
Wester Fintray Aberds 83 B10
Wester Gruinards Highld 87 B8
Wester Lealty Highld 87 D9
Wester Milton Highld 87 F12
Wester Newburn Fife 77 G7
Wester Quarff Shetland 96 K6
Wester Skeld Shetland 96 J4
Westerdale Highld 94 E3
Westerdale N Yorks 59 F7
Westerfield Shetland 96 H5
Westerfield Suff 31 D8
Westergate W Sus 11 D8
Westerham Kent 19 F11
Westerhope T&W 63 G7
Westerleigh S Glos 16 D4
Westerton Angus 77 B9
Westerton Durham 58 C3
Westerton W Sus 11 D7
Westerwick Shetland 96 J4
Westfield Cumb 56 D1
Westfield E Sus 13 E7
Westfield Hereford 26 D4
Westfield Highld 94 D2
Westfield N Lanark 68 C6
Westfield Norf 38 E5
Westfield W Loth 69 C8
Westfields Dorset 8 D6
Westfields of Rattray Perth 76 C4
Westgate Durham 57 C11
Westgate N Lincs 45 B11
Westgate Norf 38 A4
Westgate Norf 38 A5
Westgate on Sea Kent 21 D10
Westhall Aberds 83 A8
Westhall Suff 39 G10
Westham Dorset 8 G5
Westham E Sus 12 F5
Westham Som 15 G10
Westhampnett W Sus 11 D7
Westhay Som 15 G10
Westhead Lancs 43 B7
Westhide Hereford 26 D2
Westhill Aberds 83 C10
Westhill Highld 87 G10
Westhope Hereford 25 C11
Westhope Shrops 33 G10
Westhorpe Lincs 37 B8
Westhorpe Suff 31 B7
Westhoughton Gtr Man 43 B9
Westhouse N Yorks 50 B2
Westhumble Sur 19 F8
Westing Shetland 96 C7
Westlake Devon 5 F7
Westleigh Devon 6 D3
Westleigh Devon 7 E9
Westleigh Gtr Man 43 B9
Westleton Suff 31 B11
Westley Shrops 33 E9
Westley Suff 30 B5
Westley Waterless Cambs 30 C3
Westlington Bucks 28 G4
Westlinton Cumb 61 G9
Westmarsh Kent 21 E9
Westmeston E Sus 12 E2
Westmill Herts 29 F10
Westminster London 19 D10
Westmuir Angus 76 B6
Westness Orkney 95 F4
Westnewton Cumb 56 B3
Westnewton Northumb 71 G8
Westoe T&W 63 G9
Weston Bath 16 E4
Weston Ches E 43 G10
Weston Devon 7 H10
Weston Dorset 8 G5
Weston Halton 43 D8
Weston Hants 10 B6
Weston Herts 29 E9
Weston Lincs 37 C8
Weston N Yorks 51 E7
Weston Northants 28 D2
Weston Notts 45 F11
Weston Shrops 34 C1
Weston Shrops 34 F1
Weston Staffs 34 C5
Weston W Berks 17 D10
Weston Beggard Hereford 26 D2
Weston by Welland Northants 36 F3
Weston Colville Cambs 30 C3
Weston Coyney Stoke 34 A5
Weston Favell Northants 28 B4
Weston Green Cambs 30 C3
Weston Green Norf 39 D7
Weston Heath Shrops 34 D3
Weston Hills Lincs 37 C8
Weston-in-Gordano N Som 15 D10
Weston Jones Staffs 34 C3
Weston Longville Norf 39 D7
Weston Lullingfields Shrops 33 C10
Weston-on-the-Green Oxon 28 G2
Weston-on-Trent Derbys 35 C10
Weston Patrick Hants 18 G3
Weston Rhyn Shrops 33 B8
Weston-Sub-Edge Glos 27 D8
Weston-super-Mare N Som 15 E9
Weston Turville Bucks 28 G5
Weston under Lizard Staffs 34 D4
Weston under Penyard Hereford 26 F3
Weston under Wetherley Warks 27 B10
Weston Underwood Derbys 35 A8
Weston Underwood M Keynes 28 C5
Westonbirt Glos 16 C5
Westoncommon Shrops 33 C10
Westoning C Beds 29 E7
Westonzoyland Som 8 A2
Westow N Yorks 52 C3
Westport Argyll 65 F7
Westport Som 8 C2
Westrigg W Loth 69 D8
Westruther Borders 70 F5
Westry Cambs 37 F9
Westville Notts 45 H9
Westward Cumb 56 B4
Westward Ho! Devon 6 D3
Westwell Kent 20 G6
Westwell Oxon 27 H9
Westwell Leacon Kent 20 G6
Westwick Cambs 29 B11
Westwick Durham 58 E1
Westwick Norf 39 C8
Westwood Devon 7 G9
Westwood Wilts 16 F5
Westwoodside N Lincs 45 C11
Wetheral Cumb 56 A6
Wetherby W Yorks 51 E10
Wetherden Suff 31 B7
Wetheringsett Suff 31 B8
Wethersfield Essex 30 E4
Wethersta Shetland 96 G5

Wetherup Street Suff 31 B8
Wetley Rocks Staffs 44 H3
Wettenhall Ches E 43 F9
Wetton Staffs 44 G5
Wetwang E Yorks 52 D5
Wetwood Staffs 34 B3
Wexcombe Wilts 17 F9
Wexham Street Bucks 18 C6
Weybourne Norf 39 A7
Weybread Suff 39 G8
Weybridge Sur 19 E7
Weycroft Devon 8 E2
Weydale Highld 94 D3
Weyhill Hants 17 G10
Weymouth Dorset 8 G5
Whaddon Bucks 28 E5
Whaddon Cambs 29 D10
Whaddon Glos 26 G5
Whaddon Wilts 9 B10
Whale Cumb 57 D7
Whaley Derbys 45 E9
Whaley Bridge Derbys 44 D4
Whaley Thorns Derbys 45 E9
Whaligoe Highld 94 F5
Whalley Lancs 50 F3
Whalton Northumb 63 E7
Wham N Yorks 50 C3
Whaplode Lincs 37 C9
Whaplode Drove Lincs 37 D9
Whaplode St Catherine Lincs 37 C9
Wharfe N Yorks 50 C3
Wharles Lancs 49 F4
Wharncliffe Side S Yorks 44 C6
Wharram le Street N Yorks 52 C4
Wharton Ches W 43 F9
Wharton Green Ches W 43 F9
Whashton N Yorks 58 F2
Whatcombe Dorset 9 D7
Whatcote Warks 27 D10
Whatfield Suff 31 D7
Whatley Som 8 D2
Whatley Som 16 G4
Whatlington E Sus 13 E6
Whatstandwell Derbys 45 G7
Whatton Notts 36 B3
Whauphill Dumfries 55 E7
Whaw N Yorks 57 F11
Wheatacre Norf 39 F10
Wheatcroft Derbys 45 G7
Wheathampstead Herts 29 G8
Wheathill Shrops 34 G2
Wheatley Devon 7 G8
Wheatley Hants 18 G4
Wheatley Oxon 28 H2
Wheatley S Yorks 45 B9
Wheatley W Yorks 51 G6
Wheatley Hill Durham 58 C4
Wheaton Aston Staffs 34 D4
Wheddon Cross Som 7 C8
Wheedlemont Aberds 82 A6
Wheelerstreet Sur 18 G6
Wheelock Ches E 43 G10
Wheelock Heath Ches E 43 G10
Wheelton Lancs 50 G2
Wheen Angus 82 F5
Wheldrake York 52 E2
Whelford Glos 17 B8
Whelpley Hill Herts 18 A6
Whempstead Herts 29 F10
Whenby N Yorks 52 C2
Whepstead Suff 30 C5
Wherstead Suff 31 D8
Wherwell Hants 17 G10
Wheston Derbys 44 E5
Whetsted Kent 20 G3
Whetstone Leics 36 F1
Whicham Cumb 49 A1
Whichford Warks 27 E10
Whickham T&W 63 G8
Whiddon Down Devon 6 G5
Whigstreet Angus 77 C7
Whilton Northants 28 B3
Whim Farm Borders 69 E11
Whimble Devon 6 F2
Whimple Devon 7 G9
Whimpwell Green Norf 39 C9
Whinburgh Norf 38 E6
Whinnieliggate Dumfries 55 D10
Whinnyfold Aberds 89 E10
Whippingham IoW 10 E4
Whipsnade C Beds 29 G7
Whipton Devon 7 G8
Whirlow S Yorks 45 D7
Whisby Lincs 46 F3
Whissendine Rutland 36 D4
Whissonsett Norf 38 C5
Whistlefield Argyll 73 D10
Whistlefield Argyll 73 D11
Whistley Green Wokingham 18 D4
Whiston Mers 43 C7
Whiston Northants 28 B5
Whiston S Yorks 45 D8
Whiston Staffs 34 D4
Whiston Staffs 44 H4
Whitbeck Cumb 49 A1
Whitbourne Hereford 26 C4
Whitburn T&W 63 G10
Whitburn W Loth 69 D8
Whitburn Colliery T&W 63 G10
Whitby Ches W 43 E6
Whitby N Yorks 59 E9
Whitbyheath Ches W 43 E6
Whitchurch Bath 16 E3
Whitchurch Bucks 28 F4
Whitchurch Cardiff 15 C7
Whitchurch Devon 4 D5
Whitchurch Hants 17 G11
Whitchurch Hereford 26 G2
Whitchurch Oxon 18 D3
Whitchurch Pembs 22 D2
Whitchurch Shrops 33 A11
Whitchurch Canonicorum Dorset 8 E2
Whitchurch Hill Oxon 18 D3
Whitcombe Dorset 8 F6
Whitcott Keysett Shrops 33 G8
White Coppice Lancs 50 H2
White Lackington Dorset 8 E6
White Ladies Aston Worcs 26 C6
White Lund Lancs 49 C4
White Mill Carms 23 D9
White Ness Shetland 96 J5
White Notley Essex 30 G4
White Pit Lincs 47 E7
White Post Notts 45 G10
White Rocks Hereford 25 F11
White Roding Essex 30 G2
White Waltham Windsor 18 D5
Whiteacen Moray 88 D2
Whiteacre Heath Warks 35 F8
Whitebridge Highld 81 B6
Whitebrook Mon 26 H2
Whiteburn Borders 70 F4
Whitecairn Dumfries 54 D5
Whitecairns Aberds 83 B11
Whitecastle S Lanark 69 F9
Whitechapel Lancs 50 E1
Whitecleat Orkney 95 H6
Whitecraig E Loth 70 C2
Whitecroft Glos 26 H3
Whitecross Corn 3 B8
Whitecross Falk 69 C8
Whitecross Staffs 34 C4
Whiteface Highld 87 C10
Whitefarland N Ayrs 66 B1
Whitefaulds S Ayrs 66 F5
Whitefield Gtr Man 44 B2
Whitefield Perth 76 D4
Whiteford Aberds 83 A9
Whitegate Ches W 43 F9
Whitehall Blackburn 50 G2
Whitehall W Sus 11 B10
Whitehall Village Orkney 95 F7
Whitehaven Cumb 56 E1
Whitehill Hants 11 A6
Whitehills Aberds 89 B6
Whitehills S Lanark 68 E5
Whitehough Derbys 44 D4
Whitehouse Aberds 83 B8
Whitehouse Argyll 73 G7
Whiteinch Glasgow 68 D4
Whitekirk E Loth 70 B4
Whitelaw S Lanark 68 F5
Whiteleas T&W 63 G9
Whiteley Bank IoW 10 F4
Whiteley Green Ches E 44 E3
Whiteley Village Sur 19 E7
Whitemans Green W Sus 12 D2
Whitemire Moray 87 F12
Whitemoor Corn 3 D8
Whitemore Staffs 44 F2
Whitenap Hants 10 B2
Whiteoak Green Oxon 27 G10
Whiteparish Wilts 9 B11
Whiterashes Aberds 89 F8
Whiterow Highld 94 F5
Whiteshill Glos 26 H5
Whiteside Northumb 62 G3
Whiteside W Loth 69 D8
Whitesmith E Sus 12 E4
Whitestaunton Som 8 C1
Whitestone Devon 6 B3
Whitestone Devon 7 G7
Whitestone Warks 35 G9
Whitestones Aberds 89 C8
Whitestreet Green Suff 30 E6
Whitewall Corner N Yorks 52 B3
Whiteway Glos 16 B5
Whiteway Glos 26 G6
Whitewell Aberds 89 B9
Whitewell Lancs 50 E2
Whitewell Bottom Lancs 50 G4
Whiteworks Devon 5 D7
Whitfield Kent 21 G10
Whitfield Northants 28 E3
Whitfield Northumb 62 H3
Whitfield S Glos 16 B3
Whitford Devon 8 E1
Whitford Flint 42 E4
Whitgift E Yorks 52 G4
Whitgreave Staffs 34 C4
Whithorn Dumfries 55 E7
Whiting Bay N Ayrs 66 D3
Whitkirk W Yorks 51 F9
Whitland Carms 22 E6
Whitletts S Ayrs 67 D6
Whitley N Yorks 52 G1
Whitley Reading 18 D4
Whitley Wilts 16 E5
Whitley Bay T&W 63 F9
Whitley Chapel Northumb 62 H5
Whitley Lower W Yorks 51 H8
Whitley Row Kent 19 F11
Whitlock's End W Mid 35 H7
Whitminster Glos 26 H4
Whitmore Staffs 34 A4
Whitnage Devon 7 E9
Whitnash Warks 27 B10
Whitney-on-Wye Hereford 25 D9
Whitrigg Cumb 56 C4
Whitrigg Cumb 61 H8
Whitsbury Hants 9 C10
Whitsome Borders 71 E7
Whitson Newport 15 C9
Whitstable Kent 21 E8
Whitstone Corn 6 G1
Whittingham Northumb 62 B6
Whittingslow Shrops 33 G10
Whittington Glos 27 F7
Whittington Lancs 50 B2
Whittington Norf 38 F3
Whittington Shrops 33 B9
Whittington Staffs 34 G4
Whittington Staffs 35 E7
Whittington Worcs 26 C5
Whittle-le-Woods Lancs 50 G1
Whittlebury Northants 28 D3
Whittlesey Cambs 37 F8
Whittlesford Cambs 29 D11
Whittlestone Head Blackburn 50 H3
Whitton Borders 62 A3
Whitton N Lincs 52 G5
Whitton Northumb 62 C6
Whitton Powys 25 B9
Whitton Shrops 26 A2
Whitton Stockton 58 D4
Whitton Suff 31 D8
Whittonditch Wilts 17 D9
Whittonstall Northumb 62 H6
Whitway Hants 17 F11
Whitwell Derbys 45 E9
Whitwell Herts 29 F8
Whitwell IoW 10 G4
Whitwell N Yorks 58 G3
Whitwell Rutland 36 E5
Whitwell-on-the-Hill N Yorks 52 C3
Whitwell Street Norf 39 C7
Whitwick Leics 35 D10
Whitwood W Yorks 51 G10
Whitworth Lancs 50 H4
Whixall Shrops 33 B11
Whixley N Yorks 51 D10
Whoberley W Mid 35 H9
Whorlton Durham 58 E2
Whorlton N Yorks 58 F5
Whygate Northumb 62 F3
Whyle Hereford 26 B2
Whyteleafe Sur 19 F10
Wibdon Glos 16 B2
Wibsey W Yorks 51 F7
Wibtoft Leics 35 G10
Wichenford Worcs 26 B4
Wichling Kent 20 F6
Wick Bmouth 9 E10
Wick Devon 7 F10
Wick Highld 94 E5
Wick S Glos 16 D4
Wick Shetland 96 K6
Wick V Glam 14 D5
Wick W Sus 11 D9
Wick Wilts 9 B10
Wick Worcs 26 D6
Wick Hill Wokingham 18 E4
Wick St Lawrence N Som 15 E9
Wicken Cambs 30 A2
Wicken Northants 28 E4
Wicken Bonhunt Essex 29 E11
Wicken Green Village Norf 38 B4
Wickenby Lincs 46 D4
Wickersley S Yorks 45 C8
Wickford Essex 20 B4
Wickham Hants 10 C4
Wickham W Berks 17 D10
Wickham Bishops Essex 30 G5
Wickham Market Suff 31 C10
Wickham Skeith Suff 31 B7
Wickham St Paul Essex 30 E5
Wickham Street Suff 30 C4
Wickham Street Suff 31 B7
Wickhambreux Kent 21 F9
Wickhambrook Suff 30 C4
Wickhamford Worcs 27 D7
Wickhampton Norf 39 E10
Wicklewood Norf 39 E6
Wickmere Norf 39 B7
Wickwar S Glos 16 C4
Widdington Essex 30 E2
Widdrington Northumb 63 D8
Widdrington Station Northumb 63 D8
Wide Open T&W 63 F8
Widecombe in the Moor Devon 5 D8
Widegates Corn 4 F3
Widemouth Bay Corn 4 A3
Widewall Orkney 95 J5
Widford Essex 30 H3
Widford Herts 29 G11
Widham Wilts 17 C7
Widmer End Bucks 18 B5
Widmerpool Notts 36 C2
Widnes Halton 43 D8
Wigan Gtr Man 43 B8
Wiggaton Devon 7 G10
Wiggenhall St Germans Norf 38 D1
Wiggenhall St Mary Magdalen Norf 38 D1
Wiggenhall St Mary the Virgin Norf 38 D1
Wigginton Herts 28 G6
Wigginton Oxon 27 E10
Wigginton Staffs 35 E8
Wigginton York 52 D1
Wigglesworth N Yorks 50 D4
Wiggonby Cumb 56 A4
Wiggonholt W Sus 11 C9
Wighill N Yorks 51 E10
Wighton Norf 38 B5
Wigley Hants 10 C2
Wigmore Hereford 25 B11
Wigmore Medway 20 E5
Wigsley Notts 46 E2
Wigsthorpe Northants 36 G6
Wigston Leics 36 F2
Wigthorpe Notts 45 D9
Wigtoft Lincs 37 B8
Wigton Cumb 56 B4
Wigtown Dumfries 55 D7
Wigtwizzle S Yorks 44 C6
Wike W Yorks 51 E9
Wike Well End S Yorks 45 A10
Wilbarston Northants 36 G4
Wilberfoss E Yorks 52 D3
Wilberlee W Yorks 44 A4
Wilburton Cambs 29 A11
Wilby Norf 38 G6
Wilby Northants 28 B5
Wilby Suff 31 A9
Wilcot Wilts 17 E8
Wilcott Shrops 33 D9
Wilcrick Newport 15 C10
Wilday Green Derbys 45 E7
Wildboarclough Ches E 44 F3
Wilden Bedford 29 C7
Wilden Worcs 26 A5
Wildhern Hants 17 F10
Wildhill Herts 29 H9
Wildmoor Worcs 34 H5
Wildsworth Lincs 46 C2
Wilford Nottingham 36 B1
Wilkesley Ches E 34 A2
Wilkhaven Highld 87 C12
Wilkieston W Loth 69 D10
Willand Devon 7 E9
Willaston Ches E 43 G9
Willaston Ches W 42 E6
Willen M Keynes 28 D5
Willenhall W Mid 35 H9
Willenhall W Mid 34 F5
Willerby E Yorks 52 F6
Willerby N Yorks 52 B6
Willersey Glos 27 E8
Willersley Hereford 25 D10
Willesborough Kent 13 B9
Willesborough Lees Kent 13 B9
Willesden London 19 C9
Willett Som 7 C10
Willey Shrops 34 F2
Willey Warks 35 G10
Willey Green Sur 18 F6
Williamscott Oxon 27 D11
Willian Herts 29 E9
Willingale Essex 30 H2
Willingdon E Sus 12 F4
Willingham Cambs 29 A11
Willingham by Stow Lincs 46 D2
Willington Bedford 29 D8
Willington Derbys 35 C8
Willington Durham 58 C2
Willington T&W 63 G9
Willington Warks 27 E9
Willington Corner Ches W 43 F8
Willisham Tye Suff 31 C7
Willitoft E Yorks 52 F3
Williton Som 7 B9
Willoughbridge Staffs 34 A3
Willoughby Lincs 47 E8
Willoughby Warks 28 B2
Willoughby-on-the-Wolds Notts 36 C2
Willoughby Waterleys Leics 36 F1
Willoughton Lincs 46 C3
Willows Green Essex 30 G4
Willsbridge S Glos 16 D3
Willsworthy Devon 4 C6
Wilmcote Warks 27 C8
Wilmington Devon 7 G11
Wilmington E Sus 12 F4
Wilmington Kent 20 D2
Wilminstone Devon 4 D5
Wilmslow Ches E 44 D2
Wilnecote Staffs 35 E8
Wilpshire Lancs 50 F2
Wilsden W Yorks 51 F6
Wilsford Lincs 36 A6
Wilsford Wilts 17 F8
Wilsford Wilts 17 H8
Wilsill N Yorks 51 C7
Wilsley Pound Kent 13 C6
Wilsom Hants 18 H4
Wilson Leics 35 C10
Wilsontown S Lanark 69 E8
Wilstead Bedford 29 D7
Wilsthorpe Lincs 37 D6
Wilstone Herts 28 G6
Wilton Borders 61 B10
Wilton Cumb 56 E2
Wilton N Yorks 52 A4
Wilton Redcar 59 E6
Wilton Wilts 9 A9
Wilton Wilts 17 E9
Wimbish Essex 30 E2
Wimbish Green Essex 30 E3
Wimblebury Staffs 34 D6
Wimbledon London 19 D9
Wimblington Cambs 37 F10
Wimborne Minster Dorset 9 E9
Wimborne St Giles Dorset 9 C9
Wimbotsham Norf 38 E2
Wimpson Soton 10 C2
Wimpstone Warks 27 D9
Wincanton Som 8 B6
Wincham Ches W 43 E9
Winchburgh W Loth 69 C9
Winchcombe Glos 27 F7
Winchelsea E Sus 13 E8
Winchelsea Beach E Sus 13 E8
Winchester Hants 10 B3
Winchet Hill Kent 12 B6
Winchfield Hants 18 F4
Winchmore Hill Bucks 18 B6
Winchmore Hill London 19 B10
Wincle Ches E 44 F3
Wincobank S Yorks 45 C7
Windermere Cumb 56 G6
Winderton Warks 27 D10
Windhill Highld 87 G8
Windhouse Shetland 96 D6
Windlehurst Gtr Man 44 D3
Windlesham Sur 18 E6
Windley Derbys 35 A9
Windmill Hill E Sus 12 E5
Windmill Hill Som 8 C2
Windrush Glos 27 G8
Windsor N Lincs 45 A11
Windsor Windsor 18 D6
Windsoredge Glos 16 A5
Windygates Fife 76 G6
Windyknowe W Loth 69 D8
Windywalls Borders 70 G6
Wineham W Sus 11 B11
Winestead E Yorks 53 G8
Winewall Lancs 50 E5
Winfarthing Norf 39 G7
Winford IoW 10 F4
Winford N Som 15 E11
Winforton Hereford 25 D9
Winfrith Newburgh Dorset 9 F7
Wing Bucks 28 F5
Wing Rutland 36 E4
Wingate Durham 58 C5
Wingates Gtr Man 43 B9
Wingates Northumb 63 D7
Wingerworth Derbys 45 F7
Wingfield C Beds 29 F7
Wingfield Suff 39 H8
Wingfield Wilts 16 F5
Wingham Kent 21 F9
Wingmore Kent 21 G8
Wingrave Bucks 28 G5
Winkburn Notts 45 G11
Winkfield Brack 18 D6
Winkfield Row Brack 18 D5
Winkhill Staffs 44 G4
Winklebury Hants 18 F3
Winkleigh Devon 6 F5
Winksley N Yorks 51 B8
Winkton Dorset 9 E10
Winlaton T&W 63 G7
Winless Highld 94 E5
Winmarleigh Lancs 49 E4
Winnal Hereford 25 E11
Winnall Hants 10 B3
Winnersh Wokingham 18 D4
Winscales Cumb 56 D2
Winscombe N Som 15 F10
Winsford Ches W 43 F9
Winsford Som 7 C8
Winsham Som 8 D2
Winshill Staffs 35 C8
Winskill Cumb 57 C7
Winslade Hants 18 G3
Winsley Wilts 16 E5
Winslow Bucks 28 F4
Winson Glos 27 H7
Winson Green W Mid 34 G6
Winsor Hants 10 C2
Winster Cumb 56 G6
Winster Derbys 44 F6
Winston Durham 58 E2
Winston Suff 31 B8
Winston Green Suff 31 B8
Winstone Glos 26 H6
Winswell Devon 6 E3
Winter Gardens Essex 20 C4
Winterborne Bassett Wilts 17 D8
Winterborne Clenston Dorset 9 D7
Winterborne Herrington Dorset 8 F5
Winterborne Houghton Dorset 9 D7
Winterborne Kingston Dorset 9 E7
Winterborne Monkton Dorset 8 F5
Winterborne Monkton Wilts 17 D8
Winterborne Stickland Dorset 9 D7
Winterborne Whitechurch Dorset 9 D7
Winterborne Zelston Dorset 9 E7
Winterbourne S Glos 16 C3
Winterbourne W Berks 17 D11
Winterbourne Abbas Dorset 8 E5
Winterbourne Dauntsey Wilts 9 A10
Winterbourne Down S Glos 16 D3
Winterbourne Earls Wilts 9 A10
Winterbourne Gunner Wilts 17 H8
Winterbourne Steepleton Dorset 8 F5
Winterbourne Stoke Wilts 17 G7
Winterburn N Yorks 50 D5
Winteringham N Lincs 52 G5
Winterley Ches E 43 G10
Wintersett W Yorks 51 H9
Wintershill Hants 10 C4
Winterton N Lincs 52 H5
Winterton-on-Sea Norf 39 D10
Winthorpe Lincs 47 F9
Winthorpe Notts 46 G2
Winton Bmouth 9 E9
Winton Cumb 57 E9
Winton N Yorks 58 G5
Wintringham N Yorks 52 B4
Winwick Cambs 37 G7
Winwick Northants 28 A3
Winwick Warr 43 C9
Wirksworth Derbys 44 G6
Wirksworth Moor Derbys 45 G7
Wirswall Ches E 33 A11
Wisbech Cambs 37 E10
Wisbech St Mary Cambs 37 E10
Wisborough Green W Sus 11 B9
Wiseton Notts 45 D11
Wishaw N Lanark 68 E6
Wishaw Warks 35 F7
Wisley Sur 19 F7
Wispington Lincs 46 E6
Wissenden Kent 13 B8
Wissett Suff 39 H9
Wistanstow Shrops 33 G10
Wistanswick Shrops 34 C2
Wistaston Ches E 43 G9
Wistaston Green Ches E 43 G9
Wiston Pembs 22 E5
Wiston S Lanark 69 G8
Wiston W Sus 11 C10
Wistow Cambs 37 G8
Wistow N Yorks 52 F1
Wiswell Lancs 50 F3
Witcham Cambs 37 G10
Witchampton Dorset 9 D8
Witchford Cambs 37 H11
Witham Essex 30 G5
Witham Friary Som 16 G4
Witham on the Hill Lincs 37 D6
Withcall Lincs 46 D6
Withdean Brighton 12 F2
Witherenden Hill E Sus 12 D5
Witheridge Devon 7 E7
Witherley Leics 35 F9
Withern Lincs 47 D8
Withernsea E Yorks 53 G9
Withernwick E Yorks 53 E7
Withersdale Street Suff 39 G8
Withersfield Suff 30 D3
Witherslack Cumb 49 A4
Withiel Corn 3 C8
Withiel Florey Som 7 C8
Withington Glos 27 G7
Withington Gtr Man 44 C2
Withington Hereford 26 D2
Withington Shrops 34 D1
Withington Staffs 34 B6
Withington Green Ches E 44 E2
Withleigh Devon 7 E8
Withnell Lancs 50 G2
Withybrook Warks 35 G10
Withycombe Som 7 B9
Withycombe Raleigh Devon 5 C11
Withyham E Sus 12 C3
Withypool Som 7 C7
Witley Sur 18 H6
Witnesham Suff 31 C8
Witney Oxon 27 G10
Wittering Pboro 37 E6
Wittersham Kent 13 D7
Witton Angus 83 F7
Witton Worcs 26 B5
Witton Bridge Norf 39 B9
Witton Gilbert Durham 58 B3
Witton-le-Wear Durham 58 C2
Witton Park Durham 58 C2
Wiveliscombe Som 7 D9
Wivelrod Hants 18 H3
Wivelsfield E Sus 12 D2
Wivelsfield Green E Sus 12 D2
Wivenhoe Essex 31 F7
Wivenhoe Cross Essex 31 F7
Wiveton Norf 38 A6
Wix Essex 31 F8
Wixford Warks 27 C7
Wixhill Shrops 34 C1
Wixoe Suff 30 D4
Woburn C Beds 28 E6
Woburn Sands M Keynes 28 E6
Wokefield Park W Berks 18 E3
Woking Sur 19 F7
Wokingham Wokingham 18 E5
Wolborough Devon 5 D9
Wold Newton E Yorks 52 B6
Wold Newton NE Lincs 46 C6
Woldingham Sur 19 F10
Wolfclyde S Lanark 69 G9
Wolferton Norf 38 C2
Wolfhill Perth 76 D4
Wolf's Castle Pembs 22 D4
Wolfsdale Pembs 22 D4
Woll Borders 61 A10
Wollaston Northants 28 B6
Wollaston Shrops 33 D9
Wollaton Nottingham 35 B11
Wollerton Shrops 34 B2
Wollescote W Mid 34 G5
Wolsingham Durham 58 C1
Wolstanton Staffs 44 H2
Wolston Warks 35 H10
Wolvercote Oxon 27 H11
Wolverhampton W Mid 34 F5
Wolverley Shrops 33 B10
Wolverley Worcs 34 H4
Wolverton Hants 18 F2
Wolverton M Keynes 28 D5
Wolverton Warks 27 B9
Wolverton Common Hants 18 F2
Wolvesnewton Mon 15 B10
Wolvey Warks 35 G10
Wolviston Stockton 58 D5
Wombleton N Yorks 52 A2
Wombourne Staffs 34 F4
Wombwell S Yorks 45 B7
Womenswold Kent 21 F9
Womersley N Yorks 51 H11
Wonastow Mon 25 G11
Wonersh Sur 19 G7
Wonson Devon 5 C7
Wonston Hants 17 H11
Wooburn Bucks 18 C6
Wooburn Green Bucks 18 C6
Wood Dalling Norf 39 C6
Wood End Herts 29 F10
Wood End Warks 27 A8
Wood End Warks 35 F8
Wood Enderby Lincs 46 F6
Wood Field Sur 19 F8
Wood Green London 19 B10
Wood Hayes W Mid 34 E5
Wood Lanes Ches E 44 D3
Wood Norton Norf 38 C6
Wood Street Norf 39 C9
Wood Street Sur 18 F6
Wood Walton Cambs 37 G8
Woodacott Devon 6 F2
Woodale N Yorks 50 B6
Woodbank Argyll 65 G7
Woodbastwick Norf 39 D9
Woodbeck Notts 45 E11
Woodborough Notts 45 H10
Woodborough Wilts 17 F8
Woodbridge Dorset 8 C6
Woodbridge Suff 31 D9
Woodbury Devon 5 C11
Woodbury Salterton Devon 5 C11
Woodchester Glos 16 A5
Woodchurch Kent 13 C8
Woodchurch Mers 42 D5
Woodcombe Som 7 B8
Woodcote Oxon 18 C3
Woodcott Hants 17 F11
Woodcroft Glos 15 B11
Woodcutts Dorset 9 C8
Woodditton Cambs 30 C3
Woodeaton Oxon 28 G2
Woodend Cumb 56 G3
Woodend Northants 28 D3
Woodend W Sus 11 D7
Woodend Green Northants 28 D3
Woodfalls Wilts 9 B10
Woodfield Oxon 28 F2
Woodfield S Ayrs 66 D6
Woodford Corn 6 E1
Woodford Devon 5 F8
Woodford Glos 16 B3
Woodford Gtr Man 44 D2
Woodford London 19 B11
Woodford Northants 36 H5
Woodford Bridge London 19 B11
Woodford Halse Northants 28 C2
Woodgate Norf 38 D6
Woodgate W Mid 34 G5
Woodgate W Sus 11 D8
Woodgate Worcs 26 B6
Woodgreen Hants 9 C10
Woodhall Herts 29 G9
Woodhall Invclyd 68 C2
Woodhall N Yorks 57 G11
Woodhall Spa Lincs 46 F5
Woodham Sur 19 E7
Woodham Ferrers Essex 20 B4
Woodham Mortimer Essex 20 A5
Woodham Walter Essex 30 H5
Woodhaven Fife 77 E7
Woodhead Aberds 89 E7
Woodhey Gtr Man 50 H3
Woodhill Shrops 34 G3
Woodhorn Northumb 63 E8
Woodhouse Leics 35 D11
Woodhouse N Lincs 45 B11
Woodhouse S Yorks 45 D8
Woodhouse W Yorks 51 F8
Woodhouse W Yorks 51 G9
Woodhouse Eaves Leics 35 D11
Woodhouse Park Gtr Man 44 D2
Woodhouselee Midloth 69 D11
Woodhouselees Dumfries 61 F9
Woodhouses Staffs 35 D7
Woodhurst Cambs 37 H9
Woodingdean Brighton 12 F2
Woodkirk W Yorks 51 G8
Woodland Devon 5 E8
Woodland Durham 58 D1
Woodlands Aberds 83 D9
Woodlands Dorset 9 D9
Woodlands Hants 10 C2
Woodlands Highld 87 E8
Woodlands N Yorks 51 D9
Woodlands S Yorks 45 B9
Woodlands Park Windsor 18 D5
Woodlands St Mary W Berks 17 D10
Woodlane Staffs 35 C7
Woodleigh Devon 5 G8
Woodlesford W Yorks 51 G9
Woodley Gtr Man 44 C3
Woodley Wokingham 18 D4
Woodmancote Glos 16 B4
Woodmancote Glos 26 F6
Woodmancote Glos 27 H7
Woodmancote W Sus 11 C11
Woodmancote W Sus 11 D6
Woodmancott Hants 18 G2
Woodmansey E Yorks 53 F6
Woodmansterne Sur 19 F9
Woodminton Wilts 9 B9
Woodnesborough Kent 21 F10
Woodnewton Northants 36 F6
Woodplumpton Lancs 49 F5
Woodrising Norf 38 E5
Wood's Green E Sus 12 C5
Woodseaves Shrops 34 B2
Woodseaves Staffs 34 C3
Woodsend Wilts 17 D9
Woodsetts S Yorks 45 D9
Woodsford Dorset 9 E6
Woodside Aberdeen 83 C11
Woodside Aberds 89 D10
Woodside Brack 18 D6
Woodside Fife 77 G7
Woodside Hants 10 E2
Woodside Herts 29 H9
Woodside Perth 76 D5
Woodside of Arbeadie Aberds 83 D9
Woodstock Oxon 27 G11
Woodstock Pembs 22 D5
Woodthorpe Derbys 45 E8
Woodthorpe Leics 35 D11
Woodthorpe Lincs 47 D8
Woodthorpe York 52 E1
Woodton Norf 39 F8
Woodtown Devon 6 D3
Woodtown Devon 6 D3
Woodvale Mers 42 A6
Woodville Derbys 35 D9
Woodyates Dorset 9 C9
Woofferton Shrops 26 B2
Wookey Som 15 G11
Wookey Hole Som 15 G11
Wool Dorset 9 F7
Woolacombe Devon 6 B3
Woolage Green Kent 21 G9
Woolaston Glos 16 B2
Woolavington Som 15 G9
Woolbeding W Sus 11 B7
Wooldale W Yorks 44 B5
Wooler Northumb 71 H8
Woolfardisworthy Devon 6 D2
Woolfardisworthy Devon 7 F7
Woolfords Cottages S Lanark 69 E9
Woolhampton W Berks 18 E2
Woolhope Hereford 26 E3
Woolhope Cockshoot Hereford 26 E3
Woolland Dorset 9 D6
Woollaton Devon 6 E3
Woolley Bath 16 E4
Woolley Cambs 29 A8
Woolley Corn 6 E1
Woolley Derbys 45 F7
Woolley W Yorks 45 A7
Woolmer Green Herts 29 G9
Woolmere Green Worcs 26 B6
Woolpit Suff 30 B6
Woolscott Warks 27 B11
Woolsington T&W 63 G7
Woolstanwood Ches E 43 G9
Woolstaston Shrops 33 F10
Woolsthorpe Lincs 36 B4
Woolsthorpe Lincs 36 C5
Woolston Devon 5 G8
Woolston Shrops 33 C9
Woolston Shrops 33 G10
Woolston Soton 10 C3
Woolston Warr 43 D9
Woolstone M Keynes 28 E5
Woolstone Oxon 17 C9
Woolton Mers 43 D7
Woolton Hill Hants 17 E11
Woolverstone Suff 31 E8
Woolverton Som 16 F4
Woolwich London 19 D11
Woolwich Ferry London 19 D11
Woonton Hereford 25 C10
Wooperton Northumb 62 A6
Woore Shrops 34 A3
Wootten Green Suff 31 A9
Wootton Bedford 29 D7
Wootton Hants 9 E11
Wootton Hereford 25 C10
Wootton Kent 21 G9
Wootton N Lincs 53 H6
Wootton Northants 28 C4
Wootton Oxon 17 A11
Wootton Oxon 27 G11
Wootton Shrops 33 C9
Wootton Shrops 33 H10
Wootton Staffs 34 C4
Wootton Staffs 44 H5
Wootton Bassett Wilts 17 C7
Wootton Bridge IoW 10 E4
Wootton Common IoW 10 E4
Wootton Courtenay Som 7 B8
Wootton Fitzpaine Dorset 8 E2
Wootton Rivers Wilts 17 E8
Wootton St Lawrence Hants 18 F2
Wootton Wawen Warks 27 B8
Worcester Worcs 26 C5
Worcester Park London 19 E9
Wordsley W Mid 34 G4
Worfield Shrops 34 F3
Work Orkney 95 G5
Workington Cumb 56 D1
Worksop Notts 45 E9
Worlaby N Lincs 46 A4
World's End W Berks 17 D11
Worle N Som 15 E9
Worleston Ches E 43 G9
Worlingham Suff 39 G10
Worlington Suff 30 A3
Worlingworth Suff 31 B9
Wormald Green N Yorks 51 C9
Wormbridge Hereford 25 E11
Wormegay Norf 38 D2
Wormelow Tump Hereford 25 E11
Wormhill Derbys 44 E5
Wormingford Essex 30 E6
Worminghall Bucks 28 H3
Wormington Glos 27 E7
Worminster Som 16 G2
Wormit Fife 76 E6
Wormleighton Warks 27 C11
Wormley Herts 29 H10
Wormley Sur 18 G6
Wormley West End Herts 29 H10
Wormshill Kent 20 F5
Wormsley Hereford 25 D11
Worplesdon Sur 18 F6
Worrall S Yorks 45 C7
Worsbrough S Yorks 45 B7
Worsbrough Common S Yorks 45 B7
Worsley Gtr Man 43 B10
Worstead Norf 39 C9
Worsthorne Lancs 50 F4
Worston Lancs 50 E3
Worswell Devon 4 G6
Worth Kent 21 F10
Worth W Sus 12 C2
Worth Matravers Dorset 9 G8
Wortham Suff 39 H6
Worthen Shrops 33 E9
Worthenbury Wrex 43 H7
Worthing Norf 38 D5
Worthing W Sus 11 D10
Worthington Leics 35 C10
Worting Hants 18 F3
Wortley S Yorks 45 C7
Wortley W Yorks 51 F8
Worton N Yorks 57 G11
Worton Wilts 16 F6
Wortwell Norf 39 G8
Wotherton Shrops 33 E8
Wotter Devon 5 E6
Wotton Sur 19 G8
Wotton-under-Edge Glos 16 B4
Wotton Underwood Bucks 28 G3
Woughton on the Green M Keynes 28 E5
Wouldham Kent 20 E4
Wrabness Essex 31 E8
Wrafton Devon 6 C3
Wragby Lincs 46 E5
Wragby W Yorks 51 H10
Wragholme Lincs 47 C7
Wramplingham Norf 39 E7
Wrangbrook W Yorks 45 A8
Wrangham Aberds 89 E6
Wrangle Lincs 47 G8
Wrangle Bank Lincs 47 G8
Wrangle Lowgate Lincs 47 G8
Wrangway Som 7 E10
Wrantage Som 8 B2
Wrawby N Lincs 46 B4
Wraxall Dorset 8 D4
Wraxall N Som 15 D10
Wraxall Som 16 H3
Wray Lancs 50 C2
Wraysbury Windsor 19 D7
Wrayton Lancs 50 B2
Wrea Green Lancs 49 F3
Wreay Cumb 56 B6
Wreay Cumb 56 D6
Wrecclesham Sur 18 G5
Wrecsam = Wrexham Wrex 42 G6
Wrekenton T&W 63 H8
Wrelton N Yorks 59 H8
Wrenbury Ches E 43 H8
Wrench Green N Yorks 59 H10
Wreningham Norf 39 F7
Wrentham Suff 39 G10
Wrenthorpe W Yorks 51 G9
Wrentnall Shrops 33 E10
Wressle E Yorks 52 F3
Wressle N Lincs 46 B3
Wrestlingworth C Beds 29 D9
Wretham Norf 38 G5
Wretton Norf 38 F2
Wrexham = Wrecsam Wrex 42 G6
Wrexham Industrial Estate Wrex 43 H6
Wribbenhall Worcs 34 H3
Wrightington Bar Lancs 43 A8
Wrinehill Staffs 43 H10
Wrington N Som 15 E10
Writhlington Bath 16 F4
Writtle Essex 30 H3
Wrockwardine Telford 34 D2
Wroot N Lincs 45 B11
Wrotham Kent 20 F3
Wrotham Heath Kent 20 F3
Wroughton Swindon 17 C8
Wroxall IoW 10 G4
Wroxall Warks 27 A9
Wroxeter Shrops 34 E1
Wroxham Norf 39 D9
Wroxton Oxon 27 D11
Wyaston Derbys 35 A7
Wyberton Lincs 37 A9
Wyboston Bedford 29 C8
Wybunbury Ches E 43 H10
Wych Cross E Sus 12 C3
Wychbold Worcs 26 B6
Wyck Hants 18 H4
Wyck Rissington Glos 27 F8
Wycoller Lancs 50 F5
Wycomb Leics 36 C3
Wycombe Marsh Bucks 18 B5
Wyddial Herts 29 E10
Wye Kent 21 G7
Wyesham Mon 26 G2
Wyfordby Leics 36 D3
Wyke Dorset 9 B6
Wyke Shrops 34 E2
Wyke Sur 18 F6
Wyke W Yorks 51 G7
Wyke Regis Dorset 8 G5
Wykeham N Yorks 52 A5
Wykeham N Yorks 52 B4
Wyken W Mid 35 G9
Wykey Shrops 33 C9
Wylam Northumb 63 G7
Wylde Green W Mid 35 F7
Wyllie Caerph 15 B7
Wylye Wilts 17 H7
Wymering Ptsmth 10 D5
Wymeswold Leics 36 C2
Wymington Bedford 28 B6
Wymondham Leics 36 D4
Wymondham Norf 39 E7
Wyndham Bridgend 14 B5
Wynford Eagle Dorset 8 E4
Wyng Orkney 95 J4
Wynyard Village Stockton 58 D5
Wyre Piddle Worcs 26 D6
Wysall Notts 36 C2
Wythall Worcs 35 H6
Wytham Oxon 27 H11
Wythburn Cumb 56 E5
Wythenshawe Gtr Man 44 D2
Wythop Mill Cumb 56 D3
Wyton Cambs 29 A9
Wyverstone Suff 31 B7
Wyverstone Street Suff 31 B7
Wyville Lincs 36 C4
Wyvis Lodge Highld 86 D7

Y

Y Bala = Bala Gwyn 32 B5
Y Barri = Barry V Glam 15 E7
Y Bont-Faen = Cowbridge V Glam 14 D5
Y Drenewydd = Newtown Powys 33 F7
Y Felinheli Gwyn 41 D7
Y Fenni = Abergavenny Mon 25 G9
Y Ffôr Gwyn 40 G5
Y Fflint = Flint Flint 42 E5
Y-Ffrith Denb 42 D3
Y Gelli Gandryll = Hay-on-Wye Powys 25 D9
Y Mwmbwls = The Mumbles Swansea 14
Y Pîl = Pyle Bridgend 14
Y Rhws = Rhoose V Glam 14
Y Rhyl = Rhyl Denb 42
Y Trallwng = Welshpool Powys 33
Y Waun = Chirk Wrex 33
Yaddlethorpe N Lincs 46
Yafford IoW 10
Yafforth N Yorks 58
Yalding Kent 20
Yanworth Glos 27
Yapham E Yorks 52
Yapton W Sus 11
Yarburgh Lincs 47
Yarcombe Devon 8
Yard Som 7
Yardley W Mid 35
Yardley Gobion Northants 28
Yardley Hastings Northants 28
Yardro Powys 25
Yarkhill Hereford 26
Yarlet Staffs 34
Yarlington Som 8
Yarlside Cumb 49
Yarm Stockton 58
Yarmouth IoW 10
Yarnbrook Wilts 16
Yarnfield Staffs 34
Yarnscombe Devon 6
Yarnton Oxon 27 G
Yarpole Hereford 25 B
Yarrow Borders 70
Yarrow Feus Borders 70
Yarsop Hereford 25 D
Yarwell Northants 37
Yate S Glos 16
Yateley Hants 18
Yatesbury Wilts 17
Yattendon W Berks 18
Yatton Hereford 25 B
Yatton N Som 15 E
Yatton Keynell Wilts 16
Yaverland IoW 10
Yaxham Norf 38
Yaxley Cambs 37
Yaxley Suff 31
Yazor Hereford 25 D
Yeading London 19
Yeadon W Yorks 51
Yealand Conyers Lancs 49
Yealand Redmayne Lancs 49
Yealmpton Devon 5
Yearby Redcar 59
Yearsley N Yorks 52
Yeaton Shrops 33 D
Yeaveley Derbys 35
Yedingham N Yorks 52
Yeldon Bedford 29
Yelford Oxon 17
Yelland Devon 6
Yelling Cambs 29
Yelvertoft Northants 36
Yelverton Devon 4
Yelverton Norf 39
Yenston Som 8
Yeo Mill Devon 7
Yeoford Devon 7
Yeolmbridge Corn 4
Yeovil Som 8
Yeovil Marsh Som 8
Yeovilton Som 8
Yerbeston Pembs 22
Yesnaby Orkney 95
Yetlington Northumb 62
Yetminster Dorset 8
Yettington Devon 7
Yetts o' Muckhart Clack 76
Yieldshields S Lanark 69
Yiewsley London 19
Ynys-meudwy Neath 24
Ynysboeth Rhondda 14
Ynysddu Caerph 15
Ynysgyfflog Gwyn 32
Ynyshir Rhondda 14
Ynyslas Ceredig 32
Ynystawe Swansea 14
Ynysybwl Rhondda 14
Yockenthwaite N Yorks 50
Yockleton Shrops 33
Yokefleet E Yorks 52
Yoker W Dunb 68
Yonder Bognie Aberds 88
York York 52
York Town Sur 18
Yorkletts Kent 21
Yorkley Glos 26
Yorton Shrops 33
Youlgreave Derbys 44
Youlstone Devon 6
Youlthorpe E Yorks 52
Youlton N Yorks 51
Young Wood Lincs 46
Young's End Essex 30
Yoxall Staffs 35
Yoxford Suff 31
Yr Hôb = Hope Flint 42
Yr Wyddgrug = Mold Flint 42
Ysbyty-Cynfyn Ceredig 32
Ysbyty Ifan Conwy 41
Ysbyty Ystwyth Ceredig 24
Ysceifiog Flint 42
Yspitty Carms 23
Ystalyfera Neath 24
Ystrad Rhondda 14
Ystrad Aeron Ceredig 23
Ystrad-mynach Caerph 15
Ystradfellte Powys 24
Ystradffin Carms 24
Ystradgynlais Powys 24
Ystradmeurig Ceredig 24
Ystradowen Carms 24
Ystradowen V Glam 14
Ystumtuen Ceredig 32
Ythanbank Aberds 89
Ythanwells Aberds 89
Ythsie Aberds 89

Z

Zeal Monachorum Devon 6
Zeals Wilts 9
Zelah Corn 3
Zennor Corn 2